WHAT IS THE LEA FOR?

AN ANALYSIS OF THE FUNCTIONS AND ROLES
OF THE LOCAL EDUCATION AUTHORITY

Second Edition

Simon Whitbourn
with
**Robert Morris, Alan Parker, Keith McDonogh,
John Fowler, Keith Mitchell and Kenneth Poole**

First edition published in 2000

This edition published in June 2004 by EMIE at the
National Foundation for Educational Research
The Mere, Upton Park, Slough, Berks SL1 2DQ

© 2000, 2004 NFER

ISBN 1 903880 70 X

CONTENTS

PREFACE

'Daddy, what is the gentleman for?' is said to have been asked about, variously, Charles James Fox, Benjamin Disraeli and Randolph Churchill. The innocent but wide-open question was adapted as the short title of the first edition of this book in 2000: *What is the LEA for?*

The new edition is a greatly revised and expanded attempt to answer the latter question. The analysis is still law-based: LEAs are creatures of statute; Ministers continue to use legislation to entrench the Government's social policies; and both LEAs and the Secretary of State still find themselves in court.

Since the first edition there has been much change: the Learning and Skills Act 2000 has come into force; the Special Educational Needs and Disability Act 2001 has further refined the law on SEN and has applied the requirements of the Disability Discrimination Act 1995 (which it has amended) to the processes of education; and, by the monumental Education Act 2002, the Government has not only significantly altered the substance of the public education service but also has procedurally cleared the way for more of the future changes to be effected by regulations and orders than by new primary legislation. Anticipating its own Children Bill (presented, initially in the House of Lords, in March 2004), the Government appointed a Minister for Children, with interdepartmental responsibilities, but based in the DfES, and has already set about those other reforms to early-years education and childcare which were in the Green Paper *Every Child Matters* (2003) but which do not require new legislation.

Case law on education has grown. The challenge brought by Miss Phelps, whose dyslexia had not been properly diagnosed and treated while she was at school, culminated in her winning her case against her home LEA in the House of Lords in July 2000. Though she received the relatively modest compensation originally awarded by the High Court in 1997, their Lordships' speeches have greatly clarified the law on educational negligence and on the LEA's vicarious liability for acts or omissions on the part of its employees. The House of Lords added to the explication of vicarious liability in *Lister v Hesley Hall* (2001), a case concerning an independent school, but with direct implications also for the public sector.

Some dogs have not barked. There has been no spate of successful claims over alleged past deficiencies in schooling, following *Phelps*. The floodgates have not opened to claims of infringement of rights following implementation of the Human Rights Act 1998. The book explores reasons why things have been rather quiet in these areas.

The law has made itself felt in other contexts, though. The unfortunate Mrs Amos of Banbury was sent to prison for the second time for the aggravated offence of failing to secure attendance at school by one of her children (under the Criminal Justice and Court Services Act 2000). The Crime and Disorder Act 1998, elaborated by the Anti-social Behaviour Act 2003, brought in parenting orders, which may be applied in cases of exclusion from school. The 2003 Act also provides for parental contracts and (again, from early 2004) has given an education welfare officer or headteacher power to serve a penalty notice on a parent allowing his or her child to be absent from school without authorisation.

Over the same period, the Local Government Acts of 1999 and 2000 have brought about radically new ways in which local authorities (including of course LEAs) have conducted their business and have been held to specific public account for their performance. There has been talk – again – of reforming local government finance; any change here is bound to affect education as local government's largest single service. In the post-Christmas silly season, *The Independent's* front page (30 December 2003) led with a 'Cabinet clash over plan to end schools' local funding', but the narrative put the 'clash' in context, in which the Secretary of State for Education and the Deputy Prime Minister were said to oppose the old idea, revived by Downing-Street policy wonks, of transferring schools' funding from LEAs to a central agency.

Whatever the outcome of that story, or of the more sober review now being conducted of local government finance, this book vividly illustrates the range and depth of responsibilities that any new agency would acquire if it were given the funding remit.

More practically, though, the book discusses what LEAs have to do and to answer for in the real world. There is also discussion of the schools' so-called funding crisis of 2003, and how it has been tackled, including, inevitably, the issuing of new regulations.

Another new, and prominent, feature of the book is an early chapter – strictly not an appendix – on the distinctive character of the education service in Wales, the relationship between the 22 LEAs and the National Assembly, and the implications for educational administration within what is still the one jurisdiction of England and Wales.

As before, the book is designed to interest, inform and stimulate educators (LEA officers and elected members; headteachers and their senior colleagues; governors; and teachers of education management); and lawyers. It therefore not only includes the whole apparatus of the law textbook – tables of cases, statutes, statutory instruments, etc. – but also explains the legalities as it goes; and it gives a guide through the complex of public bodies that have flourished or withered over the six decades since the Education Act 1944.

The book is a team production. Simon Whitbourn, solicitor, formerly of Hampshire County Council and now in private practice (with some consultancy work for DfES), is the principal author, as he was of the first edition. His *Education and the Human Rights Act* 1998 was published by EMIE/NFER last year. He has been assisted – as the team believes – by contributions from: Dr Bob Morris, sometime Education Officer of the Association of Metropolitan Authorities and a writer on education law; Alan Parker, also formerly Education Officer of AMA, more recently Executive Director, Education and Lifelong Learning, Ealing, and now inter alia one of the school adjudicators; Keith McDonogh, until recently Director of Education and Children's Services, Flintshire; John Fowler, sometime Deputy Head of Education, Culture and Tourism at the Local Government Association and presently undertaking interim management work in local government and writing on current education policies and legislation; Keith Mitchell, a law graduate and Director of Education for Durham County Council; and Kenneth Poole, retired solicitor and a former editor of Butterworths' *Law of Education*. Bob Morris acted as editor and chaired the team's meetings.

The team is indebted to the publisher's readers – Gillian Allen, formerly of the House of Commons Library and John Bull, County Councillor, Derbyshire – whose timely and pertinent comments enhanced the pre-publication re-reading and revision. Responsibility for errors in and omissions from the text lies, however, with the writers and editor. Their aim was to bring the writing up-to-date as at the end of 2003, but so much has happened since then that (inevitably, selective) updating has been done wherever possible to May 2004.

This edition, like its predecessor, has greatly benefited from the input of Keith Mitchell's colleagues in Durham. Warm thanks go to Phil Barclay, Frank Firth, Paul Jackson, Ken Pattison, Graham Plews, Jim Robinson and Joan Teesdale, and to Victoria Ashfield, who has since moved to Cumbria as Director of Education, for all their help with the project.

The writers also record their enormous gratitude to EMIE at NFER and especially to Valerie Gee and Jeff Griffiths, the service's Head and Deputy, who have led, supported, inspired, checked, corrected and chased this project from its inception, and to Senior Information Officer Richard Downing for his contribution, most notably the preparation of the index and listings of Government circulars and guidance. They and their colleagues, including Mary Hargreaves, NFER's Media Resources Officer, Alison Riley, Service Administrator for EMIE, and Sue Woolmer and Monica Hetherington, EMIE Senior Information Officers, have worked with great enthusiasm and diligence to bring this now very solid book to completion. The assistance of editorial staff at the NFER, and of Janet May-Bowles, Pauline Benefield, Christine Taylor, Katie Longfield and Alison Jones of the NFER's Library, is also gratefully acknowledged. Lastly, thanks are due to Avril Ehrlich for compiling the Tables of Statutes and Statutory Instruments, and for her help with the Table of Cases.

But expressions of opinion herein are those of the writers and must not be imputed to the National Foundation for Educational Research or EMIE.

This work is intended to be informative and helpful. It does not, however, purport to give legal guidance or to offer any authoritative interpretation of the law. *Caveat lector.*

INTRODUCTION

It is a privilege and honour for me to be asked to provide an introduction to this fine book which, because of legislative change, needs to be updated since it was first published in July 2000.

This book is a very timely and valuable reminder of the vast range of responsibilities carried out by Local Education Authorities. It is an authoritative guide. As such, the book will be invaluable for LEA education, legal and administrative officers and those in the private sector who are involved in partnership arrangements. The book provides a comprehensive overview of the powers and duties of LEAs acting as a guide to the developing and changing role of LEAs.

The modern LEA is at the heart of the voluntary association of equal partners and has a common cause of raising achievement with the aim of fulfilling the potential of all children, young people and adults. There is potentially a wide range of stakeholders, both national and local, who can make a significant contribution to the development of a community with high expectations, self-belief and a commitment to lifelong learning. The foundation of success is undoubtedly a common sense of direction, built on mutual trust and manifested in working together positively at a local level, together with a shared understanding of mutual roles and responsibilities. Ofsted inspections of LEAs demonstrated a trend of increasing effectiveness with the majority of LEAs now receiving two or three stars in the CPA assessment process. This book sets out the statutory basis of the roles and responsibilities of an open and collaborative framework. Authorities learn to seek to understand the need of schools, through timely and thorough consultation and a commitment to meet their needs. The book also reminds us that LEAs have a full range of responsibilities which include the Youth Service, in the context of lifelong learning and the well-being of the community, linking education to cross-cutting regeneration initiatives such as social inclusion. Essentially it is the way in which LEAs exercise their powers and responsibilities, working in partnership with strong local relationships which ultimately helps all children, young people and adults fulfil their potential. Successful LEAs know their localities, have educational expertise and earn their authority.

Education does not take place in a vacuum – it is interwoven and an integral part of the local community in a network of relationships and localities. Local democratic leadership working in partnership with all who can contribute and really add value and make a difference. Likewise, if we believe in democracy, then we have to develop the powers and abilities of all children, young people and adults so that we can continue to live in a free society. As Archbishop William Temple, the guiding spirit behind the 1944 Education Act, said: 'If you want human liberty, you must have educated people.'

We live in a changing world and this book charts the various changes that have happened with LEAs since their inception over one hundred years ago. Learning is for all and LEAs have a very strong track record delivering increasing learning opportunities, raising standards in schools, making things happen so that everyone has the opportunity to fulfil their potential. As we look to the future, I believe that LEAs will continue to adapt and will lead change in the interests of their local communities.

Brian Edwards
Chair of the Association of Chief Education Officers
Director of Education – Northumberland
January 2004

TABLE OF CASES

Notes to the Table of Cases

1. Neutral Citations

Each judgment of the Court of Appeal, Administrative Court, House of Lords and Privy Council has, since 11 January 2001, had a unique Judgment Number added to it. The addition of a unique judgment number was extended to High Court judgments from 14 January 2002.

The unique or neutral citations appear as:

[Year] EWCA Civ 1 for Court of Appeal (Civil Division)

[Year] UKHL 1 for the House of Lords

[Year] EWHC 1 (QB) for the Queen's Bench Division

[Year] EWHC 1 (Admin) for the Administrative Court

[Year] ScotCS 1 for the Scottish Court of Session

[Year] HCA 1 for the High Court of Australia

2. Abbreviations of Law Reports referred to in the Table of Cases

All England Law Reports	All ER
All England Law Reports (Direct)	AllER(D)
Appeal Cases	AC
Crown Office Digest	COD
Current Law Monthly Digest	CL
Current Law Yearbook	CLY
Council of Europe; European Commission on Human Rights – Decisions and Reports	DR
Education Case Reports	EdCR
Education Law Reports	ELR
Education, Public Law and the Individual	EPLI
Employment Appeal Tribunal	EAT
Estates Gazette Case Summaries	EGCS
European Court of Justice	ECJ
European Court Reports	ECR
European Human Rights Reports	EHRR

Family Court Reporter	FCR
Family Division (Reports)	Fam
Family Law	Fam Law
Family Law Reports	FLR
Industrial Cases Reports	ICR
Industrial Tribunal Reports	ITR
Industrial Relations Law Reports	IRLR
Justice of the Peace	JP
King's Bench	KB
Law Society Gazette	LS Gaz R
Local Government Reports	LGR
New Law Journal	NLJR
Personal Injuries and Quantum Reports	PIQR
Property and Compensation Reports	P & CR
Scots Law Times	SLT
Solicitor's Journal	Sol Jo (not SJ)
Weekly Law Reports	WLR

3. Citation of judicial review cases

Much of the case law relating to education is based upon applications for judicial review brought by individuals against public bodies. However, as can be seen from the Table of Cases, law reports of these cases can be cited in a number of ways.

For historical reasons, because applicants for judicial review were asking the court to invoke a prerogative remedy, such cases were brought in the name of the Queen and were accordingly cited as R*egina v* (or shortened to *R v*) [the public body being challenged] *ex parte* (or in shortened form *ex p*) [the applicant for the review].

Thus, if a parent (Mr Jones) sought to challenge the decision of Blankshire County Council, the case would be cited as *R v Blankshire County Council ex parte Jones*.

With the implementation of the Woolf Reforms and the new Civil Procedure Rules, the citation of these cases changed. After these reforms, therefore, judicial review cases tend to be cited as: *Regina (on the application of [*the claimant]*) v [*the public body being challenged]*. 'On the application of' is, however, usually shortened to 'ota' or simply the name of the applicant.

Thus if Mr Jones now wishes to challenge Blankshire, the case would be cited as:

R (on the application of Jones) v Blankshire County Council; or

R (ota Jones) v Blankshire County Council; or

R (Jones) v Blankshire County Council.

If the claimant is a minor and an order preventing their identification is made, they are usually referred to by a single capital letter, so if Jones was a child or school pupil, the citation would be:

R (on the application of J) v Blankshire County Council; or

R (ota J) v Blankshire County Council; or

R (J) v Blankshire County Council.

See also the **Introduction to the Glossary**.

TABLE OF STATUTES

TABLE OF STATUTORY INSTRUMENTS

Statutory Instruments are listed for England and Wales. Welsh SIs have a **W** reference number.

GOVERNMENT CIRCULARS

GUIDANCE

Chapter 3, Part C offers guidance on guidance and indicates that this is a confused area. What follows are items described as guidance in this book.

2002

1. THE BIG PICTURE

A. Introduction

1.   What are 'functions' and 'roles'?

Local education authorities, the protagonists of this book, are creatures of statute. Parliament brought them into being, may multiply or refashion them and can abolish them. Parliament has laid down what they must and may do and, by implication, what they may not. As the present [2004 *ad infinitum*] public debate on local government finance has already shown, it is open to Parliament to make radical changes to local authorities' sources of income and it is at least arguable that the LEA cannot bear the full weight of its present education functions, some of which might have to be undertaken by central government (though whether the latter could cope with the financial oversight of 23,000 schools is another matter).

In any case, as public authorities, local authorities are subject to a mass of legislation on their actions, including, to some extent, how they conduct themselves.

What LEAs *are* is examined in some detail in C.2 and 3 and part D, of this chapter. For the present, a working definition is that an LEA is a principal local authority exercising its functions under the Education Acts and other relevant legislation: its education functions.

'Functions', in the context of local authorities generally, are 'all the duties and powers of a local authority: the sum total of the activities Parliament has entrusted to it. Those activities are its functions' (*per* Lord Templeman in *Hazell v Hammersmith LBC* [1991] 2 WLR 372, HL). Section 579(1) of the Education Act 1996 states that an LEA's functions include its powers and duties. The use of 'include' rather than 'comprise', which his Lordship's dictum clearly implies, raises the question what else resides within 'functions'. The matter is debatable: as this book demonstrates, LEAs are held answerable for several kinds of situation which they have not themselves brought about directly and so 'responsibilities' might rank as an additional element of 'functions'. Another could be those powers which have become discretionary duties, as explained later in this section.

A local authority can not only carry out its explicit functions but also may do anything which is calculated to facilitate, or is conducive or incidental to, the discharge of those functions (see s. 111 of the Local Government Act 1972). As a statutory corporation, the authority can do only what is expressly or impliedly authorised by statute. If it acts outside those powers (*ultra vires*), it acts unlawfully and may be challenged in the courts (see chapter 12.D.3.2) or by the district auditor (chapter 12.B.7). Even though recent law has somewhat widened local authorities' general powers (see section E.7 of this chapter), the doctrine of *vires* within which the council must operate remains.

What, then, are powers and duties?

In general terms, a power is the discretion given to a public body to do something or not to do something. In legislation, powers are usually identified by use of the verb 'may', as in '[the LEA] may arrange for [special educational] provision [for a pupil] to be made otherwise than in a school' (s. 319 of the Education Act 1996). Frequently the exercise of a power is subject to conditions and qualifications and rarely, if ever, will the LEA have unfettered discretion. Nonetheless the discretion is one for the LEA to exercise, taking account of all the circumstances, and the courts will interfere only if the LEA has acted *ultra vires* or unreasonably. (On reasonableness, see chapters 3.C.8 and 12.D.3.2.1.)

Duties, on the other hand, are mandatory requirements over, or in respect of, which the LEA has no choice. In legislation, a duty is usually signified by the verb 'shall' as in 'each local education authority shall make arrangements for the provision of suitable education at school or otherwise than at school for those children of compulsory school age who, by reason of illness, exclusion from school or otherwise, may not for any period receive suitable education unless such arrangements are made for them' (s. 19 of the 1996 Act). This section imposes on the LEA a duty which it must fulfil even if it claims that it does not have the resources to do so (see *R v East Sussex County Council ex parte Tandy* [1998] ELR 251, HL). A failure to carry out a duty can be challenged in court or by way of complaint to the Secretary of State and a mandatory order (known until October 2000 as *mandamus*) can be issued forcing an LEA to perform its duties. See chapter 12 for a more detailed discussion of the exercise of powers and duties and the potential for challenge.

There is a tendency now for duties to be signalled in legislation by 'must', perhaps because people are thought to have lost the crucial distinction between 'he shall' and 'he will'. See, for example: s.

403(1A) and (1B) of the Education Act 1996; ss. 2 and 3 of the Learning and Skills Act 2000 and clauses 7(2) and 20(1) of the 2004 Children Bill.

In addition, somewhere between powers and duties lie a number of discretionary powers which have become *de facto* duties. A power may become a duty 'if prescribed circumstances come into existence or if a failure to exercise a discretion would frustrate a statutory provision' (Poole, 1988:19). These cases normally arise from the administrative-law principle that an authority cannot fetter its discretion by adopting over-rigid rules. Thus, if a local authority has a discretionary power, it cannot decide never to use it, but must look at each request on its merits for that power to be exercised. This has been of particular importance where LEAs had the power to make discretionary awards to students. The case law established that an LEA could not fetter its discretion by failing to consider a request for a discretionary grant (see, for example, *R v Bexley LBC ex parte Jones* [1995] ELR 42 and *R v Warwickshire County Council ex parte Collymore* [1995] ELR 217).

As to 'roles', the precursor booklet to the first edition of this book (Morris, 1994: para 1.13) distinguished them from functions as being 'more metaphorical'. The term 'role':

> '…connotes also the style, political or managerial, of doing things. Nevertheless the roles are important, because they are played out in full view of the authority's taxpayers, residents and others and the performance involves the LEA's employees and institutions. People value not only what is done but how it is done.'

At the time, the distinction seemed valid. 'Functions', the hard-edged term, was proper for statutes, where it could be properly defined; the word 'roles' was more appropriate to the discourse of commentators, or for policy statements. Regrettably, however, even 'roles' may be specified in legislation: see, for example, reg 3(1) of the Education (Admissions Forums) (England) Regulations 2002 (SI 2002 No. 2900): 'The role of a forum shall be…'

2. Invitation to the Big Picture

Before going further, however, into the minutiae of education law to answer the question 'What is the LEA for?', the authors make no apology for looking at the Big Picture. Policies (and politics) precede legislation and so it is directly relevant to the theme of this book to survey statements by Governments and their agencies about the role of the LEA in the system.

The Big Picture must start with the place of education in modern British society, where the mantra 'education, education, education' has been used to assert the Government's commitment to improving the education system primarily to promote the country's prosperity and the personal welfare of individuals.

> 'Public services are direct determinants of economic prosperity and personal welfare, not only for those people who use them, but also their families, communities and employers. For example, families gain from the education of their children [...] Strong health and education systems, plus an integrated transport network, will deliver an environment in which enterprise can flourish, not least by promoting a healthy, skilled and mobile labour force.'
>
> (HM Treasury, 2003b:1)

The collective purpose of education is further spelt out by the central education department:

> 'The work of the Department for Education and Skills is of central importance to the Government's agenda. We lead on a set of challenges that are crucial both to the economic prosperity of this country and to building a fair, equal and inclusive society.'
>
> (DfES, 2002c:1)

It is in this context that the Government sees LEAs having a role in the first decade of the 21st century: local government through its LEA functions is a partner in developing the education system to meet the Government's social and economic goals. The LEA role has changed and will continue to change. Recent landmarks in the process are considered in part B of this chapter. Part C describes the LEA role today and provides a model for considering the LEA role. Part D looks at the all important relationship between the LEA and the local authority (the apparent paradox is explained in context) and Part E describes current developments which are having an effect on the future of the LEA.

B. The Developing Roles of the LEA

> 'If we are to hold LEAs to account for their performance, we owe it to them to ensure that they have a clear job description and the tools to do that job.'
>
> (DfEE, 1997a:69)

The part played by the LEA in the public education service is complex and varied, encompassing many separate roles and often expressed by different terms: duties, powers, functions, responsibilities, obligations and expectations. Some of these roles are longstanding and, despite two decades of change, continue in place both in law and in practice. Other roles relate to and build upon, the need to promote and secure educational improvement in schools and other educational settings in the local area.

A starting point to the recent changes is the Government's education Green Paper of 1984 which led to the Education (No.2) Act 1986 and defines the roles of LEA, school and headteacher. 'In the Government's view, it is essential that each LEA should have the powers it needs for discharging its duty to secure efficient school education in its area and to make its full contribution to the achievement of higher standards in our schools' (DES, 1984:para 6).

Within four years, the Government introduced local management of schools and had begun to point LEAs to their strategic management of the local school system. 'LEAs will take on a more strategic role [...] but will have a vital overall responsibility for ensuring that Local Management is effective in delivering better education' (DES, Circular 7/88:para 18).

Four years later, the Government saw a minimal role. LEAs 'may [...] have a continuing responsibility for maintaining a number of primary, secondary and special schools if parents decide not to vote for [grant-maintained] status' (DfE, 1992:para 6.2).

However, after a further four years, there was a slightly more positive tone. 'The Government sees a significant continuing role for LEAs [...] Their role should be to provide those services and undertake those functions which schools cannot carry out for themselves and which no other agency is better placed to carry out' (DfEE, 1996b: 49).

The new Government in 1997 set out to develop the LEA role: 'This new constructive role will replace the uncertainty from which LEAs have suffered in recent years' (DfEE, 1997a:28).

The LEA role was explicitly spelt out by the Government at the start of the current decade.

> 'We continue to believe that LEAs have a core role, not just in school improvement, but in assessing special educational needs,

school place supply, admissions co-ordination and school transport, educating excluded pupils, pupil welfare and the strategic management and leadership needed to underpin those functions.'

(DfES, 2001d:para 8.18).

The roles and functions of the LEA and the perception and understanding of those roles and functions have been subject to a long period of significant change, as the above extracts confirm only too clearly. A period of ambivalence, challenge and reductionism has been followed by a new agenda which has set in hand a process of reformulation and clarification. In the same period, the Audit Commission's analysis has moved through a developing perspective from *Losing an Empire, Finding a Role* (1989) to a clear and confident conclusion in *Held in Trust* (1999) that the role of the LEA is necessary, albeit likely to be markedly different in future from that of the past.

It is clear, however, that there was a turning point in the mid-1990s, supported by the new Government in 1997, that the LEA has a role in the school-improvement and innovation strategies for all maintained schools as well as continuing with the established roles of funding schools, supporting pupils with special educational needs and managing the supply of school places. The change of direction is also seen in Government's ascribing to the LEA important tasks in the social inclusion and lifelong learning agendas, the renewal of local democracy and the development of cross-departmental services for children.

What is not yet clear is whether all these changes will be allowed to consolidate or whether the changes being brought about in some LEAs in England under the guise of modernisation are a significant development in the LEA role. These 'modernisation' changes include the so-called 'innovation' found in the Education Act 2002, the Contracting Out (Local Education Authority Functions) (England) Order 2002 (SI 2002 No. 928) and the national policy in England for planning the curriculum for 14–19 year-olds. There are wider changes in local government, which affect the LEA particularly with the introduction of new democratic arrangements and the renewed corporatism and accountability following the introduction of the Comprehensive Performance Assessment. And there are also changes that Government wishes to make in society such as heightened public concern for the welfare of children. This will have a bearing on the role of the LEA. These and related issues are considered in part E of this chapter, although references are found elsewhere in this book.

The purpose of this book is to provide for the first few years of this century an answer to the question 'What is the LEA for?' Change is, though, continuous and further change will happen. There is no ultimate answer to the question 'What is the LEA for?' LEAs have been, and will continue to be, in a never-ending argument to justify the need for a local democratic tier of government between schools, families and children on one side and central government on the other.

C. The LEA Roles Today

1.   Introduction to the analysis

It is possible to analyse and define the LEA's role by various models. The Government summarised in *The Role of the Local Education Authority in School Education* (DfEE, 2000d) its view of the current law, practice and proposed future development of the LEA role. The role is set out in para 13 under the four Fair Funding categories of special educational needs, access and school transport, school improvement and tackling failure and educating excluded pupils and pupil welfare. A fifth was added: 'a degree of strategic management and local accountability', although this was described in minimalist terms of having 'the capacity to develop policy, set priorities, allocate resources and draw up plans for delivery in relation to the Authority's central functions' (p. 9). The specific strategic tasks are: provision of factual [*sic*] information and advice, auditing school expenditure and allocating spending to schools. The crucial issue of how an LEA should work with its schools is set out in the revised *Code of Practice on Local Education Authority – School Relations* (February 2001) and its sister publication for Wales (October 2001). The Code categorically states that 'the highest priority for the Local Education Authority is to promote high standards of education' through support for school self-improvement (para 6).

The Secretary of State for Education and Skills (Rt Hon Charles Clarke) in his speech to the Association of Chief Education Officers (ACEO) on 27 March 2003 gave three 'distinct but overlapping' roles for the LEA.

- **Core role**. To guarantee the infrastructure of a universal school system, by securing: that every child has a school place; that children with special needs receive appropriate education and support; that changes in the school population are planned for;

that children entitled to free school travel receive it and that large school building projects can be managed and funded.

- **Leadership role**. LEAs have a unique legitimacy. They are part of an elected authority. That gives them the authority to lead the local education community, to set a vision for education and to bring different partners together to achieve change and improvement.

- **School improvement role**. Authorities both need to offer support to head, governors and teachers but also to monitor and challenge schools' performance.

This chapter argues that there are seven major roles, ranging from strategy and policy to detail and pragmatism and from maintenance and monitoring to raising standards and continuous improvement, as shown in Figure 1. While there are similarities with the Secretary of State's 'roles', the analysis below includes the important roles that derive from being the same corporate body as the local authority and from LEAs' functions beyond schools.

2. The overall local authority role

- Leadership and Locality
- Best Value and Improvement
- Partnership and Relationships

Many strengths of the LEA come from being the local council. Parliament and Government have emphasised this point about status.

> 'An effective local democracy, with strong and accountable political leadership, is central to community leadership and the delivery of public services [...The Government] will support councils in their efforts to lead their communities and meet people's needs [...] encourage other public sector bodies to work effectively with councils; [... and ...] give councils greater freedom and more powers to meet people's needs.'
>
> (DTLR, 2001:13)

> 'A Best Value authority must make arrangements to secure continuous improvement in the way in which its functions are exercised, having regard to a combination of economy, efficiency and effectiveness.'
>
> (s. 3 of the Local Government Act 1999)

Figure 1   The overall local authority role

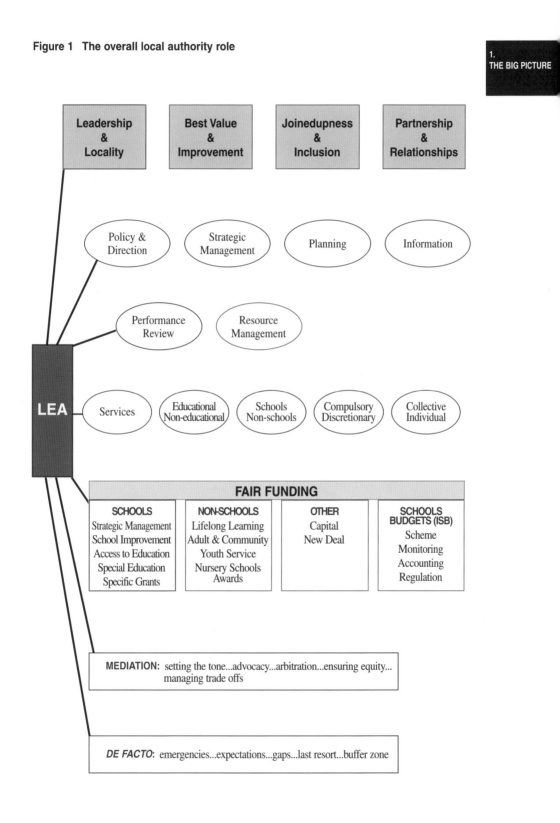

'Building on the success and potential of best value and local Public Service Agreements (PSA) the Government will put in place a comprehensive framework for continuous improvement in the quality of local government services to help councils make a real difference for their communities.'

(DTLR, 2001:23)

'The LEA's task is to challenge schools to raise standards continuously and apply pressure where they do not [... A]n effective LEA will challenge schools to improve themselves, ready to intervene where there are problems, but not interfere with those schools who are doing well.'

(DfEE, 1997a:27)

'Every local authority are [sic] to have power to do anything which they consider is likely to achieve […] the promotion or improvement of the economic […] social […] and […] environmental well-being of their area.'

(s. 2 of the Local Government Act 2000)

'Authorities have a duty to prepare community strategies […] Work to improve education standards, drawn together in Education Development Plans, will have a central role in those strategies.'

(DfEE, 2000d: para 7)

'Councils have a particular responsibility towards Local Strategic Partnerships (LSPs) […] These partnerships are the key element in developing integrated approaches to local service delivery and to tackling policy priorities in a joined-up way … [tackling] our most challenging problems – on health, crime, education, transport, housing and the local environment.'

(DTLR, 2001:18)

3.   The authority's overall role as LEA

- Policy and Direction

- Strategic Management

- Planning

- Information

'The LEA sits at the centre of the local education partnership providing strategic leadership and management. […] setting the direction of the local education system by establishing a consensus of view, articulating and communicating a vision for the education service and delivering its policies and practices.'

(Audit Commission, 1999: para 54)

'The LEA's strategic management provides the foundations for success in the quality of the leadership that it offers, the clarity of its strategic direction and vision, the tone that it sets in its LEA-school relationships and the skilfulness with which information is disseminated and communication channels managed [...] This area of LEA activity is perhaps that most intangible and difficult to measure but its importance means that it cannot be overlooked.'

(Audit Commission, 1999: para 21)

'Information is the life-blood of an LEA. Without it, none of the other LEA processes can operate effectively.'

(Audit Commission, 1998:27)

'LEAs have an essential role in securing the framework of support, challenge and cost-effective services within which schools can concentrate on the task of raising standards.'

(DfEE, 2001d:para 8.17)

A key part of the LEA's overall role is to manage the planning process for the locality and to relate that to wider regional and national agendas, both educational and otherwise. The Audit Commission's report, *Held in Trust* (1999: exhibit 17), helpfully and clearly showed the 'different plans and initiatives that have to be developed and integrated', listing some twelve strategic plans ranging from the LEA's own strategic plan to the Education Development Plan, Lifelong Learning Plan and others, to which is added the Best Value Performance Plan (BVPP). A footnote points out that this does not include plans required in respect of wider local authority responsibilities, for example, the Children's Services Plan, drugs strategy, crime and disorder reduction strategy, to which now must be added Youth Offending Team strategic activity. That picture, updated and expanded to incorporate all the strategic plans and planning processes which LEAs need to carry out, is shown in Figure 2. The planning role is likely to change as a consequence of Government policy to reduce the bureaucratic burdens on LEAs and local government generally. This will happen in two ways: local authorities will be able to combine statutory plans into a single document and high performing local authorities (as judged by the Comprehensive Performance Assessment) will be relieved of statutory planning requirements (see Freedoms and Flexibilities in E.7 of this chapter).

1.
THE BIG PICTURE

Figure 2   Strategies and plans

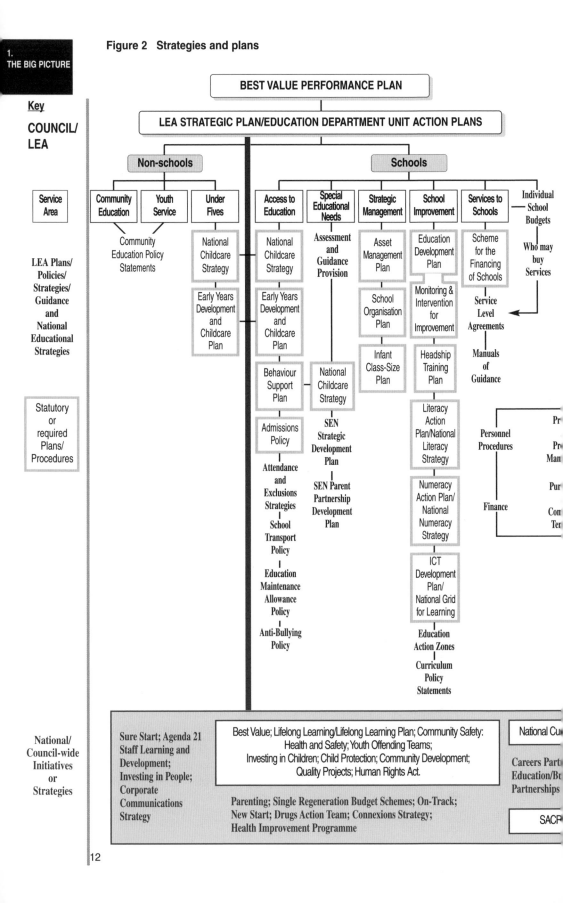

The role of the LEA also includes a significant responsibility to provide information both within the education service and outside it, locally and beyond local boundaries. This book includes, in chapter 7.C, an annotated summary of the information duties placed on LEAs.

4. Performance and resource management

- Performance Review

- Resource Management

'Setting policy and getting resources in a manner that reinforces it, are key to the development of an effective local system of education. Yet the loop would not be complete without performance review.'

(Audit Commission, 1999: para 76)

'LEAs are in a powerful position to influence and shape the provision of educational services; effective resource management is key to ensuring that this money is wisely spent.'

(Audit Commission, 1999:para 63)

The continuing role of LEAs is usefully clarified and confirmed as a result of the Government's Fair Funding settlement and the application of the Best Value regime brings further changes and duties. The exercise of these functions in future, not only against the tests of economy, efficiency and effectiveness, but in an explicit context of improved educational standards, will be particularly challenging.

5. Services

'LEAs also have other important functions, including services to schools, SEN, lifelong learning, planning school places and home-to-school transport. These other activities currently account for over 90 per cent of the expenditure retained by LEAs.'

(Audit Commission, 1999:para 98)

'A wide range of services is involved, including finance, personnel, curriculum support and premises-related services such as building maintenance and cleaning.'

(Audit Commission, 1999:para 28)

'LEAs also have an important and direct part to play in meeting the needs of individual pupils [...] LEAs have a direct and statutory responsibility for nearly one-quarter of a million children with SEN statements.'

(Audit Commission, 1999:para 44)

'We continue to believe that LEAs have a core role, not just in school improvement, but in assessing special educational needs, school place supply, admissions co-ordination and school transport, educating excluded pupils, pupil welfare and the strategic management and leadership needed to underpin those functions.'

(DfES, 2001d:para 8.18)

It remains a duty of LEAs to make provision, or to secure the provision, of appropriate services for schools under s. 13 of the Education Act 1996 and in accordance with the wider powers of local authorities by virtue of s. 111 of the Local Government Act 1972. In regard to special educational needs, the main provision is s. 321 of the Education Act 1996. It is important to recognise that statutory requirements mean that LEAs should ensure schools have access to appropriate services and the Best Value framework specifically requires that access to reflect relative need and local circumstances.

It is often assumed, wrongly, that all services are of the same standing. Some are necessary or required; some are highly desirable, some optional; some are educational, some not. Some services are best, or sensibly or by general consent, provided collectively for reasons of accessibility, equity or economy of scale. Schools and others should be able to continue to use LEA services where they wish to have access to integrated services, in a Best Value context, within a framework of trust, partnership and continuous improvement.

6. Fair Funding

- Schools
- Non-schools
- Schools' Delegated Budgets

The strategic and overall responsibilities of LEAs, as indicated above, are reflected accurately and specifically in the school and

LEA funding arrangements. Non-school funding encompasses the wider-ranging aspects of the Government's agenda and the local authority role, involving lifelong learning (with Learning and Skills Council (LSC) support – see chapter 11.A; for Wales, read National Council for Education and Training/ELWa, see chapter 2 and chapter 3.B.17.2), strengthening of communities, social inclusion, educational cohesion and a collective approach to the world of schools and beyond schools. Now that Ministers have strengthened their powers to make specific grants and have largely consolidated them in part 2 of the Education Act 2002, the LEA is both agent and actor in their administration and thus the realisation of national educational priorities. The treatment of capital funding remains an LEA responsibility (see the detailed description in chapter 6.D.17). It should also be added that the LEA retains significant duties and responsibilities with regard to the funding delegated to schools, including allocation, monitoring, accounting, regulatory and audit functions, in addition to the continuing fiduciary responsibilities of the local authority's treasurer under s. 151 of the Local Government Act 1972.

7. Mediation

- Setting the Tone
- Advocacy
- Arbitration
- Ensuring Equity
- Managing Trade-offs

'[T]here are many issues concerning the management of education that cannot reasonably be undertaken at a national level – either because of the sheer volume of decisions required or because of the need for in-depth local knowledge.'

(Audit Commission, 1998)

'The view of the Secretary of State for Education and Employment that "if LEAs did not exist, we would have to invent them" may well have arisen from years of experience in resolving a myriad of problems around school admissions, exclusions, home-to-school transport arrangements, school reorganisations, arrangements for pupils with special educational needs, student awards, etc. – many of which arise from conflicts between the interests of one party and those of another. Such problems cannot be solved fairly within an individual school (since the school is often one of the parties in conflict); nor would it be practical to tackle them in Whitehall or Westminster.'

(Audit Commission, 1998:13)

The role of the LEA as an intermediate local body for resolving systemic or institutional or individual conflicts is longstanding, well used and, according to the Audit Commission, necessary and desirable. The role includes mediation in a general sense, being a body that is perceived as sub-national, sub-regional and supra-school, which is capable of considering competing interests and striking a balance on the basis of fairness and local need. The role includes both being proactive and reactive, that is to say setting a tone and a climate within which potential disputes can be resolved before or as they occur as well as after the event.

Advancing educational opportunity has been and remains an important LEA function, particularly during periods when relative inequality has increased and includes attention to the so-called cross-cutting agenda and issues of the greatest controversy. In any complex system, there will be a need to manage the tensions and difficulties that inevitably occur. This is activity that often does not make the headlines. Indeed, the greater the invisibility, the greater the likelihood of success. But it is a role that any analysis of structure and any experience of reality would confirm as of significant importance. A well-known example relates to complaints against schools: many of these complaints, strictly in terms of local management, would be dealt with at school level but local communities seek and indeed demand the involvement of their LEAs. This is even to an extent the case with colleges of further education, where local elected members remain a conduit for complaints even though LEAs ceased to be responsible for maintaining colleges in 1993.

8.   The de facto role

- Emergencies
- Expectations (of Parliament, Government and the public)
- Last Resort
- Buffer Zone

Any comprehensive and complex system, however well designed, has gaps and so unforeseen or emergency situations occur. The *de facto* role, like that of mediation, is best performed quietly and effectively and can by definition – except in high-profile emergency situations – escape notice or proper recognition. Emergencies of such severity that they exceed or exhaust the capacity of the individual school or other public institution to handle, including school fires and threats to security and health and safety, are obvious examples. Gaps in any system often involve the handling of individual cases or difficult minority groups, often at the margins of formal provision and often at the intersection of various statutory or practical obligations by various bodies. Much LEA provision has grown up in this way, subsequently being incorporated in statute, for example, that now referred to as pupil referral units and education otherwise than at school more generally. Such activity often merges into what may be called duties or obligations of last resort, where no other partner is willing, or in a position, to handle matters, or where circumstances do not clearly fall within the responsibility of any one agency.

A clear role of LEAs throughout their history and one that certainly continues today, is to act as a local buffer between national direction or expectation and local or institutional capacity to respond. An example is the target-setting mechanisms established under the School Standards and Framework Act 1998. Because the LEA is a locally elected and accountable body, there is also a constitutional and political buffer role. This is seen in the distribution of Government grant and the annual debates on standard spending assessment or so-called 'passporting' (ensuring that money specified by Government is duly placed in the Individual Schools Budget) and the manner in which the Government immediately blamed LEAs when school funding issues hit national headlines in April 2003 (see chapter 6.D.3.4). Another example relates to school exclusions, on which, although LEAs do not exclude pupils and where Parliament has at the same time removed the previous LEA power to direct the reinstatement of an excluded pupil, the Government has determined to monitor and publish data for school exclusions at LEA, not school, level. A further example is the expectation that LEAs will help with national education policy, especially when it is found to be difficult to implement, even though the Government has legislated to remove most relevant residual LEA powers. The Director of the School Workforce Unit at DfES wrote to LEAs in August 2003 (LEA/0285/2003) to urge workforce reform: 'We expect LEAs to play a central role in ensuring that these [reforms] are made as smoothly as possible'. See also chapter 5.A.2 and 5. A.4.

D. The Synergism of Local Government: the LEA as Corporate Body

1. 'The LEA': semantics matter

This section describes the LEA as part of corporate local government and how the education functions of local authorities work together as part of corporate local government to produce an effect greater than the sum of the parts.

The character of the LEA as a corporate body of local authority elected members is crucial to its broad legitimacy and the pragmatic discharge of its role. The very term 'local education authority' and its abbreviation have been common currency in the public education service since the Education Act 1902 abolished school boards and added responsibility for elementary education to the existing education functions of county and county borough councils.

In this context, it is relevant to ask why the nominally parallel terms 'local social services authority' (and 'LSSA'), 'local housing authority', or 'local planning-control authority' are infrequently used in statute and have not caught on in common parlance. 'LEA' as a statutory term of art is both helpful and unhelpful: its positive character is to emphasise that it is precisely the authority, the county (or, if appropriate in Wales, county borough) council, unitary district council, Council of the Isles of Scilly, London borough council or the Common Council of the City of London, that has the duty to 'contribute towards the spiritual, moral, mental and physical development of the community' (s. 13 of the Education Act 1996). 'LEA' is an unhelpful appellation where it seems to connote separateness, so that the citizen may refer to the 'LEA' as something other than the council, or to the chief executive or county or borough treasurer as outside the LEA, rather than being colleagues of the chief education officer, all in the service of the LEA.

Despite, or perhaps because of, its familiarity in education, 'LEA' has often been overlooked as simply a statutory term to denote a principal council in exercise of functions under the Education Acts and other relevant legislation, detracting from the fact of the council as a multi-service authority and the aspiration (at least) for it to be for its area something more than the sum of its service parts.

The separateness of 'the LEA' – what the linguistic philosopher knows as referential opacity – is in part the fault of the legislators. As early as 1944, Beattie and Taylor criticised the new Education Act's repetition of old terminology. The LEA, if satisfied that any of its pupils 'is suffering from a disability of mind of such a nature or to such an extent that he will [...] require supervision after leaving school, shall [...] issue to the local authority for the purposes of the Mental Deficiency Act 1913 [...] a report [...]' (s. 57(5)). The commentators dryly remark that 'the report to be issued under this subsection will normally be given by the authority in one capacity to itself in another capacity' (Beattie and Taylor, 1944:193). Such linguistic problems remain, however in legislation, see, for example, s. 322 of the Education Act 1996 (Duty of Health Authority, Primary Care Trust or local authority to help local education authority [initial letters set here as in the amended Act]).

2.   Collaboration across local government

In theory and in best practice, there is much to be gained from close collaboration across local authority services at all levels. Reliance of education planning on town and country planning is obvious, most clearly so in the linkage between housing development and the provision of new school places. Education and leisure services have much in common, whether they are actually combined in one department or, at the other extreme, engaged in constant warfare over ownership of the library service, adult education or youth and community work. Collaboration is enhanced in theory when the local services are administered by the same-tier authority. Thus most LEAs have long since been on the same tier as personal social services authorities (only since 1990 in central London, upon abolition of the Inner London Education Authority), but it is only in the shire counties that education and strategic transport are part of the same authority and even then only in authorities which have not been subject to recent local government reorganisation.

Collaboration between education and personal social services has been particularly controversial. Provision of local government services for children in care, children with special education needs and children generally 'in need' has been a frequent topic of debate, legislative amendment and continuing administrative change within local government with the establishment of cross-local-authority children's services.

Collaboration of education and social services is required by statute, as in the three examples below.

1. Section 27 of the Children Act 1989 (Co-operation between authorities) and s. 28 (Consultation with local education authorities): the latter section requires consultation between the local authority and the local education authority on looked-after children. It is sad to note the comment of HM Chief Inspector of Schools (England) in his Annual Report 2001/02, at para 476, that while LEAs, including elected members, are generally now giving higher priority to these pupils: 'The development of personal education plans [to help children in public care] is too slow in some LEAs and, where they exist, their impact is not always apparent'.

2. Section 5 of the Disabled Persons (Services, Consultation and Representation) Act 1986 (Disabled persons leaving special education), which requires an officer of the local authority to give to the LEA an opinion as to whether a child is or is not a disabled person and, as noted above.

3. Section 322 of the Education Act 1996 (Duty of Health Authority, Primary Care Trust or local authority to help local education authority) requiring the local authority to help the LEA.

Other collaboration might be regarded as either a matter of common sense, such as that between education welfare officers (or education social workers) with colleagues in social services departments to support children of families with social needs, or as a manifestation of the present Government's laudable, if patronisingly-labelled, concept of 'joined-up government'. Some authorities in the name of service and administrative improvement have reorganised their services. For example, the London Borough of Bexley currently has a Directorate of Education and Community Services covering education, personal social services and housing. Others have reorganised 'horizontally' and brought all services for children within a single council directorate or department. For example, Hertfordshire County Council has a Directorate of Children, Schools and Families, described on the council's website (www.hertsdirect.org/yrccouncil/hcc/csf/) as providing services 'From money worries and relationship problems to caring for children and leaving school, this is the first place to look to find out who you can speak to for more help and what support we can provide'.

The 2003 Green Paper *Every Child Matters* (Cm 5860) and the 2004 Children Bill, which are discussed in part E.3 of this chapter and in chapters 7.B, 7C.6.2.2 and 11.B, will make mandatory the collaboration piloted in such LEAs between education and the children's divisions of social services departments; the Local Safeguarding Children Boards and a statutory appointment (eventually, in England) of directors of children's services will underpin the new arrangements.

Inter-LEA collaboration is also a matter of common sense, even though Parliament created local authorities as self-contained. But, to take examples from the most recent tranche of local government reorganisations, the Berkshire Education Literacy Service maintained by the former county council's successors and the close collaboration between unitary Telford and Wrekin with Shropshire County Council have received favourable publicity. See the study by Bannock Consulting and Indepen on *Evaluation of New Ways of Working* in Local Education Authorities (DfES, 2003) for a detailed description of how these two authorities work together on advice and inspection, special support services and other services such as a music service.

3. Greater than the sum of the parts

The LEA is part of the elected and democratically accountable council. It is subject to the constraints (such as the system of local authority finance, or the doctrine of *vires*) and open to the opportunities offered by local government such as: new ways of doing business, as in part 2 of the Local Government Act 2000; or the beneficial role of elected members in the decision-making process (HMCI, *op.cit*, para 480). Subject to the statutory duty to secure Best Value (part 1 of the Local Government Act 1999) in its services, it has recourse to considerable legal, financial, personnel and managerial expertise, largely in-house. Its accountability locally is underpinned not only by the statutory demands of audit and probity, but also in the public political debate about priorities and through its own public relations capacity.

A borough or other unitary LEA is well placed to develop civic consciousness across an identifiable community; a county LEA has the advantages of size and economies of scale also available to the larger city LEAs.

Part 1 of the Local Government Act 2000 is a response to demands by councils and their representative associations over many years to have greater scope to exercise discretion. Though the Act retains the concept of *vires*, the implied limitation of activity of the public authority to functions expressed or implied by statute, local authorities' existing *vires* have been widened. Powers under s. 137 of the Local Government Act 1972 (permitting, within capitation limits, expenditure in the interests of the authority's area) are largely replaced by a duty to act according to what the council considers will promote the economic, social and environmental well-being of its community. Time, and the readiness or otherwise of Ministers to order amendment, revocation, repeal or disapplication of constraining legislation, will show how imaginatively the new powers will be exercised or whether, as presently seems likely, these new powers will be used only to disapply statutory planning requirements on local authorities judged excellent under the Comprehensive Performance Assessment. See part E of this chapter for a further discussion on the application of these provisions.

In view of the great legislative changes which education has undergone in recent years and the commitment of Ministers to direct responsibility for the delivery of policy objectives in schooling, it seems unlikely that the Education Acts and their subordinate legislation will themselves be significantly altered by decisions taken under the Local Government Act 2000 except, as has already been mentioned, the relieving of some statutory planning requirements on some councils. There could, however, be initiatives involving LEAs' education services in, say, cultural, sporting or recreational developments led by the councils acting on their widened discretion.

And yet in matters of school effectiveness, assessment of and response to special educational needs, school attendance, funding methodology and the maintenance of the teaching force, there are signs that LEA officers may increasingly be treated as if they were the branch managers of the central department. Elected members are at the same time at risk of being:

- corralled into supervising, publicly auditing and being first-stage investigators of complaints about the work of their employees and/or

- excluded from financial decision-making which in their view meets local needs but which, in the view of Ministers, results in unacceptable variations in quality of provision from one area to another.

This process turns local authority into local office and thereby a tier of governance is unobtrusively removed from the polity. As Cllr Sir Jeremy Beecham, the Chairman of the Local Government Association (LGA) wrote in *The Guardian* (31 March 2000): 'The belittling of the role of local councillors by government is not confined to local funding decisions. Their role in leading local communities and representing the interests of their constituents is also under concerted attack.'

A telling example is found in the DfES Departmental Report 2003 (Cm 5902). The Department's relationship with local government is summed up in a chapter headed 'Some of our Partners and People that we work with'. At the very end of the chapter (p. 165), it is reported that the Department's LEA programme aims to: '…support the development of a vibrant and effective middle tier, which is critical to the delivery of a range of the Department's other programmes' (DfES, 2003e).

The chapter heading and context of this quotation are an example of a growing tendency for DfES to cast the LEA as one amongst a diversity of agencies including private companies and voluntary partnerships (education action zones, school federations etc) which exist to 'deliver' central government programmes. The categorical difference between the LEA, as a body elected by general franchise with extensive statutory powers, and the rest is glossed over.

Undeniably, there have been changes.

- New forms of participatory democracy have been inserted into the public education service: most notably, school governing bodies statutorily include parent and worker representatives and seek to embrace people from the wider community.

- Accountability has been sharpened by the transmogrification of HMI into Ofsted and Estyn (Her Majesty's Inspectorate of Education and Training in Wales) (though HMI themselves are preserved within both; on the names, see chapter 3.B.14), the work of the Audit Commission and its extension from basic audit to the promotion of good practice and the assessment of performance (chapters 3.B.15 and 12.B.7), the work of the Commission for Local Administration (3.B.16 and 12.B.4), the refinement by the courts of judicial review of administrative action (12.D.3.2), the creation in England of a Standards Board and for Wales a further extension of the duties and powers of the ombudsman with the whole apparatus of assessment and league tables of performance as the pinnacle of the new accountability.

- Society itself has changed, in part through technological change that has brought about new accountability through new and fast forms of communication.

- There has been increasing recourse to litigation (much of it assisted by the availability of legal aid to children deemed to have *locus standi* in education cases), both by way of judicial review (see chapter 12.D.3.2) and through actions in negligence (chapter 12.D.3.3.3.viii).

- Though the pace of constitutional reform has been slower, the state is now part of the European Union and law with domestic effect is made and interpreted outside the kingdom and again, in progress measurable *per decennium* rather than *per annum*, international law is being imported directly into the domestic judicature, as through the Human Rights Act 1998, fully in force since 2 October 2000.

- Wales has acquired a directly elected Assembly, with a Minister for Education and Lifelong Learning (see chapter 2) and there is the prospect of regional government in parts of England (except London), together with further local government reorganisation to produce unitary authorities following the enactment of the Regional Assemblies (Preparations) Act 2003.

And questions remain about the fitness of an essentially nineteenth-century institution to discharge the duties in, for example, ss. 13 of the Education Act 1996 (General responsibility for education) and 14 (Functions in respect of provision of primary and secondary schools) and the questions are indeed urgent as well as legitimate and timely.

The problem is that the basic questions are rarely addressed, whereas change, for better, worse or to no demonstrable effect, goes on. The reforms in the Local Government Act 2000 are designed to meet some of the wishes of advocates of more generally powerful local government, though stopping short of substituting a power of general competence for a narrow interpretation of *vires*. On the negative side, as local government apologists would see it, local authorities are used more overtly as agencies of central government and the servants of national policy.

It is salutary to recall that the Government's downgrading of the political and the emphasis on the professional at local level is not new. Alan Alexander (1985:69) took a historical perspective on the tendency in legislation from the middle of the nineteenth century onwards to specify the appointment of certain officers: 'By reducing the contribution of local politicians and increasing that of professionals whom local politicians were bound to employ, this obligation contributed to a uniformity that was conducive to centralisation and control.'

4. Conclusion

The year 2000 stands out as the high point of questioning the role of the LEA with the LGA's *Has the 'LEA' had its day?* (LGA, 2000), which questioned the very concept of 'LEA', IPPR's *A New Governance for Education* and the New Local Government Network's 2002 *Future Models of Local Education.* At the close of the year, DfES issued *The Role of the Local Education Authority in School Education.* (DfES, 2000d)

In January 2000, at the North of England Education Conference at Wigan and in answer to a questioner who 'sensed a profound ambivalence on the part of the Government to LEAs', the then Secretary of State (Rt Hon David Blunkett) issued what became known as the 'Wigan challenge':

> 'I repeat what I have said on previous occasions at the North of England Conference and elsewhere: if education authorities did not exist, we would have to invent them; but we would not invent them in the guise of 1988 or 1992, or even 1998. We would invent them for the coming century. The challenge is not to whine about what has been done by central government, but to get up and show what education authorities can do in that task, as many of them are doing, with great esteem, recognised by the inspection process, in transforming the life chances of children, rather than turning the service in on itself.'

At the May 2000 conference of The Education Network the Secretary of State restated the challenge:

> 'The question we have to ask ourselves is not whether an education authority should exist – I have said before that if we didn't have authorities we would have to invent something similar. Rather, it is in what form and for which century? What functions have to be carried out by the education authority itself?'

In answer to his own question he said:

> 'Councillors play a vital role in the success of Local Education Authorities. Good, strong and committed leadership in the

education is vital in raising standards in schools. The new role in overview and scrutiny that many councillors will have will bring more transparency and accountability to local decision-making [...] Local Education Authorities have a duty to promote high standards. What is emerging clearly is that successful Authorities – those that continually improve education standards, challenge and support poorly performing schools – have a chief education officer and senior management personally committed to raising standards and councillors with a firm commitment to education. [...] But to make this happen [...] we have to give support too.'

That message was a timely reminder of the need, as the Secretary of State put it, for 'genuine cooperation [...] schools working with schools, schools with community and schools and LEAs working together with Government to raise standards'.

Two fundamental conclusions seem to emerge: first, that LEAs (or something similar) must and will continue to exist and that they must and will continue to change. This is a prescription by no means confined to LEAs in today's ever-changing educational world but, for LEAs, the Secretary of State's insistence on 'change for a purpose', on support, genuine co-operation and partnership, is a message that is welcome and overdue. The second conclusion and the greater challenge, appears to be the need for all the educational partners to engage in that process constructively and in true partnership and, above all, with an up-to-date and properly informed understanding of the respective contributions which each partner can make to secure the best education service that the nation can afford and that all our children deserve.

E. The Future

1. Introduction

This chapter has shown how the LEA has developed over the last 20 years or so and described the main roles it performs in 2004. The particularly important corporate relationship between the LEA and the local authority is described which of necessity includes a brief outline of the LEA's key relationships with other bodies, particularly central government and schools. These relationships will be described further in later chapters.

The chapter has emphasised that the LEA role is developing and will continue to change in response to central and local government policies. This final part brings together all the changes being promoted by central government which the authors believe will shape the LEA role over the next five years. They are listed below, in no particular order and are further explained later in this chapter. They are not exclusive of each other, for example, new models of LEA organisation can help with the developing cross-public-sector managements of all services for children and the advent of regional government could enable increased micromanagement in LEAs and new ways of managing 14–19 provision. There are other changes which may in time affect the role of the LEA: new ways of learning, especially with the introduction of new technologies and the extended school. Their impact is unlikely to be felt, however, on the role of the LEA within the next five years.

2. New models of LEA organisation

There are three strands to the development of 'new models' of LEA organisation. The School Standards and Framework Act 1998 gave the Secretary of State the power when an LEA is found 'to be failing in any respect to perform any function [...] to an adequate standard' to direct that the function may be performed on behalf of the authority 'by such other person as is specified in the direction' (s. 497A of the 1996 Education Act). At the same time, local authorities were starting to try out new ways of providing services which had been made possible by the extension of compulsory competitive tendering to support and professional functions in the mid-1990s and the Best Value regime in the late 1990s. The expectation was that more financially efficient ways of providing services could be found which would also have a positive effect on raising standards. Local authorities were also considering new ways of managing services at a political level following the abolition in 1994 of the statutory requirement to have an education committee and new ways of combining responsibilities of senior staff. This has now been assisted by the novel forms of political management possible under the Local Government Act 2000. These three strands are characterised as 'service procurement or delivery', 'executive management' and 'governance' in the *Evaluation of New Ways of Working in Local Education Authorities*, the report to the DfES by Bannock Consulting and Indepen (May 2003).

Government encouragement to widen the scope of services that could be outsourced was given in *The Role of the Local Education*

Authority in School Education (DfEE, 2000d) under the heading 'New ways of discharging responsibilities in partnership'. The Department also announced its intention to fund a limited number of pilot projects to test out new models of delivering LEA services. Legal obstacles to outsourcing services to private companies and voluntary bodies (and indeed to joint arrangements with other LEAs) were removed in 2002 by the Contracting Out (Local Education Authority Functions) (England) Order 2002 (SI 2002 No. 928). Previously, an LEA could outsource functions only if directed to by the Secretary of State if it was failing to perform a function adequately. The Education Act 2002 also empowered LEAs to encourage schools to form companies to which LEA functions could be outsourced. The 2002 Act also allows LEAs to propose that education law be suspended for experiments, although none had made such a proposal by the end of 2003.

The Bannock Consulting & Indepen study reported that the DfES had identified 44 LEAs involved in new ways of working. The study clearly found difficulty in categorising the new ways: '[E]ach case seemed unique and most involved a number of components of new ways of working.' The study concludes that 'new ways of working made a material contribution to the performance of LEAs' strategic functions and in enhancing their provision of services to schools'.

The study does not and could not answer the question whether services to schools might have been enhanced more if, for example, new LEA management arrangements had been adopted. There is now a sizeable private sector, admittedly containing a considerable number of former local authority chief and senior officers, keen to develop new ways of working with LEAs. So far, Ofsted inspections have been positive about the new arrangements.

It is difficult to see how the Government could require, except in the case of a failing authority, LEA involvement in new models. Such decisions can be taken locally only by those elected to decide on the best pattern of local provision. There is likely to be an interim period when it will be hard to draw conclusions about patterns of administration in LEAs and it will mean more varied career patterns for those working in educational administration as they go between public and private bodies. At present, it seems likely that new models will only change who performs LEA functions rather than lead to a change in the function *per se*.

3. Children's services

Debate on how best to provide public services to children is not new. The changes of the early 1970s led to the vertical organisation of public services particularly in education, personal social services and health when, for example, speech therapy and health visiting were transferred from local government to the National Health Service. Although local and health authorities tried to ensure that services for children were integrated through, for example, Joint Care Planning Teams for children and, within the local authority, encouraging close working between education welfare officers and field social workers, it was clear, if for no other reason than the stream of inquiries into the deaths of children either in care or otherwise known to social services authorities, that the system needed improvement.

Apart from experiments in managing integrated services for children and families in need under new ways of working, the main policy thrust since 1998 has come from the Government through the work of the Social Exclusion Unit and decisions of the cross-cutting reviews announced in the Comprehensive Spending reviews of 1998, 2000 and 2002. Within the goal of eradicating child poverty and tackling social exclusion, a range of initiatives have been and are proposed to improve services for children. Four have direct implications for LEAs.

• Establishment of cross-Whitehall units to assist with the integration of policy nationally and co-ordinate services locally and often with power to fund initiatives, for example Sure Start, Children and Young People's Unit (with the Children's Fund) and Connexions.

• Asking for overarching Local Preventative Strategies to be developed by April 2003 in each local authority area to prevent children and young people from facing difficulties. The strategy was to cover all local authority services, the health service, the police and key criminal justice agencies; relate to other inter-agency work such as the Early Years Development and Childcare Partnerships, Youth Offending Teams, Drug Action Teams, Sure Start and Teenage Pregnancy Partnerships as well as over cross-cutting initiatives such as Neighbourhood Renewal, Tackling Health Inequalities and Crime Reduction.

- Identification, Referral and Tracking (IRT) (subsequently renamed Information Sharing and Assessment) whereby common data systems between all agencies responsible for children will be put in place for all young people at risk.

- Children's Trusts, enabling common commissioning or provision of community health and local authority children's services through greater strategic coherence, better integration of services and improved access. Pooled funding between local authorities and the health services is possible using the flexibilities under s. 31 of the Health Act 1999 and s. 2 of the Local Government Act 2000.

The Children Bill, to give statutory effect to policies in the Green Paper *Every Child Matters* (2003) requiring legislation was published in early March 2004. The outline below and in other places cross-referenced in this book is necessarily tentative: at the time of writing, little Parliamentary debate had taken place on the Bill, which was likely to be amended in both Houses before it achieved enactment, probably in late 2004. Thereafter, the programme of implementation will be signalled by commencement orders and the making and coming into force of regulations.

Separate parts of the Bill cover provisions in England and in Wales affecting LEAs and social services authorities (i.e. the principal local authorities, called in the Bill 'children's services authorities'). There are some differences of principle as well as of structure, but the basic aims of 'co-operation to improve [children's and society's] well-being' and 'arrangements to safeguard and promote [children's] welfare' are the same.

In England, the children's services authority may and, if required on a day to be appointed must, appoint a director of children's services to work for it in its exercise of education and social services functions insofar as both extend to children. Such an appointment may be made by two or more authorities jointly. There must also be within each authority a 'lead [elected] member for children's services'.

The authority must establish a Local Safeguarding Children Board (LSCB) for its area, the board to be representative of (though not in every case directly so) shire district councils (if any) and police, probation, health, vocational training and prison authorities, the Children and Family Court Advisory and Support Service, as other bodies deemed relevant by these partners.

Procedures and functions of LSCBs may be governed by regulations. The partners will be responsible for funding the boards. The LSCB's main purpose is effective co-ordination among the various bodies in the interests of children. Two or more authorities may set up a joint LSCB.

The Bill will bring about multidisciplinary inspections of children's services. Development work led by HM Chief Inspector of Schools in spring 2004 was intended to set out basic priciples and procedures. The list of inspectorate or commission partners is significant: Ofsted, Adult Learning Inspectorate, Audit Commission, Social Care Commission, Healthcare Commission and HM Inspectors of Constabulary, Probation, Prison and Court Services

For Wales, the two most striking differences in the statutory proposals are the following. First, though the authority must have a lead member and establish a LSCB, the authority's principal officer for children's services is designated 'lead director for children's and young people's services'. He may or may not also be the chief education officer; the explanatory notes to the Bill even speculate that the role could be performed by the authority's chief executive. Secondly, the Wales provisions will also put on a statutory basis the Children and Young People's Framework Partnerships and Children's Partnerships and regularise their relationship with Young People's Partnerships set up under s. 123 of the Learning and Skills Act 2000. The issues are discussed in chapters 3.B.3, 7.B and 9.D.

4. Fourteen to nineteen and the management of education and training

The legislative building blocks for the Government's policies on 14–19 education in England are in place. The Learning and Skills Act 2000 established the Learning and Skills Council as a funding and planning body with quality control being providing by Ofsted and the Adult Learning Inspectorate. The 2002 Act enhanced the planning role of the LSC so that proposals could be made to reorganise school sixth forms and enabled 14–19 area inspections to take place. LSC-led strategic area reviews of learning provision for learners from 16 up to higher education commenced in April 2003. Proposals to change the 14–16 curriculum were launched for consultation in May 2003. Yet doubts remain about whether this is an effective structure, particularly over the role of the Learning and Skills Council and its 47 local councils. Given that the 14–19 policies are crucial for the success of two key Government policies, getting half of 18–30 year-olds through higher education and significantly reducing the proportion of 16–19 year-olds who are not in education, employment or training, it is likely that further structural changes may be proposed to assist Government policy, with implications for the role of the LEA.

Arrangements for Wales are described in chapter 2. See also chapter 11.

5.   Regional government

The Regional Assembly (Preparations) Act 2003 received Royal Assent in May 2003 and enables referendums to be held in any English region outside Greater London about whether there should be an elected regional assembly. There are three implications for LEAs.

In areas where there are two tiers of local government, the shire county and district councils, a successful vote for a regional assembly will mean that the existing pattern of local authorities will be reorganised into unitary authorities. Electors will be asked to vote on their preferred form of unitary local government.

According to the White Paper *Your Region, Your Choice. Revitalising the English Regions* (Cm 5511, 2002), the assemblies will be given powers to improve the quality of life for people in their regions. The assemblies will have strategic roles on planning, housing, transport, the arts, tourism and sport.

The Deputy Prime Minister (Rt Hon John Prescott) has called for adult education to be added to the powers of regional assemblies (Peter Hetherington: 'Prescott plans to beef up regional assemblies,' *The Guardian*, 26 January 2004). The existing Regional Development Agency will be accountable to its assembly, which will play an important role in other aspects of the skills agenda and the interface with the Learning and Skills Council and the local councils. The LEA, in developing its own policies on education and skill development for 14–19 year olds, will in effect also have to take account of the policies of the regional assembly.

The Government had not published a draft Bill on the powers of regional assemblies by spring 2004. It is expected that assemblies will take over some responsibilities from the Government Offices (which have been increasingly exercising a supervisory role over LEAs). The senior members of assemblies will be full-time and paid accordingly. If assemblies do not get powers initially it cannot be long before they seek additional powers to put in place regional strategies. High on the agenda must be rationalisation of the local LSCs' arrangements and possibly powers over secondary education, given the significance of good secondary education for the prosperity of a region.

6. Micromanagement

The desire of Government to micromanage local government is not to be underestimated. The Government's Regional Offices have been taking a greater interest in the work of LEAs especially where there is an overlap with the work of the LSC and the Connexions service, for example, with the request to 'receive' LEA Youth Service Development Plans in 2003. Other examples include the role of the central department's Standards and Effectiveness Unit Schools Directorate Advisers (though the SEU will be disbanded in 2004 and its functions transferred to the Schools Directorate); the DfES website declared (in June 2003) that they 'also work closely with DfES and Government Office colleagues in "virtual teams" to address specific priorities and more widely on cross-cutting initiatives and funding streams (e.g. Neighbourhood Renewal and Local Strategic Partnerships) to make maximum impact on standards in schools.' A DfES letter to LEAs of 30 May 2003 on School Organisation asks that relevant officials be asked to register on a new website so that they can access, among other facilities, an 'Ask the Expert' feature.

The Secretary of State in a speech in June 2003 declared '[T]here is no going back to the days of big brother LEAs – it's not your job to dictate: it's to facilitate. Government needs a local partner to make raising standards a reality.' He went on to describe his wish to establish a Delivery Deal (now termed 'compact') with each LEA on the following 10 areas.

1. Raising standards in literacy, numeracy and the other key stages.

2. Tackling weaknesses and failure in underperforming schools.

3. Delivering integrated childcare and early-years education to all families to ensure every child has the best start in life.

4. Rooting out bad behaviour and non-attendance.

5. Supporting the modernisation of the workforce in every school.

6. Rolling out the National Grid for Learning so that white boards, broadband and computer access become vital learning tools in every school.

7. Challenging schools to exploit data to pinpoint strengths and weaknesses in their performance and tailor learning to every individual child.

8. Building dynamic relationships between schools, colleges and employers to offer a varied and exciting 14–19 curriculum.

9. Developing learning network between schools, teachers and subject specialists.

10. Ensuring that education provision is inclusive.

Whereas the facilitation of Government policy can be seen as a longstanding role of the LEA, the compact, which would appear to entail the agreement of detailed programmes for achieving the Government's policies in virtually every LEA area, is new (see the DfES Guidelines, LEA/0282/2003: 'Compacts – Partnership working to deliver shared priorities', 15 August 2003). It is, though, in keeping with the 'middle tier' view of the LEA role as found in the 2003 DfES Departmental report (Cm 5902) (see above).

7. Freedoms and flexibilities

The freedom and flexibilities programmes led by the Office of the Deputy Prime Minister are almost the complete opposite of the micromanagement described above. Local authorities can be given freedoms and flexibilities (sometimes referred to as 'earned autonomy'), that is, relieved of requirements of legislation and/or permitted to manage resources in locally-determined ways, by two means. The first is through the Local Public Service Agreements (LPSAs) whereby the local authority agrees local targets beyond those set for all local authorities. The EMIE publication *Public Service Agreements at the Local Level* (2003) found that 'the common relaxations for education concern the ability to vire between different categories within the School Standards Fund [...] and a commitment to work with a number of authorities on education plan rationalisation.' The other means is through those freedoms and flexibilities which will be given to authorities which achieve the highest ratings on the Comprehensive Performance

Assessment (CPA). The authorities categorised as excellent under the CPA and with three stars for performance in education will be given freedom from producing plans to a specific format except for a restyled Best Value Performance Plan (BVPP) and a Community Strategy. Thus the DfES can no longer require plans from these authorities unless there is a statutory requirement.

The effect on the role of the LEA of these changes is likely to be minimal except as regards accountability (and the possibility of reduced burdens on the staff of the excellent LEAs). A prime function of the LEA is to be accountable not only to the local electorate but also to those bodies in the local education partnership which depend on the good governance of the LEA. Pruning the planning information, because plans were being produced differently from other LEAs, could have an adverse effect on the relationship between LEAs and schools. On the other hand, the compacts described above should improve local democratic decision-making.

8. Other corporate agenda: social inclusion, community cohesion, community leadership and neighbourhood renewal

In addition to responding to the needs of children at risk, LEAs are also heavily involved in three other cross-cutting initiatives within the Government's social inclusion drive. These are: Neighbourhood Renewal, Community Cohesion and Local Strategic Partnerships.

The Neighbourhood Renewal Fund aims to help local authorities improve services in their most disadvantaged neighbourhoods, including helping them achieve Government targets and narrow the gap between deprived areas and the rest of the country. LEAs are involved in improving educational attainment and skills in the 88 local authority areas where specific funding is provided, although the ideas and lessons behind neighbourhood renewal are likely to be used outside the funded areas as part of the Government's National Strategy for Neighbourhood Renewal.

The Community Cohesion Pathfinder Programme (led by the Home Office) has been established to ensure that community cohesion is improved in a number of local authorities across England. Guidance has been produced for all local authority areas and a specific programme funds projects in 15 local authority areas. The projects aim to identify the most effective ways of finding how community cohesion can be integrated across planning and service delivery in the public, voluntary and private sectors so that all communities can play a part in their areas and minority communities are not marginalised.

There is a youth focused Community Champions Fund designed to help young people aged 18–25 to inspire others to get more involved in renewing their neighbourhoods and building cohesive communities.

Furthermore, local strategic partnerships are voluntary partnerships of local service providers from the voluntary, community and private sectors. The partnerships enable the providers to come together to agree a local strategy and priorities to tackle key social issues. It is likely that the plan will be that required of local authorities under the Local Government Act 2000 and called the Community Plan. Typically, the plan should enable partners to set out what needs to be done in their area over a longer period of time, such as 15 years and consider how the various services can work together to improve economic, social and environmental well-being over a three year planning period to address the issues which affect people at local level.

2. A NOTE ABOUT EDUCATION IN WALES:
Essential Background to Education in England and Wales

Note to the reader

For reasons set out in the text below, this chapter is designed to be of interest not only to those residing and/or working in Wales and the Marches but also to the reader based in and mainly concerned about England.[1]

Conversely, there are in the other chapters many pointers to distinctive differences of detail in structures and procedures between England and Wales. As well as giving a completely Cambrian picture of the public education service, however, chapter 2 offers some guidance to the policy differences that have led to the widening divergence.

A. The Dragon Wakes

As in several other areas of public life, education in Wales has to be considered alongside that of England, despite differences of England and Wales form one legal jurisdiction. There remains the concept of 'the law of England and Wales'; for example, the law recognizes someone who has lived all his life in, say, Caerphilly, as a resident in England and (not or) Wales. Primary legislation for England and Wales is made only by the UK Parliament. The Secretary of State (as is normal in statutes, without the name of any specific Department) still has the general duty to 'promote the education of the people of England and Wales' (s. 10 of the Education Act 1996). The Secretary of State for Education and Skills (so identified, as is normal in statutory instruments) regulates the qualification and employment of teachers in both countries.

And yet the differences are palpable and, in some cases, increasing. This chapter outlines the particular protection for and promotion of the Welsh language as a core or other foundation subject and the permeation of Welshness (Cwricwlwm Cymreig) in the school curriculum. Attention is drawn here and elsewhere in this book to differences in terminology (in English or in Welsh) as well as in the structure and functions of organisations in education. From its first

---

[1] References for this chapter can be found on page 514.

term of existence, the National Assembly for Wales (NAW) adopted educational policies (see below) which rest on political principles contrasting with those of Her Majesty's Government.

For education, the Assembly represents the latest and greatest (so far) step of the constitutional changes which started in the 1960s with the transfer of specific functions from the then Department of Education and Science to the Welsh Office. The Assembly's lawmaking powers extend no further than the making of subordinate legislation (and with some reservation of powers to the Secretary of State) but those powers are automatically strengthened by provisions within the Education Act 2002 to bring about much statutory change in education henceforward through orders and statutory instruments rather than the Acts of the Westminster Parliament.

The Local Government (Wales) Act 1994 and the subsequent local government reorganisation which took place in Wales in April 1996 transformed the pattern of eight large county councils into a network of 22 county and county borough councils, each functioning as an LEA. A Welsh Local Government Association (WLGA) replaced the Welsh County Councils Association and the Association of District Councils in the same year. In 1998 the Government of Wales Act paved the way for the creation of devolved governance for Wales, with a series of Transfer of Functions Commencement Orders and a Memorandum of Understanding setting out protocols for roles and responsibilities between national and sub-national administrations.

In May 1999 Wales elected its first National Assembly whose education responsibilities included the power to make secondary legislation and regulation and to ignore or to optimise enabling legislation. Initially its education and training functions were the responsibility of two Secretaries (in the ministerial sense of that office): one for pre-16 Education, also including responsibilities for Children and a second for Post-16 Education and Training. Designations changed in November 2000, with the creation of a single Minister for Education and Lifelong Learning in a Welsh Assembly Government.

All of the individual policy thrusts rest on the direction and corporate objectives for Wales set out in the Plan for Wales, the successor to *betterwales* (The Strategic Plan, 2000). Cross-cutting themes are also clearly articulated and find reference in the policy thrusts of each cabinet portfolio. There are thus clear interconnections at a policy and a strategic level, which require collaborative working between sectors and agencies and sponsor departments within the Assembly if they are to be implemented. Overall policy can be seen as developmental and holistic, with policy documents from different portfolios characterised by interdependence.

B. Key Policy Frameworks

The overarching strategic planning document for the newly-elected Assembly, betterwales, was published in May 2000 and drew for its education and training policies on work previously initiated by the Welsh Office and particularly:

* *Building Excellent Schools Together (the BEST programme)*, July 1997

* *An Education and Training Action Plan for Wales (ETAP)*, March 1999

* *Future Skills Wales*, March 1999.

Its successor, the *Plan for Wales*, was published in October 2001 and represented the policies of the newly created partnership government between the Labour and Liberal Democrat groups on the Assembly.

The Minister had announced the launch of a Basic Skills Strategy for Wales in April 2001 and in September published *The Learning Country* (2001), setting out a 10-year strategy for Lifelong Learning. In November, *Extending Entitlement* (2000) was published as a consultative document and resulted in proposals in July 2002 to introduce a network of Youth Support Services in each local authority area, with the creation of Children and Youth Partnerships.

An Entrepreneurship Action Implementation Plan for Wales was agreed in November 2000 to cover a three-year period. The overall Economic Development Strategy for Wales was published as *A Winning Wales* in January 2002, followed by a Skills and Employment Action Plan in February 2002 and a 10-year strategy for Higher Education in *Reaching Higher*, a month later. The health and social care strategy for Wales in *Well-being in Wales* followed in the same month.

Strands of each of these policy and strategy thrusts are woven into local authority responsibilities and activities, be it in the promotion of a welfare-focused social care agenda, as 'Children First'; or in the access and social inclusion dimensions of the education service itself. As such they involve the LEA in the delivery of the new duties of social and economic development as well as in its more traditional mainstream education agenda.

If the Assembly Government's agenda is set out as a series of interrelated and integrated strategies, so has the delivery at LEA level of those duties and responsibilities in Wales been reflected by a progressive integration of previously discrete responsibilities. An education directorate *per se* has become a rarity in the 22 unitary councils as a number of trends have emerged following local government reorganisation in 1996 and particularly the modernising agenda for local government that resulted from the Local Government Act 2000. The first trend is the creation of portfolio directorates: Lifelong Learning, which may encompass education, youth and information services and Education and Children's Services, which embraces children's social care services and permutations of these which can include aspects of Leisure and the Arts and Culture. A parallel trend has been the creation of corporate or portfolio directorates where education is the major component but whose chief officer is drawn from a different area of expertise. Distinction has had to be drawn between the chief education officer, who may be second tier, and the head of the department; and dynamics of decision-making and relationships have changed.

In contrast with the 2004 Children Bill's provisions for England, its Wales requirements include the appointment of a 'lead director for children and young people's services' in each authority, whilst the statutory requirements to have a chief education officer and a director of social services remain.

C. A Distinct Agenda for Education

It should not be surprising that the Assembly, its politicians and administrators have already exercised their powers distinctively and that the distinctions within the public education service within England and Wales reflect significant differences of substance. It was not until the Local Government Act 1972 that Welsh LEAs ceased to be located as 'in Wales and Monmouthshire'. Historically, there were examples of Parliament's legislating, on occasions, differently for Wales, as in the Welsh Intermediate Education Act 1889 which enabled counties and county boroughs to set up post-primary schools a decade before that reform was legally achievable in England. Two sections in part IV of the Education Reform Act 1988 provided for subordinate legislation to be distinctive of requirements in Wales. And part VI of the School Standards and Framework Act 1998 legalised partnership arrangements between secondary schools and further education institutions in Wales. Such examples were, however, quite rare and, from its inception, the Assembly effected a step change in thinking which has characterised its policies and initiatives over the period of its first term.

The development of a distinctive agenda for education in Wales is set out clearly in the earliest ministerial statements: the first meeting of the Assembly's Pre-16 Education, Schools and Early Learning Committee in June 1999 identified Framework Principles for Education Policy in Wales. Three references set the approach and the values.

'The National Assembly's education policy should set a clear framework which reflects the distinctive characteristics and needs of the education system in Wales and the particular circumstances of its schools and pupils.'

'Policy towards education should publicly and deliberately value consistency. It should progress without sharp changes of direction on the basis of sound, quantitative and qualitative evidence, full consultation and assessment of the impact on schools, local education authorities and others.'

'The Assembly will play its part in cultivating partnerships supporting children's education. In particular, local authorities should be fully engaged, especially in supporting weak and failing schools; investing in the renewal and replacement of school buildings; securing appropriate numbers of school places and giving strategic leadership for local school improvement which engages local partners and contributes to meeting all-Wales objectives.'

Three years on and with developed confidence, patterns of policy and provision have been seen to diverge from the England models, further creating elements of what begins to look like a separate set of policies and practices for Wales which many believe will lead eventually to a first Education Act for Wales. In the introduction to *The Learning Country*, the then Minister for Education and Lifelong

Learning, Mrs Jane Davidson, set out some principles for that divergence and places local authorities at the heart of delivery:

'We share key strategic goals with our colleagues in England – but we often need to take a different route to achieve them. We shall take our own policy direction where necessary, to get the best for Wales. It is right that we put local authorities, local communities and locally determined needs and priorities at the centre of the agenda for schools, for example. Our communities want excellent local schools for all their children. Partnership on that front is at the heart of the way we do things in Wales.'

(The Learning Country, 2001:Foreword)

And, in anticipation of the primary legislation in 2002, she warned:

'As is the case in England, we remain entirely committed to a universal, publicly funded, publicly accountable education system, free at the point of delivery. However, insofar as these new measures feature in forthcoming primary legislation and do not fit with arrangements that work well and get good results in Wales, we intend that the Assembly will have the power not to proceed with them […].'

(The Learning Country, 2001:para 40)

Paradoxically, this independence of direction is contrasted in other policy areas with an inability to depart from arrangements for England, where specific powers for both England and Wales are retained by the Secretary of State. More problematic is the impression of uncertainty and confusion which this mixture of autonomy and dependence can on occasion create as proposals are announced for England – such as that on student 'top-up' fees in January 2003 – when there was no definitive answer as to the implications of that announcement for Wales. Even more confusing can be references to education standard spending assessments – not published in Wales, and to various specific-grant funding streams to schools in England, often as part of the Chancellor's Budget statement. The Assembly Government's decisions over the application of the Wales 'share' of this resource can reflect different priorities and in a different and delayed timescale. A specific example was the allocation in 2000 of additional revenue funding to improve school buildings in England: the Assembly Government applied its share of the additional resource to meeting the costs of introducing Leadership arrangements (see part E.3, below). This can then lead to perceptions and sometimes accusations at LEA and school level of a disparity of funding for the education service between England and Wales.

D. A Partnership Culture

A particular feature of the development of Assembly policy and practice in Wales since 1999 has been the commitment of the National Assembly to place working in partnership at the heart of its policy delivery. Partnership Government itself was initiated in 2001 when the Labour and Liberal Democrats entered into a governance coalition. 'Policy Agreements' have been created between local and national government supported by a programme of Partnership Incentive Grants to Local Authorities who commit themselves to achieving a range of national targets. At the LEA level, it is reflected in relationships between the WLGA and the Assembly Government and the significance and role given by the central department to the professional contribution made by the LEAs together and by the Association of Directors of Education in Wales.

Much of this collaboration is, of course, made easier because of the relatively small sizes of the LEAs and the compactness of the country. It is routine for all 22 directors to meet regularly in order to help formulate policy and to handle consultation: such joint planning usually results in consistent implementation. It is also routine for the 22 spokespersons on education who hold executive or cabinet responsibility in the modernised unitary authorities to meet to discuss key issues. That the Minister and the senior officials also use these opportunities to highlight policy priorities and developments makes for a more coherent and corporate approach to the development and delivery of the education agenda in Wales.

Alternative arrangements for outsourcing services (now quite common among the English LEAs), together with the role of private sector companies in providing management support for the education officer, do not form part of the vision for Wales.

> 'In a small country, with relatively small unitary authorities, with so many distinctive features and circumstances, there would be real risks in a wholesale shift to extensive and untested measures delivered solely through the private or other sector discrimination and without full consideration of the implications case by case.'
>
> (*The Learning Country*, 2001:para 38)

It is also to be borne in mind that the history of education in Wales has reflected strong commitment to a public service ethos. The first comprehensive school in Wales was founded in Anglesey over half a century ago and the comprehensive principle has been endorsed throughout that period. Ministerial proposals for secondary education in the 21st century still rest upon the concept of a community school which is all-inclusive. And while the 1988 Education Reform Act brought other lasting changes, grant-maintained schools found little foothold in Wales and city technology colleges none. In looking forward to 2010:

'We remain committed to non-selective, comprehensive school provision in Wales. This pattern of provision serves us well.'

(The Learning Country, 2001:para 37)

'So too [has been ruled out] the introduction of a programme of specialist schools. In Wales, schools have for long been encouraged to build on their strengths. When a system is working and developing well it makes no sense to disrupt the productive pattern of the relationships on which it rests – so long as they remain so.'

(Jane Davidson, press statement for launch of
The Learning Country, 15.9.2002)

Later in this chapter are highlighted the principal developments which are distinct to Wales at the time of publication. As such, they need to be read with care: a second Assembly began its term of office in May 2003 and so it must be expected that other distinct initiatives will follow. Equally, what Wales did or does today may become policy for England tomorrow, as was seen in January 2003 with the Secretary of State's decision to re-introduce maintenance grants for students suffering hardship, an initiative already taken by the Welsh Assembly Government from September 2002. In February 2003 the Secretary of State announced the opening of consultation on a revised 14–19 curriculum for England a month after the Wales consultation on the Assembly Government's separate proposals closed.

These are the first manifestations of devolved education policy and practice: as such they hold inherent risks. The pursuit of either divergent or parallel tracks of development raises issues of interchangeability or relevance cross-border. Where financial support arrangements are involved, inequalities of access may develop. Future moves to devolve responsibility to the English regions will require a redefinition of roles and relationships between central and local government in England and a strategy to ensure that the risks of variations in practice and policy are managed so as not to disadvantage learners.

E. Devolution in Practice

1. Curriculum and assessment

The specific sections (97–117) of the Education Act 2002 related to the curriculum and its assessment are discussed in detail in chapter 4. They include the responsibility of the NAW for undertaking the functions in England exercised by the Secretary of State and the requirement for schools and LEAs to have regard to guidance from the Assembly. They provide the statutory basis for the National Curriculum in Wales. References to the responsibility of the Secretary of State in legislation preceding the Government of Wales Act need now to be ascribed to the National Assembly for Wales.

Distinctive developments since 1999 are set out below (with the detail in note form).

1.1. Curriculum

Following consultation, the National Assembly approved amendments to the National Curriculum subject orders under powers conferred by the Education Act 1996, transferred to the Assembly in July 1999. (The Orders comprising SI 2000 Nos. 1098–1101 (W 76–79) and 2000 Nos. 1153–1159 (W 84–90) cover individual subject areas).

Key changes:

- for Maths and English, programmes of study to be made more supportive of the distinctive Welsh strategies for Numeracy and Literacy

- for Science, no programme of study shall be taken to include HIV or Acquired Immune Deficiency Syndrome or any sexually transmitted disease, or aspects of human sexual behaviour other than biological (SI 2000 No. 1099)

- for Modern Foreign Languages, list of specific languages to be discontinued to allow free choice provided at least one EU language is studied (SI 2000 No. 1980)

- for Design and Technology, the range of materials to be used at key stages 1, 2 and 3 to be non-statutory

- for PE, health-related exercise to be specific and incorporated into each Programme of Study. Requirement to swim unaided for

25 metres at key stage 2 replaced by ability to swim unaided, competently and safely. Key stage 4 areas of activity to be grouped under four areas of experience and compulsory games dropped.

- for Welsh Second Language, model to be simplified to enable manageability.

The National Curriculum for Wales consists of:

- key stages 1 and 2: English, Welsh, Mathematics, Science, Design and Technology, Information Technology, History, Geography, Music Art and PE

- key stage 3: as above and to include a modern foreign language

- key stage 4: English, Welsh, Mathematics, Science and PE.

All pupils study religious education and all schools provide personal and social and health, careers and sex education.

Subsequent amendments to the National Curriculum and its assessment in Wales, following the publication of *The Learning Country* (DfEE, 2001) are listed below.

1.1.1 Extension of careers education to post-16 students
Resolved by the National Assembly in May 2001 (SI 2001 No. 1987 (W 138)), this legislation extends careers education to all young people aged 16–19 attending maintained schools (except special schools established in hospitals), pupil referral units and further education institutions.

1.1.2 Modern foreign languages strategy
A National Modern Foreign Languages Strategy was published in February 2002. It sets objectives for schools, LEAs and the National Council and Higher Education Council respectively. Principal thrusts are listed below.

- Creation of CILT Cymru to promote language learning, provide in-service training for teachers and good practice materials.

- Requirement on each LEA to set a local target for the take-up of languages in its Education Strategic Plan.

- Creation of better links between the teaching of Welsh and of modern foreign languages by commissioning guidance from Estyn and ACCAC (Qualifications, Curriculum and Assessment Authority for Wales).

- Sector Skills Council to take forward plans to promote languages for business.

- Allocation of Assembly funding to pilot modern foreign language learning for pupils at key stage 1 from 2003 onwards (Circular 41/02).

1.1.3   Personal and social education

A framework for PSE was issued by ACCAC in 2000. In October 2002, the Minister announced that PSE would become a statutory element within the basic curriculum for children aged 5–16 from September 2003. Supplementary guidance would be extended up to age 19.

1.1.4   Work-related education

Similarly, a framework for work-related education was issued by ACCAC in 2000. WRE will be a statutory element within the basic curriculum for pupils aged 14–16 from September 2004. Entitlement (see below) to one work experience and access to one additional activity.

1.1.5   Sex education

The framework for the provision of sex education rests on the revised guidance issued by the Assembly (Circular 11/02) which replaces Welsh Office Circular 45/94 and takes account of s. 148 of the Learning and Skills Act 2000, which requires the National Assembly to issue guidance which will secure that when sex education is targeted, schools must teach the nature of marriage and its importance to family life and the bringing up of children.

The framework and associated guidance developed by ACCAC are seen as contributing to the National Assembly's Strategic Framework for promoting sexual health in Wales.

See also the discussion of this topic in chapter 4.B.

1.2   Assessment

1.2.1   'Secondary school league tables'

In July 2001 following a public consultation, publication of LEA results was abolished. Results continue to be published at individual school level.

'[I]t is clear [...] that they do not have the support of either the teaching profession or members of the public. I propose therefore that we do something different in Wales.

The Assembly will work with LEAs and schools to develop a national value-added model which supports improvement programmes and helps schools put their targets and results in context.'

(Mrs Davidson, formal announcement of the abolition of LEA results, 20.7.2001)

1.2.2 Assessment at key stage 1

In *The Learning Country* the Minister had announced her intention to consider the need for testing at the end of key stage 1. In November 2001 she announced the abolition of testing for seven year-olds in Wales (SI 2002 No. 45 (W 4)).

1.3 Pilot arrangements

1.3.1 Single credit framework

In July 2001, speaking at the Credit and Qualification Framework for Wales Conference in Cardiff, the Minister announced plans for the introduction of a single credit-based operational framework in April 2003. Essential elements of the system are listed below:

- full unitisation of the curriculum

- values and credits assigned to each unit

- all qualifications and awards to have credit values

- system based on nine stages from entry vocational level to Ph.D

- credit transcript to provide learners with a record of learning achievement

- seamless transition from secondary to further and higher education

- facilitating lifelong learning and social inclusion.

Of the framework she said: 'Its contribution to learning cohesion and quality cannot be underestimated: it will form the central plank for all education and training in Wales.'

1.3.2. Welsh Baccalaureate pilot

In September 2003, a first wave of schools and colleges began a six-year rolling pilot of the Welsh Baccalaureate, which is designed to encompass existing A-level and vocational examinations. By 2010 the Assembly hopes to see the qualification adopted in all schools and that by then plans will be advanced to introduce an intermediate Baccalaureate incorporating GCSE, GCSEs in Vocational Studies, GNVQ or NVQ level 2 units.

It comprises a mandatory core whose components would include the following:

- elements related to contemporary Welsh life and culture
- preparation for the world of employment (including work-related education and careers education and guidance)
- community-centred activity
- key skills
- personal and social education
- European awareness, to include language modules.

Optional studies would be drawn from GCE A-level, AS level, Vocational A-level and NVQ level 3 studies.

2. Professional and management development

The Assembly targets specific national development priorities through the Grants for Education Support and Training scheme (GEST), which supports an annual programme at LEA level and, through the LEA, the individual school. Priorities for the annual programme are the subject of discussion between the sponsor department and the 22 LEAs. Funding is directed according to the Education Strategic Plan, which each LEA has to have approved by the Minister and by the School Development Plan of each institution.

Current regulations are set out in SI 2002 No. 1187 (W 135), with current guidance contained in Circular 22/02.

There is no Standards Fund operating in Wales and there are no grant schemes that apply Assembly funding direct to individual schools. Even late decisions on increases to school budget lines are 'passported' through LEAs. A limited number of Additional Grant schemes aimed at school improvement have been used sparingly during the life of the first Assembly. These are routed through LEAs, which are given discretion as to their application within guidelines provided. Provision may thus be shaped to meet locally perceived priorities.

3. Teacher development and support

The introduction of performance management in Wales has centred on the strategic role of LEAs working individually and in consortia.

Commenting on the scheme, which started in April 2001, the Minister claimed: 'We are well on the way to providing a distinctive "Made in Wales" approach to teachers...' (press release, 19 April 2002). Distinct proposals for Wales emphasise objectives related to professional development and retain the involvement of a peer headteacher in the appraisal of a headteacher.

The Assembly also provided for external advisers to schools through the existing advisory role of the LEAs, rather than employing private consultants to carry out this role. (See the School Teacher Appraisal (Wales) Regulations 2002 (SI 2002 No.1394 (W 137)) and the School Government (Terms of Reference) (Amendment) (Wales) Regulations 2002 (SI 2002 No. 1396 (W 138)).

Wales has its own National Headship Development Programme to prepare aspiring headteachers through its separate National Professional Qualification for Headship (NPQH), which has currency in other parts of the UK. It also has established from 2001 a Professional Headship Induction Programme (PHIP) to support newly appointed headteachers in addition to the Leadership Programme for Serving Head Teachers (LPSH), which addresses the ongoing needs of experienced heads.

Development work for the PHIP in particular was undertaken in partnership with working groups which included LEA advisers.

A separate training and development programme for the Leadership group was initiated by the Assembly in late 2000. A national framework of school leadership modules, devised by a working group, is developed locally and delivered by the LEAs to meet specific local and regional needs.

Pilot arrangements were also initiated in 2002 for an induction scheme for newly qualified teachers in Wales prior to making induction statutory from September 2003 (SI 2003 No. 543 (W 77)). Teachers are set specific targets to meet and each is given an induction tutor and time to address the tasks. The LEA makes the final decision taking advice from the headteacher: a one-year extension is offered to those who fail. The Assembly has planned a next phase of early professional development to meet teachers' needs in their second and third years.

3.1   GTC Wales

The General Teaching Council for Wales is the statutory self-regulating professional body for teachers in Wales (SIs 1999 No.

3185 (W 43), 2000 No. 1941 (W 139), 2000 No. 1979 (W 140), 2001 No. 1424 (W 99), 2001 Nos. 2496, 2497 (W 200, W 201), 2002 No. 326 (W 39), 2003 No. 389 (W 51) and 2003 No. 503 (W 71)). A key aspect of the Council's work is to advise the Assembly on teaching issues, including recruitment, retention and professional development.

4. The 'extending entitlement' agenda

In December 2000, the Assembly published two consultative documents, one from the Minister responsible for co-ordinating policy for children and young people, *Children and Young People: a Framework for Partnership*; the second from the Minister for Education and *Lifelong Learning – Extending Entitlement*. The first aimed to give children and young people an active part in decision-making and determining services they receive, through involvement in the community planning process. The second was targeted specifically at young people (estimated to be 12,000) who were not participating in education, work or training.

> 'In contrast to the Connexions approach being developed in England, we are building on the strengths of Careers Wales [the corporate brand for the Careers Companies set up as a consequence of the Trade Union Reform and Employment Rights Act 1993] and all partners in the Young People's Partnerships which are developing to implement Extending Entitlement in Wales.'
>
> (*Learning Pathways 14–19*, p. 26)

At the same time, financial commitments were made for a three-year period to address separate strands of the agenda set out for consultation. These included support for discrete programmes funded through local authorities, statutory agencies and the voluntary sector:

- Sure Start

- Children First

- Children and Youth Partnership Fund, including Play 2000 and Youth Access.

Additional funding was also provided to Careers Wales and to support the National Childcare Strategy, as well as to provide running costs for the office of the Children's Commissioner.

These measures were intended to contribute to a holistic approach to meeting the needs of children and young people, but they fell short of the coherent implementation agenda which came into force in September 2002 under the Youth Support Services Directions (Wales) 2002 made by the Assembly in exercise of its powers under s. 123 of the Learning and Skills Act 2000. The legislation and associated guidance in circular 37/02 direct local authorities to provide or secure the provision of youth support services having regard to guidance issued by the National Assembly. Key elements of that guidance spell out expectations and requirements of local authorities, which are to:

- work in partnership with other agencies

- establish a multi-agency Young People's Partnership in each of the 22 local authority areas to prepare a strategic plan to cover a first period from 2002 to 2008 and an annual delivery plan commencing on 1 April

- ensure that work planned complements existing provision, overcomes duplication and focuses efforts harmoniously to achieve common purpose

- develop and maintain a young-people-centred strategy, ensure delivery of entitlement and monitor effectiveness

- ensure mechanisms are in place to allow young people to contribute to the strategy

- provide and/or secure a high quality youth service which meets the principles and ethos of the Youth Work Curriculum Statement for Wales (membership is prescribed and there is an explicit interrelationship with the Community Planning process and with the overall Children and Young People's Framework Partnership of which it is part).

The ten 'entitlement elements' to be met in each LEA plan are specified:

1. education, training and work experience tailored to individual needs

2. basic skills to open doors to a full life and promote social inclusion

3. opportunities for participation in volunteering and citizenship

4. high-quality, responsive and accessible services and facilities

5. independent specialist careers advice and student support

6. personal support and advice with ground rules on confidentiality

7. advice on health and housing benefits

8. recreational and social opportunities

9. sporting, artistic, musical and outdoor experiences

10. the right to be consulted and to participate in decision-making.

Stress is placed on the environment within which services and opportunities are to be provided: accessible, safe, welcoming.

To support planning and implementation at local levels, the Assembly has contracted with an independent not-for-profit company to develop comprehensive information services for young people, covering seven elements bilingually:

1. an information handbook for all school leavers

2. distribution and promotion of the Euro under-26 Discount Card

3. access to a fully bilingual information website

4. access to telephone helplines including a legal advice line

5. support for the development and operation of a network of information points across Wales

6. access to a consultation service

7. access to a range of training opportunities.

5. Structural reform

The Learning Country and its related consultative documents, circulars and guidance set out specific proposals for the development of the phases and stages of education to be introduced over a 10-year period.

5.1 Early years

The Learning Country sets out proposals for the development of early-years approaches. These include a new statutory foundation stage for children aged 3–7, on which the Assembly began formal consultation in February 2003 with the publication of *The Foundation Phase – 3 to 7 years*.

The current principles underlying the education of children under five are set out in *Desirable Outcomes for Children's Learning before Compulsory School Age* (ACCAC, 2000). These outcomes and their associated guidance are non-statutory. Children are assessed statutorily prior to admission to reception year; this sets a learning baseline to assist teachers in planning individual learning.

The proposals are based on the premise that the present early-years curriculum is excessively formal both in the experiences provided and in the learning environment. The proposals emphasise the importance of play and the need to develop independence, decision-making, creative expression and cultural understanding. They also address adult-to-children ratios and the space required for early-years settings.

The consultation proposes a fusion of early-years and key stage 1 approaches to provide a continuum of learning, with the programmes of study and focus statements in key stage 1 adapted and integrated with the Desirable Outcomes. Bilingualism and multi-cultural understanding are added to the existing six outcomes, with 'well-being' added to personal and social development. It is accepted that there are implications for changes to the key stage 2 curriculum to ensure continuity.

The proposals set out an implementation timetable which begins with pilots for early years in 2004, extended to include key stage 1 in 2005, with full implementation in maintained and non-maintained settings in 2006 for early years and progressively from 2007 for key stage 1. Minimum adult-to-children ratios will be introduced from 2006.

The Assembly also proposes ways of bringing together provision of childcare and nursery education at key stage 1, with advice commissioned from Estyn. The Education (Nursery Education and Early Years Development and Childcare Plans) (Wales) Regulations 2003 (SI 2003 No. 893 (W 113)) required LEAs to prepare two Early Years Development Plans which include childcare and nursery provision for submission to the Assembly in July and October 2003 and by 20 October in each successive year. They require reference to be made to the LEA's transport policy.

The Assembly's objective to ensure a nursery place for every three year-old by September 2004 is underpinned by the work of an Early Years Advisory Panel to develop a national strategy and implementation plan.

Early Years Centres were to be promoted across Wales, with at least one established in each LEA area by September 2002.

5.2 Schools in general

A range of priorities for improving school effectiveness is set out in *The Learning Country* and, where necessary, provided for in the subsequent legislation:

- all secondary and feeder primary schools to form families or consortia to plan for positive transition (s.198 of the Education Act 2002)

- the piloting of a 'unique learner identifier' to assist in managing the transition from compulsory schooling, to allow more efficient access to data and to reduce the bureaucratic burden on teachers

- small primary schools to be enabled to form groups under one leadership team and one governing body

- partnership agreement protocols between LEAs and schools (s. 197 of the 2002 Act)

- schools councils to be established and linked to local authority youth forums

- a national strategy to provide behaviour support, to complement behaviour support plans maintained under existing regulations (SI 1998 No. 644, as amended by SIs 2001 No. 606 (W 29) and 2001 No. 3710 (W 306))

- radical approaches to address the transition at 16+ and to bridge the academic–vocational divide from 14+ initially

- further curriculum flexibility to be pursued through disapplication of the National Curriculum at key stage 4 and possibly key stage 3, following option advice from ACCAC.

5.3 Fourteen to nineteen

Learning Country: Learning Pathways 14–19, published in October 2002 and its subsequent implementation plan make proposals for a continuum of learning 14–19 with structured pathways to meet the needs and abilities of all learners. Working titles for the stages and curricula and qualifications are summarised below.

A Springboard 14–16, which takes in the statutory National Curriculum for Wales, together with an options menu. The learning pathway includes enhanced essential skills and real-life experience, a vocational option for all and more emphasis on community and work-focused learning opportunities. Accreditation is to foundation level 1 or intermediate level 2. Five GCSE grades D-G and GNVQ make up the former, five GCSE Grades A*–C the latter. GCSE is seen as a progress check.

For those attaining foundation level 1, progression is to a National Traineeship comprising GCSE A*–C, GNVQ and NVQ and following the framework of the Welsh Baccalaureate. Achievement at this level gives progression to the Combined Apprenticeship, or to level 3 learning via the General or the Modern Apprenticeship.

For those attaining intermediate level 2, progression is to a Combined Apprenticeship, comprising A-, AS and A-level Vocational Courses. This route is intended to be school- or college-based. Progression is to the General or Modern Apprenticeship.

The General Apprenticeship is seen as school or college based and gives progression to level 3 learning at A, AS or A-Level Vocational.

The Modern Apprenticeship is work-based, with level 3 learning at NVQ.

Central to the underpinning of this 14–19 strategy is the development of a continuum of learning 14–19, with the Welsh Baccalaureate incorporated as an overarching award. The Single Credit Framework is seen as accrediting learner experience from 14+.

Implementation of the strategy is to be planned on an area basis by 14–19 Networks. These are required to liaise with the National Council for Education and Training in Wales (see below) and also the Young People's Partnership and together with the LEA to produce an Area Option Menu. This brings together the structures already created to progress aspects of the post-16 reforms and also 'Extending Entitlement', but with no clear identification of how their overlapping remits are to be reconciled.

The LEA role is explicit: pre-16 funding will continue to be channelled through the LEA, with the LEA and the National Council seen as having partnership arrangements in place to deliver post-16 education and training. The Minister expects to see 'existing funding mechanisms […] harnessed and refined to meet the needs of developing wider and more flexible provision for 14–19 year olds.' (*Learning Pathways*, chapter 7)

5.4   Post-16

The National Council for Education and Training for Wales was established under the Learning and Skills Act 2000 and is the largest

Assembly-sponsored public body. It has adopted the brand name ELWa (short for 'Education and Learning Wales'). Its functions were first set out in The National Council for Education and Training for Wales (Interim Functions) Order 2000 (SI 2000 No. 2539 (W 162)). From 1 April 2001, ELWa took over the majority of the functions of the four Training and Enterprise Councils in Wales and also the Further Education Funding Council for Wales. Its responsibilities are for funding, planning and promoting further education, private and voluntary-sector training provision, adult continuing education and, from April 2002, sixth-form funding.

The Council has no powers to fund schools directly and its allocation to support school sixth forms is channelled through and administered by LEAs in accordance with their funding schemes.

The National Council has four regional committees which act as links with local organisations involved in learning and skills development. They advise the National Council on matters related to education and training in their areas and provide regional knowledge through regional statements of needs and priorities.

Twenty-one community consortia for education and training have been established throughout Wales. They comprise learning providers from LEA, schools and colleges, private training organisations and the voluntary sector. Their prime function is to produce for each consortium area a learning plan which meets current and future skills needs, creates opportunities for widening participation, eliminates duplication and unnecessary competition and ensures optimum use of resources. Patterns of membership vary across Wales, but LEAs and colleges have been the driving forces in the majority of community consortia to date.

The regional statement of needs and priorities is subject to consultation with the community consortia as it informs their activities. Similarly, the regional committee advises ELWa on the recommendations of the consortia.

All resource allocation decisions remain the responsibility of ELWa. The development by ELWa of its planning and funding system is intended to achieve flexible funding arrangements which encourage access to learning and which have the potential to shape learning provision to satisfy the entitlement required by the learner and expected of the provider network. The model is intended to be demand-led and learner-focused, with funding following strategy. The basis for funding is related to the achievement within the single credit framework described above.

At the heart of the planning and funding framework is the notion of a learning network which can offer a defined learning entitlement. The network may be locality-based or designed on specialism. It may or may not be coterminous with the 21 community consortia areas and, if it is not, it will require some joint working between them if it is to be viable. A further complication is the creation, in the *Learning Pathways* implementation plan, of the 14-19 consortia. There is currently an absence of joined-up planning which risks introducing the very duplication which ETAP set out to avoid and jeopardises the move towards a seamless planning, organisational and delivery base for all post-14 education and training.

5.5. Special education

Special Education has its own Code of Practice in Wales, with associated regulations (The Education (Special Educational Needs) (Wales) Regulations 2002 (SI 2002 No. 152 (W 20)) and separate regulations requiring provision of information by LEAs (SI 2002 No. 157 (W 23)). Particular emphasis is of course laid on the importance of bilingual services. The provisions are further strengthened by the Special Education Needs and Disability Act 2001 and by the proposals contained in *The Learning Country*, a number of which were covered by the Education Act 2002.

Provisions include:

- support for the LEA and schools to renew policies and procedures, using specific funding through GEST

- a strategic approach to reduce service fragmentation for low-incidence and high-dependency disability groups

- LEAs to be enabled to provide regional resources for children with complex needs and difficulties (ss. 191, 192 of the Education Act 2002,)

- common guidelines to amplify the current code of practice to eliminate assessment variations between authorities

- a separate tribunal for SEN and educational disability rights for Wales (s. 195 of the Education Act 2002).

6. Student support

The introduction in Wales in July 2002 (through the Education (Assembly Learning Grant Scheme) (Wales) Regulations 2002 (SI

2002 No. 1857 (W 181)), as amended) of support to tackle student hardship followed consideration by the Assembly of the 54 recommendations contained in the report of an independent investigation group on student hardship and funding in Wales chaired by Professor Teresa Rees. The Assembly learning grant provides means-tested additional income to Welsh-domiciled students, wherever they choose to study, in HE and first-time students in FE from September 2002. This funding complements the contingency funds to be made available to institutions of HE and FE to ensure that a level of discretionary funding remains available to support students from outside Wales.

LEAs were made responsible for administering the grants and a proportion of the funding made available by the Assembly was allocated to meeting LEA costs. The Local Education Authority (Post-Compulsory Education Awards) (Wales) Regulations 2002 (SI 2002 No. 1856 (W 180)) deal with LEA responsibility for administering the Assembly Learning Grant and redefine as a consequence LEA powers to grant awards.

7.   Inspection

Responsibilities for inspection in Wales are the province of Estyn, which carries out inspections of LEAs together with the Audit Commission under the Best Value regime initially and the Wales Programme for Improvement subsequently (see the Inspection of Education and Training (Wales) Regulations 2001 (SI 2001 No. 2501 (W 204)). There is a separate Code of Practice for LEAs in Wales and a separate inspection framework.

While Estyn (Her Majesty's Inspectorate of Education and Training in Wales) has the power to carry out full LEA inspections, practice up to the end of 2003 has been to inspect thematic areas such as numeracy or literacy and to produce a report for each LEA to contribute to its Best Value and Wales Programme of Improvement Plan corporately. Such inspections and reports are on an annual basis.

The Learning Country proposed to extend Estyn's remit to include area inspections of 14–16 provision (s. 51), aimed at assessing the coherence of pre- and post-16 learning in Wales. Regulations to bring the proposal into effect came into force on 1 August 2001 (SI 2001 No. 2501).

8. General

8.1 Welsh

Provision of Welsh first and second language and of the Cwricwlwm Cymreig is statutory within the National Curriculum for Wales and bilingualism is one of the cross-cutting themes which underpins ELWa's corporate strategy for 16+. It is one of the six current 'desirable outcomes' for early-years learning.

Responsibility for the planning and provision of school places rests with LEAs, each of whom is required to produce a Welsh Education Scheme, approved by the Welsh Language Board, which sets out a strategy for developing Welsh medium education. This scheme informs the School Organisation Plan, which the LEA must update annually and which sets out its plans for providing places in all schools, including Welsh-medium. The Education (School Organisation Plans) (Wales) Regulations 2003 (SI 2003 No. 1732 (W 190)) sets out the current regulations for planning for school places. Circular 23/02 sets out requirements relating to proposals by ELWa.

Proposals for strengthening the position of Welsh-medium education are set out in *The Learning Country* and include:

- analysis of LEAs' asset management plans to identify relative condition of Welsh-medium schools

- examination of the effectiveness of approaches to immersion language learning, particularly at ages 5–7 and 11

- support for the network of Welsh-medium NVQ practitioners

- research into the sustainable balance between supply and demand for Welsh-medium provision.

8.2 ICT

The Assembly's strategic framework Cymru Ar-lein was published in July 2001. Two specific sets of investment have created access points in all public libraries, the digitising of learning materials and associated training programmes for teachers and librarians; as well as hardware and software investment into schools, further and higher education institutions and lifelong-learning access points.

The e-learning proposals in *The Learning Country* include:

- meeting the National Grid for Learning target to have all schools on line by 2002, with further investment in hardware

- establishment of ICT learning centres in schools and community settings

- development of bilingual resources.

F. Signposts to the Future?

The Welsh Local Government Association (WLGA), in its publication *The Future Role of Local Authorities in Education in Wales* (October 2002), sets out a vision for the role of the LEA in Wales and concludes that it remains 'the agency and the influence which bind the disparate pieces together and the support which allows partners to work effectively.'

There is no doubt that many of the strategies and initiatives introduced by the National Assembly in its first term have depended upon the LEAs for their local delivery and in some cases for their co-ordination and development. Local authorities figured prominently in the first ministerial statements and remain central in Assembly Government thinking as it set out its agenda to 2010:

> 'We shall maintain the constitutional capacity of local authorities to reach balanced judgments about investment suited to their circumstances and which they are best placed to justify.'
>
> *(The Learning Country*, para 34)

> 'The commitment to enable schools to build on their strengths and overcome their weaknesses is of long standing in Wales. In large measure, this finds expression in the close partnership arrangements that exist with local education authorities [...]'
>
> *(The Learning Country*, para 29)

It is not, however, a return to a centralist or monopoly view. All the Assembly's initiatives lay store on the involvement of young people as equal partners in the services that are being designed for them. The learning agenda demands flexibility in design, access and delivery. It requires work with partners as equals and nowhere will this be tested more keenly than in the priorities and the decision-making processes within the unitary councils themselves if they are to fulfil WLGA's expectations.

Equally testing will be the relationships that the Assembly expects to be developed and strengthened between schools and the LEA as the power to require partnership agreements set out in s. 197 of the Education Act 2002 is exercised.

That Wales is intent upon pursuing its own route to excellence as a learning country is clear from developments from 1999 and intentions to 2010. The challenge for the LEA and its education professionals is to reflect strategically at a local level the coherent agenda which has emerged as the Assembly's intent. This is not a passive and servicing role: it demands – in the Children and Youth Partnership, in the development of 'learning pathways' and in the design and delivery of the post-16 agenda – a clear vision of the fit with overall community planning and the ability to exercise a lead role with other key partners in articulating and facilitating the delivery of that vision.

The population of Wales accounts for just under five per cent of the UK total and just over five per cent of that of England and Wales. Whereas a small potential readership deters textbook publishers from devoting much, if any, of their lists to educational administrative law and practice in Wales alone, the very differences of principle, practice and terminology demand wide study of the effects of devolution. Furthermore, this chapter has shown that the Assembly has been quick to innovate in education and reform in Wales may lead to reform in England. Administration in Wales presently looks more joined-up, to use the terminology in vogue, than that in England, both within LEAs and between them and the central authority. For the future, the possibilities are a matter of speculation, but constitute only one reason why the reader in England should keep an eye on what seem at first to be peculiarly Welsh developments. Also to be weighed up are the implications of devolution for the mobility of learner and teacher (and civil servant and local government officer) across Offa's Dyke; the schooling of children of families moving into and out of Wales and the cross-border differences and issues affecting the work of especially those lawyers who specialise in education.

3. THE STRUCTURE OF EDUCATION:
A Brief Introduction to Education Organisations and Providers

A. Introduction

Such is the diversity and near-universality of the public education service that the yearbooks are full of statutory, chartered, voluntary, campaigning, researching, representative, collectively-supportive, more or less charitable, learned, not-for-profit or increasingly profitable, religious or otherwise, bodies – all deeply involved in the myriad processes of education. This chapter provides a selective guide to many of those with which LEAs are frequently and unavoidably engaged, with particular reference to the statutory or statutorily recognised. The focus is on bodies within, or doing regular business with, the LEA and does not attempt a guide to the whole of quangoland.

Wherever possible, cross-reference is made to more detailed discussion elsewhere in the book, of bodies' interaction within or with LEAs. In the notes that follow, historical and other explanations of policy reasons for recent statutory changes are included.

The outline (in part B) begins with the Secretary of State because the traditional description of the public education service places the holder of that office at the apex of a pyramidal structure. Part C ('Guidance from Above') deals with the complex matter of Ministerial guidance and direction. That part of the chapter is mostly concerned with England; things are done differently in Wales, as chapter 2 has shown.

In part B, the differences between structures and entities in England and in Wales are noted wherever relevant and wherever – through timing of the making of statutory instruments – possible.

B. The Leading Players

1. Secretary of State

Section 1(1) of the Education Act 1944 (the whole statute now repealed, replaced and vastly expanded-upon) set out a simple hierarchical relationship, in words which were, however, a novel formulation, markedly different from those of earlier Education Acts:

> 'It shall be lawful for His Majesty to appoint a Minister [...] whose duty it shall be to promote the education of the people of England and Wales and the progressive development of institutions devoted to that purpose and to secure the effective execution by local authorities, under his control and direction, of the national policy for providing a varied and comprehensive educational service in every area.'

Despite their lapidary and reformist tone, the words were more aspirational than literal even when enacted: for example, the Act made only a few references to such non-LEA providers of the people's education as universities, independent schools, voluntary bodies, or specialist and industrial training establishments.

Half a century later, education had become much more complex, with, in particular, the burgeoning of quangos and diversification of colleges of further and higher education. LEAs had suffered loss of ownership and responsibility, with the departure of most of their HE under the Education Reform Act 1988 and nearly all their FE under the Further and Higher Education Act 1992. Legislation in the 1980s and early 1990s had the effect of strengthening schools, through powers to administer their budgets (see chapter 6.D) and to take over many of the employer-functions of their LEAs (chapter 6.E). Though the two parts of chapter 6 cited here demonstrate that considerable responsibilities fall upon LEAs within the overall duty to 'maintain' their maintained schools and LEAs have acquired, since 1981, progressively more detailed functions in respect of children with SEN, they have undeniably lost some education territory.

Over the years, both the Secretary of State and LEAs have faced challenge through development of judicial review (see chapter 12.D.3.2), which can be seen as detracting from the simple and authoritarian relationship implied in the 1944 Act. At the same time, quangos and other agencies have appeared on the scene, created by statute and with executive functions. By the time of the Education Act 1993, the euphuistic terms of the Secretary of State's role had been toned down to: 'The Secretary of State shall promote the education of the people of England and Wales'. That provision was subsequently repeated in the codifying statute (s. 10 of the Education Act 1996). The Secretary of State is thus deuteragonist in this book.

The 1944 Act translated the President of the Board of Education into the Minister of Education and the department was known as the Ministry of Education until 1964, when it became the Department for Education and Science (DES), its principal Minister having the title of Secretary of State.

This is an ancient title, but its modern usage simply denotes the head of a team of Ministers of State and Parliamentary Under Secretaries of State. Acts of Parliament normally do not explicitly add the departmental name, such as 'for Health' or 'for Wales' to references to a Secretary of State, the constitutional theory being that the basic title is generic and the functions are interchangeable; in practice, it is clear which Secretary of State takes action in each area.

In 1992, the designations of Secretary of State and his department changed to 'for Education' (hence DfE) and abolition of another department of state (the Department for Employment) in 1995 brought further change, to 'for Education and Employment' (and so DfEE). In 2001, designations changed again, to 'Education and Skills', hence DfES.

As this book explains *passim*, the Secretary of State discharges a range of duties and exercises perhaps a wider one of powers, affecting the functions of LEAs. His department's close interest in how those functions are carried out is explained in chapter 1.E.6 above. In broad political terms, old controversies about the extent of 'central interference' and its impingement on local discretion have been overtaken by accusations of 'micromanagement' (hence the heading to the section cited) and the fact of Governmental control (through Parliament) of the detail of the school curriculum: see chapter 4.A.

2. LEA

Local government has undergone several restructurings since the 1944 Act designated the then 145 county and county borough councils in England and Wales as LEAs (s. 6(1)). In England, the essential pattern today is that of the Local Government Act 1972, with subsequent restructuring. The present numbers of LEAs in each category are given in square brackets.

- Where there is a county council, that is the LEA. [34, the restructuring process (see below) having abolished the county councils of Avon, Berkshire, Cleveland and Humberside and having split the (1972) County of Hereford and Worcester, the latter reverting to county-council status].

- In London, the councils of the outer boroughs have been LEAs since 1965, under the London Government Act 1963 and those of the inner London boroughs plus the Common Council of the City of London became LEAs in 1990 (under the Education Reform Act 1988, which abolished the Inner London Education Authority) [33].

- In the areas of the six metropolitan counties (Tyne & Wear, South and West Yorkshire, Merseyside, Greater Manchester and West Midlands, the county councils for them now all abolished) each metropolitan district council is an LEA; a little confusingly, some MDCs have the honorifics 'city' or 'borough', but there is no difference of substance that affects education [36].

- Selective restructuring was carried out throughout the 1990s under the Local Government Act 1992. A commission reviewed all England outside the metropolitan counties and London. It considered evidence and argument for retaining the status quo: upper-tier 'shire' county council, with education, social services and strategic planning among its functions; whole county area also made up of (lower-tier) districts, whose councils' main responsibilities cover housing, environmental health and local planning control. The alternative was to adopt a 'unitary' system in all or part(s) of the area of the former shire, with DCs exercising all the functions of principal councils, on the MDC model. Ministers considered the commission's recommendations and many unitary authorities were established by statutory instrument, in a three-year programme. Again, the councils' names are differently styled: a particular unitary authority may be called a district, a borough, or a city, council, or even '[X] Council' [46].

- The Council of the Isles of Scilly continued to be an LEA [1].

The present total of LEAs in England is 150.

In Wales, the Local Government (Wales) Act 1994 replaced the eight county councils, which had been operational from 1974, all of them being LEAs, social services authorities and strategic-planning authorities, together with 37 shire district councils. Eleven county and eleven county borough councils were created, all unitary authorities with education and the other functions of principal authorities [22].

This change came into effect in April 1996. See chapter 2 for the detail and implications.

During the 1990s' restructurings, the Isle of Wight remained an LEA but became unitary (i.e the district-council tier was abolished) and the Isle of Anglesey (Ynys Môn) became a Welsh county LEA. The Isle of Man and the Channel Islands lie outwith the local administrations of England and Wales.

One criticism of the 1990s' changes and especially of the painstaking review process in England, was that there ought first to have been a national review of what local government is for (hence, in part, the title of this book). Instead, education – to take the example of local government's biggest single service – was the subject of primary legislation, much of it making fundamental changes, in 1992 (two Acts), 1993 (one substantial Act), 1994, 1996 (four Acts, including two Consolidating Acts), 1997 (two Acts, of which one enacted the scaled-down Bill of the outgoing Government) and 1998 (three Acts, of which two were major). On the other hand, constant legislative change in education, social services, criminal justice and procedure, seems to be part of the public perception of what national government is for and we may have lost forever the periods of relative legislative quietude of the 1950s and two subsequent decades. It may have been inevitable, therefore, that authorities were reviewed and some were restructured without proper examination of their functions and roles, either as they were at the time or as they might develop within a sensible planning period.

Elsewhere in this book, you will find discussion of the major Acts on education; among the most recent, the Learning and Skills Act 2000 underlies the whole of chapter 11 and the Special Educational Needs and Disability Act 2001 the whole of chapter 8. A novel and special feature of education legislation is now that the Government intends to do less by primary but more by subordinate legislation (regulations and orders); some particular consequences of this policy, enshrined in the Education Act 2002, for LEAs are discussed in chapters 1.E, 3.C, 5.A, 6.B, 6.D, 6.E and 7.C.

For discussion of the relationship between 'LEA' and local authority, see chapter 1.C. 2 and 3 and part D of that chapter.

3. Chief education officer

Each LEA is required to appoint a 'fit person' as its chief education officer (s. 532 of the Education Act 1996). That section consolidated the remains of s. 88 of the 1944 Act, which, before it was amended by the Local Government Act 1972, had also provided that the Secretary of State be consulted before any such appointment was made. Specifically, the LEA had to furnish details of the names, previous experience and qualifications of everyone on the shortlist. Beattie and Taylor (1944:225) quote the Ministerial reasoning for such a prescription, namely, objection to: '[...] a good many cases where a person who has been an ordinary clerk in the town clerk's office has been appointed chief education officer of the borough, without any experience that enables him to give the local education committee sound advice [...].'

Section 88 was new to the law of education, though Beattie and Taylor point out that there were already statutory requirements elsewhere upon appropriate authorities to appoint medical officers of health, highway engineers, or chief constables.

From time to time, there has been controversy in particular LEAs over the precise job description of, and particularly the strategic management exercisable by, the CEO. Just because an officer is designated as CEO, it has been argued, that does not mean that he or she is head of education: the particular authority might wish to have, above the CEO, a head of education and social services, or of education, culture and leisure – or whatever. See also chapter 6.E.2.

This is an area where Parliament and the law have tended not to get involved: the legislation specifies what an authority must or may do, but is often reticent about how and even more so about by whom. Earlier requirements to permit attendance by the CEO or representative at particular meetings of school governing bodies making senior appointments have been changed to the formulary in (e.g.) reg 12 of the School Staffing Regulations (England) Regulations 2003 (SI 2003 No. 1963), ascribing the right to a representative of the LEA. But when the CEO was specified in this context, the rumour was that Ministers had wanted the officer, simply to avoid a situation in which the LEA might be represented by an elected member. If that story is true, it means that present Ministers may be less inclined to see councillors as bogeypeople.

The term 'CEO' appears to imply a leading management role, but arguably there is no reason why an LEA should not appoint to a more senior position someone with the title 'senior chief education officer', by analogy with the cumbersome title of 'Senior Chief Inspector' given to the head of Her Majesty's Inspectorate before the 1992 changes (see below).

Statutory provisions on the office of CEO are to be changed once the Children Bill (2004) is enacted. It proposes repeal of s. 532 for England and provides for every principal authority in England to appoint (though there will be no requirement to do so until the Secretary of State makes an order) a director of children's services as leading officer for education and social services functions relating to children. The authority would no longer be required (under s. 6 of the Local Authority Social Services Act 1970) to appoint a director of social services, but it would have to have a director of adult social services to cover functions other than those in the prospective Children Act 2004.

The director of children's services would not necessarily be responsible for the LEA's adult education or student support, but he could be.

Section 532 would remain for Wales, but each children's services authority (LEA/social services authority) will be required to appoint a 'lead officer for children and young people's services', who could be the chief education officer, chief executive or someone else.

It is a matter for speculation how long the permissive arrangements will obtain in England. Total change could be brought about either by an order made under the forthcoming Act, or simply through pressure of new-style appointments made by the majority of authorities as time goes on. Certainly the internal character of the education department will have altered considerably from, say, the mid-1980s, when LEAs were responsible for higher education outside the universities, further and adult education, the youth service, schools and nursery education, student awards and (collectively) for the negotiation of teachers' conditions of service across England and Wales. The ethos was undeniably educational. In future, there will be problems of combining a duty to promote excellence in schooling with the raft of duties in respect of child welfare. Whether the new culture is better or worse is for judgment later. Certainly, it will be different.

See also chapter 5 and *Every Child Matters* (2003), (especially paras 5.8 and 5.9) and chapter 1.E.3 of this book.

4. Education committee

LEAs are no longer required to appoint education committees and indeed, an executive committee for education has no place in the new ways of conducting business envisaged in the Local Government Act 2000 (see chapter 1.E.2, above). But, where an LEA has a committee wholly or partly concerned with the discharge of education functions – an education scrutiny committee, for example – section 499 of the Education Act 1996 as amended requires appointment as voting members representatives of those who appoint foundation governors and of parent governors.

This has tended to mean that the typical LEA channels all 'education' business through a single scrutiny committee, to avoid proliferation of non-councillor committee members (another perceived category of bogeyperson – see above). Some commentators have seen this as frustrating the aims of making council business more 'joined-up' and scrutiny 'cross-cutting'.

See also chapter 12.B.6.

5. Standing advisory council on religious education (SACRE)

Creatures of the Education Reform Act 1988, SACREs (pronounced to assonate with 'padres') had resulted from an outburst of Parliamentary religiosity over some very modest proposals by Ministers of the day to make the law on worship in maintained schools a little more flexible. An informative and entertaining, but not unsympathetic, account of the debates and their background is given by John McLeod (1990).

Every LEA is required to have a SACRE (s. 390 of the Education Act 1996). A SACRE is made up of groups appointed by the LEA to represent:

- Christian denominations and other religions or denominations of religions which reflect the traditions in the LEA's area

- the Church of England

- teacher associations

- the LEA.

There being no established church in Wales, the second element is not applicable in Wales.

The function of the SACRE is to advise the LEA on such matters as the LEA refers to it connected with: (a) religious worship in community and foundation schools which do not have a religious character and (b) the religious education to be given in accordance with an agreed or other syllabus (s. 391). In addition, the SACRE can determine requests from headteachers of the schools in (a) above that the requirement of a daily act of Christian collective worship should not apply in their schools (s. 394).

For more detail, see chapter 4.D.

6.   School organisation committee and the Adjudicator

6.1   School Organisation Committee (SOC) (at present, England only)

Every LEA in England is required to set up a SOC (s. 24 of the School Standards and Framework Act 1998). Procedural rules are set out in sched 4 to the Act and they and requirements as to membership are greatly expanded in the Education (School Organisation Committees) (England) Regulations 1999 (SI 1999 No. 700). Membership of the SOC must include representatives of the LEA, Church of England, the Roman Catholic Church, the learning and skills council, governors of schools and such community representatives as the LEA determines. No category may be larger than seven persons.

The functions of a SOC are described in chapter 6.C, but its main tasks, in outline, are to approve the LEA's school organisation plan and to consider proposals for establishment, alteration or discontinuance of maintained schools.

6.2   Adjudicator (England)

Ministers intended that the creation of SOCs in the 1998 Act would remove from the service a historical pattern in which such proposals affecting individual schools were usually referred to the Secretary of

State for determination, with consequently inevitable delays. As referee in instances of disagreement within the SOC, s. 25 of the 1998 Act provides for the adjudicator; detailed conditions as to the appointment and functions of the adjudicator(s) are set out in schedules 5 and 6 to the Act.

The Office of the Schools Adjudicator (OSA) also acts as resolver of disputes on school admissions policies. This role presently represents the larger part of OSA's business.

See chapters 7.A and 12.B.3.

6.3   Wales

Section 27 of the 1998 Act empowers the National Assembly to establish SOCs and the office of adjudicator by regulations, with such modifications to the statutory conditions (as applying in England) as it may think fit. So far, the Assembly has introduced neither body into the system and so it discharges the appropriate functions itself.

7.   Admissions forum

By s. 46 of the Education Act 2002, a new s. 85A was inserted into the School Standards and Framework Act 1998 making it mandatory for every LEA to establish an admissions forum to advise it and other admission authorities (i.e. governing bodies as appropriate) on admission arrangements for all maintained schools. Previously, establishment of such a forum had been discretionary, though the subject of strong positive guidance in a former code of practice on admissions.

Details of a forum's role (not 'functions'), membership and procedures are given in the Education (Admission Forums) (England) Regulations 2002 (SI 2002/2900), which also provide for two or more LEAs to discharge the duty through joint forums.

Regulations for Wales came into force on 1 December 2003 (SI 2003 No. 2962 (W 279)). As in England, provision is made for LEAs to adopt joint arrangements.

On admissions, see chapter 7.A. On the 'admissions' function of the adjudicator, see section 6.2, above.

8. Schools forums

Section 43 of the Education Act 2002 imported a new s. 47A into the School Standards and Framework Act 1998, requiring every LEA (except the City of London and the Isles of Scilly) to establish a schools forum. Its purpose is to advise the LEA 'on such matters relating to the authority's Schools Budget' as may be prescribed by regulation. For England, the regulations are the Schools Forums (England) Regulations 2002 (SI 2002 No. 2114), which required establishment of forums by 15 January 2003. The regulations also prescribe membership (minimum 15, mostly representatives of the categories of schools maintained by the LEA, but allowing for not more than one-third of the membership to be from diocesan bodies or people otherwise deemed appropriate (regs 4, 5).

3.
THE STRUCTURE
OF EDUCATION

Subjects for consultation are listed as the school funding formula, contracts and other practical financial matters (regs 7–10).

The purpose of the innovation is to increase transparency in the apportionment of resources to schools and to give the latter a guaranteed forum in which to express their concerns on a perennially contentious area of schools administration.

For Wales, regulations came into force on 13 November 2003 (SI 2003 No. 2909 (W 275)), requiring establishment of forums by 15 December 2003.

See chapter 6.D on financing maintained schools.

9. Education Action Zones (EAZs) and Education Action Forums (EAFs)

Originally intended to be innovative partnerships of schools, business and local communities around schools facing 'challenging circumstances', 'in areas of educational underperformance', EAZs and their management forums were creatures of the new Government's first major Education Act, the School Standards and Framework Act 1998 (chapter III of part I of the Act, as now amended by the Education Act 2002). They were intended to 'encourage innovative approaches to tackling disadvantage and raising standards'. [The phrases above in quotation marks are from DfEE's *Education Action Zones: An introduction* (1997)]. Special, nursery and independent schools and pupil referral units are eligible for EAZ membership.

Each EAZ was set up by order made by the Secretary of State and the order specified the membership of the EAF. Proposals were intended to draw in contributions from business and industry (public administration was not excluded) and Government grant has been payable to each EAZ. See chapter 5.A.9, which alludes to evidence of difficulties in raising – even in kind rather than cash – the business contribution and to general disappointment that the EAZ has not proved to be, as Ministers repeatedly claimed during passage of the Bill, a 'test bed' for the education system in the next century. Some of the thinking behind the EAZ has, however, been re-stated in the 'powers to facilitate innovation' in part 1 of the 2002 Act.

There are no EAZs in Wales.

10. Categories of maintained schools

The School Standards and Framework Act 1998 revised, with effect from 1 September 1999, the basic framework of schools established by the settlement enshrined in the Education Act 1944 (and significantly added to only by the creation of grant-maintained (GM) schools under the Education Reform Act 1988). The new categorisation of maintained schools comprises:

- community schools (formerly county schools)
- foundation schools (formerly GM schools)
- voluntary controlled schools (no change)
- voluntary aided schools (formerly voluntary aided, special agreement, or GM schools which had been aided before they became GM)
- community special schools (formerly [maintained] special schools
- foundation special schools (formerly GM special schools).

With the exception of GM schools, which were able to choose their new category, all other schools were assigned to categories according to their existing status. There was then a one-year moratorium on change of status, proposals for which are subject to the formal procedures for change of character (on which, see 'school organisation committee' and 'adjudicator', above and chapter 6.C.8).

11. Schools

11.1 Schools proper

Schools are defined by the Education Act 1996 as educational institutions which are outside the FE and HE sectors and which provide either primary or secondary education, or both (s. 4). Maintained schools are maintained by LEAs [the banality of this statement is a reflection of the period between enactment of provisions in the Education Act 1993 and their repeal, when GM schools were statutorily not 'maintained schools'].

Independent schools are those which are not maintained but are also not 'non-maintained special schools' (s. 463 of the 1996 Act). A 'non-maintained special school' is a category of school specially organised to make provision for children with SEN (s. 342 of the Education Act 1996).

City technology colleges and Academies (the reverential initial capital is statutory) are independent schools because the law says they are: respectively, ss. 68(3) and 69 of the Education Act 2002 and s. 65 of that Act, inserting a new s. 482(1)(a) into the Education Act 1996. They are substantially funded directly by DfES, but are not 'maintained' (on maintenance in this context, see chapter 6).

11.2 Pupil referral units

Provisions relating to statutory bodies to be called pupil referral units (PRUs) were introduced into the Education Bill at Lords Committee stage of what became the Education Act 1993. The Government's proposals followed consultation on a departmental paper of November 1992 on exclusions from school and publication of figures showing a rise in already large numbers of excludees. The new specific duty placed upon LEAs was to make arrangements for full- or part-time education of children out of schooling 'by reason of illness, exclusion from school or otherwise'. This formulation, which was duly included in the consolidation at s. 19 of the Education Act 1996, has been strongly criticised only for the regrettable concatenation of children out of school for no fault of their own with excludees. Section 19 states that a PRU is a school and, on the recommendation of the Law Commission, the matter was put beyond doubt by insertion of subs. (2) into s. 4 of the Act. A PRU is not, however, a 'maintained school'.

Section 48 of the Education Act 1997 provided for management committees for PRUs.

See chapter 9.F on education otherwise than at school.

12. Governing body

By s. 19 of the Education Act 2002, every maintained school is to have a governing body: 'a body corporate constituted in accordance with regulations' (subs. (1)).

That requirement also applies to a maintained nursery school (s. 39(1)). See chapter 6.B on school government.

13. Headteacher

The main duties of headship are set out in part IX of *The School Teachers' Pay and Conditions Document*, but that is not exhaustive. An array of duties and responsibilities could be drawn up from that and from statutory requirements relating to the head of a school.

Under ss. 35(3) and 36(3) of the Education Act 2002, every maintained school and every maintained nursery school must have 'a person appointed as headteacher'.

Something of a stir was caused in December 2003, when a DfES paper entitled *Workforce Reform – Blue Skies* was leaked to the press. It looked to the period after 2006 and noted that, following 'deregulation' in the 2002 Act, a school is obliged to appoint only a headteacher to its staff: other functions could be performed by agency or seconded teachers, or by classroom assistants, the former being required by regulation where supervision of a class was involved, but the latter able to organise individual learning, e.g. through electronic communication. In response to the predictable outrage of teacher unions, Ministers distanced themselves from the views in the paper, which they alleged to be the work of a junior civil servant. (See: William Steward: 'Schools without teachers' and 'Storm out of blue skies', *TES*, 5 December 2003:1,6; and Richard Garner: 'Schools will need only a headteacher and classroom assistants, say civil servants', *The Independent* 6 December 2003.)

14. Her Majesty's Chief Inspectors

HM Inspectors of Schools have a distinguished history, antedating not only LEAs (Education Act 1902) but also the Board of Education (Board of Education Act 1899). The first HMI were appointed in 1839 as servants of the Education Committee of the Privy Council and HMI are still appointed by the Queen in Council, every appointment being promulgated in a statutory instrument in the form of an order over the signature of the Clerk of the Privy Council. This formality is widely held to be a guarantee of the inspectorate's independence, which was arguably strengthened by s. 1 (for England; s. 5 for Wales) of the Education (Schools) Act 1992, now re-enacted and replaced by the Schools Inspection Act 1996 (ss. 1 and 4, respectively).

The 1992 Act designated the heads of the service in England and Wales as HM Chief Inspectors of Schools and recognised their offices as non-ministerial departments of state. The former head of the service (styled HM Senior Chief Inspector, to whom seven chief inspectors reported) had been based at the DES, but the new department, formally the Office of HM Chief Inspector but already fashionably styled Ofsted (Office for Standards in Education), moved to separate premises.

HMCI for Wales was given a new appellation by s. 73 of the Learning and Skills Act 2000: HM Chief Inspector of Education and Training in Wales or Prif Arolygydd Ei Mawrhydi dros Addysg a Hyfforddiant yng Nghymru (the title appears in both languages in amended s.4 of the School Inspections Act 1996). The expanded title takes account of the wider responsibilities of HMCI in Wales.

The 2000 Act extended the remit of HMCI in England into some FE and adult training, including teacher training, but also created (chapter 1 of part III of that Act) the Adult Learning Inspectorate, a non-departmental corporate body, to inspect industrial training for 16+ and FE for 19+ within the scope of the Learning and Skills Council.

Both HMCIs are empowered to appoint additional inspectors, registered inspectors (who are not HMI) and other staff (s. 7 of and schedule 1 to the 1996 Act).

The schools functions of HMCI are to arrange and have oversight of inspections and to keep the Secretary of State or National Assembly informed about:

- the quality of education provided by and the standards achieved in, schools

- whether the financial resources of schools are managed efficiently

- the spiritual, moral, social and cultural development of pupils

- matters connected with schools on which HMCI advises the Secretary of State or Assembly. (ss. 2, 5)

HMCI may arrange inspections of one or more LEAs at his or her discretion or as requested by Secretary of State or National Assembly (s. 38 of the Education Act 1997).

See chapter 12.B.2 and 'Audit Commission', below.

15. Audit Commission

The Audit Commission for Local Authorities and the National Health Service in England and Wales was set up under s. 11 of the Local Government Finance Act 1982, but its functions are now more fully set out in the Audit Commission Act 1998. It is responsible for appointing each authority's external auditors; it monitors performance against published criteria and is the custodian, as it were, of Best Value (see chapter 12.B.7) and it carries out studies to enable it to issue guidance on economy, efficiency and effectiveness in services. Specifically in education, it may, at the request of HMCI, assist (under s. 38 of the Education Act 1997) in the inspection of an LEA or LEAs under s. 41 of that Act (see chapter 12.B.2).

16. Commissioners for Local Administration

John Ayto's *Twentieth Century Words* (1999) logs 1959 as the first occurrence of the Swedish word ombudsman ('commission man') in English. He explains that the *justitieombudsmannen* had a remit to guard against abuse of state power. New Zealand adopted the idea in 1962 and the UK in 1967, in the Parliamentary Ombudsman. The Commissioners for Local Administration, for England and for Wales, were established under the Local Government Act 1974.

See chapter 12.B.4.

17. Learning and Skills: the 'Councils'

17.1 Learning and Skills Council (LSC)

Created by the Learning and Skills Act 2000 (s. 1), the LSC for
England is charged with securing 'proper' facilities for education
and training of 16–19 year-olds (s. 2) and 'reasonable' facilities for
people over 19 (s. 3). The Act abolished former arrangements for
which the principal agencies had been the Training and Enterprise
Councils and the Further Education Funding Council for England
(the latter quango created by the Further and Higher Education Act
1992 to plan and fund most FE). The LSC accordingly took over the
FE function, but it also acquired from LEAs the funding powers for
school sixth forms (s. 7). The LSC is under a duty to set up local
learning and skills councils (s. 19, the lower-case initials appearing
in the statute, but the abbreviated form in common usage being
'local LSCs'); the Government initially established 47 such local
bodies.

See chapter 11, especially part A.

17.2 National Council for Education and Training for Wales

The 2000 Act established for Wales the National Council for
Education and Training for Wales or Cyngor Cenedlaethol Cymru
dros Addysg a Hyfforddiant (the title appears in both languages in s.
30). Its functions parallel those of the LSC, except that the Wales
body has no duty to set up local bodies, but may establish regional
and other committees. Originally known as CETW, the council
adopted the demotic 'ELWa' (Education and Learning Wales). It
took over the statutory FE functions from the FE Funding Council
for Wales (which was abolished).

See chapters 2 and 11.A.

18. General Teaching Councils (GTCs)

Ever since the foundation of the College of Preceptors in 1846 and
its gaining a royal charter three years later, there have been
pressures to establish for schoolteachers a professional and
registration body comparable to the General Medical Council or the
Law Society. The Board of Education Act 1899 empowered the
Board to set up a register of teachers and a council to administer it.
Attempts to construct a register foundered through administrative
and political difficulties and the project was abandoned in 1906. The
Administrative Provisions Act 1907 provided for a teachers'
registration council, eventually set up by the Privy Council in 1912.

In 1929, it became the Royal Society of Teachers, but was wound up in 1949, no provision for compulsory registration having been made in the Education Act 1944. Although a statutory General Teaching Council for Scotland was created in 1965 and an official report of 1970 recommended something similar for England and Wales, that too foundered through disunity among the teachers' unions and other bodies. In the 1980s, agreement was reached among thirty or so representative bodies, which formed a pressure group to lobby for legislation. That eventually came about, in the Teaching and Higher Education Act 1998, which provided for GTCs for England (s. 1) and for Wales (s. 8).

Operational from 1 September 2000, the GTCs are required (s. 2) to advise the Secretary of State or National Assembly (or other parties) on standards of teaching and teachers' conduct, the role of the teaching profession, training, career development and performance management, recruitment and medical fitness to teach. Teacher supply and retention and the standing of the profession were added by para 2 of sched 12 to the Education Act 2002. The GTCs must establish and maintain registers of teachers eligible for registration; may decline to register a person and may exercise disciplinary powers, including that of deletion from the register.

LEAs, along with other employers of registered teachers, are required by reg 29 of the General Teaching Council for England (Disciplinary Functions) Regulations 2001 (SI 2001 No. 1268) (reg 28 of the parallel regulations for the Wales GTC) to report to the GTC the details of any teacher dismissed by reason of professional incompetence or having resigned to avoid such dismissal. In a long article on the work of the England GTC to date, John Crace (*Education Guardian*, 2 December 2003) noted that so far only one-third of the 150 LEAs appeared to have adopted this requirement as standard practice.

19. Teacher Training Agency (TTA)

Ministers may have felt more secure in allowing proposals for GTCs (see above) to go forward into the 1998 Act once they had established the TTA, through the Education Act 1994. Under s. 1, its duties are to contribute to raising the standards of teaching, promoting teaching as a career, improving the quality and efficiency of all routes into the teaching profession (a significant phrase to appear in statute, offering an end to wrangling over whether teaching is a profession, semi-profession or a job) and securing the involvement of schools in the initial training of teachers. LEAs are among bodies eligible to receive funding from the TTA for in-school initial training.

20. Qualifications and Curriculum Authority

The Qualifications and Curriculum Authority (QCA) was established by s. 21 of the Education Act 1997 as a quango with membership appointed by the Secretary of State. The Wales equivalent, the Qualifications, Curriculum and Assessment Authority for Wales, was set up under s. 27 and is usually known by its Welsh acronym ACCAC (for Awdurdod Cymwysterau, Cwricwlwm ac Asesu Cymru, the Welsh title also given in the statute).

QCA replaced the statutory School Curriculum and Assessment Authority (SCAA, a creature of the Education Act 1993) and the non-statutory National Council for Vocational Qualifications. SCAA had replaced twin statutory quangos, the National Curriculum Council and the School Examinations and Assessment Council (Education Reform Act 1988), which had superseded the Ministerially-appointed School Curriculum Development Committee and Secondary Examinations Council. These two had replaced in 1982 the single Schools Council for Curriculum and Examinations (created 1964). Its predecessors have been the Board of Education's Secondary Schools Examinations Council (1917) and DES's internal advisory body, the Curriculum Study Group (1962). To adapt Mrs Malaprop: a nice derangement of quangos.

QCA's general function is to advance education and training and in so doing promote quality and coherence (s. 22 of the 1997 Act). It has oversight of *inter alia* school curricula and examinations and assessment and it may accredit external academic and vocational qualifications (s. 24).

See chapter 4.A for its relationship with LEAs and schools.

21. Parents

Much lip service is paid to parents as children's first educators, but the law is framed so as to give particular, if limited, rights to parents, over, for example:

- preference for schools for their children

- acknowledgement of the parent's denominational adherence (if any and as relevant)

- exclusion

- responses to children's SEN

- electing representative parent governors.

Answers, however, to the question of who is a child's parent may not always be straightforward.

A pupil's 'parent' for the purposes of the Education Acts includes any person (a) who is not a natural parent of the child but who has parental responsibility for him/her, or (b) who has care of him/her (s. 576(1) of the Education Act 1996).

'Parental responsibility' means 'all the rights, duties, powers, responsibility and authority which by law a parent has in relation to the child and his property' (s. 3(1) of the Children Act 1989). Although that Act does not go into any further detail, Department of Health guidance states that parental responsibility is concerned with 'bringing up the child, caring for him and making decisions about him, but does not affect the relationship of parent and child for other purposes' *(The Children Act 1989 Guidance and Regulations*, vol 1, Court Orders, para 2.2).

Understanding the term is therefore not easy, nor is trying to assess who may have parental responsibility and/or be a 'parent'. It can be said, however, that the following may be treated as a child's parent: the natural mother, the natural father, a resident step-parent, any person who has a parental responsibility order in respect of the child, a person with a residence order in respect of the child, a local authority where the child is subject to a care order and any person who has care of the child. A foster parent will be considered to be a parent of the child (see *Fairpo v Humberside County Council* [1997] 1 All ER 183).

The rights, responsibilities and roles of parents are touched on in this book, but particular issues are discussed under 'Admissions' (chapter 7.A), 'Education Welfare and Attendance' (chapter 9.B) and 'Civil liability' (chapter 12.D.3).

The corporate parent has to be legislated for (or against). For example, to ensure that the social services authority does not have a vote on whether a child's grammar school should continue selective admissions (s. 105 of the School Standards and Framework Act 1998), reg 4(3) of the Education (Grammar School Ballots) Regulations 1998 (SI 1998 No. 2876) excludes from eligibility to vote 'a parent who is not an individual'. A similar formulation excludes a corporate parent from being served a parenting order or fixed-penalty notice of a fine for allowing truanting (Anti-social Behaviour Act 2003, s. 24).

C. Guidance from Above

1. Classification

A Department with 'Education' in its title has long issued guidance to LEAs in the form of circulars, circular letters and miscellaneous publications difficult to categorise. Some documents are now entitled 'Guidance' as such. Of late, guidance has come partly in codes of practice which legislation obliges the Secretary of State (or, in Wales, the National Assembly) to issue. Legislation also now grants him a limited number of specific powers at his discretion (or exceptionally imposes a duty) to give guidance to LEAs and others: so-called 'statutory guidance'. This is an unfortunate term so far as it gives rise to the misconception that the guidance is itself of statutory effect: statutory guidance does not, it will be suggested, have the force of law. Codes of practice may contain statutory guidance and it is not always clear whether guidance is statutory or otherwise. It follows that although a hierarchy of status may be ascribed to guidance – codes of practice, statutory, non-statutory – a tidy three-tier model has rough edges.

2. Codes of Practice

The code of practice is a recent innovation in education law. It takes effect only on the approval of, or in the absence of a negative resolution by, Parliament. That on Special Educational Needs derives in the first place from the repealed Education Act 1993. The School Standards and Framework Act 1998 introduced Codes on School Admission Arrangements, on Admission Appeals and for Securing Effective Relationships between LEAs and Maintained Schools. (The 'other' 1998 Act, the Teaching and Higher Education Act, authorises either General Teaching Council, under regulation, to issue a code for registered teachers.)

3. Statutory guidance

'Statutory guidance', next in the hierarchy, is published under s. 571 of the 1996 Act. It has a longer pedigree than the code of practice (though not reaching back to the 1944 Act). The 1980 Act required LEAs to have regard to any guidance given by the Secretary of State about consultation on proposed establishment, alteration, etc., of schools. The 1988 Act, similarly, required LEAs, in preparing financial delegation schemes, to take guidance into account. The 1998 Act repeats both obligations. The 1997 Act, amending the 1996 Act, requires LEAs to 'have regard to any guidance given from time to time by the Secretary of State' about exceptional provision of education in pupil referral units or elsewhere. The 1998 Act places governing bodies and headteachers under the same obligation as regards their disciplinary responsibilities.

It was the 1998 Act that brought statutory guidance into bloom. There are some two dozen separate powers granted to the Secretary of State to give guidance to LEAs, or additionally or alternatively to others such as governing bodies and school organisation committees. All or most of those powers have been exercised. At a high level of generality is the guidance in Circular 10/99, given under s. 61, on school exclusions (which, with the Admission Appeals Code of Practice, superseded the non-statutory Code issued by the former Associations of County Councils and of Metropolitan Authorities). In a descent to what might be deprecated as pettiness, Guidance 180/2000 advises LEAs on how to present 'fairly' and with 'reasonableness' such factual information about the consequences of a grammar school ballot as they may wish to present.

More recently still, the Learning and Skills Act 2000, amending the 1996 Act, obliges LEAs to have regard to the guidance the Secretary of State must issue about sex education. Further guidance will be emanating as a result of the Education Act 2002.

4. Non-statutory guidance

Statutory guidance creates, by implication, a third category, 'non-statutory guidance' on the exercise of statutory functions by LEAs and others. Some examples (if any are needed) are to be found among the documents appended to the *Code of Practice on LEA – School Relations*, of which annexes 2 and 3 'do form part of the Code and have statutory force' (para A.vii), but annexes 1, 4 and 5 are included only 'for ease of reference'. The different forms of non-statutory guidance are given distinguishing descriptions, but it is by no means always apparent why one rather than another has been selected. Guidance of this kind has long been a feature of educational administration. The DfES and its predecessors have failed to find time to carry out a thoroughgoing cull of material. Its extent is beyond measurement.

It may not be quite true that, where guidance is not 'statutory', the *ultra vires* rule requires it always to be incidental to the Secretary of State's other statutory functions: according to de Smith and Brazier (1989:180), he derives his powers from the prerogative (that is, the royal prerogative exercised by one of Her Majesty's Ministers). However, in *AG v De Keyser's Royal Hotel Ltd* [1920] AC 508, it was held that so far as statutory powers co-exist with the prerogative, the former supersede the latter. It might be thought to follow that s. 10 of the 1996 Act, which provides that 'The Secretary of State shall promote the education of the people of England and Wales' and s. 11, which elaborates that duty in the case of primary, secondary and further education, together exclude any prerogative power to the same effect. But de Smith and Brazier are tentative in this area (p. 132) and it may be that the Secretary of State has inherent powers to promote education over and above his statutory functions. The provisions mentioned should, however, be broad enough to make the use of the prerogative unnecessary for giving non-statutory guidance. If, however, they are no more than declaratory and merely anticipate more specific powers, then the argument would be that giving guidance is reasonably incidental to those powers.

One way or another the non-statutory guidance the Secretary of State publishes in his official capacity is necessarily a more or less direct incident of his functions. So 'non-statutory' is best regarded as a convenient but potentially misleading description. It is also misleading if it is understood as a synonym for 'non-legal' guidance (such as that given in Circular 2/98 on reducing the bureaucratic burden on teachers), because much non-statutory guidance is about the interpretation and use of statutory powers.

5.   Guidance or direction?

While it seems plain enough that the Secretary of State has wide powers to give guidance, two further questions arise: where the line is to be drawn between guidance and the exercise of substantial power and how far the prerogative supports the latter. In *R v Secretary of State for Education and Employment, ex parte The*

National Union of Teachers [2000] EdCR 603, QBD, Jackson J held that the Secretary of State's obligation under ss. 10 and 11 of the 1996 Act to promote education did not enable him to set 'threshold' standards as a basis for performance-related pay. To do so was more than giving general guidance. And his powers in relation to pay and teacher appraisal did not extend beyond those conferred by statute. He had promulgated standards by announcement and not in accordance with statutory procedures. It was not enough that prior consultation had taken place on a Green Paper.

6.   How compelling is guidance?

The formula 'have regard to' ordinarily appears as the requirement in relation to statutory guidance as it does in relation to codes of practice. Judicial decisions indicate that a requirement to have regard to one specified consideration does not exclude the right, or perhaps   , to have regard to others. Section 76 of the 1944 Act, which lives on in s. 9 of the 1996 Act, gave rise to the leading case, *Watt v Kesteven County Council* [1955] 1 QB 408, which established that the duty of LEAs to have regard to the general principle that pupils are to be educated in accordance with their parents' wishes left them free to have regard to other matters. Indeed the reference to a 'general principle' points to the possible relevance of other considerations. See also *Cumings v Birkenhead Corporation* [1972] Ch, 12 and *Harvey v Strathclyde Regional Council* [1989] SLT 612, HL.

Where the Secretary of State gives statutory guidance there is no such hint of other considerations or obligations; but it has been held (outside the context of education law, in *Ishak v Thowfeek* ([1968] 1 WRL 1718 at 1725), that a duty to have regard is not a duty to comply: matters to which regard is to be had are to be taken into account, considered and given due weight, yet an ultimate discretion remains. For discussion of the significance of 'have regard to' see *Hansard* (545 HL Deb 485ff, 29 April 1993 and 548 HL Deb 1002ff, 26 July 1993).

More comprehensively the Court of Appeal held in *R (on the application of S) v Brent Borough Council* ([2002] EWCA Civ 693) and related cases that:

> '[G]uidance is not more than that: it is not direction and certainly not rules. Any Appeal Panel which, albeit on legal advice, treats the Secretary of State's Guidance as something to be strictly adhered to or simply follows it because it is there will be breaking its statutory remit in at least three ways: it will be failing to

exercise its own independent judgment; it will be treating guidance as if it were rules and it will, in lawyers' terms, be fettering its own discretion. Equally, however, it will be breaking its remit if it neglects the guidance [...]'

It seems probable that this conclusion, touching an (exclusion) appeal panel, applies equally to guidance given to LEAs. As Woolf J put it in *R v ILEA ex p Bradbury*, [1989] All ER 417, HL, 30 January 1980 (unreported):

'[U]nless it can be said that the circular is mandatory in form [...] disregard of [its] requirements may be evidence, but no more than evidence, that an LEA is acting unreasonably. Whether or not it is acting unreasonably in any particular case will have to be judged on the facts and the circulars will only be part of the evidence as to that matter. To suggest that merely because there is a departure from a circular or the adoption of a particular interpretation of a circular an LEA has acted in any way *ultra vires*, in my view, is not sustainable. That is elevating the circulars to a status which they just do not have. They are not more than advice and guidance from the Minister as to a course which, in general, he suggests the education authority should follow.'

See Liell, Coleman and Wolfe (1984 rev. 2003) at E[1]; also *C v Special Educational Needs Tribunal* [1997] ELR 390 at 398.

Sedley J, in R v London Borough of Islington ex parte Rixon [1997] ELR 66, said:

'In my judgment Parliament in enacting s. 7(1) [of the Local Authority Social Services Act 1970] did not intend local authorities to whom ministerial guidance was given to be free, having considered it, to take it or leave it. Such a construction would put this kind of statutory guidance on a par with the many forms of non-statutory guidance issued by departments of state. [W]hile [...] "guidance does not compel any particular decision" (*Laker Airways Ltd v Department of Trade* [1967] QB 643, at 714 per Roskill LJ) [...] in my view Parliament by s. 7 (1) has required local authorities to follow the path charted by the Secretary of State's guidance, with liberty to deviate from it where the local authority judges on admissible grounds that there is a good reason to do so, but without freedom to take a substantially different course.'

Section 7 (1) of the 1970 Act requires local authorities, in exercising social service functions, to act 'under' the general guidance of the Secretary of State. It was in this particular context that Sedley J submitted in *Rixon* that statutory guidance is more compelling than non-statutory guidance. In contrast LEAs are required to 'have regard to' statutory guidance, which, the decisions cited have shown, is a less compelling formula. They are probably under an equal, unstated, obligation where guidance is non-statutory: Lord Woolf's remarks in *Bradbury* indicate that LEAs need to have regard to all the Secretary of State's guidance. There is, for example, no particular requirement to have regard to the guidance given in Circulars 0269/2002 and 0270/2002, on governors' annual reports in primary and secondary schools, but failure to do so would, as explained below, put governors at risk. It would not be difficult to find other similar examples of non-statutory guidance.

Thus the enhanced status of statutory over non-statutory guidance is probably no more than a matter of form and carries no stronger obligation to have regard to it. Why then should the Secretary of State seek power to impose an express requirement, as exemplified in s. 61 of the School Standards and Framework Act 1998? Section 61 is headed 'Responsibility of governing body and head teacher for discipline'; in exercising its functions, the governing body is to 'have regard to any guidance given from time to time by the Secretary of State'. The answer may lie in the tags 'for the avoidance of doubt' or '*ex abundante cautela*'; it seems more likely to turn on the salience of particular issues in the educational or political arena.

7.   The Departmental view

In the year 2000 a new numbering system for Departmental communications was introduced and in 2000 and 2001 guidance to LEAs was newly entitled simply as such, but in 2002 additionally the 'Circular' reappeared. Over the past ten years guidance, previously unglossed, has carried preliminaries helpfully indicating, *inter alia*, related and superseded documents. On the evidence of more than 30 of the most recent guidance pieces reproduced in *The Law of Education* (Liell *et al.*, 2003) the preliminaries may now omit the once familiar warning that guidance 'should not be treated as a complete and authoritative statement of the law', but they commonly include a statement of its 'status'. This the lawyer would expect to be either 'statutory' or 'non-statutory' and indeed 'statutory' sometimes appears as the status of guidance, but it is not to be understood as indicating that the guidance is statutory, either by reason of the explicit power of the Secretary of State to give it, or, wrongly, that it is of binding effect. 'Statutory' in this context means that the guidance expounds the law and reminds LEAs of their powers and duties. With the same connotation 'status' is often and better, described as 'guidance on the law'. That attributed to Guidance 180/2000 is (pleonastically) 'Guidance': it is in fact statutory in the strict sense, evidently being given under s. 107 of the 1998 Act. Exceptionally, Guidance 0774/2001 is properly awarded the status of statutory guidance and in its body LEAs are reminded that it 'must not be ignored'. ('Statutory' also appears, in Circular 10/99, under the heading 'Action', which seems to imply, obscurely, that some forms of action by LEAs are more statutory than others.)

It might be thought wise to leave LEAs to assess the relevance of particular guidance to the local situation, but 'status' has also been used to specify how much weight the Department attaches to it. Thus Guidance 116/2000 is said to be 'good practice' (it is statutory guidance under the 1996 Act, s. 403 as amended). The status of another Guidance document is 'strongly recommended', a commendation prompting the fancy that compliance cures all known forms of the shortcomings addressed. *The Complaints Procedure Toolkit* (LEA/0180/2003) recites the statutory guidance provision on complaints procedures but states 'This note does not represent Statutory Guidance [...]'

Some lack of clarity and consistency may be noticed in these examples, but a helpful indication of the (or perhaps one) Departmental view is in the Guidance, unnumbered, given in January 2000, on statutory proposals for changes in schools. Guidance in that document is said to be 'of two kinds: statutory guidance, to which those concerned are required by legislation to have regard and non-statutory guidance, which is designed to inform people about the [Department's view of] legislative requirements and help them to carry out their roles as effectively as possible'. This distinction is uncontentious as far as it goes; it does not, however, indicate the likely identity of outcome on a challenge that regard has not been paid to either the one or the other type. The same Guidance also spells out the need for all proposals to be considered on their individual merits – which can be taken as recognition that LEAs are not expected to follow it slavishly.

In the codes of practice the Department walks a skilful tightrope in commenting on the status of guidance. The SEN Code states that 'all those to whom the Code applies have a statutory duty to have regard to it; they must not ignore it.' The LEAs and other bodies concerned 'must consider what the Code says'. But the 'Code is not prescriptive' (Circular 9/94 para 14). The 'Effective Relationships' Code remarks that the duty to have regard to the Code 'means for all normal purposes they [LEAs, etc.] should observe its principles and guidance, departing from it only where there is good reason'. The Code notes that the 1998 Act does not create specific sanctions or rights of appeal linked to breaches of the Code, but it refers to the Secretary of State's long established general powers of intervention under the Education Acts and in particular to the sanction against unreasonable action which now appears in s. 496 of the 1996 Act.

8.   Unreasonable action

Section 496, as explained in *Wednesbury (Associated Provincial Picture Houses Ltd v Wednesbury Corporation* [1948] 1 KB 223) essentially restricts the significance of 'unreasonable action' to the exercise of a function in a capricious, irrational or perverse manner. If the Secretary of State concludes that an LEA or governing body has acted unreasonably in failing to have regard to guidance, in a code or otherwise, he may give whatever directions he judges expedient to put the matter right. Under s. 497 'failure to have regard to guidance' would be a default – and so enable the Secretary of State to direct an LEA to perform its duty – but the direction would not of itself appear to promote correction of unreasonable action.

In construing s. 68 of the 1944 Act (precursor of s. 496) the House of Lords, in the *Tameside* judgment (*Secretary of State for Education and Science v Tameside Metropolitan Borough Council* [1977] AC 1014, HL), held that although the use of the words 'if the Secretary of State is satisfied' appear to make the decision as to reasonableness a matter solely for his judgment, if he misdirects himself on the facts his power is open to challenge. Only in cases of 'pure judgment', as Lord Wilberforce put it in *Tameside*, may he intervene under s. 496 in circumstances where the unreasonableness does not meet the *Wednesbury* tests. It is not enough for him to disagree with an LEA's policy. And since the Secretary of State would be using a statutory power he could scarcely assert against an LEA some alternative common law and less strict criterion of unreasonableness.

'These are much deeper waters than I had thought', as Sherlock Holmes puts it, and neither the *Wednesbury* concept of unreasonableness nor *Tameside* will be in the minds of most lay readers of the codes or of guidance generally: it will be up to education lawyers to enlighten them. It would be disingenuous – perhaps unreasonable even – to expect the Secretary of State to draw special attention to how his s. 496 powers are circumscribed. (To be fair, it should be added that there is a reference to *Wednesbury* in para 14 of annex B to the School Admission Appeals Code of Practice.)

See also chapter 12.B.1 of this book for further discussion of ss. 496, 497.

9. Summary and conclusion

It is plain that, whether or not given under an explicit power, guidance carries considerable weight. An LEA which departs from it needs to be ready to show that it first had regard to it and departed from it knowingly and on defensible grounds; otherwise it is at risk under the s. 496 sanction. But that sanction is a clumsy weapon: where the Secretary of State wishes to impose an obligation more demanding than under the usual rubric, Parliament has enacted accordingly. Sections 497A and 497B (added to the 1996 Act by the 1998 Act and extended by ss. 60–62 of the 2002 Act) give the Secretary of State wide powers to direct LEAs to secure performance of a function to an adequate standard; failure to follow guidance might plausibly be linked to adequacy. And there are more specific powers. For example, if it appears to the Secretary of State that an LEA has not taken his guidance sufficiently into account in preparing its financial delegation scheme for maintained schools he may substitute his own scheme (School Standards and Framework Act 1998, sched 14, para 1) and he is granted power to direct LEAs under s. 23 of the Learning and Skills Act 2000 regarding provision of education and training for those aged 19 and above.

The Secretary of State's guidance has conventionally been the subject of prior consultation with the interested parties. It is plainly expressed and often presented in an attractive format; yet sometimes patience is tried by a seemingly repetitive and 'told for the bairns' style. The dissemination of guidance may be represented as a responsible Government endeavour to raise standards by urging best practice upon LEAs; alternatively, it may be deplored as hindering their freedom to deal with particular situations not foreseen in the generality of the guidance. Interference in the exercise of proper discretions by elected bodies, the argument continues, stifles innovation from its surest source, practical experience (though it must be acknowledged that some guidance documents give examples of local achievements). And local government may not attract and retain able members and officers if it becomes little more than the executive instrument of centrally-determined policy. The clash of values is inescapable: a balance must be held. Such a glimpse of the obvious is worth revealing when the Secretary of State takes explicit power, in recent statutes, to assert his advice in such a wide range of circumstances. It may not be incautious to speculate that, in a further edition of the book, this section will be entitled 'Direction from Above'.

In an effort to embrace e-government, most guidance from the DfES is now issued on the internet on either its own site (www.dfes.gov.uk), www.teachernet.gov.uk or www.governornet.gov.uk, although there appears to be little logic or consistency as to which site is chosen to host particular pieces of guidance. There also appears to be no consistency in providing DfES references to accompany this guidance. For example, the Staffing Guidance (see chapter 6.E) appears on *governornet* but not under *teachernet* management pages and bears no reference number. Finding guidance through these sites' search engines is a lottery and there appears to be no single location where a comprehensive list of DfES guidance can be found. Perhaps worst of all, the Department is able to, indeed would probably promote it as an advantage of using the web, alter its guidance as and when it wishes and with, it would seem, little publicity. An example is the Department's alteration of its guidance on exclusions to clarify the standard of proof to be used in exclusion appeals. This of course means that if a copy of the document is printed off one day, there is no guarantee that the guidance will not have been altered the next. These problems might have been eased if these sites identify and track any changes which have been made and when, but this does not appear to happen.

This practice is frustrating to say the least; where, however, public bodies are required to have regard to the guidance on pain of being held to be in breach of duty, it is wholly unsatisfactory and renders uncertain guidance that its readers should expect to be certain.

4. SPIRITUAL, MORAL, CULTURAL, MENTAL AND PHYSICAL DEVELOPMENT

A. Curriculum

1. Background

The LEA's statutory role in shaping educational provision in maintained institutions has changed enormously over recent years. After decades in which the law was at best vague about the LEA's responsibility for the curriculum, the emphasis now is on what LEAs can do to improve the quality of what goes on in schools. The duties and powers over what is taught in schools now fall on the Government through the National Curriculum and on governing bodies and headteachers. However, LEAs retain a number of residual, though important, responsibilities. The most significant change is with the oversight of the curriculum including its assessment arrangements in maintained primary and secondary schools. Section 23 of the Education Act 1944 left the 'secular instruction' of county and voluntary schools (except aided secondary schools) under the control of the LEA, subject to provisions, if any, in articles of government for secondary schools and rules of management for primary schools. The Education (No. 2) Act 1986 defined the roles of the LEA, school governing body and headteacher in respect of the school curriculum, although this was overtaken by the Education Reform Act 1988 with the adoption of a National Curriculum. The last explicit LEA duty, to have a local curriculum statement, was removed by the School Standards and Framework Act 1998, with the exception, in theory, of the curriculum in nursery schools. The position was clarified by the Education Act 2002 with the formal introduction of the foundation stage as part of the National Curriculum.

However, the LEA can influence the shape of what is taught in schools and its assessment arrangements, in a variety of ways through being the local authority and doing things incidental to the powers and duties described below and otherwise, for example, support for environmental education using non-education resources, citizenship and road safety.

2. Overall duties

Section 13 of the Education Act 1996 imposes on each LEA a duty to 'contribute towards the spiritual, moral, mental and physical development of the community by securing that efficient primary and secondary education are available to meet the needs of the population of the [...] area'. Section 13A requires the LEA to ensure that its functions are exercised 'with a view to promoting high standards' in the provision of education for all persons of compulsory school age and for all pupils at schools maintained by the authority.

Section 13 reproduced the wording of s. 7 of the 1944 Act. The addition of 'cultural' in the heading of the present chapter is a reference to s. 78 of the Education Act 2002, which re-enacts s. 351 of the Education Act 1996 requiring the curriculum of every maintained school and maintained nursery school to promote 'the spiritual, moral, *cultural* [italics added], mental and physical development of pupils at [...] school'. By s. 79(2) of the 2002 Act (also derived from s. 351 of the 1996 Act), the LEA must exercise its functions 'with a view to securing' that s. 78 is fulfilled. And so LEAs have picked up a 'cultural' duty. But Liell *et al.* (1984, rev 2003) point out that, under s. 1(2)(d) of the Education Act 1994, the Teacher Training Agency's duties include that of securing 'that teachers are well fitted and trained to promote the spiritual, moral, *social* [italics added], cultural, mental and physical development of their pupils'. Arguably, the 'social' is otiose, as the point is covered by the requirement (also subs. (2)) that pupils be prepared 'for the opportunities, responsibilities and experiences of adult life'. That phrase, along with the rest of s. 351 of the 1996 Act, is derived from s. 1 of the Education Reform Act 1988.

3. Curriculum duties

The statutory National Curriculum was reprovided by the Education Act 2002 with separate, but very similar provisions, for England (ss. 76–96) and Wales (ss. 97–118) with the law in England commencing on 1 October 2002 and Wales (with the exception of the Foundation Curriculum) on 19 December 2002. (The Wales Assembly Government consulted in 2003 on introducing a foundation phase for children aged 3–7 years from September 2006, thus combining the foundation stage with key stage 1, although no specific new role is offered to LEAs.)

3.1 General duties

The LEA has a duty under s. 79 (s. 100 for Wales) of the Education Act 2002 to exercise its functions with a view to securing that every school it maintains (including nursery schools) and nursery education funded through the LEA, meets the 'general requirements' for the curriculum (s. 78; s. 99 for Wales). These requirements are that the curriculum taught is a balanced and broadly based curriculum which:

- promotes the spiritual, moral, mental and physical development of pupils at the school and of society

- prepares pupils at maintained schools for the opportunities, responsibilities and experiences of adult life.

The s. 79 (England) and s. 100 (Wales) 'general requirements' duties include, in particular, the National Curriculum (which now includes the foundation stage), religious education and religious worship (subs. (4)). Locally devised curriculum material will also be covered. See below for sex education. The duty is shared with the Secretary of State (in Wales, the National Assembly) and the governing body and headteacher of every maintained school. In respect of each maintained school, the LEA, together with the governing body, must exercise its functions with a view to securing that the National Curriculum as subsisting at the beginning of the school year is implemented in the school (s. 88; s. 109 in Wales). This includes the assessment arrangements. The headteacher has the primary duty to secure the implementation of the National Curriculum.

The new curriculum for key stage 4 in England commencing in September 2004 includes work-related learning. The Education (Amendment of the Curriculum Requirements for Foundation Key Stage 1 (England) Order 2003 (SI 2003 No. 2946)) inserts a new s. 85 into the Education Act 2002. Section 85(9) requires LEAs, governing bodies and headteachers to have regard to QCA guidance about work-related learning and the new 'entitlement' subjects. Although the QCA guidance does not specifically state it is guidance under s.85, the following are available: *Changes to the Key Stage 4 curriculum: Guidance for implementation from September 2004* (QCA/03/1167) and *Work-related learning for all at key stage 4: Guidance for implementing the statutory requirement from 2004* (QCA/03/1168). There are no specific references to LEAs except the need to have regard to any guidance and a note that LEA advisers might be useful in promoting education-business links.

3.2 Compliance

The means by which the LEA can exercise its functions with a view to securing that a school's curriculum complies with the law are various. The authority will have a professional education staff (see below on Education Development Plans or Education Strategic Plans in Wales), led by a 'fit' person as the chief education officer (s. 532) to advise schools on the statutory requirements. Advice can be delivered through visits by link, assessment and subject advisers and through providing courses of teacher professional development. If problems are found through adviser visits (including visits to monitor the assessment arrangements), headteacher appraisal reports or through parental complaints about the curriculum (see below), the LEA can ask the school to comply with the law. If this does not lead to compliance, the LEA in England can pursue the matter further by using the various mechanisms outlined in Annex 2 (Statutory guidance on use of Local Education Authority powers of intervention) found in the *Code of Practice on Local Education Authority – School Relations* or part 2 of the Welsh Code.

3.3 Careers education

Careers education, as distinct from careers advice from careers/Careers Wales/Connexions advisers, is a distinct subject on the school curriculum outside the curriculum provisions of the 2002 Act by virtue of s. 43 of the Education Act 1997. The LEA and the teacher in charge of a pupil referral unit have a joint duty to ensure careers education is provided for pupils in years 9–11 and in years 7–11 from September 2004 by virtue of the Education (Extension of Careers Education) (Education) Regulations 2003 (SI 2003 No. 2645).

4. Education Development Plan

The LEA can shape the direction of the local curriculum using flexibility in local funding arrangements, including the Standards Fund under s. 14 of the 2002 Act (s. 484 of the 1996 Act in Wales and called Grants for Education Support and Training) and the Education Development Plan (Education Strategic Plan, in Wales) under s. 6 of the School Standards and Framework Act. The LEA is able in the plan to make a statement of proposals (including the funding) to develop the provision of education for children in an area by raising standards and improving the performance of schools. The plan requires the approval of the Secretary of State (or National Assembly for Wales). The LEA could, for instance, use the plan to

4. SPIRITUAL, MORAL, CULTURAL, MENTAL & PHYSICAL DEVELOPMENT

improve the teaching of modern languages by providing additional advisory support and provision of out-of-school activities, or enable schools to gain access to resources to enable the curriculum to be broad and balanced.

As part of the drive to reduce unnecessary bureaucratic burdens on LEAs, the DfES had been consulting on proposals to reform the legislation governing planning requirements through the proposed introduction of a Single Education Plan (SEP) for all LEAs by April 2006. But Ministers have announced during passage of the Children Bill the substitution of a statutory plan for children, superseding the single education plan (see *Local Government Chronicle*, 25.6.2004).

The SEP would have incorporated the EDP, as well as other statutory plans, i.e. the Behaviour Support Plan, the Early Years Development and Childcare Plan and the School Organisation Plan, as well as other, non-statutory plans. The SEP would not be subject to formal approval but the Secretary of State was expected to reserve power to require changes.

See also chapter 5.A.3.

5.   National Curriculum assessment arrangements

The National Curriculum consists of the attainment targets and programmes of study for each subject but also the assessment arrangements. In England, the Secretary of State can order under s. 87(6)(d) (for the Foundation Stage) and s. 87(7)(b) (for key stages 1–3) of the Education Act 2002 that LEAs perform functions in relation to National Curriculum assessment. Current (2003) requirements include the following.

- The Education (National Curriculum) (Foundation Stage Profile Assessment Arrangements) (England) Order 2003 (SI 2003 No. 1327) requires LEAs to monitor the way in which the assessments and foundation stage profiles are being conducted by teachers to ensure consistency and proper implementation of the statutory provisions. Information about the assessments has to be provided to parents and the LEA. The LEA has to forward the information to the Secretary of State at the end of school year.

- The Education (National Curriculum) (Key Stage 1 Assessment Arrangements) (England) Order 2003 (SI 2003 No. 1037) requires the LEA to verify the 'standard task assessments' in English and mathematics in 25 per cent of schools each year.

- The Education (National Curriculum) (Key Stage 2 Assessment Arrangements) (England) Order 2003 (SI 2003 No. 1038) and the Education (National Curriculum) (Key Stage 3 Assessment Arrangements) (England) Order 2003 (SI 2003 No. 1039) both require the LEA to monitor the National Curriculum test in ten per cent of schools.

Further details of LEA duties are to be found in the annual 'assessment and reporting arrangements' published by the DfES and QCA.

4.   SPIRITUAL, MORAL, CULTURAL, MENTAL & PHYSICAL DEVELOPMENT

In Wales, although LEAs do monitoring and verification work, they are not specially mentioned in the Wales Assessment Orders. For example, The Education (National Curriculum) (Assessment Arrangements for English, Welsh, Mathematics and Science) (Key Stage 1) (Wales) Order 2002 (SI 2002 No. 45) enables the Welsh curriculum body, ACCAC, to determine monitoring arrangements, although it should be noted that the aforementioned order abolished key stage 1 SATs and thus removed the need for the LEA role which is still continuing in England.

6.   Development work and experiments

For community, voluntary controlled or community special schools, the LEA can apply (with the governing body's agreement) under s. 90 of the 2002 Act to the Secretary of State for a direction to disapply the National Curriculum, or apply it with modifications, for the purpose of curriculum development work. A school can apply with the LEA's agreement. The equivalent provision for Wales is s. 111 and applications have to be made to the National Assembly for Wales. This is a little-used provision.

7.   Temporary exceptions for individual pupils

The LEA has a duty (s. 94(5) of the 2002 Act), when informed by a headteacher that a temporary exception has been made to the National Curriculum provision for a pupil, to consider whether the pupil's special educational needs should be assessed under s. 323 of the 1996 Act. The equivalent provision in Wales is found in s. 115(5).

8.   Courses leading to external qualifications

8.1   Oversight

LEAs must use their powers to secure that no course of education or training, funded publicly and leading to an external qualification, is provided (or proposed to be provided) for pupils of compulsory school age, or for pupils who are above that age but have not attained the age of 19, unless the qualification has been approved by the Secretary of State or the National Assembly or by a body authorised by the Secretary of State or NAW (s. 96 of the Learning and Skills Act 2000).

8.2 LEA-provided qualifications

Section 190 of the Education Act 2002 enables an LEA to award or authenticate academic and vocational qualifications. LEAs may be a member of a corporate body which provides qualifications. The main purpose of this provision was to put beyond doubt the *vires* of the Welsh Joint Education Committee (WJEC) and its examination work. Apart from the WJEC, the tradition of LEAs providing, for example, language tests for 14 year-olds, appears to have lapsed, as judged by the list of approved qualifications found at www/dfes.gov.uk/section96.

9. Complaints

Under s. 409 of the Education Act 1996, each LEA shall, after consulting with governing bodies of voluntary aided and foundation schools and with the approval of the Secretary of State, make arrangements for the consideration and disposal of certain complaints relating to the curriculum and religious education. The range of complaints is limited and extends only to a complaint which is to the effect that the LEA, or the governing body of any community, foundation or voluntary school maintained by the LEA or any community or foundation special school so maintained which is not established in a hospital:

a) has acted or is proposing to act unreasonably in relation to the exercise of a power conferred on it in respect of matters such as the National Curriculum, collective worship, religious education, non-approved external qualifications or syllabuses, the provision of information, or the conduct of an appeal to the governing body about the head's direction to withdraw the provisions of the National Curriculum for a pupil; or

b) has acted or is proposing to act unreasonably in relation to the performance of, or has failed to discharge, a duty imposed on it in respect of such matters (s. 409(1)–(3)).

Such investigations can take up much officer time and expertise.

The need to seek the Secretary of State's or NAW's approval to the scheme is repealed by paragraph 47 of sched 21 of the 2002 Act in England on 1 October by the Education Act 2002 (Commencement No. 2 and Savings and Transitional Provisions) (England) Order 2002 (SI 2002 No. 2439) and Wales on 19 December 2002 by virtue of the Education Act 2002 (Commencement No.1) (Wales) Order 2002 (SI 2002 No.3185 (W 301)).

4. SPIRITUAL, MORAL, CULTURAL, MENTAL & PHYSICAL DEVELOPMENT

B. Sex Education

The law relating to the LEA role on sex education differs between England and Wales. The law as derived from the Education (No. 2) Act 1986 still applies in Wales. However, at the time that the Learning and Skills Act 2000 was going through Parliament, there was controversy over the Government's attempt to rescind 'clause 28' (see below). The Government responded by removing the last vestige of an LEA role in England but, it is understood because of opposition from the Welsh Assembly Government, the Government did not ask Parliament to extend the new law to Wales.

In Wales, s. 403(1) of the 1996 Act places a duty on LEAs, together with governing bodies and headteachers, to take such steps as are reasonable to secure that where sex education is given to any registered pupils at a maintained school, it is given in such a manner as to encourage those pupils to have due regard to moral considerations and the value of family life. In England, the Secretary of State (under s. 403(1A)) must issue guidance, to which governing bodies and headteachers must have regard (subs. (1B). This can be found in *Sex and Relationship Education Guidance* DfEE 0116/2000 and, for example, suggests that further information can be found through the LEA's Personal, Social and Health Education advisory services. Several non-school curricular issues are dealt with in the guidance such as child protection and the role of the youth service. (See chapters 9 and 10.) However, the LEA as part of the 'general requirements' duty in s. 79 (see above) has to have regard to the guidance issued under s. 403(1A) and, except as specified in the guidance, LEAs are not to take the 'general requirements' duty as imposing any duty with regard to sex education. The amendment was achieved by the Learning and Skills Act 2000 and did not apply to Wales. However, possibly because of a drafting error, the wording of s. 79 has been carried across to the 'general requirements' duty for Wales and is found in s. 100(6)–(7), i.e. Welsh LEAs have to have regard to guidance on sex education issued by the NAW and, unless specified in the guidance, cannot exercise their 'general requirement' duty over sex education.

On the status and force of 'guidance', see chapter 3.C.

Section 2A of the Local Government Act 1986, more commonly known as 'Clause 28' because it derived from clause 28 of the Local Government Bill of 1988, has exercised LEAs and local authorities in general and, on occasions, may have confused school staff over the restrictions on teaching about homosexuality. It was repealed by section 122 (Repeal of prohibition on promotion of homosexuality) of the Local Government Act 2003 with effect from 18 November 2003, two months after Royal Assent.

4. SPIRITUAL, MORAL, CULTURAL, MENTAL & PHYSICAL DEVELOPMENT

C. Political Indoctrination

LEAs, together with governing bodies and headteachers, must forbid (a) the pursuit of partisan political activities by any junior pupils at a maintained school and (b) the promotion of partisan political views in the teaching of any subject in a school (s. 406 of the Education Act 1996).

D. Religious Education

LEAs are under the 'general requirements' duty to exercise their functions with a view to securing that religious education and religious worship form part of the curriculum of every maintained school, but not nursery schools and funded nursery education (ss. 79(4) and 100(4) of the 2002 Act). A similar duty is found in s. 69 of the School Standards and Framework Act 1998. This duty specifically places religious education in the basic curriculum of ss. 80 and 101 of the 2002 Act.

Schedule 19 to the 1998 Act determines the provision for religious education which is required by s. 80 (1)(a) or s. 101 (1)(a) of the 2002 Act as part of the basic curriculum of schools:

(a) community schools and foundation and voluntary schools which do not have a religious character,

(b) foundation and voluntary controlled schools which have a religious character; and

(c) voluntary aided schools which have a religious character.

Provision of religious education in (a) and (b) should be the agreed syllabus.

4. SPIRITUAL, MORAL, CULTURAL, MENTAL & PHYSICAL DEVELOPMENT

LEAs, again together with governing bodies and headteachers, must exercise their functions with a view to securing that each pupil at a maintained school shall, on each school day, take part in an act of collective worship (s. 70 of the School Standards and Framework Act 1998). For judicial consideration of this duty, see *R v Secretary of State for Education ex p R and D* [1994] ELR 495 (and noted by Liell *et.al.*, (2003) at F[852]).

Each LEA is under an obligation to convene a conference to devise an agreed syllabus of religious education. The conference has to consist of representatives of Christian and other religious traditions in the area (in numbers reflecting their strengths) together with teacher and LEA representatives (s. 375 of and sched 31 to, the Education Act 1996). The LEA must adopt as the agreed syllabus for the area the syllabus agreed by the conference. The syllabus must reflect the fact that the religious traditions in Great Britain are in the main Christian whilst taking account of the teaching and practices of the other principal religions represented in Great Britain (s. 375(3) of the 1996 Act). An LEA must also convene an Agreed Syllabus Conference on receipt of written notification from a Standing Advisory Council on Religious Education (sched 31, para 3 to the 1996 Act).

Standing Advisory Councils on Religious Education (SACREs) are bodies which must be established by every LEA (s. 390 of the 1996 Act). Their role is to advise LEAs on such matters connected with (a) religious worship in community schools or in foundation schools which do not have a religious character and (b) the religious education to be given in accordance with an agreed or other syllabus in accordance with sched 19 to the School Standards and Framework Act 1998 as the LEA may refer to the SACRE or as the SACRE sees fit. The relevant matters include, in particular, methods of teaching, the choice of materials and the provision of training for teachers (s. 391(1) and (2)). In addition, SACREs have a duty to consider, upon request from a headteacher of any community school maintained by the LEA or any foundation school which has not been designated as having a religious character, whether it is appropriate that the requirement that there be an act of daily Christian collective worship should apply in the case of the school (s. 394).

The composition and constitution of SACREs are regulated by ss. 390–392 of the 1996 Act. For guidance on SACREs, see DES Circular 1/94 Religious Education and Collective Worship.

See also chapter 3.B.5 of this book.

E. Curriculum Information

LEAs are under a duty under s. 408 of the 1996 Act to provide information about the curriculum and assessment arrangements of maintained schools when required by regulations. The duty to publish school level key stage 2 performance was repealed by the Education (School Performance Information) (England) (Amendment) Regulations 2003 (SI 2002 No. 2135) from the principal regulations, the Education (School Performance Information) (England) Regulations 2001 (SI 2001 No. 3446) as amended. However, duties remain in relation to information about key stage 1 results and excluded pupils. There is a duty to enable the transfer of information about pupils between schools – the 'common transfer information' – as specified in the Education (Pupil Information) (England) Regulations 2000 (SI 2000 No. 297) as amended and the LEA has duties in the production of information about schools in the Education (School Performance Information) (Wales) Regulations 1998 (SI 1998 No. 1867) as amended.

5. MONITORING AND IMPROVING STANDARDS

A. The Law's Requirements

1. Introduction

Although there may be concerns at the underplaying of some of the other functions of LEAs by both the DfES and Ofsted, there is no doubt that a widely-recognised and key role of the LEA is to ensure that educational standards both in schools and amongst its own staff are monitored and improved.

2. The golden thread

The golden thread, running through everything an LEA does, is the obligation to promote and support educational improvement and high standards of achievement within the whole community as well as specifically in schools. This responsibility is based on clear general legal duties, but LEAs will achieve the noble aims only by utilising their true strengths as community leaders, facilitators and, above all, partners with other local educational interests. Recourse to legal duties and use of intervention powers can and should only be of last resort. Establishing a general ethos of improvement and high standards, pervading the whole service, is the only way that LEAs will be able to achieve these objectives and, indeed in the light of inspection, ensure their own survival.

LEAs have two paramount responsibilities, which must guide virtually all of their work.

First, each LEA is under a duty to contribute towards the spiritual, moral, mental and physical development of the community by securing that efficient primary education, secondary education and further education are available to meet the needs of the population of its area (s. 13 of the 1996 Act).

Second, the major imperative for LEAs is the duty to exercise their functions with a view to promoting high standards, so far as such functions are capable of being so exercised (s. 13A). As this duty applies to all education for persons of compulsory school age and persons above or below that age who are registered pupils at schools maintained by the LEA, the duty affects virtually all that an LEA does and, even where certain functions are outside the legal duty, it would be a foolhardy LEA which did not apply the same ambition to that work as well. In any event, those other functions will have to be subject to a Best Value review and what LEA will seriously argue that it is not prepared to promote high standards in all its work?

To support the whole concept of improvement, specific grants have been made available from the Secretary of State. Previously these were made under separate sets of Standards Fund regulations. General powers to enable the Secretary of State to provide funding for improvement are now contained in s. 14 of the 2002 Act.

5.
MONITORING &
IMPROVING
STANDARDS

3. Education Development Plans

In addition to the general duties, the 1998 Act imposes on LEAs other, more specific duties to further the aim of school improvement.

The most important of these is the requirement for an LEA to prepare an Education Development Plan (EDP) or, in Wales, an Education Strategic Plan (ESP) for its area and such further plans as may be required (s. 6(1) of the 1998 Act). An EDP should set out the LEA's proposals for the action it will take to raise the standards of education provided for the children for whom it is responsible and to improve the performance of the schools it maintains.

An EDP must consist of:

a) a statement setting out the LEA's proposals for developing provision of education for children in its area, whether by:
    (i) raising the standards of education provided for such children (whether at schools maintained by the LEA or otherwise than at school), or
    (ii) improving the performance of such schools; and

(b) annexes to that statement

both of which must contain the material prescribed by the Education Development Plans (England) Regulations 2001 (SI 2001 No. 3815, as amended by the Education Development Plans (England) Regulations 2002 (SI 2002 No. 423)), (this also provided certain flexibilities for five LEAs: Birmingham City Council; Blackburn with Darwen Borough Council; Derbyshire County Council; Stockton-on-Tees Borough Council and Warwickshire County

Council – by virtue of reg 3), or the Education Development Plans (Wales) Regulations 1999 (SI 1999 No. 1439 as amended). They may also contain such other information as the LEA considers relevant (s. 6(2) and (5)).

The statement of proposals must be submitted to the Secretary of State for approval (s. 6(4) and s. 7).

In preparing the EDP, the LEA must have regard to the education of children with special educational needs (s. 6(6)) and must also consult the governing body and headteacher of every school maintained by the LEA, the appropriate diocesan authorities and anyone else it considers should be consulted (s. 6(7)).

To assist in the preparation of EDPs, the Secretary of State may issue guidance to which (pursuant to s. 6(9)) the LEA must have regard. Very brief guidance can be found in the *Code of Practice on LEA – School Relations* (annex 1, paras 12 and 13).

Section 7 of the 1998 Act sets out the procedure for securing the approval of the Secretary of State to the EDP and the options open to the Secretary of State to approve, modify or reject it. If the EDP is approved or approved with modifications, the LEA must publish it in accordance with the regulations.

The work involved in preparing EDPs can be contracted out by LEAs in England, except to the extent that an LEA must not authorise another person to (a) approve the plan, for the purpose of its submission to the Secretary of State for his approval or (b) adopt the plan (with or without modification) (the Contracting Out (Local Education Authority Functions) (England) Order 2002 (SI 2002 No. 928), sched 2, para (a)).

See also chapter 4.A.4.

In addition to the freedoms mentioned above for the five specified LEAs, greater freedom from the restrictions of EDPs have also been granted to LEAs which are considered to be 'excellent' under the Comprehensive Performance Assessment. (See also the *Consultation on Changes to the Plans required of Local Education Authorities by the Department for Education and Skills*, DfES 14 November 2003, which proposes the removal of statutory planning requirements and the introduction of a single education plan, now, in the light of the Children Bill (2004) likely to be superseded by a single, statutory children's plan.)

5.
MONITORING &
IMPROVING
STANDARDS

4.   Literacy and numeracy strategies

Examples of non-statutory obligations imposed on LEAs (what the authors have called *de facto* duties) by DfES decree abound, but the most important in recent years include the requirements imposed in respect of the Literacy and Numeracy Strategies. As frequently the case, these *de facto* duties are tied in to the receipt of grant so that, in order to receive grant funding, LEAs are compelled to implement certain DfEE/ DfES schemes or conditions.

There was or is no statutory duty on LEAs to implement literacy and numeracy strategies in primary schools maintained by them. Instead, LEAs were able to apply for a grant from the Secretary of State under, formerly, the Education (Education Standards etc. Grants) (England) Regulations 1999 (SI 1999 No. 606), or, in Wales, the Education (Education Standards Grants) (Wales) Regulations 1999 (SI 1999 No. 521), for the support set out in the schedules to those regulations, or now generally under s. 14 of the 2002 Act and the various funding or grant schemes which will be established under that section. If successful, the LEA is under a quasi-contractual duty to implement the supported activities, failing which the Secretary of State may take action against it to recover the sums paid.

5.   Limit on infant class sizes

Another element in the Government's effort to raise standards of school education is the provision which seeks to limit infant class sizes to 30 (although the limit may subsequently be amended by the Secretary of State by order (s. 1(5) of the 1998 Act).

By virtue of s. 1 of the 1998 Act, the Education (Infant Class Sizes) (England) Regulations 1998 (SI 1998 No. 1973) and the Education (Infant Class Sizes) (Wales) Regulations 1998 (SI 1998 No. 1943), where infant class size limits apply, each LEA is under a duty to exercise its functions with a view to securing that that limit is complied with in relation to each infant class (s. 1(6)).

An 'infant class' means a class containing pupils the majority of whom will attain the age of five, six or seven during the course of the school year (s. 4).

The 1998 Act leaves much of the detailed provision to the regulations, but it provides that the limit will be 30 pupils during an ordinary teaching lesson conducted by a single qualified teacher (or a single 'school teacher' in Wales, but also in England once para 87 of sched 21 to the Education Act 2002 is brought into force: a 'school teacher' is elsewhere defined as being *inter alia* a qualified teacher).

In order to demonstrate how it intends to meet the class size limits, every LEA is required to prepare a statement setting out the arrangements which the LEA proposes to make for the purpose of securing that any limit imposed on infant class sizes is met at schools maintained by it (s. 2(1)). The statement must contain the information required by the Education (Plans for Reducing Infant Class Sizes) (England) Regulations 1998 (SI 1998 No. 1971) and, for Wales, Education (Plans for Reducing Infant Class Sizes) (Wales) Regulations 1998 (SI 1998 No. 194). Consultation must take place in accordance with the requirements of the regulations and the statement has to be submitted to the Secretary of State for his approval (s. 2(3) and (5)).

The Education (Infant Class Sizes) (Grants) Regulations 1999 (SI 1999 No. 14), make provision for the Secretary of State to pay grants to LEAs in respect of expenditure incurred or to be incurred by them for the purpose of securing that the limits are met (s. 3).

To protect the efforts to reduce class sizes, it was recognised that LEAs could not prepare plans, commit expenditure, turn down applications which would take the numbers in a class above 30, but then find schools having to admit children because they were caught by the normal duty to comply with parental preference and/or decisions made by independent appeal panels. Consequently, the rules for admission appeals (discussed in detail in chapter 12.C.4.1) have been amended so that different procedures apply in respect of appeals against decisions to refuse children admission to an infant class.

These modifications to the normal admission procedures are now found in ss. 86(4) and 94 of, together with sched 24 to, the 1998 Act. Guidance on their effect can be found in the current versions of the *Code of Practice on School Admission Arrangements* (see paras A.35–36) and the *Code of Practice on School Admissions Appeals* (see paras 4:53–60).

The result is that where a parent expresses a preference for their child to be admitted into an infant class, there is a duty on the admissions authority to comply with that preference unless compliance with the preference would prejudice the provision of efficient education or the efficient use of resources (s. 87(3)(a)) or the other two exemptions from the duty (s. 87(3)(b) and (c)).

Prejudice may, however, arise by virtue of s. 87(4) by reason of measures required to be taken in order to ensure compliance with the infant class size duty.

Where admission is refused on the grounds of such prejudice, the procedure and rules for the subsequent appeal change and the chances of a parent's succeeding are significantly reduced. This is because an appeal panel hearing such an appeal can allow the appeal only if either:

a) the decision was not one which a reasonable admissions authority would make in the circumstances of the case and/or

b) the child would have been offered a place if the admission arrangements had been properly implemented.

Guidance on the effect of this new procedure and, in particular, what is meant by reasonable in this context can be found in the *Codes of Practice*.

Somewhat surprisingly, the introduction of these new restrictions did not lead to a flood of litigation or complaints to the Ombudsman. A number of court cases were however subsequently brought in an attempt, largely, to understand what an appeal panel could or could not do. The first case was *R v Southend Borough Education Appeals Committee ex p Southend-on-Sea Borough Council* 17 August 1999, unreported, QBD, in which the judge did not address the changes to the appeal arrangements. Instead, he considered the nature of the evidence which should be presented to appeal committees (now panels) generally and, although criticising what the particular committee had considered, nonetheless held that it was justified in allowing 32 children into a reception class. In the second, *R v Richmond London Borough Council ex parte C (a child)* (2000) *Times*, 26 April, the judge held that an appeal involving infant class size issues was in no sense a rehearing, but a review, of the LEA's decision, a judgment confirmed by the Court of Appeal ([2001] ELR 21).

The biggest issue has been over the circumstances in which appeal panels could decide that the behaviour of the LEA in refusing admission was not one which a reasonable admissions authority would make in the circumstances of the case. The confusion was not helped by DfES guidance circulated following the *Richmond* case, which suggested that panels could not consider the individual circumstances of parents or their children.

Subsequently, in *R (ota South Gloucestershire LEA) v South Gloucestershire Schools Admission Appeals Panel* [2001] EWHC

Admin 732, [2001] All ER (D) 81(Aug) QBD, in the particular circumstances of the case, including a confusing admissions policy, the court upheld a panel's decision to allow infant class size appeals to succeed on the grounds of unreasonableness. Of more general importance is the decision of the *Court of Appeal in R v School Admissions Appeals Panel for Hounslow LBC ex parte Hounslow LBC* [2002] EWCA Civ 900. Refuting the idea that parental preference did not have to be taken into account in infant admissions, the court made clear that whilst an infant class size appeal was merely a review not a rehearing and that the 'unreasonable' ground implied perversity on the part of the admissions authority, not just unreasonableness in the lay sense, nevertheless, the circumstances of the case had to include the child's particular circumstances, including the preference expressed by the parents, as well as the LEA's admissions arrangements. The child's and parents' circumstances are therefore relevant albeit only in so far as they shed light on any perversity of the LEA's decision. Unlike with non-infant class size appeals, those circumstances cannot be used in an attempt to outweigh a decision made by the admissions authority which was otherwise one a reasonable admissions authority could make.

The restrictions on parental 'rights' inherent in the infant class size duty and limited rights of appeal are not incompatible with the Human Rights Act 1998 – see the *Richmond* case and *R (ota K and S) v Admissions Appeal Panel of Cardiff County Council and Cardiff County Council* [2003] EWHC 436 Admin.

6. Intervention in schools

As the *Code of Practice on LEA-School Relations* makes clear (see para 6), the highest priority for the LEA is to promote high standards of education. Key to this is its support for self-improvement in all schools. To do this, an LEA needs to monitor information about all schools, facilitate the sharing of best practice, but focus its energies and resources on schools which need further challenge or support to secure improvement. And where, we would add, the LEA (or, in this new world of contracting out, the appropriate external provider) may as a last resort have to intervene. Although the current Code does not expressly state that there is a presumption in favour of school autonomy as the old Code did, the guidance still suggests that successful schools should be given greater freedom from LEA involvement. It does, however, better recognise that such autonomy has to be matched with accountability. If schools fail, intervention may be necessary to ensure that the school's pupils do not suffer. The role of the LEA is central to this process as the means by which external support and intervention can be brought to the assistance of schools.

To facilitate this role, the 1998 Act (together with the enhanced powers in the 2002 Act, such as interim executive boards) provides LEAs with a number of powers to intervene where absolutely necessary in the governing body's and headteacher's running of a maintained school. A number of the powers may have been in existence prior to the Act, but the benefit of the 1998 legislation is that they are now set out expressly and these, together with the guidance in the *Code of Practice* (see specifically Annexes 2 and 3), help clarify the action LEAs can take in respect of schools causing concern.

Though the Education (Schools) Act 1992 set limits on an LEA's powers to inspect its own schools, the Act (and the consolidating School Inspections Act 1996) empowered an LEA to carry out an inspection in respect of any school maintained by it where (a) for the purpose of enabling it to exercise any of its functions, the LEA requires information about any matter in connection with the school and (b) it is not reasonably practicable for it to obtain the information in any other manner (s. 25 of the School Inspections Act 1996). Any LEA officer carrying out such an inspection has a right of entry to the school premises at all reasonable times (s. 25(2)). For guidance, see part III of Annex 1 of the Code of Practice.

A key provision is contained in s. 14 of the School Standards and Framework Act 1998, which provides that an LEA may intervene in a maintained school in certain circumstances. Those circumstances are outlined below.

Where, as a result of such an inspection or as a result of information from other sources, the LEA discovers that there are concerns about the conduct or organisation of a school, it can issue a formal warning notice to the governing body (s. 15 of the School Standards and Framework Act 1998).

Such a notice can, however, be issued only in certain circumstances. These are that the LEA is satisfied that:

a) the standards of performance of pupils at the school are unacceptably low and are likely to remain so unless intervention occurs; or

b) there has been a serious breakdown in the way the school is managed or governed which is prejudicing, or is likely to prejudice, such standards of performance; or

c) the safety of pupils or staff of the school is threatened (whether by a breakdown of discipline or otherwise); and

d) the LEA has previously informed the governing body and the headteacher of the matters upon which that conclusion is based; and

e) those matters have not been remedied to the LEA's satisfaction (s. 15(2)).

The LEA should give notice to the governing body and/or headteacher of its concerns and what it believes they should do. If the appropriate party has not remedied the situation satisfactorily, the LEA may give a formal warning notice to the governing body. The warning notice must be in writing and must set out the matters causing concern, the action which is required and the period within which those matters shall be rectified and action taken (s. 15(3)).

If the governing body fails to comply or secure compliance with the notice to the LEA's satisfaction within the specified period and the LEA gives reasonable notice that it intends to use its intervention powers, then it may do so.

The one case on the exercise of powers under s. 15, *R v Rhondda Cynon Taff County BC ex parte Lynwen Evans* 31 August 1999, unreported, has set down a number of principles to be followed. Where an LEA intends to rely on s. 15(2) and particularly s. 15(2)(a) or (b), the governing body and headteacher should be informed before the issuing of the notice. As the notice would be directed at those already involved who should be aware of most of the circumstances, the prior notification does not have to be particularly detailed nor be in writing. The s. 15 notice does, however, have to be clear and the time for compliance has to be reasonable in terms of the amount of teaching time available to take the necessary steps.

The ability to use the intervention powers also arises in two other situations.

1. Where a report of an inspection has been made under the School Inspections Act 1996, an opinion has been given that the school has serious weaknesses and where a subsequent inspection of the school has been made and the initial opinion has not been superseded by the inspector's making a report stating that in his opinion the school no longer has serious weaknesses; or the Chief Inspector's giving the Secretary of

State a notice that the school requires special measures. This provision has been extended by the 2002 Act (s. 55). Previously, an LEA had to wait to intervene until a subsequent report had been produced concluding that the school still had serious weaknesses; now it is not necessary to wait for the formal report. Serious weaknesses are found where, although giving its pupils in general an acceptable standard of education, the school has significant weaknesses in one or more areas of its activities (s. 15(5)).

2. Following an inspection under the School Inspections Act 1996, the Chief Inspector has given the Secretary of State notice that he agrees with the registered inspector that special measures are required to be taken in relation to the school and, in any subsequent report of an inspection, the report does not state that in the opinion of the inspector special measures were not required to be taken (s. 15(6)).

NB although inspections of schools are mainly a matter between the school and Ofsted (or, in Wales, Estyn), the LEA does have a duty to prepare a written statement of the action which it, as opposed to the governing body, proposes to take in light of the report or to produce a written statement of why it proposes no action on its part (s. 18(2)(a) of the School Inspections Act 1996).

If these situations exist at a school maintained by the LEA, the LEA may exercise the powers of intervention contained in the 1998 Act (s. 14(2)). These consist of:

a) the power to appoint such number of additional governors as the LEA thinks fit (s. 16); or

b) the power to provide that the governing body consist of interim executive members (s. 16A); and

c) the power to suspend the school's right to a delegated budget (s.17 and see also chapter 6.D, below).

In addition, the LEA may intervene, whether or not the conditions laid down in s. 14 apply, where there has been a fundamental breakdown of discipline (see s. 62 of the 1998 Act and chapter 9.G.3 of this book).

The further power to provide that the governing body comprise interim executive members (IEMs) was inserted by the 2002 Act (s. 57). It enables the LEA at any time when the circumstances permitting intervention apply, with the consent of the Secretary of State, to give the governing body written notice stating that, from a specified date, the governing body is to be constituted as a governing body consisting of interim executive members (s. 16A(1) and constituted under sched 1A to the 1998 Act). If the LEA seeks to invoke this power in respect of a school with serious weaknesses or in special measures, it can do so only if the Secretary of State has given the LEA notice under s. 16A of the School Inspections Act 1996 (that the Chief Inspector has notified him that the school has serious weaknesses or requires special measures) and at least 10 days have elapsed since the date of the Secretary of State's notice (s. 16A(2) 1998 Act) or such shorter period as the Secretary of State may determine (s. 16A(3)). Before using this power the LEA must consult the governing body of the school, where relevant, the appropriate diocesan authority, or, in the case of any other foundation or voluntary school, the persons by whom the foundation governors are appointed (s. 16A(4)).

The constitution and powers of Interim Executive Boards (IEBs), the name given to governing bodies comprising interim executive members, are set out in s. 59 of and sched 6 to the 2002 Act, which insert a new schedule 1A into the 1998 Act. Where the LEA has intervened, it is responsible for appointing the members of the IEB, who can be members of the school's governing body. A minimum of two IEMs must be appointed and the chair can be appointed by the LEA. Members can be paid; payments are made by and at the discretion of the LEA (para 9 of schedule 1A). With limited exceptions, the IEB will have the functions of the governing body. The aim is that an IEB will be a short-term entity, which will either turn round the school and allow a reconstituted governing body to take back the conduct of the school or recommend the school's closure.

A further innovation in the 2002 Act is the power given to the Secretary of State or NAW to require an LEA to obtain advisory services (s. 63 of the 2002 Act). Where one or more schools maintained by an LEA may potentially be subject to the LEA's powers of intervention because they require special measures or have serious weaknesses and it appears to the Secretary of State (or the NAW in Wales) that the LEA:

(i)   has not been effective or is unlikely to be effective in eliminating deficiencies in the conduct of the school or schools, or

(ii) is unlikely to be effective in eliminating deficiencies in the conduct of other schools which may in future fall within those categories, or

(iii) maintains a disproportionate number of schools falling within those categories

The Secretary of State or NAW may direct the LEA to enter into a contract or other arrangement with a person specified in the direction, or a person falling within a specified class, for the provision to the LEA or the governing body of any school maintained by the LEA, or both, of specified services of an advisory nature (s. 63(1) and (2)).

The direction may require the contract or arrangement to contain specified terms and conditions (s. 63(3)). Any such direction shall be enforceable by a mandatory order (s. 63(5)).

Where the Secretary of State or NAW notifies the LEA that he/it is contemplating making such a direction, the LEA must give him/it such assistance as it can reasonably give (s. 64(1)). The person brought in to provide the advisory services must have, at all reasonable times, a right to enter the LEA's premises and a right to inspect and take copies of any records or other documents kept by the LEA and any other document containing information relating to the LEA which he considers relevant to the provision of the advisory services (s. 64(3)) as well as access to computers and computer records (s. 64(4) of the 2002 Act and s. 497B(3) of the 1996 Act). Similar rights of access and inspection apply to schools maintained by the LEA (s. 63(6)).

7. The proper performance of LEA functions

If LEAs are to continue to play a central role in the provision of effective and efficient education, it is obvious that they too must strive to be effective and efficient. As has been seen (chapter 1.C.4), LEAs are required to undergo Best Value reviews across the whole range of their functions as part of the obligation placed on all local authorities. In addition, however, the Secretary of State has a number of powers in place to monitor and require improvements in the standards of LEAs.

Her Majesty's Chief Inspectors of Schools in England and in Wales have the power (or the duty, if the Secretary of State or Assembly, as appropriate, directs them to do so) to arrange for any LEA to be inspected (s. 38 of the Education Act 1997). An inspection consists of a review of the way in which the LEA is performing any of its functions which relate to the provision of education (a) for persons of compulsory school age (whether at school or otherwise) or (b) for persons of any age above or below compulsory school age who are registered as pupils at any school maintained by the LEA (s. 38(2)).

If the Secretary of State (or, as appropriate, the NAW) intends to request an inspection, he must first consult the Chief Inspector (but not the LEA) and any inspection so requested shall specify the LEA or LEAs concerned and the functions to which the inspection is to relate (s. 38(4) and (3)).

An inspection will be carried out by one of Her Majesty's Inspectors of Schools or by an additional inspector authorised under para 2 of schedule 1 to the School Inspections Act 1996 and may be assisted by such persons as the Chief Inspector thinks fit (s. 38(5)).

5.
MONITORING &
IMPROVING
STANDARDS

If the Chief Inspector requests, the Audit Commission may assist with any inspection (s. 41(1)), provided that the Chief Inspector pays the Commission's full costs.

The LEA must provide the Chief Inspector with prescribed information within such time as the relevant regulations require (s. 38(6)). At the time of writing no such regulations were in force, although that has not stopped the Chief Inspector setting out the information required from LEAs and LEAs complying with such requests.

The inspector carrying out the inspection or any person assisting him has at all reasonable times a right to enter the premises of any LEA to which the inspection relates, the premises of any school maintained by the LEA and any other premises at which education by way of exceptional provision for children in PRUs or otherwise out of school is provided (s. 40(2) of the Education Act 1997) other than a private dwelling house. The inspectors also have the right to inspect, and take copies of, any records kept by the LEA and any other documents containing information relating to the LEA, or any school maintained by the LEA, or exceptional provision, which the inspector considers relevant to the exercise of his function (s. 40(3)).

The LEA and the governing body of any school maintained by the LEA must also give the inspector and his assistants all assistance in connection with the exercise of his functions which it is reasonably able to give (s. 40(5)).

To assist in the inspection process, Ofsted issued *Framework for the inspection of LEAs* (HMI 345: until superseded by the latest version effective from January 2004 (HMI 1770)), which explains the basis upon which inspections of LEAs will be carried out and indicates to

LEAs what functions will be reviewed. The 2004 Framework lays greater emphasis on LEAs' self-evaluation and on differentiation of inspection according to LEAs' performance scores.

In Wales, Estyn has issued *Local Education Authorities in Wales. A Framework for Inspection* (April 2003), setting out inspection arrangements as part of the Wales Programme for Improvement.

Following an inspection, the inspector must make a written report on the matters reviewed and send copies of the report to the LEA (or if more than one LEA, to all the relevant LEAs) and the Secretary of State (s. 39(1)).

Upon receipt of the report, the LEA must prepare a written statement of the action which it proposes to take in light of the report and the period within which it proposes to take it. The LEA must publish the report and the statement within a prescribed period and in accordance with regulations (s. 39(2) and (3)).

The Chief Inspector may arrange for any report to be published in such manner as he considers appropriate (s. 39(4)).

The Secretary of State has always possessed general default powers to intervene where LEAs have failed to discharge any statutory duty (see s. 497 Education Act 1996 and *Meade v Haringey LBC* [1979] 2 All ER 1016; *R v Secretary of State for Education and Science ex p Chance* 26 July 1982, unreported and *Secretary of State for Education and Science v Tameside MBC* [1977] AC 1014). See chapter 12.B.1.

To deal with LEAs which are not necessarily in default of their statutory duties but which are not performing adequately, the 1998 Act gives the Secretary of State and the NAW additional reserve powers. The 2002 Act has added to these to ensure that all relevant LEA functions are covered, including those such as early years and adult education which were arguably omitted from the 1998 Act. Statutory references in the rest of this section are to the Education Act 1996 as amended.

If the Secretary of State is satisfied (either on complaint by any interested person or otherwise) that an LEA is failing in any respect to perform any function under the Education Acts, or any other functions of whatever nature which are conferred on the LEA in its capacity as an LEA, to an adequate standard or at all, the Secretary of State may:

a)   give the LEA or an officer of the LEA such directions as the Secretary of State thinks expedient for the purpose of securing that the function is performed on behalf of the LEA by a person specified in the direction. The directions may require that any contract or other arrangement made by the LEA with that person contains such terms and conditions as may be so specified (s. 497A(4)); and

b)   direct that the function shall be exercised by the Secretary of State or a person nominated by him and that the LEA shall comply with any instructions of the Secretary of State or his nominee in relation to the exercise of the function (s. 497A(4A)); and

c)   give the LEA or an officer of the LEA such other directions as the Secretary of State thinks expedient for the purpose of securing that the function is performed to an adequate standard (s. 497A(4B)).

The Secretary of State may also exercise these powers where he has given a previous direction in relation to an LEA and he is satisfied that it is likely that if no further direction were given on the expiry or revocation of the previous direction, the LEA would fail in any respect to perform that function to an adequate standard or at all (s. 497A(2A)).

Where the Secretary of State considers it expedient that the person specified in directions or the Secretary of State or his nominees, as appropriate, should perform other functions in addition to the functions which are not up to standard, the directions may also relate to the performance of those other functions (s. 497A(5)).

Where the Secretary of State is satisfied that an LEA is failing to perform a function to an adequate standard or at all or is satisfied that this would be the case if no further direction is made (i.e. s. 497A (2) or (2A)(b)), and has notified the LEA that he is so satisfied and that he is contemplating the giving of directions under s. 497A(4) or (4A), the LEA must give the Secretary of State and any person authorised by him for the purpose, all such assistance, in connection with the proposed exercise of the function by the Secretary of State or his nominee, as it is reasonably able to give (s. 497AA). This requires full co-operation prior to any direction as opposed to the other provisions which apply once a direction has been given.

Where the Secretary of State considers it expedient that the person specified in the direction should perform other functions in addition to those where there is failure, the Secretary of State may so specify (s. 497A(5)).

Any direction may either be for an indefinite period until revoked or have effect until any objectives specified in the direction have been achieved (s. 497A(6)). Compliance with directions is mandatory and any refusal to comply can be enforced by a mandatory order (s. 497A(7)). Where the direction gives power to the person specified or nominated by the Secretary of State in the direction, that person shall at all reasonable times have the right to enter the LEA's premises and its maintained schools and a right to inspect and take copies of any records or other documents kept by the LEA and any other documents containing information relating to the LEA which are relevant (s. 497B(2)). The specified or nominated person shall also be entitled at any reasonable time to have access to and inspect and check the operation of, any computer and any associated apparatus which is or has been in use in connection with the records or other documents in question. He may also require the person by whom or on whose behalf the computer is or has been so used or any person having charge of, or otherwise concerned with the operation of the computer (etc.) to afford him such assistance as he may reasonably require (including the making of information available for inspection or copying in a legible form) (s. 497B(3)). The LEA shall also give the person all assistance in connection with the performance of the function or functions which it is able to give.

5.
MONITORING &
IMPROVING
STANDARDS

8. The power to innovate

In a chapter dealing with raising standards and securing improvement, it is probably also important to consider the new power to innovate included as one of the main features of the 2002 Act.

The purpose of the power is to make it easier to implement innovative projects that may, in the opinion of the Secretary of State, or, in Wales, the NAW, contribute to the raising of the educational standards achieved by children (s. 1(1) of the 2002 Act).

In general, it was expected that schools might be more forthcoming with proposals, but the power is available equally to LEAs or to LEAs jointly with schools (s. 1(1) and (3)). In putting a proposal forward, the promoter would seek the suspension of, exemption from, modification to or relaxation of statutory requirements (s. 2) which would otherwise get in the way of or compromise the efforts to innovate. Applications for orders, which are required to give effect to the exemption etc, must be made in such form as is required (see s. 4(1)) and before making the application the applicant should consult the LEA and such other persons as appear to be appropriate, having regard to published guidance (see s. 4(2)(c)). In deciding whether the application may contribute to the raising of educational standards, the Secretary of State must have regard to the need for the curriculum for any school affected by the project to be a balanced and broadly based curriculum which promotes the spiritual, moral, cultural, mental and physical development of children and society and consider the likely effect of the project on all the children who may be affected by it (s. 1(2)). Orders may be varied or revoked, but the orders are time limited, having, at most, a life of six years (s. 2(2) and 3(2)).

The first three orders made under this provision were:

- The Langley Junior School (Change to School Session Times) Order 2002 (SI 2002 No. 3063),

- The Grinling Gibbons Primary School (Change to School Session Times) Order 2003 (SI 2003 No. 716) and

- The Norton College (Change to School Session Times) Order 2003 (SI 2003 No.1671).

These permit the named schools to extend their school day without complying with the process laid down in the Changing of School Session Time Regulations 1999 (SI 1999 No. 2733).

9. Education Action Zones

Education Action Zones were seen by the new government in 1997 as a means of raising standards and were therefore an instrumental part of the 1998 Act.

Under s. 10 of the 1998 Act, the Secretary of State may, if he considers that it is expedient to do so with a view to improving standards in the provision of education at any particular maintained schools, nursery schools, pupil referral units or independent schools, order that those schools collectively constitute an education action zone (s. 10(1) and (1A)). Such a zone will be established initially for three years, but the Secretary of State may provide for it to continue for a further two years.

Where an education action zone is in existence for a group of schools, the Secretary of State may add a school in which the LEA has intervened under s. 15 of the Act (s. 10(3)).

A school can be included in a zone only with the consent of the school's governing body (s. 10(4)) and the zone can be enlarged only with the consent of each school which forms part of the zone.

The order which establishes the zone must also establish an Education Action Forum (EAF) for the zone. An EAF is a body corporate (s. 11).The members of an EAF must include one person appointed by the governing body of each participating school and one or two persons appointed by the Secretary of State (s. 11A). Zones may be expanded by adding eligible schools (s. 11B) and schools may also be removed (s. 11C).

The main function or objective of every forum is the improvement of standards of education at each of the participating schools (s. 12(1)) and, with the consent of the Secretary of State, a forum may also carry on any other activities which it considers will promote the provision of, or access to, education whether in a participating school or otherwise (s. 12(1A)). With the agreement of the governing body of a participating school, to further these objects the forum may discharge any function of the governing body on behalf of the governing body (s. 12(2)(a)) or assume full responsibility for the full discharge of that function (s. 12(2)(b)). Governing bodies have not been keen to cede their functions (see Sarah Billington, 'Education Action Zones: a progress report', *Education Law* [2000] at p. 11) – and none has.

Schedule 1 to the 1998 Act provides further details of the composition and constitution of EAFs and the detailed provisions relating to the discharge of the functions of governing bodies were to be contained in regulations issued under s. 12(3), although the Secretary of State indicated that it was expected that within a zone all schools should transfer similar functions to the EAF.

One key feature of an education action zone is that participating schools can apply to the Secretary of State for an exemption from the conditions of employment imposed by the School Teachers' Pay and Conditions Act 1991 (s. 13). Again, though, none has.

Education action zones were seen as key instruments in improving standards especially in literacy, numeracy and basic skills in targeted areas. Seventy-four zones were established, some with optimistic names (see, for example, the Greenwich Time to Succeed Education Action Zone Order 1999, the Speke Garston Excellent Education Action Zone Order 1999, the Epicentre LEAP Ellesmere Port Cheshire Education Action Zone Order 1999 and the South of England Virtual Education Action Zone (No. 2) Order 2000). Their success in meeting these aims though is variable (see *Excellence in Cities and Education Action Zones: management and impact*, HMI, June 2003). Establishment of an Education Action Zone brought with it higher levels of funding from the Government, together with anticipated private sector fundraising. Each zone received £500,000 of Government grant, but is under a duty to raise a further £250,000 from private sector businesses operating in its area.

Zones were also intended to have a wider role than just improving standards. This was recognised by the desire to involve local businesses and not just for fund-raising purposes. The intention was that by providing improvements in basic skills, vocational skills should increase with a consequential benefit to the future workforce in the area (see 'Plenty of snap and crackle but where's the radical pop?' *The Independent*, 16.3.2000). It should also secure greater inclusion in schools and education action zones have certain responsibilities to address social exclusion in their areas and specifically to reduce truancy and exclusions.

Though there were early expectations – by Ministers if by nobody else – that EAZs could be a prototype for the LEA of the future, this has never happened. Initially established for three years, most have been extended for a further two years, giving a maximum life of five years. None, however, will continue beyond that period and the last Zone will be wound up in 2005. Instead, the objectives of the Zones will be transferred to Excellence in Cities (EiC) projects, with their mini-EiC action zones or clusters, which will be run under the umbrella of other organisations, usually LEAs. All EAFs as bodies corporate will be dissolved.

B. Good Practice Exemplified: Monitoring and Intervention for Improvement

1. Introduction

The high profile given to school improvement, both by the government and in LEA inspections has made this well-trodden

5. MONITORING & IMPROVING STANDARDS

ground. The first edition of this book included a detailed outline, drawn from the procedures of one LEA, but written also in the light of others' practices. By now all LEAs will have developed and refined their own approach in the light of local circumstances, albeit heavily influenced by the framework of law and policy outlined in section A above.

The shorter section in this edition gives a brief summary of the main elements which are usually covered in schemes adopted by LEAs. A copy of the fuller and revised version of the procedural steps outlined below is available to readers on the EMIE website (www.nfer.ac.uk/emie), as are similar documents from a number of other authorities.

2. Principles

The processes adopted by the LEA to govern its improvement strategy will be based on a number of principles for which agreement will have been negotiated with schools:

- the criteria for establishing need are clear, are implemented fairly and ensure that schools will receive the level of support they need when they need it,

- the LEA is committed to the early identification of difficulties in schools so as to intervene preventatively whenever possible,

- the LEA's processes for identification of need will build on and support schools' own processes for self-review, but will be supplemented by the LEA's analyses of data, the first hand observation by inspectors in classrooms and the feedback from other LEA officers. Schools may identify for themselves that there are weaknesses which need to be addressed and signal this to the LEA through the link inspector, and

- this partnership approach will encourage schools' independence and an understanding that they are themselves responsible for bringing about their own improvements.

The basis for seeking such LEA wide agreements is the *Code of Practice on LEA-School Relations*. The agreements are reviewed and renegotiated periodically as strategies develop in each locality. That process will include considering issues of:

- transparency;

- consultation;

- an understanding of the circumstances in which the LEA will use its new and existing powers with schools and governing bodies;

- partnerships, federations and collaborative structures; and

- involvement of the Learning and Skills Council where there are weaknesses in sixth-form provision.

3. Monitoring, review and evaluation

The success of strategies to raise standards of achievement by improving the quality of teaching, educational leadership and management depends upon the appropriateness of action plans and the willingness and the capacity to implement necessary change. The contribution of the LEA to improving quality in schools requires its officers to engage with them in processes involving judgments, evaluating, analysing and acting on a wide range of information. LEA schemes often set out explicitly what is meant by these terms, which are examined below.

3.1 Monitoring

Monitoring is the systematic and routine collection of information about a range of statistical and other performance data and first-hand observations relating to schools' performance, to activities in formal plans, particularly the EDP or (for Wales) ESP, School Improvement, Raising Attainment and Collaborative Plans and to locally and nationally set expectations or targets all within a given period of time.

Good information and intelligence about all aspects of both the LEA's and schools' performance will help to secure reliable conclusions and evaluations.

3.2 Analysis

The interpretation of information will involve gauging significant differences or changes over time and taking relevant individual circumstances into account whilst comparing against national and local benchmarks. Sensitive use of these judgments will make for sound analysis.

3.3 Evaluation

Evaluation involves judging the value of activities in terms of their impact, their sustainability and cost effectiveness. Evaluation will be most valuable when it involves the school through a process of self-evaluation, complemented by an objective judgment from external observers.

3.4 Challenge

Challenge is fundamental to all the monitoring and evaluation activities outlined above. Challenge will be provided through the LEA's programmed visits to schools to:

- agree targets;

- observe teaching; and

- validate schools' own processes of self-evaluation.

**5.
MONITORING &
IMPROVING
STANDARDS**

3.5 Monitoring through Ofsted inspection reports

Ofsted inspection provides a sustained period of direct observation that gives rise to shared judgments about leadership and management, standards, teaching and learning, pupil progress and the pastoral, administrative, professional and financial strengths and weaknesses of the school.

Following an Ofsted inspection, information from the inspection, the strengths and weaknesses of the school and major issues such as the quality of teaching become available to inform other LEA monitoring and support activities.

4. Information

Good information and intelligence are crucial to the exercise of the improvement function. Whilst there is no substitute for first-hand knowledge, as we have seen above, LEAs are expected to obtain as much information as they can by other means before undertaking school visits or direct observation. Again, LEA published strategies will be explicit about their sources of information for evaluation:

- data collection such as academic results, finance, attendance, pupil exclusions, schools' performance and assessment reports (for inspections), LEA profile, LEA's inspection databases, data from Ofsted inspections;

- direct observation of schools' activity, through visits by link, phase and subject inspectors and other LEA officers;

- judgments made by the school's self-review.

5.
MONITORING &
IMPROVING
STANDARDS

4.1 The LEA's departmental database

Most LEAs have some form of school database to record information and evaluative judgments based on the above mentioned monitoring activities. This information is then made available to decision-makers in both the LEA and schools, from a single source in an easily accessible format. Its regular maintenance with accurate, relevant and up-to-date information lies at the heart of the LEA's ability to know how well schools are performing and progressing, the areas where intervention or help is needed and the sources of successful practice. All information on individual schools is available to the headteacher of the relevant school and print-outs are frequently provided, to coincide with visits from staff (usually termed advisers or inspectors) designated as the main link with each school. No new information is entered onto the database without the headteacher's first having been informed and, in many cases, providing the information. In the vast majority of cases there will have been prior agreement between the officer and the headteacher about the entry.

5. Support

The school improvement function is characterised very much as a balance between challenge and support. In this instance LEAs have aspired faithfully to translate political rhetoric into reality.

5.1 Financial

Much of the financial resource for school improvement is built into delegated school budgets. However schools have access to additional support for planned developments, for example through Standards Fund and the Leadership Incentive Grant. This support is targeted at specified schools which, through the regular programme of monitoring and evaluation, are identified as needing to make greater improvements.

5.2 Human resources

All LEAs maintain teams of officers to undertake their school-improvement function and adopt processes to review the standards of all schools in the LEA, to identify successful practice and those schools which are causing concern. All aspects of schools' performance are taken into account, including pupils' performance, attendance and behaviour, progress in addressing key issues, quality of teaching, standards of management and governance.

Many LEA services, outside school improvement teams, have close contacts with schools and, where these are on a formal basis, information about their specialist aspect will also add to the information available on which judgments will eventually be made. Where contact is less formal the LEA representative will make a note of any issues and copy it to the school and make a note of visits on the departmental database. If the issue is serious the officer will bring this to the attention of a service head.

Where issues of concern are noted – some of which may need corroboration before being recorded – schools are categorised by grade or level according to a hierarchy of seriousness of the matters causing concern. This categorisation is then used as a trigger for appropriate action including a more intensive level of monitoring than the basic entitlement level and, where necessary, additional support.

5.3   School-specific monitoring

Where schools are identified as needing higher levels of monitoring and support, monitoring is often undertaken by a specially formed group chaired by a senior LEA officer and including the headteacher, the link inspector, appropriate governor(s) and any officer whose expertise is relevant to the identified concern. This group will meet as necessary to review progress, agree action and report back to the LEA's main monitoring structures.

6.   Categorisation of schools

As indicated above, LEAs are required to graduate their intervention in schools in inverse proportion to success. In order to ensure equity and avoid challenge under the *Code of Practice on LEA – School Relations* this needs to be done in a transparent, structured and objective manner. Whilst structures and criteria differ in detail they tend to follow a similar pattern.

There is invariably some form of 'basic entitlement' level which defines the degree of contact the LEA expects to have with all its schools. This may involve, say, two or three half-day visits per year from a specialist link inspector to focus on the outcomes of his or her desk-based review of school performance.

There will then be a category (or categories) recognising low level or temporary development issues which require a slightly higher level of LEA monitoring and possibly some extra support. Where additional factors are present, higher levels of 'concern' will be defined, with the highest usually being a school that has been placed in 'special measures' as a result of an adverse Ofsted inspection report.

Issues taken into account in making these decisions include:

- levels of pupil attainment in comparison to national averages

- levels of achievement, using national value-added comparisons, in comparison to similar schools

- progress against agreed targets, or deficiency in target-setting process

- quality and consistency of teaching across the school

- post-inspection action plan or other planning issues

- level of complaints received by the LEA from parents, staff, governors or pupils

- exclusion or attendance rates

- effectiveness of the governing body

- any other aspects of leadership and management, pupil behaviour, attendance, target-setting, curriculum organisation and management, relationships with parents and the community or provision for particular groups of pupils which are judged to be problematic – using Ofsted criteria.

In addition to judgments based on what might be termed the objective performance of schools, LEAs usually take into account contextual issues, which may be temporary in nature, but which call for additional monitoring and/or support. These may therefore occur in schools rated good, very good or excellent in other respects.

Such temporary development issues might include:

- significant staff changes – new headteacher, new deputy headteacher, a number of key teachers moving, a major reorganisation of teaching or management responsibilities or the appointment of one or more newly-qualified teachers

- significant changes to pupil population – sudden rises or falls, shifts in the population balance (rehousing, asylum seekers etc.), changes in levels of pupils with SEN and small shifts in patterns of attendance or exclusions

**5.
MONITORING &
IMPROVING
STANDARDS**

- significant building issues – unexpected damage, major repairs or redevelopment, significant internal reorganisation, amalgamation

- significant community issues – individual complex parental complaints, new community involvements (Sure Start, out-of-hours learning, etc)

- significant curriculum issues – major reorganisation, problems with national strategies

- 'schools facing challenging circumstances', as defined by DfES

- other unexpected problems – by definition unpredictable.

These lists are intended to be illustrative rather than exhaustive.

5.
MONITORING &
IMPROVING
STANDARDS

7. Intervention

The hard edge of school improvement is reached when challenge and support have not worked and the LEA is required to use its statutory powers of intervention to rectify an unacceptable state of affairs. School improvement strategies will usually outline the approach that will be adopted in these circumstances including intervention in: schools deemed by the LEA or by an Ofsted inspection to have serious weaknesses; schools which require special measures and any to which a formal warning notice has been issued by the LEA. Powers available to the LEA are set out elsewhere in this book, but it is through documents dealing with school improvement that the LEA's approach to using them is drawn to the attention of schools.

6. THE MAINTENANCE OF SCHOOLS, OR KEEPING SCHOOLS GOING

A. Introduction

A cynic might suggest that it is wholly inappropriate to use the word 'structure' in the same heading as 'education' and 'school framework', certainly in England. Is there a structure any more? It is true that schools still exist, by and large, in similar categories to those of 1944 and LEAs still exist to provide some overarching role, but it is not the same structure as was in place in 1997, let alone 1988 and certainly not 1944 or 1902. Instead, these structures have been or will be replaced by a combination of LEA provision, collaboration, federation and companies as well as contracted out functions and the LEA committed to outsourcing. And that is before innovative arrangements which may be piloted under the power to innovate start to appear.

For all the talk of self-government and autonomy, schools within England and Wales still operate, however, within a framework or structure in which the LEA is a (probably the) key participant. Even where LEA functions are outsourced or the LEA may not own school buildings or employ school staff, the LEA remains responsible for maintaining all schools in the public sector (for these purposes Academies are not considered to be schools in the public sector) and for putting in place the constitutional arrangements for their governance.

Although the main role of the LEA is changing rapidly from being a provider of education to being an enabler of school improvement, the fact cannot be ignored that LEAs remain responsible for providing, funding and staffing the majority of schools in the country.

Ofsted has, in the various editions of the *Framework for the Inspection of Local Education Authorities*, unfortunately underplayed the importance of these tasks and any reference to an LEA's maintenance responsibilities in the latest (January 2004) version is still implicit rather than express. Without a constitution and a governing body, without a building, without funds and without staff, no school could function. The authors therefore believe that the role of LEAs in providing the structure of education continues to be fundamental and deserves separate detailed analysis and consideration.

Each LEA is, after all, under a duty to secure that sufficient schools for providing primary and secondary education are available in its area (s. 14 of the Education Act 1996) and to enable them to do so is given power to establish, maintain and assist primary, secondary (s. 16) and nursery schools (s. 17).

In this chapter, therefore, the role of LEAs in constituting governing bodies and providing, supplying and physically supporting the majority of maintained schools will be examined under the following headings:

- School Governance and Related Matters
- The Provision of Schools and School Buildings
- The Financing of Maintained Schools
- Staffing of Maintained Schools.

B. School Governance and Related Matters

1. Constitution of governing bodies and instruments of government

The 2002 Act seeks to provide greater flexibility in the constitution and composition of governing bodies, in part reflecting the recommendations of the Way Forward Group following a DfES consultation exercise on a modernised framework for school governance (September 2001) and provides governing bodies with the powers to make choices as to their structures. Responsibility for approving instruments of government setting out the constitution of such bodies, however, continues to rest with LEAs.

Where proposals for the establishment of any new maintained school have been published, an LEA may make arrangements to constitute a temporary governing body in anticipation of approval of the proposals or a determination that the proposals should be implemented (reg 8(1) of the Education (New Schools) (England) Regulations 2003 (SI 2003 No. 1558) (referred to below as 'the New School Regulations'). As to who should be consulted, see reg

8(2)–(4) and for the composition of a temporary governing body see regs 10–22.

Where proposals for the establishment of any new maintained school fall to be implemented, an LEA must make arrangements providing for the constitution of a temporary governing body, which shall continue in existence until such time as the governing body is constituted for the school under an instrument of government (s. 34(1)–(2) of the Education Act 2002). In fact, the instrument of government must be secured (reg 53(1) of the New School Regulations) by the LEA in accordance with the procedure for making such an instrument under the School Governance (Constitution) (England) Regulations 2003 (see below), before the school opening date, which is the date when the school first admits pupils (s. 34(9) of the Education Act 2002). The instrument takes effect from the date of its making for the purpose of constituting the governing body but this does not affect the continuing operation of the temporary governing body (reg 53(2) of the New School Regulations).

6.
THE
MAINTENANCE
OF SCHOOLS

In the case of an existing maintained school, this will already have a governing body constituted under an instrument of government. Previously, scheds. 9 and 12 to the School Standards and Framework Act 1998 governed the composition of governing bodies and the process for reviewing such instruments and for producing and approving an instrument for a new school. The relevant provisions are now contained in the School Governance (Constitution) (England) Regulations 2003 (SI 2003 No. 348), referred to below as 'the Constitution Regulations'. Although these regulations introduced greater flexibility to permit maintained schools to select the size and composition of the governing body within broadly defined parameters, the LEA is still responsible for approving instruments of government. Governing bodies have had the option of reviewing their constitution from September 2003 onwards, but the LEA is under a duty to ensure that the new-style instruments and governing bodies are in place no later than 31 August 2006 (reg 33 of the School Constitution Regulations).

The constitution and the composition adopted is a matter for the governing body. The LEA's responsibility is to approve every draft instrument submitted to it by a maintained school, subject to a limited number of grounds upon which it may reject it (reg 30(3)). Previously, the instrument had to be made 'by order' of the LEA; to reduce the bureaucracy inherent in that formal process, the new rules simply say that it is for the LEA to approve the instrument (reg 30(3)). How an LEA does that is a matter for it to decide. It must (reg 32) also ensure that a copy of the instrument or any variation to an instrument is sent to:

- every member of the governing body of the school,

- any trustees under a trust deed relating to the school, and

- in the case of a Church of England or Roman Catholic Church School, the appropriate diocesan authority, or in the case of a new school which has not opened, the diocesan authority which will be the appropriate authority.

Apart from providing greater flexibility, the 2002 Act does not really make significant changes to the constitution and instruments of government of maintained schools in themselves. Where it does broaden the powers of governing bodies is in respect of collaboration and federation.

2. Collaboration

To a certain extent, collaboration is not a matter for LEAs. Schools have worked together in many ways in the past, whether informally or more formally, through, for example, agreements relating to the joint use of facilities. To address concerns that some of these arrangements touched at the edge of legality, the 2002 Act gives the Secretary of State power to issue regulations to enable governing body functions to be discharged jointly or by a joint committee (s. 26 and see the School Governance (Collaboration) (England) Regulations 2003 (SI 2003 No. 1962)). LEAs will have little say in these arrangements, but they are something they will have to note and deal with, especially when a joint committee starts to exert greater bargaining or purchasing power.

3. Federations

Of perhaps more significance to LEAs, although only in terms of approving their instruments of government rather than approving their creation, will be federations. Longserving LEA officers may recall the days of grouped schools, Ministerial disfavour for which was enshrined in the School Standards and Framework Act 1998. Now groupings of schools, albeit in federated structures, are back in favour, because they are seen as a means of improving standards.

Care should be taken however, as the term 'federation' has been used to cover a multitude of collaborative arrangements between schools as well as ideas for more formal amalgamations. Here we are referring only to the legal federation of governing bodies envisaged by ss. 24 and 25 of the 2002 Act. Under these provisions the governing bodies of two or more schools (or, where federations have already been created, a federation and another school or two federations) may, after complying with a procedure set out in regulations, provide for their respective schools to be federated. To date, regulations relating only to federations of community, voluntary controlled, community special and maintained nursery schools have been made (the Federation of Schools (Community Schools, Community Special Schools, Voluntary Controlled Schools and Maintained Nursery Schools) (England) Regulations 2003 (SI 2003 No. 1965)). Regulations dealing with federations of voluntary aided, foundation and mixed categories of maintained schools are to appear at some stage in the future.

The effect of federation is that the existing governing bodies are dissolved and a single federated governing body is created to conduct all the schools within the federation. It should be stressed that this is not the same as a merger of schools, as each school within the federation will continue to maintain its separate identity; it is only the governing bodies which are unified into one. Federations may comprise schools of the same or different categories; schools of different phases; mainstream schools and special schools and, indeed, between schools in different LEAs – or a combination of all of these.

Where federation does occur, it will have a single governing body constituted under a single instrument of government (s. 24(3) of the 2002 Act). The same stakeholder models of governing body and the same parameters as to size and composition apply to federated governing bodies, as they do to non-federated ones, subject to modifications set out in schedule 6 to the Federation of Schools (Community Schools, Community Special Schools, Voluntary Controlled Schools and Maintained Nursery Schools) (England) Regulations 2003. Although LEAs will have to be consulted in respect of any proposal to federate (reg 8), LEAs will not be responsible for approving the act of federation itself. The LEA's role will therefore be limited to offering its views and then, once federation is agreed, to approve the federation's instrument of government, the responsibilities for and restrictions on, which are similar to the LEA's role in making or varying 'normal' instruments (reg 24 and the modifications in sched 6). LEAs will also have a role if schools subsequently decide to leave federations or federations are wound up, in terms of putting in place new or amended instruments of government (regs 32 and 37); as a school in a federation will no longer have its own governing body, the

6.
THE
MAINTENANCE
OF SCHOOLS

regulations specify the minimum number of federation governors, parents, staff or others who can initiate a move to leave the federation.

Federated governing bodies will have the same duties and powers as separate governing bodies and special provision will be made to deal with the appointment of headteachers, the appointment of staff where federations include schools from different categories and property transfers, again, particularly difficult where different categories of schools are involved.

4. LEA governors

In addition to constituting governing bodies, LEAs are also responsible for appointing (and occasionally removing) LEA governors. The number of such governors varies between categories of school and, in light of the new flexibilities, will vary depending upon the structure chosen by each governing body. Under an earlier version of the *Code of Practice on LEA-School Relations*, LEAs were encouraged to make appointments promptly and publish the process adopted. That guidance, although no longer appearing in the 2001 version of the Code, still seems valid.

LEAs should not seek to overrule or undermine the true role of their appointees. LEA governors are not delegates and cannot be mandated by the LEA to take any particular line. Their first loyalty and responsibility should be to the school. The DfES encourages LEAs to appoint high-calibre governor candidates to schools that need most support and to appoint candidates irrespective of any political affiliation or preferences. LEAs may appoint minor authority representatives as LEA governors. See the *Statutory Guidance on the School Governance (Constitution) (England) Regulations 2003* (DfES 0323–0329/2003).

Removal of LEA governors is often a sensitive issue. Clearly, given this primary obligation to the school, LEAs should not remove governors on the basis that they do not support the LEA's view on a particular issue (see *R v ILEA ex p Brunyate* [1989] 2 All ER 417, HL). These governors can, however, be removed for good reason. In *R v Warwickshire CC ex p Dill-Russell and Another* (1990) Times, 7 December, the Court of Appeal held that maintaining the political balance after changes brought about by local elections was a lawful reason for replacing LEA nominees on governing bodies – whether this decision is still valid in light of the DfES advice referred to above may, however, be open to question.

5. Support for governors

Finally, in this section on governance proper, LEAs are required to provide governors with support and training. An LEA must therefore secure that every governor is provided, free of charge, with such information as it considers appropriate in connection with the discharge of his or her functions as a governor and secure that there is made available to every governor, free of charge, such training as the LEA considers necessary for the effective discharge of the governor's functions (s. 22 of the 2002 Act and see paras 17 and 18 of Annex 1 of the *Code of Practice on LEA–School Relations*).

6. School companies

A further new player in the educational framework for LEAs will be the school company. A number of schools had already formed companies either alone or with other schools, but, again, concern was expressed at their legality. The opportunity was therefore taken in the 2002 Act to clarify the powers of schools to establish companies and to encourage their use as a means to raise standards, achieve economies of scale and take over the performance of a number of LEA functions.

The legislation (see *Explanatory Notes, Education Act 2002*) envisaged two types of company and the regulations, in effect, create a third:

1. a purchasing company, which procures the provision of services using delegated budgets, including for example, providing or arranging the provision of the financial, technical or legal advice that schools would normally have to arrange elsewhere or procure suppliers through the use of standard contracts;

2. a service delivery company, which would enable beacon schools to share their expertise with other schools or for schools to work together to provide services to other schools and use the proceeds to invest in participating schools; and

3. a company which enters into, facilitates or otherwise enables a school to participate in, a private finance initiative.

If they ever take off and it is perhaps questionable if there is a popular demand for these entities to be created with the additional workload on governors that they entail, they could have a substantial impact on particular LEAs, especially where there is a move for them to take over LEA functions. LEAs will also have a supervisory role over these creatures, as a result of concerns that these companies might otherwise be unaccountable other than to their members or shareholders. Whilst this is a positive step to provide this monitoring, it is perhaps debatable if LEAs are really equipped to monitor private limited companies and guard against insolvency.

A governing body of a maintained school may form or participate in forming companies to provide services or facilities for any schools; to exercise relevant LEA functions; or to make or facilitate the making of, arrangements under which facilities or services are provided for any schools by other persons (s. 11(1)). A governing body may also invest in or provide staff to such a company (s. 11(2) and (5)). Only a school with a delegated budget may form or join a company and if, after the school has joined, the budget is withdrawn, the governing body must withdraw from the company (reg 13 of the School Companies Regulations 2002 (SI 2002 No. 2978)). The LEA functions which are considered relevant are any functions of an LEA as are or may become exercisable by the company in accordance with an authorisation given or direction made by virtue of any enactment (s. 11(9)). This is not the neatest of definitions, but this will extend to functions schools perform on LEAs' behalf out of delegated funds or any function which an LEA can contract out, especially under the Contracting Out (Local Education Authority Functions) (England) Order 2002 (SI 2002 No. 928)).

School companies can be either limited by guarantee or, despite opposition during the Act's passage though Parliament, limited by shares i.e. companies which may pay dividends to shareholders. Although the regulations restrict certain potential abuses, it will continue to be possible for companies limited by shares to make profits and distribute those profits to their shareholders. This is not such an issue where schools and other public bodies are the beneficiaries, but as we will see, the shareholders need not be so confined.

In addition to the restrictions imposed in the two sets of regulations relating to school companies, governing bodies must have regard to any guidance issued by the Secretary of State or NAW. A governing body wishing to form or join a company must also obtain the consent of its LEA (s. 12(1)), although the circumstances in which the LEA may refuse are limited. Thus the LEA must consent unless:

a)   the school is subject to special measures;

b)   the school has serious weaknesses;

c)   the LEA considers that the school is likely to become subject to special measures or be assessed as having serious weaknesses within the next year;

d)   the school has a deficit budget;

e)   the governing body has within the last three years been a member of a school company which became insolvent at a time when it was a member; or

f)   the governing body has been a member of a school company which failed to act in accordance with the relevant regulations within the last three years (reg 15 of the School Companies Regulations 2002).

In the case of PFI companies, consent can be refused only on grounds (d), (f), (a) and (b) (reg 7 of the School Companies (Private Finance Initiative Companies) Regulations 2002 (SI 2002 No. 3177)). In all cases, where an LEA refuses to give consent, it must provide written reasons (reg 16 of the School Companies Regulations 2002 and reg 8 of the School Companies (Private Finance Initiative Companies) Regulations 2002).

As with much of the 2002 Act, the detail on school companies is in regulations and two sets have been issued: one, the School Companies Regulations 2002 (SI 2002 No. 2978, as amended by the School Companies (Amendment) Regulations 2003 (SI 2003 No. 2049)), for non-PFI companies (in effect, categories 1 and 2 identified above) and one for PFI companies, the School Companies (Private Finance Initiative Companies) Regulations. These regulations apply only to England.

The School Companies Regulations apply to any company whose members include the governing body of a maintained school that is using its powers under s. 11 of the 2002 Act. The constitution of such a company must provide that membership is limited to: the governing body of a maintained school; a local authority in England; the proprietor or governing body of an independent school; a company which 'has as a significant proportion of its business the provision of education or educational or ancillary services or goods'; the governing body of a FE or HE institution; and any individual who is not excluded (reg 5). An excluded individual is one who would be disqualified from being a company director or from being a school governor (see schedule1). The regulations also make provision for the appointment of directors,

6.
THE
MAINTENANCE
OF SCHOOLS

interests, remuneration (see regs 6–9 as amended) and also address the application of any surplus or profits (reg 10), although this does not prevent the distribution of surpluses or profits to members of the company.

Of most interest to LEAs are the provisions dealing with the appointment and responsibilities of 'supervising authorities'. Every school company must have an LEA designated as its supervising authority (s. 12(5) and reg 17(1)). If all the participating governing bodies are from schools maintained by one LEA, that LEA is the supervising authority (reg 17(2)). If the schools are drawn from a number of LEAs, the supervising authority is the LEA, if any, which is not a member of the company (reg 17(3)). If this is not the case, the relevant LEAs should agree which one will be the supervising authority and, in the absence of agreement, the matter will be decided by the Secretary of State (reg 18). Supervising authorities may resign (regs 21 and 23) and must resign if all the governing bodies of schools maintained by the supervising authority cease to be members of the company (reg 22).

When an LEA becomes a supervising authority, it must within 28 days provide the Secretary of State with written details of the members of the company, the name and registered number of the company and the fact that it is the supervising authority (reg 25). The authority must also notify the Secretary of State within the same period of any changes to the company's membership, name and registered number or if it ceases to be a relevant LEA, i.e. if it no longer maintains any school within the company (reg 27).

The supervising authority has a duty to monitor the management and finances of the school company and to notify members of the company and relevant LEAs if it considers that the company is poorly managed or there is a risk of the company's becoming insolvent (reg 26). With all due respect to finance officers within LEAs, do they have either the time or the expertise to operate, in effect, as company auditors? To assist the supervising authority in its task, the company must provide it with certain information and accounts (reg 28). These include a copy of audited accounts, first, covering the initial six months of the company's operation from the date a governing body of a maintained school becomes a member and second, thereafter a copy of the annual audited accounts (reg 28(1) and (2)). The company must also supply a copy of its constitution i.e. its memorandum and articles of association within 28 days of the supervising authority's appointment (reg 28(3)). Any changes must also then be notified within 28 days (reg 28(4)).

As to its powers, the supervising authority may direct (reg 29):

a) the company to provide it with such information on the company's constitution, finances, management and contracts to which the company is a party, as the supervising authority requests;

b) the company to take specified steps in order to comply with the regulations;

c) the governing body of a maintained school to reduce its involvement in the management of the company (as to what steps the governing body must take, see reg 32); or

d) the governing body of a maintained school to resign as a member of the company (as to what steps the governing body must take, see reg 33).

6.
THE
MAINTENANCE
OF SCHOOLS

The supervising authority must (reg 30(1)), however, direct the governing body of a maintained school to reduce its involvement in the management of the company or resign where:

- the school is in special measures;

- the school has serious weaknesses;

- the authority considers that the school is likely to become subject to special measures or be assessed as having serious weaknesses within the next year; or

- the school has a deficit budget.

The authority must also direct all governing bodies to resign if the company fails to comply with a discretionary direction issued by the LEA under regulation 29(b) (reg 30(2)) (though whether a governing body must resign if the company fails to comply with a mandatory direction under reg 30(1) is not specified).

Where a direction to resign is issued, the supervising authority must notify the company of the direction within seven days of issuing it (reg 34(1)). A supervising authority may, however, revoke a direction at any time by informing the governing body (reg 34(2)).

The role of the supervising authority in respect of Private Finance Initiative (PFI) Companies is dealt with in the School Companies (Private Finance Initiative Companies) Regulations. These are companies whose members include the governing body of a maintained school which has exercised its powers under s. 11 of the

2002 Act to become a member of the company, where the main purpose of the members in forming the company is to enter into or facilitate agreements under the private finance initiative and one of the company's objects is to enter into or facilitate agreements under the private finance initiative (reg 4). An 'agreement under the private finance initiative' is defined in reg 3.

The designation of a supervising authority is dealt with in regulations 10–15 and the information which the supervising authority must supply to the Secretary of State in reg 17.

However, the supervising authority has no other duties i.e. it does not have to monitor the management and finance of the company nor does it have any powers, in particular to issue directions. The only obligation on the company is to provide the supervising authority with its annual audited accounts (reg 18). The rationale behind permitting an LEA to supervise a company providing, say, services, but not one entering into a multi-million pound PFI deal is perhaps difficult to fathom, but presumably it is assumed that the LEA will be a key player in such a company and will therefore have the necessary oversight through other means.

If these companies are to become common, then they may have a substantial impact on LEAs, definitely if they seek to carry out LEA functions, but also where, even if the companies are not in competition, the LEA is required to perform a monitoring and supervisory role.

C. The Provision of Schools and School Buildings

1. Introduction

Amidst the emphasis on the self-government of schools, the role of LEAs in providing the structure in which education is provided can be overlooked. Despite the period of opting out and the continuing role of foundation and voluntary aided schools, the great majority of schools are provided and maintained (in construction and repair terms, possibly with the assistance of PFI schemes) by LEAs. All are, of course, maintained in financial terms by LEAs. Or at least they are at the time of writing: the first paragraph of chapter 1.A.1 draws attention to the continuing debate over the funding role of LEAs in the context of political concern over the unsatisfactory state of local government funding as a whole.

To many, the fundamental role of the LEA, besides providing strategic leadership and a force for improvement, is its provision of schools and school buildings, the allocation of resources to extend and improve and its responsibility to ensure that schools are of a standard in which children can learn – a key part of the LEA's strategic management. Indeed, Ofsted (or, in Wales, Estyn) will criticise LEAs which fail to maintain school buildings to an appropriate, or even, in some cases, basic, standard (see, for example, the inspection report on Sheffield LEA, 2 February 2000).

There is also a considerable overlap between the strategic management function and the responsibility to secure access by providing sufficient school places and removing surplus places where necessary. Although it is in theory possible for an LEA to own no school of its own, but to supply places through schools established and maintained by other bodies, the history of state provision means that, short of a revolutionary transfer of ownership, the LEA will continue to be the main owner and builder of schools for the foreseeable future.

This section will therefore examine the duties and powers imposed upon LEAs to provide, build and keep in good repair those schools which they still legally own.

2. Establishment of schools

2.1 History

Until the 1830s, the state played little part in the development of schools, with the main responsibility being left to private bodies, charities and the churches. Only in 1833 were the first government grants paid to school promoters and inspections of schools were carried out only from 1840, though not quite in the same form as Ofsted/ Estyn inspections 150 years later.

What those inspections showed was a woeful lack of schools in many parts of the country. To meet this shortfall, legislation was passed to encourage the establishment of schools. The most important were the School Sites Acts of 1841, 1844, 1849, 1851 and 1852 and the Elementary Education Act 1870. The School Sites Acts encouraged the transfer of land for the purpose of establishing schools and building houses for schoolteachers with the incentive of allowing automatic reverter of the site to the conveyer of the land should the land cease to be used for those purposes. At that time, the problems which became apparent when the schools became too small or obsolete in the 1960s would not have been foreseen.

The School Sites Acts did not, however, provide a system of schools throughout the country and, to fill the gaps, school boards were set up under the Elementary Education Act 1870 in areas where there were not enough church schools. These boards were able to raise a rate and to acquire, by way of gift or sale, land upon which public elementary schools could be built. A number of schools were subsequently built which were owned and maintained by the school boards and which complemented the provision of voluntary schools by the churches. If, however, there were areas where the church schools were sufficient, there was no need for a school board and, hence, no need for school-board schools.

In 1902, LEAs were 'created' (or rather, pre-existing authorities were designated as LEAs) to take over the functions of school boards, including the ownership and maintenance of school board schools. They continued, however, to work alongside church schools and although by the 1940s LEAs had become the main providers of schools, the church continued to supply a significant number of school places. This fact was recognised by the Education Act 1944 and the partnership between LEAs and churches was enshrined in that legislation. (For a more detailed consideration of the work of LEAs in building and adapting school premises with incidentally profound curricular implications see Maclure (1984).)

This history therefore explains perhaps one of the most surprising elements of LEA responsibility: that whilst an LEA is under a duty to secure that sufficient school places for providing primary and secondary education are available in its area (s. 14 of the Education Act 1996), it need not itself provide a single school but has the power to do so (ss. 16–17).

This duty is discussed in more detail elsewhere, but the wording of s. 14 plainly reflects the responsibility of LEAs (as successors to school boards), not necessarily to establish schools, but to monitor and ensure that gaps are filled. Ironically, the current view of LEAs as monitors of educational standards rather than actual providers is not far removed from the role of their Victorian predecessors. Just as a school board, if satisfied that there was adequate alternative school provision in its area, could decide not to establish any schools, so an LEA could in theory come to the same conclusion.

Along similar lines, in *R v Secretary of State for Education and Science ex p Avon County Council* (1990) Times, 15 June, it was held that an LEA is entitled and required to take into account the provision of all schools (including independent schools) in its area to determine what numbers and types of schools are required to secure that there are sufficient school places available.

Schools cannot be regarded, however, as sufficient unless they are sufficient in number, character and equipment to provide all pupils with the opportunity of appropriate education (s. 14(2)). Appropriate education means education which offers such variety of instruction and training as may be desirable in view of the pupils' different ages, abilities and aptitudes and the different periods for which they may be expected to remain in school, including practical instruction and training appropriate to their different needs (s. 14(3)).

The practical reality, however, is that the providers of the majority of schools are LEAs.

2.2 Establishment of new schools

In order to fulfil their functions, LEAs have the power to establish primary and secondary schools inside or outside their administrative borders (s. 16(1) and (2) of the 1996 Act). Under s. 17 of the 1996 Act, an LEA may also establish nursery schools, although only within its area.

In recent times, however, the primacy of the LEA's role in establishing schools has been reduced by, first, the instigation of city technology colleges or city colleges for the technology of the arts and, second, by city academies, now known as Academies (s. 65 of the 2002 Act). A striking innovation in the 2002 Act is, effectively, the putting out to tender of proposals to establish additional secondary schools (s. 70). These will be considered below.

The powers that enable an LEA to acquire land, in order to build these new schools, are contained in ss. 530 and 531 of the 1996 Act. Section 531 enables an LEA to acquire land for the purposes of a community school by agreement and s. 530 allows an LEA to seek an order from the Secretary of State to purchase compulsorily any land (whether within or outside its area) which is required for the purposes of any school which is to be maintained by it or which it has power to assist, or is otherwise required for the purposes of its functions under the 1996 Act. If s. 530 is invoked, the LEA will have to comply with the authorisation procedure contained in the Acquisition of Land Act 1981 and the regulations made under that.

If an altruistic soul wishes to give land to an LEA for the purposes of a school or for a purpose connected with education, s. 529 of the

1996 Act gives the LEA power to accept such a gift on trust. To avoid any complications, s. 529(3) makes it clear that although the land would be vested in the LEA as trustee, any school which is established as a result will be a community school. Albeit now in different terms, this provision replicates the effects of the Elementary Education Act 1870 whereby school boards were able to accept gifts of land which would then be held on trust for elementary education purposes.

The only difference is that land given free of charge or conveyed at an undervalue under the 1870 Act is held on charitable trust (see *Hampshire County Council v Attorney General* (1994) NPC 62, (1994) CLY 370), whereas gifts under s. 529 should not create such trusts as they will be used to build community schools which by statutory definition cannot be charities.

An LEA is expressly prohibited from acquiring land required for the purposes of a voluntary school unless it is satisfied that the expenditure incurred will not include any sums which should have fallen to be borne by the governing body of the voluntary school (s. 532(2)).

In order to establish a community school, or a community special school, an LEA will need to comply with the formal procedures to establish such schools. The procedure is now set out in ss. 28 and 31 of and sched 6 to the School Standards and Framework Act 1998 and the Education (School Organisation Proposals) (England) Regulations 1999 (SI 1999 No. 2213, as amended by the Education (School Organisation Proposals) (England) (Amendment) Regulations 2003 (SI 2003 No. 1229)). In Wales, the Education (School Organisation Proposals) (Wales) Regulations 1999 (SI 1999 No. 1671), as amended by the Education (School Organisation Plans) (Wales) 2003 (SI 2003 No. 1732 (W 190)), will apply. Proposals are submitted to the local school organisation committee (SOC) for determination. In Wales, school organisation committees have yet to be established and the roles of the committee are performed by the National Assembly for Wales. A power of the Secretary of State to appoint adjudicators has not been used (s. 27).

Under s. 28, where an LEA proposes to establish either a community or foundation school or a maintained nursery school, it is required to publish statutory proposals in the form and in the manner prescribed by the 1999 Regulations. A copy of the published proposals should be sent to the school organisation committee for the LEA's area (s. 28(6)). Before doing so, however, the LEA must consult such persons as appear to it to be appropriate (s. 28(5)).

Before publishing the proposals and during the course of the procedure, the LEA should have regard to any guidance published by the Secretary of State.

Once the proposals are published, any person may make an objection to, or comments on, them (para 2 of sched 6), which should be sent to the promoting LEA within six weeks of the date of publication (known as 'the representation period') (reg 7 of the 1999 regulations). The LEA must then send copies of all objections and comments to the SOC, together with its comments, within one month after the end of the representation period.

If no objections are received or the objections that have been received are subsequently withdrawn, the LEA determines whether the proposals should be implemented within four months of the date of publication (para 4). If, however, objections have been received and not withdrawn or no objections are outstanding, but the LEA has failed to make a determination within four months, it is necessary for the SOC to consider the proposals (para 3). (For the rules concerning the establishment and conduct of the SOC, see s. 24 of and sched 4 to the 1998 Act and the Education (School Organisation Committees) Regulations 1999 (SI 1999 No. 700).)

The SOC has the power to reject the proposals, approve them without modification, approve them with such modification as it thinks desirable after consulting the prescribed persons and bodies or, if the SOC thinks it appropriate to do so, refer them to the adjudicator (para 3(2)). In reaching a decision, the SOC should have regard to guidance from the Secretary of State and to the LEA's School Organisation Plan.

Where the proposals are determined by the LEA or are approved by the SOC, the LEA must implement the proposals in the form in which they were determined or approved (para 5). There is, however, provision for the LEA to request that the proposals be modified after consultation with the prescribed persons and bodies or implemented at a later date (para 5(2)).

The procedure for the establishment of community or foundation special schools is set out in s. 31 of and sched 6 to the 1998 Act. At the time of writing, these procedures had not been brought into line with those applying to mainstream schools and so the old procedures, excluding, for example, references to the adjudicator and the inability to consider comments, will continue to apply. A consultation, however, took place in autumn 2003 on special school reorganisation which may lead to such reorganisations being

6.
THE
MAINTENANCE
OF SCHOOLS

brought into line or being subject to a separate regime. (See *Consultation on the Draft Education (Maintained Special Schools) (Amendment) (England) Regulations*, DfES 0531/2003.)

Procedures for the establishment of other categories of new schools by bodies other than LEAs are also set out in s. 28 and sched 6, together with details of those bodies, including LEAs, which are responsible for implementing the proposals. Relating to these proposals, there are occasions where an LEA may give assistance to the governing bodies of voluntary aided schools (para 8 of sched 3 of the 1998 Act). Where the assistance takes the form of the LEA's providing premises, the LEA comes under a duty to transfer its interest to the school trustees, or if there are no such trustees, to the foundation body (para 20). Similarly, where an LEA is to provide a site (but not playing fields) for a voluntary controlled, foundation or foundation special school, the LEA must transfer its interest in the site and buildings to the school trustees, or if none, to the foundation body, or, if that does not exist, the governing body (para 16). Where the trustees of a voluntary controlled school, to whom the interest in the site or buildings has been conveyed by the LEA, subsequently sell land which was previously used for a school, the trustees must pay so much of the proceeds of sale to the LEA as the Secretary of State may determine, having regard to the value of the interest conveyed by the LEA to the trustees. The Secretary of State does, though, have a wide discretion when considering what matters are to be taken into account when determining the value of the interest conveyed by the LEA (see *R v Secretary of State for Education and Employment ex p Rochdale MBC* [2001] EWCA Civ 248, CA).

**6.
THE
MAINTENANCE
OF SCHOOLS**

2.3 Additional secondary schools

Specific provision is now made to deal with proposals for additional secondary schools (ss. 70 and 71 of, and sched 8 to, the Education Act 2002). Where an LEA proposes to establish a community, foundation or voluntary school or an Academy as an additional secondary school, it may publish a notice identifying the possible site, specifying the date for submission of proposals and other prescribed matters and, in effect, inviting proposals from promoters. LEAs should have regard to guidance from the Secretary of State as to when competition should be sought and how. The LEA must publish any proposals received and may publish its own proposals for a community or foundation school.

The idea behind these sections (see para 5.24 of the White Paper *Schools Achieving Success*) is to encourage new ways of developing innovative schools within the state sector, so that, where an LEA proposes a new secondary school, it should invite any interested parties, including community or faith groups, LEAs or any other private or public bodies to publish proposals for the school, including proposals to establish Academies.

The first example of such a competition concerned proposals for a new secondary school in Lambeth ('Twigg encourages parents, local community and other interested parties to set up new secondary school', DfES press release 10 November 2003).

2.4 Academies

In England only, Academies are the successors, first, to city technology colleges and city colleges for the technology of the arts (deriving from the Education Reform Act 1988) and, secondly, city academies (deriving from s. 482 of the 1996 Act as amended). City colleges will continue in existence, but no new ones can be established. City academies which have been established will in future be called Academies.

The Secretary of State may enter into an agreement with any person (which can include LEAs) under which that person undertakes to establish and maintain and to carry on or provide for the carrying on of an independent school. In return the Secretary of State agrees to make payments to that person (s. 482(1) of the Education Act 1996). Academies are therefore independent schools, established by a sponsor, who is required to contribute an initial capital sum. The remainder of the capital costs and all future revenue costs are then met by the Secretary of State. Before entering into this agreement the Secretary of State must consult the LEA in whose area the school is situated or if a significant number of pupils will be from the area of another LEA, that LEA too (s. 482(3)).

The Academy must have certain characteristics (s. 482(2)): the curriculum must be broad and balanced, each Academy must have an emphasis on a curriculum area or areas and pupils have to be of different abilities and wholly or mainly drawn from the area in which it is situated.

Provision relating to the transfer of land for the use of an Academy (usually land previously used as a school and owned by an LEA) is made in schedule 35A to the 1996 Act. That schedule includes provision for the Secretary of State to make transfer schemes and restrictions on the ability of LEAs to dispose of land that has been used as a school within the last eight years without the Secretary of

State's consent. The idea behind the latter restriction is to stop LEAs disposing of land that the Secretary of State believes could be used for an Academy.

2.5 Private Finance Initiative (PFI) and Building Schools for the Future (BSF)

No consideration of the construction and maintenance of schools would now be complete without mention of the private finance initiative and its effect on school building. By 2003 over 500 schools had received some form of PFI investment.

The detail of PFI is outside the scope of this book, but given the number of schools now established or refurbished with its assistance, it is important to be aware of such schemes where the private sector will bear the costs of building or re-furbishing a capital/fixed asset and will then provide services connected with the asset, for which the public sector will make revenue payments over a period of years.

Concern has been expressed at the complexity and cost of PFI projects and, indeed, whether they have, in the education sector, achieved their objectives and/or value for money. Partly in response to these criticisms and principally to seek new ways of securing improvement to school buildings, the DfES issued *Building Schools for the Future – Consultation on a new approach to capital investment* DfES/0134/2003, which proposed a number of alternative models for securing the necessary investment, procurement and project management to enable the government's proposed capital funding for school improvement to be implemented. These proposals included establishing exemplar school designs and a national procurement vehicle which would then enable local procurement vehicles to be set up as joint ventures between central and local government and Partnerships UK. A joint venture between the DfES, Church of England and Partnerships UK has already been developed to help voluntary aided schools to secure much more efficient access to PFI funding.

3. Maintenance, control, alteration and rationalisation

LEAs are under a duty to maintain any community, community special, voluntary controlled, foundation, foundation special, voluntary aided and maintained nursery schools within their areas (s. 22(1) of the School Standards and Framework Act 1998).

In the case of a community, community special or maintained nursery school, the duty to maintain includes the duty to defray all the expenses of maintaining it and the duty to make premises available to be used for the purposes of the school (s. 22(3)).

For a foundation, voluntary controlled and foundation special school, the duty consists of the defraying of all the expenses of maintaining it, together with the duty to provide new premises in certain circumstances (s. 22(4) and see also scheds 3 and 6).

For voluntary aided schools, the duty to maintain includes defraying all expenses of maintaining the school, except those which are required to be met by the governing body under para 3 of sched 3 to the 1998 Act and the duty to provide new premises in certain circumstances (s. 22(5) and see para 4 sched 3 or para 14 of sched 6). This duty was modified by The Regulatory Reform (Voluntary Aided Schools Liabilities and Funding) (England) Order 2002 (S.I. 2002 No. 906), which, among other things, provides that governing bodies are responsible for all capital expenditure in relation to the school premises including boundary walls and fences, with the exception of playing fields and buildings thereon used in connection with the playing fields. There is a proviso that capital expenditure will not include expenditure under £2,000. Capital expenditure in consequence of the use of school premises for non-school purposes following a direction by the LEA will remain the liability of the LEA.

6.
THE
MAINTENANCE
OF SCHOOLS

4. Control and use

The control and use of maintained school premises are governed by s. 40 of and sched 13 to the 1998 Act and, when those provisions are repealed, will be governed by s. 31 and the regulations made under that section of the 2002 Act. The former provide that the occupation and use of community and community special school premises, both during and outside school hours, shall be under the control of the governing body, subject to any direction given by the LEA, any transfer of control agreement or any requirement of an enactment or regulations made under it (para 1 of sched 13). The LEA may give such direction as to the occupation and use of the premises as it thinks fit. In particular, the LEA will want to satisfy itself as to the security of tenure of premises and the controls over persons likely, in effect, to come onto school premises, as a consequence of an agreement and so come into contact with pupils.

In respect of use outside school hours, the governing body must have regard to the desirability of the premises being made available for community use. More particularly, in order to promote community use, the governing body may enter into a transfer of control agreement with any person or body. Before doing so, however, the governing body must obtain the LEA's consent (para 2(1) and (2)).

In the case of foundation and foundation special schools, the control of the premises is solely a matter for the governing body and the LEA cannot give directions as to the use of the premises, nor is its consent required before the governing body can enter into a transfer of control agreement (para 3).

With voluntary controlled and voluntary aided schools, the occupation and use of the premises are under the control of the governing body but are subject to:

- in the case of voluntary controlled schools, such direction as the LEA thinks fit, subject to allowing the governing body to decide the use of the premises on Saturdays when not required for school purposes or for a purpose connected with education or the welfare of the young and permitting foundation governors to decide the use of the premises on Sundays (paras 5–7); and

- in the case of voluntary aided schools, a direction from the LEA to require the governing body to provide accommodation on the school premises on not more than three weekdays in any week, free of charge, for a purpose connected with education or the welfare of the young and only when the premises are not required for school purposes (paras 5–7).

In spite of the principles of control set out above, LEAs are considered to be the rateable occupiers of community and voluntary controlled school premises. In *Kent County Council v Ashford Borough Council and Others* (1999) Times, 7 September, the Court of Appeal held that in the case of a voluntary controlled school, the LEA and not the governing body, was the rateable occupier of the school buildings. The court decided that the scheme of financial management adopted by the LEA did not touch on the occupation or control of the school premises. That is perhaps understandable, but what is difficult to understand is how the court ignored the sections set out above which provided that, subject to limited directions from the LEA, the occupation and use of such a school is under the control of the governing body. The consequence of the decision was that the LEA lost an entitlement to charitable rate relief amounting to £6m, but it may have wider implications in clouding what was already a fairly unclear picture of responsibility.

The position was, however, confirmed by s. 78 of the 1998 Act, which states that for the purposes of part III of the Local Government Finance Act 1988 (provisions dealing with non-domestic rating), the occupier of a maintained school shall be deemed to be the LEA in the case of community, voluntary controlled and community special schools and the governing body in all other cases.

Whoever is in control, however, maintained schools benefit from the provision in s. 547 of the Education Act 1996 which makes it a criminal offence for a person who is present on school premises, including playing fields, without lawful authority, to cause or permit a nuisance or disturbance to the annoyance of persons who lawfully use the premises. The 2002 Act has extended the provisions of s. 547 to include non-maintained special schools, independent schools and, perhaps most importantly for LEAs, establishments provided by LEAs which are used wholly or mainly in connection with the provision of instruction or leadership in sporting, recreational or outdoor activities, such as sports centres and outdoor centres (s. 547(2A) as inserted by para 1 of sched 20 to the 2002 Act).

A police constable who has reasonable cause to suspect that a person is committing or has committed this offence may remove him from the premises. The LEA (in the case of community and voluntary controlled schools and other LEA establishments) or the governing body (in the case of voluntary aided or foundation schools) may authorise a person other than a police constable to take this action, although concern for the safety of staff may suggest that the removal of trespassers is best left to the police. Proceedings under s. 547 can be brought only by a police constable, the LEA or, in the case of voluntary aided or foundation schools, a person authorised by the governing body. For the offence to be committed, it is not necessary for the persons annoyed to be on the premises at the same time as the offender causes the nuisance or disturbance. Glue sniffers who sniffed glue on a school playground and left the apparatus behind to be discovered by pupils were held to have been properly found guilty of the offence (*Sykes v Holmes* [1985] CLR 791), so it could be used equally against drug users who leave their needles behind or dog walkers whose dogs leave faeces on playing fields, although there may be evidential problems proving who left what, where and when.

6.
THE
MAINTENANCE
OF SCHOOLS

Parents do, though, cause particular problems and it was once thought that they had no more than a bare licence to enter school premises and that this could be revoked if they behaved unreasonably. This is, however, no longer the case following the Court of Appeal's decision in *Wandsworth LBC v A* [2000] EdCR 167. The LEA had obtained an injunction against a parent who had been causing a problem in one of its schools. The Court of Appeal accepted that parents have no licence to roam at will, enter classrooms during lessons or interfere with the professional work of education. However, the court did not accept that parents were in the same position as milkmen or postmen or any casual enquirer at the school. The court then considered the type of buildings to which the public may have access and the steps which a local authority could take to prevent or to terminate that access.

First, in the case of property to which members of the public are not normally invited, a local authority has the unfettered right to give or withhold permission to visitors and there is no requirement placed on the authority to give a visitor an opportunity to make representations before he is banned. The second category was identified as premises belonging to the local authority that are usually open to the public in general, although there is no statutory duty placed upon the authority to permit the public to have access. Here, before the local authority can forbid a member of the public from entering, it is required to give the individual an indication of what it is proposing to do and an opportunity to make representations why that course should not be taken. The case of a parent visiting the school their child attends was held to be within a third category, even stronger than the second one. A parent's interest, in public law terms, in being on school premises was even greater than a member of the public using a recreation ground or a library and, therefore, before he or she could be banned from the site, the headteacher had an obligation to give the parent the opportunity to make representations. Although not suggesting that the headteacher had to conduct a formal investigation or something resembling a trial, the Court of Appeal nonetheless found that the headmaster should have written to the parent asking for her [as it was in this case] comments and giving her a short time for reply. As he had not, the court concluded that the parent's licence to use the school premises had not been properly terminated.

A frequent cause of problems for school security is a public right of way passing close to or through a school site. To address this, the Education Act 2002, by amending the Highways Act, makes it easier for highways authorities to stop up highways to reduce crime or where it is expedient for protecting pupils or staff from violence, harassment, alarm, distress or other risk to their health and safety (s. 118B of the Highways Act 1980).

5. Asset Management Plan

In respect of schools which are maintained by an LEA, the LEA is under an effective obligation to prepare an asset management plan setting out the priorities for capital expenditure on schools and the approach proposed locally to dealing with them (reg 2 of the Education (Education Standards etc. Grants) (England) Regulations 1999). Standards Fund grants were available for supporting the preparation of such plans. LEAs with excellent or good asset management plans have also been given greater flexibilities in the way they use their capital formula funding. See Special Grant Report (No. 122), 7 May 2003. 'Voluntary' guidance from the DfES on these plans can be found in *Asset Management Plans* DfEE 095/2000.

6.
THE
MAINTENANCE
OF SCHOOLS

6. Standards of premises

Under s. 542 of the 1996 Act and the Education (School Premises) Regulations 1999 (SI 1999 No. 2), LEAs are under a duty to secure that maintained school premises conform to prescribed standards. The only exceptions to this duty occur where the Secretary of State has directed that the standards may be relaxed, for example, if the nature of the site makes it unreasonable to require conformity or, if a school is to have an additional or new site, certain circumstances apply (for all the circumstances, see s. 543). Guidance on the standards can be found in DfEE Circular 10/96 *The 1996 School Premises Regulations*, albeit in the context of the 1996 Regulations, the predecessors to the 1999 version.

The duty is an absolute one (see *Reffell v Surrey County Council* [1964] 1 All ER 743), which can cause LEAs some problems. The duty applies to all maintained schools, so will include voluntary aided and foundation schools. The question may be rhetorical, but how can an LEA ensure that the duty is met in schools which it neither owns nor controls and into which it has no right of access for maintenance purposes? The problem is not necessarily limited to voluntary aided and foundation schools, for, although the LEA may own community and voluntary *controlled* schools, it does not – paradoxically in the case of voluntary controlled schools – control them. In addition, given the division of responsibility for repairs first established under local management, LEAs do not have responsibility for many factors which may affect the standard of the premises. Fair Funding has further prejudiced the LEA's position by enabling governing bodies to take the money delegated to them for repair and maintenance and use outside contractors rather than the LEA's own architects or buildings staff. It may not be long therefore before an LEA is held responsible for injury caused by a breach of its absolute duty under s. 542 in circumstances where it could not have prevented the accident because it does not own, control or inspect the premises in question. It is true that in the case of community schools, LEAs may still give directions, which could encompass a direction as to the standard of the premises, but nonetheless it is a worrying potential liability for LEAs.

By way of some assistance, the Regulatory Reform (Voluntary Aided Schools Liabilities and Funding) (England) Order 2002 increases from 85 per cent to 90 per cent the amount of grant that the Secretary of State should provide for expenditure which is necessary to ensure that voluntary aided school premises conform to standards prescribed under s. 542 of the Education Act 1996.

In addition to the duty to ensure that premises meet the prescribed standards, occupiers of premises owe duties to users of sites under the Occupiers' Liability Acts 1957 and 1984, the Health and Safety at Work etc. Act 1974 and the Environment Act 1990.

Under the Occupiers' Liability Acts in particular, the occupier, or person having control, of premises is under a duty to take such care as in all the circumstances of the case is reasonable to see that a visitor will be reasonably safe in using the premises for the purpose for which he is invited or permitted to be there (s. 2(2) of Occupiers' Liability Act 1957). The Occupiers' Liability Act 1984 imposes a duty of care (usually a lesser duty) in respect of persons other than visitors (see especially *Tomlinson v Congleton BC and Another* [2003] UKHL 47, [2003] 3 All ER 1122). Parents are more than mere visitors and have certain rights to enter schools (see *Wandsworth LBC v A*, above).

Invariably, in the case of community schools, it is the LEA which will be sued for any breach of the Acts, although it is possible that the governing body may fall within the definition of occupier by virtue of the provisions of sched 13 to the 1998 Act and s. 31 and regulations to be made under that section, of the 2002 Act. The *Kent County Council* case may, however, direct liability back on to the LEA as, according to the Court of Appeal, *de facto*, even if not *de jure*, occupier of community and voluntary controlled schools. The point may however be academic, as the cost of any claim made against the governing body of a community or voluntary controlled school will be an expense of maintaining the school and hence should be payable by the LEA.

For some cases on the responsibility of LEAs for accidents caused by defective premises, see, for example, *Ching v Surrey County Council* [1910] 1 KB 736 (pothole in playground); *Morris v Caernarvon County Council* [1910] 1 KB 840 (heavy door on spring unsuitable for use by young children); J*ackson v London County Council and Chappell* (1912) 76 JP 217 (contractor leaving dangerous materials in playground); *Gillmore v London County Council* [1938] 4 All ER 331 (highly polished floor used for PE); *Lyes v Middlesex County Counci*l (1962) 61 LGR 443 (unstrengthened glass panel in door) and *Reffell v Surrey County Council* [1964] 1 All ER 743 (use of untoughened glass in door).

**6.
THE
MAINTENANCE
OF SCHOOLS**

Under the Health and Safety at Work Act 1974, a duty is imposed on all persons having control of premises to any extent to ensure, so far as is reasonably practicable, that the premises, means of access and any plant or substance are safe and without risk to health (s. 4). Although it has not been tested in the courts, as in the case of the Occupiers' Liability Acts, both the LEA and the governing body of community and voluntary controlled schools may fall within the ambit of the Act. In *Moualem v Carlisle City Council* (1994) Times, 8 July, a local authority was held to owe a duty under s. 4 towards children at an indoor play centre, so the precedent is probably there for a similar claim to be made against an LEA in respect of similar activities at schools.

Under the Management of Health and Safety at Work Regulations 1992 (SI 1992 No. 2051), the LEA must arrange to organise, control and review how the health and safety measures in schools are managed. For assistance on health and safety duties and the responsibility as between LEA and governing body, see *Health and Safety Responsibility and Powers* (DfES 2001).

One consolation for LEAs, though, is that it is the governing body which is responsible under the Environmental Protection Act for keeping school land clear of litter and refuse (s. 89 Environmental Protection Act 1990). So clearing up dog faeces, although many LEA officers will feel it to be within their job description, is a matter for governing bodies.

In addition, LEAs clearly need to be conscious of the obligations imposed by the Disability Discrimination Act 1995. The Act applies to the access to and use of any place which members of the public are permitted to enter (s. 19(3) of the Disability Discrimination Act 1995). Consequently, there may an obligation to ensure that disabled parents or other users of school premises, particularly community facilities, are not denied access because of their disability.

7.   Alteration and rationalisation

Similar provisions to those applying to the procedure for establishing schools apply in the case of proposals to alter maintained schools. Thus, where an LEA proposes to make a prescribed alteration to a mainstream community school or a prescribed alteration to a foundation school, being an enlargement of the school premises, the LEA must publish proposals (s. 28(1)(b) and (c) of the School Standards and Framework Act 1998). For a judicial consideration of what is meant by significant changes as defined by s. 573 of the 1996 Act, see *R v Downes ex parte Wandsworth LBC* [2000] ELR 425. The proposals must be in the form and manner prescribed by the Education (School Organisation Proposals) (England) Regulations 1999 (SI 1999 No. 2213, as amended), or, in Wales, the Education (School Organisation Proposals) (Wales) Regulations 1999 (SI 1999 No.1671).

The process for dealing with objections and comments and determining applications is the same as for the establishment of schools set out above, with the ultimate decision, if objections are received, being for the school organisation committee or adjudicator. A new provision in the 2002 Act is the ability given to schools of a 'prescribed description' to appeal to the adjudicator if a proposed alteration is rejected by the SOC, the intention being to allow successful and popular schools to appeal if they are prevented from expanding by the SOC.

Alterations to community and foundation special schools are dealt with under s. 31 of the 1998 Act. At the time of writing, however, because the procedure for altering special schools has not been brought into line with the new procedure applying to mainstream maintained schools, there are some variations in the process. For example, there are different timescales for objections and no ability for a School Organisation Committee (SOC) to choose to refer proposals to the adjudicator. A consultation, however, took place in autumn 2003 on special school reorganisation, which may lead to s. 31 proposals being brought into line or a separate regime established.

Most LEAs, as part of their school organisation planning, will seek to rationalise the provision of school places. If, however, the Secretary of State takes the view that the provision for primary or secondary education in maintained schools in the area of any LEA or in any part of such an area is excessive, he may direct an LEA to exercise its powers to make proposals for the establishment, alteration or discontinuance of schools (s. 34 of and para 2 of sched 7 to the 1998 Act). In respect of any foundation, voluntary or foundation special school, the Secretary of State may direct that the governing body shall issue proposals for the alteration of its school (para 2(2)(b)).

If the contrary situation applies and the Secretary of State believes that the provision for primary or secondary education in maintained schools in the area of an LEA or part of an LEA's area is insufficient, he may make a direction requiring an LEA to exercise its powers to make proposals for the establishment, alteration or discontinuance of schools or inviting proposals for the establishment of additional secondary schools (s. 71 of the Education Act 2002). Similar directions may be made in respect of foundation, voluntary and foundation special schools as apply in the case of excess places.

If no proposals are forthcoming, the Secretary of State may make such proposals as might have been made by the LEA or governing body (para 5 of sched 7 to, and s. 71(4) of, the 2002 Act) and the procedure for such proposals by the Secretary of State is governed by schedule 7 to the 1998 Act. If, however, the LEA or governing body does publish proposals, they are dealt with in the same way as all other proposals to establish, alter or discontinue, i.e. under s. 28, sched 6 and the 1999 Regulations.

The 2002 Act makes two further changes to the provisions dealing with alterations.First, governing bodies of community and voluntary controlled schools are given the same powers as foundation and voluntary aided governing bodies to enlarge or alter their schools (s. 28 of the 1998 Act as amended by s. 73 of the 2002 Act). The Explanatory Note to the 2002 Act indicates that these schools may now propose to enlarge their premises, to increase by 27 or more pupils the number in the relevant age group or to add a sixth form.

Second, provision is made (s. 113 of and sched 7A to the Learning and Skills Act 2000, as amended by s. 72 of and sched 9 to the 2002 Act) for the Learning and Skills Council to make proposals for the establishment, alteration or closure of maintained school sixth forms.

6.
THE
MAINTENANCE
OF SCHOOLS

These proposals must:

(i) follow on from an area-wide inspection (under s. 65 of the 2000 Act);

(ii) promote one or more of the 'relevant objectives' (i.e. an improvement in the educational or training achievements of persons who are above compulsory school age but below 19; an increase in the number of such persons who participate in education or training suitable to the requirements of such persons; or an expansion of the range of educational or training opportunities suitable to the requirements of such persons – see s. 72 of the 2002 Act); or

(iii) are made in addition to proposals relating to education or training other than in schools and the combined proposals are made with a view to promoting one or more of the relevant objectives (see above) (s. 113(1)(c) of the 2000 Act).

8. Change of category

An analogous process to the alteration of premises applies to proposals to change the categorisation of a school. Under the School Standards and Framework Act 1998, new categories of school were introduced (s. 20 and sched 2). Former county schools were allocated the new category of community school, aided and special agreement schools were deemed to be voluntary aided schools, controlled schools became new voluntary controlled schools. Maintained special schools similarly became community special schools. Only former grant-maintained and grant-maintained special schools had any freedom to choose their new category. These schools were given an indicative category by the DfEE, normally foundation or foundation special school or voluntary aided in the case of grant-maintained schools which had formerly been aided or special agreement before acquiring grant-maintained status (para 4 of sched 2 and see the Education (Allocation of Grant-maintained and Grant-maintained Special Schools to New Categories) Regulations 1998 (SI 1998 No. 1969)). They could, though, elect to accept their indicative category or choose to be allocated a different category. A few did, but most chose to accept their categorisation as foundation schools.

The 1998 Act makes provision for schools to change their categories subsequent to their original categorisation (s. 35 and sched 8), although initially a moratorium was imposed on any changes (except in the case of voluntary aided schools wishing to become voluntary controlled) until 31 August 2000 (reg 3 of the Education (Change of Category of Maintained Schools) (England) Regulations 1999 (SI 1999 No. 2259)).

From that date on, maintained schools have been allowed to propose to change their categories and, if they do so, must follow the procedures laid down in para 2 of sched 8 and the Education (Change of Category of Maintained Schools) (England) Regulations 2000 (SI 2000 No. 2195, as amended by the Education (Change of Category of Maintained Schools) (Amendment) (England) Regulations 2003 (SI 2003 No. 2136). These, in effect, require LEAs or governing bodies, once they have decided to publish proposals to change category, to follow the procedures for alteration or discontinuance under ss. 28 and 31 discussed above and below, with the ultimate decision normally resting with the SOC or, as appropriate, the adjudicator. (Unlike other reorganisation proposals, the procedure relating to the change in category of special schools has been updated so that the procedure here is the same as for all other maintained schools.)

Where a change of category is approved, the regulations make provision for the transfer of land (in the case of a community school becoming foundation, for example, the LEA will be required to transfer its ownership of the school site to the new governing body) and staff. The LEA will also have to make the instrument of government for the school under its new category.

9. Discontinuance and disposal

For many reasons, LEAs wish to close schools, for example, through their own rationalisation plans or in consequence of a direction from the Secretary of State under sched 7 to the 1998 Act.

The procedure for closing community, foundation, voluntary schools or maintained nursery schools is contained in s. 29 of and sched 6 to the 1998 Act. Proposals to discontinue community and foundation special schools are governed by s. 31 and sched 6.

The principles are similar to those applying to establishment and alteration. If an LEA proposes to discontinue a maintained school or maintained nursery school, it must first publish statutory proposals (s. 29(1), see above). The proposals shall be in the form and manner prescribed by the relevant regulations (the 1999 regulations, as amended) and the LEA must consult such persons as appear to it to be appropriate (for the extent of consultation required and the steps to be taken by an LEA in response, see *R v Leeds City Council ex p N* [1999] ELR 324, QBD and CA). In so doing, the LEA must have regard to the guidance of the Secretary of State. Copies of the proposals, together with prescribed additional information about the proposals, must be sent to the SOC for the area (s. 29(5)).

Once the proposals are published, any person may make an objection to, or comment on, them (para 2 of sched 6) which should be sent to the promoting LEA or the governing body within six weeks of the date of publication (reg 7 of the 1999 regulations) except where the school is one to which s. 15 of the 1998 Act applies (i.e. one subject to a warning notice). The LEA must then send copies of all objections and comments to the SOC together with its comments on the objections within one month of the end of the representation period or two weeks if the school is subject to a warning notice.

If no objections are received or the objections which have been received are subsequently withdrawn, the LEA is responsible for determining whether the proposals should be implemented and must do so within four months of the date of publication (para 4). If, however, (1) objections have been received and not withdrawn or (2) no objections are outstanding, but the LEA has failed to make a determination within four months, it is necessary for the SOC to consider the proposals (para 3).

The SOC has the power to reject the proposals, approve them without modification, approve them with such modification as it thinks desirable after consulting the prescribed persons and bodies or, if it thinks it appropriate, refer the proposals to the adjudicator. In reaching a decision, the SOC should have regard to guidance from the Secretary of State and the LEA's school organisation plan.

Where the proposals are determined by the LEA or are approved by the SOC, the LEA must implement the proposals in the form in which they were determined or approved (para 5). There is however provision for the LEA to request that the proposals be modified after consultation with the prescribed persons and bodies or implemented at a later date (para 5(2)).

Similar provisions apply to the discontinuance of community and foundation special schools (s. 31) although as noted above, the most recent changes to the procedures do not apply to such schools.

The discontinuance of a school often leads to an LEA establishing a new school on the same site, for example if the LEA discontinues an infant and junior school on the same campus and then creates a new primary school in their place. On other occasions, however, as a consequence of discontinuance, the LEA may be faced with having to dispose of the site.

In principle, the LEA has the general power, available to all local authorities, to dispose of school sites and obtain capital receipts under s. 123 or s. 127 of the Local Government Act 1972. This power is, however, subject to a number of restrictions.

First, following national concern at the widespread disposal of school playing fields, s. 77 of the 1998 Act imposes controls on the ability to dispose of any playing fields which are, immediately before the date of disposal, used by a maintained school for the purposes of the school or which are not then so used, but have been so used at any time within the period of ten years ending with that date (s. 77(1). Playing fields are defined as land in the open air, which is provided for the purposes of physical education or recreation, other than any prescribed description of land (s. 77(7)).

6.
THE
MAINTENANCE
OF SCHOOLS

Consequently, before disposing of the playing fields or former playing fields, the LEA must obtain the consent of the Secretary of State. Guidance on the use of s. 77 and the criteria to be adopted by the Secretary of State can be found in DfEE Circular 3/99 *The Protection of School Playing Fields*. The number of school playing fields sold to developers was claimed to have decreased from 40 per month to three per month after the introduction of these measures (*The Independent*, 14 March 2000).

Similar controls are exercised by the Secretary of State over any proposal by an LEA to change the use of current playing fields or land used as playing fields within the last ten years. Unless the Secretary of State's consent is obtained, the playing fields cannot be used for purposes which do not consist of or include their use as playing fields by a maintained school for the purposes of the school (s. 77(3)). This control does not, however, apply where the land will become used in connection with the provision by the local authority of educational facilities for a maintained school or any recreational facilities (s. 77(4)).

Restrictions on disposal are also imposed in connection with the provision of land for Academies (see sched 35A to the Education Act 1996). Unless land previously used by an LEA as a school within the previous eight years is to be transferred for use by an Academy, the Secretary of State's consent to its disposal must be obtained.

Second, where an LEA wishes to dispose of schools originally built under the Elementary Education Act 1870, particular issues may arise. If the conveyance of the original land to the school board stated that the land was to be held upon trust for the purposes of an elementary school within the meaning of the Elementary Education Act 1870 or used similar words, the land may be held subject to a charitable trust. This may mean that any proceeds of sale will not belong absolutely to the LEA, but will be held on trust for charitable, educational purposes. This restriction arises from the decision of Morritt J in *Hampshire County Council v Attorney General* (1994) NPC 62, (1994) CLY 370, where it was held that land originally conveyed to a school board either by way of gift or at a discounted price, using the wording set out above, was subject to a charitable trust. His decision left open the possibility that land conveyed at full value was not so encumbered, although the Charity Commission has maintained that these sites too are charities. The consequence is that if land affected in this way is sold, either the charitable trusts will have to be transferred to the site of any new school established to replace the old school or a Charity Commission scheme will be required to set up a charitable fund from which awards and grants can be made.

Third, if school land has been obtained by compulsion under s. 530 of the 1996 Act, the *Crichel Down* principle will apply. This requires a local authority, when considering disposing of land acquired under a compulsory purchase order, to first offer the land back to the original owner.

Fourth, there are the rules relating to the reverter of sites. As this chapter started with an examination of how state schools were first established in the 19th century, it is ironic that as the section comes to an end, it is necessary to look back to those same times. However much education is modernised, the reality is that the structure is still based on the foundations of schooling built between 1841 and 1880.

As mentioned when looking at the history of schooling, under the series of School Sites Acts between 1841 and 1852, individuals were encouraged to provide land for schools with the incentive being that, if land ceased to be used for a school, the land would revert back to its original owner. (Land ceases to be used for the purpose for which it was originally granted under the 1841 Act when it ceases to be used as a school, but also where a denominational school changes in character to a non-denominational school, see *Fraser and Fraser v Canterbury Diocesan Board of Finance* [2001] 2 WLR 1103, CA.) What the creators of these Acts had perhaps not envisaged was that the land would continue to be used well into the next century and that when, eventually, the school closed, ascertaining the original owner would prove a nightmare for LEAs. Even where a revertee could be found, it was discovered that they frequently had no power to dispose of or even use the land, leading to a number of sites falling into disrepair. As a result, the Reverter of Sites Act 1987 was passed. This Act provides that where land should have reverted to the successor to the original owner, the land, instead of reverting back, is held on trust by, usually, the LEA (s. 1(1)). The statutory trust requires the trustee to sell the land and stand possessed of the net proceeds of sale upon trust for the persons who would have otherwise been entitled to the ownership of the land upon reverter (s. 1(2)) (but see *Bath and Wells Diocesan Board v Jenkinson* [2002] EWHC 218 (Ch), [2002] 4 All ER 245, [2002] 3 WLR 202 for consideration of the effect of the passing of such proceeds by will or other devise).

If the LEA is unable to locate the person to whom the land should have reverted, it may apply to the Charity Commissioners for a scheme which extinguishes the rights of the person to whom the land should have reverted and requires the LEA to hold the proceeds on sale for such purposes as the Commissioners permit (s. 2). Before making an application, the LEA must have taken such steps as are reasonably practicable to locate the revertee, including placing notices in two national newspapers and one local newspaper and on the relevant land. A period of not less than three months must be given for the revertee to come forward, after which, if no claim has been made, the LEA can apply to the Charity Commissioners (s. 3).

Where the Commissioners make an order, public notice must be given and a copy must be available for public inspection in the locality of the land. An appeal to the High Court against the order can be made by the Attorney General, the trustees of the statutory trust, a beneficiary or any two or more local inhabitants (s. 4).

Problems arose under the 1987 Act where land, originally conveyed under the 1841 Act, had formed part of a larger piece of land. In *Marchant v Onslow* [1994] 2 All ER 707, the court held that, when a site which had been conveyed pursuant to the 1841 Act ceased to be used for school purposes, the site reverted to the same ownership as that of the other land or estate of which it originally formed part. Where, however, the land conveyed was a freestanding site and did not form part of a larger estate or parcel of land, it reverted to the original grantor or his successors in title. The 1987 Act has also generated litigation in respect of entitlement to the proceeds of a fire insurance policy following the destruction by fire of a school conveyed under the 1841 Act (*Habermehl v HM Attorney General* (1996) EGCS 148).

In addition to disposal of school sites by LEAs, it is also possible for governing bodies of voluntary and foundation schools to sell their land. Because of the provisions governing the establishment of these schools, the LEA enjoys certain rights in connection with the disposal of the property. Section 76 of and sched 22 to the 1998 Act govern the disposal of land used for the purposes of foundation, voluntary and foundation special schools. Where the land is held by the school's governing body, the consent of the Secretary of State is required before the land can be sold and, as a condition of disposal, the Secretary of State may order either that the land be transferred to the LEA for such sum as he may determine or that the LEA is entitled to the whole or part of the proceeds of sale (para 3 of sched 22). (Different rules apply to the disposal of land by a foundation body or trustees of foundation, voluntary or foundation special schools – see paras 2 and 3.)

The wisdom of the 1987 legislation was demonstrated as the *Fraser* case went on. In January 2004, the Court of Appeal determined that the purpose in the defunct school's trust deed had ceased long before 12 years prior to the Act's having come into force, the site has automatically and irrevocably reverted to the grantor's successors and the doctrine of adverse possession allowed the diocesan board to take the proceeds of its sale (*Fraser and Another v Canterbury Diocesan Board of Finance and Another* [2004] EWCA Civ 15, (2004) Independent, 6 February).

D. Financing of Maintained Schools

1. History

1.1 Financial 'maintenance'

The obligation upon LEAs to 'maintain and keep efficient' schools originates from s.18 (Maintenance by school board of schools and sufficient school accommodation) of the Elementary Education 1870 when the duty was placed on school boards. The Education Act 1902, s. 7 (Maintenance of schools), placed the duty on the local education authority and extended it to cover all public elementary schools in the area, that is, not just the schools provided by the school boards but also the voluntary schools provided the average attendance was not less than 30. There were other conditions over maintaining voluntary schools particularly, as far as financing of schools is concerned, a requirement on the managers of voluntary schools to make the school buildings available 'free of charge' and keep them in 'good repair' while the LEA would be responsible for 'fair wear and tear'. The 1944 Act, s. 114(2)(a), while retaining the responsibility of the governors of voluntary aided schools for their buildings, describes the LEA role as a 'duty of defraying all the expenses of maintaining the school'.

1.2 Delegation of funding

In the 40 years following the 1944 Act various schemes were tried for delegating to schools decisions about specific school expenses such as non-teaching costs. Section 29 of the Education (No. 2) Act 1986 required the LEA to provide a financial statement to each school once every year 'with a view to assisting the governing body to judge whether expenditure in relation to [its] school represents economic, efficient and effective use of resources'. The LEA also had to make a sum available to the school to spend on 'books, equipment, stationery and such other heads of expenditure as specified' by the LEA or prescribed by the Secretary of State.

6.
THE
MAINTENANCE
OF SCHOOLS

A Written Answer (*Hansard*, 24 July 1987, col. 495, Mr Dunn, Parliamentary Under Secretary of State) listed some 23 English LEAs that were known to be operating their own schemes of financial delegation.

But before the 1986 Act provision was fully implemented, ss. 35–51 of the Education Reform Act 1988 introduced Local Management of Schools (LMS) and ss. 52–104 introduced grant-maintained schools (GMs). With LMS, only a proportion of a school's expenses was initially delegated although in time this became a very high proportion covering nearly all school-based decisions. If a school opted-out of an LEA and so became GM, all, in theory, of the school's expenses were met by funds supplied by the then DES including the LEA's expenses of supporting local schools and pupils. The DES made generous estimates of the costs of these LEA services and removed the money from the local authority's block grant. The Education Act 1993 created the Funding Agency for Schools (FAS), a quango for funding GM schools. Such schools were free to buy back central services and the LEA continued to provide some services such as school attendance and school transport.

The rest of this section considers developments since 1998 on the LEA responsibilities for the revenue funding of maintained schools. Information on capital funding is found in section 17 of this part of chapter 6.

2. Fair Funding

The School Standards and Framework Act 1998 swept away the then divisions between schools, bringing all 'maintained' schools back to LEA maintenance. Section 20 defines the categories of schools that LEAs have to maintain and s. 22 requires the LEAs to maintain them. Sections 45–53, part II, chapter IV (Financing of Maintained Schools), now significantly amended by the Education Act 2002 by the addition of five sections, specify how schools will be funded.

An LEA has therefore been required to maintain from 1 April 1999 with the abolition of the FAS:

- community schools
- voluntary controlled schools
- community special schools
- maintained special schools
- voluntary aided schools
- foundation schools
- foundation special schools.

This applies even though the LEA does not own the land or employ the staff at the three latter types of school. LEAs are also required to maintain pupil referral units under s. 19 of the Education Act 1996.

To provide for the financing of all maintained schools under the framework introduced by the 1998 Act, new arrangements, known as Fair Funding, were introduced with effect from 1 April 1999. These were intended to produce a clearer division of responsibility between LEAs and schools and to ensure further delegation of funds to governing bodies. A DfEE Consultation Paper, *Fair Funding: Improving Delegation to Schools*, was issued in May 1998 and the implementing regulations, the Financing of Maintained Schools Regulations 1999 (SI 1999 No. 101), which applied to both England and Wales, soon followed. Subsequent amendments to and replacement of, the regulations are territorially specific. See below for the 2003 regulations.

The aims of the new financial framework included raising standards, developing the self-management of schools, increasing accountability and transparency, achieving equality in distribution and ensuring value for money. To promote the other main aim of providing clarity in the division of responsibility between LEAs and maintained schools, the 1999 regulations sought to identify those areas for which the LEA must still retain responsibility for expenditure and those areas where schools should be given freedom to spend. However, problems with the new arrangements began to emerge in 2000 particularly with the relationship to local government finance overall. These are described in section 3 below.

When considering the specific rules governing Fair Funding, it should be remembered that these arrangements do not operate in isolation, but form part of the general financial management of local authorities. These general provisions are outside the scope of this work, but it should never be forgotten that the arrangements for education finance continue to fall within the responsibilities of the chief financial officer, who is charged with the proper administration of the authority's financial affairs (s. 151 of the Local Government Act 1972). An excellent analysis and summary of the law relating to local government finance can be found in the now unfortunately somewhat out of date Arden *et al.* (1999).

In addition to explicit statutory functions, it should be noted that LEA finance teams spend a great deal of time not only monitoring budgets but also in providing advice and support. LEA assistance covers how to handle accounting systems, budget review and helping schools through licensed deficits.

The sources of funds to schools have been diversified over the years, so that by April 2003 the LEA was the distribution agent for: lump-sum allocations to schools via the DfES- [part-] funded Standards Fund system; resources to schools with sixth forms via the LSC funding formula; devolved capital (principally to deal with school-building repair and improvement); and numerous grants – all these on top of the basic annual budget share.

Advice and guidance on devolved capital uses and the way in which Standards Fund grants are distributed and the conditions attached to them, are matters for routine contact between the LEA and its schools.

Since 2002/2003 a 'consistent financial reporting' system has been in force. This requires all schools to account for their income and expenditure in a standard format. The LEA advises schools on how to construct the accounts. In addition, most LEAs support financial software used by schools; typically, that will include budgetary control, commitment accounting, ordering and invoice payments.

For four out of the five most recent financial years, the size of year-end financial balances has risen considerably. LEAs take an active role in identifying any large unallocated amounts within school budgets and offering guidance to headteachers and governing bodies on the most effective uses of such 'spare' resources. As part of the financing schemes, LEAs can regulate the permissible size of uncommitted balances so as to enable redirection of excess balances within the Schools Budget.

Creative use of school balances, for example by deploying 'loans' for schools to equip ICT suites or other school improvements, has been an increasing practice.

3. New, new school funding (England)

3.1 Evolution

In September 2000 the (then) Department of Transport, Local Government and the Regions (DTLR) published a Green Paper on local government finance *Modernising Local Government Finance* (see www.local.dtlr.gov.uk/greenpap/index.htm). That document contained a short chapter suggesting that the Government wished to change the part of the system responsible for funding education (or more properly schools) and addressing three key issues (para 6.6):

- how best to ensure that funding is properly matched to the separate responsibilities of local authorities and schools

- how best to ensure that the funds allocated by the central government for education are used for that purpose

- how to ensure a fair allocation of funding between authorities and between schools in authorities to reflect pupil needs.

In January 2001 the Education Finance Strategy Group (EFSG) was set up by DfES, bringing together representatives of all the major stakeholders with an interest in LEAs and schools and including HM Treasury and DTLR (later the office of the Deputy Prime Minister (ODPM)). The Strategy Group reported at the end of May 2002, shortly before the government's proposals for revision to the overall funding system were published at the beginning of July. DfES undertook a parallel consultation exercise on the detail of the education dimension and subsequently consulted on the regulations necessary to implement its proposals in the autumn of 2002. The report and proceedings of the EFSG can be found from its home page: www.dfes.gov.uk/efsg/.

In parallel with these changes appropriate clauses had been included in the Education Bill and are now found at ss. 41–43 of the Education Act 2002. The previous decisions to transfer resources from adult and continuing education and for sixth-form pupils in schools to the Learning and Skills Council (and, in Wales, to ELWa) were implemented from the 2001/02 and 2002/03 financial years respectively under the Learning and Skills Act 2000. See chapter 11.

3.2 The debate on funding systems

The two-year debate before April 2003 leading up to the new funding system was effectively the culmination of a campaign led by headteacher trade unions drawing attention to apparent disparities between the level of funding enjoyed by apparently similar schools in different LEAs and the alleged 'funding fog' which made it impossible for anyone to understand the system that had brought about this state of affairs. The debate was also fuelled by a campaign promoted by the 'F40 Group' of less well-funded local authorities. From early in the debate, it had been made clear that the Government did not intend to remove the responsibility of the LEA for devising and maintaining a formula-based system for distributing resources to schools in its area and explicitly rejected the option of directly managing a national funding formula for schools. See www.teachernet.gov.uk/management/schoolfunding/.

6.
THE
MAINTENANCE
OF SCHOOLS

The focus of the debate was on the mechanisms used to determine each LEA's 'need to spend' in order to achieve a notional equivalent level of education service. It was therefore about distribution between LEAs, rather than direct impact on individual schools. Whilst the principles of the Fair Funding system were to be maintained, there would be some inevitable knock-on effects on the detail of the scheme.

3.3 National funding arrangements – England

There is new terminology: the former standard spending assessment (SSA) became formula spending shares (FSS), with the consequence that education standard spending (ESS) is now education formula spending (EFS) and education SSA is now education FSS.

The main difference in structure between SSA and ESS is that the former was organised into five blocks (under-five, primary, secondary, post-16 and other), whilst EFSS is divided into two blocks, one for schools and one for the LEA (schools formula spending share and LEA formula spending share respectively).

This apparent simplicity did not produce the effect which many who had been lobbying for change desired insofar as the 'schools block' could not be used to read off the amount of money that an individual school might expect its LEA to pass on to it. There are a number of reasons for this, not least the fact that the local discretion built into the 1988 legislation allowed LEAs, in consultation with their schools, to determine (within limits) which responsibilities were to be delegated to schools and which held centrally. After more than a decade schools and LEAs in different localities have arguably arrived at a stable position which suits local conditions and preferences. A national system which allowed the 'schools block' to be equivalent to the total amount delegated to schools would logically require every LEA to have a uniform scheme of delegation. Introducing this would have had the result of forcing some LEAs to delegate additional functions and others to withdraw delegation of different functions and possibly some LEAs to do both. Both kinds of change would be likely to be unpopular with both LEAs and schools and would increase the turbulence that would inevitably follow the introduction of any new system. The net result of this is that the term 'schools block' is something of a misnomer. It is more properly understood as a block of expenditure to be devoted to direct spending upon pupils of school age.

The upshot of this is that, despite good intentions and raised expectations, there will still be expenditure in the 'Schools Budget' that is not delegated to schools. As a device to mitigate the disappointment of those who had been lobbying for both greater transparency and (incidentally) an overall increase in the level of delegation to schools, the Government invented the schools forum. See section 8 below.

3.4   The 2003 funding crisis

Notwithstanding the two-year debate, there was a widely-perceived crisis in school funding in summer 2003 leading to intense scrutiny of LEAs by the DfES about passing on money to schools and the dropping of planned changes to the funding system from 2004 onwards. See the statement by the Secretary of State to the House of Commons on 17 July 2003 (*Hansard*, cols 454–8). DfES itself came in for heavy criticism in the media and also by the House of Commons Education and Skills Committee (First Report of Session 2003–04, *Public Expenditure: Schools' Funding,* HC 112, 18.12.2003). The reasons for the alleged crisis are beyond the scope of this book, although the authors believe that the problems over school funding had little to do with the new legislation and much more to do with: the impact of a four per cent increase in employers' national insurance contributions; the recalculation of the formula to take account of 2001 census data and adjustments to take account of social and educational need and the differential impact of the transfer to local government funding, or deletion, of some large Standards Fund grants – as well as overly high expectations about what an 11.6 per cent increase in funding could achieve.

4. Early-years and youth service expenditure

From April 2003 other changes occurred in the funding of LEAs, particularly in regard to early years and the youth service. In the case of early years the new funding system allocates resources to LEAs on the basis of the number of individuals for whom provision is made (rather than according to population as was the case under SSA). The specific Nursery Education Grant is transferred to general local government funding.

6.
THE
MAINTENANCE
OF SCHOOLS

The LEA block is sub-divided to include a separate sub-block for youth and community provision. Paradoxically, one of the simplifications of the SSA, compared to the previous regime (grant related expenditure assessments) had been that a separate element for youth and community service had been removed. The re-inclusion of a separate centrally determined sum for this service can be linked to the creation of Connexions. Because the Connexions service is separately funded with new money, but partially integrated with youth service provision, central government was concerned that LEAs would take the opportunity to reduce their own expenditure and expect the Connexions service to take up the slack in provision. The identification of a new sub-block was clearly intended to send a signal to LEAs about how much the Government expects them to spend. This has two effects. Where LEA spending has historically been lower, authorities will no doubt be under pressure to spend more but could do so only at the expense of other services. Conversely, where historic expenditure has been higher than the indicative level, there will no doubt be internal pressures within those authorities to redirect that 'excess' resource elsewhere.

5. LEA funding of schools from April 2003 – England

The aim of Fair Funding, as under its predecessor LMS, is to ensure that each maintained school within an LEA's area has an allocated budget share (s. 45 of the School Standards and Framework Act 1998). The process and calculations required to arrive at that budget share are specified by ss. 45A (inserted by s. 41 of the 2002 Act) and 47 of the 1998 Act and, for the 2003/04 financial year, the LEA

Budget, Schools Budget and Individual Schools Budget (England) Regulations 2002 (SI 2002 No. 3199) and the Financing of Maintained Schools Regulations (England) Regulations 2003 (SI 2003 No. 453).

5.1 Definitions of LEA Budget, Schools Budget and Individual Schools Budget

Under s.45A, in keeping with the new definitions of expenditure blocks, LEAs must allocate the money spent on education according to the:

- LEA Budget (for LEA functions)

- Schools Budget (the total amount of money spent on schools and children)

- Individual Schools Budget (the aggregate amount of money received by schools), which is the amount remaining to distribute to schools after deductions have been made from the Schools Budget in accordance with regulations.

The LEA Budget, Schools Budget and Individual Schools Budget (England) Regulations 2002 (SI 2002 No. 3199) prescribe the classes or descriptions of expenditure comprising the budgetary categories. An explanatory letter (ref: LEA/0432a/2002) about the new regulations was sent to CEOs on 20 December 2002 and can be found at www.dfes.gov.uk/fairfunding/docs/CEOLet.doc. The regulations came into force on 10 January 2003. They define four expenditure areas: the Schools Budget, the LEA Budget, the Exceptions – items outside education budgets and the Individual Schools Budget.

5.1.1 Schools Budget

Regulation 2 defines the Schools Budget as planned expenditure:

- on maintained schools and maintained nursery schools;

- on the education of pupils registered in those schools;

- on the education of pupils at independent schools, non-maintained special schools, pupil referral units, at home and in hospital; and in any other form of provision of primary and secondary education for pupils otherwise than at schools maintained by the authority; and

- all other expenditure incurred in connection with the authority's functions in relation to primary and secondary education.

5.1.2   LEA Budget

Regulation 3 defines the LEA Budget and schedule 1 lists the items. Associated administrative costs and overheads are included. The regulation makes clear that where expenditure is chargeable to a school's budget share by a statutory provision or some provision in the LEA's school financing scheme, the expenditure lies in the Schools Budget even though it may be expenditure listed in schedule 1. The list is based on the summary of the education authority role found in *The Role of the Local Education Authority in School Education* (DfEE, 2000d, pp. 7–10)

The main items are:

- **Special educational provision**, including
  - educational psychologists
  - costs associated with making, maintaining and reviewing statements
  - monitoring provision and disseminating good practice
  - collaboration with other bodies to provide support for children
  - parent partnership services and arrangements for avoiding or resolving disagreements with parents
  - behaviour support plan
  - functions in relation to child protection
  - provision under s. 31 of the Health Act 1999 (approved arrangements for NHS bodies and local authorities to act on each other's behalf)
  - medical support for individual pupils not met by health bodies.

- **School improvement**, including:
  - preparation, review and implementation of the Education Development Plan (EDP)
  - contracted advisory services following a direction under s. 63 of the 2002 Act
  - action taken under ss. 14 to 17 of the 1998 Act (powers of intervention, etc. in respect of schools with serious weaknesses or requiring special measures)
  - the appointment and remuneration of members of interim executive boards.

- **Access to education**, including:
  - management of the authority's capital programme, the asset management plan and costs associated with PFI transactions

- planning and managing the supply of school places, including the school organisation plan and establishment, alteration or discontinuance of schools
- the exclusion of pupils (but not provision for such pupils in the Schools Budget), but including advice to their parents
- school organisation committees
- home to school transport
- grants to individuals (clothing, boarding etc)
- the education welfare service and school attendance functions
- outdoor education centres
- and a variety of support, grants and payments for specified purposes.

- **FE and training**, including a variety of specified provision for young people and adults.

- **Strategic management**, including:
  - expenditure as the LEA, such as on the chief education officer and his/her staff (infelicitously called 'personal staff' in the regulations)
  - planning for the education service as a whole
  - functions of the authority related to Best Value and advice to governing bodies on procuring goods and services, revenue budget preparation, etc,
  - administration of grants to the authority
  - some 20 further specified functions and activities; and
  - a further list of around a dozen varied expenditures, such as computer systems linked to schools, the standing advisory council on religious education, maternity leave, the appointment of governors, and insurance not falling within the Schools Budget.

5.1.3   Exceptions

Regulation 4 defines the exceptions: items which are not to be included in the LEA Budget or Schools Budget. They include capital expenditure other than CERA (the acronym is defined and used in the text of the regulations, that is, capital expenditure which an authority expects to charge to a revenue account); expenditure on school crossing patrols and expenditure of extended school services.

5.1.4   Individual Schools Budget

Regulation 5 defines how the Individual Schools Budget – the total amount of money delegated to schools through budget shares – is reached. An LEA may deduct the items listed in schedule 2 from the Schools Budget, with associated administration costs and overheads. The main items are:

- **expenditure on support grants** (other than that listed elsewhere in that schedule or in schedule 1) which the LEA is obliged to incur;

- **special educational provision**, including:
  - that specified in pupils' statements of SEN (subject to certain provisos)
  - some specialist support to governing bodies
  - encouragement of inclusive provision in mainstream schools
  - education otherwise than at school
  - provision at pupil referral units
  - services required to implement for children with behavioural difficulties (excluding expenditure incurred under schedule 1 or elsewhere in schedule 2)
  - fees at independent schools or non-maintained special schools
  - recoupment for children with statements of SEN;

- **access to education,** including:
  - administration of the admissions system (subject to the allocation to each governing body which is an admission authority of a reasonable sum to meet their costs
  - admission forums
  - milk, meals and other refreshment, with certain caveats and repair and maintenance of associated kitchens
  - grants, fees or other payments in respect of pupils at a school not maintained by an LEA, under s. 18 of the 1996 Act; and

- **other expenditure**, including:
  - nursery education other than at a maintained school
  - school and premises insurance if not funded through schools' budget share
  - services to schools provided by museums and galleries
  - library services for primary and special schools, with caveats
  - licence fees and subscriptions for schools (to a maximum of 0.2 per cent of the LEA's Schools Budget)
  - schools forum
  - recoupment payments to another LEA
  - exceptional payments to schools to avoid serious prejudice to pupils' education
  - increases to a school's budget share in specified circumstances
  - expenditure not covered elsewhere in the schedule to a maximum of 0.1 per cent of the authority's Schools Budget
  - and CERA for purposes not covered elsewhere in that schedule or in schedule 1.

6. Secretary of State's power to set a minimum Schools Budget

Section 45A also requires the LEA to submit to the Secretary of State (or NAW) by the end of January its proposed Schools Budget for the following financial year. The Secretary of State (or NAW) has a reserve power to set a minimum Schools Budget for each LEA under ss. 45B and 45C, as substituted by s. 42 of the Education Act 2002, if the Secretary of State (or NAW) considers the Schools Budget 'is inadequate'. Section 45C sets out a process for the Secretary of State (or NAW) to set a minimum Schools Budget. This was part of the compromise with headteachers to ensure that money allocated by the Government is 'passported' to schools.

The new power was not used for the 2003/04 financial year although contemplated. See DfES news www.dfes.gov.uk/pns/DisplayPN.cgi?pn id=2003_0020 which stated that the Secretary of State was proposing to use the new power against Westminster and Croydon in February 2003. The new power was not used, as the LEAs agreed to make changes voluntarily.

As part of the package of changes announced in July 2003 in response to the funding 'crisis' (see section 3.4 above), para 66 of sched 7 to the Local Government Act 2003 amends s. 45A to require LEAs in England to submit their proposed Schools Budget by the end of December. At the beginning of 2004, the Secretary of State gave details of the kind of pressure he was putting on LEAs which had fallen short of the 'passporting' targets for 2004/05; the press statement (13 January 2004) is remarkable for its revelation of the closeness of the scrutiny and for the publication of detail on every LEA.

7. School budget shares

Each school's budget share is determined by the LEA, dividing up the ISB among the maintained schools in its area under s. 47, but subject to the rules laid down – the formula – in the Financing of Maintained Schools (England) Regulations 2003 (SI 2003 No. 453). In particular, the regulations set out the factors the LEA must take into account when determining each school's budget share and the procedure for consultation on the allocation methods the LEA proposes to use.

The LEA must strike the right balance of distribution which ensures that: small schools, which otherwise would probably not attract sufficient funds through a funding formula based on pupil numbers, continue to be viable; there are enough places in LEA-funded special schools and SEN bases to support the most complex special needs and the LEA can deliver enough funds to very large secondary schools to meet their curricular and other demands. In practice the majority of funding is linked to pupil numbers, but LEAs use a variety of lump sums, floor-area formulae, socio-economic factors and other mechanisms to maintain the best possible balance.

Thorough consultation is important for any formulary changes, as it is inevitable that there will be different and competing interests and the LEA is required to take a considered and impartial view about the optimum distribution of available funds and indeed is the only body able to do so. It is important to be open about the financial implications for schools – hence the significance of the schools forum in the whole process.

6.
THE
MAINTENANCE
OF SCHOOLS

8.   Schools forums

Section 47A, as inserted by s. 43 of the 2002 Act, placed a duty on every LEA (except the City of London and the Isles of Scilly) to establish a schools forum to advise, as prescribed in regulations, on the distribution of money between schools and how much should be spent on certain LEA-wide functions. Regulations may require the LEA to have regard to advice from the schools forum.

The Schools Forums (England) Regulations 2002 (SI 2002 No. 2114) came into force on 2 September 2002. The DfES published guidance to LEAs on 12 August 2002 *Schools Forums: Constitutional, Procedural and Administrative Matters* (see www.dfes.gov.uk/fairfunding/docs/forumguide113amended2.doc) along with a letter (see www.dfes.gov.uk/fairfunding/docs/CEO-Forums.Let.doc) stating that a policy note would be sent to schools forums setting out the issues which forums should consider before giving advice. This had not appeared by the end of 2003.

DfES letter Academies and School Forums, of 10 January 2003 (see www.dfes.gov.uk/fairfunding/docs/forumsacademieslet.doc), asked that Academies should have observer status on forums. The letter stated that the Schools Forums Regulations would be amended to guarantee observer status for Academies (see the Schools Forums (England) (Amendment) Regulations 2004 SI2004 N0. 447)).

The practical outcome of the first round of schools forum activity seems to have been the emergence of a well-informed and powerful lobby of stakeholders who are prepared to take issue with the Government over any ambiguity in statements issued about school funding.

8.1 Regulations and guidance

The main requirements are summarised below.

8.1.1. Establishment and membership

- Each LEA had to establish a schools forum for its area by 15 January 2003 (reg 2).

- Each forum should have at least 15 members. At least four-fifths of the members must come from schools; the remainder are 'non-schools' members, but the LEA can choose to have no 'non-school' members.

- Schools members are appointed in accordance with reg 4. They must be headteachers or governors and must represent primary and secondary schools and the relative number representing each sector should take account of the relative numbers of pupils in those sectors in the LEA's schools. There must be at the least one schools member who is representative of special schools, should the LEA maintain any. The LEA determines how and by whom the school representatives are elected. The guidance suggests that the LEA may wish to enable representation according to category of school – community, foundation, aided and controlled – but there is no requirement to do so (para 1.2).

- Non-school members are appointed in accordance with reg 5. LEAs are required to seek nominations from organisations if there are to be non-school members. The way in which this is done and a decision as to whether to accept the person nominated, are matters for the LEA. If non-school members are appointed then nominations must be sought from local Church of England and Roman Catholic Church diocesan bodies. The Secretary of State has a reserve power to remove from the forum any non-school member representing an organisation which the Secretary of State believes should not be in membership.

- The LEA determines the term of membership. A member will cease to be a member should he or she leave the position which enabled him/her to be eligible for appointment, i.e. if a governor retires then the governor must leave the forum.

- An observer from the local LSC has to be invited to each meeting of the forum.

8.1.2   Conduct of meetings

- The quorum is 40 per cent of the total membership (reg 6). The guidance advises (para 2.3), that it is for the LEA to decide whether a quorum can include substitute members.

- No other provision is made in the regulations regarding the timing and frequency of meetings of the forum. Paragraph 2.1 of the guidance states:

  'The LEA must arrange meetings so that the forum can be consulted on issues listed in the regulations in time for its views be taken into account in deciding on the disposition of the Schools Budget for the following financial year. Failure to do so will render the LEA vulnerable to a complaint of unreasonableness.'

- The guidance advises a minimum of three meetings a year of which two may be needed in the autumn term.

- The guidance also advises that it is for the LEA to determine what rules should apply for the forum to reach decisions as to what its advice should be. LEAs can also determine whether meetings should be held in public or private and where they should be held. The LEA should consider whether declarations of interest should be made (paras 2.4–2.6).

8.1.3   Forum costs

- LEAs could charge costs to the Local Schools Budget in 2002/03 financial year and the Schools Budget in 2003/04 (reg 11, see also s. 4 of the guidance).

- The LEA can pay reasonable expenses to forum members (reg 12, see also s. 5 of the guidance).

8.1.4   Functions

The LEA must consult the forum on:

- the LEA school funding formula (reg 7), including changes to the factors and criteria which are taken into account and the methods, principles and rules that have been adopted, in the LEA formula to distribute money to schools. Consultation must take place in sufficient time for views to be taken into account by the LEA before determining arrangements for the following financial year

- contracts (reg 8) which are proposed for the supply of services paid out of the LEA's Schools Budget where the value of the contract is above a specified threshold. Consultation has to occur at least one month prior to the issue of invitations to tender

- financial issues relating to the Schools Budget (reg 9) in connection with special educational needs provision; pupil referral units; early-years education and insurance

- prospective revisions of the scheme for financing schools; administrative arrangements on the allocation of central government grants to schools via the LEA and arrangements for free school meals.

The regulations as drafted require the LEA to have regard to the forum's guidance on the school funding formula and not the other matters, although the fact that the LEA has to consult implies a requirement to consider the response.

The LEA can consult the forum on such other matters concerning the funding of schools as it sees fit.

6.
THE
MAINTENANCE
OF SCHOOLS

The forum must give an account of its deliberations to schools (reg 10).

9. LEAs' financial schemes

To regulate the distribution of school budget shares and also to provide a mechanism by which the Secretary of State can monitor an LEA's compliance with the Act and regulations, s. 48 of the 1998 Act imposes a duty on each LEA to prepare a scheme dealing with such matters connected with the financing of schools maintained by the LEA as are required to be dealt with in the scheme or by regulations, currently the Financing of Maintained Schools (England) Regulations 2003. The regulations may include details of how surpluses and deficits may be carried forward into the next financial year, amounts which may be charged by the LEA against a school's budget share, the terms on which services and facilities are to be provided to schools by the LEA and the imposition of conditions, which must be complied with by schools, in relation to the management of their delegated budgets.

In theory, an LEA has some discretion as to what conditions and rules it may impose in its scheme, but in reality the scheme, in order to obtain the approval of the Secretary of State, must contain the information prescribed by the regulations and, although some flexibility is allowed in respect of the imposition of local conditions, for example, to address insurance arrangements, s. 48(3) ensures that the Act and the regulations will always prevail in the event of any inconsistency or ambiguity.

The procedure for preparing and publishing the scheme is set out in sched 14 to the 1998 Act. This schedule re-emphasises the central control mechanism of the Secretary of State by requiring that, first, all schemes must be submitted to the Secretary of State for approval (para 1(1) and (4) of sched 14) and, second, that LEAs should have regard not only to the regulations but also to any guidance issued by the Secretary of State as to the provisions he regards as appropriate for inclusion in the scheme (para 1(2)). See *Schemes for Financing Schools: Section 48 of the School Standards and Framework Act 1998 and Schedule 14 to the Act, Statutory Guidance for Local Education Authorities: Issue 2(Rev)* found at www.dfes.gov.uk/fairfunding/docs/sguiderev2003.doc.

Before submitting the scheme to the Secretary of State, the LEA must consult the governing body and headteacher of every school maintained by the LEA (para 1(3)(b)).

The scheme cannot come into force until approved by the Secretary of State (para 1(4)), who may modify the scheme as he thinks fit after consulting the LEA. In the event of the LEA's failing to submit a scheme within the time limits set by the Secretary of State or submitting a scheme which the Secretary of State does not believe accords with the guidance, the Secretary of State may, after consulting the LEA, impose a scheme which makes such provision as he thinks fit.

The approved scheme must be published by sending a copy to the governing body and headteacher of every school maintained by the LEA and making a copy available for reference at all reasonable times and without charge at each school maintained by the LEA and at the LEA's principal office (reg 30 of the 2003 Regulations).

10. Three-year budgets and control of school balances

In October and December 2002 DfES issued guidance to LEAs about Ministers' wish to see 3-year budget plans being prepared for schools. At the same time a system for the control of school balances was introduced. In May 2004, the Prime Minister re-affirmed commitment to the 3-year budget, but declined to say how this would affect the LEAs. (see *Local Government Chronicle*, 7 May)

The logic of 3-year budgeting relies heavily on advance DfES decisions associated with teacher pay awards, treatment of specific grants, levels of devolved capital and the anticipated revenue growth available from year to year.

As long as there remains the considerable link between pupil numbers and school budget shares, as a basis for funding, it will always be difficult for many schools to go forward with any certainty and make significant decisions, particularly on staffing, without an element of risk. Most governing bodies tend to adopt a cautious approach in such situations.

LEAs were advised in December 2002 that they could revise their schemes for financing schools to allow some control over levels of individual school balances. This was contingent on LEAs being able to issue 3-year budgets to schools. In 2001 the national total of school balances stood at £1,040m. The Government had concerns that this amount was rising year on year and some individual schools had very large sums, which was not seen as desirable especially if allowed to grow unchecked. Whilst acknowledging that it is prudent for all schools to have a level of reserves, the intention was to ensure monies are mainly spent on pupils already in school, unless there is a planned saving for a specific project.

Model text that LEAs could insert in schemes for financing schools was produced in December 2002 and this sought to define a 'surplus balance' and how this could be identified and redeployed each year. The text can be found in s. 4 of the model scheme for financing schools (reference above). The logic is that by 31 May, after the end of the preceding financial year, the LEA should be able to calculate whether a school had a surplus balance after accounting for the previous year's finance commitments, unspent Standards Fund grant and amounts 'assigned for a special purpose'. It is the latter category over which debate will inevitably arise as there needs to be some agreement reached between the governing body and the LEA, probably after consultation on the principles with the schools forum, about what can reasonably discounted before deciding whether a school has a genuine surplus balance. Assuming an agreement on the stages described can be reached then, if the residual amount is greater than five per cent of a secondary school's current budget share, or eight per cent for a primary or special school, the excess can be deducted by the LEA for redistribution within the Schools Budget of the authority.

However, the DfES guidance advises:

> 'The purpose of such provision is to allow LEAs to monitor excessive balances, not institute a general regime of control. There

6.
THE
MAINTENANCE
OF SCHOOLS

is no intention to introduce provision for capping balances or allowing them to be taken into account in calculating budget shares.'

The intention was that this undoubtedly contentious change to schemes for financing schools could be consulted on and be with the DfES by October 2003, to allow operation from January 2004 i.e. for the first time in relation to the 2003/04 financial year's outturn.

11. Delegated budgets

Having calculated each maintained school's budget share and having published its scheme to show how the share was calculated, the LEA is under a duty to provide every maintained school with a delegated budget (s. 49(1)). The only exception is if the governing body's right to a delegated budget has been suspended under s. 51 (see below).

It must be remembered, however, that, by delegating a budget to a school, the LEA does not give or transfer the ownership of that money to the governing body. As s. 49(5) makes clear, any amount made available to the governing body by the LEA remains the property of the LEA until spent by the governing body or headteacher. When the budget is spent, it is taken to have been spent by the governing body or headteacher as the LEA's agent. This position was confirmed in *R v Yorkshire Purchasing Organisation, ex parte British Educational Suppliers Ltd* [1998] 2 ELR 195, CA, where the Court of Appeal held that a maintained school with a delegated budget, even though incorporated, was an agent of the LEA. Thus any contract entered into by the governing body using money from its delegated budget is in law a contract between the LEA and the supplier and the governing body is not a contracting party. Any enforcement action is therefore taken against the LEA, not the governing body.

This does, however, mean that an LEA can be held responsible for a contract entered into by a governing body of a voluntary aided or foundation school using delegated funds. Whether governing bodies of foundation schools or, indeed, the contractors with whom they contract appreciate this is debatable.

The only exceptions to this principle are in respect of the repayment of the principal or interest on a loan taken out by the governing body, provided that their LEA's scheme allows such schools to take out loans, and expenditure which has to be met by the governing body of a voluntary aided school.

12. Effect of financial delegation

The effect of financial delegation is set out in s. 50 of the 1998 Act, which defines the respective powers and duties of the LEA and governing body in relation to a school's budget share. As so often, it will be no surprise that the duties fall on the LEA, the powers on the governing body.

Where a maintained school has a delegated budget in respect of the whole or part of a financial year, the LEA has the duty to secure that there is available to be spent by the governing body a sum equal to the school's budget share for the year (or if it only has delegation for part of that year, a sum equal to that portion of the school's budget share for the year which has not been spent). The amounts must be made available to the governing body in accordance with the timings in the scheme.

The governing body then has the power to spend the amounts made available for any purposes of the school or for such purposes as may be prescribed in regulations (s. 50(3)). The governing body may delegate to the headteacher its powers to spend, but s. 50(3) does not allow it to pay allowances to governors otherwise than in accordance with the statutory scheme for governors' expenses and allowances contained in para 6 of sched 11 to the 1998 Act.

Although the governing body is an incorporated legal entity and thus, in the absence of fraud or bad faith, personal liability should not fall on individual governors anyway, s. 50(7) expressly states that governors shall not incur any personal liability in respect of anything done in good faith in the exercise or purported exercise of their powers to spend the sums made available to them by the LEA. In the absence of fraud by an individual governor, it is hard to understand when in law governors might be personally liable and this provision has always appeared to serve no purpose other than perhaps to provide a reassurance to prospective governors that they will not be bankrupted because of decisions which they may take as governors. The provision serves no purpose as, first, any liability should fall on the incorporated governing body and, secondly, but most importantly, as the governing body acts as the LEA's agent for the purposes of spending the delegated budget (see s. 49(5)(b)), the LEA will remain liable to meet any claim which may be made as a result of the governing body's spending its delegated budget. As this will apply even if the governing body has incompetently or negligently exercised its powers, this might be described as a *de facto* duty on the LEA to meet the cost of a governing body's commercial ineptitude.

A number of LEAs, having experienced such difficulties, now make specific provision in their schemes to address these potential problems. It has also been suggested that the scheme may make clear that governing bodies should seek advice before entering into certain contracts, with the proviso that, if that advice is not taken, the governing body will be treated as if it had acted in bad faith and thus the governors might leave themselves open to personal liability. The issue of school companies is dealt with separately: see B.6 of this chapter.

13. Suspension of financial delegation

As the delegation of budget sums to schools increases and the LEA has become more of a cheque processor than a controller of expenditure, its role to regulate and ensure effectiveness in education expenditure has diminished. With schools now being responsible for upward of 90 per cent of an LEA's revenue expenditure, an LEA can have little influence over how and upon what, schools spend their money.

Nonetheless, under local management, it was recognised that there needed to be some check on a governing body's ability to spend the LEA's public money and so, under the Education Reform Act 1988, LEAs were given the responsibility for monitoring the management of delegated budgets by governing bodies. Those provisions, slightly strengthened to allow an LEA to address standards through withdrawal of the delegated budget (see ss. 14 and 17 of the 1998 Act), can now be found in s. 51 of and sched 15 to the 1998 Act.

Under para 1 of the schedule, the LEA may suspend the governing body's right to a delegated budget where it appears to the LEA that the governing body of a school which has a delegated budget (a) has been guilty of a substantial or persistent failure to comply with any delegation requirement or restriction or (b) is not managing in a satisfactory manner the expenditure or appropriation of the school's delegated budget share. The schedule was amended from 2 September 2002 for England and 1 September 2003 for Wales to include mismanagement of funds delegated to the school for extended school/community-focused school purposes under s. 27 of the Education Act 2002.

Where an LEA does suspend a governing body's delegated budget, it does not mean that the LEA must take over all the governing body's functions. The LEA may decide to devolve back to the governing body such decision-making powers as it feels the governing body can manage. For example, the LEA may wish to retain responsibility for staffing expenditure, if that is where the problem has arisen, but may be happy to allow the governing body to be responsible for non-staff related expenditure.

The most significant effect of the suspension of a school's delegated budget relates to the governing body's staffing powers. This is discussed below in part E.3.2 and 4.2 of this chapter.

13.1 Guidance on suspension of delegation

In order to ensure that LEAs do not use this power in an arbitrary fashion, in considering whether or not to suspend a governing body's right to a delegated budget, the LEA must have regard to the *Code of Practice on LEA – School Relations (England)* (DfEE, 2001). Annex 1 provides information on the legal framework in paras 36–38. Annex 2 gives guidance in para 7 on the use of the two LEA powers to suspend delegation: s. 51 of, and sched 15 to, the School Standards and Framework Act 1998 (financial mismanagement etc) and s. 17 of the Act (suspension of delegation as a result of an LEA warning or a special measures or serious weaknesses finding by Ofsted).

Paragraph 7 of Annex 2 sets out the principles which LEAs must have regard to in exercising its powers to suspend delegation. These include:

a) suspension of delegation should happen only in exceptional circumstances; the LEA must be clear in its notice to explain to the governing body if it is acting under its powers of intervention to improve standards (s. 17) or to address financial mismanagement or non-compliance with scheme requirements (s. 51);

b) an explanation for the reasons for the suspension must be given including the evidence used to reach the conclusion and how suspension will help the school; and

c) delegation should be restored as soon as practicable and legally possible after the problem has been resolved and the governing body can safely be relied on to consolidate and build on the improvements which have been made.

13.2 Requirements of schedule 15 on suspension of delegation

The LEA should give the governing body not less than one month's notice in writing of the suspension, unless, by reason of any gross

6.
THE
MAINTENANCE
OF SCHOOLS

incompetence or mismanagement on the part of the governing body or other emergency, it appears to the LEA to be necessary to give the governing body a shorter period of notice or to give the governing body notice suspending their right to a budget with immediate effect (para 1(2) of sched 15). The notice must specify the grounds for the suspension, giving particulars of:

a)   any alleged failure on the part of the governing body to comply with any delegation requirement or restriction;

b)   any alleged mismanagement; and

c)   if applicable, the grounds upon which the LEA has decided to give less than one month's notice (para 1(3)).

The notice must also be given to the headteacher of the school and a copy must be sent to the Secretary of State (para 1(5) and (6)).

Once the right of a governing body to a delegated budget has been suspended, the LEA may review the suspension at any time it thinks appropriate (para 2(1)(b)). The LEA must, however, review every suspension before the beginning of the next financial year, unless the suspension took effect less than two months before the beginning of that financial year (para 2(1)(a)). When reviewing suspension, the LEA must give the governing body and headteacher of the school an opportunity to make representations. Having reviewed the suspension, the LEA may:

a)   revoke it with effect from the beginning of the next financial year following the review (if the review takes place before the new financial year);

b)   revoke it with effect from such time as the LEA may determine, if the LEA has held the review at any other time (para 2(3)); or

c)   decide not to revoke the suspension.

In any case, the LEA must give the governing body and headteacher notice in writing of its decision (para 2(4)).

In the case of a decision to suspend the budget or not to revoke the suspension, the LEA must include in the written notice details of the fact that the governing body, but not the headteacher, may appeal to the Secretary of State against the imposition of the suspension or the decision not to revoke the suspension (para 3(1)). Such an appeal must be brought within two months of the LEA's decision. The Secretary of State may allow or reject the appeal and in determining the appeal must have regard to the gravity of the default on the part of the governing body and the likelihood of it continuing or recurring (para 3(4)).

14. Expenditure incurred for community purposes

Sections 27 and 28 of the Education Act 2002 enable schools to provide community facilities called extended schools in England and community-focused schools in Wales. Schedule 3 of the 2002 Act inserts s. 51A into the 1998 Act to provide for the management of expenditure provided by the LEA and third parties for the provision of community facilities. In case of a claim by a third party against the school, the LEA may recover the costs from the school but not from the school's budget share.

15. Financial statements

Further to regulate the delegation of budget shares to schools, LEAs are required to produce financial statements before the beginning of each financial year ('the budget statement') and after the end of each financial year ('the outturn statement') (s. 52 of the 1998 Act). The outturn statement should contain details of the LEA's planned expenditure in that year and, taken from the budget statement, the expenditure actually incurred by the LEA in the year and any other resources allocated by the LEA in that year to maintained schools. Again, the detail and form of these statements are left to regulations. For the 2003/04 financial year see the Education (Budget Statements) (England) Regulations 2003 (SI 2003 No. 475). For the Outturn Statements for the 2002/03 financial year see the Education (Outturn Statements) (England) Regulations 2003 (SI 2003 No. 1153). These regulations will have to be replaced or amended for successive financial years.

The LEA must supply the governing body and headteacher of each maintained school with a copy of the relevant parts of every budget and outturn statement (s. 52(4)) and shall publish the statements by supplying a copy to the Secretary of State and making a copy available for reference by parents and other persons at all reasonable times and without charge at each education office of the LEA (reg 4 of the budget regulations and reg 5 of the outturn regulations). The budget statement had to be published before the beginning of the financial year and the outturn statement by 10 October 2003.

DfES revised the layout of the financial statements for April 2003, so as to include the total education spending plans for each LEA including the youth service. The layout is split between the schools budget and the LEA budget.

If the Secretary of State directs, an LEA must require the Audit Commission to make arrangements for certifying either part or all of an LEA's budget or outturn statement as the Secretary of State may specify under s. 53.

16. Consistent Financial Reporting (CFR)

Consistent Financial Reporting (CFR) is the accounting system which schools in England have used to collect information about their expenditure decisions since the 2002/03 financial year. Section 44 of the 2002 Act enables a detailed scheme to be prescribed although this has not been done except for s. 44(5) which enables regulations to be prescribed for reporting purposes. This has been done by the Consistent Financial Reporting (England) Regulations 2003 (SI 2003 No. 373). LEAs had to report to the Secretary of State each school's audit data by 22 August 2003 for the 2002/03 financial year. The data to be collected is specified on the DfES Value for Money website: www.dfes.gov.uk/valueformoney/ including the CFR Framework and Guide. The Value for Money website reported on 26 September 2003 that 145 LEAs (out of 150) had submitted data, of which 127 had submitted 100 per cent of their schools' data. Section 45 amends s. 52 (financial statements by LEAs) of the 1998 Act to enable resources not provided by LEAs to be included in the accounts.

6.
THE
MAINTENANCE
OF SCHOOLS

17. Capital funding for new building and major maintenance in England

17.1 History

Up until 1997 education capital funding was fairly simple in its allocation. LEAs were funded for education expenditure including capital works on an annual basis by an education allocation included within the revenue support grant funded by central Government to allow LEAs to carry out their services. LEAs could also apply for basic credit approval (borrowing powers) to raise additional capital funding in expenditure bids called annual capital guidelines. By 1996 the emphasis had changed from removal of surplus places to basic need. 'Basic need' is to provide capital for the provision of additional school places in areas of population growth.

17.2   Current position

Central Government education strategy changed in 1997 and since then there has been a growth in the number of funding channels available to LEAs in accordance with *Building Schools for the Future*. Funding channels available to LEAs and schools can comprise any of the following funding sources:

1) basic credit approvals

2) target capital funding

3) capital support for the expansion of popular schools

4) 'condition' and modernisation

5) devolved formula capital

6) 'seed challenge'

7) access initiative

8) staff workplaces

9) LEA co-ordinated voluntary aided programme (LCVAP)

10) *Building Schools for the Future.*

17.3   Funding channels

17.3.1   Basic credit approvals

Basic need is the requirement for additional school places in areas of population growth, where there is no more capacity in schools in the surrounding area. The funding is delivered to LEAs in the form of basic credit approvals. (Sometimes supplementary credit approvals are awarded on a one-off basis at any point in a financial year if funding becomes available.)

17.3.2   Target capital funding

This is a form of capital funding for which LEAs have to make a bid on an annual basis. It is a relatively limited programme and is intended to support projects which contribute directly to meeting Government's educational priorities and which might not otherwise be supported through formulaic funding allocations to LEAs and schools (e.g. 'condition' and modernisation funding for LEAs and devolved formula funding for schools). The first year of this funding allocation was in 2003/04.

17.3.3   Capital support for the expansion of popular schools

This funding channel was first introduced in 2003 and is available to support the expansion of successful and popular schools and to ensure that where school organisation committees or the adjudicators are considering proposals to expand a successful and popular secondary school, they are not prevented by lack of capital funding from agreeing to proposals.

17.3.4 'Condition' and modernisation funding

'Condition' and modernisation funding streams are intended to assist in raising educational standards by contributing towards meeting the capital investment needs of school buildings, according to locally agreed priorities in each LEA's asset management plan. 'Condition' has been a Standards Fund grant, allocated to LEAs using a formula that is partially targeted at repairs, as well as pupil numbers. From 2003/04 this funding has been paid as part of the so-called 'single capital pot', giving LEAs greater flexibility in using these resources. This funding is issued on conditions similar to those for 'condition' funding, but it also takes into account suitability issues. The intention is that LEAs will join up these funding streams to meet the most appropriate school building priorities, whether related to 'condition' or wider improvement needs.

17.3.5 Devolved formula capital

This is a DfES Standards Fund grant which gives maintained schools direct funding to help support the capital needs of their buildings. It is allocated to LEAs, who then allocate the funding directly to schools using a formula. The funding is intended to be invested in priorities agreed locally and identified in the local asset management plan. This funding can be rolled forward for up to three years to allow schools to plan larger projects. During the year 2003/04, because of the school funding difficulties nationally, schools have been allowed to use devolved formula capital to support revenue expenditure.

17.3.6 'Seed challenge'

This funding is in the form of a grant and its aim is to increase pupil achievement through the improvement of school buildings. It is allocated to LEAs and operates on the principle of generating matched funding, where 'new money' can be raised. It is intended to support innovative investment in school buildings and recognises that raising funds from private sources generally offers exceptional value for money.

17.3.7 Access initiative

The schools access initiative is intended to provide funding to make mainstream schools more accessible to children with disabilities and special educational needs. It is allocated by pupil-related formula to all LEAs, which then decide how it should be allocated to schools.

17.3.8   Staff workplaces

This grant is intended to enable school staff to work more effectively by contributing towards the investment needs of buildings at maintained schools. This investment is standards-focused and is to be used to make more effective use of professional time which should have a positive impact on pupil achievement. It is allocated by pupil-related formula to LEAs, which are then responsible for determining allocations to schools in line with the needs identified in local asset management planning processes.

17.3.9   LEA co-ordinated voluntary aided programme (LCVAP)

This is the main funding programme available to the VA sector in the financial year 2003/04. There are no limits on the size of a project that can be supported via LCVAP, nor any restrictions on the type of capital project, as long as the capital work is governors' liability.

Each LEA is asked to co-ordinate, in consultation with local partners, the allocation of the programme according to local needs and priorities. This allocation process takes into account the priorities identified in the asset management plan. When deciding which new projects should be funded through LCVAP, local partners must also consider the amount of devolved formula capital (DFC) held by schools. Some schools may be asked to contribute some, or all, of their allocation towards the cost of the LCVAP project, in order to ensure that schools do not hold large amounts of unallocated DFC and that the LCVAP programme funds as much work as possible.

17.3.10   *Building Schools for the Future*

The *Building Schools for the Future* proposals were published, with very challenging deadlines, in mid-2003. They include the modernisation or replacement of the whole secondary school stock over a period 15–20 years and will be for the most part funded through the PFI. The main aims are to:

- continue existing successful programmes for primary and secondary schools, but use the extra capital investment available in 2005/06 for a major programme of secondary school building;

- collaborate better with other funders to create schools that are community assets

- target the extra investment on geographical areas, covering groups of schools;

- develop exemplary designs to ensure consistently high standards of design for all new schools;

- establish a national body to support local authorities in ensuring that new schools are well designed, built on time and at a reasonable cost to the taxpayer and are properly maintained over their lives; and

- look carefully at the availability and balance of capital funding across the system, so that there is significant investment to address the urgent building needs of primary schools and secondary schools that are not included in the early phase of *Building Schools for the Future*.

The Government's guidance indicates that:

'[…] local authorities and local people will play a central role in drawing together this new approach. *Building Schools for the Future* is about Government support for local visions and the new procurement body should be seen in that context. The new approach will also help us plan together long-term and improve on the old culture of annual, win-lose bidding.'

**6.
THE
MAINTENANCE
OF SCHOOLS**

17.4 Private Finance Initiative and the future of 'capital'

A key development in Government policy in capital finance in recent years has been the development of the PFI in the public services (see also part C.2.5 of this chapter). The principle behind PFI is that private sector funding can be levered in to support publicly-funded capital expenditure by the private sector's providing the buildings and at the same time, for a guaranteed period of 30 years or so, managing, at a profit, the services which will be provided in those buildings. It is too early to come to a final view either on the policy or its implementation, especially since it is a development which, by definition, entails so long a period of operation. The practical view appears to be that, since it is Government policy that the bulk of capital expenditure in the public sector should increasingly be provided by this route and that all other routes have ceased or have been very significantly scaled down, this is an approach which must be pursued *faute de mieux* or, as the cliché has it, as 'the only game in town' whatever the advantages, disadvantages and consequences may be.

The other important development is that local authorities will be required to operate under new Prudential Guidelines for capital borrowing in future. The previous borrowing regime has been abolished and the Government has put in place provision for local authorities to regulate their own borrowing on the principle of 'affordability'. The Government has not yet set out full details of the new arrangements, but CIPFA has devised guidelines to help local authorities come to a view on what is 'affordable', although the arrangements are very complex and the Secretary of State retains a power to cap expenditure.

18. Wales

For the 2003/04 financial year, Wales continued to use the financial arrangements specified in the School Standards and Framework Act 1998 prior to amendment by the 2002 Act. However, the Welsh Assembly Government consulted in Summer 2003 on introducing the amended legislation for the 2004/05 financial year. See *Consultation on the Replacement of the Financing of Maintained Schools Regulations 1999 (as amended)* which ran from 31 March to 13 June 2003. The document can be found at www.wales.gov.uk/subieducationtraining/content/Consultation/ maintained-schools-consultation-e.pdf. The March consultation document proposed a similar categorisation of the LEA Budget, Schools Budgets and Individual Schools Budget as England. The Welsh Assembly Government will take the power to determine an LEA's Schools Budget. The amended legislation commenced in Wales for the 2004/05 financial year by way of the LEA Budget, Schools Budget and Individual Schools Budget (Wales) Regulations 2003 (SI 2003/3118 (W 296)). The School Budget Shares (Wales) Regulations and the Scheme for Financing Schools (Wales) Regulations had not been made at the time of writing.

18.1 Schools forums – Wales

The schools forum provisions commenced in Wales on 1 November 2003 and the Schools Forums (Wales) Regulations 2003 (SI 2003 No. 2909 (W 275)) came into force on 13 November 2003. Although differently formulated in places, the effect of the regulations is similar to those for England. Each LEA had to establish a schools forum by 15 December 2003. The LEA appoints members; there must be at least 15 and they must be representative of the different categories of schools: non-schools' members must not be more than a quarter. The LEA must ensure as far as is practicable that one of the schools' members must be a parent governor. The LEA, in addition to church representatives, must seek nominations from 'teaching and other trade unions with members working in Wales'. The quorum, as in England, is 40 per cent of the membership. The regulations make it explicit that the chair of the forum has to be elected from members of the forum, who would hold the office for one year but may be reappointed. The regulation (reg 7) on consultation on financial issues is more widely drawn than the equivalent for England (reg 9).

18.2 Community-focused schools – Wales

Section 51A (Expenditure incurred for community purposes) was inserted into the 1998 Act for Wales on 1 September 2003, the day that the provisions relating to community-focused schools commenced, principally ss. 27 and 28 of the 2002 Act.

E. Staffing of Maintained Schools

1. Introduction: why there is confusion

Of all the divisions of responsibility between LEAs and schools, the understanding of the respective duties and liabilities towards staff probably causes most confusion. Before the advent of local management, the situation was comparatively clear. LEAs appointed and dismissed both non-teaching and teaching staff in county, voluntary controlled and special agreement schools. In voluntary aided schools, the situation has always been different as the governing body was the employer, but, by and large, in all other schools, both the staff and, perhaps more importantly, the law could easily identify the employer.

Following the introduction of local management in the Education Reform Act 1988, the position was considerably confused. Ask most teaching staff in schools and they would point to either the headteacher or the governing body as their employer. Local management did indeed mean that the governing body took on responsibility in county and voluntary controlled schools for advertising, interviewing, appointing, promoting and disciplining and dismissing the majority of school staff, but in law the employer nonetheless remained the LEA, despite the fact that it had little control over the process. The situation in voluntary aided and grant-maintained schools was different, with the governing body being solely responsible. This difference has continued under the School Standards and Framework Act 1998 in respect of voluntary aided and foundation schools, which will be discussed separately below.

As a consequence of this confusion, there has been considerable litigation, mainly in the employment tribunals and regulations to try and clarify the situation, but, as will be seen below, clarity is at times still lacking.

The other problem in the area of staffing is that people think of headteachers and teaching staff as being the only employees about whom issues arise (often with belated acknowledgement of schools' non-teaching staff), but it must of course not be forgotten that the LEA employs a considerable number of other people outside of school who are necessary to perform the whole range of its educational and/or administrative functions. Even though they are not literally part of the 'Staffing of Maintained Schools', this category will be considered first, before attention is drawn to the far more complex and potentially more litigious field of responsibility for school-based staff.

2. LEA staff

The first appointment for all LEAs is the chief education officer. Section 532 of the Education Act 1996 requires the LEA to appoint a fit person to be the chief education officer of the authority (see chapter 3.B.3 for the origins of this requirement). Interestingly, the Local Authority Social Services Act 1970 requires a (principal) local authority to appoint 'an officer, to be known as the director of social services' (s. 6(1)) and secure that there are 'sufficient staff for assisting him in the exercise of his functions' (s. 6(6)). Pointing out that the 1970 Act required not only these appointments but also laid down that there should be a social services committee and that the authority should act under general Ministerial guidance in the exercise of social services functions, Professor Richards (1980:78) called it 'the most authoritarian piece of local government law [...] in recent years'. He conjoined the requirement on the LEA to appoint a chief education officer in the same adverse critique. But at least the education legislation did not prescribe the actual job title.

When the 2004 Children Bill is enacted, both s. 532 of the 1996 Act and s. 6 of the 1970 Act are to be respectively repealed and very substantially amended, for England. See chapters 1.E.3 and 3.B.3 of this book.

The present requirement, however, is not necessarily to appoint somebody as the chief education officer, provided that there is somebody designated with that function within the authority. Hence a number of LEAs, particularly following the modernising agenda, have decided that the role of chief education officer should fall within strategic directorates or other departments which have perhaps not traditionally been seen as part of the education function, such as libraries, culture and leisure services. Some have been anticipating the requirements in the Children Bill.

The powers by which the chief education officer is appointed by the LEA are the same general powers that enable local authorities to appoint staff to carry out their functions. Section 112 of the Local Government Act 1972 permits a local authority to appoint such staff on such terms and conditions as it considers appropriate to carry out its functions, provided that such appointments are always made on merit (see s. 7(1) Local Government and Housing Act 1989). In employing such staff (and indeed this will apply to school staff as well), the local authority is not able to act altruistically, for example by imposing out of the ordinary pay rises (see *Roberts v Hopwood [1925] AC 578, HL and Pickwell v Camden LBC* [1983] 1QB 962, HL) and obviously, except where exemptions are allowed in the legislation, the local authority cannot discriminate on grounds of race, disability or sex. From December 2003, the types of unlawful discrimination were extended to include sexual orientation discrimination and discrimination on the grounds of religion or beliefs (see the Employment Equality (Sexual Orientation) Regulations 2003 (SI 2003 No. 1661) and the Employment Equality (Religion or Beliefs) Regulations 2003 (SI 2003 No. 1660)). The general principles relating to unfair dismissal, redundancies etc. apply to such local authority staff.

Thus an LEA will employ a number of administrative staff from the chief education officer downwards, including education officers, education psychologists, education welfare officers and inspectors and advisers under their general powers. Only where other statutes make express reference to the employment of specific staff will they be employed under other powers.

3. Community and voluntary controlled school staff

Having covered the relatively simple area of employment in LEAs, it is now necessary to turn to the more complicated arrangements for the employment of staff (both teaching and non-teaching) in community and voluntary controlled schools. The employment of staff in voluntary aided and foundation schools is considered separately.

Perhaps the first point to consider is what duty an LEA has to employ staff in the first place. The answer to a layman would appear obvious, but in legal terms that would be too simple and a general duty needs to be found under which LEAs and school governing bodies can make provision for the employment of staff within schools.

The starting point, therefore, before considering the individual details of staff employment, was, perhaps bizarrely, reg 4 of the Education (Teachers' Qualifications and Health Standards) (England) Regulations 1999 (SI 1999 No. 2166). Under this regulation, each LEA was under a duty to ensure that at any school there was employed a staff of teachers suitable and sufficient in numbers for the purpose of securing the provision of education appropriate to the ages, abilities, aptitudes and needs of the pupils, having regard to any arrangements for the utilisation of the services of teachers employed otherwise than at the school in question. The regulations also required that a headteacher was appointed for each school (reg 4(2)(a)).

The obligation to include a person appointed as headteacher is now found in s. 35(3) of the Education Act 2002, (s. 36(3) sets out the equivalent requirement in voluntary aided and foundation schools); see also the Education (Head Teachers' Qualifications) (England) Regulations 2003 (SI 2003 No. 3111). This means that whilst a headteacher post can be shared between one or more individuals, a school cannot have more than one headteacher post designated and acting as such. The explanation is simple: the headteacher of a school has a number of statutory powers and duties so it is important that it is clear who in a school is exercising those functions and is responsible for them.

6.
THE
MAINTENANCE
OF SCHOOLS

The obligation to ensure that a staff of teachers is employed, on the other hand, appears to have disappeared, at least in England, with the revocation of the 1999 Regulations by the Education (School Teachers' Qualifications) (England) Regulations 2003 (SI 2003 No. 1662), but s. 35(2) of the Education Act 2002 continues to provide that all staff employed in community, community special, voluntary controlled and maintained nursery schools are to be employed by the LEA. See reference in chapter 3.B.13 to some 'blue skies' thinking deep within DfES on school staffing for the future and a Ministerial rebuttal.

Despite all the misconceptions to the contrary, an incorporated governing body of a community or voluntary controlled school cannot enter into contracts of employment (para 3(7) of schedule 1 to the Education Act 2002) and so cannot in law be an employer.

The exact nature of the relationship of the LEA with school staff is dependent upon whether or not the school has a delegated budget.

3.1 Schools with delegated budgets

In the most common case, where a community, voluntary controlled or community special school has a delegated budget, the governing body has the responsibility for appointing staff, filling vacancies, disciplining, suspending and, where necessary, dismissing staff. But as stated above, the LEA will, in law, be the employer.

3.1.1 Appointment of staff

Where a vacancy arises for the post of headteacher or deputy headteacher, the governing body must notify the LEA of the vacancy in writing before taking any steps (reg 13(1) of the School Staffing (England) Regulations 2003 (SI 2003 No. 1963) – referred to below as 'the Staffing Regulations').

The governing body must advertise the vacancy in such manner as it considers appropriate (reg 13(2) of the Staffing Regulations) and must appoint a selection panel consisting of at least three of its members to:

6.
THE
MAINTENANCE
OF SCHOOLS

- select for interview such applicants as it thinks fit and notify, in the case of the headteacher, the LEA of the applicants selected;

- interview the applicants; and

- where it considers it appropriate, recommend to the governing body for approval one of the applicants interviewed (reg 13(3)).

There may, however, be occasions where the governing body had good reason not to advertise and conduct a selection process (reg 13(7)). Suggested 'good reasons' are described in paras 2.15 and 2.16 of the DfES Staffing Guidance issued under ss. 35(8) and 36(8) of the Education Act 2002 ('the Staffing Guidance'). LEAs, governing bodies and headteachers are required to have regard to the Staffing Guidance in discharging any staffing function conferred by the Staffing Regulations; see ss. 35(8) and 36(8) of the Education Act 2002.

Following notification of the applicants selected for interview, the LEA has seven days in which it can make written representations to the selection panel that any applicant is not a suitable person for appointment. The principles applying to the LEA's role and types of concern which might appropriately trigger representations are set out in para 3.2 of the Staffing Guidance. Appropriate triggers might include the fact that the school of which the candidate is headteacher or senior teacher is currently in special measures, the candidate has never worked in the same phase of school as the appointing school and the candidate's experience is inadequate (for these and other triggers see para 3.2f of the Staffing Guidance). The selection panel must consider those representations and where it decides to recommend for appointment someone about whom representations have been made, notify the governing body and the LEA in writing of its reasons (reg 13(4) of the Staffing Regulations).

If the person recommended by the selection panel is approved by the governing body, the LEA must appoint that person provided they meet all relevant staff qualification requirements (i.e. requirements as to qualifications and registration under the Education (School Teachers' Qualifications) (England) Regulations 2003 (SI 2003 No. 1662) and the Education (Specified Work and Registration) (England) Regulations 2003 (SI 2003 No. 1663) and any regulations made under s. 135 of the Education Act 2002; conditions as to health and physical capacity under the Education (Teachers' Qualifications and Health Standards) (England) Regulations 1999 (S.I. 1999 No. 2166) or under s. 141 of the 2002 Act – see the Education (Health Standards) (England) Regulations 2003 (SI 2003 No. 3139) and is not subject to direction under s. 142 of that Act that he is prohibited from teaching (reg 13(5) of the Staffing Regulations).

It is for the governing body to determine if the person selected should be appointed under a contract of employment with the LEA, by the LEA otherwise than under a contract of employment or by the governing body otherwise than under a contract of employment (regs 11(2) and 13(5)).

A representative of the LEA has the right to attend and offer advice at all proceedings relating to the selection of a headteacher and any advice offered must be considered by the governing body or the person(s) to whom the relevant function has been delegated (reg 12). In practice, the appointment of a headteacher is a significant and rare event. Few governors have recent experience of the exercise and so they will tend to seek advice from the LEA. The structure of the legislation encourages a collaborative approach, which allows the LEA to help the governing body through the process.

One of the changes brought about by the Staffing Regulations is the greater emphasis on delegation of staffing functions from the governing body to committees of governors, individual governors or the headteacher (reg 4 and see below). The appointment of a headteacher or deputy head, however, cannot be delegated; the whole governing body must approve the appointment (regs 4(1) and 13(3)(c)).

The procedure for the appointment of other teachers is broadly similar. Where a vacancy in any teaching post (whether full-time or part-time) at the school arises and which will be for a period of more than four months, the governing body must draw up a specification for the post and send a copy to the LEA (regs 14(1) and (2)).The post must be advertised unless it is decided to accept a teacher already working at the school or a teacher nominated by the LEA (para 5.3 Staffing Guidance).

In contrast to headteacher and deputy headteacher appointments, the appointment of other members of staff can be delegated to the headteacher, an individual governor or a group of governors with or without the headteacher (reg 4 and see s. 1of the Staffing Guidance). The Staffing Guidance (para 1.2) contains the expectation that headteachers will normally lead in determining all staff appointments outside the leadership group. It should be noted that the headteacher cannot delegate his or her delegated responsibility to another person (para 1.5 of the Staffing Guidance).

6.
THE
MAINTENANCE
OF SCHOOLS

A representative of the LEA may attend and offer advice at all proceedings relating to teacher appointments and such advice must be considered by the governing body or the person(s) to whom the decision has been delegated (reg 12).

Where the governing body either recommends to the LEA or notifies the LEA that it accepts for appointment any person nominated by the governors, the LEA shall appoint that person unless (a) he or she is to be appointed by the LEA or governing body otherwise than under a contract of employment (reg 11(1)) and/or (b) he or she does not meet such staff qualification requirements as are applicable in relation to that appointment (reg 14(3)).

A key development over the last couple of years has been the attempts at school workforce reform which culminated in January 2003 in what was described by the DfES as 'the historic agreement on the reform of the school workforce': the Raising Standards and Tackling Workload agreement. This proposes the reduction of teachers' workload through the increasing use of school support staff.

The agreement requires LEAs, nationally and individually, to develop the capacity to support schools in remodelling their workforces. Schools have to take ownership of this significant agreement, but DfES guidance is clear that many will need a degree of external support and collaboration, differentiated to take account of particular circumstances, from LEAs. A DfES grant is available to LEAs for this purpose.

The DfES expectation is that LEAs will identify a facilitator or champion [*sic*, *sic*] – a lead person to work directly with schools and their senior managers.

As support staff tend to be on conditions of service which are different from those of teaching staff and which apply to staff across an authority's entire workforce, not just in education, it is important for the authority to have greater influence over their appointment in order to ensure consistency and prevent discriminatory treatment. Whilst recognising the importance of giving governing bodies greater flexibility, it is equally important, therefore, to recognise the continuing role of the LEA as employer and the obligations it owes not only to those staff but also to the others it employs. The Staffing Regulations and the Guidance do therefore appropriately deal with the employment of support staff in light of the workforce agreement.

Thus, the Staffing Regulations have made a number of changes to the process for appointing support staff (i.e. any member of a school's staff other than a teacher – reg 3(1)). Previously, where the governing body required the appointment of a person to work in a non-teaching post at the school, it could recommend a person to the LEA for appointment to the post, but before doing so, however, the governing body had to consult, in addition to the headteacher, the chief education officer.

In order to encourage more flexible and innovative use of support staff, the Staffing Regulations have removed the obligation imposed on governing bodies to consult in all cases. Instead, the governing body need not consult the LEA before recommending a person for appointment. When it does recommend such a person, however, the governing body (or person to whom the function has been delegated) must send a job specification for the post to the LEA, which must include the governing body's recommendations as to the duties to be performed, the hours of work (if part-time), the duration of the appointment, the grade and the remuneration (reg 15(1) and (2) and see paras 5.3–5.15 Staffing Guidance).

Where the LEA has a discretion with respect to the remuneration to be paid, the LEA must exercise that discretion in accordance with the governing body's recommendation. The LEA will have discretion if any provisions regulating the rates of remuneration or allowances payable to persons in the LEA's employment do not apply in relation to that appointment or leave to the LEA a degree of discretion as to the rate of remuneration (reg 15(4)).

The LEA does however retain the ability, within seven days of receiving the job specification, to make representations to the governing body relating to the grade or remuneration to be paid and, if it does, the governing body must consider those representations and, where it decides not to change the grade or remuneration to be paid, notify the LEA in writing of its reasons (reg 15(5)). An LEA should, according to the Staffing Guidance (para 5.10), make use of this provision only where it believes the governing body's recommendation is inconsistent with the LEA's obligations under equal pay legislation. It should be noted that a representative of the LEA does not have the right to attend and offer advice in respect of support-staff appointments.

Where a recommendation is received by the LEA, the LEA shall appoint that person unless he does not meet such staff qualification requirements as are applicable in relation to that appointment (reg 15(6)).

School meals staff are treated slightly differently (reg 18 and paras 5.13– 5.15 of the Staffing Guidance) in that they are appointed as well as employed by the LEA, although the LEA must consult the governing body when exercising its staffing functions to such extent as the LEA thinks fit (reg 18(1)). (But see section 8 below on delegation and outsourcing of school meals staff.)

In addition to ensuring that teachers and non-teaching staff meet the staff qualification requirements, the LEA is also under a duty to carry out pre-employment checks to ensure that it does not employ anyone barred from teaching by the Secretary of State and it should also check the criminal backgrounds of staff whose posts involve substantial unsupervised access to children (para 5.16 of the Staffing Guidance). In the case of teachers, checks should be made to ensure that they are registered with the GTC, have qualified teacher status and have completed their induction. (For further information on the procedures for checking staff see DfES Circulars *Child Protection: Preventing Unsuitable People from Working with Children* and *Young Persons in the Education Service* and *Managing the Demand for Disclosures*. Both documents, like much recent DfES Guidance, bear no reference numbers but can supposedly be located on the www.teachernet.gov.uk website. See also the joint Department of Health and other agencies guidance *What to do if you're worried a child is being abused*, DoH 2003/31553.)

Furthermore, it should also not be forgotten that, in addition to the specific Staffing Guidance, in exercising their powers in respect of staffing and with respect to advising governing bodies, LEAs must have regard to the *Code of Practice on LEA-School Relations* (particularly Annex 1, paras 19–21).

Upon appointing staff, the normal obligations on an employer to send particulars of the employment to the employee under the Employment Rights Act 1996 will apply and this obligation will be solely on the LEA. As s. 1(3) of the Employment Rights Act requires the particulars to include the name of the employer, it is surprising that there is still confusion over the identity of a teacher's employer, but nonetheless confusion exists, especially when it comes to terminating employment (see below). The written particulars must also include such matters as the date when the employment began or the date upon which the period of the person's continuous employment began and the terms of employment, such as remuneration, hours of work, holiday entitlement, sick leave, pension details and notice. Although often considered as the contract of employment, the written particulars are in fact only evidence, albeit very strong evidence, of the actual contract (see *Parkes Classic Confectionery v Ashcroft* (1973) 8 ITR 43).

The appointment of the clerk to the governing body is subject to slightly different principles. Under the Education (School Government) Regulations 1999 (SI 1999 No. 2163), in an established community, voluntary controlled and community special school with a delegated budget, the LEA was under an express duty to appoint the person selected by the governing body to be its clerk (reg 23). This express provision has now, however, been removed from the successor School Governance (Procedures) (England) Regulations 2003 (SI 2003 No. 1377). Instead, these regulations provide (reg 8) in effect that the governing body of any maintained school is responsible for appointing and removing the clerk. Where the school does not have a delegated budget, the LEA may remove the clerk and appoint a substitute. These provisions are stated (reg 8(1)) to be without prejudice to any rights and liabilities which the clerk may have under any contract of employment with the governing body or the LEA. Effectively, what this does is place the clerk in the same position as any other member of support staff employed or engaged to work at a school.

As has been seen (sections B.2 and 3 of this chapter), the 2002 Act encourages collaboration and federation between governing bodies. In many cases, a reason for collaboration or federation may well be a wish to share staff or to benefit from another governing body's experience or expertise in appointing staff. Consequently, the Staffing Regulations (regs 28–30 and see paras 9.1–9.5 of the Staffing Guidance) deal with staff appointments in collaborating schools. Where a headteacher or deputy head is to be appointed by two or more governing bodies discharging their functions jointly, the selection panel must consist of at least three governors taken from any of the collaborating schools and the selection panel must make a recommendation to the governing body of the school or schools at which the person will be appointed (reg 29(1)). In the case of other staff, the collaborating bodies may delegate the appointment to the headteacher of one or more of the collaborating schools, one or more governors from any of the collaborating schools or one or more headteachers with one or more governors from any of those schools (reg 30(1)). Any decision, where it can be unanimous, i.e. the decision is not delegated to one person, must be unanimous (reg 30(2)). Where the headteacher of the relevant school does not have the decision delegated to them, he or she has the right to attend and offer advice, which must be considered (reg 30(3)). The representative of the LEA has the same entitlement to offer advice as in the case of individual governing bodies (reg 32).

3.1.2 Performance, discipline, suspension and dismissal

At a community, voluntary controlled or community special school with a delegated budget, the responsibility for supervising the performance and discipline of staff rests primarily with the governing body. The governing body must establish procedures for the regulation of the conduct and discipline of staff at the school and by which staff may seek redress for any grievance (reg 6(1) of the Staffing Regulations). The governing body must also establish procedures for dealing with lack of capability on the part of school staff (reg 7).

Within this control is the power both on the part of the governing body and the headteacher to suspend any person employed, or engaged otherwise than under a contract of employment, to work at the school where his or her exclusion from the school is required (reg 16(1)). When exercising such power of suspension, the governing body or headteacher is under a duty to inform the LEA, the headteacher or the governing body as the case may be. A suspension can be ended only by the governing body (reg 16(3)), which must immediately notify the LEA and the headteacher of its decision to end it. A suspension can be imposed only for reasonable and proper cause (*Gogay v Hertfordshire CC* [2000] IRLR 703 and *Evans v Monmouthshire CC* 9 March 2001, unreported, QBD) and the member of staff must be informed of the disciplinary procedures which will be adopted. The *Evans* case also illustrates the importance of governing bodies' formally adopting, rather than just noting, personnel codes and disciplinary rules and procedures and then ensuring that the proper steps are taken to ensure that they are incorporated into the contracts of employment of the relevant staff.

Where the governing body, having properly investigated, determines that any person employed by the LEA to work at the school should cease to work there, it must notify the LEA in writing of its determination and the reasons for it (reg 17(1)).

If that person is employed or engaged to work solely at the school (and he/she does not resign), the LEA shall, before the end of the period of 14 days beginning with the date on which notification was given by the governing body, either (a) give him/her notice terminating the contract of employment, or (b) terminate the contract without notice if the circumstances are such that the LEA is entitled to do so by reason of that person's conduct (reg 17(2)). (If the person concerned is not employed to work solely at the school, the LEA shall require him or her to cease to work at the school – reg 17(3).) In the case of the clerk to the governing body, the governing body may remove him or her from office (reg 8(5) of the School Government (Procedures) (England) Regulations 2003 (SI 2003 No. 1377)).

A representative of the LEA has a right to attend for the purpose of giving advice all proceedings of the governing body relating to a determination that a person be dismissed. The governing body is under an obligation to consider that advice before making a determination. The representative does not have to attend on every occasion (see *R v Secretary of State for Education and Employment ex p McNally* [2002] ICR 15).

Under the School Standards and Framework Act 1998, before notifying the LEA of its determination, the governing body was required to make arrangements for giving any person in respect of whom it proposed to make a determination an opportunity of making representations as to the action the governors proposed to take (including, if he or she so wished, oral representations to such person or persons as the governing body appointed for the purpose) and to have regard to any representations made by him/her (para 27(1) of sched 16 to the Act). The governing body was also required to make arrangements for giving any person in respect of whom it had made a determination an opportunity of appealing against it before the governing body notified the LEA.

6.
THE
MAINTENANCE
OF SCHOOLS

In two cases, the point at which a person was dismissed exercised the courts. In *Howard v Brixington Infants School and Devon County Council* [1999] ELR 91, the governing body determined that a teacher should be summarily dismissed from the school and notified the LEA. The teacher appealed to the governing body, but the LEA went ahead and notified the teacher of his summary dismissal. The Employment Appeal Tribunal held that this was unlawful and that the LEA should have awaited the hearing of the teacher's appeal before dismissing him in the way it had done. The tribunal recognised, however, that this could prevent school staff being summarily dismissed even in circumstances, such as in the case itself, where such action may have been justified.

In *Drage v Governors of Greenford High School* (2000) *Times*, 28 March, CA, the Court of Appeal had to decide the effective date of termination of a teacher's employment. The teacher had been dismissed for gross misconduct and had appealed. The Court of Appeal held on the facts that the effective date of termination was the date when the decision was confirmed on appeal, not the date of the original decision to dismiss, as the dismissal was not to be implemented until after the appeal was heard.

The Staffing Regulations attempt to deal with these points and, at the same time, bring the rules relating to school staff in line with the general rules on dismissal and appeals which will be found in the Employment Act 2002, when the relevant provisions of that Act are brought into force (see also ss. 6 and 7 of the Staffing Guidance).

Until the Employment Act 2002 does come into force, the transitional provisions contained in the Schedule to the Staffing Regulations will apply. Thus, before the governing body (or the person with delegated responsibility) determines that a member of staff should cease to work at the school, it must give that person an opportunity to make representations as to any action it proposes to take (including, if he or she so wishes, oral representations) and have regard to any representations made by him (para 2(2) of the schedule to the Staffing Regulations).

Where the governing body has determined that a member of staff should cease to work at the school, it must make arrangements for enabling that person an opportunity to appeal at a hearing before at least three governors and notify the LEA of the outcome (para 2(3) of the schedule). This hearing may take place before the LEA is notified of the governing body's determination that the person should cease to work at the school, but, in contrast to the old appeal process as seen in *Howard*, it does not have to do so.

When s. 29(1) of the Employment Act 2002 comes into force (which sets out statutory dispute resolution procedures), the procedures outlined in that Act and which will apply to employers generally, will have to be put in place.

The standard procedure specified in the Employment Act (part 1, chapter 1, of sched 2)) is as follows.

1. The employer must set out in writing the employee's alleged conduct or characteristics, or other circumstances, which lead him to contemplate dismissing or taking disciplinary action against the employee.

2. The employer must send the statement or a copy of it to the employee and invite the employee to attend a meeting to discuss the matter.

3. The meeting must take place before action is taken, except in the case where the disciplinary action consists of suspension.

4. The meeting must not take place unless:

    a) the employer has informed the employee what the basis was for including in the statement under para 1(1) the ground or grounds given in it and

    b) the employee has had a reasonable opportunity to consider his response to that information.

5. The employee must take all reasonable steps to attend the meeting.

6. After the meeting, the employer must inform the employee of his decision and notify him of the right to appeal against the decision if he is not satisfied with it.

7. If the employee does wish to appeal, he must inform the employer.

8. If the employee informs the employer of his wish to appeal, the employer must invite him to attend a further meeting.

9. The employee must take all reasonable steps to attend the meeting.

10. The appeal meeting need not take place before the dismissal or disciplinary action takes effect.

11. After the appeal meeting, the employer must inform the employee of his final decision.

In cases of summary dismissal resulting from gross misconduct, a modified procedure is required (part 1, chapter 2, of sched 2) which is set out below.

1. The employer must:

   a) set out in writing:

      i. the employee's alleged misconduct which has led to the dismissal;

      ii. what the basis was for thinking at the time of the dismissal that the employee was guilty of the alleged misconduct; and

      iii. the employee's right to appeal against dismissal; and

   b) send the statement or a copy of it to the employee.

2. If the employee does wish to appeal, he must inform the employer.

3. If the employee informs the employer of his wish to appeal, the employer must invite him to attend a meeting.

4. The employee must take all reasonable steps to attend the meeting.

5. After the appeal meeting, the employer must inform the employee of his final decision.

6.
THE
MAINTENANCE
OF SCHOOLS

There is, of course, nothing to stop governing bodies simply carrying over the procedures under the Staffing Regulations as these should comply with the statutory procedures. (See also s. 7 of the Staffing Guidance.)

These provisions may be brought within the revisions to the Education (Modification of Enactments Relating to Employment) Order (see section 9.3 below) to clarify who, in community and voluntary controlled schools, is the employer for these purposes and who is responsible for taking the relevant action. It is suggested, however, that in all practical cases it will be the governing body or the person or persons to whom it has delegated the function who will be the 'employer'.

A representative of the LEA has the right to attend and advise at all proceedings relating to the dismissal of a teacher, including the headteacher and deputy (reg 12(1)). They do not have the right to do so in the case of the dismissal of support staff, although schools might be well advised to seek appropriate advice. Care needs to be taken, however, to ensure that the representative's attendance does not infringe the principles of natural justice. In *R v Secretary of State for Education and Employment ex p McNally* ([2002] ICR 15), Dyson LJ expressed concern where the LEA representative, who could have been regarded as a member of the team presenting the case against the teacher, subsequently retired with the members of the appeal panel to offer them advice.

Similar arrangements need to be made in the case of collaborating schools, although the three governors hearing the appeal can be drawn from any of the collaborating governing bodies (para 2(5) of the schedule to the Staffing Regulations), potentially a useful device if otherwise governors from the member of staff's school might be tainted.

So far as payments in respect of dismissal are concerned, it is for the governing body to determine:

a)   whether any payment should be made by the LEA in respect of the dismissal, or for the purpose of securing the resignation, of any member of the staff of the school; and

b)   the amount of any such payment (s. 37(1) of the Education Act 2002).

This does not, however, apply in relation to a payment which the LEA is required to make by virtue of any contract other than one made in contemplation of the impending dismissal of the member of staff or any statutory provision (s. 37(2)).

The LEA shall take such steps as may be required for giving effect to any determination of the governing body under s. 37(1) and shall not make, or agree to make, a payment in relation to which that subsection applies except in accordance with such a determination (s. 37(3)).

Costs incurred by the LEA in respect of any premature retirement of a member of the staff of a maintained school (other than a person employed for community purposes (s. 37(7)) shall be met from the school's budget share for one or more financial years except in so far as the LEA agrees with the governing body in writing (whether before or after the retirement occurs) that they shall not be so met (s. 37(4)).

Costs incurred by the LEA in respect of the dismissal, or for the purpose of securing the resignation, of any member of the staff of a maintained school shall not be met from the school's budget share for any financial year except in so far as the LEA have good reason for deducting those costs, or any part of those costs, from that share (s. 37(5)). Thus, if the LEA considers that a dismissal is likely to be found to be unfair by an Employment Tribunal, the LEA may deduct the whole or part of those costs from the school's budget share (see also paras 27 and 28 of Annex 1 of the *Code of Practice on LEA – School Relations*).

3.2 Schools without delegated budgets

The above sets out the position in the normal case where a community, voluntary controlled or community special school has a delegated budget. If, however, such a school does not have a delegated budget, the provisions of the Staffing Regulations do not apply (s. 35(7) of the Education Act 2002). Instead, the arrangements for staffing at the school shall be determined by the LEA and the LEA may appoint, suspend and dismiss teachers and other staff at the school as the LEA thinks fit (paras 1 and 2 of sched 2 to the 2002 Act) subject to consulting the governing body to such an extent as the LEA thinks necessary. The LEA may remove the clerk to the governing body and appoint a substitute, subject to appropriate consultation (reg 8(6) of the School Governance (Procedures) (England) Regulations 2003 (S.I. 2003 No. 1377)).

6.
THE
MAINTENANCE
OF SCHOOLS

4. Staff at voluntary aided and foundation schools

4.1 Schools with delegated budgets

As the governing bodies of foundation, voluntary aided and foundation special schools do, in contrast to those of community and voluntary controlled schools, have the power to enter into contracts of employment, the regime for the employment of staff at these schools is significantly different. Under s. 36 of the Education Act 2002, part 3 of the Staffing Regulations applies where these schools have delegated budgets.

The LEA's role in respect of these schools is significantly reduced. In order, however, to recognise their relationship with the LEA as maintaining authority, advisory rights in respect of selection and dismissal can be granted to the LEA.

A representative of the LEA does not automatically have rights to advise the governing body. Instead, the governing body of the foundation, voluntary aided or foundation special school has the power to agree with the LEA that the LEA has an entitlement to advise the governing body in relation to the exercise of some or all of its staffing functions (reg 21(2) of the Staffing Regulations). If the governing body cannot agree to give such rights, it is for the Secretary of State to determine the extent to which such advisory rights should be accorded to the LEA (reg 21(3)).

Similar provisions apply for the appointment and dismissal of staff at these schools, with appropriate modifications to reflect the fact that the governing body employs the staff and can dismiss them (rather than just recommend that a person cease to work at the school) (regs 22–25). These governing bodies also have similar powers to delegate their functions, except for the appointment of a headteacher and deputy (reg 4(1)).

Where no advisory rights are granted, nonetheless the LEA still has the responsibility for determining whether a person is suitable for appointment. In so doing, the LEA must have regard to guidance given from time to time by the Secretary of State.

Thus, where a selection panel of a governing body selects for interview applicants for the post of headteacher or deputy headteacher, the panel must notify the LEA in writing of the names of the applicants selected and the LEA has a period of 14 days to make written representations that any of the applicants is not suitable for the appointment. Such a person shall not be recommended for appointment by the governing body unless the selection panel has considered those representations and notified the LEA in writing of its response (reg 22(4)). The LEA is also responsible for carrying out criminal record checks.

If advisory rights have been granted, the chief education officer or the nominee may attend meetings relating to the dismissal of staff at such schools, but apart from this, the LEA has no involvement in the dismissal of staff employed by the governing body of the school.

4.2 Schools without delegated budgets

If, however, the delegated budget of the school has been withdrawn, the Staffing Regulations cease to apply (s. 36(7) of the 2002 Act) and the number of teachers and non-teaching staff to be employed at the school is determined by the LEA (para 5 of sched 2). Except with the consent of the LEA, the governing body shall not appoint any teacher to be employed at the school or engage, or make arrangements for the engagement of, any person to provide services as a teacher at the school or dismiss any teacher (para 6 of sched 2). In return, the LEA may give the governing body directions as to the educational qualifications of the teachers to be employed for providing secular education or require the governing body to dismiss any teacher at the school (para 7 of sched 2).

Although no issue has arisen yet, this power does raise implications with regard to responsibility for proceedings relating to dismissal.

For example, if a teacher dismissed by the governing body following a direction from the LEA claims unfair dismissal, who should be liable? On general principles (see below) the employer would retain responsibility, i.e. the governing body, but it does seem somewhat unfair if the governing body has no choice in acting upon the direction of the LEA.

5. Federations

The Staffing Regulations generally apply to federated schools in the same way as they do to other maintained schools, subject to certain modifications (see reg 26 of and sched 8 to the Federation of Schools (Community Schools, Community Special Schools, Voluntary Controlled Schools and Maintained Nursery Schools) (England) Regulations 2003 (SI 2003 No. 1965)).

The key differences are:

a) suspensions – the governing body of the federation and the headteacher of the federation or a federated school have the power to suspend any person employed to work at the federation or at that federated school;

b) the provisions of the Staffing Regulations relating to dismissal and disciplinary procedures apply, except that the federated governing body takes responsibility (or the person or persons given delegated responsibility where appropriate) for establishing the relevant procedures in respect of staff employed at the federation or a federated school.

At the time of writing, regulations enabling federations between voluntary aided schools, foundation schools, or a mixture of schools of different categories had not yet been made. These types of federations will be particularly complex, but especially with regard to the appointment and dismissal of staff and greater modification of the Staffing Regulations will therefore be required.

6. Underperformance of headteachers

Prior to the School Standards and Framework Act 1998, the LEA's responsibility was limited to responding to requests from the governing body to implement disciplinary and dismissal determinations. That response is still part and parcel of the LEA's role, but following concerns that LEAs were powerless to intervene where schools were underperforming because of the activities of their staff, the 1998 Act introduced a mechanism by which the LEA can bring to the governing body's attention underperformance by the headteacher and require the governing body to take action.

Where the LEA has any serious concerns about the performance of the headteacher of a school, whether community, voluntary controlled or foundation, it must make a written report of its concerns to the chairman of the governing body, at the same time sending a copy to the headteacher. The chairman of the governing body must notify the LEA in writing of the action which he proposes to take in the light of that report (reg 5 of the Staffing Regulations). In determining whether to make a report, the LEA must have regard to any guidance given from time to time by the Secretary of State which is currently contained in the Staffing Guidance (section 8) and the *Code of Practice on LEA – School Relations* (paras 3 and 4 of Annex 3,). In summary, the LEA should make such reports only in rare cases where it has grounds for concluding that the headteacher's performance is having a detrimental effect on the performance, management or conduct of the school or would have such an effect if action were not taken. The report should not come as a surprise and, before issuing any report, the LEA should always consider whether its concern would be better pursued through the appraisal mechanism; specific, if limited, provision is made for this by reg 20(4) of the Education (School Teacher Appraisal) (England) Regulations 2001 (SI 2001 No. 2855) and reg 17(2) of the Wales regulations (SI 2002 No.1394 (W 137)). The Secretary of State (Staffing Guidance, para 8.2d and *Code of Practice*, para 4d) has indicated that concerns which might appropriately trigger the making of the report by the LEA include (the following are primarily taken from the *Code of Practice*, para 4d):

a) the school has been found following inspection to require special measures or to have serious weaknesses and the LEA considers that the post-inspection plan is seriously deficient;

b) standards of performance in National Curriculum assessments or public examinations have worsened significantly for reasons attributable to the headteacher's performance;

c) the school is falling a long way short of the performance targets agreed with the LEA or standards can be shown by analysis of benchmark information to be well below those achieved by comparable schools, for reasons attributable to the headteacher's performance;

d) there has been a pattern of repeated and serious complaints over a period of time from parents, staff, governors or pupils which has not been satisfactorily addressed;

6.
THE
MAINTENANCE
OF SCHOOLS

e) there is significant evidence of continuing and systematic weaknesses in the management of the school or in its financial controls which, if not tackled, risk serious disruption to the school's continuing operation; or

f) (in the Staffing Guidance), serious concerns about the discharge of staffing responsibilities delegated to the headteacher, including failure to consider appropriate disciplinary action in relation to a member of staff.

The report must state the grounds for the LEA's concern and the evidence upon which it relies (para 8.3f of the Staffing Guidance,). The LEA should also advise the chairman of governors on action which it may be appropriate to take. The LEA must also allow the headteacher the opportunity to make representations to the chairman of the governing body and to the LEA about the report, if necessary being accompanied by a friend.

In practice, these powers will often be used in conjunction with those to suspend delegation, as a good governing body will deal unprompted with a failing headteacher and good headteachers can manage their governors. It is mainly when both headteacher and governing body are weak that the LEA is forced to intervene.

7. Newly qualified teachers

In respect of the arrangements for the induction of newly qualified teachers, each LEA is the appropriate body under the Teaching and Higher Education Act 1998 for maintained schools and non-maintained special schools within its area (s. 19 of the Teaching and Higher Education Act 1998 and reg 5 of the Education (Induction Arrangements for School Teachers) (Consolidation) (England) Regulations 2001 (SI 2001 No. 2897)). As such, it has responsibility for deciding whether newly qualified teachers have met the relevant induction standards. Together with headteachers, the LEA is also responsible for a newly qualified teacher's training and supervision during induction. In order to fulfil these responsibilities, LEAs will therefore need to ensure that headteachers and governing bodies know their duties for monitoring, supporting, guiding and assessing newly qualified teachers and are capable of meeting them. Guidance on the respective tasks involved in induction can be found in DfEE Circular 5/99, *The Induction Period for Newly Qualified Teachers.*

In the case of independent schools, the appropriate body will be either the LEA for the area in which the school is located or the Independent Schools Council Teacher Induction Panel.

In addition to the guidance in Circular 5/99, the LEA, when acting as an appropriate body, must have regard to the relevant regulations (the Education (Induction Arrangements for School Teachers) (Consolidation) (England) Regulations 2001 (SI 2001 No. 2897)). Teacher induction should also be covered within the relevant sections of the LEA's Education Development Plan.

At the end of the period of induction, the headteacher must complete a formal assessment of the new teacher and make a recommendation to the LEA on whether the teacher has met the professional standards required for the successful completion of that induction period.

The LEA will decide whether or not the new teacher has successfully completed the induction period or whether there are exceptional circumstances which would justify the period being extended. It is expected that governing bodies and headteachers will allow the LEA access to the school, where necessary, to enable it to perform this task properly.

LEAs must notify the Secretary of State (by providing electronic lists) and the General Teaching Council of their decisions. Appeals against the LEA's decision are made to the GTC.

In Wales, the relevant regulations are the Education (Induction Arrangements for School Teachers) (Wales) Regulations 2003 (SI 2003 No.543 (W 77)).

8. School meals staff

Differences between teaching staff and non-teaching support staff have been briefly considered above. To add further complication to a chaotic situation, the position of school meals staff employed to work in schools is again different from those of both teaching staff and other types of support staff. What was especially confusing was, however, confused even more, first as a consequence of the competitive tendering of school meal contracts and then by the 1998 Act, under which the responsibility for providing school meals can be transferred to governing bodies.

In many cases, the provision of meals will have been contracted out and the contractor will be responsible for the employment of the catering staff. Where, however, such arrangements have not been made, specific provisions in the Staffing Regulations will apply.

The Staffing Regulations (reg 18) provide that in general the LEA is responsible for appointing, disciplining, suspending and dismissing school meals staff at community and voluntary controlled schools. Before taking such action, however, the LEA should consult with the governing body (reg 18(1)).

If, however, the Secretary of State has made an order requiring the governing body of a school to take over the responsibility of the LEA to provide school lunches and, where necessary, to provide school lunches free of charge, the governing body may either agree with the LEA that the LEA will supply the lunches or else may decide to supply the lunches itself.

If the governing body agrees that the LEA will supply the lunches, the LEA will be responsible for the appointment, disciplining, suspension and dismissal of school meals staff at the school, subject to consulting the governing body beforehand (reg 18(2)). The governing body in this situation may, however, decide that a member of the school meals staff should cease to work at the school. If it does, it must give written notice and details of its reasons to the LEA and the LEA shall thereupon require the person to cease to work at the school (reg 18(3)).

If the governing body has not agreed with the LEA that the LEA should supply the lunches, the governing body will be responsible for appointing, disciplining, suspending and dismissing school meals staff in the same way as it is responsible for other school-based staff, although, of course, the LEA will remain the employer in law of the staff (regs 6 and 15–17), except where the governing body has contracted out the provision of school meals.

In the case of voluntary aided, foundation and foundation special schools, the position is more straightforward as, in most cases, the governing body will be responsible for appointing, disciplining, suspending, dismissing and employing school meal staff, except where the provision of school meals has been contracted out.

9.   Other education-related employment issues

Discussion of the general responsibilities of an employer is beyond the scope of this work, but a number of issues of wider application do have an effect on the employment of school-based staff. These are briefly discussed below, but it is not the authors' intention that issues such as sexual, racial or disability discrimination should be dealt with in detail, as those topics are far better covered elsewhere in specific texts on employment law. In this section, we will deal only with issues which are related to the principles of staffing discussed above.

9.1. Continuity of employment

Under normal employment principles, if an employee moves from one employer to another, unassociated employer, there is a break in his employment which means that when calculating his entitlement to various benefits or when calculating time periods before he can make statutory claims, for example for unfair dismissal, he cannot include the time spent in his previous employment.

In the school environment, this could have led to an unwillingness amongst staff in maintained schools to move on and between schools. Within county and voluntary controlled schools, as they were prior to the 1998 Act, there was no problem, as the staff were always employed by the same employer and therefore, if a member of staff transferred from one county school to another, there was no change in employer and no break in continuity.

The problem was, however, that, if staff moved between county or voluntary controlled schools and voluntary aided or grant-maintained schools, there was a change of employer and hence a possibility that there would be a break in the continuity of employment. Consequently, to meet this problem, provision was made to allow teachers to move within the different types of state school within, in effect, the area of an LEA without breaking their continuity of employment. This provision can now be found in s. 218(7) of the Employment Rights Act 1996. If either an employee of the governors of a school maintained by an LEA is taken into the employment of the LEA or an employee of an LEA is taken into the employment of the governors of a school maintained by the LEA:

a) his period of employment at the time of the change of employer counts as a period of employment with the second employer; and

b) the change does not break the continuity of the period of employment.

9.2 Transfer of undertakings

Related to continuity of employment is the problem facing staff in undertakings which are taken over by or transferred to another employer. The Acquired Rights Directive 77/187/EEC (OJ L61/26) and the Transfer of Undertakings (Protection of Employment) Regulations 1981 (SI 1981 No. 1794), which were introduced to meet the United Kingdom's obligations under the directive, provide certain protection to staff affected by the transfer of the business to which they belong. In general, the directive and regulations aim to ensure that members of staff are not dismissed simply by virtue of the transfer and that they continue to be employed by the transferee employer on the same terms and conditions of employment that they enjoyed prior to the transfer.

Substantial case law has established that the regulations apply to the public sector, for example to protect school cleaning and catering staff who were employed by LEAs, but who transferred into the private sector when the work was put out to competitive tender.

In the school context, the regulations have had little impact, partly because transfers hardly ever arise and partly because of the provisions governing continuity of employment. In respect of the closure of schools and the establishment of new schools, however, the regulations have been used in an attempt to protect the position of teachers at a closing school.

In *National Union of Teachers v Governing Body of St Mary's Church of England (Aided) Junior School* ([1996] EWCA Civ 1194, (1996) Times, December 16), a voluntary aided school was closed and replaced by a new school. The teachers at the closed school were made redundant. The Transfer of Undertaking Regulations could not apply on the facts so the union sought to rely on the directive itself. The directive would have direct effect in the circumstances only if the governing body was considered to be an emanation of the state under European law. The Court of Appeal accepted that the governing body·was an emanation of the state and so the protection set out in the directive could have a direct effect on the actions in respect to the closure of the school. Thus, in principle, where an aided or foundation school closes and a new school is created with a new governing body, the staff may be protected by the 1981 regulations and the directive.

Where, however, a community or community special or voluntary controlled school closes in similar circumstances and a new school is created, neither the directive nor the 1981 regulations can apply as there is no change in the employer (i.e. the LEA) even if there is a change in the governing body that appoints the staff. This is evident from the Court of Appeal's decision in *Governing Body of Clifton Middle School and Others v Askew* [1999] ELR 425, [1999] EdCR 800. In that case, Mr Askew was employed by the LEA to teach at a middle school sharing a site with a first school. The LEA decided to cease to maintain the two schools and established a single primary school instead. As a result Mr Askew was dismissed by reason of redundancy. He then tried to argue that he was protected by the directive and 1981 regulations as there had been a transfer of the school and that he had therefore been unfairly dismissed as his employment did not carry over into the new school. The court

6.
THE
MAINTENANCE
OF SCHOOLS

dismissed this argument and made clear that teachers were employed under contracts of service with LEAs and not by governing bodies. Consequently, when the new school opened, there could not have been any change of employer as the LEA had employed the staff at the old school and would employ the staff at the new school. There was thus no qualifying transfer between employers and Mr Askew could therefore not rely on either the directive or the 1981 regulations.

This continues to remain the position and no attempts have been made in the Education Act 2002, the Staffing Regulations or the 2003 Modification Order to alter this situation.

9.3 The Education (Modification of Enactments Relating to Employment) Order 2003

Despite the legislation and now, following the *Askew* decision, the case law making clear that governing bodies are not the employers of school-based staff, for certain purposes governing bodies can be deemed to be the employer. It is perhaps not surprising that some confusion remains.

The Education (Modification of Enactments Relating to Employment) Order 2003 (SI 2003 No. 1964), the successor to the Education (Modification of Enactments Relating to Employment) Order 1999, modifies a number of pieces of legislation where governing bodies have delegated budgets, with the effect that any reference to an employer in that legislation is deemed to be a reference to the governing body (art. 3(1)). The legislation affected is set out in the schedule to the Order and includes certain parts of the Sex Discrimination Act 1975, the Race Relations Act 1976, the Disability Discrimination Act 1995 and the Employment Rights Act 1996.

In addition, where a person employed at a school with a delegated budget is dismissed by the LEA following the procedure set out in the Staffing Regulations, provisions relating to dismissal in the Employment Rights Act 1996 (for example the right of an employee to be given reasons for his dismissal by his employer) are to be read as if the governing body is the employer (art. 4(1) of the 2003 order).

If an employee at school wishes to make an application to an employment tribunal in respect of his employment, the application should be issued and proceedings should be carried on against the governing body, not the LEA (Article 6(1) and (2)). The governing body is, however, required to notify the LEA within 14 days of receiving notification of the application and the LEA is then entitled to apply and be added as an additional party to the proceedings. This may be important as even though the governing body may be the true respondent to any application, any decision of the tribunal (except a direction that the employee be reinstated or re-engaged) has effect against the LEA, not the governing body (Article 6(3), but see also s. 37(5) of the Education Act 2002 for the LEA's power to deduct the costs of an action for unfair dismissal from the school's budget share).

The 2003 order does not apply to voluntary aided and foundation schools as they are clearly the sole employer of the staff at the school and there is therefore no need for the order to deem that they, not the LEA, should be treated as the employer for the purposes of the respective legislation.

It should be noted, however, that the order does not deem governing bodies of community or voluntary controlled schools to be employers for the purposes of the Equal Pay Act 1970. Although there was some confusion whether such governing bodies could or could not be deemed to be the employer where a claim of constructive dismissal was made (because of the decision of the Employment Appeal Tribunal in *Green v Governing Body of Victoria Road Primary School and Kent County Council* [2003] ELR 455, [2003] ICR 713, EAT), it is now clear, after the Court of Appeal reversed that decision, that the order will deem the governing body to be the employer in such a case (*Kent County Council v Green* [2004] EWCA Civ 11, *sub nom Green v Governing Body of Victoria Road Primary School and Another* (2004) *Independent* (case summary), 1 March 2004).

The 2003 order was enacted in order to update the 1999 Modification Order in line with the changes brought about by the Staffing Regulations. Consequently, the list of enactments in its schedule repeats the legislation in the 1999 order and does not include legislation or regulations enacted since 1999. This means that for all legislation not mentioned, the LEA continues to be the employer. The DfES is, it is understood, proposing to consult on making substantive changes to the list of legislation.

9.4   Discrimination

As mentioned above, a detailed consideration of the law against discrimination is outside the scope of this work. Nonetheless, it is perhaps worth reminding readers of the main principles and prohibitions as, clearly, the amount of litigation against discrimination in the employment field is increasing.

Discrimination against employees or potential employees is prohibited on grounds of sex or gender reassignment or marital status by ss. 1 to 3 of the Sex Discrimination Act 1975. The definition of 'sex' in the 1975 Act does not, however, extend to sexual orientation, so it has not been, until recently, unlawful to discriminate against a person by reason of their homosexuality alone (see *Grant v South West Trains Ltd* [1998] 1 All ER (EC) 193, *Smith v Gardner Merchant Ltd* [1998] 3 All ER 852 and *Pearce v Governing Body of Mayfield School* [2003] UKHL 34 [2003] ELR 655). However, from December 2003, such discrimination has become unlawful when the Employment Equality (Sexual Orientation) Regulations 2003 (S.I. 2003 No. 1661) came into force.

Discrimination on the grounds of colour, race, nationality or ethnic or national origin is banned by s. 3 of the Race Relations Act 1976. Discrimination on the grounds of religion or belief has been unlawful since December 2003 under the Employment Equality (Religion or Belief) Regulations 2003 (S.I. 2003 No. 1660): 'religion or belief' is defined as any religion, religious belief, or similar philosophical belief (reg 2(1). It is also unlawful to discriminate against any disabled person on the grounds of disability (s. 1 of the Disability Discrimination Act 1995). For guidance on the implications of the 1995 Act for LEAs and schools, see DfEE Circular 3/97 *What the Disability Discrimination Act (DDA) 1995 Means for Schools and LEAs*.

The law prohibits two types of discrimination: direct and indirect. Direct discrimination occurs in this context where an employer treats an applicant for a job or an employee less favourably on grounds of sex or marital status (s. 1(1)(a) of the Sex Discrimination Act 1975) or race (s. 1(1)(a) of the Race Relations Act 1976) than the employer would treat other persons and there is no objective justification for that treatment. Less favourable treatment on grounds of disability is also unlawful, but only if the employer cannot show that the treatment in question is justified (s. 5(1) of the Disability Discrimination Act 1995).

Indirect discrimination occurs where an employer applies a requirement or condition, which would be applied to persons of either sex or marital status (in the case of the Sex Discrimination Act 1975) or to persons of any racial group (in the case of the Race Relations Act 1976), but which is such that the proportion of persons of a particular sex, marital status or racial group who can comply with the requirement or condition is considerably smaller than the proportion of persons not of that sex, marital status or racial group who can do so. The aggrieved person must be able to show that he or she suffers detriment by reason of not being able to comply with the condition or requirement and the employer can produce a defence to the claim if it can be shown that the condition or requirement is justifiable, irrespective of the sex or racial group of the person to whom it is applied (s. 1(1)(b) of the Sex Discrimination Act 1975 and s. 1(1)(b) of the Race Relations Act 1976). An example of indirect discrimination under the 1975 Act concerns part-time employees, where the majority of part-time employees in certain jobs are female. To prevent part-timers from enjoying certain benefits, such as the right to belong to an occupational pension scheme, therefore disadvantages more women than men and is therefore indirectly discriminatory (see *R v Secretary of State for Employment ex p Equal Opportunities Commission* [1994] 2 WLR 409, HL).

Indirect discrimination is not, however, prohibited by the Disability Discrimination Act 1995.

One discrimination issue of particular relevance for LEAs is the responsibility of a school and the LEA for the acts of pupils as opposed to employees. What if, instead of the typical case of a teacher being subjected to less favourable treatment on the grounds of sex, race or disability by the employer or a fellow employee, the treatment is meted out by pupils or their parents?

In *Bennett v Essex County Council and the Chair and Governors of Fryern's School* 5 October 1999, unreported, EAT, the LEA was held liable for the racial abuse directed against a teacher by pupils. The Employment Appeal Tribunal held that a teacher could succeed in a claim for racial discrimination if she could show that the racial harassment by pupils was something which was sufficiently under the control of the LEA and governing body that they could, by the application of good education practice, have prevented the racial harassment or reduced the extent of it. Similarly, in *Go Kidz Go v Bourdouane* EAT/1110/95, unreported, the employer of a member of staff at a playgroup was held responsible under the same principles for the sexual harassment committed by a parent of a child at the group.

More recently, in *Pearce v Governing Body of Mayfield School* ([2003] UKHL 34, [2003] ELR 655), the House of Lords limited the occasions where schools would be liable for the acts of their pupils and stated that the decision which had previously been relied upon to establish liability on the grounds of control (*Burton v De Vere Hotels Ltd* [1997] ICR 1) as well as the *Go Kidz Go* case, had been wrongly decided. The House of Lords emphasised the wording of the legislation and that to be liable, the employer had to be shown to have 'subjected' the employee to discrimination. The question of control was therefore imposing too wide an obligation on an employer, where, as in *Pearce*, it was third parties who were committing the acts of discrimination. In effect, the employer will have to be shown to have directly discriminated or committed the act of discrimination, rather than merely failing to take action to address another person's discrimination. This is not to say that schools should not act against discriminatory conduct whether towards staff or pupils, but it means that it is unlikely that governing bodies will be held liable for compensation in the tribunals.

9.5   Terms and conditions of employment

The statutory conditions of employment of headteachers and teachers are contained in a pay and conditions order made by the Secretary of State and contained in the *School Teachers' Pay and Conditions Document* (annually revised and reissued) (ss. 122–124 of the Education Act 2002). This document forms part of a teacher's contract of employment and places statutory duties on, and gives statutory rights to, teachers. In Wales, this function, together with that of pensions oversight and regulation, has not been devolved upon the National Assembly.

Only the salaries and pay scales set out in the document can be applied to teaching staff (except in the case of schools exempt from the document in Education Action Zones (s. 128 of the 2002 Act)) or schools which are exempted by order (see, for example, the Education (Islamia Primary School Brent) (Exemption from Pay and Conditions) Order 1999 (SI 1999 No. 2879)). Some flexibility is given to governing bodies, in the case of those with delegated budgets, or to the LEA, in respect of schools without delegated budgets or in respect of teaching staff within a centrally provided service. Where governing bodies are empowered by the document to make decisions, the LEA is under a duty to act on the governing body's decision.

It must be remembered that where a pay and conditions order and the *Pay and Conditions Document* applies, a term of a teacher's contract shall have no effect insofar as it is prohibited by the order or is otherwise inconsistent with a provision of the order (s. 122(2)(c) of the 2002 Act). Thus, in *Governing Body of The Plume School v Langshaw and Thomas* ([2003] ELR 97, EAT), a case under the equivalent provisions in the predecessor legislation to s. 122, the EAT held that a governing body could not impose a temporal limitation on a salary protection to which the teachers were entitled under the pay and conditions document where that limitation was not authorised and conflicted with the provisions of the *Pay and Conditions Document*.

Exemption or modification of pay and conditions provisions is one of the flexibilities that may be granted to schools under 'earned autonomy' (ss. 6–10 of the 2002 Act). If this concept is ever brought into reality, the governing body of a qualifying school (i.e. one which meets the prescribed criteria in respect of performance of the school, quality of leadership and quality of management) may request the Secretary of State that designated pay and conditions provisions should not apply to schoolteachers employed at the school (s. 7). In making an application schools should have regard to any guidance issued by the Secretary of State (or NAW) (s. 7(4)) and should have consulted the LEA, each schoolteacher employed at the school and such other persons as appear appropriate (s. 8(2)). Exemptions or modifications that have been granted by order can subsequently be removed (s. 9). Where an order has been made, it does not in itself effect changes to teachers' terms and conditions: instead it is enabling in the sense that the governing body may then determine the remuneration and other conditions of employment of each schoolteacher to the extent that by virtue of the order the pay and conditions provisions do not apply (s. 10(1)(a)). The governing body cannot use the order to vary unilaterally the teacher's contract; it must still be negotiated in the usual way. The LEA must do anything necessary to give effect to the governing body's determination (s. 10(1)(b)). Pending the governing body's making a determination, the terms of employment remain as contained in the relevant pay and conditions document at the time the order was granted (s. 10(1)(c)), i.e. any subsequent pay and conditions documents will not have effect.

The pay and conditions of non-teaching staff employed by an LEA will depend upon the nature of the employment and the appropriate local government conditions of service which apply to the particular post. Earned autonomy cannot apply to non-teaching staff. The DfES, through the National Agreement, is keen, however, for greater use to be made of support staff in schools and expects LEAs to show greater flexibility when schools propose appointing such staff (hence the reason for the changes to the procedure for appointing support staff in community and voluntary controlled schools: see reg 15 of the Staffing Regulations and Staffing Guidance paras 5.3–5.12).

6.
THE
MAINTENANCE
OF SCHOOLS

9.6 Pensions

LEA staff and school-based staff are eligible to participate in pension schemes authorised under the Superannuation Act 1972, if they elect to do so. The scheme for teachers is governed by the Teachers' Pensions Regulations 1997 (SI 1997 No. 3001) and the scheme for other local government employees by the Local Government Pension Scheme Regulations 1997 (SI 1997 No. 1612). The teachers' scheme is administered by the central Teachers' Pension Agency (which is in turn outsourced to SERCO), whilst the local government scheme is administered locally by a number of pension fund authorities.

The detail of these schemes is outside the scope of this work. However, it should be noted that following a number of pensions scandals, the regulation of all pension funds, including those applying to LEA staff, is now far more stringent.

The other relevant development concerns the ability of part-time employees to join the two pension schemes. Following changes to the relevant regulations, most part-time employees are now and have been for some time, eligible to belong to the schemes, but this was not always the position. Because more women tend to be employed on a part-time basis, it was argued that this amounted to indirect sexual discrimination. In *Vroege v NCIV Instituut voor Volkshuisvesting BV and Another* ([1994] ECR 1-4541, (1994) *Times*, 7 December, ECJ) the Court of Justice of the European Communities held that where part-time workers were excluded from occupational pension schemes, sexual discrimination, in that case based upon Article 119 of the EEC Treaty on equal pay for men and women, could arise during the period when those part-time employees were prevented from belonging to the schemes.

This decision led to a flood of claims to the employment tribunals in England and Wales, with many part-time or former part-time employees seeking retrospective membership of occupational pension schemes and/or increased benefits. A number of test cases proceeded through the employment tribunals, up to the House of Lords ([1998] UKHL 6, [1998] 1 All ER 528, [1998] 1 WLR 280 HL) and then to the European Court of Justice before being finally considered by the House of Lords again (*Preston and Others v Wolverhampton Healthcare NHS Trust and Others* ([2001] 2 WLR 448, [2001] IRLR 237, [2001] ICR 217, [2001] 3 All ER 947). In this case, it was held that claims for retrospective admission to pension schemes should not be limited simply to a period of two years dating back from the date of claim. Instead, a claimant could seek admission for a period dating back to April 1976. A claimant did, however, have to issue their claim within six months of the termination of their employment with the employer who denied them access to the relevant pension scheme. Where part-time employees were in a stable employment relationship resulting from a succession of short-term contracts concluded at regular intervals in respect of the same employment to which the same pension scheme applied, the six-month period ran from the end of the final contract in that relationship, not from the end of each individual contract. This latter finding is of particular significance to LEAs that employed and still employ, many part-time staff, such as supply teachers and school secretaries, under a succession of short-term, often termly, contracts.

Since these decisions, the Government, local authorities and the employment tribunal have been working out the implications of the decision on claimants and those still in employment. Agreement appears now to have been reached on the method of calculating retrospective contributions where employers accept liability. However, even after eight years of litigation several issues still remain outstanding and test cases are still proceeding through the system. Of particular relevance to the education sector is the position of staff who have changed employer either through statutory transfer (such as staff within the further education sector, who were employed by LEAs prior to 1 April 1993 and subsequently by the newly-incorporated colleges) or non-statutory transfers, usually by agreement or under TUPE. In the case of FE staff, it now appears accepted that a series of contracts before the transfer counts for continuity purposes and the liability for meeting any retrospective contributions rests with the FE college employer, not the former employing LEA (see Employment Tribunal Information Bulletin Nos. 7 and 8). In the case of other transfers, however, the decision of the Employment Tribunal, that staff subject to TUPE transfers should have made a claim within six months of the transfer, in effect saying that there was a break in employment, has recently been overturned (*Preston and Others v Wolverhampton Healthcare* [2003] EAT 1069).

A further outstanding issue concerns the appropriate comparator. As will be seen in the next section, a part-time claimant has to show that they were, in effect, treated less favourably than a person of the opposite sex employed to do the same work or work of equal value. Some employers have accepted that there are such comparators, whilst others are arguing that there are not. This too remains an outstanding issue and, as will be seen, the method of selecting the appropriate comparator is still a matter to be resolved by the employment tribunal.

9.7   Comparators under the Equal Pay Act

The equal pay and anti-discrimination legislation does not impose obligations on employers to treat staff fairly; what it does is ensure that staff are not treated less favourably. This means that in most cases a claimant has to point to a comparator and show that they have been treated less favourably than that person.

In the case of Equal Pay Act claims, and this is an issue still perplexing the employment tribunal over part-time pensions claims (see Employment Tribunal Information Bulletin Number 8), the comparator has to be a man (or woman if the claimant is male) in 'the same employment' as the claimant (s. 1 of the Equal Pay Act 1970). Men are stated to be in the same employment with a woman if 'they are men employed by her employer or any associated employer at the same establishment or at establishments in Great Britain which include that one and at which common terms and conditions of employment are observed either generally or for employees of the relevant classes' (s. 1(6)).

Where, therefore, employees are employed on common terms and conditions (for example teachers employed on the terms set out in the *Teachers' Pay and Conditions Document*), it is arguable that a comparator can be found in a different school or even a different LEA.

This problem was first highlighted in the Scottish case of *South Ayrshire Council v Morton* ([2002] IRLR 256, [2002] ICR 956, Court of Session). The claimant was a primary school teacher whose claim was founded on the principle that primary school headteachers (who were predominantly female) were generally paid less than secondary school teachers (who were predominantly male). She therefore sought to use three male secondary school headteachers as appropriate comparators. One of the headteachers chosen was, however, employed by a different education authority from that which employed the claimant. The authority challenged this, but was unsuccessful. The court considered that because the terms and conditions of employment of headteachers were derived from common terms and conditions, i.e. the pay and conditions document, it was possible for a headteacher employed by a different authority to be used as a comparator. It would follow that the same argument could be used in respect of other common terms and conditions, including for example, those based on National Joint Council for Local Government/Single Status conditions as well as those applying to teaching staff. This could have considerable impact on a school's or authority's salary grading processes if an employee can 'cherry pick' a comparator not only from within the same authority but also from outside.

A potential limit on this problem was imposed by the ECJ in *Lawrence and Others v Regent Office Care Ltd and Others* (17 September 2002, unreported, ECJ). That case concerned former local authority cleaning staff who had been transferred into the employment of private contractors. The cleaners, in making an equal pay claim, argued that the appropriate comparators were cleaners still employed by the local authority. The ECJ held that the pay conditions of the workers could not be attributed to a single source (although the cleaners had transferred under TUPE, they were employed under the private contractors' conditions of employment), there was no one body which was responsible for the inequality and which could restore the equal treatment. The cleaners therefore could not compare themselves with the staff employed by the authority.

6.
THE
MAINTENANCE
OF SCHOOLS

The *Lawrence* decision was relied upon in *Rawlinson v Board of Governors of Blessed Edward Jones High School* ([2003] All ER (D) 271 (Jul), EAT). A female bursar at the school attempted to compare herself with two male bursars employed at other schools maintained by the LEA. The EAT was critical of the *Morton* decision and held that she could not claim comparison with the individuals employed in the other schools. However, care needs to be taken with this decision as, although the claimant initially thought she was employed by the LEA, she was in fact employed by the governing body of the school. The decision may therefore be authority that an employee of a voluntary aided or foundation school cannot compare themselves with an employee of the maintaining LEA and vice versa; it is not authority for saying that a member of staff at community school A cannot compare themselves with a member of staff at community school B or, indeed, any other employee of that LEA. The *Rawlinson* decision does, however, suggest that comparison with staff employed by another LEA would not be permitted.

The matter may be resolved when the ECJ considers whether equal pay comparisons can be made between employees of different employers operating in the same employment sector (*Allonby v Accrington and Rossendale College* [2001] EWCA Civ 529).

This topic is likely to continue to exercise tribunals and not just in the part-time pension cases. It will of course still be available to the employer to show objective justification for any less favourable treatment, but it may still be the case that a claimant, certainly one in LEA employment, can look beyond their immediate place of employment in order to find the appropriate comparator.

9.8 Vicarious liability

Although the liability of LEAs is discussed elsewhere (see chapter 12), the issue of vicarious liability often arises in connection with the employment of staff. In general terms vicarious liability is the liability an employer owes for the acts of his employee during the course of the employee's employment with the employer.

In the context of an LEA, the principle therefore extends to the responsibility of an LEA for the actions of its staff, including, because it is in law the employer, the actions of staff employed at community and voluntary controlled schools.

In the school setting, it is usually obvious that an LEA is vicariously liable for the negligent act of a teacher supervising a PE lesson (for example, *Gibbs v Barking Corporation* [1936] 1 All ER 115, *Ralph v London County Council* (1947) 111 JP 548 and *Affutu-Nartoy v Clarke* (1984) *Times*, 9 February) or a chemistry lesson (for example, *Crouch v Essex County Council* (1966) 64 LGR 240).

Previously, LEAs were not held liable for the acts of teachers who had been guilty of deliberate criminal misconduct, on the grounds that such acts were outside the scope of the employee's employment. (See, for example, *Trotman v North Yorkshire County Council* [1998] ELR 625, now overruled, in which an LEA was held not to be vicariously liable for a sexual assault by a deputy headteacher on a handicapped teenager in his charge whilst on a school trip abroad). Since the House of Lords decision in *Lister v Hesley Hall Limited* ([2001] UKHL 22, [2001] 2 All ER 769, [2001] ELR 422), however, an LEA is likely to be held vicariously liable for the acts of teachers and other employees, even if they amount to criminal misconduct, where there is a sufficiently close connection between the misconduct and the employment involved. In *Lister*, a warden employed by the proprietor of an independent school for maladjusted and vulnerable children, sexually assaulted some pupils. He was subsequently convicted and the children sued the proprietor. The proprietor was held liable on the basis that there was a close connection between the guilty party's misconduct and the nature of his employment: the proprietor had undertaken to care for the children; in doing so it had employed the abuser and put him in the position where he could commit the abuse; the acts had been committed in the time when and on the premises where the abuser was employed to perform his duties. It follows, therefore, that if a similar situation were to occur in the maintained sector, the LEA (in the case of a community or voluntary controlled school) or governing body (in the case of a voluntary aided or foundation school) is also likely to be held liable so long as there is that close connection between the act and the nature of the employment. In Australia, the High Court carried out a detailed analysis of the law post-*Lister* in a similar case which, to a certain extent, clarifies the rationale underlying the imposition of vicarious liability on public authorities in these type of cases, but draws back from, in effect, making public authorities liable on all occasions for the criminal misconduct of employees (*New South Wales v Lepore; Samin v Queensland; Rich v Queensland* [2003] HCA 4 and 'Australian School Authorities' Liability (Without Fault) for Sexual Abuse of Students by Employees', D. Stewart and A. Knott [2003] Education Law 170).

9.9 Indemnity

Although the principle of vicarious liability will mean that most legal actions will be issued against the employing LEA or governing body, there is nothing to prevent a claimant's suing the individual they believe was responsible for their injury or loss. To protect staff in this position from personal liability and having to take out their own insurance, s. 265 of the Public Health Act 1875 (as amended by the Local Government (Miscellaneous Provisions) Act 1976) provides that 'no matter or thing done and no contract entered into by any local authority […] and no matter or thing done by any […] officer of such authority or other person whomsoever acting under the direction of such authority shall if the matter or thing were done or the contract were entered into *bona fide* […] subject them or any of them personally to any action liability claim or demand whatsoever'. Thus the staff of an LEA should benefit from this protection if acting *bona fide*.

9.10 Health and safety responsibilities

Just as an LEA is responsible for the breach of duties by its staff, it is under a direct duty to its staff both under the health and safety legislation and also at common law to protect them from harm. Under ss. 2 and 3 of the Health and Safety at Work etc. Act 1974, an employer is under a duty to ensure, so far as is reasonably practicable, that the health and safety and welfare of employees are protected. The employer in these circumstances is the LEA in the case of community and voluntary controlled schools, the governing body in the case of voluntary aided and foundation schools.

For an illustration of a case where the LEA has been held in breach of its duties to ensure the safety of staff see, for example, *Moore v*

6.
THE
MAINTENANCE
OF SCHOOLS

Kirklees MBC [1999] EWCA Civ 1326. The LEA was found liable for an injury to a dinner lady caused by a statemented child where the lady had not been forewarned of the pupil's behaviour and had not been given appropriate training in dealing with it. Along similar lines, in *Waugh v Newham LBC* ([2002] EWHC 802 (QB)), an LEA, which failed to provide information and instruction to an escort responsible for looking after a child with severe special educational needs, was held liable when the pupil escaped from the escort and assaulted a teacher at the school the child attended. In contrast, in *Purvis v Buckinghamshire County Council* ([1999] ELR 231, [1999] EdCR 542), a welfare assistant in a school's special educational needs department suffered a back injury after restraining a five-year-old pupil with behavioural and learning difficulties. Her claim for damages was dismissed as the pupil had been appropriately placed, the claimant had been in the department for two years and was experienced and it was unclear how training might have helped her deal with the situation. Though there had technically been a breach of the LEA's duties under the Manual Handling Operations Regulations 1992 (SI 1992 No. 2793), in that no assessment had been made of such an incident, that had not contributed to the accident. If it had contributed, the outcome might have been different.

Stress claims are becoming increasingly common and important. The general principles applying to stress-related claims will of course apply (see, for example, *Walker v Northumberland CC* [1995]1 All ER 737, [1995] ICR 702 and *Sutherland (Chairman of Governors of St Thomas Becket RC High School) v Hatton and Others* [2002] EWCA Civ 76, [2002] 2 All ER 1, [2002] IRLR 263) and an LEA has been held liable for failing to monitor the condition of a teacher once it became aware that she was suffering from stress (*Unwin v West Sussex CC* 13 July 2001, unreported QBD).

As a general principle, responsibility for health and safety matters resides at all levels of management. In other words, every individual employee is under a duty to conduct him- or herself in a safe manner and every layer of management is required to take proper cognisance of health and safety matters in exercise of its particular responsibility. At senior management levels, this includes taking active steps to ensure that others are aware of and appropriately trained to discharge these duties (see *Purvis*, above).

However, although individuals are in part responsible for their own health and safety, an LEA will be vicariously liable for the conduct of a headteacher who breaches her duty of care to a member of staff. In *Powys v Neath Port Talbot County Borough Council and the Governors of Coedffranc Junior School* (4 January 2002, unreported, Swansea County Court), the school's headteacher was found to have failed to provide the claimant with support, showed a lack of sensitivity to his position and took an early uninformed view of his performance to the extent that she undermined him and caused a breakdown of their professional relationship which led to his suffering depression. The LEA was therefore held liable for the psychiatric condition the teacher suffered as a result of the headteacher's conduct.

**6.
THE
MAINTENANCE
OF SCHOOLS**

7. ADMISSIONS, EARLY YEARS, INFORMATION

A. Admissions to Maintained Schools

1. Introduction

The LEA's responsibility for securing sufficient school places and enabling children to access schools within its area is another of its key functions. Research produced by the DfES (and mentioned in its consultation document on school admission (September 2001)) showed that an LEA's admission practices could have a significant impact on parental satisfaction. Indeed, in many cases, the only contact parents may have with their LEA is when they seek to get their children into school.

In his introduction to the School Admissions *Code of Practice* (DFES/0031/2003), the Secretary of State identifies two key roles of the LEA: first, a central role in coordinating and rationalising admission arrangements: 'Our aim is more co-ordination between admission authorities to produce admission systems parents will find simpler and more streamlined' and, second, the now mandatory admission forums organised by LEAs will have important roles of giving advice to their admission authorities and promoting local consensus on admission arrangements.

Reflecting the importance attached to this role, the area of admissions has been subject to a number of legislative changes culminating in the School Standards and Framework Act 1998 and, now, further 'improvement' through the Education Act 2002.

As has been seen (chapter 6.C.2), every LEA has the general duty under s. 14 of the Education Act 1996 to secure that there are available in its area sufficient schools in number, character and equipment to provide for all pupils the opportunity of appropriate education (s. 14(2)). That general duty has been characterised as a target duty in *Meade v London Borough of Haringey* [1979] 2 All ER 1016, rather than absolute, though the LEA must be able to show reasonable cause (such as an emergency) why it cannot in a particular instance fulfil the duty and it must take all statutory steps to overcome obstacles to its fulfilment (per Woolf LJ, as he then was, in *R v Inner London Education Authority ex parte Ali and Another* [1990] COD 317).

The general duty is restricted to provision for the LEA's area and so the LEA is under no duty to secure provision of schooling for pupils at large from outside its area (although as will be seen, an LEA cannot discriminate in its admission arrangements against pupils from outside its area).

In addition, LEAs have general obligations in respect of individual children of compulsory school age (which are set out in detail in chapter 9) to see that they are receiving full-time education in school, or other institutional setting, through LEA-provided tuition, or otherwise. They have, moreover, an explicit duty to make arrangements for the education of sick children, expellees and others, otherwise than at school, for example in a pupil referral unit (s. 19 of the Education Act 1996) - but this duty does not extend to children who are out of school because they have been voluntarily withdrawn by their parents – see *R (ota G) v Westminster City Council* [2003] EWHC 2149 (Admin), confirmed in the Court of Appeal ([2004] EWCA Civ 45, (2004) *Independent*, 8 January).

On the admission of children with statements of special educational needs (see chapter 8), it should be noted that the standard admission arrangements generally do not apply to such children (s. 98(7) of the School Standards and Framework Act 1998). On the effects of the statutory limitation of infant class sizes, see chapter 5.A.5.

As to the particular duties imposed on LEAs to facilitate the admission of individual children into schools, every LEA must make arrangements for enabling the parent of a child in the area of the authority (a) to express a preference as to the school at which he [or she, passim] wishes education to be provided for his child and (b) to give reasons for his preference (s. 86(1) of the 1998 Act). Except in the case of children excluded from two or more schools (see s. 87 and chapter 9.G below)), the relevant admission authority must comply with any preference expressed in accordance with these arrangements (s. 86(2)), subject to the exceptions considered below.

We will consider the two aspects of this duty: (1) the arrangements and how they should be produced and (2) complying with preference. In respect of all functions relating to admissions, however, LEAs, admission authorities and appeal panels must have regard to any relevant provisions of the code or codes of practice made by the Secretary of State (s. 84(3)). The two relevant codes are *The School Admissions Code of Practice* (DFES/0031/2003) and *The School Admission Appeals Code of Practice* (DFES/0030/2003) in England. Different versions of both Codes apply in Wales.

2. Admission arrangements

The admission authority for a maintained school (i.e. LEA for community and voluntary controlled schools or governing body for foundation and voluntary aided schools, as appropriate) is required, before the beginning of each school year, to determine the admission arrangements which are to apply for that year (s. 89(1)). The detailed rules for the determination of these arrangements are now contained in the Education (Determination of Admission Arrangements) (England) Regulations 1999 (SI 1999 No. 126), as amended by the Education (Determination of Admission Arrangements) (Amendment) (England) Regulations 2002 (SI 2002 No. 2896).

In England, before determining the admission arrangements which are to apply for a particular school year, the admission authority must consult the following about the proposed arrangements by 1 March in the determination year:

a) whichever of the governing body and the LEA is not the admission authority;

b) the admission authorities for all other maintained schools in the relevant area or for such class of such schools as may be prescribed;

c) the governing bodies for all community and voluntary controlled schools in the relevant area (so far as not falling within paragraph (a) or (b));

d) the admission authorities for maintained schools of any prescribed description (s. 89(2)); and

e) in the case of Church of England schools, the relevant diocesan authority.

In the case of faith schools, it should be noted that the effect of the 2002 Act (s. 49) is that foundation and voluntary aided faith schools will no longer be able to make special admission arrangements to preserve their religious character. Such schools with a religious character will not therefore be able to keep places empty if they do not have enough applications from their particular faith or denomination. It does not, of course, mean that the school's admission arrangements cannot reflect its denomination or faith and impose appropriate criteria.

In Wales, before determining the admission arrangements which are to apply for a particular school year, the admission authority must consult the following about the proposed arrangements:

a) the LEA (where the governing body is the admission authority),

b) the admission authorities for all other maintained schools in the relevant area or for such class of such schools as may be prescribed, and

c) the admission authorities for maintained schools of any prescribed description.

Once the admission authority has carried out this consultation, it must:

a) determine that its proposed arrangements (either in their original form or with such modifications as it thinks fit) shall be the admission arrangements for the school year in question; and

b) (except in such cases as may be prescribed) notify the bodies whom it consulted of those admission arrangements (s. 89(4)).

If an admission authority considers that the arrangements should be varied within year in view of a major change in circumstances occurring since they were determined, it shall (except in a case where their proposed variations fall within any description of variations prescribed – see the Education (Variation of Admission Arrangements) (England) Regulations 2002 (SI 2002 No. 2898) refer the proposed variations to the adjudicator (in Wales, initially it was to the Secretary of State, but references to adjudicator below should be read, for Wales, as referring to the NAW) and shall (in every case) notify the bodies whom it consulted of the proposed variations (s. 89(5)). Where the LEA is the admission authority for the school, it must consult the governing body before making a reference (s. 89(9)). The adjudicator will then consider whether the arrangements should have effect with those variations until the end of that year and, if he determines that the arrangements should so have effect or that they should so have effect subject to such modification as he may determine, the arrangements shall have effect accordingly as from the date of his determination and the admission authority shall (except in such cases as may be prescribed) notify the bodies whom it consulted of the variations subject to which the arrangements are to have effect.

According to the *Explanatory Note to the Education Act 2002*, the main change to this procedure brought about by that Act was to provide governing bodies of community and voluntary controlled schools with a right to be consulted about the admission arrangements which admission authorities for other schools in their areas propose to make. This, in turn, will give such governing bodies the right to refer objections about proposed admissions arrangements to the adjudicator to the extent permitted by regulations. Admission authorities may also be required to publish their proposals in certain circumstances, such as where they intend to admit fewer pupils than the school has capacity for (as calculated under a formula); this is for the purpose of enabling groups of ten or more parents to refer an objection to the adjudicator about the proposed admission number.

In addition, where the admission authority is a school's governing body, the new s. 89(2A) allows for regulations to provide that the duty to consult may be disapplied in certain circumstances (for example, where the admission arrangements have not been the subject of previous objection to the adjudicator and remain unchanged).

One key aspect of any school's admission arrangements is its admission number and how that number is determined. Accordingly, the determination of the admission arrangements must include a determination of the number of pupils in each relevant age group that it is intended to admit to the school in that year (s. 89A(1) and (2) for boarding schools). *The Explanatory Notes to the Education Act 2002* state that s. 89A requires admission authorities to consider, amongst other factors, the current capacity of the school (as determined under a new formula) when setting an admission number and allows admission authorities for schools which provide boarding accommodation to have separate admission numbers for their day and boarding places respectively. The requirement for schools to have a standard number is therefore removed and instead each school should have a current indicated admission number, which must be taken into account by the school's admission authority in determining the school's admission arrangements. Guidance on assessing capacity can be found in the *DfES document* Assessing the Net Capacity of Schools (DfES/0739/2001Rev).

If, in England, an admission authority determines an admission number for a relevant age group which is lower than that indicated by the school's net capacity assessment, the authority must undertake additional publication (reg 9 of the 1999 Regulations). A notice must be placed in a local newspaper explaining what has been done and advising parents of their right to object to the adjudicator. Any group of ten or more parents will be allowed to lodge such objections.

3. Co-ordination

Another key function of an LEA is to seek to ensure that admission arrangements are coordinated. With the potentially high number of different admission authorities within an LEA's area, previous attempts to secure voluntary co-ordination had met with some, but not total, success.

Consequently, the 2002 Act attempted to put co-ordination on a more prescriptively mandatory footing. Thus regulations may require an LEA to formulate, for any academic year in relation to which prescribed conditions are satisfied, a qualifying scheme for coordinating the arrangements for the admission of pupils to maintained schools in its area and to take prescribed action with a view to securing the adoption of the scheme by itself and each governing body which is the admission authority for a maintained school in the area (s. 89B(1)). In effect, LEAs must attempt to negotiate agreement between all maintained schools in their areas for a coordinated application process for local parents. Each LEA will be responsible for the administration of the coordinated arrangements. In the absence of the LEA's securing the coordinated scheme, the Secretary of State has power to intervene and make such a scheme (s. 89B(2)). Provision as to the procedure and content of these schemes is contained in the Education (Coordination of Admission Arrangements) (Primary Schools) (England) Regulations 2002 (SI 2002 No. 2903), as amended by the Education (Coordination of Admission Arrangements) (Primary Schools) (England) (Amendment) Regulations 2003 (SI 2003 No. 2751) and the Education (Coordination of Admission Arrangements) (Secondary Schools) (England) Regulations 2002 (SI 2002 No. 2904).

The primary school regulations require admission arrangements for primary schools to be coordinated by each LEA for admissions in the school year 2006/07 (the original regulations had required these arrangements to be in place for 2005/06), although LEAs may do so if they wish for 2005/06. The LEA should formulate a qualifying scheme for each primary school by 1 January in each relevant year (reg 3). The LEA must refer the proposed scheme to the admission forum for advice or recommendations before it then consults the governing body to which it applies. Other LEAs should be consulted so that schemes are compatible. By 15 April in each year (reg 5) the LEA must notify the Secretary of State that it has adopted a qualifying scheme, otherwise the Secretary of State may impose a scheme (reg 6). At the time this chapter was completed, the Secretary of State had imposed two coordinated schemes: for Kent and Dorset (details at www.dfes.gov.uk/sacode).

The scheme is to be administered by the LEA.

The scheme must set out the eligibility of children to be granted admission to a primary school and the criteria to be used in determining whether a child is offered a place. Procedures for dealing with late applications and applications outside the normal admission round must feature in the scheme. A governing body that is an admission authority must notify the LEA of any applications made directly to it and must rank all applications according to the school's admission criteria. The LEA will then make a single offer of a school place for each child. All offers are to be made on the same day, to be designated by each LEA (reg 7).

The secondary school regulations are broadly similar, except they can apply two years earlier i.e. 2004/05 (LEAs are not under a duty to adopt qualifying schemes in the first year, although they are encouraged to do so in the Code of Practice). Schemes should be adopted by 1 January in each year (from 2004 onwards) (reg 4) and the Secretary of State should be notified by 15 April. Otherwise he can impose a scheme.

Guidance on coordinated arrangements can be found in chapter 6 of the *Code of Practice on School Admission Arrangements*. It fleshes out the nature of the application form and process, so that, for example, schemes must allow parents to express a minimum of three preferences on a common application form that the LEA must make available to all parents resident in its area. The common application form can be supplemented, but not replaced, by additional forms where a particular school needs extra information, such as denominational commitment or in relation to testing. Parents who are resident in one LEA but who wish to apply for a place at a school maintained by another LEA will apply through the maintaining LEA's common application form. If a parent applies for a place at a school maintained by an outside LEA, that LEA must tell the LEA in whose area the child resides if it intends to offer a place. The home LEA can then decide not to offer a place at one of its own schools. If this is to be done, parents must be informed in the relevant LEA's composite prospectus.

4. Admission forum

Closely aligned with co-ordination is the role of the admission forum. Under the 1998 Act these forums were encouraged as a means of achieving co-ordination and advice but were not compulsory. After the 2002 Act, however, LEAs are required to establish them (s. 85A of the School Standards and Framework Act, as inserted by s. 46 of the 2002 Act).

An LEA must therefore establish for its area a body, in accordance with regulations (see the Education (Admission Forums) (England) Regulations 2002 (SI 2002 No. 2900), to be known as an admission forum. The purpose of the forum is to advise the LEA on such matters connected with the exercise of its admission functions as may be prescribed and to advise the admission authorities for maintained schools in the area for which the forum is established on (a) such matters connected with the determination of admission arrangements and (b) such other matters connected with the admission of pupils as may be prescribed (s. 85A(1)). The LEA and admission authorities must have regard, in carrying out their functions, to any relevant advice given to them by an admission forum (s. 85A(4)). The LEA must make arrangements for the forum (and any sub-committee) to be provided with accommodation and with such services as it considers appropriate. Guidance on the role and operation of forums is contained in chapter 5 of the *Code of Practice*.

The LEA may decide the overall size of its forum. The forum is to be made up of core members appointed by the relevant LEA and those members have the power to appoint other members to represent the interests of any section of the local community (reg 5). These represent stakeholder groups, including at least one and not more than five members of the LEA. Groups of schools should be represented as core members, but these are appointments for each category of school, not representatives for each school. Each school representative should be a headteacher or a governor who is not an LEA member (reg 4). Nominations for appointment should also be made for members representing dioceses, Academies and city technology colleges. It is recommended that neighbouring LEAs be included. Members, who are appointed for up to four years (reg 6), can appoint alternates (reg 10).

The role of the forum is set out in reg 3. It should meet at least three times in its first year and at least twice in each subsequent year. The forum must consider how well existing and proposed admission arrangements serve the interests of children and parents within the area of the relevant authority. It should also consider the effectiveness of the LEA's proposed co-ordination arrangements and promote agreement on admission issues. The forum must also consider how actual admissions relate to the admission numbers published for schools and also monitor the admission of children who move into an LEA area and who are admitted to schools outside the normal admission process. The forum must also promote admission arrangements for children with special educational needs, looked-after children and children excluded from school (reg 3).

Regulations may authorise or require an admission forum to give advice to the governing body of any Academy in the LEA's area and the governing body of that Academy shall have regard to any relevant advice so given (s. 85B and see reg 11 of the Education (Admission Forums) (England) Regulations 2002 (S.I. 2002 No. 2900).

Regulations for Wales came into force on 1 December 2003 (Education (Admissions Forums) (Wales) Regulations 2003 (SI 2003 No. 2962 (W 279)).

5.   Objections to admission arrangements

As has been seen, parents may object to the adjudicator where the LEA proposes adopting an admission number lower than the school's assessed capacity. Other objections to admission arrangements can be made by governing bodies of community and voluntary schools or any other consultee (s. 90). Such objections are subject to a number of limitations contained in the Education (Objections to Admission Arrangements) Regulations 1999 (SI 1999 No. 125, as amended by the Education (Objections to Admission Arrangements) (Amendment) (England) Regulations 2002 (SI 2002 No. 2901)). These regulations also set out the procedure to be adopted for dealing with and determining such objections. The adjudicator can be involved only in respect of general arrangements; he cannot be involved in disputes over the application of the arrangements in respect of individual cases.

On involvement of the adjudicator, see also chapter 12.B.3.

6.   Information

The LEA must publish certain information about admissions and admission arrangements in its area: see the Education (School Information) (England) Regulations 2002 (SI 2002 No. 897). A composite prospectus should be produced (regs 8 to 10 and sched 2) by the LEA, giving detailed particulars of the admission policy for each school, including the coordinated admission arrangements. If a school has adopted a lower admission number than its assessed net capacity, that should be mentioned and explained. Details about school transport and obtaining further information should be set out.

7. Parental preferences

Once admission arrangements are in place, except in the case of children excluded from two or more schools (see s. 87 and chapter 9.G and below) and children in accommodation centres (see s. 36 of the Nationality Immigration and Asylum Act 2002), the relevant admission authority must comply with any preference expressed in accordance with these arrangements (s.86(2)) subject to the exceptions outlined below.

Points to note about this general duty include the following.

* The LEA is responsible for making the arrangements for preferences to be expressed, even in respect of schools for which it is not the admission authority. An LEA is (unless it has transferred the function to the governing body of the school) the admission authority for community and voluntary controlled schools; the governing body is the admission authority for voluntary aided and foundation schools (s. 88). The admission authority is, however, responsible for complying with the parental preferences expressed under those arrangements.

* The LEA must enable the parent to give reasons for their preference. This would, *inter alia*, enable it to consider if any religious or philosophical convictions are being expressed for a child to attend a particular school (see *R (K) v Newham LBC* [2002] EWHC 405 (Admin)).

* An LEA cannot allow a preference to be expressed by inertia or give priority to those who do not express a preference. In *R v Rotherham MBC ex p Clark* [1998] ELR 152, CA, the LEA's policy was that parents within a school's designated area would be assumed to have expressed a preference for that school, unless they expressed a preference for another one. Parents who, however, expressed a preference for a particular school, but then discovered they were given lower priority than parents in the area who had not stated a preference, challenged the LEA's policy. The Court of Appeal held that the arrangements were unlawful; parents who had expressed a preference should have been given priority over those who had not.

* The arrangements may allow the parent of a child to express preferences for more than one school; but the admission authority for a maintained school for which a child's parent has expressed a preference is not required to offer the child admission to the school if, in accordance with a scheme adopted or made by virtue of s. 89B (see above), the child is offered

admission to a different school for which the parent has also expressed a preference (s. 86(2A)).

The duty to comply with the preference need not apply in the following specified circumstances (s. 86(3) to (3B)):

- if compliance with the preference would prejudice the provision of efficient education or the efficient use of resources; or

- (in England) in relation to a preference expressed by a parent as to the school at which he wishes secondary education suitable to the requirements of pupils who are over compulsory school age to be provided for his child, the duty to comply with the preference does not apply if the relevant selection arrangements are wholly based on selection by reference to ability or aptitude and compliance with the preference would be incompatible with selection under those arrangements (s. 86(3A)). 'The relevant selection arrangements' mean (a) the arrangements for admission to the school for secondary education suitable to the requirements of pupils who are over compulsory school age, or (b) those arrangements and the arrangements for entry to the sixth form of children who have been admitted to the school;

- (in Wales) if the preferred school is a foundation or voluntary aided school and compliance with the preference would be incompatible with any special admission arrangements to preserve the religious character of a foundation or voluntary aided school or if the arrangements for admission to the preferred school (i) are wholly based on selection by reference to ability or aptitude and (ii) are so based with a view to admitting only pupils with high ability or with aptitude and compliance with the preference would be incompatible with selection under those arrangements.

Prejudice of the kind referred to under the first bullet point above may arise by reason of measures required to be taken in order to ensure compliance with the duty imposed by s. 1(6) (duty of local education authority and governing body to comply with limit on infant class sizes). See chapter 5.A.5 for detailed consideration of the infant class size legislation.

In Wales, no prejudice shall be taken to arise from the admission to a maintained school in a school year of a number of pupils in a relevant age group which does not exceed (a) the relevant standard number, or (b) the admission number fixed in accordance with s. 93, whichever is the greater (s. 86(4)).

In England, however, the 2002 Act abolished the standard number and so instead no prejudice shall be taken to arise from the admission to a maintained school in a school year of a number of pupils in a relevant age group which does not exceed the number determined (under s. 89) as the number of pupils in that age group that it is intended to admit to the school in that year i.e. the indicated admission number. This does not, though, apply if the school is one at which boarding accommodation is provided for pupils and certain other conditions set out in s. 84 and s.89 are met.

If the parent of a child resident outside the LEA's area expresses preference for a school maintained by the LEA, that LEA must treat the preference on the same footing as if the application came from one of its residents, i.e. it must comply with it unless one of the standard specified exceptions applies (s. 86(8)(a)). This principle was confirmed by the *Court of Appeal in R v Greenwich London Borough Council ex p Governors of the John Ball Primary School* [1990] Fam Law 469. The judgment declared unlawful a decision by the newly-created Greenwich LEA to give priority to its own residents for admission to a secondary school, thus excluding applicants (other than siblings who were already pupils at the school) from the neighbouring LEA. Following *Greenwich*, there was concern among LEAs whether school catchment areas (as distinct from the sibling rule, or relative proximity of home to preferred school) were lawful. Advice from the then DfE (Annex C of Circular 6/93, since withdrawn) was very cautious; it recommended that any catchment should be drawn by reference to physical barriers, such as a river or motorway. But the courts subsequently confirmed the lawfulness of the catchment area: in a judgment on a case in which racial discrimination had been alleged (*R v Bradford MBC ex p Sikander Ali* [1994] ELR at 312B) and even where the LEA boundary happened to form a substantial part of the school catchment boundary (*R v Wiltshire CC ex p Razazan* [1997] ELR 370, CA and R v Rotherham MBC ex p LT [2000] ELR 76, [2000] EdCR 39, CA).

Where admission arrangements for a school provide for all pupils admitted to the school to be selected by reference to ability or aptitude, those arrangements shall be taken for the purposes of this section to be wholly based on selection by reference to ability or aptitude, whether or not they also provide for the use of additional criteria in circumstances where the number of children in a relevant age group who are assessed to be of the requisite ability or aptitude is greater than the number of pupils which it is intended to admit to the school in that age group (s. 86 (9)).

**7.
ADMISSIONS,
EARLY YEARS,
INFORMATION**

As part of the admission procedure, an LEA must make arrangements for enabling a parent to appeal against any decision made by or on behalf of the LEA as to the school at which education is to be provided for the child and, in the case of a community or voluntary controlled school maintained by the LEA, any decision made by or on behalf of the governing body refusing the child admission to the school (s. 94(1)). In voluntary aided and foundation schools, the governing body is responsible for putting in place appeal arrangements (s. 94(2)). Joint appeal arrangements may be established (s. 94(3) and (4)).

In three cases, children are taken outside the 'normal' admission procedure outlined above.

First, the duty to comply with a parental preference does not apply where the child has been permanently excluded from two or more schools and the last of those exclusions was less than two years ago (s. 87(1) and (2)). This does not apply, however, to children who were below compulsory school age when excluded, pupils who were reinstated following a permanent exclusion or pupils who would have been reinstated following a permanent exclusion but it was impracticable to do so i.e. a decision under reg 6(6)(c) of the Education (Pupil Exclusions and Appeals) (Maintained Schools) (England) Regulations 2002 (see para 7.4 of the *Schools Admissions Code of Practice*).

An admission authority may still decide to admit the child under the normal procedures, but it does not have to do so. Where such a child is refused admission, the relevant admission authority is not required to allow the parent to appeal against the decision (s. 97(1)). It may do so if it wishes. Further, if the LEA has, despite being under no obligation to do so, permitted the child to be admitted, it must make arrangements for enabling the governing body of the school to appeal against the decision to an appeal panel (s. 97(2) and sched 25).

Second, children with statements of special educational needs or who are applying for admission to special schools fall outside the standard admission arrangements outlined above (s. 98(6) and (7)).

Third, the normal arrangements do not apply in relation to nursery schools or children under compulsory school age at the time of their proposed admission, except where a maintained school has made arrangements for the admission of children under that age for education which is not nursery education (s. 98(1) to (4)).

8.   Power to direct

One further admission power available to LEAs to assist in securing places for all children is the power contained in s. 96 of the 1998 Act to give a direction to (in England) a governing body of a school for which the LEA is not the admission authority or (in Wales) any governing body if, in the case of any child in its area, in relation to each maintained school which is a reasonable distance from his home and provides suitable education, he has been refused admission to the school or he is permanently excluded from the school (s. 96(1)). Such a direction should specify a school in the LEA's area that is a reasonable distance from the child's home and from which the child is not permanently excluded (s. 96(2) and (3)). A school cannot, however, be specified if it would lead to prejudice because of infant class size measures being taken by the school. Once a direction is issued, the governing body of the specified school must admit the child (s. 96(5)), although he can subsequently be excluded on valid grounds (s. 96(6)).

Before issuing a direction, the LEA must consult the child's parent and the governing body of the school it proposes to specify (s. 97(1)). Before making a direction, the LEA must give notice in writing to the governing body and the headteacher and cannot give its direction until the period in which the governing body can refer the matter to the Secretary of State has expired or, if so referred, the Secretary of State has made a decision (s. 97(2)). Thus the governing body can stay the direction if it refers the matter to the Secretary of State within 15 days (s. 97(3)). The Secretary of State may determine which school should admit the child and if he does so, where the LEA is the admission authority for that school, it shall admit the child to the school and give notice in writing to the governing body and headteacher of the school of the Secretary of State's determination. Where the LEA is not the admission authority, the Secretary of State will specify the school in the direction. In Wales, the NAW may determine which school is to be required to admit the child and, if it does so, that school shall be specified in the direction (s. 97(4)). Any direction must be given in writing and a copy given to the governing body and headteacher.

9.   Selective admission arrangements

Admission arrangements based on selection are often contentious. The 1998 Act prohibits selection by ability unless it makes provision for a 'permitted form of selection' or the school is a grammar school (s. 99(1)). 'Permitted forms of selection' are, in summary, pre-existing permitted arrangements, selection by banding and sixth form admission on grounds of ability (s. 99(2)). Selection by aptitude may operate only where there are pre-existing arrangements or the selection is authorised by s. 102 of the 1998 Act.

A school that practised selection by ability or aptitude at the beginning of the 1997/98 school year and continued doing so, may continue to do so, so long as there is no increase in the proportion of selective admissions in any age group and no significant change in the basis of selection. This rule does not apply to grammar schools (s. 100(1)). Selection by ability is permissible if admission arrangements are designed to secure that the pupils admitted in any age group are representative of all levels of ability among applicants in that age group, no level being substantially over- or under-represented (s. 101). The introduction of banding arrangements is a prescribed 'alteration' that is subject to the procedure for statutory alterations or reorganisation. Schools with banding arrangements which also select by aptitude may apply aptitude tests at any stage in the admission process and give priority to an 'aptitude' applicant irrespective of his level of ability. Such schools may either allocate up to 10 per cent of places by aptitude and the remainder under banding arrangements, or band all applicants and then admit 10 per cent of each band by aptitude (s. 101). Schools with a specialism may select up to 10 per cent of any admission age group by reference to aptitude in a prescribed subject or subjects, but the admission arrangements are not to include a test of ability (otherwise than for banding at the same school) or of aptitude in another subject or subjects (s. 102). For further guidance on this area see paras 3.21–3.31 *School Admissions Code of Practice*.

Grammar schools which at the beginning of the 1997/98 school year had selective admission arrangements based on general ability and designed to admit only pupils of high ability, have been designated by the Secretary of State and may continue to offer selective admission arrangements (see s. 104). The Education (Grammar School Ballots) Regulations 1998 (SI 1998 No. 2876) and the Education (Proposals for Grammar Schools to Cease to have Selective Admission Arrangements) Regulations 1999 (SI 1999 No. 2103) enable parents to ballot on whether grammar schools should retain their selective admission arrangements. A ballot may relate to all grammar schools within a prescribed LEA or other prescribed area, to a prescribed group of grammar schools, or to any other grammar school. LEAs and governing bodies of LEA schools are not to incur expenditure on publishing, or assisting the publication of, material designed to influence whether a ballot should be requested, or its outcome, or on using or supporting any other means of influence. But expenditure may be incurred on factual information fairly presented, a fair and reasonable assessment of the likely consequences of the abandonment of selective admission arrangements and an accurate statement of the intentions of the LEA or governing body in that event. Regard should be had to any guidance given by the Secretary of State about what is 'fair' and 'reasonable' (s. 107). See also chapter 3.C.3.

Where the result of a ballot is that one or more grammar schools should end selective admission, the admission authority is to devise new non-selective admission arrangements (s. 108). Selective admission arrangements of a grammar school may be varied (otherwise than as the result of a ballot) so as to substitute either no provision at all for selection by ability, or selection by banding, or selection by aptitude or selection by ability of pupils over compulsory school age (s. 109). Such variations are, however, alterations to the school's character and statutory proposals will need to be published. The governing body rather than the LEA is, however, to publish the proposals where the grammar school is a community school.

**7.
ADMISSIONS,
EARLY YEARS,
INFORMATION**

B. Early-Years Education and Childcare

1. Introduction

LEAs have a distinguished record of providing early-years education, that is, education for children below the statutory school age. Though the principal local authority, as LEA and social services authority (see chapter 1.D), has played separate but parallel roles, its education department has had an increased part to play in the provision of day care for children, or childcare, since the early 1990s. Given the variety of different management arrangements within local authorities in 2004 and the lack of a recent survey, making general statements is perhaps unwise, but it is likely that where a director of education and a director of social services can be identified, the director of education's responsibilities include childcare as well as early-years education. Commensurate with the local change, the Government transferred the function from the Department of Health to the DfEE/DfES in the late 1990s. With the further changes proposed in the Green Paper *Every Child Matters* (Cm 5860) and embodied in the 2004 Children Bill, it will fall clearly within the remit of the director of children's services.

2.   History

The Education Act 1870 (s. 74: As to attendance of children at school) gave school boards the power to make school attendance compulsory for children between the ages of five to 13 and the Education Act 1876 placed a duty on parents to ensure their children in that age-range received efficient elementary instruction. It is likely, though, that many schools catered for younger children. Matthew Arnold HMI, in his report for 1878, refers to educating four-year-olds in elementary schools (Arnold 1908). Nursery schools outside the responsibility of school boards/LEAs appeared from the 1890s and their numbers increased during the First World War. The Education Act 1918 gave power to LEAs to make arrangements for supplying or aiding the supply of nursery schools and nursery classes for children over two and under five years of age (s. 19). Although nursery schools were not classed as public elementary schools, LEAs could grant-aid them provided they were open to LEA inspection and the LEA was represented on the body of managers.

The local authority role for the care, welfare and development of children can be traced back to the Elizabethan Poor Laws. The Maternity and Child Welfare Act 1918 empowered local authorities using their health functions to establish crèches and day nurseries for children from birth to the age of five. The provision, now cast as a duty, can be found in s.18 (Day care for pre-schools and other children) of the Children Act 1989. The local authority role was reduced by the transfer of the registration and inspection of childcare provision including childminding to Ofsted by the Care Standards Act 2000. The Education Act 2002 transferred from the local authority to the LEA the duty to provide an information service on childcare and related services.

The interwar period was not a beneficent time for local authorities to use their powers. Dent (1944) reports that in 1939 there were only 115 nursery schools in England and Wales, with accommodation for 10,000 children, and only 104 day nurseries, with accommodation for 3,700 children, with the largest provision being made in nursery classes, with more than 170,000 children: a total of nearly 200,000 out of two million in the birth to five age group. By 1943, Dent estimated that the number in some sort of provision was not much more, although there had been a massive shift towards day care and nursery schools.

The Education Act 1944 clarified the position: LEAs could establish, maintain or assist nursery schools and the LEA-maintained nursery school was defined. The White Paper

Educational Reconstruction (Cmd 6458, 1943) supported the creation of the self-contained nursery school as a transition from home to school as the most suitable form of provision for children under five. Section 8(2)(b) of the 1944 Act requires LEAs to have regard to the need to secure provision for pupils who have not attained the age of five or 'where the authority consider[s] the provision of nursery schools to be inexpedient, by the provision of nursery classes'.

The expansion of nursery provision did not occur during the first 20 years after the war. Ministry of Education Circular 8/60 on nursery education noted that the circumstances were such that it is 'impossible to undertake any expansion in the provision of nursery education' as no resources could be spared for the expansion of nursery education and no teachers could be spared who might otherwise work with children of compulsory school age. The Education Act 1980 abolished the 1944 Act duty, replacing it with a power. There was, though, expansion in nursery provision from the early 1970s mainly due to falling rolls and the desire of primary schools to make part-time provision. Although the number of full-time places went up from 240,000 to 320,000 in the 20-year period to 1986, the part-time places increased from 11,000 to 290,000. In 2002, 96 per cent, over 1.1 million of three and four year-olds, were in early-years provision, of whom just over one million (85 per cent of the cohort) were in funded nursery education with the resources managed by the LEA. The Government set itself the objective that by April 2004, there would be a free early-years education place for every three year-old whose parents wanted it.

7.
ADMISSIONS,
EARLY YEARS,
INFORMATION

A full explanation of this significant expansion of the LEA role is beyond the scope of this book. The expansion, however, of early-years provision became Government policy only in January 1996 with the publication of *Nursery Education Scheme: The Next Steps*, which announced the short-lived nursery education voucher scheme and the legislation which became the Nursery Education and Grant-maintained Schools Act 1996. Credit therefore must go to the large number of LEAs which led expansion locally: many were providing education for nearly all four year-olds and a significant proportion of three year-olds from the late 1980s. The 1996 Act gave the LEA responsibility for funding early-years education, initially for four year-olds via vouchers, in social services day care and the independent, private and voluntary sector. Although the incoming Government abolished the paper vouchers in 1997, it used funding powers in the Act to establish the Nursery Education Grant to stimulate early-years provision in public, private and voluntary settings. The specific grant was finally transferred to mainstream local authority funding from 1 April 2003. The DfES's specific-funding powers have also been used to develop a series of initiatives which support the role of the local authority/LEA, particularly Sure Start and Early Excellence Centres, which are described further below.

The Government announced its broad policy approach to early-years services in May 1997. The key element of the policy is that these services should be planned in each local authority area through an Early Years Development Plan (referred to as the Plan or the EYDP), drawn up by the local authority in full co-operation with a body representing all the relevant early-years interests in the area. These bodies were initially called Early Years Development Partnerships (referred to as EYDPs or the Partnership) were set up in late 1997. All bodies submitted draft EYDPs to the Secretary of State for approval in February 1998. This arrangement was given legislative backing in the School Standards and Framework Act 1998.

On 19th May 1998, before the 1998 Act had reached the statute book, the Government published a Green Paper *Meeting the Childcare Challenge* (Cm 3959) which proposed a National Childcare Strategy covering children from birth to 14 years. Acknowledging the vital links between care and education, especially in the early years, the Green Paper proposed that the national strategy should be planned and delivered by local childcare partnerships, building on the existing Partnerships, each of which would thus become an Early Years Development and Childcare Partnership (referred to as the EYDCP or the Partnership) and produce an Early Years Development and Childcare Plan. The Government's guiding principles, outlined in the Strategy, for the future developments of early-years and childcare services are: quality, affordability, diversity, accessibility and partnership.

The partnerships took on the role of planning and coordinating childcare from April 1999. This new role was given legal sanction by the Education Act 2002 and specifically gave the LEA new duties to:

- review the sufficiency of childcare with the EYDCP; and

- provide an information service on childcare and related services, a role transferred from the local [social services] authority (for which it had previously been a duty under the Children Act 1989).

The LEA also gained a duty under the 2002 Act to ensure the providers of 'funded nursery education' comply with relevant requirements and guidance, for example the teaching of the foundation stage of the National Curriculum and health and safety legislation. If the requirements are not met, the LEA can reclaim any financial assistance given to the nursery. This replaces the provisions of the Nursery Education and Grant-maintained Schools Act 1996, which was repealed in England from 1 April 2003. A date for its repeal in Wales had not been announced by spring 2004. Providers of funded nursery education are the private and voluntary sector, i.e. playgroups, nurseries etc. and the local authority social services sector. LEA-maintained provision is excluded from the sanction, as recourse lies in the accountability framework described elsewhere in this book.

A further development of the LEA planning and delivery arrangements took place from 1 April 2004 with the deregulation of many planning requirements originally imposed on partnerships from their inception. See *Sure Start Guidance 2004–2006: Overview and Local Delivery Arrangements* (DfES, November 2003) that brings Sure Start into the arrangements for planning early-years provisions. The objective is to enable LEAs to 'develop partnership working and planning in a way that makes sense locally'. Plans do not have to be submitted annually to the Secretary of State and much regulation on the operation of EYDCPs has been removed.

7.
ADMISSIONS,
EARLY YEARS,
INFORMATION

For the most significant of the likely changes in respect of childcare to be brought about after the 2004 Children Bill is enacted, see chapter 1.E.3.

3. The law

Prior to the Nursery Education and Grant-maintained Schools Act 1996, there was a clear division between the LEA and local authority roles for publicly-funded early-years provision, i.e the LEA provided the statutory basis for maintained school education including maintained nursery schools and the local authority provided the rest, mainly under the Children Act 1989. Since then, LEAs now fund, though not necessarily entirely, the education of three and four year-olds in local authority day care and in the independent and voluntary sector. LEAs also have a planning and information role with the Early Years Development and Childcare Partnerships. Although this is not the place to describe the remaining local authority functions in part III (Local Authority Support for Children and Families) of the

Children Act 1989, there is a catch-all provision in s.27 (Co-operation between authorities), which enables the local authority to request help from the local education authority (and other bodies) and the request must be complied with if it is compatible with the LEA's statutory or other duties. Section 17 (Provision of services for children and families) places a general duty on the local authority to safeguard and promote the welfare of children and s. 18 (Day care for pre-school and other children) contains the powers to provide early-years day care provision of which education is a part. The duties in s. 19 (Review of provision for day care, child minding etc.) have now transferred to an LEA duty found in s. 118A of the School Standards and Framework Act 1998.

The law can be found in the Education Act 1996, the School Standards and Framework 1998 and the Education Act 2002. The (now-repealed for England) Nursery Education and Grant-Maintained Schools Act 1996 provided the statutory basis for the funding provisions of the Nursery Education (England) Regulations 2000 (SI 2000 No. 107). The resource is now provided through general grant on local government expenditure and central control over the level of allocation to particular projects is exercised through statutory guidance on the Early Years Development and Childcare Plan and subsequent approval of the plan by the Secretary of State.

Section 117 (Definition of 'nursery education') of the 1998 Act defines 'nursery education' as full-time or part-time education suitable for children who have not attained compulsory school age (whether provided at schools or elsewhere). Section 118 (Duty of LEA as respects availability of nursery education) requires the LEA in subs (1) to secure sufficient nursery education for children who have attained a prescribed age. The Education (Nursery Education and Early Years Development) (England) Regulations 1999 (SI 1999 No. 1329) as amended by the Education (Nursery Education and Early Years Development) (England) (Amendment) Regulations 2003 (SI 2003 No. 2939) define the 'prescribed age' as three from 1 April 2004, in keeping with Government policy that every three-year-old should have access to an early-years education place from April 2004. In Wales, the Education (Nursery Education and Early Years Development and Childcare Plans) (Wales) Regulations 2003 (SI 2003 No. 893 (W 113)) define the age as four.

In deciding whether there is sufficient nursery education available, the LEA can take account of available provision outside its area and the LEA must have regard to any guidance given by the Secretary of State in England of NAW in Wales (s.118(2)).

The LEA has several powers to make new nursery provision if it finds that provision is not sufficient. It can:

- open maintained nursery schools under section 17 (Powers in respect of nursery education) of the 1996 Act;

- open a nursery class in an existing primary school or establish a new primary school with a nursery class under s. 16 (Power to establish, maintain and assist primary and secondary education) and s. 17(2) (continuing power to establish and maintain primary schools at which education is provided for children under compulsory school age and for older children including schools at which there are nursery classes for children under compulsory school age); and

- develop new provision with private and voluntary providers of nursery education, or use the local authority's social services powers. Such provision is governed by s. 153 (Powers of the LEA in respect of funded nursery education) of the 2002 Act which enables LEAs to make arrangements 'in consideration of financial assistance' with providers of nursery education subject to conditions which would enable the LEA to reclaim financial support if children were not taught the foundation stage of the National Curriculum.

7.
ADMISSIONS,
EARLY YEARS,
INFORMATION

While it might be theoretically possible for an LEA fully to meet its early-years duties by making provision only in maintained schools, no LEA has attempted to do so. As can be inferred from s. 14(4) (LEA functions in respect of provision of primary and secondary schools), the LEA is not required to secure sufficient schools to meet its early-years duties but to secure sufficient provision in maintained schools or otherwise.

Section 118A of the 1998 Act (Duties of the LEA in respect of childcare) requires the LEA to review annually the sufficiency of childcare for its area taking account of available provision outside the LEA area which the LEA expects to become available and guidance from the Secretary of State or NAW. The LEA, of course, has no power to provide childcare unless it is incidental to the provision of education. The local authority can provide 'appropriate' childcare under s. 18 (Day care for pre-school and older children) of the Children Act 1989. There is no requirement that the provision is made without charge as is the case for maintained school education.

Section 119 (Early years development and childcare partnerships) requires the LEA under subs (1) to establish a partnership for its area. In carrying this out, the LEA is one of a number of members of the wider group promoting effective partnership working and supporting that work through management of the resources attached to the planning mechanisms. The LEA must have regard to any guidance by the Secretary of State or NAW in establishing the partnership and determining its constitution (s. 119(2)). The LEA also has the power to establish a sub-committee of the partnership for any part of its area (s. 119(3)). Responsibility for convening, servicing and facilitating meetings and proceedings of the partnership is the duty of the LEA (s. 119(4)). The partnership, in conjunction with the LEA, has a duty to review the sufficiency of nursery education and childcare in the area and to prepare the Early Years Development and Childcare Plan (s. 119(5)). Additional functions may be conferred on partnerships (s. 119(6)).

Section 120 (Early years development and childcare plans) requires the LEA to prepare the Early Years Development and Childcare Plan and develop further such plans, in conjunction with the Early Years Development and Childcare Partnership (s. 120(1)) at prescribed intervals. In England, the Education (Nursery Education and Early Years Development) (England) (Amendment) Regulations 2003 (SI 2003 No. 2939) removed the requirement to prepare plans at intervals of one year from 1 April 2004. In Wales, the Education (Nursery Education and Early Years Development and Childcare Plans) (Wales) Regulations 2003 (SI 2003 No. 893 (W 113)) require plans to be submitted to the NAW by 20 October each year. Subsections (2) to (4) of s. 120 prescribe what the development plan should consist of.

The LEA has a duty to submit the plan by a specified date to the Secretary of State or NAW for approval under s.120 (Approval, modification and review of early-years development and childcare plan). The Secretary of State may require modifications to the plan. It is the duty of the LEA to implement an approved plan (s. 121(3)). The Secretary of State and NAW may keep the plan and its implementation under review and approval can be withdrawn. Reports to the DfES are required of the LEA, in order for the proposals and their implementation to be kept under review (s. 121(5)). The LEA has the power, with the agreement of the partnership, to submit modifications of an approved plan to the Secretary of State for approval (s. 121(8)). The LEA shall publish the plan (s. 121(9)).

Section 123 (Children with special educational needs) places a duty on any LEA or other person providing nursery education and their employees to have regard to the provisions of the *SEN Code of*

Practice. Subsection (3B) inserted by the Special Educational Needs and Disability Act 2001 requires the LEA or other person concerned to inform parents if special educational provision is being made for their child in funded nursery education. Section 124 (Travel arrangements for children receiving nursery education otherwise than at school) inserts a s. 509A into the 1996 Act to enable the LEA to provide assistance with travel arrangements for children receiving nursery education otherwise than at school.

A number of authorities identified as 'excellent' by the 2002 comprehensive performance assessment exercise began pressing government to deliver on its promise of lightening the burden of the requirement to produce separate statutory plans for related areas of policy. Joining-up policy for the benefit of the children became an early focus for such activity and some local authorities pressed to be allowed to adopt a single strategy with respect to children and not to be required to submit plans under existing legislation.

4. Central initiatives

Following the comprehensive spending review in 2000, the government set up the Children and Young People's unit as a cross-governmental agency to oversee the promotion of the government's priority for joining up policies on children. At the same time a line of funding, called the Children's Fund, was set up to resource programmes championed by the unit. The unit was physically and administratively located within the DfES, but had a government-wide remit and reported through the Minister for Children (a junior minister within the Home Office). Grants from the Children's Fund were channelled through local partnerships in each LEA, but there was a degree of flexibility and in many areas they were fully integrated with the Early Years Development and Childcare partnerships. There were also links in some areas to wider community partnership arrangements.

The remit of the CYPU covered children and young people from birth to age 19 and therefore went beyond the early-years agenda. It maintained close links with the Sure Start Unit that was more focused on promoting projects for children from birth to three and, again, used a partnership structure to administer its projects. Following an internal DfES reorganisation in 2002 the Sure Start Unit absorbed the formerly separate directorates for early-years education and childcare – which themselves reflected the split responsibilities between the former Departments for Education and for Employment prior to their merger in the 1990s.

In addition to the new source of funding for child-related and young-person-related projects, the unit was made responsible for developing an overarching strategy for children and young people. Consultation on a draft for this strategy was concluded in 2002, but publication of the strategy itself was overtaken by the announcement of *Every Child Matters* (on which see also chapter 9.D below). The strategy finally saw the light of day, in much reduced form, within chapter 1 of the Green Paper: 'The Challenge'. As noted below, the Green Paper also led to the winding-up of the CYPU as a cross-departmental agency, its functions being subsumed in a new directorate general within the DfES reporting to a higher-profile Minister of State for Children and Families (Rt Hon Margaret Hodge) from June 2003. The Sure Start Unit retained its integrity within the new structure. DfES also absorbed staff from the Home Office and the Department of Health.

The reorganisation brought into DfES responsibility for the related, but previously separate, Children's Trust initiative. The Department of Health had invited expressions of interest to pilot the concept of a 'children's trust' to be submitted in the spring of 2003. Such a body would be set up to provide integrated service delivery for children across health, education and social services. Department of Health and DfES were formally partners in developing this scheme, which was characterised by an open-ended approach. The organisation of a children's trust and its scale of responsibilities were deliberately left vague in the hope that different models would emerge to be tested in pilot areas.

A major change with respect to the funding of early-years provision is noted in chapter 6.D. From the 2003/2004 financial year, the bulk of funding for early-years and childcare provision has been made available to LEAs through the mainstream local government finance system in the under-fives sub-block of the schools block of the education formula spending share. LEAs now receive funding according to the level of provision made or funded, rather than on the basis of a population allocation topped-up according to a calculation of expanded provision since the baseline year of 1996. This marks the final disappearance of the effects of the nursery voucher scheme (underlined by the repeal of the relevant legislation). For practical purposes, the Early Years Development and Childcare Partnerships have become a consultation mechanism to influence the exercise of a local government function – as opposed to a vehicle for spending specific grants as they were originally conceived.

C. Information Collection and Data Sharing

1. Introduction

A prominent role of an LEA nowadays is as a creator of plans and strategies and a collector and distributor of information and statistics. In this book, the, at times seemingly infinite, number of required plans and strategies have, wherever possible, been addressed and analysed in the relevant sections dealing with the substantive areas of education work: for example, education development plans are considered at chapter 4.A.4 and elsewhere, behaviour support plans at chapter 9.E and asset management plans at chapter 6.C.5. This section will therefore look at the role of the LEA in collecting information and forwarding this to schools and the DfES and also at the duties imposed on LEAs in the increasingly important and complex area of data sharing.

2. Information collection

One of the original aims of the previous edition of this work had been to produce an exhaustive list of the informational requirements imposed on LEAs. The authors, however, had to admit defeat, as such a list would be seemingly unending, unreadable and most probably out of date within a few months.

This edition does not even attempt to rectify that omission: if anything, the volume and type of information which LEAs are required to gather, collate and distribute have grown. A brief search of Butterworths' *The Law of Education* produces 5330 references to the word 'information' in the education legislation including regulations. An exhaustive list, even if such a beast were possible, might therefore not be wholly desirable.

The other difficulty is that, in addition to the statutory obligations to provide information, much LEA information collection is required by Departmental circular or as part of grant conditions, either general or specific. The latter is likely to become even more common as the DfES increases the use it makes of its general grant-giving powers under s. 14 of the 2002 Act.

The commentary below therefore seeks to group in broad categories and contextualise the information which LEAs must collect, collate, submit (e.g. to the Secretary of State and/or, in Wales, the National Assembly), interpret or publish. Particular emphasis is laid on the purposes of processing the information.

3. General duties

First, the power of the Secretary of State to require information is nothing new. Section 92 of the Education Act 1944 has survived and now appears, with extensions, in the consolidatory Education Act 1996. But the 1944 formulation: 'Every [LEA] shall make to the Minister [of Education, as he then was] such reports and returns and give him such information as he may require for the purpose of the exercise of his functions under this Act' is itself a re-enactment of provision consolidated in the Education Act 1921.

Under s. 29 of the 1996 Act (as amended), the duty is imposed on LEAs to make such reports and returns to the Secretary of State and give to him such information as he may require for the purpose of the exercise of his functions (s. 29(1)). An LEA must also compile such information and make such provision for conducting, or assisting the conduct of, research, as may be required for the purpose of providing the Secretary of State, in such form and at such times as may be prescribed, with such information relating to the provision of primary or secondary education in the authority's area as may be prescribed (s. 29(3)). In particular, the Secretary of State must exercise these powers so as to secure the provision of information relating to the provision of education for children with special educational needs (s. 29(4)). An LEA is also required to publish, at such time or times and in such manner as may be required by regulations, such information as may be so required with respect to its policy and arrangements in respect of any matter relating to primary or secondary education (s. 29(5)).

This section therefore imposes a number of obligations on LEAs: a requirement to produce such information as is prescribed in regulations (s. 29(5)), but also an obligation to respond to requests for information which the Secretary of State may require for his functions, either through regulations or merely through Departmental request or demand and without any need for Parliamentary endorsement.

As indicated above, it would be impossible to provide a list of the circumstances where the DfES requires information under the general and/or ad hoc powers, but an illustrative sample of regulations specifically aimed at information gathering would include:

- the Education (School Hours and Policies) (Information) Regulations 1989 (SI 1989 No. 398) but only in relation to Wales

- the Education (Information as to Provision of Education) (England) Regulations 1999 (SI 1999 No. 1066), as amended

- the Education (Pupil Information) (England) Regulations 2000 (SI 2002 No. 297), as amended

- the Education (School Performance Information) (England) Regulations 2001 (SI 2001 No. 3446)

- the Education (School Information) (England) Regulations 2002 (SI 2002 No. 2897)

- the Education (Special Educational Needs) (Information) Regulations 1994 (SI 1994 No. 1048)

- the Special Educational Needs (Provision of Information by Local Education Authorities) (England) Regulations 2001 (SI 2001 No. 2218)

- the Special Educational Needs (Provision of Information by Local Education Authorities) (Wales) Regulations 2002 (SI 2002 No. 157 (W 23)).

7.
ADMISSIONS,
EARLY YEARS,
INFORMATION

These are, though, regulations the primary purpose of which is to impose information-gathering obligations. The list does not include regulations in which information gathering is a secondary or ancillary purpose. For example, an LEA must forward any information the Secretary of State requests concerning exclusions (reg 7A of the Education (Pupil Exclusions and Appeals) Maintained Schools (England) Regulations 2002 (SI 2002 No. 3178)).

Information may also be required by the Secretary of State in response to general or individual grants, hence, where the Secretary of State makes a grant to an LEA under s. 14 of the 2002 Act, he may impose and most usually will, requirements on the grant recipient to provide certain information at certain times or on request.

And, of course, the Secretary of State is not the only body which will demand information from LEAs. For Ofsted inspections of the LEA, the latter is required: a) to provide HM Chief Inspector with such information as may be prescribed, in such format, at such notice, or at such times as may be prescribed (s. 38(6) of the Education Act 1997) (at the time of writing no regulations had been made); and b) to publish the inspection report and its action plan drawn up in response (s. 39(3) of the Education Act 1997).

The Education (Publication of Local Education Authority Inspection Reports) Regulations 1998 (SI 1998 No. 880) prescribe the manner and timing of such publication by LEAs in England and Wales. The original Ofsted *Framework for the Inspection of Local Education Authorities 1999, Appendix 2*, published by the Office of HM Chief Inspector in conjunction with the Audit Commission, gave a non-exhaustive list of 74 items of information that HM Chief Inspector for England required for an inspection of the LEA. That level of detail is now absent from the most recent guidance published by the Chief Inspector (*Framework for the Inspection of Local Education Authorities* January 2004), but, although it may not be explicit, it is implicit that such amounts of information, if not more when including statistics and information relating to Best Value, will still have to be produced to demonstrate the effectiveness of the LEA.

An LEA also clearly has duties to publish and provide information to schools, for example, the scheme of financial delegation for the schools the LEA maintains (s. 48 of the 1998 Act) and the publication of budget and outturn statements (s. 52 of the 1998 Act and see the Education (Budget Statements) (England) Regulations 2003 (S.I. 2003 No. 475) and the Education (Outturn Statements) (England) Regulations 2003 (SI 2003 No. 1153) and also chapter 6.D of this book). In the summer of 2003, DfES consulted on a revised 'Performance Data Framework for LEAs', in what turned out to be a generally welcomed attempt to set standards against which LEAs could judge their provision of data (theirs, schools', the QCA's and the department's) to schools. The exercise could be listed as an example of inter-agency good practice at a technical level, without the need for specific legislation but within the duties outlined above. The completed Framework was published in February 2004.

Finally, there are the obligations to a wider public, in part including the information considered above, but also including such matters as:

a) information to inform those qualified to stand and vote that parent governor representatives are to be elected to LEA committees wholly or partly for the purposes of education which are conferred on the LEA (s. 499(6) of the 1996 Act); and

b) the duty to publish statutory proposals in connection with the school organisation plan and proposals of significant changes to schools themselves (ss. 26, 28–29 and 31 of the 1998 Act).

4. Performance indicators

In what the Audit Commission has called 'the developing performance culture in local government', performance indicators (PIs) are now widely accepted. This was not always the case: the three Es, of economy, efficiency and effectiveness (s. 26 of the Local Government Act 1982) originally incurred suspicion, especially in education, where outcomes were held not to be susceptible to crude accountancy. Over time, however, the accountancy has become less crude and more selective. Even though numbers collected and collated in a reasonably objective spirit cannot define an educated person, or educated society, PIs and performance standards have become inevitable facts of local-government accountability, management and funding. A solidly-standardised foundation of measurable achievement is essential for systematic inspection by Ofsted as well as for the purposes of audit, financial and otherwise. Any remaining recusants can be rebuked by Socrates: the unexamined life is not worth living.

Following enactment of the Local Government Act 1999, the then Department for the Environment, Transport and the Regions issued on behalf of itself, the Audit Commission and the Home Office, *Best Value and Audit Commission Performance Indicators for 2000/2001: vol 1 The Performance Indicators*, in December 1999. This was the first combined guidance to local authorities on producing and publishing the now-complementary: (a) Best Value performance indicators (BVPIs) to be specified under s. 4 of the Act; and (b) Audit Commission performance indicators as prescribed by ss. 44 and 46 of the Audit Commission Act 1998 and based on experience of the preceding seven years.

The above book set out statutory guidance on BVPIs, under s. 5 of the 1999 Act, relating to England only (except in respect of housing, council-tax benefit and police and fire authorities), other matters being within the responsibility of the National Assembly for Wales. The first statutory order setting out the BVPIs, was the Local Government (Best Value) Performance Indicators Order 2000 (SI 2000 No. 896); it applied to England (and Wales, though not for LEAs in Wales, for whom the National Assembly legislates separately).

The most recent order, the Local Government (Best Value) Performance Indicators and Performance Standards Order 2003 (SI 2003 No. 530), covers all principal authorities and therefore LEAs, in England but only police and fire authorities in Wales. Though the general pattern is similar to that of the 2000 order, there has been rationalisation. In 2003, there were only 17 education PIs, as against 27 in the original order. The newer list (sched 3) covers: youth-service expenditure; vacant school places; early-years education; attainment in schools; timescale of SEN statementing; exclusions from school and tuition for excludees and schools in special measures.

Performance Indicator number 5 is 'How the authority's schools budget compares with its Schools Funding Assessment'. This is evidence of the huge cultural change in local government since the 1960s and 1970s, when the Government's unhypothecated grant to authorities was immune, in constitutional doctrine, to disaggregation; specific grant was anathema and education committees were suspected of an heretical yearning for pre-1958 percentage and specific grants for education. The theological metaphors are wholly appropriate here, but the orthodoxy has changed in the past five years across all local government and its services. See chapter 6.D for discussion of the present arrangements for education funding.

As in previous orders, that of 2003 reflects educational values not only in the 'education' schedule but also in: social services (sched 4), where two PIs relate to young people's attainments on leaving public care (on which, see chapter 9.H) and 'Cultural and Related Services' PIs (sched 13) include 'the number of pupils visiting museums and galleries in organised school groups'.

On Best Value, including recent policy developments, see also chapter 12.B.7.2.2. On comprehensive performance assessments, see chapter 12.B.8.

5. The significance and utility of information

There are considerable demands for good and timely information to enable the fulfilment of broad general duties such as those of the Secretary of State to promote the education of the people (s. 10 of the Education Act 1996); or to enable him to exercise his powers with a view to improving standards, encouraging diversity and increasing opportunities for choice (s. 11(2) of the Education Act 1996). Similarly, the LEA's broad duties to secure the provision of efficient education (s. 13 of the Education Act 1996) or of sufficient schools (s. 14) rely on an intelligence capacity without which planning is ineffective. But there are numerous specific duties (see, for example, those discussed in chapters 1, 2, 5 and 9), for which total mastery of the basic information is prerequisite.

The information and intelligence functions are an important element of what goes on; they are linked – arguably, very closely – with the exercise of political discretion and local democratic accountability and – by definition – with good management of services to pupils and their parents, adult learners, schools and other establishments. The managerial and the political are connected and both depend crucially on accurate factual intelligence.

LEAs also, and necessarily, have a strong relationship with the Government and, in Wales, with the National Assembly and their departments and agencies.

There must, however, be a concern that these information requirements are excessive or contained in too many disparate pieces of legislation. To be fair to the DfES, it appears keen to address these difficulties: see *Making a Difference: Reducing Red Tape and Bureaucracy in Schools*, DfES and Cabinet Office, March 2003 and *Trust in the Future: The Report of the Bureaucracy Task Force*, November 2002, which relates to the FE sector. There is a wholly laudable aspiration that information collection should be rationalised across departments and agencies of Government so that LEAs and schools should be asked for each item of information only once, the data then being pooled.

6. Information collection and disclosure

Once an LEA gains possession of information under the various obligations and powers, there arises the potentially trickier issue of what it can or cannot do with that information. That therefore brings us on to the subjects of freedom of information, data protection and, perhaps most importantly in the context of an LEA's functions, the ability to share data with other parts of 'its' authority and with other agencies.

6.1 Freedom of Information Act 2000

Consideration of the detail of the Freedom of Information Act could take up a book in its own right and does (see, for example, Birkinshaw (2001)) and the best freely-available guidance can be obtained from the Information Commissioner (*The Freedom of Information Act 2000: An Introduction, June 2003* (referred to in this section as 'the Guidance'), see www.dataprotection.gov.uk/dpr/foi.nsf). As the effects of the Act will be felt by local authorities and schools, especially from January 2005 onwards, it is important that we give some consideration to its impact on their work.

In summary, the Act creates two broad obligations on local authorities:

- first, the publication of schemes setting out what information they hold and how/where the information is available to an interested individual; and

- second, by giving an individual who makes a request for information the right (subject to certain exemptions) to be told whether the body holds such information and if it does, the right to have that information communicated to him. This individual right of access to information will be brought into force for all public authorities (including schools) in January 2005.

6.1.1 Publication schemes

Although in reality the secondary object of the Act, by dint of timetabling the requirement to produce a publication scheme has become the first priority for local authorities.

It is therefore the duty of every public authority (for the meaning of 'public authority' see below) to adopt and maintain a scheme which relates to the publication of information by the authority and have that scheme approved by the Information Commissioner (s. 19 (1)(a) of the Act). The authority must also then publish information in accordance with its scheme and from time to time ensure that it is reviewed (s. 19(1)(b) and (c)). The publication scheme must specify classes of information which the authority publishes or intends to publish, specify the manner in which information of each class is, or is intended to be, published and specify whether the material is, or is intended to be, available to the public free of charge or on payment (s. 19(2)). In adopting or reviewing a scheme, the authority must have regard to the public interest in allowing public access to information held by the authority and in the publication of reasons for decisions made by it (s. 19(3)).

'Public authorities' which are subject to the Act are defined in schedule 1 and include local authorities (thus including LEAs) and the governing bodies of maintained schools (s. 3 and schedule 1). The duties will also extend to 'publicly owned companies' which are companies having no members except for a public authority or companies owned by that public authority (s. 6). Companies wholly owned by LEAs or school governing bodies will therefore be caught by the Act.

Local authorities were obliged to adopt publication schemes from February 2003. The governing bodies of maintained schools had until 29 February 2004 to produce and obtain approval of their publication schemes.

To assist public authorities, whilst each may produce its own bespoke scheme, the Information Commissioner has power to approve model publication schemes (s. 20(1)). If an authority adopts such a model without modification, no further approval from the Information Commissioner is required (s. 20(2)).

Publication schemes, if those published to date are anything to go by, are intended to serve a useful purpose, even if their bulk and content may at times be off-putting to a casual reader. They may prove to be helpful in illustrating what an authority does and what information is available to the public. They may also assist members of the public in making requests for information and they may provide reasons for denying access where previous or future publication is a ground for refusing access (see ss. 21 and 22).

6.1.2   Right to information

From January 2005, any person making a request for information to a public authority is entitled (a) to be informed in writing by the authority whether it holds information of the description specified in the request ('the duty to confirm or deny') and (b) if that is the case, to have that information communicated to him (s. 1(1)).

A request must be in writing (including transmission by electronic means, e.g. e-mail or fax), be received in legible form, be capable of being used for subsequent reference and should state the name of the applicant and an address for correspondence and describe the information requested (s. 8). An LEA may charge a fee for complying with the request (s. 9 and subject to any regulations which may be made prescribing the circumstances in which fees may be charged and, if so, their level) and should comply with the request promptly and, in any event, not later than 20 working days following receipt of the request (s.10), although where a fee notice is issued, the period effectively runs from the date when the fee was paid (s.10(2)). An authority is also under a duty to provide such advice and assistance, so far as reasonable, to persons who have made, or propose to make, requests for information to it (s. 16). A public authority that complies with the Access Code in this respect is regarded as having complied with this duty.

The *Code of Practice on the discharge of public authorities'
functions under Part I of the Freedom of Information Act 2000*
(LCD November 2002), known as the Access Code, is one of two
codes of practice which have been issued by the Lord Chancellor
(ss. 45 and 46). It sets out the Lord Chancellor's views of desirable
practice for public authorities and covers:

* the provision of advice and assistance by public authorities to
  any applicant seeking information

* the transfer of requests by one public authority to another public
  authority which may hold the information

* consultation with anyone to whom the information relates or
  those likely to be affected by a disclosure of information

* the inclusion of terms relating to disclosure of information in
  contracts entered into by public authorities

* the provision of a complaints procedure.

The second Code, the *Code of Practice on the management of
records* (LCD November 2002), known as the Records Management
Code, sets out the Lord Chancellor's views on desirable practice for
keeping, management and destruction of records.

**7.
ADMISSIONS,
EARLY YEARS,
INFORMATION**

Unlike the educational Codes of Practice with which LEAs are
familiar, there is no express obligation on an authority to have
regard to these Codes. However, if it appears to the Information
Commissioner that the practice of a public authority does not
conform to either Code of Practice, he may give the authority a
written 'practice recommendation'. This must include reference to
the provisions of the Code with which the public authority's practice
does not conform and the steps which he considers should be taken
to conform (s. 48). A failure to comply with a practice
recommendation may lead to adverse comments in a report to
Parliament by the Commissioner. It may also indicate a failure on
the part of the public authority to comply with the Act; in which
case, the Commissioner may consider the enforcement powers
available to him (Guidance, para 4.2.3) which include the issue of
enforcement notices (s. 52).

The key issues for LEAs though will be the circumstances in which
they have to comply with a request for information. A public
authority may refuse to comply with a request for information only
in the following circumstances:

- where a statutory exemption applies;

- where the public authority reasonably requires further information to identify and locate the information requested and has requested such information but the applicant has failed to supply it (s. 1(3));

- where the request is vexatious (s.14(1)) – a request will not be vexatious just because it is difficult to see why the applicant would want the information requested, or because considerable effort is required to retrieve the information, notwithstanding that this might cause annoyance or embarrassment to the public authority in receipt of the request (Guidance, para 2.10);

- where the public authority has previously complied with an identical or substantially similar request from the same applicant and a reasonable time has not elapsed between compliance with the previous request and the making of the current request (s. 14(2)); or

- where the public authority estimates that the cost of complying with the request would exceed the 'appropriate limit' (ss. 12 and 13 – the limits will be prescribed by order).

The statutory exemptions fall into two categories: absolute and qualified.

The exemptions conferring an absolute exemption include:

- information accessible to the applicant by other means (s. 21)

- information supplied by, or relating to, bodies dealing with the security services (s. 23)

- personal information (s. 40)

- information provided in confidence (s. 41)

- information prohibited from disclosure (s. 44).

The list of qualified exemptions is longer and includes:

- information intended for future publication (s. 22)

- investigations and proceedings conducted by a public authority (s. 30)

- law enforcement (s. 31); audit functions (s. 33); health and safety (s. 38)

- personal information (part of s. 40)

- legal professional privilege (s. 42)

- commercial interests (s. 43).

If information falls within the absolute exemptions, as the name implies, the information need not be disclosed and, in many cases, the authority is not even required to confirm or deny whether the information exists. If information may be subject to a qualified exemption, the authority must consider first whether the exemption applies and, second, if it does, whether the public interest in maintaining the exemption or exclusion from the duty to confirm or deny outweighs the public interest in communicating information or confirming or denying that the authority has such information. This is known as 'the public interest test' (s. 2 and ss. 21– 44 and see, in particular, chapter 3 of the Guidance). The Information Commissioner's Guidance is likely to provide the best advice to LEAs on how these exemptions will be interpreted and applied.

The following glosses on absolute exemptions may prove helpful.

a) Information accessible to the applicant by other means (s. 21 and para 3.2.1 of the Guidance). This is not defined and will be a question of fact in each case. It is accessibility to the individual applicant which is important and information may be regarded as reasonably accessible even if it is accessible only on payment. Information which a public authority or another person is obliged by virtue of any enactment to communicate to members of the public on request (other than by making the information available for inspection) is to be taken as reasonably accessible to the applicant. If there is no statutory duty to communicate the information requested, or if the duty is only to make the information available for inspection, the availability of the information from the public authority on request can be regarded as 'reasonably accessible to the applicant' only if it is made available in accordance with the authority's publication scheme. The requirement for any payment must then be stated in the scheme.

b) Investigations and proceedings conducted by public authorities (s. 30 and para 3.2.9). Information held by a public authority is exempt information if it has, at any time, been held by the public authority for the purposes of an investigation of an offence or in relation to any criminal proceedings the authority has the power to conduct. This is possibly of limited relevance to the work of LEAs, but potentially applicable to education welfare investigations and non-attendance prosecutions.

c) Personal information (s. 40 and Guidance, para 3.2.19 and the Annex). This exemption applies to any information which constitutes personal data as defined by the Data Protection Act 1998 (and see below). This is likely therefore to be the most important exemption for local authorities. The information involved could be divided into two categories: personal data which relate to the individual who is applying for information (the data subject) and personal data which relate to an identifiable living individual other than the applicant.

d) Information provided in confidence (s. 41 and Guidance, para 3.2.20). Information is exempt information if: (a) it was obtained by the public authority from any other person, including another public authority and (b) the disclosure of that information to the public (otherwise than under the Act) by the public authority would constitute a breach of confidence actionable by any person.

The duty to confirm or deny does not arise if, or to the extent that, the confirmation or denial would constitute an actionable breach of confidence.

Information is exempt information under s. 41 only where it is obtained by the public authority from another person, including another public authority, under a duty of confidence. For the exemption to apply, it must still be an actionable breach of confidence to disclose the information at the time the application is made. The exemption will not apply where the information passes between different parts of the same public authority. Simply because a document is marked 'Confidential' does not mean that this exemption will apply. Information that is in the public domain or that is useless or trivial information will not be protected by the law of confidence.

An actionable breach of confidence will arise either under a contract or where no contract exists, where:

a) the material communicated had the necessary quality of confidence (in that it is of limited public availability and of specific character capable of clear definition);

b) it was communicated or became known to the original recipient in circumstances entailing an obligation of confidence; and

c) there has been an unauthorised use or disclosure of that material.

Information to which an obligation of confidence applies may, in certain circumstances, be disclosed by the recipient of the information where it is in the public interest to do so. Prohibitions on disclosure (s. 44 and Guidance, para 3.2.23) apply where disclosure of the information is prohibited by or under any enactment, is incompatible with any European Community obligation or would amount to contempt of court.

The qualified exemptions, which must be subject to the public interest test, include the following.

a) information intended for future publication (s. 22 and Guidance, para 3.2.2). This will apply where the information is held by a public authority with the intention that it or some other person will publish it in the future, whether or not the date for future publication has been determined; the information was already held with the intention of such publication at the time when the request for information was made and it is reasonable in all the circumstances that the information should be withheld from disclosure until such time as the information is published;

b) information relating to law enforcement (s. 31 and Guidance, para 3.2.10). This applies where disclosure might prejudice the investigation of crimes or the taking of other similar enforcement action;

c) audit functions (s. 33 and para 3.2.12). Information held for audit purposes is exempt if its disclosure would, or would be likely to, prejudice the exercise of any of the functions of a public authority in relation to the audit of accounts or the examination of the economy, efficiency and effectiveness with which it or other public authorities use their resources;

d) health and safety (s. 38 and para 3.2.17). Information is exempt information if its disclosure would, or would be likely to, endanger the physical or mental health or the safety of any individual;

e) legal professional privilege (s. 42 and para 3.2.21); and

f) commercial interests (s. 43 and para 3.2.22). Information is exempt if it constitutes a trade secret or if its disclosure under the Act would, or would be likely to, prejudice the commercial interests of any person, which includes the public authority holding it.

6.1.3 Dealing with requests for information

When a request for information is received, the authority must consider whether it should meet the request or refuse it. If it decides that it should refuse, the authority must:

a) where it considers the request to be vexatious, repeated or involving costs exceeding the appropriate limit, give the applicant a notice setting out the reasons for the refusal (s.17(5)). This must be done within the stipulated timescale for complying with the duties to confirm or deny and to communicate information; or

b) where the authority is relying to any extent upon a claim that one of the statutory exemptions applies, it must, within the timescale for complying with s. 1(1), give the applicant a notice which:

   (i) states that one of the exemptions in the Act relating to the duty to confirm or deny is relevant, or that the information is exempt information;

   (ii) specifies the exemption in question; and

   (iii) states (unless otherwise apparent) why the exemption applies (s. 17(1)).

In addition, where the public authority is obliged to apply the public interest test and has not yet reached a decision whether to confirm, deny or disclose, the notice must also state that no decision has been reached, together with an estimate as to the date by which the authority expects to have reached such a decision (s. 17(2)).

If a decision has been made as to the application of the public interest test, the notice (or a separate notice given within such time as is reasonable) must further state that the public interest in maintaining the exclusion of the duty to confirm or deny or in maintaining the exemption (as applicable) outweighs the public interest in disclosing whether the public authority holds the information, or in disclosing the information (s. 17(3)).

A public authority is not obliged to state why an exemption applies, having applied the public interest test, or why it has decided not to disclose or to refuse to confirm or deny if, or to the extent that, the statement would involve the disclosure of information which would itself be exempt information (s. 17(4)).

Notices refusing a request must set out the authority's complaints process and inform the applicant of his right to apply to the Information Commissioner for a decision notice (s. 17(7)).

6.2 Data Protection Act 1998

One of the key exemptions under the Freedom of Information Act 2000 concerns personal data held under the Data Protection Act 1998. That Act though, in its own right, imposes important obligations on LEAs and schools and, in turn, has important consequences when we consider the ability of LEAs and other public agencies to share such data.

Detailed consideration of the Act's provisions is beyond the scope of this work, but guidance can again be obtained from the Information Commissioner, in particular, *The Data Protection Act 1998 – Legal Guidance* which is available on the Information Commissioner's website, free of charge. There was much publicity late in 2003 to two stories. In the first, a police force was said – wrongly, as its chief constable subsequently acknowledged, though the initial statement excited much adverse commentary on the Act by the media – to have interpreted the Act so as to lead it to delete records of allegations of sexual attacks carried out by a man who later and as caretaker at a school in another area, murdered two young girls. The second story was of an elderly couple who were found to have died after their gas supply had been disconnected for non-payment; the gas supplier had assumed that the Act precluded it from informing the social services authority of the risk to the couple in cold weather. The implications of the first case were considered by the Bichard Inquiry, which reported on 22 June 2004 (www.bichardinquiry.org.uk). In the second, the Information Commissioner published a note relating to circumstances such as occurred in the gas-supply case and denied that there was a statutory obstacle to disclosure. But the Commissioner did promise *inter alia* to issue 'more practical and user friendly guidance for organisations' and an improved data protection helpline (press release, 14 January 2004).

6.2.1 Summary

In summary, the Act requires that anyone (not just public authorities) must, when processing personal data or sensitive personal data, comply with the eight data protection principles (schedule 1 to the Data Protection Act 1998). These are that data must be:

1. fairly and lawfully processed;

2. processed for limited purposes;

3. adequate, relevant and not excessive;

4. accurate;

5. not kept for longer than necessary;

6. processed in accordance with the data subject's rights;

7. secure; and

8. not transferred to countries without adequate protection.

The first principle applies to those processing 'personal data'. This is defined as data which relate to a living individual who can be identified from those data, or from those data and other information in, or likely to come into, the possession of, the data controller. It includes any expression of opinion about the individual and any indication of the intentions of the data controller or any other person in respect of the individual (s. 1 of the Act). It should be noted, however, that the mere mention of a data subject in a document does not necessarily amount to personal data (see *Durant v Financial Services Authority* [2003] EWCA Civ 1746 – a very recent judgment which contains important guidance on the whole area and the implications of which, at the time of writing, were still being considered).

7.
ADMISSIONS,
EARLY YEARS,
INFORMATION

A further, more restricted, type of data under the Act is 'sensitive personal data'. This comprises information as to:

- the racial or ethnic origin of the data subject;

- his or her political opinions;

- religious beliefs or beliefs of a similar nature;

- membership of a trade union or non-membership;

- physical or mental health or condition;

- sexual life;

- the commission or alleged commission of an offence; or

- proceedings for a committed or allegedly committed offence (s. 2).

Ensuring compliance with the second to eighth data protection principles (which are set out in full in schedule 1 to the Act) is obviously of importance – but the biggest current issue facing authorities which handle sensitive personal information tends to be the sharing, or in the Act's terms processing, of personal data or information.

6.2.2 Data sharing

The distinction between personal data and sensitive personal data becomes important when considering the processing of the data. Under the first data protection principle, personal data must be processed fairly and lawfully and, in particular, shall not be processed unless at least one of the conditions in sched 2 to the Act is met and, further, in the case of sensitive personal data, at least one of the conditions in sched 3 is met.

The menu of six conditions, any or all of which are applicable under schedule 2, is listed below.

1. The data subject has given his consent.

2. The processing is necessary:
    a) for the performance of a contract to which the data subject is a party; or
    b) for the taking of steps at the request of the data subject with a view to entering into a contract.

3. The processing is necessary for compliance with any legal obligation to which the data controller is subject, other than an obligation imposed by contract.

4. The processing is necessary in order to protect the vital interests of the data subject.

5. The processing is necessary:
    a) for the administration of justice;
    b) for the exercise of any functions conferred on any person by or under any enactment;
    c) for the exercise of any functions of the Crown, a Minister of the Crown or a Government department; or
    d) for the exercise of any other functions of a public nature exercised in the public interest by any person.

6. The processing is necessary for the purposes of legitimate interests pursued by the data controller or by the third party or parties to whom the data are disclosed, except where the processing is unwarranted in any particular case by reason of prejudice to the rights and freedoms or legitimate interests of the data subject.

The menu of ten further additional conditions, any or all of which are applicable under schedule 3, is listed below.

1. The data subject has given his explicit consent to the processing of the personal data.

2. The processing is necessary for the purposes of exercising or performing any right or obligation which is conferred or imposed by law on the data controller in connection with employment.

3. The processing is necessary:
   a) in order to protect the vital interests of the data subject or another person, in a case where:
      i. consent cannot be given by or on behalf of the data subject; or
      ii. the data controller cannot reasonably be expected to obtain the consent of the data subject; or
   b) in order to protect the vital interests of another person, in a case where consent by or on behalf of the data subject has been unreasonably withheld.

4. The processing:
   a) is carried out in the course of its legitimate activities by any body or association which:
      i. is not established or conducted for profit, and
      ii. exists for political, philosophical, religious or trade-union purposes;
   b) is carried out with appropriate safeguards for the rights and freedoms of data subjects;
   c) relates only to individuals who either are members of the body or association or have regular contact with it in connection with its purposes; and
   d) does not involve disclosure of the personal data to a third party without the consent of the data subject.

5. The information contained in the personal data has been made public as a result of steps deliberately taken by the data subject.

6. The processing:
   a) is necessary for the purpose of, or in connection with, any legal proceedings (including prospective legal proceedings);
   b) is necessary for the purpose of obtaining legal advice; or
   c) is otherwise necessary for the purposes of establishing, exercising or defending legal rights.

7. The processing is necessary:
   a) for the administration of justice;

**7.
ADMISSIONS,
EARLY YEARS,
INFORMATION**

b) for the exercise of any functions conferred on any person by or under an enactment; or

c) for the exercise of any functions of the Crown, a Minister of the Crown or a government department (the Secretary of State may exclude this condition in prescribed circumstances).

8. The processing is necessary for medical purposes and is undertaken by:

a) a health professional;

b) a person who in the circumstances owes a duty of confidentiality which is equivalent to that which would arise if that person were a health professional. ('Medical purposes' includes the purposes of preventative medicine, medical diagnosis, medical research, the provision of care and treatment and the management of healthcare services.)

9. The processing:

a) is of sensitive personal data consisting of information as to racial or ethnic origin;

b) is necessary for the purpose of identifying or keeping under review the existence or absence of equality of opportunity or treatment between persons of different racial or ethnic origins, with a view to enabling such equality to be promoted or maintained; and

c) is carried out with appropriate safeguards for the rights and freedoms of data subjects.

10. The personal data are processed in circumstances specified in an order made by the Secretary of State.

Guidance on these conditions can be found in the Information Commissioner's Guidance (see para 3.13 for sensitive personal data).

6.3 Obstacles to information sharing?

Significant issues for LEAs and what are increasingly becoming seen as a potential fetter on the legitimate sharing of personal data, are the duties which are apparently imposed under the legislation considered above, the common law duty of confidence and, potentially, the Human Rights Act 1998. Add onto these the question of the rights of the data subject and the powers under which authorities are able to share information, then combine it with a considerable degree of misunderstanding, myth and, on occasion, absence of plain common sense and it is not hard to see why this area has become incredibly complex. If, however, the complexity cannot be overcome, it is an area with potentially significant and tragic effects.

> 'Throughout this Inquiry it was said repeatedly that when there is professional concern about the welfare of a child, the free exchange of information is inhibited by the Data Protection Act 1998, the Human Rights Act 1998 and common law rules on confidentiality. The evidence put to the Inquiry was that unless a child is deemed to be in need of protection, information cannot be shared between agencies without staff running the risk that their actions are unlawful. This either deters information sharing, or artificially elevates concern about the need for protection - each of which is not compatible with serving well the needs of children and families. Clearly these matters are complicated. There must be a balance struck between the protection of a child and the right to privacy.'
>
> (The Victoria Climbié Inquiry Report, January 2003 (Cm 5730), para 17.115)

The Inquiry report therefore pressed the Government to 'issue guidance on the Data Protection Act 1998, the Human Rights Act 1998 and common law rules on confidentiality. The Government should issue guidance as and when these impact on the sharing of information between professional groups in circumstances where there are concerns about the welfare of children and families' (recommendation 16).

These recommendations were picked up in the Green Paper *Every Child Matters*, which focuses on information sharing between agencies (see section 4 'Early Intervention and Effective Protection'). The answer put forward in the Green Paper is the integration of information across services, to ensure that professionals share concerns about children at an early stage, through the development of local information hubs in every authority. This 'hub' will consist of a list of all the children living in an authority's area and include basic details about these children (see paras 4.3–4.12). The information should, it is intended, follow national standards to enable the full exchange of information and avoid breakdowns because of variations in information stored or incompatibility of systems. An agency coming into contact with a child would then be able to check the list of information about him or her. It is further hoped that information recording concerns about particular children could be flagged. Though there is something Orwellian about systems holding records for every child in an authority's area – the Green Paper does not say what happens to this sensitive data when a child reaches adulthood – there clearly have been instances in the past of children slipping through the net and, hopefully, these hubs if fully and properly implemented might avoid this in the future. 'Trailblazing' identification, referral and tracking projects are being tested in 15 local authorities and the Green Paper proposes steps to remove the legal and technical barriers to effective information sharing systems.

Chapter 4 of the Green Paper, 'Early Intervention and Effective Protection', focuses on the need for improved sharing of information between professionals and across different services to facilitate better joint working in the interests of children. It promises:

> "The government intends to legislate at the first opportunity to enable information sharing to happen at an earlier stage to prevent problems escalating. In anticipation of legislative change, in August 2003 we issued guidance on how to apply current legislation.'

The guidance alluded to is that issued by the Children and Young People's Unit (CYPU) at DfES (see the preceding section of this chapter). As will be seen from this chapter, legal obstacles to information sharing are sometimes more apparent than real. In most cases where common sense dictates information should be shared a legal justification for such action can be found, although its location in statute or regulations differs according to the professional group(s) concerned. However, greater attention has been paid to recent legislation designed to protect individual rights and limit inappropriate disclosure of confidential information. The complexity of the position, combined with natural caution on the part of those called upon to give legal advice, has led to a tendency to err on the side of confidentiality. There is also some truth in the contention that administrative inertia or professional resistance to collaboration has been cloaked in the language of legal difficulties.

The first print of the 2004 Children Bill contained no amendments to the Data Protection Act or Human Rights Act. As noted above and below, there are already sufficient exceptions in this legislation to allow information sharing in appropriate circumstances and to weaken it further would be neither acceptable nor effective. A more likely approach is to look at the legislation governing the actions and responsibilities of the various professional groups who come into contact with children. Much of the genuine (as opposed to perceived) legal difficulty arises from the limited scope and inconsistent framing of specific legislation applying to different functions and services. Thus medical practitioners will be confident in their dealings with the health authority and schools know what information can be provided to the LEA, but there is less clarity over what information could, or should, be shared between doctors and teachers.

'Information sharing' is a prominent feature of the Bill. Clause 8 for England and clause 23 for Wales are separate only because the administrative structures existing or proposed for the two countries differ. The principles relating to data are the same. The Secretary of State (or NAW) will be empowered: (a) to make regulations by which children's services authorities (LEAs/social services authorities) will set up and operate databases; or (b) to operate or establish a quango to operate one or more databases. The regulations are to cover the type of data, its input and disclosure and authorities' duties to participate in the operation of any national database. The regulations will also safeguard users against common law liability for disclosing specified types of data otherwise falling within the duty of professional confidentiality. In addition, the Secretary of State or NAW may give guidance or direction on, for example, technical specifications or security of a database.

Although this legislation is pending, a number of changes to the machinery of government that will have an impact on local authorities are already being implemented (see also chapters 9 and 11). A single focus on children's issues has been created within the DfES under a new Director General for Children and Families. The new Directorate starting from relevant DfES units (Sure Start, CYPU, Connexions, etc) has absorbed staff and functions relating to children's social services from the Department of Health and the family policy and teenage pregnancy units from the Home Office (although youth justice remains separate). The most significant outcome in relation to information exchange is the merger of three previously separate governmental initiatives. These are:

- CCIS – the Connexions Customer Information System (the 'tracking' aspect of Connexions set up after the social inclusion unit report *Bridging the Gap* and formerly the responsibility of DfES Youth Directorate);

- ICS – The Integrated Children's System (a project sponsored by DoH to define a standard data set and approach to record keeping for use by children's social services); and

- IRT – Identification, Referral and Tracking (the approach to information sharing outlined in chapter 4 of *Every Child Matters*, previously being developed by the CYPU as part of the Children at Risk strategy; now called Information Sharing and Assessment (ISA)).

In future these will be managed together. The new legislation (primary and subordinate) to facilitate information exchange may therefore build on ss. 117, 119 and 120 of the Learning and Skills Act 2000, which empower the Connexions service to gather information about 13–19 year-olds from various sources, in order to establish a national register of clients for its services.

The concerns set out in the Green Paper were not, however, new. Prompted by earlier fears about public data sharing, the Performance and Innovation Unit (PIU) in the Cabinet Office had produced a report in April 2002 *(Privacy and Data Sharing – The way forward for public services)*, outlining the main issues and making recommendations. The Lord Chancellor's Department or, as it has now become, the Department for Constitutional Affairs, was given the responsibility for implementing those recommendations too, although, again, at the time of writing it has yet to do so. The former Children and Young People's Unit in the DfES has, however, issued its own guidance, which is helpful and fills at least part of the gap in government advice. This guidance comprises three documents: *IRT: Information Sharing to Improve Services for Children – Guidance on Information Sharing*; *IRT: Guidance on Information Sharing and Information Sharing Protocols* and *IRT: Information Sharing to Improve Services for Children – Technical Issues Report* (all accessible at www.dfes.gov.uk/publications/key).

This guidance demonstrated that the Trailblazer projects had already run ahead of the slightly simplistic model outlined in the Green Paper before it was published. The projects quickly rejected the notion of a massive central database containing a full record on every child. This would not only be technically difficult and expensive but would raise genuine concerns about large numbers of people having access to sensitive information. The function of the 'hub' would be to facilitate communication between professionals working with the same child and to ensure that no individuals fall through the net – particularly when families move within and between areas. This would require only minimal information to be held centrally – name, age address and unique identifier(s) (e.g. NHS number) and contact details for a key worker if allocated. All sensitive case information would continue to be held and controlled by individual professionals and agencies and shared bilaterally only if and when appropriate.

One solution which has been considered is that legislation may be introduced permitting certain specified data sharing; the PIU recommendation was that there should be such legislation to give authorities the power to share personal data with the consent of the individual concerned. With respect, that may not solve the problem and could make it worse. Currently there are arguments for saying (and some of these are set out below) that local authorities, despite what any Cabinet Office report or the Information Commissioner may say, have wide powers to share information where it is in the public interest to do so, with or without the consent of the data subject. Introducing specific legislation would therefore (a) not make any difference to this situation, (b) might suggest that any sharing outside the specified circumstances might make illegal what had been otherwise permissible data sharing and (c) in many cases, the problem is that the consent of the data subject cannot be obtained and requiring it might frustrate the proper sharing of information where, again, the public interest would demand it.

Nonetheless, it must be recognised that, relevant personal and sensitive personal data is likely to be held by authorities subject to duties of confidence and/or [but most probably 'and'] subject to duties under the Data Protection Act. There may also be human rights issues for, if the information is disclosed, there might arguably be an infringement of an individual's right to have their private and family life respected.

Consequently, to be able to process that information (i.e. pass it onto another person) an authority is going to have to show that:

a) it has the power to do so and, where the data subject does not consent (in the case of personal data) or explicitly consent (for sensitive personal data);

b) in doing so it does not breach the duty of confidence;

c) it does not infringe the right of that person to have their private and family life respected or, if it does, that the infringement is justified and proportionate; and

d) it does not infringe a data protection principle (especially the first principle, that of fair processing).

As noted above, the Children Bill (at clauses 8(7) for England and 23(7) for Wales) seeks to over-ride the common law duty of confidence by providing for regulations explicitly permitting disclosure upon the exercise of professional judgment. As the Bill proceeds through Parliament, these clauses are likely to be keenly debated and will probably be much amended.

6.4 Powers

In her *Advice Note – Local Authorities and Data Sharing* (February 2001), the then Information Commissioner summarised the position as:

> 'For public bodies such as local authorities […] if personal data are processed for purposes which are prohibited by statute or which are ultra vires then that processing will automatically breach the First Data Protection Principle. Similarly, if personal data are processed in breach of an obligation of confidence (which would be unlawful) then that processing would also breach the First Data Protection Principle.
>
> The issue for a local authority is, therefore, whether it has the powers to process personal data obtained for one statutory purpose for another purpose, or whether it is prevented from doing so by virtue of an obligation of confidence or any statutory prohibition on processing (including disclosure).'

The question of powers or *vires* to pass on information has therefore troubled the Information Commissioner and was of concern to the PIU. Clearly, where there are express statutory powers to pass information, no issue should arise. The *vires* will be apparent; it should be in the public interest to disclose it (Parliament has effectively said so); it is likely to be permitted under the Data Protection Act and as long as the action is proportionate, there should be no Human Rights Act breach. An example is s. 115 of the Crime and Disorder Act 1998 which authorises any person to provide information to the police, local authorities, probation authorities and health authorities in connection with the purposes of that Act.

Unfortunately, there is a woeful lack of express power in legislation, hence the PIU recommendation for the Lord Chancellor/Secretary of State for Constitutional Affairs to create some. However, even where there are no express powers, it is suggested that other powers may be available to an authority and the problem may not be as great as perhaps the Information Commissioner or PIU suggest. As the CYPU guidance helpfully points out, the law should not be seen as a barrier to the proper sharing of necessary information to protect children. And see above, on the 'information sharing' provisions of the Children Bill.

The courts, at least, appear already to have recognised the danger of imposing overly technical and bureaucratic barriers. For example, in *R (A) v Hertfordshire County Council* [2001] ELR 666, [2001] All

ER (D) 259, the Court of Appeal accepted that there was implied statutory power to share data under the Children Act 1989. In that case, the local authority had notified the director of education that there was reasonable cause for suspecting that a particular headteacher posed a risk of significant harm to children in his care. Section 47 of the Children Act provides that where a local authority has reasonable cause to suspect that a child in its area is suffering or is likely to suffer significant harm, the authority shall carry out enquiries to enable it to decide whether it should take action to safeguard or promote the child's welfare. Where 'as a result of any such inquiries, it appears to the authority that there are matters connected with the child's education which should be investigated, [it] shall consult the relevant LEA' (s. 47(5)). The court considered that it was necessarily implicit in s. 47(1) of the Children Act 1989 that the LEA, in making enquiries in the performance of its duty under s. 47 of that Act, was entitled to conclude that a particular individual presented a risk of significant harm to children in its area. The LEA had the power to communicate that conclusion by implication from the responsibilities conferred on local authorities for the welfare and protection of children. Keene LJ (at [2001] ELR p 677) stated that he considered that the general duties under the Children Act gave rise to 'a power to communicate such a belief [i.e. about a child's welfare] where the authority genuinely and reasonably believes that such a step is necessary to protect children in its area from the risk of sexual abuse, but where it does not need to go so far as to seek a court order.'

The decision therefore suggest that the courts will be willing to read implied powers into the legislation, particularly where there is a pressing social need that data be shared.

Even if this is not to be the case, it is suggested that s. 111(1) of the Local Government Act 1972 could also provide the necessary powers in certain situations. The section states:

'Without prejudice to any powers exercisable apart from this section but subject to the provisions of this Act and any other enactment passed before or after this Act, a local authority shall have power to do any thing (whether or not involving the expenditure, borrowing or lending of money or the acquisition or disposal of any property or rights) which is calculated to facilitate, or is conducive or incidental to, the discharge of any of their functions.'

Is not data sharing incidental to much of what an LEA does? The difficulty with using this section, however, is the fact that it is subject to any other enactment, which would include the Data Protection Act. Utilising this provision to share information would therefore be possible only where it did not conflict with the Act.

In addition, a local authority also has power under s. 2 of the Local Government Act 2000 to promote well-being, including the power to do anything which it considers is likely to achieve, amongst other aims, the promotion or improvement of the social well-being of its area (s. 2(1)(b)), which must, it is suggested, include the protection of children for whom it is or may be responsible. This power, like s. 111, does not enable an authority to do anything which it is unable to do by virtue of any prohibition, restriction or limitation on its powers which is contained in any enactment, whenever passed or made (s. 2(1)). That would, again, include the Data Protection Act where it is relevant.

The key therefore tends to be that implied powers can be found so long as they do not conflict with other legislation, including the DPA. That might lead to some degree of circularity, but, given the court's position in the *Hertfordshire* case, it is likely that in the majority of cases where, for legitimate reasons, LEAs need to share information they will have either the express or implied power to do so.

6.5 Duty of confidence

The second potential problem is whether LEAs owe duties of confidence in respect of information in their possession. As has been seen, in summary, a duty is owed where a person receives information in circumstances where he knows or can be taken to know that the information is to be treated as confidential. This creates a legal duty to respect the confidentiality of the information provided and not disclose it to anyone else without the consent of the person to whom the duty is owed or where the overriding public interest requires it. Inherent within the duty and any decision to disclose is a duty to act reasonably and in a manner that is proportionate to the authority's objective. Thus any disclosure must not be to any greater extent (both in terms of the amount of information disclosed or the number of people to whom the information is communicated) than is necessary in the interests of the child or other person in whose interests the authority is acting.

This common law duty will be overridden by any express statutory duty to disclose information, for example, to help in the detection of crime or to prevent serious harm to a child, including, for example, the duty to co-operate with a local authority making enquiries under

s. 47 of the Children Act or the duty under s. 115 of the Crime and Disorder Act 1998. The principle is also enshrined in the Children Bill (see above).

As examples of the operation of the overriding public interest, decisions of the Court of Appeal are of help. In *Re L* (1999) 1 LGLR 316, a local authority asked for the court's permission in care proceedings to disclose the address of a known child abuser who operated as a football coach to a football club and its league. Here, the Court of Appeal held that the authority's duty of confidence was not outweighed by the public interest in passing that information on. In contrast, in *Woolgar v Chief Constable of Sussex Police* [2000] 1 WLR 25, (2000) 2 LGLR 340, the Court of Appeal allowed police to disclose to a registered nurse's professional body details of an interview conducted following the death of a patient. In the latter case, the court felt the public interest did outweigh the police's duty of confidence.

6.6 Human rights

As to Human Rights Act implications, here too, the courts have adopted what seems to be a sensible and workable solution which enables consistency to be found between this issue and that of confidentiality and data protection. Article 8(1) of the European Convention (incorporated through the Human Rights Act 1998) provides that everyone has the right to respect for his private and family life. The right is qualified so that 'There shall be no interference by a public authority with the exercise of this right except such as is in accordance with the law and is necessary in a democratic society in the interests of national security, public safety or the economic well-being of the country, for the prevention of disorder or crime, for the protection of health or morals, or for the protection of the rights and freedoms of others' (Article 8(2)).

It is important to note that the concept of private life extends to aspects of a person's relationship with others and can include a person's business activity. Disclosing of private or confidential information is therefore likely to bring article 8 into play. Consequently to justify disclosure under Article 8(2) an LEA will need to show that it is in accordance with the law and is necessary for one of the stated reasons. The disclosure will also have to be proportionate, i.e. there will need to be a balancing exercise, weighing the individual's rights against the public interest – and so, in reality, the same balancing exercise will apply for both confidentiality and human rights issues - and any disclosure should be only to the extent that is necessary.

As the CYPU Guidance states (at para 42):

'There are of course many circumstances where the fact that someone's right to privacy would be infringed must not be allowed to prevent you from taking appropriate action. If for example you suspect that a child is being mistreated by a member of his family you may have a duty to intervene to protect the child. This will inevitably interfere with the person's privacy and respect for his family life. But the circumstances clearly justify the interference.'

LEAs should also be aware of Article 2, which protects a person's right to life and Article 3, which provides that no one should be subjected to torture or inhuman or degrading treatment. These impose positive obligations. In some circumstances, therefore, not disclosing information which could prevent this type of 'abuse' could place an LEA in breach of the Human Rights Act. Certainly, if this is the situation, reliance on these articles should demonstrate that the disclosure is proportionate for Article 8 purposes.

6.7 Conclusion: a beam of light through a grey area

The social workers who dealt with Victoria Climbié were wrong. Although the Climbié Inquiry recognised that there was confusion and misunderstanding, it is suggested that that was due more to the policies and attitudes adopted by the social services staff involved. For once, the law should probably not take the blame for preventing the proper exchange of information for, as we have seen, the obstacles are more perceived than real.

All three issues are closely interrelated – if an authority complies with the Data Protection Act it will meet its obligations of confidentiality and will not infringe the Human Rights Act. Similarly, what is permissible under the Human Rights Act will be lawful under the Data Protection Act and should not breach any duty of confidence. Apart from the cases already mentioned, when challenges are brought in the courts all three issues tend to have arisen on the same facts. When these cases have reached the courts, pragmatic approaches appear to have been taken which tend in the main to be supportive of necessary information sharing.

For example, in *R v Chief Constable of North Wales Police ex p AB & CD* [1998] 3 WLR 57, [1998] 3 All ER 310, [1998] 2 FLR 571, the police became aware that two male sex offenders had, after being released from prison, rented a caravan on a North Wales site. Reports from another police force and probation services were that the men were extremely dangerous so, after a meeting with social services, the men were told that the site owner would be told if they did not move on. They did not move and the police informed the site owner. Of course, the convictions were in the public domain although the report from the other police force was known to be incorrect in some respects. The Court of Appeal held that whilst the men should have been given the opportunity to respond to the incorrect report, North Wales Police had acted reasonably. The court considered Article 8, but concluded that, especially in light of the reasonable actions of the police officers concerned, the infringement of the men's rights was justified and the action proportionate.

In *R v A local authority in the Midlands ex p LM* [2000] FLR 612, (2000) 2 LGLR 1043, QBD, however, Dyson J held that, on the facts, disclosure of information would be irrational. In that case, a man was seeking a contract with an LEA to run a school bus service. Allegations of sex abuse had been made against the man seven and ten years before. Police had interviewed him but no proceedings had ever been brought but the fact that those allegations had been made was disclosed to the LEA. Dyson J, following the Court of Appeal decision in the North Wales case, set out his guiding principles for the exercise of the power to disclose:

> 'Each of the […] authorities had to consider the case on its own facts. A blanket approach was impermissible. Having regard to the sensitivity of the issues raised by the allegations of sexual impropriety made against LM, disclosure should be the exception and not the rule. That is because the consequences of disclosure of such information for the subject of the allegations can be very damaging indeed. The facts of this case show how disclosure can lead to loss of employment and social ostracism, if not worse [...] The same principle applies regardless of the identity of the person or persons to whom disclosure is to be made.'

Applying that test, the judge concluded that disclosure should not have been made. Even if the correct test had been applied, though, Dyson J considered that the decision to disclose would have been unlawful: 'Disclosures of allegations of child sex abuse can have grave consequences and so there must be real and cogent evidence of a pressing need for disclosure.' In the case, there was no such evidence and so the decision to disclose was held to be unlawful.

Although that decision is highly relevant to LEAs, it should be considered as relating purely to its facts. It did not say that disclosure could never be achieved; instead, it laid down a test which had to be applied in each case.

As an example and in contrast to ex p LM, in *R v the Chief Constables of C and D ex p A* [2001] 1 WLR 461, QBD, Turner J allowed similar disclosure. There A was a homosexual schoolteacher about whom complaints had been made concerning his conduct towards pupils. This led to police investigations but not to criminal proceedings. He applied for a post with an LEA and was provisionally offered a job. During the vetting checks, however, the police passed details of the previous police investigations to the LEA. The offer of employment was then withdrawn. The judge held that the Data Protection Act did not prevent the disclosure, which would in any event have been permitted under one of the conditions in sched 3. The challenge was against the decision of the police forces, not the LEA in relying on that information. This somewhat technical distinction allowed the judge to find that there had been no infringement of the teacher's rights when the information was passed by the police to another public body. If the challenge had been made to the LEA's decision to rely on the information, the judge stated:

> 'There cannot be the slightest doubt that the education authority had a lawful interest and a "pressing" need to receive the information which was in the possession of the County police since it was or could be important as affecting the decision which it was required to make. In one sense, the education authority was the body qualified to decide what, if anything, it would make of the information with which it was being provided. If it was uncertain about the strength of the complaints and needed to know more in order that it could make an informed decision, it was always at liberty to ask for assistance from that communicating police force for its opinion about that matter. It would thereafter be for it [i.e. the LEA] to decide whether, or to what extent, the non-conviction material should inform its decision. Before it did, it would, of course, have to provide the applicant with at least the gist of that information and offer him the opportunity to make representations about it.'

This whole area is complex and confusion amongst practitioners is perhaps understandable. But, in practice, as long as the relevant and correct questions are asked and answered (and preferably recorded so the rationale for disclosure can subsequently be produced if challenged), the task is not as difficult or frustrating as might otherwise appear.

The recommendations of the Green Paper, if practically achievable, should go some way to address the difficulties by removing the actual or perceived legal barriers (see para 4.8 of Cm 5860). In the meantime, where LEAs wish to disclose information and the data subject has not provided the necessary consent, it needs to answer the following questions.

1. Under what powers is it acting when disclosing this information?

2. Do these powers provide express authority to disclose or, if not, can that authority be implied?

3. Is it personal data or sensitive personal data? If so, do one of the conditions in schedule 2 and, if necessary, schedule 3 of the Data Protection Act apply?

4. Is it held in confidence? If so, is disclosure in the public interest and is the disclosure proposed proportionate?

5. Is disclosure going to infringe the data subject's right to have his or her private or family life respected? If so, is the action lawful, justified and proportionate?

Provided LEAs do so and ensure that their staff are aware of the steps they need to go through, it is hoped that the legal issues in this field should not impose an undue burden or even a barrier to the proper disclosure of information which should be shared in the public interest.

8. SPECIAL EDUCATIONAL NEEDS AND DISABILITY DISCRIMINATION

A. Special Educational Needs (SEN)

1. Introduction

Of all areas of LEA responsibility, the most litigated must be the field of special educational needs (SEN). Partly because of the specific and individual nature of the duties owed, partly because of effective campaigning organisations, the legislation relating to children with SEN has been closely and frequently examined by the courts.

Although the Human Rights Act 1998 has not brought the spate of litigation some pessimists expected, the changes brought about by the Special Educational Needs and Disability Act 2001 have heightened awareness of the rights of these children and their parents and have imposed further obligations on LEAs. At the time of writing the effect of these changes had not become fully apparent, but there is no doubt that the duties imposed on LEAs both in terms of SEN provision and, more particularly, disability discrimination are likely to raise the prospect of an increasing number of claims being brought by parents. One optimistic aim in the Special Educational Needs and Disability Act 2001 is the introduction of compulsory dispute resolution which may at least reduce the number of appeals proceeding to the Special Educational Needs and Disability Tribunal (SENDIST). The change of name from 'SEN Tribunal' was made by s.17 of the 2001 Act, inserting a new s. 28H into the Disability Discrimination Act 1995.

A separate Tribunal operates in Wales, the Tribiwynlys Anghenion Addysgol Arbennig Cymru or the Special Educational Needs Tribunal for Wales (s. 336ZA of the Education Act 1996) – in this section, references to SENDIST will include references to the Welsh Tribunal.

Special educational provision, however budgets may be allocated, delegated or apportioned by LEAs, affects a significant number of pupils. As at January 2003, some 17 per cent of pupils had SEN; this comprised 14 per cent who did not have SEN statements and three percent who were statemented. SEN therefore will continue to be a key function of the LEA, albeit one which may be considered for inclusion within care trusts or children's trusts given the interrelationship between these particular children's educational, health and social service needs.

The importance of this field has therefore correctly been recognised by Ofsted in identifying special educational provision as one of its five groups of functions (*Framework for the Inspection of Local Education Authorities*, January 2004, para 22). In the first edition of our book, the authors took issue with Ofsted for including within special educational provision looked-after children and joint working with Social Services to improve the educational attainment of looked-after children. That ceased to be the case with the January 2002 Framework for LEA Inspection and under the current framework (2004) children in public care are considered under social inclusion (para 33). The importance of addressing the needs of looked-after children is therefore correctly emphasised, but it is no longer assumed that, almost by definition, these children have SEN. It is pleasing to see that Ofsted now deals with these children under the same heading as we did. Similarly, the authors questioned whether the management of pupil referral units should have been included by Ofsted under the special educational provision heading. The 2002 framework included this provision within its heading of 'promoting social inclusion', changed to 'support for school inclusion' in the 2004 version.

For Ofsted purposes, with which the authors are now in agreement, the areas of LEAs' support for SEN to be examined (see paras 30 and 31 of the Ofsted 2004 Framework) are as follows:

- the effectiveness of the LEA's strategy for SEN

- the effectiveness of the LEA in meeting its statutory obligations in respect of SEN

- the effectiveness of the LEA in exercising its SEN functions to support school improvement

- the extent to which the LEA has exercised its SEN functions to secure value for money.

The various aspects of these responsibilities will be considered in this chapter. In addition, it will examine the additional obligations placed on LEAs under the Disability Discrimination Act 1995 (as amended by Special Educational Needs and Disability Act 2001) as those duties, though separate and applicable to children without SEN, will to a certain extent overlap with special educational provision.

8.
SPECIAL
EDUCATIONAL
NEEDS

2.   Definitions

A child has SEN for the purposes of the 1996 Act if he has a learning difficulty which calls for special educational provision to be made for him (s. 312(1)). A child has a learning difficulty if either:

a)   he has a significantly greater difficulty in learning than a majority of children of his age,

b)   he has a disability which either prevents or hinders him from making use of educational facilities of a kind generally provided for children of his age within the area of the LEA, or

c)   he is under compulsory school age and is, or would be if special educational provision were not made for him, likely to fall within (a) or (b) when of that age (s. 312(2) of the Education Act 1996).

Special educational provision means (a) in relation to a child who has attained the age of two, educational provision which is additional to, or otherwise different from, the educational provision made generally for children of his age in schools maintained by the LEA and (b) in relation to a child under that age, educational provision of any kind (s. 312(4)).

An exceptionally gifted child does not have SEN simply by reason of being intellectually abler than his or her peers. Only where a gifted child has learning difficulties such as dyslexia will such a child have SEN within the 1996 Act (see *R v Secretary of State for Education ex p C* [1996] ELR 93).

8.
SPECIAL
EDUCATIONAL
NEEDS

3.   The Code of Practice

In exercising their functions in respect of children with SEN, LEAs must have regard to a statutory code of practice issued by the Secretary of State under s. 313 of the 1996 Act. The current *Special Educational Needs Code of Practice* (the SEN Code) was issued by the Secretary of State in November 2001 and came into effect on 1 January 2002. A separate Code of Practice has been issued for Wales and came into effect on 1 April 2002.

4.   General principle: children with SEN normally to be educated in mainstream schools

Inclusion has long been statutorily encouraged. The Education Act 1981 set out a presumption that a child with SEN would be educated in an 'ordinary' school wherever that was appropriate and that principle was strengthened by the 1993 Act and consolidated into the 1996 Act. An LEA was required, in exercising its functions in respect of a child with SEN who should be educated in a school, to secure, subject to certain conditions, that the child was educated in a school which was not a special school, i.e. was a mainstream school, unless incompatible with the wishes of his parents (the original s. 316 of the 1996 Act). The conditions were that educating the child in a school which was not a special school was compatible with (a) his receiving the special educational provision for which his learning difficulty called, (b) the provision of efficient education for the children with whom he would be educated and (c) the efficient use of resources.

The amendments to the 1996 Act brought about by the Special Educational Needs and Disability Act 2001 go further in placing the emphasis on the principle that children with SEN should normally be educated in mainstream schools. The provisions of the 2001 Act reflected the Consultation Document: *SEN and Disability Rights in Education Bill* (March 2000). The consultation was worded:

> 'The principles of the new provision would be that a child with SEN shall be educated within a mainstream setting unless:
>
> (a) this is incompatible with the wishes of his or her parents; or
>
> (b) a school or local authority [presumably this meant LEA] cannot take reasonable steps to adapt its provision to secure a place for them in a mainstream setting without:
>
> > (i) prejudicing the efficient education of the children with whom he or she will be educated; or
> >
> > (ii) incurring unreasonable public expenditure.'

8.
SPECIAL
EDUCATIONAL
NEEDS

The eventual provision introduced into the 1996 Act by the 2001 Act carried through this ambition, but not wholly in the way envisaged in the consultation. A child with SEN but no statement must be educated in a mainstream school (s. 316(2)). If a statement is made, the child must be educated in a mainstream school unless that is incompatible with the wishes of his parent or the provision of efficient education for other children (s. 316(3)). Interestingly, in contrast to the consultation document, incurring unreasonable public expenditure is, on the face of the Act, no longer a reason to preclude placement (but see below).

5. General principle: children should be educated in accordance with parents' wishes

Until recently, the general obligation on LEAs imposed by s. 9 of the 1996 Act to have regard to the principle that pupils are to be educated in accordance with the wishes of their parents, so far as that is compatible with the provision of efficient instruction and training and the avoidance of unreasonable public expenditure, was thought to apply only to functions other than special education on the basis that the parts of the Act dealing with special education stood apart from the remainder of the Act. This belief was, however, shown to be mistaken in *C v Buckinghamshire County Council and the SEN Tribunal* [1999] ELR 179.

In the B*uckinghamshire* case, the Court of Appeal held that there was nothing in the 1996 Act to suggest that the general principle that pupils were to be educated in accordance with the wishes of their parents was intended to be disregarded in the case of children with SEN. The result of this is that, in exercising their SEN functions, LEAs should have regard to the principle that pupils are to be educated in accordance with the wishes of their parents, so far as that is compatible with the provision of efficient instruction and training and the avoidance of unreasonable public expenditure.

What is or is not unreasonable public expenditure has caused some judicial confusion. In *Edwards v Cornwall County Council and SENT* [1997] ELR 390, it was conceded that social services expenditure could be included as 'public expenditure' when calculating the cost to an LEA of a particular form of provision. In contrast, however, in *S v Somerset County Council* [2001] EWCA Civ 1358, (2002) LGR 279, the Court of Appeal considered that the concession in Edwards was incorrectly made and held that only LEA expenditure should be taken into account – presumably only expenditure falling within the local Schools Budget – and not social services expenditure. This decision also appears to confirm that 'unreasonable public expenditure' is the same as 'inefficient use of resources'.

It needs to be remembered, however, that notwithstanding s. 9, specific provision is made to enable parents to express a preference for a maintained school. Thus, a parental preference for a maintained school is binding in the absence of the LEA's showing that such a placement is not compatible with the two qualifications (i.e. that the school is unsuitable to the child's age, ability or aptitude or to his SEN, or the attendance of the child at the school would be incompatible with the provision of efficient education for the children with whom he would be educated or the efficient use of resources (sched 27, para 3(3)(a) and (b)). Consequently, s. 9 tends to be most important where parents make representations for their child to attend an independent or non-maintained special school.

It is clear, however, that parental preference cannot prevail if the preferred school is unsuitable. In *Forbes v Brent LBC and Vassie* 30 September 1999, unreported, QBD, the court held that parents did not have a veto on mainstream education and could not override the LEA's primary duty to make proper and adequate provision for the child's needs. If the school put forward by the parents was unsuitable, that should be the end of the matter and their preference could not override the proper educational placement.

A preference, or more strictly, parental representations, for a non-maintained or independent school must also be considered by the LEA, together with the qualifications to s. 9, but the representations are not binding as such. Instead it is an important relevant consideration for the LEA and on appeal the SENDIST, to take into account. (For further judicial consideration of the relationship between s. 9 and SEN, see also *Lane v Worcestershire County Council and Hughes* [2000] All ER (D) 333, CA, where the court held that parental wishes were relevant but not an overriding factor.)

8.
SPECIAL
EDUCATIONAL
NEEDS

6. The LEA's duties

6.1 The general and the specific

An LEA's responsibilities for special education fall into two categories: general duties owed towards all children and specific duties owed towards individual children and/or their parents. It is the number and precision of the latter type of duties which have caused so much difficulty for LEAs in the courts and have also enabled parents to obtain far greater redress through the SENDIST and, on appeal, the High Court.

The first of the responsibilities imposed on LEAs is the duty in s. 315 of the Education Act 1996 to keep under review the arrangements made by the LEA for special educational provision.

In carrying out this duty (as with all other duties and powers towards children with SEN), the LEA must have regard to the SEN Code. It must also, to the extent that it appears necessary or desirable for the purpose of co-ordinating provision for children with SEN, consult the governing bodies of maintained schools in the LEA's area.

This obligation to keep arrangements under review is general and does not apply to specific pupils, whose progress and review of needs is covered by s. 328(5) of the 1996 Act. It does not therefore impose a duty on an LEA, for which damages can be recovered, to, in effect, keep an eye on specific children placed by an LEA in residential schools (see *P v Harrow LBC* [1993] 2 FCR 341).

6.2   Children with SEN

Children with SEN fall into two categories. First, there are those children who have SEN, but for whom it is not necessary for the LEA to determine the special educational provision which any learning difficulty they have calls for. Secondly, there are those children with SEN for whom it is necessary for the LEA to determine the special educational provision which any learning difficulty they have calls for.

It is to the second category of children that LEAs owe specific duties enforceable through SENDIST, the courts or the Secretary of State. That does not, however, mean that duties are not owed to children in the first category (in effect, children without statements of SEN). Those children are owed duties, not by the LEA, but by the governing bodies of maintained schools. Section 317 of the 1996 Act provides that the governing body of a maintained school or a maintained nursery school shall:

a)   use its best endeavours, in exercising its functions in relation to the school, to secure that, if any registered pupil has SEN, the special educational provision which his learning difficulty calls for is made;

b)   secure that, where the headteacher or designated SEN governor has been informed by the LEA that a registered pupil has SEN, those needs are made known to all who are likely to teach him; and

c)   secure that the teachers in the school are aware of the importance of identifying and providing for, those registered pupils who have SEN (s. 317(1)).

Further, where a child who has SEN is being educated in a maintained mainstream school, those concerned with making special educational provision for the child shall secure, so far as is reasonably practicable and is compatible with:

8.
SPECIAL
EDUCATIONAL
NEEDS

a) his receiving the special educational provision which his learning difficulty calls for;

b) the provision of efficient education for the children with whom he will be educated; and

c) the efficient use of resources,

that the child engages in activities of the school together with children who do not have SEN (see s. 317(4)).

Governing bodies also have a duty to notify parents of a decision by the school that their child has SEN (s. 317A). The duty also applies to children in PRUs, so that the LEA must ensure that the unit's headteacher informs the parent (s. 317A(2)).

To strengthen the information available to parents, s. 332A of the 1996 Act imposes an obligation on LEAs to arrange for the parent of any child in its area with SEN to be provided with advice and information about matters relating to those needs. In making these arrangements, LEAs must have regard to guidance from the Secretary of State or NAW and must take such steps as they consider appropriate for making these services known to the parents of children in their areas, headteachers in their areas and such other persons as they consider appropriate (s. 332A(1) to (3)).

To encourage the resolution of disputes without parents having to resort to the tribunal, courts or ombudsman, the 2001 Act also introduced a requirement on LEAs to make arrangements with a view to avoiding or resolving disagreements between LEAs and parents of children in their areas about the exercise of SEN functions (s. 332B(1)). Each LEA must also make arrangements with a view to avoiding or resolving, in each relevant school, disagreements between the parents of a child with SEN who is a registered pupil at the school and the proprietor of the school about the special educational provision made for that child (s. 332B(2)). This applies to maintained schools, PRUs, CTCs, CCTA, Academies, independent schools named in statements and non-maintained special schools. The arrangements must provide for the appointment of independent persons with the function of facilitating the avoidance or resolution of these disagreements (s. 332B(3)). In making arrangements LEAs must have regard to guidance from the Secretary of State or NAW (s. 332B(4)) and must make the arrangements known to parents, headteachers and others in their areas as they consider appropriate (s. 332B(5)). Seeking disagreement resolution does not affect a parent's right to appeal to SENDIST.

6.3 Children with special educational needs for whom the LEA is responsible

The above duties will apply to all children with SEN whether or not they have a statement. More specific and precise duties are, however, imposed on LEAs in respect of the second category of children, namely those who have SEN and it is necessary for the LEA to determine the special educational provision which any learning difficulty the child may have calls for.

In respect of these children, the responsible LEA must exercise its powers with a view to securing that such children are identified (s. 321(1)). For this purpose, an LEA is responsible for children who are in its area and who are:

a) registered pupils at maintained schools and maintained special schools; or

b) pupils at non-maintained or independent schools where the fees are paid by the LEA; or

c) where a) or b) do not apply, registered pupils at a school and have been brought to the attention of the LEA as having, or probably having, SEN; or

d) not registered pupils at a school, but are not under the age of two or over compulsory school age and have been brought to the LEA's attention as having, or probably having, SEN (s. 321(3)).

For a consideration of when the LEA's responsibility comes to an end, see *R v Dorset County Council and the Further Education Funding Council ex p Goddard* [1995] ELR 109, *R v Oxfordshire County Council ex p B* [1997] ELR 90 and *Wakefield MDC v Evans [2001] EWHC Admin 508*, [2001] All ER (D) 94 (Jul). See also 6.10 of this section, below.

Alleged failures on the part of LEAs or their staff to identify a child's SEN have been the source of much litigation in recent years. In theory, following the decisions of the House of Lords in *X v Bedfordshire County Council* [1995] ELR 404 and, more particularly after *Phelps v Hillingdon LBC* ([2000] ELR 499) a negligent failure by the staff of an LEA to identify a child's needs could lead to a pupil's recovering compensation from the LEA (see chapter 12.D.3.3.3.viii).

8.
SPECIAL
EDUCATIONAL
NEEDS

6.4 Assessments of SEN

Where an LEA is of the opinion that a child for whom it is responsible has, or probably has, SEN and it is necessary for the authority to determine the special educational provision which his learning difficulty may call for, the LEA is under a duty to carry out an assessment of the child's SEN (see s. 323(1) and (2)). To initiate an assessment, the LEA must serve notice on the child's parent informing him (or, as appropriate, her or them: see chapter 3.B.21) that it proposes to make an assessment of his educational needs, of the procedure to be followed, the name of an officer who can provide information and of his right to make representations and submit written representations to the LEA within a specified period.

Where the specified period has expired and the LEA remains of the opinion that, having taken into account any representations made and evidence submitted, the child has, or probably has, SEN and it is necessary for the authority to determine the special educational provision which his learning difficulty may call for, the LEA is under a duty to make an assessment of his educational needs and to notify the parents accordingly.

Parents may also request that the LEA carry out an assessment of their child's SEN under s. 329 of the 1996 Act. The LEA is under a duty to comply with such a request where all of the following apply:

a) the LEA is responsible for the child but no statement is maintained;

b) no assessment has been made within the period of six months ending with the date on which the request is made; and

c) it is necessary for the LEA to make an assessment because the child has, or probably has, SEN and it is necessary for the LEA to determine the special educational provision which any learning difficulty he may have calls for (s. 329(1)).

If the LEA determines not to comply with the request, it must give notice of that decision to the parent and inform him that he may appeal to the SENDIST against the determination (s. 329(2)).

In response to concerns that parents could not appeal against refusals to assess where the child's headteacher had requested an assessment, the 2001 Act amended the 1996 Act to provide that headteachers may now request that an LEA carry out an assessment. The LEA must inform the child's parents of the request (s. 329A(3)).

The LEA must comply with the request where:

8.
SPECIAL
EDUCATIONAL
NEEDS

a) the child is a registered pupil at a relevant school (i.e. a maintained school, maintained nursery school, PRU, independent school or non-maintained special school approved under s. 342 of the 1996 Act) and the LEA is responsible for the child but no statement is maintained;

b) no assessment has been made within the period of six months ending with the date on which the request is made; and

c) it is necessary for the LEA to make an assessment because the child has, or probably has, SEN and it is necessary for the LEA to determine the special educational provision which any learning difficulty he may have calls for.

If the LEA refuses the request, the parents may appeal to the SENDIST (s. 329A(8)).

The procedure and requirements in respect of the making of an assessment are set out in sched 26 to the 1996 Act and in the Education (Special Educational Needs) (England) (Consolidation) Regulations 2001 (SI 2001 No. 3455). It should be noted that parents cannot appeal against the LEA's decision to carry out an assessment.

6.5   Statements of SEN

After carrying out an assessment, the LEA may decide that, although the child has SEN, it is not necessary for it to determine the special educational provision which any learning difficulty he may have calls for, i.e. the child's ordinary school should be able to meet his needs without any intervention from the LEA. This decision may be reached even if the LEA has originally proposed to issue a statement, but has changed its mind following representations made in response to the proposed statement or evidence received subsequently to the service of the proposed statement on the parents (see *R v Isle of Wight Council ex p S* 30 September 1992, unreported, QBD). If, however, the LEA decides not to issue a final statement, it must give notice of this fact to the parents and inform them of their right to appeal to the SENDIST (s. 325).

If, on the other hand, following an assessment, the LEA concludes, in light of the representations made and evidence produced, that it is necessary for it to determine the special educational provision which the child's learning difficulty calls for, the LEA shall make and maintain a statement of the child's SEN in the prescribed form (s. 324 and the 2001 Regulations). In particular, the statement must

8.
SPECIAL
EDUCATIONAL
NEEDS

give details of the LEA's assessment of the child's SEN and specify (as to what specification means, see the following three sections of this chapter) the special educational provision to be made for the purpose of meeting those SEN, including:

a) the type of school or other institution which the LEA considers would be appropriate for the child;

b) if the LEA is not required to specify the name of a school for which the parents have expressed a preference under sched 27 to the 1996 Act, in the statement, the name of any school or institution which the LEA considers appropriate for the child; and

c) any special educational provision for which arrangements shall be made by the LEA otherwise than in school and which the LEA considers should be included in the statement (s. 324(3) and (4)).

When serving the statement on the child's parents, the LEA must also give them notice that they have the right to appeal to the SENDIST against the description of the LEA's assessment of the child's SEN, the special educational provision specified in the statement (including the name of a school so specified) or, if no school is named in the statement, that fact (s. 326(1A)).

Where such a statement is maintained by the LEA, the LEA must, unless the child's parents have made suitable arrangements, arrange that the special educational provision specified in the statement is made for the child and may arrange that any non-educational provision specified in the statement is made for him in such manner as the LEA considers appropriate (s. 324(5)(a)). If the name of a maintained school is specified in the statement, the governing body of that school is under a duty to admit him or her into the school (s. 324(5)(b)). This obligation applies even if the LEA responsible for the child is different from the LEA responsible for the school (see *R v Chair of Governors and Headteacher of a School ex parte T* [2000] EdCR 223).

6.6 Educational or non-educational provision

The 2001 Regulations require that a statement of a child's SEN shall (see sched 2):

a) in part 3, specify the special educational provision which the LEA considers appropriate to meet the needs of the child set out in part 2 of the statement and to meet the objectives specified in part 3 and in particular, specify:

(i) any appropriate facilities and equipment, staffing arrangements and curriculum,

(ii) any appropriate modifications to the application of the National Curriculum,

(iii) any appropriate exclusions from the application of the National Curriculum in detail, and

(iv) where residential accommodation is appropriate, that fact; and

b) in part 5, specify the non-educational needs of the child for which the LEA considers provision is appropriate if the child is to benefit properly from the special education provision specified in part 3; and

c) in part 6, specify any additional non-educational provision which the LEA proposes to make available or which the LEA is satisfied will be made available by a health authority, a social services authority or some other body, including the arrangements for its provision, together with the objectives of the provision and the arrangements for monitoring it.

The distinction between special educational provision, which must therefore be arranged for the child by the LEA and non-educational provision, which the LEA may arrange, has provided much debate and resulted in a number of cases in the courts, commencing with the decision of *R v Lancashire County Council ex parte M* [1989] 2 FLR 279 and culminating in the Court of Appeal's decision in *Bromley LBC v Special Educational Needs Tribunal and Others* [1999] ELR 260, CA.

8.
SPECIAL
EDUCATIONAL
NEEDS

The *Lancashire* case involved a child who required intensive speech therapy as a result of a congenital speech deformity. After considering the history of speech therapy provision, the Court of Appeal held that the identity of the provider of the therapy was immaterial. The crucial test was whether the nature of the provision itself could be characterised as educational or non-educational. Finding that the speech therapy in that case was educational in nature and therefore should have appeared under part 3 of the statement, Balcombe LJ (at p. 580) set out a method of comparison which has subsequently been adopted in a number of decisions.

To teach, he said, an adult who has lost his larynx because of cancer might well be considered as treatment rather than education. But to teach a child who has never been able to communicate by language, whether because of some chromosomal disorder or because of some social cause (e.g. because his parents are themselves unable to speak and thus he cannot learn by example as normally happens) seems just as much educational provision as to teach a child to communicate by writing.

Although the judgment left open the possibility that some forms of speech therapy could be non-educational, the reality of Balcombe LJ's analysis is that most forms of speech therapy, whether implemented by speech therapists or teachers/special needs assistants, are likely to be educational and should appear in part 3 of a statement.

The decision caused problems for most LEAs. Under the National Health Service Reorganisation Act 1973, educational speech therapists had transferred to the NHS together with their funding, so the *Lancashire* case left LEAs with the duty to provide the therapy but without the resources to do a proper job. A further flaw in the decision was that the court considered the role of only speech therapists in providing speech therapy. In concluding that speech therapy could be provided only by a speech therapist, the court omitted to consider the role of teachers and learning support assistants (particularly in special schools) in delivering speech therapy or improving communication skills as an integral part of the teaching task.

As a consequence, some LEAs started to employ their own therapists. Others tried to frame parts 3 and 6 of statements so as to ensure some input from speech therapists in part 6, but with the majority of programmes being implemented by school staff under part 3. In many cases, this ensured that a child could receive therapy throughout the school day, which occasional visits from NHS speech therapists could not achieve, but it was still unsatisfactory for parents, especially when the re-prioritisation of NHS resources meant that no speech therapists were available.

Such a situation arose in Harrow in 1996, where the local health authority, for reasons of financial stringency, was able to provide only one half of the therapy (in this case, this included speech, occupational and physiotherapy) specified in a child's statement. When the parents became aware of the reduction in provision, they launched a judicial review against the LEA and the LEA in turn initiated judicial review proceedings against the health authority. The two cases came before *Turner J in R v London Borough of Harrow ex p M* and *R v The Brent and Harrow Health Authority ex p London Borough of Harrow* [1997] ELR 62, CA.

Acknowledging that the dispute arose from the chronic underfunding of public bodies who have a statutory duty to fulfil, but only a limited budget out of which to meet, their statutory obligations, the judge held that the duty on an LEA under s. 324 was personal. If the LEA's education department requested help from a health authority or a social services department and that help were provided, the LEA would have made the required arrangements. If, however, that help was not, for whatever reason, available, the LEA was under a continuing obligation to ensure that the provision was made available. The duty on the LEA was not an ultimate one, but it was a duty for which the LEA was and continued to be primarily responsible.

Although a number of cases subsequent to the *Lancashire* case have pointed out that the Court of Appeal said only that speech therapy is capable of being special educational provision, not that it has to be (see *re L* [1994] ELR 16 and *C v SEN Tribunal* [1997] ELR 390), the reality for LEAs is that most cases of speech therapy will, in law, be special educational provision and should appear in part 3 of statements.

The question, however, of whether occupational therapy, physiotherapy, nursing care and social welfare provision are special educational provision or non-educational provision is still not resolved and the case law, certainly pre-*Bromley*, was inconsistent.

In some cases, judges have been reluctant to interfere in educational, or perhaps more correctly, non-educational, decisions unless the LEA has acted irrationally or unreasonably. See, for example, *C v SEN Tribunal* [1997] ELR at p. 400 and *Bromley*, below.

In other cases, however, judges have been prepared to state categorically that certain types of provision cannot, as a matter of law, be considered educational. In *B v Isle of Wight Council* [1997] ELR 279, McCullough J concluded that the occupational therapy and physiotherapy envisaged in that case were not capable of amounting to educational provision.

In *R v London Borough of Lambeth ex p MBM* [1995] ELR 374, Owen J held that the provision of a lift to enable a child to access the upper floors of her school was non-educational provision. If, he said, the provision of a lift is necessary, it is necessary to assist M's mobility and not as special educational provision. The installation of a lift would be no more special educational provision than was the provision of M's wheelchair.

In *Bradford Metropolitan Council v A* [1997] ELR 417, the issue was whether nursing care for a child who was severely visually impaired, epileptic and had cerebral palsy, was educational or medical. Brooke J held that although certain types of provision fell in a borderline area where it was a matter of discretion for the LEA into which part of the statement they placed the provision, nursing care was not such a provision. In his view, such care fell fairly and squarely into the category of non-educational needs, which are the needs of the child for which the authority considers that provision is appropriate if a child is to benefit properly from the special educational provision.

In *C v SEN Tribunal* [1997] ELR 390, Dyson J considered occupational therapy and physiotherapy in respect of a child with limited movement, epilepsy and poor visual awareness and who could not stand or take steps without assistance. In the event, the judge did not find it necessary to decide whether occupational therapy or physiotherapy was lawfully placed in part 5 of the statement. Instead, he adopted the position that there was room for a difference of opinion as to which side of the line the therapy specified for the child in part 5 fell. 'In borderline cases where the tribunal does not interfere with the LEA's classification, I think that the court should be very slow to find that the tribunal has erred in law. [I]t is only in the clearest cases that the court should find an error of law arising from a failure by a tribunal to interfere with an LEA's classification of provision' (at p. 399). Nonetheless, he went on to express the opinion that occupational therapy and physiotherapy were not special educational provision (at p. 400).

Residential care and the provision of a 24-hour curriculum have also become areas of contention. In *G v Wakefield City MBC* (1998) 96 LGR 69, G suffered from profound and multiple learning difficulties, but her biggest problem was her home environment. Her home was not suitable for her needs and her mother was disabled and therefore incapable of carrying or lifting her. Laws J concluded that the provision of, in effect, residential and/or respite care was not special educational provision. Economic problems faced by the child's parents, where for example different and perhaps more spacious living accommodation would in an ideal world be suitable for the family because of the child's physical difficulties, he held, are not ordinarily within the remit of the SEN Tribunal. Nor are difficulties associated with a parent's disabilities, where the effect is that the child is, in physical terms, more difficult to look after.

In view of this, it is very hard to draw any conclusions from the case law or, indeed, any true principles to assist in determining whether a particular type of provision is educational or non-educational. With one or two exceptions identified above, there is clearly no hard and fast rule, no hard edge between educational and non-educational. All that can perhaps be said is, as per Laws J in G, that there must be a direct relation between the therapy or provision and the child's learning difficulties in order for it to be regarded as educational.

It was hoped that the decision of the Court of Appeal in *Bromley LBC v Special Educational Needs Tribunal and Others* [1999] ELR 260 would settle the point, but unfortunately, though probably for the very valid reason that the judiciary felt unwilling to interfere in areas of educational judgment, this did not happen and the law is still very uncertain. According to Sedley LJ:

> 'Special educational provision is, in principle, whatever is called for by a child's learning difficulty. A learning difficulty is anything inherent in the child which makes learning significantly harder for him than for most others or which hinders him from making use of ordinary school facilities [...] the LEA is required to distinguish between special educational provision and non-educational provision [...] Two possibilities arise here: either the two categories share a common frontier so that one stops where the other begins; or there is between the unequivocally educational and the unequivocally non-educational shared territory of provision which can intelligibly be allocated to either [...] to interpose a hard edge or common frontier does not get rid of definitional problems; it simply makes them more acute. And this is one of the reasons why, in my judgment, the second approach is the one to be attributed to Parliament. The potentially large intermediate area of provision which is capable of ranking as educational or non-educational is not made the subject of any statutory prescription precisely because it is for the local authority and if necessary the SENT, to exercise a case-by-case judgment which no prescriptive legislation could ever hope to anticipate. [...] It is true that the LEA's functions (which include both powers and duties: see s. 579(1)) will include the elective making of arrangements for non-educational provision as well as the mandatory making of arrangements for educational provision pursuant to s. 324(5)(a); but it is the fact that health, social services and other authorities can be enlisted to help in the making of

8.
SPECIAL
EDUCATIONAL
NEEDS

special educational provision which gives some indication of a possible breadth of the duty. [Consequently] the Tribunal's conclusion that physiotherapy, occupational therapy and speech therapy were all measures which related directly to [the child's] learning difficulties and therefore amounted to a special educational provision was a conclusion properly open to it provided that it is not read as meaning that these therapies were exclusively educational.'

(at pp. 295–6)

Having considered all this case law, therefore, perhaps the best advice for an LEA is to fall back on McCullough J's comments in *B v Isle of Wight Council*: all that anyone can do when judging whether a provision is educational or non-educational is to recognise that there is an obvious spectrum from a clearly educational (in the ordinary sense of the word) at one end to the clearly medical at the other, take all the relevant facts into account, apply common sense and do one's best.

In such circumstances, however, it is inevitable that disputes between LEAs and parents will continue, particularly as the more complex types of provision are developed and more holistic approaches to a child's needs are encouraged. Although the 2001 *Code of Practice* has provided greater clarity (see paras 8:44–8:53), so long as the various agencies involved have different statutory obligations and responsibilities, the educational/non-educational dichotomy is likely to continue to exercise tribunals and courts.

6.7 Content of statements

It is not just the educational/non-educational dichotomy which has exercised the courts. Even more litigation has been generated over the content or legality of statements issued by LEAs.

Many LEA officers will recall the bad old days of SEN when statements could amount to one or two sentences of bland generalisations which were of no use to either the child or the school. That practice should now hopefully have died out as it is clear from the legislation, the SEN Code and case law that statements must be detailed enough to enable all concerned in a child's education to understand what special educational provision is required. The point was first considered in *R v Secretary of State for Education ex p E* (1991) *Independent*, 8 May, when Nolan J at first instance compared the substantive parts of a statement of SEN to a doctor's diagnosis (part 2: the assessment of the child's SEN) and a doctor's prescription (parts 3 and 4: the special educational provision and placement). That analogy was adopted by the Court of Appeal which went on to lay down general principles applicable to the content of statements. The Court of Appeal ([1993] 2 FCR 753) recognised that if the special educational provision, which the child requires for all his needs, can be determined and provided by his ordinary school, then no statement of SEN is necessary. If, however, the LEA decides that it, as opposed to the school, is required to make arrangements itself for the special educational provision which he requires, the LEA is under an obligation to make a statement. That statement must then set out all the child's SEN and all the special educational provision that he requires whether provided by his ordinary school or the LEA.

This decision led to what could be described as a radical change in practice by LEAs and most statements post-*E* followed the guidance provided by the Court of Appeal. There was, however, always argument over the degree of specificity required in a statement, especially with regard to the special educational provision. LEAs argued that the provision needed to be recorded in terms which allowed both the LEA and schools a degree of flexibility in teaching the child; parents, on the other hand, believed that their children would not receive the education to which they were entitled unless the provision was detailed with precision. Surprisingly, the issue was not further litigated until 1997 when the case of *L v Somerset County Council* [1998] ELR 129 came before Laws J.

'In *L*, it was held that a statement had to be sufficiently specific and clear so as to leave no room for doubt as to what has been decided is necessary in the individual case. Although in some cases flexibility should be retained, in most others greater detail, including the specification of the number of hours per week, will be required of the LEA. *L* concerned a pupil with SEN placed at a mainstream school. It may be possible that, where a pupil is placed in a special school, the degree of specificity required in the statement may be less to ensure greater flexibility within an environment specifically designed to meet the needs of such children.'

Specificity became an issue when the new *Code of Practice* was placed before Parliament and when the DfES produced its *SEN Toolkit* (DfES 558/2001) to assist LEAs in assessing and drawing up statements of SEN. The first draft of the *Code of Practice* laid was withdrawn after objections were made to its alleged weakening of the requirements for LEAs to be specific. The version approved was more acceptable in saying that (*Code of Practice*, paras 8:36 and 8:37):

8.
SPECIAL
EDUCATIONAL
NEEDS

'8:36 A statement should specify clearly the provision necessary to meet the needs of the child. It should detail appropriate provision to meet each identified need. It will be helpful to the child's parents and teachers if the provision in this sub-section is set out in the same order as the description of needs in Part 2.

8:37 LEAs must make decisions about which actions and provision are appropriate for which pupils on an individual basis. This can only be done by a careful assessment of the pupils' difficulties and consideration of the educational setting in which they may be educated. Provision should normally be quantified (e.g. in terms of hours of provision, staffing arrangements) although there will be cases where some flexibility should be retained in order to meet the changing SEN of the child concerned. It will always be necessary for LEAs to monitor, with the school or other setting, the child's progress towards identified outcomes, however provision is described. LEAs must not, in any circumstances, have blanket policies not to quantify provision.'

The DfES then produced the *SEN Toolkit* designed to help everyone working with children and young people with SEN by providing practical day to day guidance on the same matters as the Code of Practice (*SEN Toolkit*, s. 1, para 1). The Independent Panel for Special Education Advice (IPSEA; a charity) took issue, complaining that the *Toolkit* undermined the duty to make statements specific. IPSEA sought judicial review of the Secretary of State's decision to issue the Toolkit. This case was heard together with an appeal brought against a decision of the SEN Tribunal which raised similar issues about the detail to be included in a statement.

In the appeal *E v Newham LBC* [2003] EWCA Civ 06, [2003] ELR 286, the SEN Tribunal had concluded that the child had a need for a number of therapies as part of his daily programme but that it would not be in his interests to limit it by specifying the number of hours. It also left the amount and way of delivering the therapies to be determined by the therapists within the school setting. The Court of Appeal held that in the circumstances, which included a school with considerable specialism and expertise, the provision was lawful. 'The degree of particularity should be determined in the context of the case [...] the degree of flexibility which is appropriate in specifying the special educational provision to be made in any particular case is essentially a matter for the tribunal [and, it is suggested, beforehand, the LEA], taking into account all relevant factors' (paras 63 and 64).

In the *IPSEA* case ([2003] EWCA Civ 07), the same court, in a decision of more general application, gave similar guidance.

'If Parliament had meant specification to mean numerical quantification no doubt it would have said so [...] However, the statement clearly has to spell out the provision appropriate to meet the particular needs of and objectives identified for, the individual child. It must be addressed to the needs of the child rather than to the needs of the system [per Hale LJ at paragraph 14] [T]he needs of the child cannot be seen in a vacuum. They may fluctuate for a wide variety of reasons. Some of these will be related to the child's own state of fitness and health. Some of these will be related to the interaction between the child and his environment. It is, of course, possible to diagnose his learning difficulties without reference being made to cater for them. But it is not always possible to prescribe that provision without taking into account the context (at para 15).'

6.8 Placement

An equally contentious area is the placement specified in part 4 of the statement. LEAs have the power to specify a maintained or maintained special school in part 4 or, where appropriate, an independent school or non-maintained special school. (Placing a child in a residential school is not in itself an infringement of the child's right to have his or her family life respected – see *CB v Merton LBC and SEN Tribunal* [2002] EWHC 877 (Admin), [2002] ELR 441). Where it is inappropriate for the special educational provision to be made in a school, the LEA also has power to arrange for the provision, or part of it, to be made otherwise than in a school (s. 319). In extreme cases, an LEA may arrange for the provision to be made outside England and Wales in an institution which specialises in providing for children with SEN (s. 320).

Frequently, disputes arise where parents wish their children to attend specialist independent or non-maintained schools, whereas the LEA believes that either a mainstream maintained or maintained special school is appropriate for the child.

The argument is important, not only in terms of finding the right school for the child, but also in respect of ascertaining responsibility for funding the placement. If a non-maintained or independent school is named either initially by the LEA, or on appeal by the Tribunal, the LEA becomes responsible for meeting the fees under s. 324(5).

**8.
SPECIAL
EDUCATIONAL
NEEDS**

Cases on this point include *R v Hackney LBC ex p C* (1995) *Times*, 7 November, *R v Kent County Council ex p W* [1995] ELR 362, *C v SEN Tribunal* [1997] ELR 390, *Surrey County Council v P and P* [1997] ELR 516 and *White v Ealing LBC, Richardson v Solihull MBC, Solihull MBC v Finn* [1998] ELR 203 and [1998] ELR 319, although not all with consistent results.

The Surrey case is important as a reminder that LEAs are not obliged to make the best possible education available, but only to meet the needs of the child. *C v SEN Tribunal* reiterated the point that an LEA was entitled to conclude that educating a child at the parents' preferred school was an inefficient use of resources when that school, while suitable, was much more expensive than the LEA's preferred option. In calculating the cost, the costs of provision specified in part 5 of the statement should be excluded since, in that case, they were to be borne by the health authority. The reasoning in this decision was followed by the *House of Lords in B v London Borough of Harrow and Others* [2000] ELR 109. Overturning the decision of the Court of Appeal, the House of Lords held that, in determining whether placement of a child in a school maintained by an adjoining LEA was incompatible with the efficient use of resources, only the resources of the placing LEA should be considered and not the resources of the LEA responsible for the maintenance of the school which the child would attend.

Whilst it is the costs of the responsible LEA which need to be considered, what costs can be included? Assuming that the provision is solely educational, the decision of the Court of Appeal in *Oxfordshire County Council v GB and Others* ([2001] EWCA Civ 1358, (2002) LGR 279, CA) nonetheless provides that not all 'resources' should be included in the calculation. Whilst independent school and non-maintained school costs would ordinarily equate to the fees charged, in the case of maintained provision the decision suggests that the only costs which can be considered are the additional costs incurred by the LEA and not costs which would be incurred with or without the proposed placement. Where a maintained special school is funded on the basis of places and will be funded in that way irrespective of whether or not those places are filled, the logic of the *Oxfordshire* case is therefore that the cost to the LEA will be nil.

Normally, the annual cost will be the one which is used in the calculation. However, where it is argued that an initially more intensive and therefore costlier, provision is proposed or, conversely, the parents' preferred placement would see the child in education longer than if placed in another school, the LEA and tribunal are entitled to calculate the costs over the relevant period rather than just on an annual basis (see *Southampton City Council v G and Stanton* [2002] EWHC 1516 Admin).

One issue which remained, though, was whether the resources of other departments than education within the one authority, particularly social services, should be taken into account in deciding what is incompatible with the efficient use of resources. The reasoning in C was thought to apply, in that social service provision is usually non-educational provision, albeit provided by the same authority and its cost should be excluded from consideration.

Despite certain comments in *B v London Borough of Harrow and Others* [2000] ELR 109 and the concession in *Edwards v Cornwall County Council*, the position now appears to be, following *S v Somerset County Council* ([2001] All ER (D) 395 (Jul), that only the LEA's costs can be taken into account. However much it would have been thought that a social services department's costs should be counted as part of public expenditure or the use of resources, it would appear that such costs cannot be counted, the LEA and Tribunal being limited to considering only costs which, in effect, fall to be borne from the Local Schools Budget.

Reverting to a consideration of the issue of placement, in *R v Hackney LBC ex p C*, the Court of Appeal held that naming a school in part 4 of a statement did not automatically render the LEA liable for all the fees at the school. The parents wanted their child to attend a non-maintained school, which the LEA considered suitable, but only with additional support, which the LEA was willing to provide. The court held that the naming of the school in these circumstances did not impose a duty on the LEA to fund all the fees. Whether this is correct is debatable in light of *R v Kent County Council ex parte W*, where Turner J appeared to take the opposite view. In this case, it was held that the LEA had failed to make suitable arrangements to make the necessary special educational provision for the child; the LEA could not in the circumstances argue that this was a case of the parents' having made arrangements. The LEA therefore had an obligation to fund the entire cost of the placement.

The result of these cases is that an LEA, contemplating naming the parents' preferred school in such circumstances, needs to be very careful how it words part 4 of the statement. This doubt is supported by the decision of Dyson J in the White case. There it was held that although there was no absolute duty to name a school in a statement,

8.
SPECIAL
EDUCATIONAL
NEEDS

if a school was named, the LEA was under a duty to arrange and pay for the placement. The normal solution, therefore, is, first, to name the maintained school that the LEA believes to be appropriate and then to record that the parents have chosen to place their child at the non-maintained school for which they are making suitable arrangements, other than for the support which the LEA is willing to fund.

Similar problems over wording have arisen with respect to school transport. In *R v Havering LBC ex p K* [1998] ELR 402, the LEA agreed to name the parents' preferred school, on condition that the parents met the transport costs. This was not, however, recorded in the statement. Later, the parents could not afford to pay the transport costs and the LEA attempted to alter the placement and require the child to attend its originally preferred school. This was held to be unlawful by the court as the non-maintained school was the named school in part 4 and, in the absence of the LEA's lawfully amending the statement, the LEA continued to be responsible for the placement, together now with the transport costs. The moral of the case is that if an LEA is prepared to name a school on the basis that the parents will meet the transport costs, that agreement needs to be recorded in the statement along the following lines: part 4: X School, provided that Mr and Mrs Z will meet the costs of transporting A to and from school. In the event that Mr and Mrs Z are no longer able to meet these costs, B School is the appropriate school.

8.
SPECIAL
EDUCATIONAL
NEEDS

Another issue relating to placement concerns the ability of an LEA or the SENDIST to place a child in a school beyond its designation. To a certain extent the problem has been resolved by the implementation of the two separate sets of regulations relating to maintained and non-maintained special schools (the Education (Maintained Special Schools) (England) Regulations 1999 (SI 1999 No. 2212) and the Education (Non-Maintained Special Schools) (England) Regulations 1999 (SI 1999 No. 2257)), but the issue may still arise in respect of certain placements (draft regulations to amend both these sets were published for consultation in September 2003; DfES/0506/2003 and 0531/2003).

Under s. 324(4), the LEA is required to name the type of school and, subject to certain conditions, to name the school which it considers would be appropriate for the child. That appears to provide a wide discretion to the LEA to name the school which it believes will best meet the child's needs. In *City of Sunderland v SEN Tribunal and Others* [1996] ELR 283, however, the judge took a more restrictive view of the LEA's powers based on his interpretation of the regulations then applying to both maintained and non-maintained special schools (Education (Special Schools) Regulations 1994 (SI 1994 No. 652)). In that case, the issue concerned whether or not a child could be placed at a maintained special school when that school had not been approved by the Secretary of State to take children of the child's age.

The regulations stated that a governing body could not admit a child to a school unless he fell within the category specified in the arrangements approved by the Secretary of State in respect of (a) the number, age and sex of day and of boarding pupils and (b) their respective educational needs (paras 1 and 7 of part II of the schedule to the 1994 Regulations). Brooke J held that a child whose age was beyond the approved age range for the school could not lawfully be admitted by the school's governing body.

Similarly, in *In re B* 4 August 1999, unreported, Latham J held that an LEA could decline to name a special school if to do so would lead to the approved number of places for the school being exceeded.

In contrast, however, in *Ellison v Hampshire County Council* 30 July 1999, unreported, Tucker J held that where the issue was not a child's age or sex (i.e. the objective criteria under (i) above), but was the subjective assessment of the child's SEN, the Sunderland case could be distinguished. The question of what school is appropriate is not necessarily determined by the designation of a particular school although that is obviously a factor to be taken into account. If other or extra provision can be made for a child's educational needs as recognised in the statement, then a school may, despite certain initial apparent disadvantages, be an appropriate school.

The position was therefore that a child could not be placed in a school if he or she was not of the same sex or age as the designation or their admission would put the school above its designated number, but a child could be admitted if the school was appropriate, even if the child's SEN did not match the type of need for which the school was approved. Tucker J's judgment was upheld by the Court of Appeal (*Ellison v Hampshire County Council* 24 February 2000, unreported), although the court preferred to find that placement was a question of educational judgment properly left to the LEA and SENDIST.

These provisions still apply in the case of admission to non-maintained special schools as paras 1 and 7 of Part II of the schedule to the 1994 Regulations now appear in the same form in the Education (Non-Maintained Special Schools) (England) Regulations 1999 (see paras 1 and 7 of the schedule).

In the case of admission to maintained special schools, however, the regulations have changed significantly and the only restrictions on a child's admission to such a school are found in reg 19 of the Education (Maintained Special Schools) (England) Regulations 1999. These provide that no child is to be admitted into a maintained special school unless:

a)   a statement of SEN is maintained for him;

b)   he is admitted for the purposes of an assessment of his SEN and his admission is with the agreement of the LEA, the headteacher of the school, the child's parent and any person whose advice is sought as part of that assessment; or

c)   he is admitted following a change in his circumstances, with the agreement of the LEA, the headteacher of the school and the child's parent (reg 19(1)).

Thus, the only real condition attached to a child's admission to a maintained special school is that he has a statement naming that school. Although an LEA must clearly have regard to his age and sex, the numbers at the school and the special educational provision which the school provides (otherwise the LEA's decision could be challenged on normal administrative law principles of unreasonableness), the important factor in future will be the appropriateness of the placement. If, with additional support, a child with particular needs can be accommodated at a school designated for a different type of need it will not be unlawful for that school to admit him.

6.9   Review of statements

Once the statement is made, the LEA is under an obligation to keep the statement under review (s. 328(5)) and must review it within 12 months of the making of the statement or a previous review. In addition, parents or the child's school may ask the LEA for a further assessment at any time provided that an assessment has not been made within the period of six months prior to that request and it is necessary for the LEA to make a further assessment (s. 328(2) and s. 329A).

8.
SPECIAL
EDUCATIONAL
NEEDS

6.10 Amending and ceasing to maintain statements

A statement of SEN is not a rigid or permanent document; it should change to reflect the changing needs of the child. Consequently, the legislation makes provision for the amendment of statements or, where the child's needs have changed to the point where it is no longer necessary for the LEA to determine the special educational provision which the child's learning difficulty may call for, the cessation of the statement.

The procedures are governed by para 9 of sched 27 to the 1996 Act and paragraphs 8:125–8:133 of the SEN Code. The 2001 Act introduced new procedures, including the service of amendment notices, to enable parents to understand more easily what changes are being proposed to their child's statement (see para 9 of sched 27 to the 1996 Act as amended).

Particular issues have arisen in respect of the termination of an LEA's responsibility when a child with SEN moves into the post-16 sector. The SEN Code provides some assistance in paragraphs 8:117 to 8:124, with greater clarity than was apparent under the old *Code of Practice* and which led to a number of decisions attempting to interpret the various responsibilities.

Thus it was left to the courts to find some semblance of order. The first case was *R v Dorset County Council ex p Goddard* [1995] ELR 109. This case involved a young person whose needs required him to be educated in an independent school. In these circumstances, it was unlawful for the LEA to try to claim that, as he was over 16, it ceased to have responsibility for the pupil, that his statement should therefore lapse and that the Further Education Funding Council should take over the liability to fund the placement. The LEA was therefore forced to maintain a statement whilst he remained at school.

If, however, the pupil moves into a further education institution, such as an FE college and his SEN can be met by that institution, it is no longer necessary for the LEA to maintain a statement and its responsibility ceases: see *R v Oxfordshire County Council ex p B* [1997] ELR 90.

An LEA does not, however, have a duty to provide a statement and special educational provision for a child who attends university. In the case of *R v Portsmouth City Council ex p Faludy* [1999] ELR

**8.
SPECIAL
EDUCATIONAL
NEEDS**

115, a child with dyslexia obtained a place at Cambridge University. The parents argued that his SEN should have been met by the LEA. The court disagreed and held that the LEA had no power to provide support in a higher education institution. Although s. 319 of the 1996 Act, which gives an LEA power to make special educational provision otherwise than in a school, could in principle apply to a university, s. 1(4) of the 1996 Act had the effect of ensuring that an LEA had no power or duties with regard to higher education and thus could not fund special educational provision at university.

The new *Code of Practice* now, as indicated, provides somewhat clearer guidance which might, hopefully, avoid some of these costly differences of opinion.

> '8:121 A statement will generally remain in force until and unless the LEA ceases to maintain it. A statement will lapse automatically when a young person moves into further or higher education. Therefore, if the young person, the parents, the LEA and the further education institution are all in agreement about the young person's transfer, there is no need to formally cease the statement since the young person will cease to be a pupil for whom the LEA is responsible after leaving school and so the statement will lapse.
>
> 8:122 A young person may leave school at age 16 plus to seek employment or training; again, there is no need to formally cease to maintain the statement since the young person would cease to be a pupil for whom the LEA is responsible once they leave school. By contrast, where there is agreement all-round that the pupil should stay at school post-16 and the LEA or other LEAs, have appropriate school provision, the LEA should normally continue to maintain the statement.
>
> 8:123 Where parents want their child to remain at school post 16, but the LEA considers that the young person's SEN would be better met in a further education institution, the LEA cannot know whether the child still requires a statement until it has contacted the FE institution in question and confirmed that it is both able to meet the young person's needs and has offered a place. The LEA should satisfy itself on both counts before taking formal steps to cease to maintain the young person's statement. At that time, the LEA must also notify the parents of their right of appeal to the Tribunal and the time limits for lodging the appeal, the availability of parent partnership and disagreement resolution services and the fact that the parent's right of appeal cannot be affected by any disagreement resolution procedure. It is not sufficient for LEAs to have a general expectation that an FE institution should be able to meet a young person's needs.

8:124 Where the young person's present school does not cater for children aged 16 plus, the LEA should consider whether to amend the statement to name another school or cease the statement if an appropriate FE course is identified. The LEA should formally propose to amend the statement to name the alternative school or formally propose to cease the statement. In both cases the LEA must also notify the parents of their right to appeal to the Tribunal and the time limits for lodging the appeal.'

(SEN Code of Practice paras 8:121–8:124)

6.11 Parental request for reassessment

It is also possible for parents to request that, where a statement is maintained for their child, the LEA carry out a reassessment of his SEN. The LEA must comply with such a request unless an assessment has been made within the period of six months ending with the date on which the request is made and where it is necessary for the LEA to make a further assessment (s. 328(2)). If the LEA refuses to comply with the request, the LEA must give notice of that fact to the child's parent and must inform the parent of his right to appeal to the SENDIST against the LEA's decision (s. 328(3)). This power is also now given to the headteacher of the child's school (s329A).

6.12 The role of the social services department

Before leaving special education, for completeness, reference should be made to the responsibility of social services authorities towards children with SEN. The wider role of the local authority in respect of social services is discussed elsewhere (see chapter 1.D.2 and chapter 9), but in respect of children with SEN there is one particular responsibility which must be considered.

Where it appears to an LEA (in this context, its education officers) that a local authority (in principle, any local authority, but in this context specifically the social services department) could, by taking any specified action, help in the exercise of any of the LEA's SEN functions, the LEA may request the help of the authority (s. 322(1) of the 1996 Act). The social services department whose help is so requested shall comply with the request unless it considers that:

a) the help requested is not necessary for the purpose of the exercise by the LEA of those functions; or

b) the request is not compatible with its own statutory or other duties and obligations or unduly prejudices the discharge of any of its functions (s. 322(2) and (3)).

Although the duty placed on the social services department is, in effect, a duty secondary to that of the LEA, if help is requested by the LEA the social services department must justify any decision to refuse to help by pointing to one of the grounds contained in s. 322(3)(b). The duty also applies internally. Although it was initially thought that s. 322 could apply only to a request from an LEA to another LEA or the social services department of another local authority, it is now established (see *G v Wakefield MDC* 96 LGR 69) that the section can apply to a request from an authority's LEA to the same authority's social services department.

6.13 Removing Barriers to Achievement

In February 2004, the DfES launched a new action plan for SEN throughout England. It admitted that, despite the Special Educational Needs and Disability Act 2001 and the new *Special Educational Needs Code of Practice,* the Audit Commission's report *Special Educational Needs – a mainstream issue* (2002) had drawn attention to shortcomings in practice. In summary, the defects amounted to: bureaucracy and delay; mainstream schools' unpreparedness to meet SEN; special schools' uncertainty over their future and geographical unevenness of SEN provision. This last item is in part an inevitable function of the circularity of definitions of SEN and special provision, which are related to relative learning abilities and a concept of what is normally provided by appropriate schools in the area (see s. 2 of part A of this chapter). Furthermore, the commonly-voiced, but factually incorrect and insulting, critique of the 'postcode lottery' – regrettably, used by DfES in its document – is a natural outcome of the unresolved tension between national (or at least nationally-expressed) standards and the exercise of local discretion.

8. SPECIAL EDUCATIONAL NEEDS

Nevertheless, the Audit Commission has been just one source of evidence that there are unacceptably wide disparities in responses to SEN and the Department was right to draw attention to the wide consultations and consensus which produced the 2004 document. In it, the Government: looks forward to implementing the changes proposed in Every Child Matters, locally and nationally; seeks to use the powers of agencies for improvement, such as the Teacher Training Agency (see chapter 3.B.19), Ofsted, Connexions and the LSC (see chapter 12), the Disability Rights Commission (part B of this chapter), the National College for School Leadership and SEN regional partnerships and to exploit information and communication technology to lessen the perceived bureaucracy of SEN processes, while improving the quality of information to parents and of performance data in SEN work.

The eleven SEN regional partnerships were set up in 1998/99 and 1999/2000 following the 1997 Green Paper *Excellence for All Children* (Cm 3785), replacing earlier arrangements for regional planning and co-ordination, which had presented a patchy picture of achievement. With advice from the centre, some funding and a National Steering Group, the partnerships have aimed to disseminate good practice, rationalise the availability of scarce specialist expertise across their regions and facilitate communications among the professions engaged in responding to SEN. Perhaps inevitably, the partnerships have a strongly professional character and their structure emphasises that side of LEA activity, as distinct from the political nature of the LEA as local authority. The subject of the partnerships' work more or less dictates this, but it is noteworthy that – as the February 2004 launch demonstrated – the exercise of political judgment is prominent nationally, i.e at Ministerial level.

Less controversially, the regional network can be viewed as an example of inter-authority collaboration without the specific sanction of statutory requirement. As such, it can be compared with the initiative on performance data (see chapter. 7.C.3).

B. Disability Discrimination

1. Introduction

The Disability Discrimination Act 1995 provided, for the first time, statutory protection to disabled persons against discrimination in the workplace and in the provision of certain goods and services. It did not, however, impose any liability for discrimination against disabled pupils in the classroom, the assumption being that these children received sufficient protection through the SEN legislation. Thus, disabled teachers could bring claims against their employers and disabled parents could bring claims if they were prevented from accessing services provided by LEAs or schools, such as parent evenings, meetings etc, but a disabled pupil was without remedy if, for example, an admission authority refused to admit him/her into one of their schools because of disability.

This position was severely criticised by the Disability Rights Task Force, which reported in December 1999 (From *Exclusion to Inclusion: A report of the Disability Rights Task Force on Civil Rights for Disabled People* DfEE, 1999). Recognising that 'the inclusion of disabled people throughout their school and college life is one of the most powerful levers in banishing stereotypes and negative attitudes amongst the next generation', the Task Force made a number of recommendations, the majority of which were accepted and implemented in the Special Educational Needs and Disability Act 2001.

As a result, with effect from 1 September 2002, the 1995 Act was amended to prohibit discrimination against disabled pupils and students in schools, further education and higher education as well as those participating in adult education and receiving youth services.

In broad terms, the amended 1995 Act now imposes duties on the bodies responsible for conducting educational institutions and LEAs:

a)   not to treat disabled pupils less favourably, without justification, for a reason which relates to their discrimination;

b)   to make reasonable adjustments so that disabled pupils are not put at a substantial disadvantage compared to pupils who are not disabled; and

c)   to plan strategically and make progress in increasing accessibility to schools' premises and to the curriculum and in improving the ways in which written information provided to pupils who are not disabled is provided to disabled pupils.

Duties are also placed on FE and HE institutions and LEAs in respect of adult education and youth services.

The duties imposed by the amended 1995 Act on schools are (strictly) outside the scope of this work, although LEAs should not ignore them as it is likely that schools will seek support and advice from their LEAs in meeting their obligations or dealing with claims. We will, though, concentrate on the areas where LEAs are 'responsible bodies' for the purposes of the Act and as such have duties towards disabled pupils.

In a similar way to SEN, in carrying out their functions in this area LEAs must have regard to *Codes of Practice* issued by the Disability Rights Commission (s. 53A of the Act). Two such Codes are relevant to LEAs: the *Code of Practice for Schools: New duties (from 2002) not to discriminate against disabled pupils and prospective pupils in the provision of education and associated services in schools and in respect of admissions and exclusions* (the Schools Code) and the *Code of Practice for providers of post-16 education and related services: New duties (from September 2002) in the provision of post-16 education and related services for disabled people* (the Post-16 Code). Both may apply to the work of LEAs: the Schools Code in matters such as admissions and pupil referral units and the Post-16 Code in matters such as the provision of evening classes, youth service work or Connexions.

Though a detailed analysis of the meaning of 'discrimination' is also beyond the scope of this work, as the definition of disability does vary from statute to statute and, thus, the meaning for social services purposes can be different from the meaning for education purposes, it is perhaps worth briefly considering which pupils, potential pupils or service users are protected.

A person is disabled within the 1995 Act, therefore, if he or she has a physical or mental impairment which has a substantial and long-term adverse effect on their ability to carry out normal day-to-day activities (s.1(1)). Provision is made to deal with past disabilities (s.2); impairments which are not to be regarded as disabilities (see, for example, the Disability Discrimination (Meaning of Disability) Regulations 1996 (SI 1996 No. 1455)) and impairments which are deemed to be disabilities (see, for example, the Disability Discrimination (Blind and Partially Sighted Persons) Regulations 2003 (SI 2003 No. 712)). Further guidance on the meaning of disability and the constituent elements of the statutory definition can also be found in *Guidance on matters to be taken into account in determining questions relating to the definition of disability 1996*, HMSO.

8.
SPECIAL
EDUCATIONAL
NEEDS

LEAs have two types of duty: what might be termed strategic (sections 2 and 3 below) and the individual (section 4).

2. Accessibility strategies

In strategic terms, each LEA is required to prepare, in relation to schools for which it is the responsible body (i.e. maintained schools, pupil referral units and maintained nursery schools) an accessibility strategy and further such strategies at such times as may be prescribed (s. 28D(1)). An accessibility strategy is a written strategy for, over a prescribed period:

a) increasing the extent to which disabled pupils can participate in the schools' curriculum;

b) improving the physical environment of the schools for the purpose of increasing the extent to which disabled pupils are able to take advantage of education and associated services provided or offered by the schools; and

c) improving the delivery to disabled pupils within a reasonable time and in ways which are determined after taking account of their disabilities and any preferences expressed by them or their parents, of information which is provided in writing for pupils who are not disabled.

The first strategy had to be prepared by April 2003 for a three year period extending to 31 March 2006 (see reg 2 of the Disability Discrimination (Prescribed Periods for Accessibility Strategies and Plans for Schools) (England) Regulations 2002 (SI 2002 No. 1981)). The regulations for Wales are in SI 2003 No. 2531 (W 246).

In preparing its accessibility strategy, an LEA must have regard to:

a) the need to allocate adequate resources for implementing the strategy; and

b) any guidance issued as to

    i.   the content of an accessibility strategy,

    ii. the form in which it is to be produced, and

    iii. the persons to be consulted in its preparation (s. 28E(1)).

Guidance on accessibility strategies is not contained in the Schools Code but can be found in separate guidance issued by the Secretary of State (see below).

Every LEA must have regard to any guidance issued by the Secretary of State (see *Accessible Schools: Planning to increase access to schools for disabled pupils* DfES July 2002 and *Accessible Schools: Summary Guidance* DfES 10 June 2002; DfES/0462/2002) with respect to the review and, if necessary, revision of its accessibility strategy (s. 28E(2) of the amended 1995 Act). Thus, every LEA must keep its accessibility strategy under review during the period to which it relates and, if necessary, revise it. Once an LEA has produced an accessibility strategy, it is the duty of the LEA to implement it. Inspections by Ofsted will include the performance by an LEA of its functions in relation to the preparation, review, revision and implementation of its accessibility strategy (s. 28D(6)).

If the Secretary of State, or, in Wales, the National Assembly, asks for a copy of the accessibility strategy, a copy must be provided by an LEA (s. 28E(5) and (6)). If asked to do so, an LEA must also make a copy of its accessibility strategy available for inspection at such reasonable times as it may determine (s. 28E(7)). The Secretary of State (or NAW) has reserve powers to ensure that LEAs have complied with their duties to produce, review and revise accessibility strategies. Where the Secretary of State or NAW is satisfied (whether on a complaint or otherwise) that an LEA:

a) has acted, or is proposing to act, unreasonably in the discharge of a duty in respect of an accessibility strategy; or

b) has failed to discharge a duty imposed in respect of such a strategy,

he/it may give that responsible body such directions as to the discharge of the duty as appear to him/it to be expedient (s. 28M(1)). Such directions may be varied or revoked by the Secretary of State (or Assembly) and may be enforced, on the application of the directing authority, by a mandatory order obtained in accordance with s. 31 of the Supreme Court Act 1981 (s. 28M(7)).

3. Accessibility plans

The main document LEAs will have to concern themselves with is the accessibility strategy. Accessibility plans, however, which normally have to be prepared by the responsible body for a school i.e. the governing body, will have to be produced by LEAs in respect of pupil referral units.

An accessibility plan is a written plan for, over a prescribed period (the initial period is 1st April 2003 to 31st March 2006: see reg 3 of the Disability Discrimination (Prescribed Periods for Accessibility Strategies and Plans for Schools) (England) Regulations 2002 (SI 2002 No. 1981):

a) increasing the extent to which disabled pupils can participate in the PRU's curriculum;

b) improving its physical environment for the purpose of increasing the extent to which disabled pupils are able to take advantage of education and associated services provided or offered there; and

c) improving the delivery to disabled pupils (i) within a reasonable time and, (ii) in ways which are determined after taking account of their disabilities and any preferences expressed by them or their parents, of information which is provided in writing for pupils who are not disabled (s. 28D(9) and (10)).

When preparing an accessibility plan, the LEA must have regard to the need to allocate adequate resources for implementing the plan (s.

8.
SPECIAL
EDUCATIONAL
NEEDS

28D(12)). Once the plan is produced, it is the duty of the LEA to implement it and keep it under review and, if necessary, revise it (s. 28D(11)). When a pupil referral unit is inspected by Ofsted, that inspection may extend to the preparation, publication, review, revision and implementation of the accessibility plan (s. 28D(13)). The Secretary of State retains powers similar to those he has in relation to accessibility strategies to ensure that LEAs have complied with their duties to produce, review and revise accessibility plans (s. 28M(1)).

4. Obligations to individual disabled pupils

In addition to strategic accessibility planning duties, responsible bodies owe duties not to discriminate against individual disabled pupils. In many cases, duties owed to school pupils or prospective pupils will be the responsibility of governing bodies. However, LEAs had this responsibility in maintained nursery schools until such schools gained formal governing bodies in September 2003, and bear them in pupil referral units and for admissions in community and voluntary controlled schools.

Further, by virtue of the obligation not to discriminate in respect of the admission of pupils to schools for which the LEA is admissions authority, LEAs have duties towards children seeking admission to such schools (s. 28K). Finally, LEAs have residual duties not to discriminate against disabled pupils, which effectively extends the protection of the 1995 Act to any pupil or person who falls under any of an LEA's functions (see s. 28F).

Two types of discrimination are effectively made unlawful in respect of these functions: discrimination which involves treating a person less favourably than a person who is not disabled ('discrimination through less favourable treatment') (s. 28B) and failing to take reasonable steps to ensure that a disabled person is not placed at a substantial disadvantage in comparison with persons who are not disabled (s. 28C).

In the case of claims relating to admission decisions, claims against an LEA should be brought before the LEA's independent admission appeal panel; in all other cases, claims are made to the SENDIST.

The residual duties, whilst imposing the obligation not to discriminate, do not require an LEA to remove or alter a physical feature or to provide auxiliary aids or services (s. 28G(3)). As with the duties imposed on governing bodies, a number of defences are available to an LEA including: where the LEA did not know of the disability, or where the pupil concerned had made a confidentiality request and where avoiding the discrimination would contravene that request. The other important defence available to LEAs is the one of justification, i.e. that although there may have been discrimination, it was justified in the circumstances. LEAs should, however, be wary of relying too heavily on the defences as the Schools and Post-16 Codes make clear the expectation that LEAs should not discriminate in the first place, that they should be proactive in both identifying children with disabilities and meeting their needs and that LEAs will therefore have to show in some detail why they felt their actions were justified.

8.
SPECIAL
EDUCATIONAL
NEEDS

9. INCLUSION

A. Introduction

Earlier in this work (chapters 1.A.1 and 3.C), we have talked of *de facto* duties imposed on LEAs by the Secretary of State, usually through departmental circular or letters from the DfES.

Perhaps the area where most *de facto* legislating (as it were) occurs is in respect of the LEA functions that broadly fall within the ambit of the term 'inclusion'. For the purposes of this work, the term will not include special education, which warrants a chapter of its own (see chapter 8), but does include the LEA's responsibilities to deal with discipline in, and exclusion from, schools, attendance and education welfare, behaviour support, education otherwise than at school and a miscellany of welfare functions. Some other functions, such as school transport, school lunches and clothing grants, might also be considered as part of the LEA's responsibility to achieve social inclusion, but are discussed in chapter 10, as they can more commonly apply to a broader range of children than just the socially excluded. The youth service, Connexions, careers, work experience and juvenile employment are examined in chapter 11.

Having set out what might be included under inclusion and what might not, for the purpose of this work, only the following functions will be considered in this chapter:

- education welfare and attendance

- Youth Offending Teams

- local co-ordination of strategies for children in England and the Green Paper

- behaviour support

- education otherwise than at school

- discipline and exclusion

- children in public care.

B. Education Welfare and Attendance

This is a classic area in which the duty of an LEA to ensure children have access to an appropriate education (*de jure*) overlaps with the DfES's view that LEAs also have an obligation to promote good attendance (*de facto*). There is no question that promoting good attendance is preferable to exercising enforcement powers, both from the interest of the LEA in costs terms and that of ensuring that parents and children are persuaded to work within the system, rather than being confronted with, and punished by, it. However, such tactics have not always worked and so the latest guidance, combined with the increasing penalties imposed on guilty parents, seeks to remind the LEA that enforcement may or, in certain circumstances, should play a key part in its steps to reduce non-attendance. The role of the education welfare officer over the last few years has thus developed from truancy officer to social worker and back, in part, to truancy officer again.

Irregular attendance prevents children properly benefiting from their years of education and often leads to low attainment. Children who are not in school are also more easily drawn into criminal or anti-social behaviour. The Government has committed and continues to commit, itself to reducing unauthorised absence from school although it is thought about 50,000 pupils are absent from school without authorisation each day (see 'Mother's jail term cuts school truancy numbers', *The Independent*, 22 November 2003). In addition to the powers outlined below, the DfES launched a fast-track prosecution system in January 2003, under which parents of persistent truants are given only 12 weeks' warning before being taken to court.

The Secretary of State has issued guidance to LEAs as to how they should exercise their functions relating to the promotion and enforcement of attendance (*Ensuring Regular School Attendance* DfES/0432/2003).

In legal terms, LEAs have clearly defined responsibilities where it becomes apparent that children are not receiving proper education. It should be noted, however, that the Government has been proposing for some time to transfer the responsibility for education welfare from LEAs to schools (see for example 'Schools to take on truancy control', *TES*, 5 November 1999). This has not yet happened and the relevant funding is not yet required to be delegated to schools, but it is understood that the idea has not been dismissed totally and some LEAs have adopted the scheme on their own initiative. What steps have been taken, however, have met with mixed success: the Chief Inspector reported in June 2003 (*Key Stage 4: towards a more flexible curriculum*, HMI 517) that 'despite concerns being raised in the past about "missing" pupils, we estimate that 10,000 15 year-olds are unaccounted for on education rolls in England.'

Parents of children of compulsory school age are under a duty to secure that their children receive suitable education by regular attendance at school or otherwise (s. 7 of the Education Act 1996). Where it becomes apparent to the LEA that a child of compulsory school age in its area is not receiving suitable education, either by regular attendance at school or otherwise, the LEA is under a duty to serve a notice in writing on the parent of the child requiring him to satisfy the LEA that, within the period specified in the notice, the child is receiving suitable education (s. 437(1) of the Education Act 1996). Suitable education for these purposes means efficient full-time education suitable to his age, ability and aptitude and to any special educational needs he may have (s. 437(8)).

If the parent fails to satisfy the LEA that the child is receiving suitable education and the LEA believes it is expedient that the child should attend school, the LEA shall serve on the parent an order (known as a school attendance order) requiring the parent to cause the child to become a registered pupil at a school named in the order (s. 437(2)).

Before issuing a school attendance order, the LEA must first serve a written notice on the parent informing him of its intention to serve the order, specifying the school which the LEA intends to name and, if it thinks fit, suitable alternatives and informing the parent of his ability to apply for places at alternative schools (s. 438(2) and (3)). If the parent applies for the child to be admitted to one of those alternative schools, that school will generally be named in the order. If the parent does not put forward such a school, then the school which the LEA indicated it intended to name will be named in the order.

Where the LEA intends to name a school, it must first consult the governing body (s. 439(5)(a)) and if the school is the responsibility of another LEA, that LEA (s. 439(5)(b)). A school cannot be named in an order if (a) the effect of admitting the child would be to take the school above its fixed admissions number and (b) the LEA is not responsible for determining the admissions arrangements at the school, i.e. is not the admissions authority, unless there is no other maintained school within a reasonable distance of the child's home (s. 439(1) to (3)).

Once the school attendance order is made, it continues in force for so long as the child is of compulsory school age unless it is revoked by the LEA or a court directs that it should cease (s. 437(4)). The LEA must inform the governing body and headteacher of the maintained school named in the order that the order has been made and the governing body is then under a duty to admit the child (s. 437(5) and (6)).

Once a school attendance order is in force, the parent of a child without a statement of special educational needs may request that the order be amended or revoked.

If at any time the parent applies for the child to be admitted to a maintained school other than the one named in the order, the child is offered a place and the parent requests that the order be amended accordingly, the LEA must comply with the request (s. 440(2)).

If the parent applies to the LEA for education to be provided at a school which is not maintained by an LEA, the child is offered a place under arrangements made by the LEA under which it pays the fees and the parent requests that the LEA amends the order, the LEA shall comply with the request (s. 440(3)).

If the parent applies for the child to be admitted to a non-maintained school, where the LEA is not responsible for the arrangements, the child is offered a place and the school is suitable to his age, ability, aptitude and to any special educational needs he may have and the parent requests that the order be amended, the LEA shall comply with that request (s. 440(4)).

If the parent applies to the LEA requesting that the order be revoked on the ground that arrangements have been made for the child to receive suitable education otherwise than at school, the LEA is obliged to comply with the request unless it is of the opinion that no satisfactory arrangements have been made for the education of the child (s. 442(2)). If the LEA refuses to revoke the order, the parent may refer the question to the Secretary of State (s. 442(3)), who may give such direction as he thinks fit. A parent cannot apply for the order to be revoked if his child has a statement of SEN and the name of the school in the order is the school specified in the statement (s. 442(5)).

If a parent on whom a school attendance order is served fails to comply with the requirements of the order, he is guilty of an offence under s. 443 of the Act, unless he proves to the court that he is causing the child to receive suitable education otherwise than at school.

School attendance orders work only where the child is not a registered pupil at a school. Where a child of compulsory school age is a registered pupil, if he fails to attend regularly, his parent is guilty of an offence (s. 444(1) and (1A)).

The offence under s. 444(1) is committed by a parent if their child, of compulsory school age, who is a registered pupil at a school, fails to attend regularly at the school. This is an offence of strict liability (see *Bath and North East Somerset District Council v Warman* [1999] ELR 81 and *Jarman v Mid-Glamorgan Education Authority* [1985] LS Gaz R 1249). The strict nature of the offence does not however deprive the parent of their right to a fair trial under Article 6 of the European Convention on Human Rights as incorporated by the Human Rights Act, see *Barnfather v Islington LBC* [2003] EWHC 418 (Admin).

That offence has been around for many years. In an attempt to crack down on truancy, however, an additional and more serious offence was introduced by the Criminal Justice and Court Services Act 2000. A parent is thus guilty of this offence if, in the circumstances mentioned in subsection 444(1) (i.e. a child of compulsory school age who is a registered pupil at a school fails to attend regularly at the school), the parent knows that his child is failing to attend regularly at the school and fails without reasonable justification to cause him to do so (s. 444(1A)).

A parent prosecuted on either charge does have, however, a number of defences available. First, a child should not be taken to have failed to attend regularly by reason of his absence from the school:

a)   with authorised leave;

b)   at any time when he was prevented from attending by reason of sickness or any unavoidable cause; or

c)   on any day exclusively set apart for religious observance by the religious body to which his parent belongs (s. 444(3)).

Second, the child shall not be taken to have failed to attend regularly at the school if the parent proves:

a) that the school at which the child is a registered pupil is not within walking distance of the child's home; and

b) that no suitable arrangements have been made by the LEA for any of the following:

    (i) his transport to and from the school,

    (ii) boarding accommodation for him at or near the school, or

    (iii) enabling him to become a registered pupil at a school nearer to his home (s. 444(4) and see *Essex County Council v Rogers* [1987] AC 66, [1986] 3 All ER 321).

Specific provision is made to protect children of traveller families (s. 444(6)).

With both types of prosecution (s. 443 and s. 444), there is no duty on the LEA actually to prosecute. The LEA always has the discretion to prosecute or not and, although prosecution is the only way of promoting good attendance in certain cases, in many cases it is not. For example, although parents may be separated and one parent be absent from the home and child and so have no ability to influence attendance, he or she will in principle be as guilty as the person with whom the child resides. In other cases, the parents may do all they can to get the child to school, but the child may be stronger than the parents and there is no physical way in which the parents can secure that the child attends. In these circumstances, fairness might persuade an LEA not to exercise its discretion to prosecute.

A new procedure relating to the s. 444(1) offence has been introduced by s. 23 of the Anti-social Behaviour Act 2003, inserting into the Education Act 1996 a new s. 444A. Under it, an authorised officer may issue a penalty notice to a person who has failed to secure regular attendance at school by the child for whom he or she is responsible. 'School' here means maintained school, PRU, Academy, CTC or CCTA. 'Authorised officer' comprises a police officer, LEA officer, headteacher, or member of school staff (as authorised by the headteacher and specified in the regulations – see below – as a deputy or an assistant head). Payment of the penalty to the LEA avoids liability to criminal proceedings under s. 444(1A) in respect of the relevant omission to secure attendance. The Education (Penalty Notices) (England) Regulations 2004 (SI 2004 No. 181) prescribe the form and content of penalty notices and set the penalty at £50 if paid within 28 days or £100 within 42 days.

The regulations, which came into force on 27 February 2004, provide that penalty notices may be issued only in accordance with a code of conduct drawn up by the LEA after consultation (regs 12–14). Regulation 21 requires that the LEA must apply the penalty revenues 'in meeting the costs of issuing and enforcing notices, or the cost of prosecuting recipients who do not pay.' By reg 6, the LEA must prosecute if the payment has not been made within the time limit, unless it withdraws the notice e.g. for error (reg 7).

News reports at the end of 2003 (e.g 'Parents of holiday truants face £100 fine', *The Guardian*, 27 December 2003) gave prominence to the Ministerial intention that the procedure should be used to deter or punish *inter alios* parents who withdraw their children for holidays in term time without the headteacher's permission. The Government's campaign against truancy was said to be only partly successful, as local 'sweeps' and DfES's enquiries revealed the extent of parental condonation.

In any event, before instituting any proceedings against a parent, the LEA must consider whether it would be appropriate (instead of or as well as instituting proceedings) to apply for an education supervision order with respect to the child (s. 447(1)).

Previously, apart from ordering education supervision orders, magistrates could consider only a range of fines upon the conviction of a parent, although on one occasion the Greenwich stipendiary magistrate imposed a bail condition requiring a mother to escort her non-attending 13 year-old to school (see James Montgomery 'Truant's parents feel force of law', *TES*, 10 May 1996). With the introduction of the additional offence in 2000, the level of punishment available was increased. A parent convicted of an offence under s. 444(1) can be sentenced only to a fine not exceeding level 3 on the standard scale (s. 444(8)). A person convicted of the more serious offence can, however, now receive either a fine, not exceeding level 4 on the standard scale, or imprisonment for a term not exceeding three months (or both) (s. 444(8A)). If a parent is charged with the more serious offence and the court finds the defendant not guilty of that offence but is satisfied that he is guilty of the lesser offence under s. 444(1), the court may find him guilty of that offence. The increased penalties seem to have some effect (see, for example, 'Truancy falls after jailing of mother', *TES*, 17 January 2003 and 'Mother's jail term cuts school truancy numbers', *The Independent*, 22 November 2003) especially after the jailing of a mother, Patricia Amos, in 2002, for repeatedly failing to secure her daughters' attendance. Though relatively few cases have been determined so far, the publicity given to such convictions in courts of first instance is great: see 'Mother jailed for teenage son's truancy', *The Independent* 15 April 2003, noting sentences of 28 days (Llanelli) and six months (Cambridge), after *Amos*, whose sentence had been 60 days, but that was reduced on appeal. The unfortunate Mrs Amos was convicted of a further offence in 2004 ('Mother may face prison again over daughter's truancy,' *The Independent* 11 February 2004).

When naughty Rupert Truant plays, Mummy Bear gets 60 days.

In addition, the courts also have the power through parenting orders (s. 8 of the Crime and Disorder Act 1998) to require parents to attend for counselling or guidance sessions for up to three months and may include other requirements to help prevent further pupil absence. Further provisions have been introduced by the Anti-Social Behaviour Act 2003 to enable residential counselling and guidance programmes to be ordered where these are likely to be more effective and any interference with family life they cause is proportionate (see now s. 8(7A) of the Crime and Disorder Act 1998). In addition, the 2003 Act has also given LEAs or the governing bodies of schools the ability to enter into parenting contracts where a child has failed to attend regularly (s. 19(2)). A parenting contract will contain a statement by the parent that he agrees to meet certain requirements, including attending counselling or guidance programmes and one by the LEA or school that it will make certain support available, the cost of which will be borne by whichever of the two provides the support. The contract does not, however, give rise to contractual or tortious obligations or liability (s. 19(8)). It is also entirely voluntary, although the guidance (see below) suggests that a parental refusal to enter into a contract, or to fail to comply with one, should be taken into consideration and may support an application for a parenting order. *Guidance on Education-Related Parenting Contracts, Parenting Orders and Penalty Notices* (DfES, 2004) deals specifically with the use of parenting contracts in the case of truancy at paras 30–50 and 223–250, to which LEAs and governing bodies will have to have regard (s. 19(9)). Principally, the guidance advises that in deciding whether a contract will be appropriate, consideration should be given to whether parental influence could be better brought to bear in improving the child's attendance, whether the support provided through a parenting contract could help in doing this and, if so, what form the support should take.

As part of the general effort to reduce non-attendance and the consequential anti-social behaviour that can result (the typical example being the absent children who make a nuisance of themselves at shopping centres), the Government introduced a new police power to deal with truants in the Crime and Disorder Act 1998.

If a police officer has reasonable cause to believe that a child or young person found by him in a public place is of compulsory school age and is absent from school without lawful authority, the officer may remove him to designated premises or to the school from which he is absent (s. 16(3) of the Crime and Disorder Act 1998). Public places include private premises to which the public may have access, such as shops, shopping centres and amusement arcades (s. 14).

This power is available only in certain circumstances and does not apply to all children found absent from school. First, a police officer above the rank of superintendent must direct that the powers can be used within a specified area and for a specified time. Second, the local authority must designate premises to which the children and young persons may be removed and inform the chief officer of police of these premises (s. 16(1)).

9.
INCLUSION

These powers are very much to be used in areas where there are particular problems with truanting and to enable a multi-agency approach involving the police, LEA and Youth Offending Team to identify suitable areas and suitable times. In particular, the powers will be used in areas where schools have high levels of unauthorised absence, including significant levels of post-registration truancy, in areas where schools are experiencing difficulty with high levels of parentally-condoned unjustified absence and in areas where juvenile crime is prevalent, especially during the day.

Co-operation between LEA officers and police will be vital to ensure that the powers are used only against children who are truanting and not against those who are absent with permission. The LEA will also have to find suitable premises to be designated. In most cases, children will be returned to local schools – either their own (which does not necessarily have to be designated) or to another school chosen as a reception centre (which will require designation). Other places can be used, such as LEA offices or offices within shopping centres, but the children must not be taken to police stations.

The Secretary of State has issued guidance to LEAs as to how they should exercise their functions relating to the promotion and enforcement of attendance (see Circular 11/99 *Social Inclusion: the LEA Role in Pupil Support*, especially its chapters 1 and 2, 'Managing Attendance' and 'Legal Action to Enforce Attendance').

C. Youth Offending Teams (YOTs)

Local authorities with responsibility for education and social services are required by s. 39 of the Crime and Disorder Act 1998 to establish multi-agency Youth Offending Teams (YOTs) to act in conjunction with the police, probation and health services. YOT members must include at least one of each of the following: a probation officer; a police officer; a social worker; a person nominated by the health authority and a person nominated by the chief education officer (s. 39(5)). Other appropriate persons, including representatives from the voluntary sector, may be invited on to the YOT.

YOTs have a duty to co-ordinate the provision of youth justice services and to carry out functions outlined in the youth justice plan for the area (s. 39(7)). The latter are plans drawn up annually by each local authority working in co-operation with the chief officer of police, probation committee and the health authority (s. 40). Each plan must be submitted to the Youth Justice Board for England and Wales, which is also responsible for monitoring the operation and performance of YOTs.

The intention is that the various members of the YOTs will work in partnership to develop a consistent and unified approach to working with young offenders and so prevent offending by children and young persons. Some transitional funding in the form of a grant tapered over three years was made available to 'pump prime' the initiative but long-term funding was expected to come from the s. 40 partners. Early tensions emerged with some partners, health in particular, finding it difficult to contribute their expected share of the costs of the team. The main burden of funding the new teams fell on local authorities and in particular their social services departments.

Core staff were provided by the probation service and social workers drawn from teams that had previously dealt with youth justice issues.

The Youth Justice and Criminal Evidence Act 1999 introduced a new approach to intervention with first-time offenders, emphasising personal responsibility, reparation and the role of the family, friends and other responsible adults in tackling offending behaviour. Under ss. 16–20 a referral order can be made for first time offenders who plead guilty and do not require custodial sentence. They are referred to a Youth Offender Panel (ss. 21–22) comprising one member of the YOT and at least two drawn from the community, one of whom takes the chair. The panel looks at the causes of offending and draws up a contract (ss. 23–27) with the young offender and their parents to tackle these. The panel takes responsibility for monitoring the contract facilitated by the YOT (under an extension to its functions under s. 29). These arrangements were piloted during 2000 and deemed a success (see the second interim evaluation report (July 2001) on the Introduction of Referral Orders into the Youth Justice System: and the Home Office guidance *Referral Orders and Youth Offenders Panel – Guidance for Courts, Youth Offending Teams and Youth Offender Panels* (www.homeoffice.gov.uk/yousys/youth.htm).

Additional project funding was made available through the Youth Inclusion Programme (YIP) and to pilot Youth Inclusion Support Panels (YISPs). From 2003, a quarter of the Children's Fund grant to each local partnership was hypothecated to approved crime prevention activities to be planned by the local children's fund partnerships in consultation with the YOT in their area. The decision to disband the Children and Young People's Unit (see below) called into question the sourcing of this funding from the Children's Fund which had been created at the same time. At the time of writing no decisions had apparently been taken but it seems likely that funding for diversionary projects for young people considered to be at risk of offending will continue to be available from one source or another.

D. Local Co-ordination of Strategies for Children in England and the Green Paper

At the turn of the century the Children and Young People's Unit was set up as a cross departmental agency to promote the government's aspiration to make society more child-friendly. It was charged with developing an overarching strategy for children and given control of resources (the Children's Fund) to support its work.

Following the 2002 expenditure review the chief executive of every principal local authority was asked to co-ordinate a Local Preventative Strategy across its area to be in place from April 2003 and drawing in all public statutory and voluntary agencies working with children. This grew out of earlier policies and initiatives related to social exclusion, but sought to achieve coherence across all opportunities to intervene early where children may be deemed to be at risk of adverse outcomes (whether for themselves or society at large). The strategy was expected to bring together all previous and current activity, including the invitation to pilot 'Children's Trusts' announced by the Department of Health at about the same time to encourage an integrated approach to service delivery for children across health, social services and education. No new funding, structures or agencies were envisaged, contrary to the approach when, for example, the SEU report *Bridging the Gap* (Cm 4405, 1999) with a similar, if more limited, aspiration gave rise to the creation of Connexions. A small amount of funding was made available by the Children and Young People's Unit to assist the development of 'Identification, Referral and Tracking' (IRT) mechanisms to support the strategy.

In the autumn of 2002, the Prime Minister announced the preparation of a Green Paper on children at risk, which was published as *Every Child Matters* (Cm 5860) on 8 September 2003. The long gestation reflected the scope of its ambition to map out how the management and delivery of all public services could be transformed to place children at the centre of the enterprise. Much of it was descriptive of initiatives that were already in place or in development, with some reframing in an attempt to achieve greater coherence across previously disparate initiatives.

- The CYPU work on its overarching strategy (which had been put out for consultation during 2001) was summarised in chapter 1 'The Challenge'.

- Chapters 2 and 3 outlined a range of current initiatives aimed at improving children's services and parenting.

- The IRT strand of activity was covered in chapter 4 'Early Intervention and Effective Protection' (see chapter 7.C of this book).

- 'Local Preventive Strategy' disappeared as a term of art, but the idea was reflected in chapter 5, 'Accountability and Integration – Locally, Regionally and Nationally'. This announced plans to place local authorities firmly in the lead with explicit responsibility for 'improving children's lives' and integrating local services 'within a single organisational focus'.

The Children Bill (2004) proposes to require each local authority with education and social services responsibilities to have a lead member (presumably with cabinet rank) for children. There will also be a new statutory post of director of children's services replacing (in England) the existing requirements for each appropriate local authority to employ fit people as chief education officer and director of social services. See chapters 1.E.3 and 3.B.3.

The new director of children's services would be 'accountable for education and [children's] social services and for overseeing services delegated to the local authority by other services'. The expected leadership of the local authority in this regard is thus made clear. However, the mechanism for achieving it is left vague. The Government's 'preferred model for achieving its long term vision' is through Children's Trusts, which are expected to be in place in most areas by 2006. In addition to relevant local authority functions a Children's Trust is expected to include 'community and acute health services – such as community paediatrics, services commissioned by drug action teams, teenage pregnancy co-ordinators and locally commissioned and provided Child and Adolescent Mental Health Services'. Other services that may be subsumed include: speech and language therapy; health visitors; occupational therapy; YOTs and Connexions. There are also references to working with other public, private and voluntary organisations.

The Bill will also create new statutory Local Safeguarding Children Boards (see chapter 1.E.3). These will replace the present Area Child Protection Committees; this is a response to the recommendations on vulnerable children in *Safeguarding Children* (October 2002), the first of a planned series of triennial joint Chief Inspector's Reports promised in the 1998 White Paper *Modernising Social Services* (Cm 4169). The department of health published guidance in 2003, *What To Do If You're Worried A Child Is Being Abused*, which also formed part of its response to the Victoria Climbié report.

These proposals represent another round of centrally-driven structural change. They also continue the trend, previously observed in early-years services, for 'joining–up' exercises to result in education's absorbing social services rather than the other way round. This trend is also reflected at national level. The 'machinery of government' changes have largely been to strengthen the DfES at the expense of other parts of Whitehall. The new Minister for Children and Families is located within DfES – replacing portfolios in the Home Office, Lord Chancellor's Department and the Treasury. The freestanding CYPU is abolished in favour of a new directorate within DfES which also absorbs officials previously located in the Home Office and Department of Health.

The loss of the CYPU's non-departmental focus is compensated for by the introduction of a Children's Commissioner. This person will be expected to act as an independent champion for all children, but particularly the disadvantaged, advising Government and engaging on their behalf with others such as business and the media.

E. Behaviour Support

Subject to the exceptions noted below, every LEA is under a duty to prepare and from time to time review a statement setting out the arrangements it is making or proposing to make in connection with the education of children with behavioural difficulties (s. 527A of the Education Act 1996).

The arrangements that must be covered by the statement include:

a) the arrangements made or to be made by the LEA for the provision of advice and resources to schools maintained by the LEA and other arrangements made or to be made by it with a view to:

   (i) meeting requests by such schools for support and assistance in connection with the promotion of good behaviour and discipline on the part of their pupils, and

   (ii) assisting such schools to deal with general behavioural problems and the behavioural difficulties of individual pupils;

b) the arrangements made or to be made by the LEA for the provision of suitable education at school or otherwise than at school for those children of compulsory school age who may not receive such education unless such arrangements are made for them (see s. 19 of the Education Act 1996); and

c) other arrangements made or to be made by it for assisting children with behavioural difficulties to find places at suitable schools (s. 527A(2)).The statement should also deal with the interaction between these arrangements and the arrangements made by the LEA for children with special educational needs (s. 527A(3)).

The statement must be prepared following consultation prescribed by the Secretary of State and, once produced, must be published as and when prescribed by regulations. The regulations shall also make provision for when and how the statement needs to be revised (s. 527A(4) and (5)).

The relevant provisions can be found in the Local Education Authority (Behaviour Support Plans) Regulations 1998 (SI 1998 No. 644). Thus, in the course of preparing the Behaviour Support Plan, the LEA must consult the headteacher and governing body of every maintained school and the teacher in charge and, where in place, the management committee of pupil referral units and also trade unions and persons representative of teachers and staff other than teachers employed in the LEA's schools, parents' representatives, FE principals, the director of social services, every diocesan authority, health authority, probation committee, chief constable, careers service organisation, learning and skills council and clerk to the justices, together with representatives of voluntary organisations working with disaffected children and young persons within the LEA's area (reg 3).

Every consultee should receive a draft of the plan and a letter containing prescribed information as to what the consultee is being asked to do.

Once the plan has been produced, it must be made available for inspection by members of the public at public libraries and such other places as may be reasonable. Copies must also be sent to the Secretary of State, HM Chief Inspector and every consultee, as well as to anyone else who asks for one (reg 4).

In preparing the Behaviour Support Plan and implementing it, LEAs must have regard to any guidance issued by the Secretary of State (s. 527A(6)). The current guidance is contained in DfEE Circular 1/98 *LEA Behaviour Support Plans*.

LEAs which have been categorised as excellent in the Comprehensive Performance Assessment in 2003 and which achieved a 3-star rating for performance in education and those LEAs preparing pilot single education plans are not required to publish revised behaviour support plans (Local Education Authority (Behaviour Support Plans) (Exception) (England) Regulations 2003 (SI 2003 No. 3082).

Behaviour support has a large element of *de facto* duty about it. Behind the explicit requirement to maintain a plan is a recognition that positive promotion of good behaviour amongst the young whilst they are attending school can do much to head off the undesirable consequences of exclusion and the anti-social behaviour that is associated with it (see parts B and G in this chapter). This policy approach became more important in 2002 when headteacher resistance led, after some initial success, to the abandonment of direct measures and targets further to reduce exclusions from school. The focus shifted away from attempting to restrict heads' ability to exclude and towards removing the reasons for their finding the need to do so.

The Green Paper *Every Child Matters* lists the initiatives that together comprise the 'national behaviour and attendance strategy' including programmes to fund:

- key workers for children at risk
- learning mentors
- training and support in all secondary (through the key stage 3 strategy) and some primary schools
- learning support units
- truancy sweeps
- creating multi-agency Behaviour and Education Support Teams (BESTs).

F. Education Otherwise than at School

Section 19 of the 1996 Act imposes an obligation on every LEA to make arrangements for the provision of suitable education at school or otherwise than at school for those children of compulsory school age who, by reason of illness, exclusion from school or otherwise, may not for any period receive suitable education unless such arrangements are made for them (s. 19(1)). Suitable education is defined as efficient education suitable to a child's age, ability and aptitude and to any special educational needs he may have (s. 19(6)).

In the case of *R v East Sussex County Council ex parte Tandy* [1998] ELR 251, it was held that, in respect of such children, s. 19(1) imposes a duty which is owed to each individual child who falls within the ambit of the subsection. The child in that case suffered from myalgic encephalomyelitis and found it difficult or impossible to attend school. The LEA provided home tuition under s. 19, but as a result of financial pressure, decided to reduce that tuition from five hours to three hours per week. The House of Lords held that such a cut was unlawful. The duty under s. 19(1) was owed not to all children within the class, but to each such child individually. In

9.
INCLUSION

those circumstances, the pressures on the LEA's financial resources were not a relevant factor in determining what was suitable education for the child and therefore, because the LEA had acted solely for financial reasons, its decision to reduce the hours was unlawful. To permit an LEA to avoid performing its statutory duties on the grounds that it preferred to spend its money in other ways would, in the Lords' view, downgrade a duty to a mere power and could not be accepted.

Thus, when considering what arrangements to make for children out of school within s. 19(1), LEAs have an individual duty to each child to provide suitable education and what is suitable will be based solely on educational grounds; financial difficulties in making the provision cannot lawfully be taken into account.

Excluded pupils, as well as sick ones, fall within the same duty, but 'or otherwise' does not extend to children who are voluntarily withdrawn from school by their parents, for example, because they believe their child is being bullied (*R (ota G v) Westminster City Council* [2004] EWCA Civ 45). The guidance from the DfES now makes clear that pupils out of school should receive about five hours of supervised education or other activity a day and LEAs have been obliged to provide this with effect from September 2002 (DfEE *Circular 11/99*, para 5.19). In effect, therefore, LEAs should provide 25 hours of tuition a week to those children out of school and they will have to show educational reasons why they do not believe that they should do so. The fact that they claim not to be able to afford to do so or do not have enough home tutors is, *per Tandy*, irrelevant. It is also noteworthy that in *Tandy* the LEA found that it could not afford five hours of home tuition per week, let alone the 25 now required. Unfortunately, it seems that the Government's aim has not yet been achieved. In his report in June 2003 (*Key Stage 4: towards a more flexible curriculum*, HMI 517), the Chief Inspector found that although since September 2002, every LEA was supposed to have been able to provide a full-time education in a PRU for children expelled from other schools, whilst some of these were making a 'significant difference', generally the quality of provision varied widely.

LEAs have a duty to make arrangements for children, i.e. persons not over compulsory school age. For those over this age (young persons), there is only a power.

In either performing their duty under s. 19(1) or exercising their power under s. 19(4), LEAs must have regard to guidance given by

**9.
INCLUSION**

the Secretary of State (s. 19(4A)), which is currently found in DfEE *Circular 11/99* and, in particular, its chapter 4, which provides guidance on LEA responsibility for arranging education outside school.

As part of their responsibilities to children outside school, LEAs have the power to establish pupil referral units to provide education specially for such children (s. 19(2)) and can secure the provision of boarding accommodation at such units (s. 19(3)). Schedule 1 to the 1996 Act provides for the conduct of these units and the differences from normal schools. Chapter 6 of DfEE *Circular 11/99* also sets out in detail information on the conduct of the units and guidance on how they should operate. The key differences between PRUs (which are legally both a type of school and education otherwise than at school) and schools are that: PRUs have management committees, not governing bodies; there can be dual registration of pupils at PRUs and schools; PRUs have teachers in charge, who may or may not be designated headteachers; the curriculum need not be the full National Curriculum and premises requirements are modified.

G. Discipline and Exclusion

1. The main principles illustrated

The role of the LEA in respect of pupil discipline has been much diminished in recent years. Before 1 September 1999, the LEA had the power to reinstate excluded pupils at county or voluntary controlled schools and so could assist inclusion by ensuring that children were not inappropriately excluded either because the school had acted too harshly or because there would be no alternative provision available.

From 1 September 1999, however, an LEA's power to reinstate an excluded pupil was removed. Instead, all it has is, first, the right to be informed by the headteachers of all maintained schools of all permanent exclusions or fixed-term exclusions of more than five school days in any one term or where the pupil would lose the opportunity to take a public examination (see the Education (Pupil Exclusions and Appeals) (Maintained Schools) (England) Regulations 2002 (SI 2002 No. 3178) made under s. 52 of the 2002 Act). (Provision to deal with the exclusion of pupils from PRUs, bringing them broadly into line with exclusions from schools, can be found in the Education (Pupil Exclusions and Appeals) (Pupil

Referral Units) (England) Regulations 2002 (SI 2002 No. 3179)). The regulations for Wales are in SI 2003 No. 3227 (W 308) in respect of maintained schools and SI 2003 No. 3246 (W 321) for PRUs.

The LEA has a role as a neutral adviser or provider of information to pupil discipline committees or exclusion appeal panels.

The emphasis of the statutory guidance *Improving Behaviour and Attendance: Guidance on Exclusion from Schools and Pupil Referral Units* (available on www.teachernet.gov.uk) is on intervention before the need to exclude arises and the key role of the LEA is in offering support to schools, but there will be occasions where a school will consider an exclusion to be necessary.

In Wales, guidance on PRUs, replacing chapter 6 and annex E of Circular 3/99, is found in Circular 1/2004.

Each governing body should enable a parent to make representation against a pupil's exclusion (reg 5 of the Education (Pupil Exclusions and Appeals) (Maintained Schools) (England) Regulations 2002, cited above). Where a headteacher has resorted to exclusion, the governors should decide whether or not to confirm a permanent exclusion or fixed-term exclusions totalling more than 15 school days in any one term, or five school days where the relevant person makes representations, or where a public examination will be missed. The LEA has the right to make representations to the governors about the exclusion and to have those representations considered by them (reg 5(2)(b)). In addition, the LEA must be allowed to attend the meeting and make oral representations which the governors must take into account (reg 5(2)(c)). But however strongly the LEA feels about a particular exclusion, it cannot direct the headteacher to reinstate the pupil.

Guidance on the use of the exclusion, the circumstances in which permanent exclusion may be appropriate and the role of the governing body can be found in *Improving Behaviour and Attendance: Guidance on Exclusion from Schools and Pupil Referral Units*.

Where pupils are permanently excluded, the LEA is under a duty to make arrangements for enabling parents, or the excluded child, to appeal against the decision of the governing body not to reinstate the pupil (reg 6). The arrangements must be made in respect of permanent exclusions from all maintained schools, including those, such as voluntary aided and foundation schools, for which the LEA is not admission authority.

The rules and procedures under which appeal panels operate are set out in the regulations with guidance, to which appeal panels must have regard (reg 7) contained in *Improving Behaviour and Attendance*. These provide that, although the appeal is against the decision of the governing body and that therefore the parties are the parents and the governing body, the LEA has the right to make written representations, attend the hearing and make oral representations and that those representations must be taken into account by the panel (para 10(2) of the schedule to the regulations).

The extent of this role has been considered by the courts in the light of a number of challenges to decisions of independent appeal panels, largely under the Human Rights Act 1998: see *R (ota S) v Brent LBC*; *R (ota T) v Headteacher of Wembley High School*; *R (ota P) v Oxfordshire County Council Exclusion Appeals Panel* [2002] EWCA Civ 693, [2002] All ER (D) 277 (May), [2002] ELR 556, referred to collectively in this work as 'The Brent Case'.

In the *Brent* case, the Court of Appeal held that exclusion appeal panels were compatible with the Human Rights Act (although in a recent report *School Admission and Exclusion Appeal Panels – Special Report* (Cm 5788), the Council on Tribunals has questioned the independence as well as the competence of these panels). However, the court in reaching this decision relied on the fact that it thought that the LEA had a neutral role in these appeals and therefore the fact that the LEA arranged the appeal did not matter. To ensure that future appeals are not challenged, though, this does mean that LEAs should adopt what the Court of Appeal saw as its proper and limited role.

'[T]here is no question but that [...] the LEA must maintain a completely objective stance [...] The statutory scheme brings the LEA into the process in a series of important and potentially conflicting roles [...] There is nothing wrong in the LEA informing the Appeal Panel of the situation in various schools in its area and providing other factual information. Self-evidently the school exclusions officer, or other limbs of the LEA, are likely to have information relevant to the issues which the Appeal Panel has to decide [...] It should be noted that Parliament has not provided a right of appeal to the LEA even if [the LEA] considers that the head teacher should not have excluded the pupil. It is no part of the function of the LEA to press for a particular conclusion in relation to a particular pupil. A clear instance would be a direct submission that the pupil ought or ought not to be permanently excluded'.

(extracts from the judgment of Schiemann LJ at paras 22–24)

The *Brent* case also provided useful assistance on the weight to be given to DfES Guidance. Although regard must be had to the Guidance and an appeal panel would act unlawfully if it did not, the Court of Appeal made clear that appeal panels had independent judgment and their discretion could not be fettered by the content of such guidance. Thus use of the word 'normally' meant just that – it could not mean or should not be taken as meaning 'always' in the context of describing the circumstances in which a child should be excluded or reinstated.

Exclusions and their legality or the legality of the appeal arrangements have exercised the courts frequently in recent years and, with the introduction of the Human Rights Act, are likely to continue to do so. Most of the cases have been decided on their individual facts, but consideration of some of the decisions may be useful in providing guidance on what to do or not to do in the future.

Another important case, as it was decided by the Court of Appeal, was *R v Camden LBC and the Governors of Hampstead School ex parte H* [1996] ELR 360. In this case, a child had been attacked with an air pistol, but the attacker was reinstated on appeal. The Court of Appeal held that, before reinstating an excluded pupil, the appeal body must investigate the effect that the proposed reinstatement would have on the victim. This has now been made a mandatory consideration for all appeals, together with the determination of whether permanent exclusion was used in accordance with the Secretary of State's guidance, the broader interests of staff (in addition to other pupils) at the school, the school's published discipline policy and, where other pupils were involved in the same incident, the fairness of the permanent exclusion in relation to the sanctions imposed on the other pupils involved. The *H* case also made clear that although there need not be, on every occasion, searching inquiries involving the calling of masses of oral evidence, the inquiries which were carried out had to be reasonably thorough and impartial.

However, in contrast, though probably justified on its facts, in *R (ota K) v Governors of The W School and West Sussex County Council* [2001] 3 ELR 311, the decision to exclude was quashed because the pupil had not been given sufficient evidence of the case against him

**9.
INCLUSION**

to prepare a proper defence; too low a standard of proof had been applied and the headmaster had improperly reported hearsay from the police. Hidden J therefore found the decision to have been unfair, unlawful and procedurally improper and considered these defects sufficiently serious as to warrant quashing the decision.

On the standard of proof, for a long time the courts had indicated that exclusion should be considered under the normal civil standard i.e. on the balance of probabilities. However, that position was then qualified where courts, recognising that an exclusion could have a severe effect on a child's education and life, raised the threshold so that, whilst the civil standard applied, decision-makers should ask whether it was 'distinctly more probable' that the pupil committed the offence, rather then just 'more probable than not' (see, for example, *R v Head Teacher of Alperton School* [2001] All ER (D) 312 (Mar) Newman J as endorsed by Kay J in *R (ota S) v the Governing Body of YP School* [2002] EWHC 2975 (Admin), [2003] ELR 578).

However, on appeal in the YP case, the Court of Appeal ([2003] EWCA Civ 1306) appears to have lifted the threshold further to the criminal standard of proof, i.e. beyond reasonable doubt, equating the standard for imposing an anti-social behaviour order under the Crime and Disorder Act 1998 (which the House of Lords said was the criminal standard – see *R (ota) McCann v Manchester Crown Court* [2002] UKHL 39) – with that for exclusions. 'In dealing with a disciplinary matter where the accusation amounts to a crime under the general law, the headteacher and governors must be sure that the child has done what he has been accused of before so finding' (Laws LJ at para 5). The judgment might cause some concern for headteachers, who are not used to carrying out criminal investigations and providing evidence to secure this threshold is reached, but it may be seen as an attempt to ensure that due process is followed and as another means of protecting these appeals from Human Rights Act challenges. The judgment should, though, be treated with some caution: the school involved conceded the appeal and so no argument was heard on the point; the views expressed are, therefore, probably *obiter* and in some respects it was strange that their Lordships' views were even reported. It may also be limited to its facts: Laws LJ made clear that the offence for which the pupil was excluded was a criminal offence, i.e. theft, and so this decision may apply only where a pupil is excluded for an offence which amounts to a crime. However, that may cause practical difficulties for heads, governors and panels in deciding when a pupil may or may not have committed a criminal offence and then having to apply different standards of proof. The Court of Appeal's judgment is therefore unlikely to be the end of the matter.

Indeed, at the time of writing, the DfES was proposing to ensure that the Court of Appeal's comments were not adopted by panels, changing (though with limited publicity) its guidance (see www.teachernet.gov.uk/wholeschool/behaviour/exclusion/guidance /part4) to say that the standard was the balance of probabilities and, at one stage, proposing regulations to clarify the matter.

In *R v Board of Governors of Stoke Newington School and others ex p M* [1994] ELR 131, the court made clear that the principles of natural justice had to apply to the exclusion appeal process. In this case, the decision challenged was that of the governors' exclusion panel, but the same principle would apply to independent LEA-arranged appeal panels. A member of the panel was the excluded child's subject teacher and head of year and had knowledge of the child's behaviour. This, the court held, rendered the panel decision unlawful as there was a real likelihood of bias against the pupil.

9.
INCLUSION

The courts have, however, more recently indicated that even if there is a defect at the stage of the pupil disciplinary hearing stage, this can be corrected on appeal to an independent appeal panel *(R (ota A) v Kingsmead School Governors* (2002) *Times*, 16 May, QBD). In this case the judge held that defects in the discipline committee's hearing had been cured by that of the panel. He did, however, make clear that even so, every hearing at every level should be free of unfairness and procedural irregularity, permanent exclusion was an exceptionally grave decision and amenability to judicial review was a permanent reminder to committees hearing appeals of the genuineness of their duty to act as a statutory and independent review body.

R v Neale and Another ex parte S [1995] ELR 199 is an interesting decision in that the judge, though not strictly being required to do so, indicated that it might be lawful to exclude a child or at least decide not to reinstate a child on the basis of his parent's behaviour. In contrast in *R v Board of Governors and Appeal Committee of Bryn Elian High School ex parte Whippe* [1999] ELR 380, the judge found that the behaviour of a parent (who was the school's former headteacher) could be relevant to a decision to exclude but only in respect of the effect that that behaviour might have on his child, normally well-behaved, to go on behaving badly in any future situations where her father's dismissal as a headteacher would come up as an issue.

In *R v Newham LBC and Another ex parte X* [1995] ELR 303, the judge, though considering a decision to exclude a 15 year-old boy in his GCSE year to be worthy of review by the court, dismissed a suggestion by the boy's barrister that a headteacher had no jurisdiction to discipline a child in relation to behaviour off the school premises. His Lordship said that it would be a very sad thing if that were the case.

Although the need to take care when relying upon identification evidence has been stressed (*R v Roman Catholic Schools ex parte S* [1998] 3 ELR 304), the courts had been reluctant to impose rules of criminal evidence on headteachers and appeal panels. This trend away from unduly onerous evidence gathering still applies, although the Court of Appeal, in *R v Headteacher and Independent Appeal Committee of Dunraven School ex parte B* [2000] ELR 156, went further than before in imposing stricter rules of evidence in exclusion appeals. The court held first that school governors (the case involved an internal appeal committee, although the principles should apply to all exclusion appeals) were there to provide an essential independent check on the judgment of a headteacher. They therefore could not simply review the headteacher's decision to check that it was not unreasonable. They had to establish the primary facts and reconsider the decision to exclude. Second, the parents had to know the case being presented against their child. Third, although a decision to exclude was not a criminal proceeding, the consequences that follow could be as serious as a criminal trial. The governors had therefore acted incorrectly in preventing the parents knowing what was in a witness statement and what was said by a witness to the governors.

The problem was that the school wished to protect the identity of an informant. The Court of Appeal said that if the governors had wanted to consider the informant's evidence, they should have considered whether his identity could have been concealed and, if it could not, they should have continued without his evidence. The court did, however, dismiss a claim that the Codes of Practice under the Police and Criminal Evidence Act 1984 should have prevented the headteacher from interviewing the excluded pupil without another adult present. Those codes, the court held, could not act as more than a touchstone outside the criminal justice process, although, perhaps giving warning for future cases, they did indicate that the Codes might be used as an aid to determining whether improper pressure had been brought by the headteacher on the pupil.

In the *Brent* case (see above), the Court of Appeal also considered how a panel should deal with anonymous evidence.

'As to anonymised witness statements [...] elementary fairness requires the pupil and his parent to know in some adequate form what is being said against the pupil: to know if the source has been inconsistent and to have access to all relevant material to which the decision-maker has had access [...] There may be very good reasons, especially in cases involving bullying, for anonymising such statements, but the injustice of using them may be even greater than the injustice of not using them. Appeal panels (and governing bodies too) should be prepared to disregard anonymised statements of evidence if they are damaging to the pupil in ways which the pupil cannot be expected to deal with without knowing who has made the statement.'

(per Schiemann LJ at para 29)

An appeal panel has no power to delegate any of its functions to its chairman (*R v Schools Appeal Tribunal of the Wakefield Diocesan Board of Education ex parte J* [1999] EdCR 566).

With regard to issues of racial discrimination and exclusion, in *R v Governors of McEntee School ex parte Mbandaka* [1999] EdCR 656, the challenge to a decision to uphold an exclusion was dismissed on technical grounds, but the judge made clear that, if there had been substance in an allegation that there was racial discrimination in the disproportionate nature of the punishment, he would have considered the exclusion unlawful. This is likely to be even more the case following the coming into force of the Race Relations (Amendment) Act 2000.

What most of the cases indicate is that, if panels act in accordance with the relevant guidance, use common sense and apply natural justice, their decisions should be safe. An example of how not to do it came from a governing body of a city technology college. In *R v Governors of Bacon's City Technology College ex p W* [1998] ELR 488, the judge criticised breaches of natural justice in the governors' proceedings which included arbitrary time limits, lack of control of the business, failure to give reasons for rejecting the appeal, one-sided presentation of the facts and a failure to allow the parent a fair hearing. Although he accepted that the child had been involved in a nasty incident, the judge quashed the decision to uphold the exclusion.

One recent development in the field of exclusions is the effect of 'teacher power' on exclusion appeals and the ability of appeal panels to reinstate pupils. In a number of cases, where it has been ordered that a pupil be reinstated, teachers have threatened industrial action and effectively prevented his or her reintegration into normal classes. This action has effectively been legitimised by the cases of *In Re P and In Re L* ([2003] UKHL 8 and 9) in which a majority of the House of Lords held that it was not unlawful for a school to decline to place a reinstated child back into a 'normal' class, if to do so would cause the teaching staff to take industrial action. Provided the industrial action was lawful, all a school would be required to do would be reinstate the pupil-school relationship, not return the child to the *status quo* which existed before he or she was excluded. Although the school should seek to reintegrate the child into normal school life as soon as possible, it was permissible for the school to isolate the child and provide separate tuition upon his return to the school.

The dissenting Lords were clearly unhappy with the situation arising (see, for example, the judgment of Lord Bingham) but it is perhaps symptomatic of the weight given to objections expressed by headteachers about the whole appeal process. This led, in part, to revisions to the constitution of appeal panels, the factors they must take into account and the remedies available to them in the Education (Pupil Exclusions and Appeals) (Maintained Schools) (England) Regulations 2002 (SI 2002 No. 3178). Thus, whilst panels may still uphold decisions to exclude permanently, or direct reinstatement, they may also decide, because of exceptional circumstances or for other reasons, it is not practical to give a direction requiring reinstatement, but that it would otherwise have been appropriate to give such direction (reg 6(6)). This could apply, for example, where the panel thinks reinstatement is appropriate, but know that directing this would prompt the staff to take industrial action which would affect other children in the school.

It is questionable whether, in the absence of specific mention in the regulations, the threat of strike action is a legitimate factor for the panel to take into account. This, together with the new constitution of panels requiring the membership of a headteacher, does raise doubts about the fairness of the process for the excluded child and the independence and impartiality of the panel. This has been recognised by the Council on Tribunals (see *School Admission and Exclusion Appeal Panels, Council on Tribunals Special Report,* May 2003 (Cm 5788)) and the next few years may see a conflict between the wishes of headteachers to have their decisions questioned only in limited circumstances and the views expressed by those such as the Council that 'there are concerns about the lack of independence of admission and exclusion appeal panels; concerns about the constitution of admission and exclusion appeal panels and particularly the over-representation of teachers on the panels and the Department's recent decision to increase the numbers of teachers on exclusion appeal panels' (*Executive Summary – School Admission and Exclusion Appeal Panels*).

2. Parenting contracts and orders

In addition to being available in cases of truancy, the Anti-social Behaviour Act 2003 (ss. 19 and 20) also enables LEAs and the governing body of schools to enter into parenting contracts and the LEA to apply for a parenting order in a case where a child has been excluded for a fixed term or permanently.

A parenting contract contains a statement by the parent that he agrees to comply with requirements specified in it, including attending a counselling or guidance programme (s. 19(5)) for a specified period and a statement by the LEA or school that it agrees to provide support (s. 19(4)). The contract does not, however, create any binding obligations in contract proper or in tort (s. 19(8)), nor, would it appear, can signing one be a condition of admission to a school or breach of one be a reason for exclusion in the future. This is suggested in paras 138 and 235–6 of the DfES's 2004 *Guidance on Education-Related Parenting Contracts, Parenting Orders and Penalty Notices*, to which LEAs and governing bodies must have regard (s. 19(9)). It would, however, be possible for the governing body of a school taking an excluded child to consider arranging a parenting contract (para 138). The cost of the support offered in the contract will be met by whichever of the LEA or governing body provides it (para 214).

Alternatively, or in cases where steps to arrange parenting contracts fail, the LEA can consider applying for a parenting order in the magistrates' court (s. 20 of the Act). Regulations prescribe the conditions in which this may be possible (s. 20(2)). The Education (Parenting Orders) (England) Regulations 2004 (SI 2004 No 182) provide that this procedure will be applicable to a child who receives two fixed-term exclusions within 12 months or is permanently excluded. An order will be appropriate only where the exclusion has been made in response to serious misbehaviour, where parenting is a significant factor in the child's behaviour and where a parenting programme could remedy the situation. An order can be made where it would be desirable in the interest of improving the behaviour of the pupil (s. 20(3)) and is an order which requires the parent to comply, for a period up to 12 months, with requirements specified in it and to attend, for a period up to three months, specified counselling or guidance programmes (s. 20(4)) which may be residential if these are likely to be more

9.
INCLUSION

effective and any interference this may have with family life is proportionate in all the circumstances (s. 20(6) to (8)).

Regulation 5 provides that the costs of parenting orders, including those of counselling or guidance programmes, are to be borne by the LEA.

3.   General breakdown of discipline

That deals with the behaviour of individual pupils. One power which LEAs have retained in respect of behaviour is found in s. 62 of the 1998 Act. This provides the LEA with the power to take such steps in relation to a maintained school as it considers are required to prevent the breakdown, or continuing breakdown, of discipline at the school (s. 62(1)).

The power may be exercised only where, in the opinion of the LEA (a) the behaviour of registered pupils at the school or (b) any action taken by pupils or their parents is such that the education of any registered pupils at the school is, or is likely in the immediate future to become, severely prejudiced and the governing body has been informed in writing of the LEA's opinion (s. 62(2)).

Alternatively, the power may be used where the governing body has been warned that the safety of pupils or staff of the school is threatened (whether by a breakdown of discipline or otherwise) under s. 15(2) of the 1998 Act, the governing body has failed to secure compliance to the LEA's satisfaction with the warning and the LEA has given reasonable notice to the governing body that it proposes to exercise its power to take steps to prevent the breakdown, or continuing breakdown, of discipline (s. 62(3)).

Steps to be taken are at the discretion of the LEA, but may include giving directions to the governing body or headteacher (s. 62(4)).

Because of the sensitivity of such intervention, the LEA, before exercising this power, is required to have regard to the *Code of Practice on LEA–School Relations*. Limited guidance can be found in paras 42 and 43 of annex 1 and para 8 of annex 2. The power is therefore one of last resort and, on the rare occasions when it is used, it should be exercised in accordance with the following criteria (para 8 of annex 2), all of which are to apply.

There must be, either currently or in immediate prospect, a breakdown of discipline at the school. Breakdown implies problems such that the school can no longer function in an orderly way, that staff cannot maintain discipline, that large numbers of pupils are truanting or that the safety or welfare of pupils or staff is at risk.

The LEA must inform the governing body in writing before it acts. Where there have been warning signals that a problem is developing, such a notice should not come as a surprise to the governing body because the LEA should already have been drawing those signals to its attention and that of the headteacher. But there must be no delay where pupils or staff may be at risk. In such cases the LEA has a right and responsibility to act urgently.

The LEA should indicate the changes it believes the school should make and any support it will provide, with a view to restoring full responsibility to the school as quickly as possible.

When issuing a notice under s. 62, the LEA must make clear upon which statutory ground it is relying. Where an LEA based its s. 62 notice upon prejudice to education, but relied upon the contention that the safety and welfare of staff and pupils were at risk, the notice was invalid (*R v Rhondda Cynon Taff County Borough Council ex p Lynwen Evans* 31 August 1999, unreported).

H. Children in Public Care

Although looked-after children (LAC), i.e. children looked after by the social services department, are not necessarily an inclusion issue, there are frequently problems in ensuring that these children receive an efficient education and therefore discussion falls most naturally under this chapter.

In 2000 the Department of Health, as part of its aim to improve children's social services launched a programme under the generic title of 'Quality Protects', which focused on issues concerning fostering, adoption and children looked after by local authorities. An important strand within this was a pressure on local authority elected members to take seriously their responsibilities, individually and collectively, as 'corporate parents' of the children in their care and to have higher aspirations for their educational achievement. The programme challenged (and provided funding to support) education and social services committees and departments to work more closely together to this end.

A looked-after child is defined in s. 22 of the Children Act 1989 as a child in the care of a local authority or who is provided with accommodation by the authority in the exercise of any social services functions. Accommodation means accommodation that is provided for a continuous period of more than 24 hours (s. 22(2) of the Children Act 1989).

It is the duty of any local authority which is looking after a child to: (a) safeguard and promote his welfare and (b) make such use of services available for children cared for by their own parents as appears to the authority to be reasonable in his case (s. 22(3)).

The Green Paper *Every Child Matters* (p. 68) proposes to add an additional duty 'to promote the educational achievement of children in care' and this is duly provided for in the Children Bill.

These duties do not however give rise to a right for a looked-after child to sue should they be performed negligently. In *Holtom v Barnet LBC and Another* [1999] ELR 255, the Court of Appeal held that it would be contrary to the public interest and not just and reasonable to impose a duty of care on a local authority exercising parental responsibilities for a child in care.

Where the local authority proposes to provide accommodation for a looked-after child in an establishment at which education is provided for children accommodated there, it must, so far as is reasonably practicable, consult the LEA before doing so (s. 28(1)). Where such a proposal is implemented, the local authority must inform the LEA of the arrangements and, if the child ceases to be accommodated, the LEA must again be told. Targets within the Quality Protects programme were designed to improve the stability of placements for LAC so that they experienced greater continuity in where they lived and avoided disruption to their education.

Looked-after children are thus not, with the law as it stands, an LEA function, being a social services responsibility, but clearly the Quality Protects programme provides a strong incentive for LEA education department staff to ensure, together with their social services colleagues, that such children in care are properly included within the education system. The policy thrust of *Every Child Matters* is to place that joint working under single political and managerial supervision.

Guidance on the education of looked-after children is now to be found in the comprehensive joint DfEE and Department of Health document *Guidance on the Education of Children and Young People in Public Care*. A similar version of this guidance is to be issued in Wales.

10. ANCILLARY AND MISCELLANEOUS FUNCTIONS

A. Introduction

The phrase 'ancillary functions' in any legislation usually conjures up images of the unimportant and obscure: what the draftsman could not fit in elsewhere and, therefore, chose to place together at the back of the statute, just before sections which define certain words or explain when the Act comes into force.

In the education context, however, a significant number of functions are included within the category of ancillary or miscellaneous functions in both the 1996 and 1998 Acts. So far as possible, the authors have considered these functions in specific chapters. For example, the *Code of Practice on LEA-School Relations* appears under part VII of the 1998 Act headed 'Miscellaneous and General', yet the effects of the Code are so important that, as will have been seen, it is referred to throughout all the chapters dealing with the substantive functions of LEAs.

Nonetheless, a number of functions remain which are incapable of being shoe-horned into any of the other categories, but it would be a mistake to treat them as peripheral. It is true that some of the functions considered below may be unimportant, unused and, in certain cases ignored by Ofsted, but others, particularly school transport, constitute a vitally important responsibility, which in many cases can have significant resource implications. The main areas dealt with below are:

- school transport (part B)

- milk and meals (part C)

- clothing (part D.1)

- board and lodging (part D.2)

- expenses and scholarships and maintenance allowances (part D.3)

- medical inspection and cleanliness of pupils (part D.4)

- miscellaneous funding powers (part D.5)

- duty to promote the welfare of children (part D.6).

B. School Transport

Probably the most important responsibility that the draftsman has seen fit to designate as ancillary is the responsibility of an LEA to arrange transport in certain cases, including, assessing the need for and providing, free home-to-school transport. As will be seen, the role is wider than just considering free transport, but as it can involve expenditure and, often over-expenditure, running to millions, it is proper for Ofsted to rate it highly as an 'access' issue.

Under s. 509 of the 1996 Act, an LEA is under a duty to make arrangements for the provision of transport and otherwise as it considers necessary, or as the Secretary of State may direct, for the purpose of facilitating the attendance of persons not of sixth-form age receiving education:

a)   at schools;

b)   at any institution maintained or assisted by the LEA which provides further education or higher education or both; or

c)   at any institution within the further education sector; or

d)   at any institution outside both the further and higher education sectors, but only if the LSC or ELWa has secured the provision of education or training at the institution and the provision of boarding accommodation under ss. 13 or 41 of the Learning and Skills Act 2000 (s. 509(1A) and (1B) of the Education Act 1996).

In considering whether or not it is required to make such arrangements in respect of a particular person, the LEA must have regard, amongst other things, to:

a)   the age of the person and the nature of the route, or alternative routes, which he could reasonably be expected to take; and

b)   any wish of his parent for him to be provided with education at a school or institution in which the religious education provided is that of the religion or denomination to which his parent adheres (s. 509(4)).

Any transport provided under these provisions must be provided free of charge (s. 509(2)).

The duty to provide such transport is inextricably linked with the duty on parents to secure the attendance of their child and, in particular, the defence under s. 444(4) and (5) of the 1996 Act which may be available in any non-attendance prosecution (see *George v Devon County Council* [1988] 3 All ER 1002, HL). Under this defence, a child is not to be taken to have failed to attend regularly if the child's school is not within walking distance (3.218688km for a child who is under eight and 4.828032 km for a child who has reached eight, in each case measured by the nearest available route) and no suitable arrangements have been made by the LEA for his transport to and from the school (s. 444(4)(b)(i)). The precision of the measurement results from the laws having gone metric; in the original formulation, the distances were respectively two and three miles.

A DfES press notice (17.9.2003) announced an action plan promoted by the Secretary of State for Education and Skills and his Transport colleague to encourage walking, cycling and bussing to school in place of the parents' 'school run' by car; it also promised a pilot scheme in some LEAs to test some more flexible arrangements than those implied by the present distance criteria. In March 2004, DfES and Wales Office Ministers jointly launched a consultation including the draft of a School Transport Bill which would exempt LEAs in the pilot schemes from the present statutory requirements and allow them to test new arrangements, including charging policies.

As to the present law, what may or may not be 'suitable arrangements' have been considered in *R v Rochdale MBC ex parte Schemet* [1993] 1 FCR 306, *R v East Sussex County Council ex parte D* [1991] COD 374, *R v Essex County Council ex parte C* (1993) *Times*, 9 December and *Re S (Minors)* [1995] ELR 98, especially in the context of parental preference. In *ex parte D*, the child had been allocated a place at a school within walking distance of his home, but his parents expressed a preference for him to attend a school 12 miles away, for which the LEA was not prepared to provide transport. Although finding the legislation surprising, the judge held that the LEA's decision was not irrational and that the suitability in the context of s. 509 relates to the suitability of the arrangements for transport or for attendance at a school nearer home. It does not require consideration of the suitability of the preferred and/or alternative schools. As Rose J said, 'If Parliament wishes free transport to be provided for those children who have to travel long distances in order to enable them to attend the school in accordance with their parents' preferences, Parliament must say so. In my judgment it has not yet said so and it is not for me to say so.' A similar conclusion was reached in *ex parte C* and *Re S* by the Court of Appeal.

**10.
ANCILLARY &
MISCELLANEOUS
FUNCTIONS**

If free transport is not provided to a child who lives beyond walking distance of his school, in principle the LEA could never enforce that child's attendance. Consequently, the practical reality of s. 509(1) is that LEAs will provide free transport to children of compulsory school age who live beyond walking distance from their school (although frequently conditions are attached if the parents have expressed a preference for a school which is not their catchment school and which is further away than that catchment school) and whose attendance the LEA will therefore be facilitating.

Walking distance is not, however, the geographical extent of the duty to provide transport under s. 509(1) because of the obligation to have regard to the age of the child and/or the nature of the route. Thus in certain circumstances where a child is particularly young or vulnerable or where the only available route is unsafe, the LEA will be under a duty to arrange transport under s. 509(1) even if the child lives within walking distance of the school (see *Essex County Council v Rogers* [1987] AC 66, where the House of Lords held that for a route to be available under s. 444(5) it must be a route along which a child accompanied as necessary can walk and walk with reasonable safety to school).

Any arrangements made must be for the full distance: an LEA cannot provide transport just for the journey from the child's home to a point which is within walking distance of the school and then require the child to walk that distance or require the parents to pay for that part of the journey (*Surrey County Council v Ministry of Education* [1953] 1 All ER 705).

Transport for pupils with SEN can occasionally cause difficulties, especially where the nature of their needs requires them to travel longer distances than other pupils. As has been seen (see chapter 8.A.5), a placement can be made conditional on a child's parents' agreement to meet the transport costs (*R v Havering LBC ex p K* [1998] ELR 402). Ordinarily, however, LEAs cannot refuse to pay for transport to a school named in a child's statement of SEN unless there is a suitable closer school which he or she could attend (see *R (ota H) v Brent LBC* [2002] EWHC 1105; [2002] All ER (D) 348 (Apr)).

Where arrangements are made, the transport must be non-stressful (*R v Hereford and Worcester County Council ex parte P* [1992] 2 FCR 732). The journey must not therefore be too long or circuitous nor the vehicle overcrowded. It must allow a child to reach school without undue stress, strain or difficulty such as would prevent him from benefiting from the education the school has to offer. For a decision on the obligation to provide seat belts, prior to the change in the law on the fitting of seat belts in school coaches and minibuses, *see R v Gwent County Council ex p Harris* [1995] ELR 27.

Where the LEA is not under a duty to provide transport, it has the power to do so for persons not of sixth-form age under s. 509(2) of the Education Act 1996.

LEAs have lesser duties in respect of nursery children. An LEA may provide a nursery-age child with assistance with transport (either by making arrangements for the purpose of facilitating the child's attendance or by paying the whole or any part of his reasonable travel expenses) if it is satisfied that without such assistance he would be prevented from attending at any premises, which are not a school or part of a school, but at which relevant nursery education is provided (s. 509A(1) and (2)). He must be attending these premises for the purpose of obtaining relevant nursery education. Relevant nursery education comprises nursery education provided by an LEA or by any other person who is in receipt of financial assistance from the LEA or which receives grants under s. 14 of the Education Act 2002 (s. 509A(5) of the 1996 Act). When considering whether to provide this assistance, an LEA may have regard to whether it would be reasonable to expect alternative arrangements to be made for him to receive relevant nursery education at any other premises, whether nearer to his home or otherwise (s. 509(3)). The assistance may also be made conditional on the child's parents or nursery education provider agreeing to make a contribution to the transport costs as the LEA may determine (s. 509A (4)).

Specific provision is now made for pupils of sixth-form age (i.e. persons over compulsory school age but who are under the age of 19 or who have begun a particular course of education or training before attaining the age of 19 and continue to attend that course (s. 509AC(1)), whether in school or in FE provision (s. 509AA). For each academic year, an LEA must prepare a transport policy statement specifying the arrangements for the provision of transport or otherwise that the LEA considers it necessary to make for facilitating the attendance of these persons receiving education or training at schools, institutions maintained by the LEA which provide FE or HE or both, any institution within the FE sector or at any establishment supported by the LSC or ELWa. The statement must specify the arrangements the LEA considers it necessary to make for the provision of financial assistance in respect of reasonable travelling expenses and also what arrangements are to be made by governing bodies providing sixth-form education and FE institutions to provide transport for facilitating the attendance of persons of sixth-form age (s. 509AA(3) and (4)). The statement should specify any travel concessions provided under the Transport Act 1985.

The arrangements made by LEAs must make provision for persons receiving full-time education or training at an institution within the FE sector (or outside the FE and HE sector where those students have learning difficulties) which is no less favourable for pupils of the same age at schools maintained by the LEA (s. 509(5)).

The policy must also state to what extent the specified arrangements include arrangements for facilitating the attendance of disabled persons and persons with learning difficulties (s. 509AB(1)). The statement should ensure that the arrangements are no less favourable to persons receiving education at institutions other than schools maintained by the LEA than to pupils of the same age or to pupils of the same age with learning difficulties attending such schools (s. 509AB (2)).

In addition to having regard to any guidance produced by the Secretary of State (s. 509AB(5)), an LEA must also have regard to: the needs of those for whom it would not be reasonably practicable to attend a particular establishment to receive education or training if no arrangements were made; the need to secure that persons in their area have reasonable opportunities to choose between different establishments at which education or training is provided; the distance from the homes of persons of sixth-form age in their area of relevant establishments and the cost of travel to the establishments in question and of any alternative means of facilitating attendance (s. 509AB (3)). In considering whether it is necessary to make arrangements, the LEA must consider the nature of the route or alternative routes and any wish of the person's parent for him to be provided with religious education or training at a school, institution or other establishment in which the religious education provided is that of the religion or denomination to which his parent adheres (s. 509AB(4)).

10.
ANCILLARY &
MISCELLANEOUS
FUNCTIONS

A transport policy statement should be published on or before 31 May in respect of the following academic year and must ensure that effect is given to the published arrangements (s. 509 AA (7)). Before publication, the LEA must consult other appropriate LEAs, governing bodies at schools providing education to persons over compulsory school age, the LSC or ELWa and, where appropriate, passenger transport authorities or, in London, Transport for London (s. 509AB(6) and (7)).

Provision of school transport will also continue to be affected by other developments relating to transport generally and already transport plans have to be produced as part of the planning process for new school development or the extension of existing schools. In the future, school transport may be affected by other developments. For example, local authorities are required to set out an integrated strategy for reducing car use and improving children's safety on the journey to school within their local transport plans and, in the transport White Paper issued in July 1998, *A New Deal for Transport: Better for Everyone* (CM 3950), it was envisaged that local authorities would be required to develop an integrated transport policy which encourages more children to get to school other than by car (see also *Travelling to School: A Good Practice Guide* DfES/0520/2003 and the note earlier in this part of the chapter about the draft School Transport Bill (2004)).

C. Milk and Meals

An LEA may provide registered pupils at any school maintained by it, any other persons who receive education at such a school, or children who receive funded nursery education, with milk, meals and other refreshment, either on the school premises or anywhere else where such education or nursery education is provided (s. 512(1) and (2) of the Education Act 1996, as amended by s. 201 of the Education Act 2002). There is no power analogous to that in respect of clothing (see D.1. below) to provide for otherwise eligible pupils at independent schools.

10.
ANCILLARY &
MISCELLANEOUS
FUNCTIONS

Although this is phrased as a power, an LEA can be required to provide school lunches for any person if any prescribed (i.e. prescribed by statutory order) requirements are met, a request has been made by or on behalf of that person to the LEA and either that person is eligible for free lunches or in the case of a registered pupil, it would not be unreasonable for the LEA to provide the lunches (s. 512(3)).

The current prescribed requirements are set out in the Education (School Lunches) (Prescribed Requirements) (England) Order 2003 (SI 2003 No. 382) and in the order for Wales (SI 2003 No. 880 (W 111)) and these apply only to registered pupils who are receiving nursery education and who receive either full-time education or attend school for a period which spans the lunch break.

If an LEA decides not to provide school lunches, it can be compelled to do so. Where an LEA receives a request by or on behalf of registered pupils at a school maintained by the LEA, it shall provide school lunches for those pupils, unless:

a)   in the circumstances it would be unreasonable for it to do so; or

b)   the pupil making the request is not of compulsory school age and is being provided with part-time education (s. 512 (1A)).

If lunches are provided as result of a request from or on behalf of a pupil, the lunches may be provided either on the school premises or anywhere else where education is provided and take such form as the LEA thinks fit (s. 512(4)).

A school lunch is defined as food made available for consumption by the pupil as his midday meal on a school day, or, in relation to a nursery child otherwise than at a school, food made available for consumption by the child as his midday meal on a day on which he receives such education, whether involving a set meal or the selection of items by him or otherwise (s. 512(6)).

The new provisions, allowing requests to be made, are intended to meet concerns that if meals were not available at midday some children might be deprived of proper nutrition. To support this aim, the LEA, or governing body where the function has been transferred (see below), is now under a duty to secure that where it provides school lunches, the food meets prescribed nutritional standards or other nutritional requirements (s. 114 of the 1998 Act). These standards are now contained in the Education (Nutritional Standards for School Lunches) (England) Regulations 2000 (SI 2000 No. 1777) or, in Wales, the Education (Nutritional Standards for School Lunches) (Wales) Regulations 2001 (SI 2001 No. 1784 (W 126)).

**10.
ANCILLARY &
MISCELLANEOUS
FUNCTIONS**

Except in the cases of children whose parents are in receipt of the benefits set out below, the LEA must charge for any milk, meal or refreshment provided and charge every pupil the same price for the same quantity of the same item (i.e. prices must be the same throughout the LEA and cannot differ in different types of school) (s. 512ZA(1) and (2) of the 1996 Act).

The LEA is under a duty to ensure that school lunch is provided free of charge to children whose parents are in receipt of income support, an income-based jobseeker allowance, or support provided under part 6 of the Immigration and Asylum Seekers Act 1999 or are in receipt of any other benefit or allowance or entitled to any tax credit under the Tax Credits Act 2002 or any other benefit which may be prescribed. If it provides milk, that milk must be free as well (s. 512(3)). A pupil may also be so eligible if he is personally in receipt of income support, an income-based jobseeker's allowance or is in receipt of any other benefit or allowance or entitled to any tax credit under the Tax Credits Act 2002 or any other benefit which may be prescribed (see the Education (Free School Lunches) (Prescribed Tax Credits) (England) Order 2003 (SI 2003 No. 383) and in SI 2003 No. 879 (W 110) for Wales). A request must, however, be made by that parent or pupil or on his behalf to the LEA before the duty arises (s. 512ZB (2), (3) and (4)).

LEAs must provide such facilities at any school maintained by them as they consider appropriate for the consumption of any meals or other refreshment brought to the school by registered pupils (s. 512(5)).

Under the School Standards and Framework Act 1998, the Secretary of State was given power to transfer to governing bodies some or all of the duties of LEAs to provide school lunches, provide free school lunches and provide milk free of charge (see s. 512A of the 1996 Act). The Education (Transfer of Functions Concerning School Lunches) (England) (No 2) Order 1999 (SI 1999 No. 2164) was made in July 1999 and effected this transfer in all English LEAs and the Education (Transfer of Functions Concerning School Lunches) (Wales) and (Wales) (Number 2) Orders 1999 (SIs 1999 Nos. 610 and 1779) achieved the same effect in Wales. As a result, the duties to provide free school lunches and paid school lunches transfer to those governing bodies whose budget share includes an amount in respect of meals and other refreshments. Where such duties are imposed on governing bodies, LEAs are no longer subject to the corresponding obligations.

For school-meals staffing, see chapter 6.E.8.

D. Other Functions

1. Clothing

An LEA may provide clothing for any pupil who is a boarder at an educational institution maintained by it, any pupil at a nursery school maintained by it and any child in a nursery class maintained by it (s. 510(1) of the 1996 Act). Clothing includes footwear (s. 579(1)).

In addition, an LEA has the power to provide clothing for any pupil for whom it is providing board and lodging elsewhere than at an educational institution maintained by it and for whom special educational provision is made in pursuance of arrangements made by the LEA (s. 510(2)).

In other cases, if it appears to an LEA that a pupil at a school maintained by it or a special school (whether maintained by it or not) is unable by reason of the inadequacy or unsuitability of his clothing to take full advantage of the education provided at the school, the LEA may provide him with such clothing as in its opinion is necessary for the purpose of ensuring that he is sufficiently and suitably clad while he remains a pupil at the school (s. 510(3)).

An LEA may also provide clothing for:

a) pupils at a school maintained by the LEA or at an institution maintained by the LEA which provides further or higher education or both;

b) persons who have not attained the age of 19 and who are receiving education at an institution within the further education sector; and

c) persons who make use of facilities for physical training further to the LEA's functions in respect of recreation and social and physical training

with such articles of clothing as the LEA may determine suitable for the physical training so provided (s. 510(4)).

**10.
ANCILLARY &
MISCELLANEOUS
FUNCTIONS**

Finally, an LEA may, with the consent of the proprietor of a school not maintained by the LEA (other than a special school) and on such financial and other terms, if any, as may be agreed between the proprietor and the LEA, make arrangements, in the case of any pupil at the school who is unable by reason of the inadequacy or unsuitability of his clothing to take full advantage of the education provided at the school, to provide him with such clothing as in the LEA's opinion is necessary for the purpose of ensuring that he is sufficiently and suitably clad while he remains a pupil at the school (s. 510(5)). Any such arrangements must, however, secure, so far as is practicable, that the expense incurred does not exceed the expense which would have been incurred by the LEA if the pupil had been a pupil at a school maintained by the LEA (s. 510(6)).

These powers are subject to the conditions laid down in the Education (Provision of Clothing) Regulations 1980 (SI 1980 No. 545). These provide the LEA with the power, where it makes clothing available, to require the parent to pay such sum as the LEA thinks the parent can pay without financial hardship (reg 3).

Clothing tends to become a controversial issue in three cases:

- whether there are any different rules for primary or secondary pupils or, indeed, whether school uniform policies should legally differ between those imposed in secondary schools and primary schools;

- in respect of the power to provide clothing, whether the LEA has the power to make clothing grants; and

- most importantly, in the enforcement of school uniform policies.

The first point can be dealt with fairly easily. The belief, often among education welfare officers and schools, that the LEA can provide clothing only to secondary school pupils, is erroneous; there is no such restriction.

The second point is trickier and, strictly, the power allows only the provision of clothing, not the payment of a grant for a parent to purchase clothing. The concern is clearly that if a parent receives money, there is no guarantee that the clothing will be purchased. In practical terms, however, an LEA cannot keep a stock of clothing and it is probably reasonable to say that the LEA has power under s. 2 of the Local Government Act 2000 or s. 111 of the Local Government Act 1972 to make a grant to a parent to buy clothing, on the grounds that it facilitates the exercise of the LEA's powers. To avoid misuse of the money, an LEA could either pay only on receipt of an invoice or issue vouchers for use in clothing stores for certain clothing.

10.
ANCILLARY &
MISCELLANEOUS
FUNCTIONS

The issue of school uniforms and uniform policies is less easy to address and is, to a certain extent, outside the scope of this work as it is a matter for individual governing bodies. Nonetheless, it can have an effect on LEAs when the enforcement of a policy leads to non-attendance or the LEA is asked for guidance on what policies may contain.

Advice issued by the DfES makes clear that, as part of the governing body's responsibility for the conduct of the school (see DfES Guidance on school uniforms issued in February 2002 and available on www.teachernet.gov.uk (though with no reference)), the governing body should decide whether school uniform is to be worn or not. Provided that it takes account of all relevant factors, including the LEA's policy on uniform grants, the imposition of a reasonable uniform policy is lawful.

What can a school do, though, if a parent refuses to send their child to school in accordance with the policy? Based on the old case of *Spiers v Warrington Corporation* [1954] 1 QB 61, the answer would be that the school can refuse to admit the child and that the parents can be prosecuted for the non-attendance. That decision might now, though, be questioned, especially as it was heard at a time when the rules on exclusion were virtually non-existent. As it stands, however, it remains authority for allowing an LEA to prosecute parents for non-attendance if they refuse to abide by the school's uniform policy. What is clear, though, is that a pupil should not normally be excluded for breaching the school's uniform policy (see DfEE Circular 10/99 Social Inclusion: Pupil Support, para 6.4 and the February 2002 DfES Guidance).

Some assistance may be gleaned from the unreported decision in *R (ota G) v Chair and Governing Body of Cwmfelinfach Primary School* ((2001) EPLI vol 6, issue 2, pp:49–50, QBD), which held that a governing body's decision to refuse to allow a pupil to wear earrings in PE lessons was lawful, as its rule against jewellery in such lessons was a permissible regulation on health and safety grounds.

The *Spiers* case is also of questionable value because the rule in question involved a girl who wanted to wear trousers to school, but the school's policy insisted that girls must wear skirts. Nowadays that might not be considered a reasonable or indeed lawful rule as it may amount to sex discrimination. Surprisingly, given the number of schools which still maintain such policies, the point has not been tested in the courts, although a case was to be brought against the governing body of Whickham Comprehensive School, Gateshead ('Once more unto the breeches', *TES*, 4 June 1999). This case was, however, resolved before reaching court with the governing body's agreeing to allow the pupil to attend in trousers. If it had gone to trial, it would have been highly probable that the rule would have been considered unlawful under the Sex Discrimination Act 1975 (just as in the same way that a ban on female teachers wearing trousers would equally infringe the 1975 Act).

In similar vein, schools and LEAs, in enforcing non-attendance, should be aware of traditional dress among certain ethnic or racial groups. Any rules which discriminated against dress such as turbans

**10.
ANCILLARY &
MISCELLANEOUS
FUNCTIONS**

worn by Sikh boys or the need for Muslim girls to cover their legs would be unlawful under the Race Relations Act 1976.

Clothing and uniform may also be a problem for disabled pupils, as policies have to make allowances for their needs (for a claim made against a school which had an inflexible rule as to the material its uniform had to made from, see 'Eczema pupil's case for wearing wrong trousers', *The Times*, Education, 7 March 2003).

2. Board and lodging

Where an LEA is satisfied with respect to any pupil that:

a) primary or secondary education suitable to his age, ability and aptitude and to any special educational needs he may have can best be provided for him at a particular maintained or maintained special school, but

b) such education cannot be so provided unless boarding accommodation is provided for him otherwise than at school

the LEA may provide such board and lodging for him under such arrangements as it thinks fit (s. 514(1)).

Where an LEA is satisfied with respect to a pupil with special educational needs that provision of board and lodging for him is necessary to enable him to receive the required special educational provision, it may provide such board and lodging for him under such arrangements as it thinks fit (s. 514(2)).

Where an LEA makes board or lodging arrangements, it must, so far as practicable, give effect to the wishes of the pupil's parent as to the religion or religious denomination of the person with whom the pupil will reside (s. 514(3)).

Where such boarding provision is made, however, the LEA must charge the pupil's parents such sum, if any, in respect of the board and lodging as in the LEA's opinion the parents are able to pay without financial hardship, but the LEA may not charge if education suitable to the pupil's age, ability and aptitude or special educational needs could not otherwise be provided for him (s. 514(4) and (5)). If a charge is made, however, the LEA may not make a profit and if the parent defaults, the sum is recoverable as a civil debt (s. 514(6) and (7)).

Any board and lodging provision made available should comply with the requirements of the Children Act 1989 with regard to the care and supervisory arrangements for the pupil. It is also important to note that the function is that of the LEA; there is no power for the governing body of a maintained school to make its own board and lodging arrangements. Though outside the scope of this work, provision in boarding schools is also subject to the Care Standards Act 2000.

3. Expenses, scholarships and maintenance allowances

LEAs retain a residuary power, significantly modified as a result of the abolition of the Assisted Places Scheme and the changes to discretionary student awards, to pay expenses and make awards or scholarships in certain cases. Under s. 518 of the 1996 Act, an LEA may, for the purpose of enabling persons to take advantage of any educational facilities available to them:

a) pay such expenses of children attending community, foundation, voluntary or special schools as may be necessary to enable them to take part in any school activities, or

b) grant scholarships, exhibitions, bursaries and other allowances in respect of persons over compulsory school age (s. 518(1)).

In exercising this power, however, the LEA must follow the relevant regulations, which include the Scholarships and Other Benefits Regulations 1977 (SI 1977 No. 1443), the Local Education Authority (Post-Compulsory Education Awards) Regulations 1999 (SI 1999 No. 229) and the Local Education Authority (Payment of School Expenses) Regulations 1999 (SI 1999 No.1727).

Before 1998 an LEA could not legally adopt a policy of not making such awards; instead, the LEA had to ensure that it considered any applications on merit (see *R v Hampshire County Council ex p W* [1994] ELR 460). That is no longer the case and an LEA may, in accordance with the legislation, determine the extent to which it will exercise these powers in each financial year and may determine not to exercise the powers at all (s. 518(2)).

Of some interest to LEAs, as new statutory provision may cut across some of the above powers, is the Secretary of State's now wide power to make grants under s.14 of the Education Act 2002 including enabling any person to undertake any course of education, or any course of higher education provided by an institution within the further education sector or providing for a person's maintenance while he undertakes such a course. This in part continues grants for specialist education (see, for example, the Education (Grants) (Music, Ballet and Choir Schools) (England) Regulations 2001 (SI 2001 No. 2743); the Education (Grants etc) (Dance and Drama) (England) Regulations 2001 (SI 2001 No. 2857)), but without the need for the grants to be made under regulations, their availability (etc.) now being a matter solely for the Secretary of State's discretion.

LEAs claim credit for the reported success of pilot schemes in 56 authorities' areas (see the Education Maintenance Allowances (Pilot Areas) Regulations 1999 (SI 1999 No. 2168) and 2001 (SI 2001 No. 2750). These allowances are aimed at encouraging young people to participate in further education. The pilots were introduced under ss. 518 and 569(4) of the Education Act 1996. To enable these allowances to be available nationally from September 2004 and to clarify the enabling powers, express provision is now made for them under s. 181 of the 2002 Act. Though the actual administrative responsibility has been given to the LSC and the operation has been contracted-out, some LEA officers have reported in early 2004 that their authorities have had to take on part of the burden in order to make the scheme workable.

Regulations may make provision authorising or requiring the Secretary of State or NAW to pay an allowance to or in respect of any eligible person who is over compulsory school age (but not in higher education (s. 181(2)) in connection with his undertaking education or training of a prescribed description (s. 181(1)). The regulations will also set out such matters as eligibility requirements, periods of payment, the amount of the allowance and appeal rights (s. 181(3)). Governing bodies of schools and FE colleges will be required to monitor the scheme's operation. Conditions will be imposed on the students set out in what will be called 'learning agreements' (s. 182(1)), including targets relating to attendance, conduct or attainment (s. 182(4)).

The Secretary of State may determine that a function relating to EMAs may be exercisable instead by LEAs or the LSC (s. 183(1)) or, in Wales, by ELWa or LEAs (s. 183(2)), subject to whatever directions may be given (s. 183(3)). The Secretary of State's functions may also be delegated to other bodies (s. 184). Where the Secretary of State or NAW's functions have been transferred or delegated, the body carrying out the function may be paid such amounts as are considered appropriate (s. 185(2)).

**10.
ANCILLARY &
MISCELLANEOUS
FUNCTIONS**

4. Medical inspection and cleanliness of pupils

LEAs are required to make arrangements for encouraging and assisting pupils to take advantage of the provision for medical and dental inspection and treatment made for them under the National Health Service Act 1977 by the relevant health authority (s. 520(1)). If a parent gives notice to the LEA that he objects to the pupil's availing himself of such provision, the pupil must not be encouraged or assisted to do so (s. 520(2)).

And an old case had established how unwise it was to examine an unwilling child: *Fox v Burgess* (1922) 1KB 623, discussed in Barrell (1970: 151–3). A girl, who might have been dirty or verminous, had indicated by gesture that she was unwilling to be examined. Counsel had suggested that compulsion should have been applied, but Avory J opined that 'that would put upon the school authorities a responsibility which was never intended by [...] Parliament. It would lead to scenes, possibly of violence and disorder in the school and most probably summonses in the police court, in every case where such disciplinary powers were attempted to be exercised alleging that an assault had been committed on the child. Such summonses are all too frequent at present when ordinary corrective discipline is applied in [...] schools.'

Although now little used because the problems they were designed to address have by and large disappeared with changes in society, LEAs still retain the powers to take action to deal with children infested with vermin or in a foul condition. Aficionados of this subject will wish to note the circumstances in which it is unreasonable to refuse a child admission (*Bowen v Hodgson* (1923) 93 LJKB 76).

An LEA may, by directions in writing, authorise a medical officer of the LEA to examine the persons or clothing of pupils in attendance at schools maintained by the LEA whenever, in the medical officer's opinion, such examinations are necessary in the interests of cleanliness (s. 521). If it is necessary to examine a female pupil, the examination must not be made by a man unless he is a registered medical practitioner (s. 521(3) of the Education Act 1996).

A 'medical officer' is defined as a registered medical practitioner who is employed or engaged (whether regularly or for the purposes of any particular case) by the LEA or whose services are made available to the LEA by the Secretary of State (s. 579(1)). Thus in

**10.
ANCILLARY &
MISCELLANEOUS
FUNCTIONS**

order lawfully to examine a pupil, the doctor or nurse must be employed or engaged beforehand by the LEA so that the LEA can call them 'theirs'. If not, there is a danger that any person examining a child will be guilty of either civil or criminal assault.

If, after the medical officer has examined the pupil, the person or clothing of that pupil is found to be infested with vermin or in a foul condition, any officer of the LEA may serve a notice on the pupil's parent requiring him to cleanse the pupil's person and clothing within a specified period (s. 522(1)). The notice should warn the parent that, unless satisfactory cleansing takes place, the pupil will be cleansed under arrangements made by the LEA (s. 522(2)).

If the medical officer remains unsatisfied as to the child's cleanliness at the end of the period, he can order that the pupil be cleansed under arrangements made by the LEA (s. 522(4)). Such an order authorises any officer of the LEA to cause the pupil to be cleansed and, for that purpose, to convey the child to and detain him at, any premises provided by the LEA for the cleansing (s. 522(5)). Thus the order will provide a defence to any claim of assault or false imprisonment.

The LEA has a duty to make arrangements for securing that any pupil required to be cleansed may be cleansed (either at the request of the parent or under a medical officer's order) at suitable premises, by suitable persons and with suitable appliances (s. 523(1)). Where a female pupil is to be cleansed, only a registered medical practitioner or a woman authorised for the purpose by the LEA may perform the task (s. 523(2)).

10. ANCILLARY & MISCELLANEOUS FUNCTIONS

If the medical officer believes that a pupil's clothing is infested or in foul condition, but action cannot be taken immediately, the medical officer may direct that the pupil be suspended from the school until such action is taken if he considers it necessary to do so in the interests either of the pupil or of other pupils at the school (s. 524).

If, after the pupil's person or clothing has been cleansed, he is again infested with vermin or in a foul condition at any time when he is attending the school and that condition is due to the neglect on the part of his parent, the parent is guilty of an offence under s. 525 of the Act.

These powers are rarely, if ever used, for a variety of reasons. The infestations and conditions which they were designed to address are, fortunately, no longer prevalent, but there are also practical difficulties in performing these types of examinations. There is naturally a fear of action for assault should an examination be carried out without meeting the exact conditions and, as the conditions are ambiguous, those fears are well grounded.

First, there is no definition of what is meant by 'infested with vermin' or 'in foul condition'. Dictionary definitions are inconsistent. *Chambers* defines 'vermin' as obnoxious insects such as bugs, fleas and lice, troublesome animals such as mice, rats, animals destructive to game such as weasels, polecats, also hawks and owls: a wide range of pests but, assuming few pupils are infested with polecats nowadays, it implies that the legislation should deal primarily with fleas and lice. Similarly, there is no definition of 'infested'. *Chambers* suggests a besetting or swarming about, which is not helpful and, although the terminology may appear pedantic, it is not when an incorrect application of the powers could lead to criminal prosecution.

'Examination' is not defined, which leads on to perhaps the biggest problem in the legislation: what can a headteacher or teacher do by way of checking a pupil? An 'examination' can be performed only by an authorised medical officer, so the head cannot 'examine' the child. But what does examination involve? A cursory glance or a good rummage around?

Again, this sounds pedantic, until we consider the biggest bugbear which affects many schools and to which these powers on the surface would appear to apply: headlice or the dreaded nits. These creatures would appear to fall within the definition of 'vermin', but they are not considered to be unclean. This has led medical officers to decline to carry out examinations as they feel that a search to check for headlice is not necessary in the interests of cleanliness. Without that initial examination, the LEA has no further power to take action to cleanse the child. Nor can anyone else, including the headteacher, carry out the examination. Thus headteachers are left in a very unsatisfactory situation. But could the headteacher check a child's head without the process's being an examination and does the headteacher have the ability to do so under common law (the old *in loco parentis*) powers? The issues are outside the scope of this work, but, because it is doubted if there is any clear answer, it does suggest that the provisions on cleanliness require considerable re-examination.

Though some of these considerations are of largely historical interest today, the whole issue of 'examination' has been newly raised by the wish of the Prime Minister (interview in *The News of the World*, 22 February 2004) to see random testing of school pupils for illegal drugs. Questions of consent or otherwise by parents and pupils, responsibility for bearing the costs, consequences of positive tests and, conceivably, human rights issues, spring to mind. Second-order and non-legal, implications include the probability of pupil ingenuity in exchanging or adulterating samples.

5. Miscellaneous funding powers

5.1 Research, conferences and trusts

An LEA can make such provision for conducting, or assisting the conduct, of research as appears to it to be desirable for the purpose of improving the educational facilities provided for its area (s. 526).

An LEA may organise, or participate in the organisation of, conferences for the discussion of questions relating to education and expend such sums as may be reasonable in paying, or contributing towards, any expenditure incurred in connection with conferences for the discussion of such questions including the expenses of any person authorised by it to attend such a conference (s. 527).

An LEA can accept, hold and administer any property on trust for purposes connected with education (s. 529).

5.2 Financial assistance to non-maintained schools

On the principle that an LEA need not actually provide schools itself, but could provide sufficient school places through the non-maintained sector and/or in recognition of the need to place some children with special educational needs outside the maintained sector, LEAs have power to assist any primary or secondary non-maintained school (whether inside or outside the LEA's area) and make arrangements for pupils to be provided with primary or secondary education at such schools (s. 18).

By s. 128 of the School Standards and Framework Act 1998, a revised s. 18 provides that such assistance cannot be provided other than in accordance with regulations made by the Secretary of State.

Incidentally, the heading to s. 18 is a rare instance of the law's use of 'non-maintained' synonymously with 'independent'.

5.3 Supply of teachers to day nurseries

Tucked away in s. 515 is the power to enable LEAs to make available to a day nursery (i.e. a day nursery provided by local authorities for pre-school and other children under the Children Act 1989) the services of any teacher who:

a)   is employed by it in a nursery school or in a primary school having one or more nursery classes; and

b)   has agreed to provide his services for the purposes of the arrangements.

6.   Duty to promote the welfare of children

Finally, but not least, are the two new duties imposed on LEAs, to look after pupils' welfare and to consult them. These are fundamental duties and should be considered in respect of the exercise of all an LEA's functions. As they were inserted into the 2002 Act under the heading of 'Miscellaneous and General', however, for convenience we are considering them here.

Following a number of incidents where schools in particular, but also LEAs, had not shone brightly in dealing with reports of child abuse (see, for example, the inquiry into the death of Lauren Wright, 'A Lifetime of Abuse', BBC News 1.10.2001), the Government decided to make explicit the duties on LEAs and schools to protect children within their care. Arguably, these duties were already present under the Children Act 1989 and the various *Working Together* documents, but it was considered that greater focus needed to be given and the roles and responsibilities made more explicit. Accordingly, during the passage of the Education Act 2002, a new duty was introduced.

An LEA must now make arrangements for ensuring that the functions conferred on it in its capacity as LEA are exercised with a view to safeguarding and promoting the welfare of children (s. 175 of the Education Act 2002). This is not, therefore, by any means a minor power; it relates to every function of an LEA. So, in theory and in effect, whenever it acts or does not act, an LEA must take its decisions in accordance with arrangements put in place for safeguarding and promoting the welfare of pupils.

In carrying out this duty, an LEA must also have regard to any guidance issued from time to time by the Secretary of State or NAW.

These obligations are likely to be further strengthened by the Children Bill, implementing the Green Paper *Every Child Matters*. The duty will be placed not only on children's services authorities (i.e. LEAs/social services authorities) but on shire district councils

**10.
ANCILLARY &
MISCELLANEOUS
FUNCTIONS**

and health, police, probation and custodial authorities, training providers and YOTs, in respect of all their relevant functions.

Equally concerned with the rights of children and building on good practice nationwide as well as the specific requirements to involve children with SEN in their education, is the provision in s. 176 of the Act, imposing a duty on an LEA, when exercising its schools functions (i.e. functions relating to maintained schools, PRUs or the provision of education for children of compulsory school age otherwise than at school), to have regard to any guidance issued by the Secretary of State or NAW about consultation with pupils in connection with the taking of decisions affecting them. This is someway shy of the moves during the passage of the Act to impose a duty to consult pupils directly, but will require LEAs to consider what consultation they will need to put in place and when before taking certain decisions affecting children for whom they are responsible.

DfES consulted on appropriate guidance in July 2003: *Working together: Giving children and young people a say (The Participation Guidance)* DfES/0492/2003, but the outcome has not yet been published. A consultation paper on implementation in Wales also suggested that school councils might be made compulsory: *Pupil Involvement in Decisions that Affect them and Establishment of School Councils in Primary Secondary and Special Schools* NAW, October 2003. See also chapter 2.E.5.2 of this book.

10.
ANCILLARY &
MISCELLANEOUS
FUNCTIONS

11. LEARNING AND SKILLS

A. Education from 16+

1.   The 16+ milestone

Over 65 years ago, the Spens Report asserted: 'The adoption of a minimum leaving-age of 16 years may not be immediately attainable, but in our judgment must even now be envisaged as inevitable' (*Secondary Education*, 1938 HMSO, reprinted 1950, chapter IX, para 19).

Provision for raising the leaving-age to 16 when 'practicable' was enshrined in s. 35 of the Education Act 1944 but achieved only on 1 September 1972 by the Raising of the School Leaving Age Order (SI 1972 No. 444) made under that section of the Act. Eventual triumph over the vicissitudes of war, post-war reconstruction, austerity and demography contributed much to the symbolic status of the new upper age of compulsory schooling.

Similarly, the connotations of 'sixth form', deriving largely from independent and grammar schools, have made the institution, in many people's view, a hallmark of the successful comprehensive school. Very few schools, it appears, have followed through the 'key stages' of the Education Reform Act 1988 and adopted the non-statutory and unofficial term 'key stage 5' in place of 'the sixth'. Unsurprisingly, one of the controversial features of the new policies is the involvement of school sixth forms both in new and separate funding and planning arrangements and in the purview of vocational training interests.

The aspirational words used by Spens and quoted above resonate in a new context in the Prime Minister's Foreword to *Bridging the Gap* (Cm 4405), Social Exclusion Unit, 1999:

> 'A few decades ago only a minority stayed in education until 18 or 21. But as we move into an economy based more on knowledge, there will be ever fewer unskilled jobs. For this generation and for young people in the future, staying at school or in training until 18 is no longer a luxury. It is becoming a necessity.'
>
> (p. 6)

This and some more tentative predictions in the White Paper *Learning to Succeed* (Cm 4392), were translated in the Connexions strategy document of early 2000 into: '[O]ur clear goal that all young people should stay in learning until 18 and beyond.' (para 1.3).

2. Recent legislation

The Learning and Skills Act 2000 was the legislative expression of a number of related policy strands in post-compulsory education. In addition to introducing major structural changes to funding agencies, it provided the legislative basis for Connexions (see below); dealt with approval powers for public funding of external qualifications; created 'Individual Learning Accounts'; removed some of the barriers to interchange (for both staff and students) between 16+ provision in schools and FE; enabled the establishment of city academies and made changes to legislation governing sex education in schools.

Based closely on policies for England outlined in the Green Paper *The Learning Age* (Cm 3790) (1998) and the White Paper *Learning to Succeed* (Cm 4392) (1999), the Act was an attempt, by no means the first by Governments of recent years, at radical change in 16+ education and training. In the *Learning and Skills Council Prospectus* (December 1999), published shortly before the Bill itself, Ministers stressed the forward-looking nature of the proposed arrangements, 'a new system of post-16 learning [...] which is coherent and accessible and is notably responsive to the needs of individuals, businesses and communities' (Secretary of State Mr Blunkett, in the Foreword), involving a cultural shift in attitudes to learning.

On the one hand, the *Prospectus* argued that 'the new framework must cater for the future needs of individuals, employers and the economy, [and] not perpetuate historic [*sic*] irrelevant patterns of delivery' (para 3.6). On the other hand, the document acknowledges *passim* the achievements of the several actors, whether continuing (e.g. LEAs, colleges) or retiring (e.g. the FE Funding Councils), on whose successes the new systems were expected to build.

The early operation of the new arrangements has not yet shown whether this latest attempt at substitution of a form of client empowerment for capture or dominance by the provider or producer – to use terms common in the discourse of the Conservative administrations of the 1980s and early 1990s – will succeed where at least by implication earlier initiatives have failed. The dichotomy between provider- and consumer-led provision, though, is itself illusory: consumers' needs are often expressed by reference to what is currently provided, albeit with modifications and indeed it would do a disservice to providers of education and training to assume that their programmes have been largely unresponsive to clients' needs and aspirations.

And there is a tension, exemplified also throughout the schools system, between national standards and requirements and the local articulation of priorities, in a geographically small country within a large and growing European Union, at a time when communications are good and workforces are expected to be unprecedentedly mobile and adaptable.

The key to the new structure is the representative (and largely business-led) and responsive character of the local learning and skills councils in England and ELWa and its regional structure in Wales, within the new structures, as briefly described below.

3. New structures

The structures of the FE Funding Councils and Training and Enterprise Councils (TECs) were replaced by the Learning and Skills Council (LSC), s. 1 of and schedule 1 to the Act, for England and s. 30 and sched 4 for Wales.

The council's main duties include securing the provision of 'proper' (as defined) facilities for education and training for the 16–19 age group (s. 2) and of 'reasonable' (as defined, including having regard to resources) facilities for education and training for people aged 19+ (s. 3). The LSC has an explicit duty to encourage greater participation by individuals and employers (s. 4). These duties exclude higher education. The LSC must establish local learning and skills councils (sched 2) which will be *inter alia* conduits for pump-priming moneys from the national body and will be allowed some freedom to adapt national programmes. In the first years of operation of the new system this freedom has translated into an ability to run additional small-scale local programmes rather than a power to change the terms of, or step outside, the national funding framework, which has remained rigidly controlled from the centre.

The LSC is answerable to, and subject to directions of, the Secretary of State. It is required to appoint two committees, for young people's and adult learning (sched 3). Initial appointments to the committees were managed by DfES alongside the process of

11.
LEARNING
& SKILLS

appointing the national council itself, according to 'Nolan' principles of public sector appointments. Forty-seven local LSCs replaced the TECs and the regional offices of the FEFC. When the abolition of TECs was announced, a significant number of (particularly industry-based) non-executive TEC directors dropped out immediately. Whilst a number of the individuals who remained were appointed to local LSCs, there was a further round of resignations when it became apparent that lay membership of a local LSC was a position of significantly less influence than a TEC non-executive directorship.

The constitutional difference between the non-departmental public bodies is that the LSC will be answerable to, and subject to directions of, the Secretary of State and ELWa will be responsible to the National Assembly for Wales, as an Assembly-sponsored public body. ELWa replaced the four TECs in Wales; it is under a duty to appoint regional committees (sched 5).

4. New arrangements for inspection

The Act created an Adult Learning Inspectorate (ss. 52–59 and sched 6), a new non-departmental public body, responsible for inspecting FE and training 19+ (and 16+ LSC-funded training on employers' premises) and the remit of HM Chief Inspector of Schools was extended to cover FE (ss. 60–68). Sections 69 to 71 require the two inspectorates to create a common inspection framework to cover all post-16 education and training and provide for them to undertake joint inspections including 'area inspections' (this last procedure to apply to education and training from 15+, in an amendment made by the Education Act 2002). This new structure is designed to take account of the blurring of the distinctions and increased complexity of funding mechanisms for post-compulsory education taking place in schools or FE institutions or on employers' premises.

In Wales, the expanded role of HMCI is reflected in the change of title to HMCI of Education and Training in Wales.

5. Territorial loss

The White Paper suggested there would be a saving of £50m arising from reduced administrative overheads in the new structure. This claim was repeated in the Explanatory Notes to the Bill (HL Bill 96–EN, paper 52/3, 24.03.2000), which suggested a 15–20 per cent overall reduction in staff funded by public money to administer 16+

11.
LEARNING
& SKILLS

education and training. The FE Funding Councils, creatures of the Further and Higher Education Act 1992 and their inspectoral and regional structures, were abolished on implementation of the Act in April 2001, as were the TECs and the Training Inspectorate of the Training Standards Council (TSC). The TECs were not statutory corporations but private companies established in 1989 by the then Secretary of State for Employment under general powers in the Employment and Training Act 1973; most of the TECs' work was founded upon contracts for particular services. Similarly, the TSC was a private company limited by guarantee, operating under an annual contract with Government. The claim that the new set-up would be cheaper is difficult to check given the two years' lapse of time between White Paper and implementation and the discontinuities between the functions of the abolished bodies and the new; but there has been some scepticism as to whether the promised benefits either in cash or effectiveness have actually been delivered.

There was significant upheaval on what may legitimately be called the training side, comparable to that attendant on the abolition of the Manpower Services Commission and its regional and sub-regional structures in 1987/88. In particular this is because the LSC has no role in direct delivery. Thus the capacity of TECs to act as a managing agent for organising training on behalf of employers did not pass to a coherent network of public institutions with comprehensive geographical coverage. The role was transferred variously to FE colleges, private training providers or new companies set up by former TEC employees who would otherwise have had a choice between redundancy or transfer to other work within a local LSC. Thus the gradual privatising of this former Manpower Services Commission function was complete.

For their part, LEA members and officers are likely to be keenly interested in the (metaphorically) territorial changes and the new statutory functions and more informal roles which their authorities are now expected to perform:

- positively, because of Ministers' emphasis on local responsiveness, consultation and collaboration (particularly with regard to participation in the creation of new sixth form colleges) within the new arrangements, but also

- negatively, because the legislation of the past 15 years has significantly reduced LEA *vires* in post-16 education, notably:

    - removal of local authority HE, initially to the régime of the Polytechnics and Colleges Funding Council, under the Education Reform Act 1988 (including abolition of the

National Advisory Body for Public Sector HE and removal of the statutory function of the Regional Advisory Councils (RACs) for FE in respect of advanced FE);

– removal (and incorporation) of not only mainstream FE colleges but also sixth-form colleges (previously in law, schools) to the new FE sector presided over by the FEFCs, under the Further and Higher Education Act 1992 (including the final *de facto* abolition of the national framework of RACs);

– substitution of a power to participate in provision of the careers service by not-for-profit or private companies under the Trade Union Reform and Employment Rights Act 1993, for the duty to provide the service under the Employment and Training Act 1973; and

– reduction of the responsibilities of the LEA as principal grant-awarding body for HE students, as an incidental result of legislation from the Education (Student Loans) Act 1990 (repealed 1998) and the Teaching and Higher Education Act 1998.

6. The LEA in the new framework

The powers and duties of the respective actors are set out in so far as they affect or directly interest LEAs and so what follows is not an exhaustive list of functions of the LSC/ELWa and inspectoral bodies.

6.1 Powers

The Learning and Skills Act empowers:

a) **the LSC** [and **ELWa**] to make grants to an LEA for 16+ education in schools, the money to be channelled to the schools through the Local Schools Budget (ss. 7, 36, respectively). LEAs have discretion to give additional funds to their schools. Following consultations the new funding arrangements were implemented for the financial year 2002/03. Despite the Government's commitment in the consultation paper to maintaining sixth forms' funding levels in real terms, implementation caused significant turbulence. DfES and LSC failed to anticipate the complex interaction between assumptions on which general Government grant was made and the operation of local funding schemes. In the event some LEAs were forced by the new regulations to deprive schools of expected increases in 5–16 funding in order to fund significant increases in sixth-form funding demanded by the new regulations;

b) **the LSC** [only] to forge links between education/training and employment for young people aged 15–19, with the intention that the LSC will work with Education Business Partnerships to secure appropriate work experience in the last two years of compulsory schooling (s. 8);

c) **any LEA** to establish and maintain a secondary school exclusively for 16–19 year-olds (effectively, reinstatement of a power exercisable before the Further and Higher Education Act 1992), subject to statutory publication and as appropriate approval, of proposals (s. 110) (with a corresponding protection of properly-established LEA-maintained 16–19 schools from being incorporated into the LSC/ELWa sector without agreement of the governing body and LEA (ss. 111, 112));

d) **the LSC/ELWa** to publish proposals in respect of any 'inadequate sixth form' (this is the term used in headings and side notes of the Act) at, or constituting, an LEA-maintained school that it cease to provide 16–19 education ('inadequacy' as it is defined in the Act and resting essentially on two seriously adverse inspection reports) (s. 113 and sched 7), the actual closure (or otherwise) to be determined through the machinery of part II of, and sched 6 to, the School Standards and Framework Act 1998, that is, after the opportunity for statutory objection: in England, reference to the school organisation committee and if necessary the adjudicator; in Wales, to the National Assembly;

e) **the Secretary of State** in England (by ss. 114–122, outlining a power, but amounting virtually to a duty through the *de facto* commitments in the Command papers to 'secure provision of an integrated support service for youngsters aged 13–19'), by directing LEAs or making arrangements through a variety of bodies including LEAs, to 'encourage, enable or assist (directly or indirectly) effective participation by young persons in education or training' (s. 114). As the Explanatory Notes put it:

> '[T]he Secretary of State intends to use these new powers to integrate and build on the existing range of services currently provided at the local level by careers service companies, youth service and other statutory and voluntary services for young people.'

(Section 116 specifically empowers LEAs to make arrangements, comply with Ministerial directions and provide or collaborate in the supply of services);

**11.
LEARNING
& SKILLS**

f) **a further or higher education corporation** to provide or collaborate in secondary education at key stage 4, after consultation with the LEA (s. 142) (a relaxation of previous controls, it loosens the LEA's control over the education of some secondary-aged pupils who may attend FE or HE colleges);

g) **any LEA** to provide FE 'in connection with local LSC plans'. The quotation is from the Explanatory Notes to the Act (para 193), but the phrase appears not to be justified on the face of the Act. Section 137 amends section 508 of the Education Act 1996 (as detailed in sched 9, paras 52–55) but makes no reference to 'LSC plans'. Presumably the Government assumes that LEA compliance with LSC plans would be sufficiently enforced by its transfer of funding from revenue support grant to the LSC as from the 2001/02 financial year.

As to the generality of the provisions here, there has been some downgrading as well as extension of functions:

- the LEA's duty to provide (since the 1992 Act, what amounted to non-vocational) FE has become a power;

- its providing 16–19 education has continued as a power, though with the addition of part-time to the existing power in respect of full-time and a power to provide full-time or part-time FE from 19+ (sched 9, paras 54–55);

- and, interestingly, the LEA's former duty to provide facilities for recreation and social and physical training – by convention, one of the statutory bases of the youth service – has been reduced to a power (s. 137). The Connexions document's reassurance to LEAs should be read against that background: 'It remains the Government's intention, that LEAs continue to provide youth services and retain the powers to do so' (p. 52).

At House of Commons Committee stage, the Government brought forward an amendment empowering the National Assembly for Wales to direct local authorities to provide, secure and participate in youth support services for 11–25 year-olds.

6.2 Duties

The Learning and Skills Act places duties on:

a) **ELWa only**, to promote education and training and employers' participation therein (s. 33);

b)   **the LSC** (and ELWa) to have regard to the needs of persons with learning difficulties, to statements of special educational needs and to assessments of SEN made by an LEA in the young person's final year of schooling (s. 13, with s. 140);

c)   **the LSC only**, to appoint local LSCs (formally regarded as its committees), whose duties include preparation of annual plans, on which any LEA in each local LSC's area is a statutory consultee (s. 22(5)(b));

d)   **every LEA** in England to make provision of 16+ education and training in accordance with the local plan, upon direction of the Secretary of State and given reasonable financial support therefore by the (national) LSC (s. 23); and

e)   **every LEA** in England to have regard to the local LSC's plan when it prepares its school organisation plan. The school organisation committee and, if appropriate, the adjudicator, are to have analogous duties (sched 9, para 81).

7.   Conclusion on 16+

Where the Learning and Skills Act 2000 differs from previous policies is in:

a)   the strong interconnection of all publicly-funded 16+ education with all publicly-funded training. Repeal (sched 11 to the Act) of the much-criticised schedule 2 to the 1992 Act, which drew a sharp distinction between FE leading to recognised and mostly vocational qualifications and essentially non-vocational FE, is a manifestation of the new integration. So also is the mandatory collaboration at local level, seen more clearly in the proposals for England; and

b)   the hands-on responsibilities assumed by present Ministers for service delivery. This is underpinned by a commitment to a corporate approach (though never labelled as such) exemplified in:

   (i)   the existence and continuation of the interdepartmental Ministerial Group;

   (ii)   the judgment of seven senior Ministers that:

> 'Teenagers, and those who try to work with them, are still all too often let down by a system which tends to treat the problems that young people face in isolation and to deliver a piecemeal response down separate channels and through professionals only able to deal with issues one by one.'
>
> (Foreword to Connexions document, p. 4)

11.
LEARNING
& SKILLS

Within the mandatory collaboration, LEAs have the duties and powers outlined earlier in this chapter. But the way in which the parties to the statutorily compulsory partnership fulfil their functions, including matters of attitude and style of working, will determine the success or otherwise of the new arrangements – as will the willingness of Ministers in England to keep much of the operation at arm's length in their directions to the LSC and the lightness (or otherwise) of touch which the LSC applies in its dealings with its agents, the local LSCs. Early experience suggests that the extent to which good progress has been made locally is patchy.

In Wales, the development of the National Assembly and its relationships with quangos, their regional committees and totally restructured local government, will be equally critical to the outcomes for 16+ education and training.

And, as in so much of the Government's thinking about new ways of delivering services locally, it is much easier to identify functions and roles of LEAs as professional organisations than as corporate bodies of elected members.

B. The Youth Service

1. Introduction

Since publication of the first edition of this book, youth work and the provision of careers advice have become more closely integrated with the new Connexions service. Further changes may be on the way as a result of the Green Paper *Every Child Matters* (see chapter 9). However, for the time being, their history, legislative basis and functions remain distinct and so this chapter retains separate sections – although they should be read together.

The youth service is a term familiar to its millions of participants and to the community at large but is unknown to statute. Such statutory reference as there is avoids even faintly contemporary language such as 'social education' (see below), preferring 'social training' and yet the service is an excellent example of the LEA as both provider (ironically, of the 'statutory' service) and enabler (of some voluntary youth organisations in its area). The stark fact is that youth work has always been, in statute law, very much an adjunct to the LEA's functions (originally, as a major provider of further education). The Learning and Skills Act perpetuates the modest status of this element of the public education service at s. 137 which amends s. 508 of the Education Act 1996 but retains the formulation 'may provide facilities for recreation and social and physical training' (RSPT).

2. Demands for specific duties

The Thompson Report (*Experience and Participation* (Cmnd 8686) (1982)) was one of many authoritative documents to criticise the vagueness of the statutory basis for the youth service; it also attacked the 'anaemic' recognition of the voluntary sector. Attempts had been made in 1973, 1974, 1975 and 1979 by Private Members' Bills and again in 2000 by tabled amendments to the Learning and Skills Bill, to define in statute the LEA duty in respect of the youth service. These foundered, to the chagrin of youth-service lobbyists, mainly on the rocks of Governmental nervousness about the cost implications of a properly-defined duty and, to a lesser extent, local government's dislike of being told in prescriptive detail by Parliament what to do.

3. Statutory basis

The service itself, as a nationally recognised entity, originated in emergency measures taken in or in anticipation of both the World Wars. The two bases of youth work as LEA functions in the Education Act 1944 were:

- s. 41 (general duties of LEAs with respect to FE): a duty to secure 'adequate facilities', including 'leisure-time occupation, in such organized cultural training and recreative activities as are suited to their requirements, for any persons over compulsory school age who are able and willing to profit by the facilities provided for that purpose'; and

- s. 53 (duty to secure provision of facilities for recreation and social and physical training): a duty in connection with duties in respect of primary, secondary and further education; such facilities to include adequate facilities for RSPT; LEAs empowered, with specific Ministerial approval, to establish, maintain and manage, or assist therewith 'camps, holiday classes, playing fields, play centres and other places (including playgrounds, gymnasiums and swimming baths [...] and [they] may organise games, expeditions and other activities', having regard (subs. (2)) 'to the expediency of cooperating with [...] voluntary societies and bodies.'

4. Language and origins

The label 'Youth Service' came from reports by the Youth Advisory Council: *The Youth Service After the War (1943) and The Purpose and Content of the Youth Service* (1945). The 'RSPT' formulation, quaint by today's standards, derives from powers in s. 17 of the Education Act 1918, consolidated into the Act of 1921 and amplified by the Physical Training and Recreation Act 1937.

5. Statutory destinations

Section 41 was restated, still in terms of duty, by s. 120 of the Education Reform Act 1988, mainly because, as the old s. 41 depended on either an approved LEA development plan or association with a county college, LEAs no longer technically had *vires* to provide most FE, including such of the youth service as might be purported to be under that section. Amended substantially by the Further and Higher Education Act 1992 to take account of the establishment of the then FE Funding Councils and the division of FE into (broadly) vocational and non-vocational, the law still required LEAs to make the sort of provision under the latter category as they had before. The amended requirement was consolidated into s. 15 of the 1996 Act which was repealed under the Learning and Skills Act 2000. The 2000 Act inserted into the existing s. 15A (for 16 to 18 year olds) LEA powers to provide 'vocational, social, physical and recreational training and [...] organised leisure time occupation', adding a new s. 15B (for persons over 19 years).

Section 53, again phrased as a duty, was consolidated into the Education Act 1996 (as s. 508). As noted earlier in this chapter, the Learning and Skills Act reduced the non-school provision of s. 508 to a power.

The Government has stated its view on the application of these LEA powers and duties in England in *Transforming Youth Work: Resourcing Excellent Youth Services* (December 2002). Annex 2 describes s. 508 as providing LEAs with a duty 'to secure the provision of youth service facilities in respect of primary and secondary education in their area'. Under the same section, they have the power to provide youth service facilities for further education. A wide range of facilities may be provided by the local authority including such things as 'playing fields, play centres, playgrounds, swimming baths, youth clubs, organised holiday activities and sports facilities'. The s. 15B power, to provide similar facilities for persons age 19 or over, is also mentioned. The duty is described here and elsewhere, e.g. p. 8, as a 'duty to ensure the provision of a sufficient youth service'. The reason for this confident claim is explained further below. However, it is first necessary to consider the parallel development of the Connexions service and the youth service since the year 2000.

The creation of Connexions in 2000 raised the issue of its relationship to the youth service and whether the youth service would merge into the Connexions. The Government set out its view on 'how the youth work and Youth Services can play their part in the Connexions Service' in March 2001 in *Transforming Youth Work: developing youth work for young people*. The Government's priorities for the youth service were stated:

> 'We must deliver a service which young people will want to use. It must be focused on young people's personal, social and educational development; their voice and influence and their inclusion and engagement in society. We must offer quality support and promote intervention and prevention. We must deliver equality of opportunity for all young people.'
>
> (p. 13)

Although references to 'Youth Services' in the document were meant to cover all publicly-supported youth work, the clear aim of the policy is to transform the local authority service. In the overall context that 'The Youth Service will be the source of expertise and champion of youth work and personal development, both as a service in its own right and as a key partner of and contributor to, the Connexions Service', responses were sought to questions on the relationship to the Connexions service, improving and guaranteeing quality and improving participation. Information was given on the variation in local authority funding, examples of good practice and evidence from Ofsted.

In mid-2002, two further documents were produced: *Working Together: Connexions and the Statutory Youth Service* and *Transforming Youth Work: Planning for the Local Authority Youth Service in 2003–04: Guidance*. The former document was a joint production with service and professional organisations: Connexions, the Local Government Association, National Youth Agency and Association of Principal Youth and Community Officers. It was also very prescriptive about the remit of the local authority youth service:

> 'The priority age group for the youth service is 13–19 year olds but the target age range group may extend to 11–25 year olds in some cases.'
>
> [p. 7]

**11.
LEARNING
& SKILLS**

393

'[…] we want to encourage Local Authorities to work towards concentrating not less than 80 per cent of the available youth work on 13–19 over the next two years to 2003 […] we would expect to see ALL 13–19 youth work and resources planned, managed and delivered as part of a joint working agreement between the Youth Service and the Connexions Partnership underpinned by respective service plans.'

[p. 13]

In discussing 'approaches to Joint Working' between services for young people an example is given 'whereby the Youth Service and the Careers Service reorganise themselves into a single organisation under the Connexions Partnership umbrella' (p. 15). Another model has all youth workers becoming Connexions personal advisers for part of their work. A third structure emerged from the phrase 'joint working agreement', whereby Connexions and youth services remained largely independent of each other but the youth service signed up to help deliver Connexions service targets and identified specifically the resource that it agreed to align with Connexions activity.

Transforming Youth Work: Planning for the Local Authority Youth Service in 2003–04: Guidance confirmed the Government's priorities for the youth service with the addition of ensuring that it 'is well planned with clear aims and objectives and focused on achieving outcomes that relate to the needs and priorities of young people at local level.' Each LEA was asked to prepare a plan for the Youth Service from 2003/04 according to a common national framework and to consider developments for the years 2004/05 and 2005/06. The document required youth services to demonstrate how they had involved the voluntary sector in developing priorities and activities within the youth service plan. It did not, however, contain a requirement by the Secretary of State for each local authority to produce a plan for approval as could have been done under s. 29 (Provision of information by local education authorities) of the 1996 Act. To the chagrin of the youth service lobby, any intention to do so was overtaken by the cross-Government initiative to reduce the number of planning requirements on local authorities and other bodies. Thus the document stated that the DfES was interested in working with LEAs who wish to rationalise and integrate youth service planning with the Connexions Plan and the Children's Services Plan. However, the document does state that the future distribution of the specific grant 'Transforming Youth Work Development Fund' would be dependent on a comprehensive approach to planning and that LEAs should seek further advice from their regional Government Office (GO). It is understood that all

11.
LEARNING
& SKILLS

LEAs were contacted by their GO in autumn 2002 asking about progress and requesting that the approved plan be submitted to the GO before the start of the 2003-04 financial year.

The final piece of the jigsaw of recent youth service changes was published in December 2002: *Transforming Youth Work: Resourcing Excellent Youth Services*. Local authorities were asked to work to the service standards for youth work provision developed by the NYA in the context of the local government financial settlement. The expectation is that these standards will be reached by 2005. The standards include specific resource targets for each LEA, for example:

- Youth Standard 7: Number of contacts per thousand (13–19) population: 25 per cent of total youth population

- Youth Standard 8: Number of individuals participating: 15 per cent of total youth population

- Youth Standard 9: Number of individuals worked with intensively: 5 per cent of total population

- Youth Standard 14: YS spending per head of population aged 13–19 years [at least £100 per head per annum, with additional funding for intensive work and disadvantage, including sparsity]

- Youth Standard 15: One full-time equivalent staff per 400 of 13–19 population.

The Government took the opportunity of the new funding distribution mechanism for 2003/04 to have a Youth and Community sub-block within the Education Formula Spending. Annex F of DfES letter *School and LEA Funding in 2003/04: Guidance Letter No.2* (LEA/0395a/2002), of 10 December 2002, gave further explanation. The sub-block stands at an increase of 5.9 percent over the DfES estimate of expenditure in 2002/03 (save that the sub-block also included expenditure on community education and FE student support). The sub-block used a distribution mechanism based on the number of 13–19 year-olds and measures of deprivation for each authority. The new financial reporting mechanisms would be changed to 'allow local authorities to demonstrate the investment they are making', which should 'bring about increased investment in every Youth Service'. The Government believes that settlement provided LEAs with the resources required to meet the 'new Youth Service targets' and contribute to a range of cross-cutting targets, in other words: LEAs were being funded to provide a sufficient youth service which can meet the 22 prescribed targets.

11. LEARNING & SKILLS

In order to ensure that LEAs use their local discretion to passport the additional money to the youth service and improve the service to meet the prescribed targets, Annex 2 of *Resourcing Excellent Youth Services* stated that the Secretary of State would use the 'supervisory powers' over LEAs in the 1996 Act, s. 114 (Provision of services) of the Learning and Skills Act 2000 and new powers of intervention inserted into the 1996 Act by the 2002 Education Act. The 'supervisory powers' presumably refers to s. 497 (General default powers). This would apply where the Secretary of State is 'satisfied' that an LEA has 'failed to discharge' the s. 508 duty. The Secretary of State can give directions 'for the purpose of enforcing the performance of the duty', although given the imprecise nature of s. 508, in spite of the reinterpretation in *Resourcing Excellent Youth Services*, it might be difficult to hold up should an LEA challenge a direction in the courts.

Section 114 of the 2000 Act was designed to give the Secretary of State the power to establish the Connexions service. The *Explanatory Notes* to the Act state that its purpose is to give the Secretary of State 'a new power to secure the provision of support for all 13 to 19 year olds for the purpose of encouraging and enabling young people to stay on and participate effectively in education and training'. Subsection (2) enables the Secretary of State to direct, after consultation, an LEA to provide or secure the provision of services which will encourage, enable or assist young people to participate in education or training. Reducing the youth service to a service which helps young people to participate in education or training would be against the principles in Transforming Youth Work and it is difficult to see how it would be effective.

The third form of intervention is likely to be the most effective way of securing a 'sufficient' youth service although it may be seen as heavy-handed especially as the LEA may be able to show that increased expenditure on the youth service will lead to reduced expenditure on schools. This recalls events in 2003/04, when the financial turbulence created by the new distributional mechanism and a chorus of complaint from schools diverted Ministerial attention toward exhorting LEAs to divert all available funds to bolster schools' delegated budgets. Section 60 of the Education Act 2002 amends s. 497A (Power to secure proper performance of functions of local education authority) of the 1996 Act such that the Secretary of State now has the power over any LEA function 'to issue directions, including the power to direct that a function be exercised by an agency other than the LEA'. There is a planned programme of Ofsted inspection of LEA youth services which in time will show, on inspection, some youth services to be ineffective and not meeting the high standards set out in *Resourcing Excellent Youth Services*. Arguably, those standards could be set as minima for any statutorily-required level of youth service provision. And certainly the inclusion of the service into Ofsted's 4-yearly LEA inspection cycle has reasserted its educational character.

See also part D, below.

6.　Wales

Little of the above applies to Wales. Wales does not have a Connexions service but has, under separate powers in ss. 123–129 of the Learning and Skills Act 2000, developed Young People's Partnerships in close co-operation with the local authority youth service. See chapter 2 for details.

C. Careers

To a certain extent, the fate of careers education and guidance is another example of the decreasing role of LEAs as service providers and the centralisation of education functions.

Under the Employment and Training Act 1973, LEAs were responsible for the provision of a careers service within their administrative areas. With effect from 10 August 1993, however, that role was diminished when the Trade Union Reform and Employment Rights Act 1993 transferred the responsibility for providing careers advice and guidance to the Secretary of State and now the LEA's role, with one or two exceptions, is limited to assisting in the provision of careers services through joint ventures or partnership arrangements.

**11.
LEARNING
& SKILLS**

Thus it is the duty of the Secretary of State to secure the provision of services for assisting persons undergoing relevant education to decide:

a)　what employments, having regard to their capabilities, will be suitable for and available to them when they cease undergoing such education, and

b)　what training or education is or will be required by and available to them in order to fit them for those employments and for assisting persons ceasing to undergo relevant education to obtain such employments, training and education (s. 8 of the Employment and Training Act 1973).

The services required to be provided include:

a) giving of assistance by collecting, or disseminating or otherwise providing, information about persons seeking, obtaining or offering employment, training and education,

b) offering advice and guidance, and

c) other services calculated to facilitate the provision of such services (s. 8(2)).

In order to enable him to carry out his duties, the Secretary of State, under s. 10, may make arrangements with (a) LEAs or (b) persons of any other description, or (c) LEAs and persons of any other description acting jointly, under which they undertake to provide, or arrange for the provision of, services in accordance with the arrangements (s. 10(1)). The Secretary of State may also by giving directions to LEAs require them to provide, or arrange for the provision of, services in accordance with the directions and in doing so the Secretary of State shall have regard to the requirements of disabled persons. Such directions may require LEAs:

a) to provide services themselves or jointly with other authorities or persons,

b) to arrange for the provision of services by other authorities or persons, or

c) to consult and co-ordinate in the provision, or in arranging for the provision, of services with other authorities or persons (s. 10(3)). These arrangements may allow charges to be made for the provision of services in accordance with the approved arrangements (s. 10(5)).

Careers service providers must comply with any guidance given by the Secretary of State and shall furnish the Secretary of State, in such manner and at such times as he may specify in the arrangements or directions or in guidance given, with such information and facilities for obtaining information as he may so specify (s. 10(6)).

LEAs have the power:

a) to provide services or arrange for the provision of services in accordance with arrangements made, or directions given (including services provided outside their areas) by any such means (including by the formation of companies for the purpose) as they consider appropriate, and

b)   to employ officers and provide facilities for, and in connection with, the provision of the services or arranging for the provision of the services but, where directions are given to LEAs, the power conferred on them must be exercised in accordance with the directions (s. 10(8)).

With the consent of the Secretary of State, where an LEA is providing careers services, it may provide, or arrange for the provision of, more extensive services than under the arrangements with the Secretary of State and may employ more officers and provide more facilities accordingly (s. 10(9)).

To assist in the provision of careers services, the functions of an LEA are (s. 10A) specifically stated to include the power to enter into any agreements for the supply of goods and services with any person (other than another local authority) who provides, or arranges for the provision of, careers services. The supply of goods authorised under s. 10A can last for only two years from the day the careers service provider starts providing services in the area and must be on such terms as can reasonably be expected to secure that the full cost of making the supply is recovered by the LEA (s. 10A(5) and (6)).

The supplies authorised include the supply by the LEA to the person of any goods, the provision by the LEA of any administrative, professional or technical services, the use by the person of any vehicle, plant or apparatus belonging to the LEA and the placing at the disposal of the person of the services of any person employed in connection with the vehicle or other property in question and the carrying out by the LEA of works of maintenance in connection with land or buildings for the maintenance of which the careers services provider is responsible. The LEA may purchase and store any goods which in its opinion it may require for these purposes.

11.
LEARNING
& SKILLS

Within maintained schools, responsibility for ensuring that pupils receive proper careers education and have access to guidance materials and to up-to-date reference materials within their last three years of compulsory schooling rests with the governing body. In the case of Pupil Referral Units, however, the LEA, together with the teacher in charge, is under a duty to ensure that pupils at the unit receive such advice (s. 43 of the Education Act 1997). For guidance on careers education in schools, see DfEE Circular 5/98 *Careers Education in Schools: Provision for Years 9–11.*

D. Connexions

Spanning both careers education and guidance and work experience, as well as a number of other areas, is the Government's Connexions service. It was developed as a response to the Social Exclusion Unit report *Bridging the Gap: New opportunities for 16-18 year olds not in education, employment or training* (July 1999). It comprises a new youth support service for all 13–19 year-olds (but, for those with learning difficulties and disabilities, up to their 25th birthday), bringing together advice and support agencies to create a single point of access for young people. Its original *raison d'être* was to co-ordinate the work of the various professional groups who might be expected to contribute to the prevention or remediation of teenage problems leading to drop-out from education and training. A Connexions service national unit was set up at the DfES in Sheffield and London to administer and monitor the scheme. Both the original idea and the mechanisms for its delivery, have been overtaken by the more ambitious and inclusive approach embodied in the Green Paper *Every Child Matters* (see chapter 9).

The service is delivered locally through partnerships based on the geographical areas covered by the local offices of the Learning and Skills Council. The partnerships were established on a rolling programme between 2001 and 2003 on the basis of a three-year business plan and under contract with the national unit. The main partners include the various careers service providers and local authorities particularly through the youth services, Youth Offending Teams and education welfare services they provide. The form of the partnership varies across the country, partly for reasons of geography (between one and 11 LEA areas covered) but also in legal status. Some operate informally with one partner (usually a local authority) acting as the accountable body to receive and distribute funds, employ staff etc; whilst others are incorporated as companies limited by guarantee or by shares. Initially it was proposed that the partnership should be expressed through a local management committee chaired by the LEA chief executive or person of similar status. In practice the local authority representative was usually the chief education officer but in many cases it was found preferable for the chair to be taken by a person independent of the main partners (the planning guidance requires that they are drawn from membership of the Connexions partnership board). In some areas, particularly those covering several LEAs, two-tier structures emerged.

As has been seen elsewhere (e.g chapter 1.C.8), the opportunity for LEA leadership here produces a *de facto* influence well beyond the

11.
LEARNING
& SKILLS

new statutory functions. However the companies formed to deliver the careers service after 1992 had a powerful incentive to seek a controlling influence as the resources upon which they depend are subsumed entirely into the Connexions programme, whereas the LEA agencies (youth work, education welfare, etc) are merely contributors to it.

The focus of Connexions is to increase participation in learning up to the age of 19, prevent disaffection and promote social inclusion and give practical support to overcome personal, family or social obstacles. The core of the service is a national network of personal advisers to support and advise teenagers who need help, attached to the Connexions partnership and 'deployed' in schools, FE/training/employment, community and voluntary bodies, social services departments and Youth Offending Teams. They have been drawn from the previous careers service and the contributing agencies with some new direct recruitment. However, there was some initial confusion arising from the fact that a number of individuals with a similar role and function were deployed as a result of separate initiatives, for example learning mentors in schools within Excellence in Cities areas. The Government's aspiration to create 'A new Profession of Personal Adviser', all members of which would be seconded to or employees of Connexions partnerships, was therefore left to local co-operation. At the time of writing convergence is being promoted but has not yet been fully achieved. As noted above, Connexions is likely to be affected by the wave of change following the introduction of children's trusts and local directors of children's services.

Ofsted will play a leading part in the audit and inspection of the service and target-setting and benchmarking will be developed to enable the quality of the delivery to be monitored.

Further information on the scheme can be found at www.connexions.gov.uk. See also part B.5, above.

**11.
LEARNING
& SKILLS**

E. Work Experience

As will be seen below, strict rules apply to the employment of children. In order, therefore to enable and encourage children at school to attend authorised programmes of work experience, specific provision has been made to allow children in their last two years of compulsory education to take on such work. (A child is in his last two years of compulsory schooling from the beginning of the last two school years during the whole or part of which he is of compulsory school age (s. 560(2) of the Education Act 1996)).

Consequently under s. 560, an LEA, or a governing body acting on behalf of an LEA, with a view to providing a pupil with work experience as part of his education, may lift the statutory restrictions where employment is arranged or approved by the school or the LEA for a pupil in his or her last two years at school. These arrangements cannot, however, override the statutory prohibition (including byelaws) on children working in certain areas of work or avoid the restrictions imposed in other areas of juvenile employment in respect to, for example, the minimum age for particular work (s. 560(3) and (4)).

Advice on work experience was originally provided in DES Circular 7/74 *Work Experience*, although that advice is now somewhat out of date. More recent advice was provided in guidance issued by the (then) DfEE on 12 May 1999 entitled *Work Experience: Legal Responsibility and Health and Safety*. Revised versions of the DfES's publications on work experience were published in February 2002: *Work Experience: A guide for schools* SPD/WES/01/02(rev) and *Work Experience: A guide for employers* SPD/WES/01/1199 (rev).

Work experience is encouraged as part of the general social inclusion agenda (see para 4.25 of DfEE Circular 10/99 *Social Inclusion: Pupil Support*). To this end, pupils may spend some of the week on work-related learning programmes in school, FE colleges or with an employer. The extra time for work-related learning is freed by dropping two of the pupil's other subjects. Some FE colleges offer tailored programmes for secondary pupils at key stage 4, part-time or full-time as agreed with the school which may be combined with work-related learning. These themes were taken up and extended in the policy document *14–19: Opportunity and Excellence* (DfES 0744/2002) published in January 2003.

F. Juvenile Employment

Every LEA is responsible for enforcing the legislation which affects the employment of children and, where the employment of children is permitted, each LEA can issue byelaws to regulate that employment.

The starting point for juvenile employment is that no child under the age of 13 can be employed in any way (s. 1 of the Children Act 1972). The employment of other children (who are defined as persons who are not over compulsory school age (s. 558 of the Education Act 1996)), where not specifically controlled by other legislation, is subject to byelaws issued by LEAs under s. 18 of the Children and Young Persons Act 1933. In order to comply with the UK's obligations under the European Community Directive on the Protection of Young People at Work 1994 (1994/33/EC), the Department of Health introduced model byelaws for adoption by LEAs in 1998.

An LEA also has the power, by notice served on an employer, to prohibit or restrict the employer employing a pupil registered at a maintained school if it considers the employment to be prejudicial to health or otherwise to render him unfit to obtaining the full benefit from the education provided for him (s. 559(1) of the Education Act 1996).

In order to enable the LEA to decide whether it should exercise this power, the LEA may compel the employer to provide the LEA within a specified period with such information as the LEA considers necessary to allow it to ascertain if the child is being employed in a manner as to render him unfit to benefit from the education provided for him (s. 559(2)). The LEA's power to enter premises under s. 28(1) and (3) of the Children and Young Persons Act 1933 applies to these provisions as much as it applies to its general enforcement role under that Act (s. 559(5)).

Specific occupations which are prohibited by other legislation include:

- employment in any industrial undertaking, including mines and quarries, manufacturing industry, construction and the transfer of passengers or goods by road, rail or inland waterway (s. 1(1) of the Employment of Women, Children and Young Persons Act 1920);

- employment involving a child riding on or driving a vehicle, machine or agricultural implement (s. 7 of the Agriculture (Safety, Health and Welfare Provisions) Act 1956);

- cleaning machinery where doing so may expose children to injury (s. 18 of the Offices, Shops and Railway Premises Act 1963);

11.
LEARNING
& SKILLS

- effecting any betting transaction, or being employed, in a licensed betting office (s. 21 of the Betting, Gaming and Lotteries Act 1963);

- employment of children in the bar of licensed premises (s. 170 of the Licensing Act 1964);

- employment on a ship registered in the UK, except as permitted by regulations (s. 51 of the Merchant Shipping Act 1970);

- handling any load likely to cause a child injury (Manual Handling Operations Regulations 1992).

No child may be engaged in street trading unless authorised to do so by local authority byelaws (s. 20 of the Children and Young Persons Act 1933).

Detailed provisions regulate child performances in the entertainment industry. Section 37 of the Children and Young Persons Act 1963 provides that no child shall take part in:

a) any performance in connection with which a charge is made,

b) any performance in licensed premises,

c) any broadcast performance or performance included in a programme service, or

d) any performance recorded by whatever means with a view to its use in a broadcast or such a service or in a film intended for public exhibition

unless a licence has been granted by the local authority in whose area he resides or, if he does not reside in Great Britain, by the local authority in whose area the applicant or one of the applicants for the licence resides or has his place of business (s. 37(1) and (2)).

A licence is not, however, required if:

a) in the six months preceding the performance he has not taken part in other performances covered by s. 37 on more than three days; or

b) the performance is given under arrangements made by a school or made by a body of persons approved for the purposes of this section by the Secretary of State or by the local authority in whose area the performance takes place

and no payment in respect of the child's taking part in the performance is made, whether to him or to any other person, except for defraying expenses (s. 37(3)).

Under the Children (Performances) Regulations 1968 (SI 1968 No. 1728), the Secretary of State has prescribed conditions to be observed with respect to the hours of work, rest or meals of children taking part in performances. Guidance on the 1968 Regulations can be found in *The Law on Performances by Children: A Guide to the Children (Performances) Regulations 1968 and Related Provisions,* Home Office (1968). A licence issued by the LEA granting approval to the performance must specify the times, if any, during which the child in respect of whom it is granted may be absent from school for the purposes authorised by the licence. A child absent during the times specified in the licence is treated as being authorised to be absent for the purposes of pupil registration (s. 37(6) and (7)).

An LEA cannot, however, issue a licence to a child under 14 unless:

a)   the licence is for acting and the application therefore is accompanied by a declaration that the part he is to act cannot be taken except by a child of about his age; or

b)   the licence is for dancing in a ballet which does not form part of an entertainment of which anything other than ballet or opera also forms part and the application for the licence is accompanied by a declaration that the part he is to dance cannot be taken except by a child of about his age; or

c)   the nature of his part in the performance is wholly or mainly musical and either the nature of the performance is also wholly or mainly musical or the performance consists only of opera and ballet (s. 38(1) of the Children and Young Persons Act 1968).

12. ACCOUNTABILITY AND CHALLENGE

A. Introduction

"My client burnt her mouth on your unattended porridge"

Although the increasing trend for litigation and the greater emphasis on the inspection of LEA services are seen as fairly recent innovations, LEAs have always been subject to checks and outside scrutiny and have never been free to act without restraint.

Litigation in particular is seen as a recent problem with the apparent Americanisation of the English legal system leading to claims against LEAs that would never have been countenanced in the past. But LEAs have always been subject to legal action and the case law on the liability of school staff dates back to *King v Ford* (1816) 1 Stark 421, when a schoolmaster who encouraged an infant pupil under his care to use fireworks was held responsible for the mischief which ensued (see Barrell (1970:256)).

There is no doubt, though, that there has never been such close scrutiny of the work of an LEA, partly through the political emphasis on education, education, education and partly because, to a certain extent, LEAs are on probation and, for many within national politics, are still required to justify their continuing existence.

Similarly, there is also no doubt that the number of claims brought against LEAs through the courts has increased, in terms of both civil actions for damages and judicial review of LEA decisions. This is partly a reflection of the greater willingness amongst parents and pupils to resort to the courts to resolve disputes, but also reflects the trends in judicial thinking which has led to the courts' exercising greater control over the actions of public authorities.

A further perception on the part of LEAs and schools may be that the increasing number of cases is related to the ease with which children appear to be able to obtain legal aid, or as it is now known, public funding. The courts have, however, been critical of lawyers who bring claims in the name of a child, when in reality it is the parent who should be bringing the action (see for a recent example, *Wandsworth LBC v K* [2003] EWHC 1424 and 1629 (Admin);

[2003] ELR 554) and from an early stage appeals against decisions of the, as it was, SENT have had to be brought by and against the parents rather than the child (see *S v SENT and City of Westminster* [1996] ELR 228, CA)). In addition, the current guidelines issued by the Legal Services Commission (see www.legalservices.gov.uk/old-docs/lsc/index.htm) ensure that the question of who should bring a claim is properly considered before public funding of a case is granted, which may reduce the number of cases which can be publicly funded.

As public authorities, LEAs are subject to the doctrine of *vires*. This means that they cannot do anything other than that which the law, through statute and regulation, permits. Local authorities currently lack the power of general competence (although developments in the future may enable high performing councils to be given this power or something approximating to it) and consequently, to justify any action, the authority must be able to point to the statutory duty or power which allows it to carry out the particular act. If it cannot do so, it acts *ultra vires* or outside its powers and the court may intervene in the course of a judicial review. The restriction on the powers of local authorities by recent Governments, together with a greater enthusiasm for challenging decisions through the courts, has been a significant factor in the increasing amount of litigation affecting LEAs. Although not having such a significant impact as some commentators initially anticipated, the Human Rights Act 1998 has also led to LEAs' facing even closer scrutiny by the judiciary.

This chapter will therefore consider the mechanisms by which LEAs can be held accountable by parents, pupils and others involved in their work and will also examine in detail the judicial remedies now available against LEAs.

B. Statutory Accountability

1. Secretary of State for Education and Skills

Although there has been criticism of the apparent recent trend towards centralisation in education with more and more powers being reserved to the Secretary of State, that Minister has, certainly since 1944, always retained reserve powers to deal with abuses committed by LEAs. These powers are now found in the 1996 Act. In this section of the book, references to the Secretary of State apply in England. For Wales, please substitute NAW (see the National

Assembly for Wales (Transfer of Functions) Order 1999 (SI 1999 No. 672).

Under s. 495 of the 1996 Act, any dispute between an LEA and a governing body of a school as to the exercise of any power conferred or the performance of any duty imposed by or under the Education Acts may be referred to the Secretary of State (who may intervene despite any enactment which makes the exercise of a power or the performance of a duty contingent upon the opinion of the LEA or of the governing body). The Secretary of State has a discretion to determine any dispute referred to him in this manner (s. 495(2)).

This dispute resolution mechanism applies both ways. Thus if a governing body is dissatisfied with the exercise of an LEA's powers, it can complain to the Secretary of State, just as in the same way an LEA can complain to the Secretary of State about the exercise of a governing body's power. Section 495 cannot, however, be utilised unless the dispute is referred to the Secretary of State; it does not allow the Secretary of State to intervene of his own volition.

Under s. 496 of the 1996 Act, if the Secretary of State is satisfied (either on a complaint by any person or otherwise) that a body to which s. 496 applies has acted or is proposing to act unreasonably with respect to the exercise of any power conferred or the performance of any duty imposed by or under the Education Acts, he may give such directions as to the exercise of the power or the performance of the duty as appear to him to be expedient (and may do so despite any enactment which makes the exercise of a power or the performance of a duty contingent upon the opinion of the body) (s. 496(1)).

Section 496 applies to any LEA and the governing body of any maintained or maintained special school.

Under s. 496, it is not necessary for a complaint first to be referred to the Secretary of State; instead the Secretary of State can act of his own volition.

12. ACCOUNTABILITY & CHALLENGE

Although in the past there have been concerns that the Secretary of State has not acted as quickly as the situation may warrant, recourse should really be had to s. 496 before any court action is contemplated. Although the case law is inconsistent, a number of decided cases have indicated that before considering judicial review, an aggrieved individual should first complain to the Secretary of State. Similarly, a complaint to the Secretary of State is not necessarily precluded where an LEA is alleged to have acted *ultra vires* or contrary to natural justice (see *Herring v Templeman* [1973] All ER 581). Here, the courts have recognised that the Secretary of State is equally capable of considering the unreasonableness of an LEA's or school's actions as a court. The question of when the statutory procedure should be invoked and when an aggrieved parent or pupil should seek judicial review will be discussed below.

It is important to remember, however, that the question of deciding whether or not the LEA has acted or is proposing to act unreasonably is to be decided in accordance with the legal definition of unreasonableness as opposed to the lay understanding of the phrase. Thus in order to intervene, the Secretary of State must show that the LEA was acting in a way in which no reasonable LEA would act (see *Secretary of State for Education and Science v Tameside MBC* [1977] AC 1014).

In addition to s. 496, the Secretary of State has a general default power where, if he is satisfied (either on a complaint by any person interested or otherwise) that either an LEA or a governing body of a maintained school or special school has failed to discharge any duty imposed on it by or for the purposes of the education legislation, he may make an order:

a) declaring the LEA or governing body to be in default in respect of that duty; and

b) giving such directions for the purpose of enforcing the performance of the duty as appear to him to be expedient (s. 497(1)).

Any direction given shall be enforceable, on an application to the court made on behalf of the Secretary of State, by a mandatory order, i.e. a court order requiring the LEA or the governing body to comply with the direction.

The s. 497 power is slightly different from the s. 496 power in that it applies only to the discharge of duties, whereas s. 496 allows the Secretary of State to intervene if he believes the LEA is unreasonably exercising a power. Because of the importance of the discharge of duties, however, s. 497 does provide the Secretary of State with a far more effective means of enforcing his decision, first by direction and second by court order if necessary.

Again, a person may complain under s. 497(1) before taking action through the courts, although the judiciary is somewhat inconsistent in deciding when the availability of this complaint mechanism

**12.
ACCOUNTABILITY
& CHALLENGE**

means that an application for judicial review should be rejected. For example, in *Meade v Haringey LBC* [1979] 2 All ER 1016, it was held that the existence of the complaint mechanism did not exclude an application to the courts for damages or an injunction by a parent who suffered damage when an LEA failed to perform its statutory duty. However, that case was not a judicial review. Where parents ask the court to invoke its discretionary jurisdiction to grant relief against the action of a public body by way of judicial review proceedings, there may be circumstances where the courts will prefer the parents to have gone through the statutory process beforehand, rather than going immediately to court.

As has been discussed in connection with the monitoring and improvement of education, to meet the concern that whilst some LEAs might be complying with their statutory duties they were not performing to the maximum standard, the School Standards and Framework Act 1998 introduced into the 1996 Act a power for the Secretary of State to issue directions if an LEA is failing in any respect to perform any function to an adequate standard (or at all) (s. 497A(2)).

If the Secretary of State is satisfied (either on complaint by any interested person or otherwise) that an LEA is failing in any respect to perform any function under the Education Acts, or any other functions of whatever nature which are conferred on the LEA in its capacity as an LEA, to an adequate standard or at all, the Secretary of State may:

a) give the LEA or an officer of the LEA such directions as the Secretary of State thinks expedient for the purpose of securing that the function is performed on behalf of the LEA by such person as is specified in the direction and such directions may require that any contract or other arrangement made by the LEA with that person contains such terms and conditions as may be so specified (s. 497A(4)); and

b) direct that the function shall be exercised by the Secretary of State or a person nominated by him and that the LEA shall comply with any instructions of the Secretary of State or his nominee in relation to the exercise of the function (s. 497A(4A)); and

c) give the LEA or an officer of the LEA such other directions as the Secretary of State thinks expedient for the purpose of securing that the function is performed to an adequate standard (s. 497A(4B)).

12.
ACCOUNTABILITY
& CHALLENGE

The Secretary of State may also exercise these powers where he has given a previous direction in relation to an LEA and he is satisfied that it is likely that if no further direction were given on the expiry or revocation of the previous direction, the LEA would fail in any respect to perform that function to an adequate standard or at all (s. 497A(2A)).

Where the Secretary of State considers it expedient that the person specified in directions or the Secretary of State or his nominee, as appropriate, should perform other functions in addition to the functions which are not up to standard, the directions may also relate to the performance of those other functions (s. 497A(5)).

Where the Secretary of State is satisfied that an LEA is failing to perform a function to an adequate standard or at all, or is satisfied that this would be the case if no further direction is made (i.e. s. 497A (2) or (2A)(b)) and has notified the LEA that he is so satisfied and that he is contemplating the giving of directions under s. 497A(4) or (4A), the LEA must give the Secretary of State and any person authorised by him for the purpose, all such assistance in connection with the proposed exercise of the function by the Secretary of State or his nominee, as it is reasonably able to give (s. 497AA). This requires full co-operation prior to any direction as opposed to the other provisions which apply once a direction has been given.

Any direction may either be for an indefinite period until revoked or have effect until any objectives specified in the direction have been achieved (s. 497A(6)). Compliance with directions is mandatory and any refusal to comply can be enforced by a mandatory order (s. 497A(7)). Where the direction gives power to the person specified or nominated by the Secretary of State in the direction, that person shall at all reasonable times have the right to enter the LEA's premises and its maintained schools and a right to inspect and take copies of any records or other documents kept by the LEA and any other documents containing information relating to the LEA which are relevant (s. 497B(2)). The specified or nominated person shall also be entitled at any reasonable time to have access to and inspect and check the operation of, any computer and any associated apparatus that is or has been in use in connection with the records or other documents in question. He may also require the person by whom or on whose behalf the computer is or has been so used or any person having charge of, or otherwise concerned with, the operation of the computer etc to afford him such assistance as he may reasonably require (including

**12.
ACCOUNTABILITY
& CHALLENGE**

the making of information available for inspection or copying in a legible form) (s. 497B(3)). The LEA shall also give the person all assistance in connection with the performance of the function or functions which it is able to give.

If a complaint is made to the Secretary of State under two or more of these sections, the Secretary of State is required to consider and respond to each section so raised (see *R v Secretary of State for Education and Employment ex p T* 7 July 2000, unreported, QBD).

2. Inspection of LEAs

Following, or perhaps more pertinently, preceding, the default power of the Secretary of State to deal with inadequate performance is the regime for the inspection of LEAs. See also chapter 5.A.7.

In summary, Her Majesty's Chief Inspector of Schools in England, or his equivalent in Wales, may arrange for any LEA to be inspected or shall arrange for such an inspection if requested to do so by the Secretary of State (s. 38(1) of the Education Act 1997).

An inspection carried out by the Chief Inspector will consist of a review of the way in which the LEA is performing any of its functions (of whatever nature) which relate to the provision of education, either for persons of compulsory school age (whether at school or otherwise) or for persons of any age above or below that age who are registered as pupils at schools maintained by the LEA or early-years education or adult education.

The LEA is required to provide the Chief Inspector with such information as may be prescribed and within such a period and in such a form as regulations may lay down (s. 38(6)).

Any inspector appointed to carry out an inspection of an LEA and any person assisting him shall have at all reasonable times a right of entry to the premises of the LEA, including, now, schools and premises used to provide education otherwise than at school and a right to inspect and take copies of any records kept by the LEA and any other documents containing information relating to the LEA which the inspector considers relevant to the exercise of his functions (s. 40(1)).

An LEA, governing body and staff employed at an 'inspected' school are required to give the inspector and any person assisting him all assistance in connection with the inspection which the body or individual is reasonably able to give (s. 40(2)).

When an inspection has been completed, the inspector is required to make a written report on the matters reviewed and to send copies to the LEA and the Secretary of State (s. 39(1)). Where an LEA receives a copy of a report, it is under an obligation to prepare a written statement of the action which it proposes to take in the light of the report and the period within which it proposes to take it (s. 39(2)). The LEA is also required to publish the report and its statement in response in accordance with the Education (Publication of Local Education Authority Inspection Reports) Regulations 1998 (SI 1998 No. 880). The Chief Inspector may also arrange for the report to be published in such manner as he considers appropriate (s. 39(4)).

When carrying out an inspection, the Chief Inspector may request the assistance of the Audit Commission and the report of the Inspector can be produced in conjunction with the Audit Commission (s. 41).

See also chapters 3.B.14 and 5.A.7.

3. Adjudicator

Although perhaps not strictly falling under accountability or challenge, the adjudicator does play a role in dealing with objections to certain decisions of LEAs (in Wales, there is no adjudicator; the role is performed by the NAW).

The Secretary of State is under an obligation to appoint such number of persons to act as adjudicators for the purposes of the 1998 Act as he considers appropriate (s. 25(1) of the 1998 Act).

Schedule 5 to the Act sets out the provisions concerning the appointment, tenure of office, remuneration of and staffing for adjudicators, together with certain rules regarding the procedure to be adopted by the adjudicator in determining matters referred to him (para 5). There is in fact a chief adjudicator, who leads a team of adjudicators, but the collective is normally referred to in the singular.

The adjudicator's role was widened by the 2002 Act so, as appropriate, the adjudicator has a role in the following areas of LEA responsibility.

1. If a school organisation committee (SOC) cannot unanimously agree either a school organisation plan (or subsequent revised plan) or any proposal for the establishment, alteration or discontinuance of a maintained school, the matter should be referred to the adjudicator.

2. The SOC can refer a matter to the adjudicator without deciding on the proposal (para 3(2) of sched 6 to the 1998 Act).

3. Promoters of new foundation or voluntary schools (who are not represented on the SOC, i.e. promoters other than Church of England or Roman Catholic promoters) may require the SOC to refer their proposals to the adjudicator if their proposal is turned down by the SOC (para 3(6A) of sched 6).

4. Where the governing body of a school of a prescribed description set out in regulations presents proposals for alteration which are rejected by the SOC, the governing body can require the SOC to refer the proposals to the adjudicator (paragraph 3(6C) of sched 6).

5. LEAs are required to establish admission forums as a vehicle for consultation and discussion of issues arising from proposed admission arrangements (s. 85A of the 1998 Act) as well as advising the LEA on prescribed matters (see reg 11 of the Education (Admission Forum) (England) Regulations 2002 (SI 2002 No. 2900)). Most disputes over admission arrangements will therefore be discussed by admission forums, but, where an admission authority objects to the admission arrangements determined by another admission authority and all attempts to resolve the matter locally between admission authorities or through the admissions forum have failed, the admission authority may refer the objection to an adjudicator (s. 89 of the 1998 Act). Parents may refer objections over existing partial selection in a similar fashion.

6. Under s. 89 of the 1998 Act, admission authorities are required to consult the governing bodies of community and voluntary controlled schools prior to determining admission arrangements (s. 89(2)). Objections to the arrangements that are subsequently determined can now be made by the governing body to the adjudicator (s. 90(1)(b)).

Adjudicators exercising their admissions functions are not able to consider objections about aspects of admission arrangements to which other statutory procedures apply. For example, the adjudicator is able to consider disputes about the admission arrangements for grammar schools, but not about the principle that a grammar school selects its pupils on the basis of high academic ability. The Secretary of State retains the power to consider and determine disputes on admission criteria relating to religious or denominational issues.

The adjudicator is, however, able to determine that an admission authority seeking to continue to make provision for partial selection should cease to do so even where that selection was introduced following the approval of statutory proposals under earlier legislation. The 1998 Act prevents new selection by ability being introduced (or selection by aptitude of more than 10 per cent of the intake) and allows objections, following petition, to be made to existing selective arrangements. The adjudicator can therefore, for example, make a determination on an objection by an admission authority that another admission authority is seeking to give priority to some pupils on the basis of aptitude.

In all cases, the procedure for referrals to adjudicators is set out in the Education (References to Adjudicator) Regulations 1999 (SI 1999 No. 702).

The adjudicators were initially involved in disputes concerning selective education (see *TES*, 30 July 1999; 6 August 1999; 10 September 1999; 5 November 1999; and 21 January 2000). A ruling of the adjudicator concerning selection in Wandsworth was overturned by the High Court (*R v Downes ex p Wandsworth LBC* [2000] ELR 425), though a challenge to another decision of an adjudicator by Wirral MBC was unsuccessful (*R v The Schools Adjudicator ex parte Wirral MBC* [2000] ELR 621). In the *Wandsworth* case, the adjudicator was held to have acted unlawfully in making a decision without having regard to the fact that the consequence of his decision could have been a significant change to the character of a school. Specific statutory procedures were in place to govern such a change and the adjudicator should not have sought to secure such a change by a back-door route. The adjudicator should also not simply rely on information provided by a school or LEA; he may be required to be more proactive in identifying and addressing particular issues (*R v John Clark ex parte JD, LC and CW* 27 March 2000, unreported, QBD). The adjudicator is also precluded from dealing with each and every aspect of admission arrangements when dealing with a specific objection (*R (Watford Grammar Schools) v Schools Adjudicator* [2004] 1 ELR 40).

See also chapter 7.A.2.

**12.
ACCOUNTABILITY
& CHALLENGE**

4. The Commissioner for Local Administration (otherwise known as the Ombudsman)

The Commissions for Local Administration were established by the Local Government Act 1974 and their powers extended by the Local Government and Housing Act 1989.

Their jurisdiction relates to complaints of injustice in consequence of maladministration in connection with action taken in the exercise of administrative functions by or on behalf of a local authority (s. 26(1) of the Local Government Act 1974).

Their jurisdiction is thus not restricted to educational powers and duties but extends across the broad range of local authority functions, albeit, as stated above, limited to those which are administrative in nature.

Although the definition of administrative functions may be pedantic, it is nonetheless important and it has been held that administrative functions include the decision-making function (see *R v Local Commission for Administration ex p Croydon* [1989] 1 All ER 1033) but not the decision itself. In effect, the jurisdiction is to examine the procedure rather than the merits of a decision and is to a certain extent akin to the High Court's supervisory functions in respect of judicial reviews. Although neither maladministration nor injustice is defined, a working definition of maladministration includes bias, neglect, inattention, delay, incompetence, ineptitude, adversity, turpitude, arbitrariness and so on as *per* Lord Denning in *R v Local Commissioner for Administration ex p Bradford MBC* [1979] 1QB 287. Thus maladministration is concerned with faulty administration or inefficient or improper management of affairs. If the ombudsman, having investigated, believes personally that the decision was wrongly taken, but is unable to point to any maladministration, he is prevented from questioning the decision (see *ex parte Bradford*).

Maladministration by itself will not do: the aggrieved complainant must also show that the maladministration has caused injustice. But because of the ombudsman's *raison d'être* – providing as informal and/or non-legalistic means of resolving complaints as possible – injustice has a wide meaning and may include a sense of outrage caused by unfair and incompetent administration even where no legal loss has occurred (see *R v Parliamentary Commissioner ex p Balchin* [1997] COD 146). Another hazard for the complainant is that the ombudsman may not investigate where a remedy is available at law, except in the limited circumstances to which reference is made later in this section.

As a result of the vagueness of the definitions, however, there is the opportunity for individual ombudsmen to take different interpretations of their function, which unfortunately can lead to some uncertainty. Areas where, for example, there is uncertainty as to what constitutes maladministration would include the failure to comply with a code of practice or where there has been a failure to honour an existing commitment. Failure to comply with the National Code of Local Government Conduct has previously been within the ombudsman's jurisdiction, (see, for example, *R v Local Commissioner for Administration in North and North East England ex parte Liverpool City Council* [1999] 3 All ER 85). Indeed, in such cases, the ombudsman could be required to name the person in breach (s. 30(3A) LGA 1974). This role has now been eclipsed, in legislation at least, by the creation of Standards Boards.

On the other hand, it does not necessarily follow that if a local authority acts unlawfully, it will be guilty of injustice in consequence of maladministration.

Examples of circumstances where the ombudsman has found maladministration in the education context are (some recent decisions can be found rehearsed in the *Digest of Cases 2001* and *2002/03*, see below):

- failure to keep parents informed during the course of the assessment of their child's special educational needs (see numerous complaints)

- failure to issue a statement of special educational need, which led to a child being denied appropriate education for a school year (Complaint No. 95/B/2431 against Dorset County Council)

- delay in dealing with a child's statement of special educational needs (see numerous complaints)

- failure to ensure speech therapy support was provided as specified in a statement (Complaint No. 95/A/2849 against Islington LBC)

- failure to establish an admissions limit which accurately reflected the capacity and resources of the school (Complaint No. 96/C/1237 against Bury MBC)

**12.
ACCOUNTABILITY
& CHALLENGE**

- failure to follow the *Code of Practice on Admission Appeals* (Complaint No. 96/C/1448 (and others) against Kingston upon Hull City Council in respect of the old Code of Practice)

- including disqualified persons on appeal panels, flaws in procedure and lack of training of members (Complaints Nos. 99/0228/A01/000 and 99/0288/A01/001 against the Appeal Committee of Corpus Christi Roman Catholic High School)

- failings in admission information, use of waiting lists and inconsistencies in measuring distances (Complaints Nos. 98/C/2464, 98/C/2770 and 98/C/2753 against Wirral Metropolitan Borough Council)

- failings in admission arrangements and their publication (see numerous complaints)

and two rare examples of complaints investigated by the ombudsman into non-school-related matters:

- insecure (i.e. leaky) handling of grant application by prominent member of the local community (Complaint No. 98/A/1835 against the London Borough of Tower Hamlets)

- failure to give timely advice (result of late information from the then DfEE) to a student on liability to pay tuition fees (Complaint No. 98/C/2809 against Birmingham City Council).

Other examples of findings in respect of education used, until late 2002, to be found in Butterworths' *Law of Education* bi-monthly Bulletin. Selective summaries of reports of the ombudsman appear regularly in *Education Law Journal* (Jordans). More recent examples can also be found on the ombudsman's website (www.lgo.org.uk/educ.htm).

The office of the CLA for England will also supply, on payment of an annual fee, hard copies of reports by category, e.g. 'all education'. The office of the CLA for Wales can arrange, for instance, for education reports to be sent as they are published to an individual subscriber, who pays for each one received.

The ombudsman's *Annual Report* and *Digest of Cases* also provide a useful insight into the work of the ombudsman and decisions made. The Digest for 2001 drew particular attention to the ombudsman's concern at the way school admissions and admission appeals are handled. The ombudsman recommended:

- clear, fair and objective criteria

- adherence to only those criteria that have been published

- avoidance of improper interviewing
- giving adequate reasons for refusal of places
- providing proper information to appellants
- ensuring training for clerks and panel members
- systematic and proper consideration of grounds of appeal.

Similar and other concerns are identified in the *Digest* for 2002/03 and the summary of cases at www.lgo.org.uk.

As will be seen, these concerns are also reflected in the Council on Tribunals' recent report *School Admissions and Exclusion Appeal Panels.*

The ombudsman's annual reports also provide a number of education case studies. These have included the following investigation reports.

- Admissions:
  - inadequate consideration of prejudice test, lack of training, insufficient role for clerk, rushed timetable (01/C/3800 and others)
  - procedural faults in decision and appeal (00/B/3812)
  - Anglican school used more stringent faith criterion than that published, clerk to governing body had private discussion with appeals panel (local settlement)
  - unlawful operation of catchment area 'guarantee' (00/B/4686 and others)
  - Roman Catholic school's unclear and unfair application of criteria, interviews assessing more than the published faith criteria (local settlement)
  - Roman Catholic school failed to follow published arrangements and criteria, interviews held outwith the published arrangements (local settlement)
  - family re-housed in council's area, but no liaison between housing and education services, or, within education, between welfare and admissions (local settlement).

- School reorganisation:
  - inadequate consultation on revised proposal (local settlement)

- SEN:
  - two-year delay in providing speech and language therapy specified in statement (00/A/9964)

  - LEA's failure to act promptly over securing suitable placement for child with Asperger's syndrome (00/A/11940)
  - family moved from one LEA's area to another, but new LEA failed to maintain or amend SEN statement naming the residential school attended (local settlement)
  - statemented child changed secondary school but LEA failed to continue provision of speech and language therapy (99/C/4727).

- Transport:
  - LEA found that it had allowed free school transport in error for two years, but then withdrew it without considering circumstances of the case (local settlement)
  - unreasonable and unfair application of policy on free transport in relation to parental preference (00/C/12531).

The jurisdiction of the ombudsman extends to any member or officer of the local authority or anyone to whom the authority has delegated its functions. It is perhaps a moot point whether any person carrying out the functions of the LEA, in response to a determination by the Secretary of State or NAW that a function is being inadequately performed (s. 497A of the 1996 Act), falls within the jurisdiction of the ombudsman as it is not clear that in this case the authority has delegated its functions to that individual. Similarly, it would appear that the jurisdiction does not extend to Education Action Zones and Education Action Forums, but it does include school organisation committees (para 4 of sched 30 to the 1988 Act). Adjudicators are not subject to the jurisdiction of the local government ombudsman but are subject to the central-Government equivalent, the Parliamentary Commissioner (para 9 of sched 5 to the 1998 Act).

Paragraph 4 of sched 30 to the 1998 Act amended the Local Government Act 1974 so that the ombudsman's jurisdiction extends to admission appeals panels set up by the governing bodies of foundation or voluntary schools as well as admission and exclusion appeal panels established by LEAs.

**12.
ACCOUNTABILITY
& CHALLENGE**

The ombudsman cannot investigate a matter in respect of which the complainant has, or had, a right of appeal or review to a tribunal, a Minister or a remedy by way of proceedings in court unless the ombudsman is satisfied that in the particular circumstances of a case it is not reasonable to expect the person aggrieved to resort, or have resorted, to those procedures.

In *R v Commissioner for Local Administration ex parte H* [1999] ELR 314, parents complained to the ombudsman in an attempt to obtain compensation. The parents had previously issued judicial review proceedings against their LEA, but those proceedings had been compromised by an agreed settlement. The consent order reflecting this settlement, because it was in judicial review proceedings, apparently could not order compensation for past loss and therefore the parents had attempted to recover this compensation through the ombudsman procedure. The ombudsman declined to investigate the complaint and the court upheld this decision on the basis that the parents had already obtained a remedy by way of proceedings in a court of law and Parliament clearly intended that the ombudsman should investigate only where such a route was not open.

In contrast, in *R v Local Commissioner for Local Government for North and North East England ex parte Liverpool City Council* [2000] LGR 571, [2002] 1 All ER 462, the Court of Appeal declined to overturn a report of the ombudsman on the basis that the complainants had alternative remedies available to them, in particular through judicial review. The ombudsman had decided that it would be very difficult, if not impossible, for the complainants to obtain the necessary evidence in judicial review proceedings, whereas her powers allowed her to compel the disclosure of documents, interview staff and conduct a fact-finding investigation. She had also taken the view that the complainants were a group in modest housing, unlikely to have the means to pursue the remedy. The Court of Appeal saw nothing wrong in this approach and felt that the ombudsman had correctly exercised her discretion in concluding that it would have been unreasonable for the persons aggrieved to have had to resort to judicial review.

Certain items are specifically excluded from the ombudsman's jurisdiction and those relevant to education include:

a) the commencement or conduct of civil or criminal proceedings before a court of law;

b) action taken in relation to contractual or commercial transactions and any other transactions in the discharge of functions under a Public General Act other than those required for the procurement of goods and services;

c) the appointment, removal, pay, discipline, superannuation of staff and any other personnel matters;

**12.
ACCOUNTABILITY
& CHALLENGE**

d)   secular instruction in maintained schools, teaching and conduct of the curriculum, internal organisation and management or discipline in such schools.

Complaints must be in writing identifying the action alleged to constitute maladministration and must be made by or on behalf of a member of the public who claims to have sustained injustice in consequence of maladministration. The complaint may be made by an individual or a body corporate or non-corporate, but not by a local authority or any other public authority or body, which includes the governing body of a maintained school. The complaint must normally be made within 12 months of the time when the person aggrieved first had notice of the matters he believes constituted maladministration, although the ombudsman may dispense with this time limit if it is reasonable to do so.

Before investigating, however, the ombudsman must be satisfied that the complaint has been brought to the notice of the local authority and that the local authority has been afforded a reasonable opportunity to investigate and reply to a complaint itself (s. 26(5) of the Local Government Act 1974).

Currently, investigations are conducted in private, although there were suggestions that, with the introduction of the Human Rights Act 1998, there would be a need for the ombudsman to conduct public hearings. This is probably unlikely to be required, given the trend of litigation since the Human Rights Act was introduced, but, nonetheless, the ombudsman must provide an opportunity both to the authority and to the individual to comment on any allegation contained in the complaint and the authority's response. If the ombudsman makes notes of interviews with authority officers and members, it would appear that the ombudsman cannot refuse to disclose those notes to the complainant (*R (Turpin) v Commissioner for Local Administration* [2003] LGR 133).

The ombudsman has all the powers of the court in relation to the attendance and examination of witnesses and the production of documents (for example, to issue a witness summons or subpoena); he may require members and officers of the authority and anyone else whom he considers is able to furnish information or produce documents relevant to his investigation, to produce such information and documents. The ombudsman cannot, however, be given information or documents which are legally privileged or protected by the privilege against self-incrimination (s. 29 (7) of the 1974 Act).

If the ombudsman decides not to conduct an investigation, he must give a statement of his reasons for not doing so to the complainant. Where, for example, an ombudsman discontinues an investigation because the authority has adequately compensated the complainant, he is not obliged to produce a report (*R (ota Maxhuni) v Commissioner for Local Administration* [2003] LGR 113). If, however, he decides to issue a report, the report will not normally identify any individual. Within two weeks of receipt of the report, the authority must give public notice by way of newspaper advertisement or otherwise that the report is to be made available to the public for inspection without charge for a period of three weeks starting no later than one week after first notification. Anyone can take copies or extracts from the report during this period and the authority is obliged to provide copies on payment of the authority's reasonable charge. Obstruction of the right to inspect or copy the report is a criminal offence (s. 30(6)).

The authority must consider any report that concludes that injustice had been caused by maladministration (s. 31(1)), although the duty at this stage may be delegated, within three months of receipt of the report, or such longer period as the ombudsman allows. The authority must notify the ombudsman what action it has taken or proposes to take (s. 31(2)). It is implicit that the authority is not bound to accept the ombudsman's conclusions and could consider other reports, for example, from an officer.

If, however, the ombudsman does not receive the necessary notification or if he is not satisfied with the authority's actual or proposed course of action, or if within a further three months, he does not receive confirmation that the authority has taken action which satisfies him, he must make a further report setting out these facts and making his recommendations. The recommendations are within the discretion of the ombudsman and should relate to the action that the authority should take both to remedy the injustice caused to the individual complainant and to prevent similar injustice in the future (s. 31(2B)). In addition, the ombudsman may also require the authority by notice to arrange for publication of a statement, to be agreed between himself and the authority, containing details of any recommendations he has made in the further report which the authority has not taken, together with supporting material as to his reasons and any statement from the authority as to why it proposes to take no action or other action to that recommended. Publication will be in two editions of a newspaper circulating in the authority's area and, if the authority does not arrange publication, the ombudsman can step in and do so

**12.
ACCOUNTABILITY
& CHALLENGE**

himself. If such a further report is issued, it must be considered by the full authority and cannot be delegated as can the first report.

As far as the actual recommendations are concerned, the ombudsman has considerable freedom. This should clearly provide an adequate remedy for any injustice found and can include financial compensation. Often an award is made for time, distress and inconvenience caused to the complainant and for expenses properly incurred. Section 1(3) makes it clear that the authority does have the power, whether or not recommended to do so, i.e. in an attempt to resolve the complaint amicably, to incur expenditure in making payments to a person who has suffered injustice in consequence of the maladministration.

5. Monitoring officer

A general power or means of challenging unlawful decisions, the monitoring officer is a statutory appointment that must be made by each local authority (s. 5 of the Local Government and Housing Act 1989).

The monitoring officer is under a duty to prepare a report to the authority in respect of:

- any proposal, decision or omission of the authority or committee, sub-committee, or officer, or employee of the authority which appears to the monitoring officer to have given rise to, or be likely to, or would give rise to contravention by the authority or any committee or sub-committee of the authority, or by any person holding any office of employment under the authority, of any enactment or rule of law or of any code of practice made or approved by or under any enactment; or

- any injustice in consequence of maladministration in connection with administrative functions.

Thus, if it came to the attention of the monitoring officer that the LEA, whether through its members or officers, were proposing to act in any of the above ways, he should prepare a report to the authority.

6. Scrutiny and standards

The Local Government Act 2000 made substantial changes to the way a local authority could take decisions, with much decision-making being taken under executive arrangements, usually by an executive portfolio holder or an executive committee or cabinet (see part II of the 2000 Act). A number of options are available, but whatever is adopted, the 2000 Act provides that an authority's executive arrangements should include the appointment of one or more overview and scrutiny committees (s. 21 of the 2000 Act – although different names have been adopted by different authorities). Apparently in an attempt to replicate the function of Parliamentary select committees in a local authority context, these committees have power to review or scrutinise decisions taken by the executive of the authority and other decisions taken by those who have responsibility for functions which are not the responsibility of the executive. They can also make reports and recommendations about these decisions. Political balance should be maintained and members of these committees can require that matters of concern be included on an agenda and be considered by the committee. These committees can require executive officers and members to attend to answer questions and may invite others to do so (s. 21(13) of the 2000 Act).

These committees, where they operate effectively, should provide a check and balance to executive decision-making and provide an additional and new means of holding to account the leadership and management of local authorities. They will, of course, apply to decisions and functions relating to education as they will to all other functions of the local authority (and also provide for scrutiny of National Health Service bodies in an authority's area. See ss. 7–10 of the Health and Social Care Act 2001 which may be an important role if LEA functions transfer into primary care, or care trusts).

A particular problem for LEAs, under the new constitutional arrangements for local authorities, was what to do with parent-governor and church representatives who had previously been guaranteed places on the authority's education committee. The new executive arrangements under part 2 of the 2000 Act preclude their involvement in decision-making, so, instead, their role is confined to sitting on the authority's overview and scrutiny committee(s). Hence, in the case of parent-governor representatives, each overview and scrutiny committee or sub-committee dealing with education functions must include between two and five parent governor representatives (reg 3 of the Parent Governor Representatives (England) Regulations 2001 (SI 2000 No. 478)). In the Isles of Scilly and the City of London, those authorities' education committees must continue to include such representatives. The LEA remains responsible for arranging the elections of these representatives (regs 4–7 of the Parent Governor Representatives (England) Regulations 2001 (SI 2000 No. 478)). In

**12.
ACCOUNTABILITY
& CHALLENGE**

the case of diocesan and other church representatives, the Secretary of State made a direction under s. 499 of the Education Act 1996, accompanied by guidance (*Church Representatives on Local Authority Committees Dealing with Education* DfEE Circular 19/99) which sets out the expectation that diocesan representatives would also sit on the relevant overview and scrutiny committee (para 13). These representatives are able to vote on any decisions which relate to schools maintained by the local authority and pupils who attend schools maintained by the local authority, or who are educated by the local authority in some other way, as well as on matters which affect how funds, already earmarked for education, are spent (paras 15 and 16).

To meet concerns about the standards and conduct of councillors, the Local Government Act 2000 also introduced new measures to strengthen standards of conduct and to provide for penalties to be imposed against offending councillors. Before the 2002 Act, councillors were supposed to abide by the *National Code of Local Government Conduct*, but compliance with the code, apart from occasional interventions by the ombudsman, was a matter for councils themselves. The 2000 Act therefore imposed certain duties on authorities to comply with a model code of conduct and establish standards committees. Although of general application, these duties and procedures will obviously affect members of LEAs.

Under the 2000 Act, the Secretary of State (or NAW) is empowered (s. 49 of the Local Government Act 2000) to specify principles that are to govern the conduct of members in relevant authorities (including councils which are LEAs) in England and police authorities in Wales. In Wales, responsibility for all authorities, other than police authorities, rests with the NAW. The principles apply to both elected members and co-opted members. The latter include persons who are not members of an authority but who are members of any committee or sub-committee of the authority, joint committees or joint sub-committees and are entitled to vote on any question which falls to be decided at a meeting of that committee or sub-committee (s. 49(7) of the Act).

The Secretary of State and NAW are also able to issue model codes setting out the conduct expected of members and co-opted members (s. 50). Once the Secretary of State (or NAW) has issued a model code, each authority has six months in which to pass a resolution of the full council adopting it (s. 51). If the model is subsequently revised, this duty applies to such subsequent versions too. Each authority's code must adopt any mandatory provisions in the model code, may include specified optional provisions and may also include any other provisions which are consistent with the model code. The current code, in England, was issued under the Local Authorities (Model Code of Conduct) (England) Order 2001 (SI 2001 No. 3575) and, in Wales, the Conduct of Members (Model Code of Conduct) (Wales) Order 2001 (SI 2001 No. 2289 (W.177)).

Every member and co-opted member must, within two months from the date the Code of Conduct is adopted, give the authority a written undertaking that in performing his functions he will observe it. If that undertaking is not given within two months, that person ceases to be a member or co-opted member at that point (s. 52(1)).

In tandem with the obligations placed on individual members, the 2000 Act also set up standards committees as the main means of securing high standards amongst those members. Consequently, each authority must establish a standards committee, comprising at least three members, of whom at least two must be members of the authority and at least one must not be (s. 53). The standards committees may not include the elected mayor or executive leader. Further provisions relating to the composition and proceedings of standards committees are contained in the Relevant Authorities (Standards Committees) Regulations 2001 (SI 2001 No. 2812) and in the Relevant Authorities (Standards Committees) (Dispensations) Regulations 2002 (SI 2002 No. 339).

The functions of standards committees are:

a) promoting and maintaining high standards of conduct by the members and co-opted members of the authority, and

b) assisting members and co-opted members of the authority to observe the authority's code of conduct (s. 54(1) of the 2000 Act).

In addition, the committees must advise their authority on the adoption or revision of a code of conduct, monitor the operation of the authority's code of conduct and advise, train or arrange to train members and co-opted members of the authority on matters relating to the authority's code of conduct (s. 54(2)). The committee may also exercise such other functions as the authority considers appropriate (s. 54(3)).

The standards committee also plays a role in imposing sanctions on members found guilty of disciplinary offences, although the primary role in investigating breaches lies with the Standards Board for

**12.
ACCOUNTABILITY
& CHALLENGE**

England (or, in Wales, the Commission for Local Administration). The Standards Board is a corporate body established under s. 57 of the 2000 Act. Its functions include: appointing ethical standards officers; issuing guidance on matters relating to the conduct of members and co-opted members and the qualifications or experience monitoring officers should possess; and investigating allegations or complaints that a current or former member or co-opted member has failed, or may have failed, to comply with the authority's code of conduct (s. 58(1)). The Board will receive complaints and, if it considers that an investigation is required, it will be referred to one of the ethical standards officers (ESOs) to investigate and report as appropriate (s. 58(2)). If matters come to his attention as a result of carrying out an investigation, the ESO may also investigate other members or co-opted members (s. 58(3)).

The ESO has fairly wide powers to obtain information etc and conduct the investigation (ss. 60–62). He must, however, provide the person he is investigating with the opportunity to comment on the allegation and no person can be compelled to give any evidence or produce any document which he could not be compelled to produce as a result of civil proceedings in the High Court (s. 62(7)). An investigation does not, however, preclude the authority from taking action in respect of the matter under investigation (s. 61(4)).

The purpose of the ESO's investigation (s. 59(4)) is to determine whether:

a) there is evidence of any failure to comply with the code of conduct of the relevant authority concerned;

b) action needs to be taken in respect of the matters which are the subject of the investigation;

c) the matters which are the subject of the investigation should be referred to the monitoring officer of the relevant authority concerned; or

d) the matters which are the subject of the investigation should be referred to the President of the Adjudication Panel for England for adjudication by a tribunal falling within section 76(1).

If the ESO reaches a decision that c) or d) above is appropriate, the ESO must produce a report, which should be sent to the authority's monitoring officer. An ESO may produce an interim report where he considers it necessary in the public interest (s. 65(1)). This might arise where there is a concern that an individual might repeat their actions or if the matter were particularly serious.

Interim and final reports of the ESO in which the ESO recommends that the matters should be referred to the Adjudication Panel are considered by interim case tribunals and case tribunals set up under and by the Adjudication Panel. The Adjudication Panel is an independent tribunal consisting of a President, Deputy President and members appointed by the Lord Chancellor (or the Secretary of State for Constitutional Affairs), with the consent of the Secretary of State, or the NAW (ss. 75 and 76). An interim case tribunal must decide either that the individual referred to in the report should not be suspended or partially suspended from being a member or that he should be suspended or partially suspended for a period of up to six months or the remainder of his term of office, whichever is the shorter (s. 78(1)). A notice of the decision must be sent to the authority's standards committee, with a copy to the monitoring officer and the individual. The authority must comply with the order of suspension.

A case tribunal considers the final report of the ESO and any representations etc from the individual concerned. If it finds there has been no breach of the code, it must notify the standards committee. If it finds misconduct has occurred, it must decide whether the nature of the failure is such that the person should be:

a) suspended or partially suspended for a period of up to one year or the remainder of their term of office, whichever is the shorter; or

b) disqualified for up to five years from being or becoming a member or co-opted member of that or any relevant authority (s. 79(4)).

The decision is notified to the standards committee. The authority must comply with the suspension. In the case of disqualification, this takes effect once the standards committee is notified and a copy of the decision must also be sent to the Standards Board.

7.   Audit

The audit of local authority accounts is another general mechanism to provide a check on financial expenditure by local authorities and (for the purposes of this book) LEAs in particular.

There are two types of audit: internal audit and, perhaps more importantly in terms of most challenge, external audit.

7.1 Internal audit

The chief finance officer of every local authority must maintain an adequate and effective internal audit (reg 5 of the Accounts and Audit Regulations 1996 (SI 1996 No. 590)).

In order to carry out the audit, the chief finance officer (or his/her authorised representative) has a right of access at all times to any documents he requires relating to the accounts of the authority and has a power to require from any officer or member such information and explanation as he thinks necessary.

Guidance on the performance of internal audit is found in the Auditing Practices Board's *Guidance for Internal Auditors* and CIPFA's *Application of the APB's Guideline Guidance for Internal Auditors in Local Government*. The latter document defines internal audit as an independent appraisal function established by the management of an organisation for the review of the internal control system as a service to the organisation. It objectively examines, evaluates and reports on the adequacy of internal control as a contribution to the proper economic, efficient and effective use of resources.

With a few exceptions, the internal audit function is performed by an authority's own internal audit department, although a number of authorities have voluntarily contracted out the activity. Usually the department is located within the finance department, which ensures it does fall within the chief finance officer's responsibilities.

In addition to the general objectives, internal audit also specifically addresses value for money and the prevention and detection of fraud.

7.2 External audit

In the context of this work, the most important audit function with respect to LEA functions is the role of the external auditor.

The accounts of all local authorities must be externally audited (see the Audit Commission Act 1998) and the role of the external auditor forms one of the oldest means of accountability. Although the principal work of external auditors does relate to the annual accounts, their role continues throughout the financial year.

The external auditor is appointed by the Audit Commission and may be an officer of the Commission (known as the District Auditor) or an individual or firm of individuals such as an accountancy firm.

The duties of the auditor, set out in s. 5 of the Audit Commission Act 1998, require the auditor to satisfy himself that:

- the accounts prepared by the local authority have been prepared in accordance with the appropriate Regulations and comply with other statutory provisions;

- proper practices have been observed in the compilation of the accounts; and

- the local authority has made proper arrangements for securing economy, efficiency and effectiveness in the use of its resources and has published such information in relation to this as is required by the Audit Commission Act 1998.

In carrying out his task, the auditor must comply with the current *Code of Audit Practice* and must also follow the relevant auditing standards published by the Auditing Practice Board. In the course of the audit, the auditor is required to consider whether, in the public interest, he should make a report on any matter coming to his notice in order that it may be considered by the local authority or brought to the attention of the public. If such a matter does come to his attention, he must consider whether to report immediately or at the conclusion of the audit.

To enable the audit to be carried out, the auditor has a right of access at all reasonable times to any documents of the authority which appear to him to be necessary for the purposes of the audit and is empowered to require any necessary information and explanation from the person holding or who is accountable for the document. Where necessary, he may require a person to appear before him to provide the information or explanation or to produce the document (s. 6 of the 1998 Act). Non-compliance with a request from the auditor can be a criminal offence (s. 6(6)).

**12.
ACCOUNTABILITY
& CHALLENGE**

In addition to the audit of the accounts for a financial year, if a local government elector so applies or if the auditor produces a public interest report, the Audit Commission may direct that an extraordinary audit be held (s. 25(1)) and, in addition, the Secretary of State may also direct the Commission to direct that an extraordinary audit be held if it appears to him to be desirable to do so in the public interest (s. 25(2)).

Where the auditor makes a public interest report, it must be sent to the local authority concerned and, once received, must be considered by the authority. Similarly, any document short of a report, such as a management letter which contains recommendations, must also be considered. Consideration must occur within four months of receipt of the report, or such other time as the auditor allows, but at a meeting the authority must decide whether the report requires any action or whether the recommendation is to be accepted and what, if any, action is to be taken in response. This duty may not be delegated.

If an immediate public interest report is received, the authority must publicise the fact in at least one local newspaper identifying the subject matter of the report and state that the public may inspect the report and take copies. All members of the authority must also be supplied with copies.

At each audit, any person interested (which includes anyone with a financial interest in the accounts (see *Marginson v Tildsley* (1903) 67 JP 226)) may inspect the accounts to be audited and all books, deeds, contracts, bills, vouchers and receipts relating to them and make copies.

Where requested, the auditor must give a local government elector or his representative an opportunity to question him about the accounts, provided that no questions can be asked about personal information relating to staff.

Any local government elector may object to the accounts on two grounds (s. 16 of the 1998 Act), that:

- the matter is one on which the auditor could take action under either s. 17 or s. 18 of the 1998 Act; or

- it is any other matter in respect of which the auditor could make a public interest report.

Section 17 provides the auditor with power to apply to the court for a declaration if he believes that an item of account is contrary to law. Section 18 allows the auditor to take action if he believes that any person has failed to bring into account a sum which should have been brought into account (which failure has not been sanctioned by the Secretary of State), or that a loss has been incurred or deficiency caused by the wilful misconduct of any person.

If the auditor refuses to apply to the court for a declaration, the objector may within six weeks of the notification of the decision require the auditor to state in writing his reasons for that decision. The objector may also appeal against the decision to the court and on appeal the court has the same power as on an auditor's application.

If the auditor does not certify that a sum or amount is due, the objector may require the auditor to state his reasons in writing and again may also appeal to the court against the decision (ss. 17 and 18 of the 1998 Act).

Following the Westminster City Council case (*Porter v Magill* (1997) 96 LGR 157, QBD, [1999] LGR 375, Court of Appeal, and [2001] UKHL 67, House of Lords), the role of the auditor in recent years in local government has taken on a significantly increased profile. Not only have auditors been querying items found in annual accounts, but they have also been giving views on the legality or otherwise of action taken or proposed to be taken by local authorities.

In many cases, that quasi-advisory role is helpful to authorities, but on occasion it has led to disputes, particularly where legal advice differs and it is therefore important to understand what powers the auditor does have in respect of unlawful items of account and/or failure to account and wilful misconduct.

7.2.1 Unlawful items of account

Under s. 17 of the 1998 Act, where it appears to the auditor carrying out an audit that an item of account is contrary to law and the item is not sanctioned by the Secretary of State, the auditor may apply to the court for a declaration that the item is contrary to law (s. 17(1)).

'Contrary to law', although having been considered in a number of cases, has not been clearly defined. It must include items of expenditure which are *ultra vires* the authority (see, for example, *North Tyneside MBC v Allsop* (1992) 90 LGR 462) and may also include items relating to the exercise of a discretionary power which is contrary to the principles of administrative law. In other words, the auditor could consider an item of account to be contrary to law if:

a) the authority had taken into account matters which it ought not to have taken into account, or

b) it had refused or neglected to take into account matters which it ought to take into account, or

12.
ACCOUNTABILITY
& CHALLENGE

c) it had come to a conclusion so unreasonable that no reasonable authority could ever have come to it (*Giddens v Harlow District Auditor* (1972) 70 LGR 485).

Examples of items contrary to law include a decision to pay local authority employees a higher minimum wage than was otherwise prevalent in the area (*Roberts v Hopwood* [1925] AC 578) or a decision to pay a landlord of a requisitioned property a higher amount than might otherwise have been necessary (*Taylor v Munrow* [1960] 1 All ER 455).

If a local authority charges an item of expenditure to the wrong account, then that too may be contrary to law.

If the auditor does believe that an item is contrary to law, he can apply to the court and the court may make the declaration sought or refuse to do so. Previously, if it made the declaration, the court could also order that any person responsible for incurring or authorising the expenditure should repay it in whole or part. If the unlawful expenditure exceeded £2,000 and the person responsible was a member of the local authority, the court could also order him to be disqualified from being a member for a specified period. Given the controversy over the *Westminster* case and general concern at the sums involved and potential penalties that could therefore be imposed on members and officers, the Local Government Act 2000 amended these provisions. Consequently, if a court makes a declaration that an item is contrary to law, the court can now order only that the accounts should be rectified (s. 17(2)(c)). It cannot order a person to repay it or be disqualified. Instead, action against the individual concerned will be taken within the new standards framework (see section 6 above).

In addition, the auditor has power to apply for judicial review of any decision of a public body he is appointed to audit which it is reasonable to believe would have an effect on the accounts of the body (s. 24).

7.2.2 Best Value

As indicated above, the role of the auditor is changing from one of enforcer to one of adviser. This has been increased by the removal of the powers of the auditor to surcharge officers. The trend was made even more evident by the Local Government Act 1999 and the introduction of Best Value inspections. Under Best Value, local authorities are obliged to secure continuous improvement in the way their functions are exercised having regard to a combination of economy, efficiency and effectiveness. Performance indicators are produced by the appropriate Secretary of State (currently housed within the Office of the Deputy Prime Minister) based upon recommendations made by the Audit Commission (see chapter 7.C.4).

Where local authorities are required to produce Best Value plans, these plans will have to be audited by the authority's external auditor. In addition, the Audit Commission may carry out an inspection of an authority's compliance with the requirements of the Best Value regulations at its own discretion, but may also do so if prompted by an external auditor's recommendation or if the Secretary of State so requires.

Inspections for all completed best value reviews (BVR) began to be introduced as the first cycle of Ofsted LEA inspections was drawing to a close and a new framework was being considered. It was deemed appropriate that each full inspection by Ofsted should also report on any education-related BVR completed in the previous twelve months. In practice this proved difficult to operate, partly because the prevalence of cross-cutting reviews led to doubt as to what was covered, but also because inspection teams, already burdened with a tight work schedule, were understandably reluctant to go out of their way to add to it.

As Government wrestled with the implications of overlapping inspection regimes promoted by different departments of state, it looked as if LEAs might have to suffer at least one of three different types of inspection every year. Fortunately the costs of inspection overload were recognised and proposals were pruned. Best Value is now integrated within the *Framework for the Inspection of LEAs*. In the 2004 version of the *Inspection Framework*, the fifth question to be answered in an organisational inspection is 'Does the LEA manage its functions in such a way as to secure continuous improvement and best value?' Completed BVRs are identified as part of the evidence base for inspection but they no longer need to be addressed in isolation.

12.
ACCOUNTABILITY
& CHALLENGE

8. Public Service Agreements and Comprehensive Performance Assessments

For completeness, we include a note on public service agreements (PSAs) and comprehensive performance assessments (CPAs): these play an important role in securing and monitoring improvement within local authorities and they include key education targets. Meeting those targets may provide LEAs with greater freedoms and rewards; failure to do so will be a further factor in holding the authority to account.

Local PSAs set out a local authority's commitment to deliver specific improvements in key target areas and the Government's commitment across a number of departments, including the DfES, to provide certain rewards, usually in terms of flexibilities or grants if they do so. The White Paper *Strong Leadership – Quality Public Services* (December 2001) proposed that each authority should adopt one target from each of the Prime Minister's public service delivery priorities and authorities choose an additional two targets from the national PSA for local government. PSAs are, however, non-statutory, a factor that may have led to difficulties within government in providing the relaxations or flexibilities promised. For more information on PSAs, see Clark (2003).

CPAs are a key element of the Government's performance framework for local government. They are supposed to support improvement planning in local authorities and lead to co-ordinated and proportionate audit and inspection followed by increased freedoms and flexibilities for local government. The Audit Commission has the task of forming judgments on the performance and corporate capacity of every local authority. Again, this is non-statutory but for some observers the process of assessment and the publication of results can have a far greater impact on a local authority than many of the statutory checks and balances.

C. Statutory Appeals

1. Introduction

To deal with a wide range of disputes, Parliament has created a number of statutory administrative tribunals with the intention of keeping disputes out of the courts and providing an alternative mechanism for seeking resolution.

A number of these may impact generally upon the responsibilities of the LEA, such as the Lands Tribunal or the Social Security Tribunal, but in this work we propose to deal only with the three categories of tribunal which tend to have the most direct impact on the functions of LEAs.

The first, the Employment Tribunal, is obviously of wider application, dealing with the whole range of employment issues, but the other two, the Special Educational Needs and Disability Tribunal and two kinds of independent appeal panels, are specifically created under the education legislation to deal with educational disputes.

2.   Employment Tribunal

The employment tribunals, formerly known as industrial tribunals, operate under the Employment Rights (Dispute Resolution) Act 1998 and in accordance with the Employment Tribunals (Constitution and Rules of Procedure) Regulations 2001 (SI 2001 No. 1171), as amended. The President of the employment tribunals has overall responsibility for their organisation, but a number of regional chairmen, appointed by the Lord Chancellor, have a responsibility for the administration of justice by the tribunals within specified areas. The general administration of the employment tribunals is carried out by the Employment Tribunal Service, an executive agency set up by the Department of Trade and Industry.

The membership of each individual employment tribunal normally comprises a legally qualified chairman and a representative from each side of industry: all three are selected from separate panels.

The jurisdiction of employment tribunals is derived from a significant amount of legislation, although they are normally seen as dealing primarily with complaints of unfair dismissal (under the Employment Rights Act 1996), unlawful discrimination on the grounds of sex or marital status (Sex Discrimination Act 1975), unlawful discrimination on the ground of race (Race Relations Act 1976) or unlawful discrimination on the ground of disability (Disability Discrimination Act 1995). There are other claims which can be brought, such as complaints regarding equal pay under the Equal Pay Act 1970 and a whole raft of less common types of application, such as complaints relating to payment of unpaid contributions to occupational pension schemes (Pension Schemes Act 1993). There are also a number of claims which have the potential to develop and increase, such as complaints by employees relating to time off for dependants, complaints by workers relating to detriment in working time and complaints relating to time off for young persons for study or training, all under the Employment Rights Act 1996, which implemented European Community law.

In addition, since 1994 the employment tribunals have jurisdiction to hear and determine certain claims for damages for breach of contract of employment (see the Employment Tribunals

**12.
ACCOUNTABILITY
& CHALLENGE**

Extension of Jurisdiction (England and Wales) Order 1994 (SI 1994 No. 1623)).

3.   Special Educational Needs and Disability Tribunal

The Special Educational Needs Tribunal as it was known between 1994 and 2002 was set up under the Education Act 1993 and started work on 1 September 1994. (In Wales, however, the tribunal is known as the Special Educational Needs Tribunal for Wales – s. 336ZA of the Education Act 1996. This tribunal secured full 'independence' from the English tribunal in September 2003. The functions of the two tribunals are broadly the same. Reference in this section is therefore to both the English and Welsh Tribunals.)

The constitution and principal rules for the operation of the tribunal, together with details of the rights of appeal which it can consider, are now set out in the Education Act 1996, as amended by the Special Educational Needs and Disability Act 2001 and the Special Educational Needs Tribunal Regulations 2001 (SI 2001 No. 600), as amended by the Special Educational Needs Tribunal (Amendment) Regulations 2002 (SI 2002 No. 2787) and the Special Educational Needs and Disability Tribunal (General Provisions and Disability Claims Procedure) Regulations 2002 (SI 2002 No. 1985), hence the new acronym SENDIST in England.

Prior to the 1993 Act, parents of children with special educational needs had limited rights of appeal against decisions taken in respect of their children to local appeal panels and there was concern that the powers of the panels did not always provide a suitable remedy for dissatisfied parents.

Consequently, the 1993 Act created a new national independent tribunal with power to consider a wide range of appeals, wholly independent of LEAs and with the power to order LEAs to take certain action. The intention of creating an informal tribunal whose decisions would be accepted by all parties has, unfortunately, not been realised. Steps were therefore taken by the Special Educational Needs and Disability Act 2001 to improve the operation of the tribunal. At the same time it was given the jurisdiction to deal with most school-based claims for disability discrimination.

As a result, requirements were imposed on LEAs to establish independent conciliation arrangements for resolving disputes with parents (s. 332B of the Education Act 1996). Express duties are now imposed on LEAs to comply with tribunal orders (s. 336A) and the views of the child have much greater prominence (see, for example, reg 13(2)(e) of the Special Educational Needs Tribunal Regulations 2001).

The SENDIST comprises a President, a chairmen's panel appointed by the Lord Chancellor and a lay panel appointed by the Secretary of State for Education and Skills (s. 333 of the 1996 Act). Members of the chairmen's panel must be legally qualified for at least seven years and no person may be appointed to the lay panel unless they have knowledge and experience in respect of children with special educational needs (regs 3–5 of the Special Educational Needs and Disability Tribunal (General Provisions and Disability Claims Procedure) Regulations 2002).

Each individual tribunal will consist of a member from the chairmen's panel who will chair the tribunal, together with two members of the lay panel. The President may sit as chairman and may also make decisions in respect of applications made during the course of the tribunal proceedings.

The tribunal has jurisdiction to consider appeals against the following decisions:

- a refusal to comply with a parental or school's request for an assessment of the child's education needs (s. 329(2) and s. 329A(8) of the 1996 Act)

- a decision, the LEA having made an assessment, not to make a statement of special educational needs (s. 325(2))

- the description in an SEN statement made by an LEA of the child's special educational needs, the special educational provision specified in the statement or, if no school is named in the statement, that fact (s. 326(1))

- a refusal to carry out another assessment of a child for whom the LEA maintains a statement of special educational needs (s. 328(2) and s. 329A(8))

- a refusal to comply with a parental request for the school named in a statement of special educational needs to be substituted with the name of a maintained school specified by the parent (sched 27, para 8)

- the description of the LEA's assessment of a child's special educational needs, the special educational provision or, if no school is named, that fact in an amended statement of special educational need made by the LEA (sched 27, para 10)

**12.
ACCOUNTABILITY
& CHALLENGE**

439

- a decision to cease to maintain a statement of special educational needs (sched 27, para 11).

The law concerning special educational needs generally is discussed in more detail in chapter 8.

It is important to note, however, that tribunals are required (or perhaps, more correctly, advised, as the President has no power to compel a tribunal to do something) to look at the child's needs and provision at the date of the hearing and not look back to the needs at the date the statement was issued, which could be some time beforehand, nor to question the actions of the LEA (see guidance note issued by the President in March 1996).

An appeal to the tribunal cannot postpone the LEA's decision pending the outcome of the appeal (*Camden LBC v Hadin* [1996] ELR 430) and so a statement made by an LEA that is challenged comes into effect unless and until overturned by the tribunal. However, a decision to cease to maintain a child's statement is now frozen if the parents appeal against that decision (para 11(5) of sched 27).

The decision of a tribunal is binding on the parties and refusal on the part of the LEA to comply with the tribunal's order can lead to a complaint to the Secretary of State. Whether the express duty in s. 336A imposing an obligation on an LEA to comply with the order before the end of prescribed time limits adds anything is perhaps a moot point (see the Education (Special Educational Needs) (England) (Consolidation) Regulations 2001 (SI 2001 No. 3455) and, in Wales, the Special Educational Needs Tribunal (Time Limits) (Wales) Regulations 2001 (SI 2001 No. 3982)). If, however, an LEA, due to a genuine mistake, incorrectly records the terms of the tribunal's decision when it issues a revised statement to parents in a manner more favourable to the parents, there is no obligation on the LEA to meet that incorrect provision (*R v Wirral MBC and Governors of Elleray Park School ex parte B* [2000] ELR 703). This does not, of course, allow an LEA to choose to put its own interpretation on a tribunal's decision and amend a statement in a way that is at variance with the tribunal's order and/or wording.

12.
ACCOUNTABILITY
& CHALLENGE

Two means of challenging the decision of the tribunal are available.

First, a party can ask that the tribunal's decision be reviewed (reg 37 of the Special Educational Needs Tribunal Regulations 2001). The Tribunal, however, has power to review only on the grounds that:

- its decision was wrongly made as a result of an error on the part of the tribunal staff;

- a party who was entitled to be heard at a hearing, but failed to appear or be represented, had good and sufficient reasons for failing to appear;

- there was an obvious error in the decision of the tribunal which decided the case; or

- the interests of justice require it.

The President issued guidance in 1996 (see [1996] ELR 278) on the circumstances in which a tribunal would agree to review a decision. He made clear that the purpose of the review is to reconsider a decision which is technically flawed and not to raise errors of law. Review will therefore be used only where there has been a fundamental procedural error, fraud or simple cases of minor error or omission.

Second, given these parameters, very few cases of review succeed and the only other option open to parties is to appeal to the High Court on a point of law under s. 11 of the Tribunals and Inquiries Act 1992. The parties can either ask that the tribunal state a case for determination by the High Court (but only during the course of proceedings, see *Brophy v SENT* [1997] ELR 291), or by bringing an appeal directly to the High Court.

4. Independent admission and exclusion appeal panels

As briefly discussed in the sections on admissions and exclusions (see, respectively, chapters 7.A and 9.G), one of the duties of an LEA is to make arrangements for the establishment of independent appeal panels to consider appeals against the refusal to admit children to community and controlled schools and against decisions to exclude children from all maintained schools.

There is a certain irony in an LEA's being required to make arrangements for panels to consider appeals against its own decisions (in the case of admissions). That irony has so far survived the implementation of the Human Rights Act 1998, which requires an impartial and fair tribunal when a person's civil rights are determined. The courts have considered that such panels, as long as certain safeguards are preserved, can be considered sufficiently independent or impartial. The ombudsman and the Council on Tribunals have not, however, been so kind to these panels. The

12.
ACCOUNTABILITY
& CHALLENGE

ombudsman's report in 2001 highlighted concerns, especially in respect of ensuring training for clerks and panel members and the systematic and proper consideration of grounds of appeal. The Council on Tribunals also expressed concern at the quality and appropriateness of such panels in its report: *School Admission and Exclusion Appeal Panels – Special Report* (Cm 5788), May 2003.

Nonetheless, at the moment, appeal panels still have a role to play. Given that panel members are all volunteers, unpaid (indeed, this was a factor which helped the courts consider them sufficiently independent) and carrying out an increasingly complex and legalistic task, the criticism from press, Secretaries of State and headteacher is, at times, a little more than ill-founded. LEAs can take steps to preserve this situation as far as possible by, for example, ensuring that panels comply with the law, follow guidance where appropriate, distance themselves from the LEA so far as possible and ensure that there are no conflicts, ensuring for example, that the authority's lawyers do not advise both the panels and the LEA and/or school which appears before them.

These panels also have jurisdiction to deal with claims of disability discrimination relating to admissions or exclusion decisions (ss. 28 K and 28 L of the Disability Discrimination Act 1995).

4.1   Admission appeals

Under s. 94 of the School Standards and Framework Act 1998 (as amended by s. 50 of the 2002 Act), an LEA is required to make arrangements for enabling the parent of a child to appeal against:

- any decision made by or on behalf of the LEA as to the school at which education is to be provided for the child, and

- in the case of a community or voluntary controlled school maintained by the LEA, any decision made by or on behalf of the governing body refusing the child admission to the school.

The constitution of admission appeal panels and the procedure relating to the making and hearing of such appeals is now contained in the Education (Admissions Appeals Arrangements) (England) Regulations 2002 (SI 2002 No. 2899) (referred to below as 'the 2002 Regulations').

The decision of an appeal panel is binding on the LEA or the governing body as appropriate (s. 94(6)).

These appeal panels must consist of either three or five members appointed by the LEA from persons who are lay members and from persons who have experience in education, are acquainted with educational conditions in the area of the LEA, or are parents of registered pupils at a school (paras 1(1) and 2(1) of schedule 1 to the 2002 Regulations). On each appeal panel one member must come from each group (para 1(2) and 2(2)). Members of the LEA or of the governing body of the school in question and any person employed by the LEA other than a teacher are disqualified from membership. In addition, any person who has or at any time has had any connection with the LEA or the school or a person employed by the LEA or the school of a kind which might reasonably be taken to raise doubts about his ability to act impartially in relation to the LEA or the school, is also disqualified (paras 1(6) and 2(6)).

The LEA may pay certain allowances to members of appeal panels (reg 7), is under an obligation to advertise for lay members (reg 4) and must provide an indemnity to members of any appeal panel against any reasonable legal costs and expenses incurred in connection with any decision made by them in good faith (reg 8).

Brief rules of procedure are set out in sched 2 to the 2002 Regulations. These require an appeal panel to give the appellant an opportunity of appearing and making oral representations and to be accompanied by a friend or be represented (para 1(3) of sched 2). An appeal is heard in private unless the LEA or governing body direct otherwise, but a member of the LEA or the governing body may attend if the panel so directs (para 1(5)). In the event of disagreement between members, the matter shall be decided by a simple majority vote and in the case of an equality of votes, the chairman of the panel shall have a second or casting vote (para 1(7)). The decision and grounds on which it is made shall be communicated by the panel in writing to the appellant and the LEA (para 1(8)). Apart from the obligations set out above, all matters relating to the procedure, including the time within which appeals are to be brought, are determined by the LEA or the governing body (para 1(10)). This, though, appears odd: the procedure should surely be governed by the panel and not one of the parties to the appeal. It is this type of provision which probably correctly caused the Council on Tribunals to be concerned about the fairness and perceived independence of these panels.

Appeals brought by the governing bodies of schools against decisions that they admit children who have previously been excluded twice (under s. 95 of the 1998 Act) are dealt with by an

12.
ACCOUNTABILITY
& CHALLENGE

appeal panel arranged by the LEA and which operates in broadly the same way as with other appeals (reg 5(1)). The differences are that a panel member may not have been previously involved in any previous consideration of whether the child should have been reinstated (reg 5(2)) and, fairly obviously, the governing body should be notified of the panel's decision (para 1(8)(b) of sched 2).

Further guidance, to which all appeal panels must have regard, is contained in the *School Admission Appeals Code of Practice* (DfES/0030/2003 February 2003).

One particular point, which all appeal panels, with the exception of those for which the reduction of infant class sizes is an issue, must consider, is the need for a two-stage process in all prejudice appeals.

The courts (see *R v South Glamorgan Appeals Committee ex parte Evans* 10 May 1984, unreported and *R v Commissioner for Local Administration ex parte Croydon LBC* [1989] 1 All ER 1033) have held that there are two distinct stages involved in an appeal other than one in respect of admission to an infant class:

1. a factual stage for the appeal panel to decide as a matter of fact whether prejudice would arise were the child to be admitted; the onus at this stage is on the representative of the admissions authority, and

2. a balancing stage for the appeal panel to exercise its discretion balancing between the degree of prejudice and the weight of the parental factors before arriving at a decision (see paras 4:61 and 4:68–4:72 of the *Code of Practice*).

If the appeal panel is not satisfied at the first stage that there would be prejudice if a child were admitted, the appeal panel should allow the appeal (in the case of an appeal from a single child). If it is satisfied that there is prejudice, the appeal panel need to go on to the second stage and balance the prejudice against the merits of the parental case.

12.
ACCOUNTABILITY
& CHALLENGE

The *Code of Practice* (paras 4:68 to 4:72) provides guidance on the conduct of multiple appeals.

Where the reduction in infant class sizes is an issue, the nature of the appeal changes and the two-stage process is unnecessary. Appeal panels may allow an appeal only if either (a) the decision was not one which a reasonable admissions authority would make in the circumstances of the case and/or (b) the child would have been offered a place if the admission arrangements had been properly implemented. The appeal is therefore not a rehearing of the parents' case, but a review in light of the parents' circumstances, on limited grounds, of the admission authority's decision: see, *R v Southend Borough Education Appeals Committee ex p Southend-on-Sea Borough Council* 17 August 1999, unreported QBD, *R v Richmond London Borough Council ex parte C (a child)* (2000) *Times*, 26 April, *R (South Gloucestershire LEA) v South Gloucestershire Schools Panel* [2001] EWHC Admin 732 and *R (Hounslow LBC) v School Admissions Appeals Panel for Hounslow LBC* [2002] EWCA Civ 900, CA and see chapter 7.A above. See also paras 4.53–4.60 of the *Code of Practice*.

4.2 Exclusion appeals

Under s. 52(3)(c) of the 2002 Act and the Education (Pupil Exclusions and Appeals) (Maintained Schools) (England) Regulations 2002 (SI 2002 No. 3178) (referred to below as 'the Maintained Schools Regulations'), an LEA is required to make arrangements for enabling a parent (or if the excluded pupil is over 18, the pupil) to appeal against any decision of a governing body not to reinstate a permanently-excluded pupil from a maintained school. Provisions requiring an LEA to make arrangements to enable a parent or pupil to appeal against permanent exclusions from a pupil referral unit are now contained in the Education (Pupil Exclusions and Appeals) (Pupil Referral Units) (England) Regulations 2002 (SI 2002 No. 3179) ('the PRU Regulations').

The procedure for the making and hearing of appeals against decisions of governing bodies of maintained schools is now governed by reg 6 of and the schedule to the Maintained Schools Regulations or, in the case of exclusions from PRUs, that Schedule as modified by the schedule to the PRU Regulations. In addition, appeal panels must have regard to the guidance issued by the Secretary of State (reg 7 of the Maintained Schools Regulations and reg 8 of the PRU Regulations) which is now contained in *Improving Behaviour and Attendance: Guidance on Exclusion from Schools and Pupil Referral Units* (available at www.teachernet.gov.uk) and, in particular part 4. However, it is important that appeal panels appreciate what 'having regard to guidance' actually means.

> '[G]uidance is no more than that: it is not direction and certainly not rules. Any Appeal panel which […] treats the Secretary of State's Guidance as something to be strictly adhered to or simply follows it because it is there will be breaking its statutory remit in at least three ways: it will be failing to exercise its own independent judgment; it will be treating guidance as if it were

**12.
ACCOUNTABILITY
& CHALLENGE**

rules and it will, in lawyers' terms, be fettering its own discretion. Equally, however, it will be breaking its remit if it neglects the guidance. The task is not an easy one' (*per* Schiemann LJ in *S, T, P v Brent LBC and Others* [2002] EWCA Civ 693 ('the *Brent* case') at para 15). See also chapter 3.C of this book.

The decision of an appeal panel is binding on the pupil and/or the parent, the governing body (or management committee of a PRU), the headteacher (or teacher in charge of the PRU) and the LEA (reg 6(5) of the Maintained Schools Regulations and reg 7(5) of the PRU Regulations).

The composition of exclusion appeal panels is now different from those for admission appeal panels. After much debate and argument, the Secretary of State bowed to demands from headteacher unions and accepted that panels must contain headteachers or former headteachers and others with knowledge of school management. Consequently, panels must have either three or five members, made up of three categories (paras 2(2) and (3) of the schedule to the Maintained Schools Regulations). The categories and main requirements are summarised below.

- A lay member, who must chair the panel. For these purposes a 'lay member' is a person who has not worked in a school in a paid capacity, although they may have been a school governor or worked as a volunteer.

- One person (or, in a five-member panel, two persons) who must be, or have been, a governor of a maintained school, provided that they have served in this capacity for at least 12 consecutive months in the last six years. The Guidance (part 4, para 4.1(b)) stated that these individuals must not be or have been a teacher or headteacher. This qualification is not, however, contained in the Maintained School Regulations, but was probably sensible precautionary advice to avoid panels becoming overburdened with teachers and susceptible to challenge – see below.

**12.
ACCOUNTABILITY
& CHALLENGE**

- One person (or in a five-member panel, two persons) who must be, or have been within the last five years, a headteacher of a maintained school (for an exclusion from a PRU this member could also be a teacher in charge of a PRU).

- Disqualifications from membership are similar to those for admission appeal panels, i.e. membership of the LEA or governing body of the excluding school; an employee of the LEA or governing body, other than as a headteacher or teacher in charge; having, or at any time having had, any connection with an interested party which might reasonably be taken to raise doubts about their ability to act impartially; or being the headteacher of the excluding school or having been the headteacher within the last five years (para 2(7) of the schedule to the Maintained Schools Regulations).

- As para 4.4 of part 4 of the Guidance makes clear, particular care beyond the statutory disqualifications needs to be taken to ensure that the impartiality and independence of the panel is preserved. Thus: 'Doubts about impartiality may arise from the panel member having worked closely with the headteacher or governing body of the excluding school, or from being the headteacher or governor of a school to which the pupil might be admitted if the exclusion is confirmed. Small LEAs may have difficulty finding serving headteachers and governors who feel they are able to act impartially and may need to recruit panel members from a neighbouring LEA if they cannot find retired headteachers and governors to take on the role.'

- Nonetheless, despite this precautionary advice, there continue to be concerns expressed about the independence and impartiality of these panels. The Court of Appeal (in the *Brent Case*) considered that exclusion appeal panels were independent and impartial, albeit its decision related to a panel constituted under the old rules now replaced by the Maintained School Regulations. In reaching its conclusion, the court took account of the fact that the then panels were carefully constituted to be independent of the excluding school, the pupil and the LEA, were subject to scrupulous provisions about eligibility and were subject to the supervision of the Council on Tribunals (*per* Schiemann LJ, para 11). The court considered the potential conflict between the role of the LEA in arranging, appointing, training and servicing the appeal panel, but took the view that provided the LEA maintained an objective stance and did not press for a particular conclusion, that conflict did not compromise the panel's independence or impartiality (*per* Schiemann LJ, paras 22–24). This conclusion does, however, mean that LEAs must perform an entirely objective and neutral role in front of the panel. Gone are the days when an LEA officer could urge a panel to uphold an exclusion or press for reinstatement. 'There is nothing wrong in the LEA informing the appeal panel of the situation in various schools in its area and providing other factual information… [But] it should be noted that Parliament has not provided a right of appeal for the LEA even if it considers that the headteacher should not have excluded the pupil. It is no part of the function of the LEA to press for a particular conclusion in relation to a particular pupil. A clear instance would be a direct submission that the pupil ought or ought not to be permanently excluded.'(*per* Schiemann LJ, para 24). Panels must also 'be careful not to let a point be reached where they appear to be acquiescing in an endeavour by the LEA – or anyone else for that matter – to determine or influence their final decision [...] An example might be a submission by the LEA that the Panel's decision should not be such as to undermine a headteacher's authority' (*per* Schiemann LJ, para 25).

- The court also rejected arguments that the composition and conduct of such appeal panels was an infringement of the right to a fair trial (article 6 of the European Convention on Human Rights) under the Human Rights Act 1998. The court followed previous jurisprudence and considered that these panels do not determine a pupil's civil rights and therefore article 6 has no application. However, in a warning for the future, Schiemann LJ (at para 30) hinted that with modern developments a court might today or in the future consider that the right not to be permanently excluded without good reason is a civil right. As the court found that the panels as then constituted were independent and impartial, the point was irrelevant; but, were a court to take a different view in the future, the outcome might be altogether different.

- It is important therefore to recognise that the changes brought about by the latest regulations do produce a quite different panel from that considered by the Court of Appeal. What is perhaps most significant is that the Council on Tribunals, whom the court saw as one of the guardians of the panel's independence, is now expressing concerns at the changes and the independence of the panels (the Council had 'concerns about the constitution of admission and exclusion appeal panels and particularly the over-representation of teachers on the panels and the Department's recent decision to increase the numbers of teachers on exclusion appeal panels', *Executive Summary, School Admission and Exclusion Appeal Panels – Special Report* (Cm 5788) May 2003) and is pressing for the determination of exclusion appeals to be passed to the SENDIST (para 3.12 of the *Special Report*). Until that happens, questions about the role of exclusion appeal panels as currently constituted may continue to be raised in court.

12.
ACCOUNTABILITY
& CHALLENGE

- So long as these panels continue in their current guise, however, the LEA is under an obligation to pay certain financial loss allowances to their members, advertise for lay members and provide the necessary indemnity (paras 3, 4 and 5 of the schedule to the Maintained Schools Regulations).

The jurisdiction of exclusion appeal panels is also different from that of admission appeals. Admission appeal panels arranged by the LEA deal only with appeals relating to community and voluntary controlled schools (unless other arrangements have been agreed); in the case of exclusion appeal panels, they are arranged by the LEA, but consider appeals against decisions not to reinstate a pupil at all maintained schools, including foundation and voluntary aided schools.

The procedure for making an appeal and conducting an appeal is set out in the schedule to the Maintained Schools Regulations and see also part 4, paras 6.1–12.6 of the Guidance.

Prior to the Maintained Schools and PRU Regulations, a panel could make one of two decisions: uphold the appeal or order that the child be reinstated, either immediately or on a date in the future. That seemed to provide the correct range of remedies, or, at least it did until, in a series of well-publicised cases, school staff refused to accept panel decisions and threatened industrial action if pupils were reinstated. Alternatively, a number of other schools decided that 'reinstatement' could mean simply readmitting the child to the school, not returning him or her to his old class and lessons.

In both cases, the courts took what might be described as a non-interventionist approach, preferring to recognise the difficulties faced by schools if staff threatened industrial action rather than looking to the strict letter of the law. Thus, the courts considered that, provided the correct processes were followed by unions, the threat by staff to refuse to teach a reinstated pupil could constitute a trade dispute, as it would relate to their terms and conditions of employment and would thus be lawful industrial action *(P v NASUWT* [2003] UKHL 8, [2003] 2 WLR 545; [2003] 1 All ER 993; [2003] IRLR 307, [2003] ELR 357). That threat could also be a factor for an appeal panel to take into account in deciding whether to reinstate.

As to what exactly constitutes reinstatement, the House of Lords by a majority of 3:2 (Lord Bingham presenting a powerful dissenting judgment) decided that all it required was a readmittance to the

**12.
ACCOUNTABILITY
& CHALLENGE**

school, a reinstatement of the pupil-school relationship. It did not require the school to return the reinstated child to the exact position he or she had been in prior to their exclusion. Thus, the requirement of reinstatement could be met if a child was forced to spend the school day in isolation from his peers and staff, taught only by a home tutor and restricted to remaining in a confined area. The House of Lords did, though, express the view that this should be part of a phased reintegration and should not become a permanent arrangement (*L v J* [2003] UKHL 9; [2003] 2 WLR 518; [2003] 1 All ER 1012).

In an attempt to address the problems caused by this sort of reaction from school staff, as well as covering other ambiguities such as the parent who wanted to clear their child's name but was not after reinstatement, the Maintained Schools and PRU Regulations offer a third order or direction. Panels may still decide to uphold the exclusion or direct reinstatement (either immediately or by a date specified in the direction), but they may also decide that 'because of exceptional circumstances or for other reasons it is not practical to give a direction requiring a pupil's reinstatement, but that it would otherwise have been appropriate to give such a direction' (reg 6(6) of the Maintained Schools Regulations). The available remedies are slightly different in the PRU Regulations, where a panel, if it determines the pupil should not have been permanently excluded, can either direct that a pupil is to be reinstated (either immediately or by a date specified in the direction) or 'in cases where it would not be practical to give a direction requiring a pupil's reinstatement, determine that it would otherwise have been appropriate to do so' (reg 8 of the PRU Regulations). The PRU cases, apparently, do not require there to be 'exceptional circumstances' making it impractical to reinstate.

The Guidance (part 4, paras 10.4 and 10.5) suggests that the circumstances where this new type of order is appropriate could include: 'situations where there has been an irretrievable breakdown in relations between pupil and teachers; between the parents and the school; or between the pupil and other pupils involved in the exclusion or appeal process. Balancing the interests of the pupil and the whole school community may suggest that reinstatement would not be the most sensible outcome in such cases. In considering whether such exceptional circumstances exist, the panel should consider representations from the governors, the head teacher and from the parent (or pupil if 18 or over).' If the panel decides to adopt this remedy, it should indicate this in its decision letter and give details of the circumstances that made it decide not to direct reinstatement. Such a letter should be added to the pupil's school record for future reference (para 10.5).

Although the existence of exclusion appeal panels has so far withstood judicial scrutiny, more and more cases are being brought challenging panel decisions. Whilst attempts to require exclusion appeal panels to follow criminal court procedures (see for example *R v Head Teacher and Independent Appeal Committee of Dunraven School ex parte B (a child)* [2000] ELR 156, QBD and CA) have failed, there is no doubt that exclusion appeal panel members will need to be more rigorous in considering appeals and ensuring that fairness and natural justice prevail at all times. In the *Brent* case, the Court of Appeal recognised this by endorsing earlier comments from Brooke LJ in *Dunraven School* that, whilst not saying that the criminal standard applies, the standard of proof that is required is not the ordinary balance of probabilities, but something higher. It has to be shown that it was distinctly more probable than not that the pupil was involved in the incident. (See however the *YP* case below and the comment in chapter 9.G.1.)

The decisions of the courts and the ombudsman over the last few years, together with the latest Guidance from the Secretary of State, emphasise the importance of panels' acting in accordance with the principles of natural justice: allowing all parties a fair hearing; being clear as to the type of evidence which may be presented and considered; recognising the importance of their decisions on the child excluded and on other pupils and staff at the school and establishing the facts of the matter.

Cases in which the courts have examined exclusions and, more particularly, exclusion appeals include the following.

- *R v Board of Governors of Stoke Newington School and Others ex parte M* [1994] ELR 131. (a) There had been a breach of natural justice when a person who was in a position to give evidence about the excluded pupil's conduct sat on the appeal panel; and (b) appeal panels perform a quasi-judicial function (not an administrative one).

- *R v Neale and Another ex parte S* [1995] ELR 198. A parent's attitude or behaviour towards staff and governors could be relevant to a decision to turn a fixed-term exclusion into a permanent one. Education was a three-way partnership among the pupil, the school and the parent(s).

12. ACCOUNTABILITY & CHALLENGE

- *R v Governors of St Gregory's RC Aided High School and Appeals Committee ex parte M* [1995] ELR 290. (a) It was not necessary for the appeal panel to hear evidence directly from the primary witnesses, provided the excluded pupil knew the nature of the allegation against him and so the headteacher was allowed to recite the evidence he had obtained from other witnesses; and (b) the excluded pupil should be allowed to give his account of events.

- *R v Newham LBC and Another ex parte X* [1995] ELR 303. (a) Rules of fairness must apply to the appeal panel procedures; and (b) it was not unlawful for a headteacher, in appropriate circumstances, to use disciplinary action in relation to the behaviour of pupils towards one another off school premises.

- *R v Camden LBC and the Governors of the Hampstead School ex parte H* [1996] ELR 360. (a) It was not necessary, on every occasion, for searching inquiries to be carried out, involving the calling of bodies of oral evidence, but once it was decided what factual issues needed to be resolved, the consideration of those issues by the appeals panel needed to be reasonably thorough; and (b) consideration had to be given to the effect a direction to reinstate might have on the victim of the excluded pupil.

- *R v Solihull MBC ex parte W* [1997] ELR 489. (a) The obligation on the appeal panel was to ask the right question and to take reasonable steps to acquaint itself with the relevant information to enable it to answer that question correctly; and (b) in appropriate cases, the appeal panel should take account of social difficulties and the previous behaviour of the excluded child.

- *R v Board of Governors and Appeal Committee of Bryn Elian High School ex parte Whippe* [1999] ELR 380. (a) The behaviour of a parent towards a headteacher could be a relevant factor in a decision to exclude but only so far as it may have affected the future behaviour of the pupil; and (b) guidance contained in DfEE circulars should be taken into account, but the mere fact that the guidance was not specifically referred to would not be a problem if it was clear from the appeal panel's decision that a particular factor was taken into account.

- *R v Head Teacher and Independent Appeal Committee of Dunraven School ex parte B* (a child) [2000] ELR 156. Although appeal panels were not criminal courts, the principles of natural justice required that they should ensure that pupils, through their parents, should know the allegations against them. It would also

12.
ACCOUNTABILITY
& CHALLENGE

be a breach of natural justice for the appeals panel to have access to material which had not been shown to the pupil.

- *R (A) v Westminster City Council [2002] EWHC 2351 (Admin)*, [2002] All ER (D) 260 (Oct). The court permitted anonymous statements to be taken into account by a panel in circumstances where the headteacher had been cross-examined as to whether or not the witness could have been mistaken and where the headteacher had said the statement had been made in a climate of fear, in which other witnesses had been threatened.

- *R (N) v The Head Teacher of X School* [2001] EWHC 747 Admin, [2002] ELR 187. The court held that it was not unfair for the panel to have typed and unsigned copies of statements by other pupils alleging bullying by the excluded pupil in circumstances where the child and her parents had been given copies and had the chance to rebut what they said.

- *R (S) v Head Teacher of C High School* [2001] EWHC 513 (Admin), [2002] ELR 73. It was held that there was no violation of article 6 of the European Convention right to a fair trial because the clerk to the panel, a solicitor, was an LEA employee. However, LEA advisers should still be aware of potential conflicts of interest: if that solicitor had advised the school, it is doubted that he or she could also have been able to act as the clerk to the panel.

- *R (A) v Enfield LBC* [2002] EWHC 395 (Admin) [2002] ELR 631. Whilst the judge found flaws in the process, i.e. documents were made available to the pupil only on the day of the pupil disciplinary hearing and the headteacher was allowed to remain in the room after the hearing, they were curable by following the appeal panel process.

- *R (K) v Governors of the W School and West Sussex County Council* [2001] ELR 311. This was a difficult case involving allegations of sexual assault by the excluded pupil that did not reach the appeal panel stage. Nonetheless, the court held that the headteacher and pupil discipline committee had failed to provide the child with sufficient detail of the case against him, too low a standard of proof had been applied and the headteacher had improperly retold hearsay evidence from the police; the court quashed their decisions.

- *R (B) v Independent Appeal Panel of SMBC* [2002] EWHC 1509 (Admin). This judgment highlighted the importance of a panel's having regard to the current version of guidance issued by the Secretary of State.

- *R (ME) v Head Teacher of Whitton High School and Others* [2001] EWHC Admin 899. Incidents that might not have been considered particularly serious if taken in isolation assumed greater significance when they revealed that the pupil was so disruptive and abusive that it had become impossible to teach him at the school and could therefore justify permanent exclusion.

- *R (AC) v Sefton MBC Independent Appeals Panel and Others* 21/12/2000 unreported, QBD. The court decided an exclusion for a one-off offence to be justified where the headteacher had followed the relevant guidance.

- *S, T, P v Brent LBC and Others [2002] EWCA Civ 693*, [2002] ELR 556. In addition to the points considered above, the Court of Appeal considered difficulties with witnesses who did not attend and with anonymised evidence. Accepting that panels have no power to compel witnesses to attend, the court felt that where there is a material conflict of evidence involving an adult witness, there is no legal reason why the witness could not be invited to attend and be questioned. 'If such a witness declines to come for a reason which the panel finds acceptable, well and good; if for no reason or an unacceptable one, the panel is entitled to draw whatever inference seems sensible in the circumstances' (Schiemann LJ at para 28). With anonymised witness statements, the court considered that there may be very good reasons, especially in cases involving bullying, for anonymising them, but the injustice of using them may be even greater than the injustice of not. 'Appeal panels should be prepared to disregard anonymised statements of evidence if they are damaging to the pupil in ways which the pupil cannot be expected to deal with without knowing who has made the statement' (Schiemann LJ at para 29).

- *R (DR) v Head Teacher of St George's Catholic School and Others; R (AM) v Governing Body of Kingsmead School and Others* [2002] EWCA Civ 1822, [2003] ELR 104. Where there had been unfairness in the proceedings before the headteacher and the pupil discipline committee, but the hearing before the independent appeal panel had been fair, the court declined to quash the earlier decisions. In effect, a fair hearing by the appeal panel could cure earlier defects.

- *R (T by her litigation friend A) v Head Teacher of Elliott School and Others* [2003] EWCA Civ 1349 [2003] ELR 160. In principle, an appeal panel was entitled to look at statements that were anonymised and consider them. But the court recognised this meant the pupil could not cross-examine their author, who may have been an unreliable witness or have been biased. There were also difficulties as to how the pupil could call evidence to rebut the statements. The court, however, felt that it had to be presumed that a headteacher would not place statements before the panel which were made by pupils known to him to have been unreliable. Moreover, schools and local authorities had a duty to highlight unreliable authors of statements. Therefore, whilst it was wrong and unfair to give weight to statements that were damaging in regard to issues which a pupil was unable to deal with, more general allegations made in statements, as in this case, although always requiring caution, could be admitted if the panel made an informed judgment in relation to fairness.

- *Abdul Hakim Ali v Head Teacher and Governors of the Lord Grey School* [2003] EWHC 1533, [2003] ELR 517, QBD. A claim for damages against a school for what the judge found to be an unlawful exclusion was dismissed. Nor did a claim for damages for breach of the pupil's right not be denied education under article 2 of the First Protocol of the European Convention succeed. Neither the school's decision to exclude the pupil whilst awaiting the outcome of a police investigation nor the LEA's failure to provide tuition, in circumstances where the pupil's family declined its offer, gave rise to any liability for a denial of his education.

- *R (ota S) v YP School* [2003] EWCA Civ 1306 (for more detailed discussion see chapter 9.G.1). Where a pupil is excluded for what is, in effect, a criminal offence, the degree of probability required may equate with the criminal standard of proof, i.e. the headteacher, pupil disciplinary committee and the panel must be sure that the child has done what he has been accused of before so finding.

- *R (ota J) v Head Teacher of The School and College and Birmingham City Council Exclusion Appeals Committee* [sic] *and Others* [2003] EWHC 1747 (Admin), [2003] ELR 743. Davis J endorsed the comments of the judges in the Dunraven case (see above) that the parent's right to be heard is worthless unless the parent knows in some adequate form what is being said against the child and where what has been said has taken different and inconsistent forms: '[F]airness will ordinarily require enough disclosure to reveal the inconsistency'. But on the facts of the case, the parent did know the nature of the case against his child. The parents also, in effect, complained that

**12.
ACCOUNTABILITY
& CHALLENGE**

teachers who made statements were not available for cross-examination, but the court considered that this could simply have led to a fishing trip in order to try to throw up inconsistencies. The claim was therefore dismissed.

D. LEAs and the Courts

1. Introduction

LEAs and schools may feel that never before have they been subject to such close scrutiny by the courts and the perception that more and more time is being spent defending educational actions or decisions extends throughout much of the education profession. In fact, the perception is probably greater than the reality, although there is no doubt that the type and number of claims that may be brought have increased substantially over the last fifteen years and each case tends to attract significant press interest.

Decisions of the courts clearly do play a significant part in both guiding LEAs as to what they can and cannot do and in holding LEAs to account where they either infringe a public law right or else commit a wrong in private law that leads to a claim for compensation from an aggrieved parent or pupil.

Although the present amount of litigation has probably never been matched, it would be untrue to say that litigation against teachers, governing bodies and LEAs is a recent phenomenon. From around 1910 onwards, LEAs have been sued with increasing regularity and the courts were required to consider such matters as injuries caused by defects in playgrounds (*Ching v Surrey County Council* [1910] 1 KB 736) and 14 year-olds attending to a teacher's fire (*Myth v Martin and Kingston upon Hull Corporation* [1911] 2 KB 775).

The courts have therefore been involved, almost since the inception of LEAs, in assessing claims for compensation. It would be wrong, however, to suggest that courts were involved only in claims for damages. Albeit rarely, LEAs have found themselves before the criminal courts and, with the relatively recent evolution of judicial review, LEAs are now more likely to be challenged in the High Court for following incorrect procedures or acting outside their powers, or, since October 2000, for failing to comply with the Human Rights Act 1998.

In recognition of these three types of cases, the interrelationship between the courts and LEAs will be dealt with under three headings:

– Criminal liability

– Civil liability – enforcement of public law rights

– Civil liability – enforcement of private law rights.

2. Criminal liability

Fortunately, the occasions where LEAs and their chief education officers or council chief executives find themselves in front of criminal courts are rare. Nonetheless, more frequently than is perhaps thought, local authorities are brought before the courts on criminal charges. Prosecutions under the Environmental Protection Act 1990 for statutory nuisances are not uncommon and LEAs have been found guilty following incidents such as the leaking of fuel oil from school storage facilities. In Liverpool, some of the LEA's pupils even went so far as to prompt the prosecution of the LEA over the state of disrepair of their school.

The responsibilities as between LEAs and governing bodies under the health and safety legislation have been discussed above (see chapter 6.C.6 and 6.E.9.10), but it is not inconceivable that charges could be laid against either the LEA (its members or officers) or a governing body if an accident were to occur which infringed the criminal provisions of the Health and Safety at Work etc. Act 1974 or the regulations made under it.

The responsibility of incorporated bodies, such as local authorities and their senior officers and members for both direct and vicarious criminal acts is notoriously complex and outside the scope of this book. Although chief education officers should not panic, it is possible that in certain cases they could be held responsible for more serious offences, particularly in the event of a fatal accident. The charge of corporate manslaughter, although fortunately rarely arising, can be levelled against local authorities and their senior officers and it is the area of outdoor activities in particular where it may be used were an accident to occur. The operators of the activities centre responsible for the children involved in the Lyme Bay canoeing tragedy were tried and found guilty; it is not inconceivable that, were an accident to occur in an LEA-maintained centre, similar charges might be brought. That tragedy prompted the introduction of the Activity Centres (Young Persons Safety) Act 1995 which attempts to ensure that similar accidents do not arise. But even so, there have been a sad but regular number of fatalities since then, which have led to staff, primarily headteachers and teachers, facing charges. See, for example, the death of Elizabeth Bee, a pupil at a private school: 'Teacher took party on leaking boat in awful weather, girl's inquest is told', *The Independent* 6 June 2001; the death of Bunmi Shagaya on a school trip to France, *The Independent* 4 August 2001 and the death of Jason Dalton, a pupil at Ystrad Mynach College, *The Independent* 26 October 2002. In September 2003, the teacher in charge of a school trip during which a 10 year-old boy drowned in a swollen stream was sentenced to a year in prison after pleading guilty to manslaughter. The Crown Court judge called his conduct 'unbelievably negligent and foolhardy' (*The Guardian*, 24 September 2003).

The Government is currently committed to reviewing the law on corporate homicide and, at the time of writing, proposals were being prepared for the law to be amended to ensure that corporate management could be more easily held accountable. This new offence will apply equally to LEAs and governing bodies as to other, more commercial organisations and LEAs will therefore be potentially liable for death caused by their employees, including staff in community and voluntary controlled schools. However, the new legislation is likely to place emphasis on risk assessments and, so, given the good practice already in place in education settings, it should still be rare for an LEA or its 'directing minds' to be held criminally liable.

3. Civil liability

3.1 Introduction

The distinction between public law and private law rights has been the subject of considerable judicial thought and academic debate, which could take up a textbook in itself. For our purposes, we will adopt a simplistic distinction. Public law actions are those where an individual seeks to enforce statutory rights or challenge statutory powers. Private law actions are those where an individual seeks to secure compensation for a breach of a statutory or common law duty that the LEA owes directly and personally to that individual. An even more simplistic distinction might be between those cases where a person seeks to obtain a court order requiring an LEA either to do something or cease doing something (public) and those cases where a person seeks damages or compensation for injury he or she has suffered at the LEA's hands (private). In practice, this distinction

12.
ACCOUNTABILITY
& CHALLENGE

is not so clear-cut: damages can be sought in judicial review proceedings and injunctions and declarations are part of private law actions. But for our purposes, it should provide a helpful structure to the following discussion.

3.2 Civil liability – enforcement of public law rights

Throughout this book, we have been identifying and considering the various statutory duties and powers which Parliament has given to LEAs. Where LEAs either fail to perform a statutory duty or exercise a statutory power in breach of normal administrative law principles, the only option in most cases open to an aggrieved parent or pupil, apart from the statutory complaints procedures outlined above, is to seek judicial review of the LEA's action or inaction.

3.2.1 Judicial review

Judicial review is the means by which the High Court exercises a supervisory jurisdiction over the activities of public bodies. It needs to be remembered that judicial review is not an appeal mechanism or an opportunity for the court to examine the merits of a decision. Those are matters for statutory appeal.

As the courts cannot intervene in the merits of a particular case, it is important to recognise the circumstances when a court can interfere. Often reference is made to principles of *'Wednesbury* unreasonableness'. This means that the courts can intervene only where an LEA has acted outside its powers (*ultra vires*). It does not, however, mean that an LEA acts unlawfully only when it fails to comply with a particular duty; the principles have been interpreted to ensure that when exercising discretionary powers the court has an equal supervisory jurisdiction.

The summary of the principle was first set out in *Associated Provincial Picture Houses Ltd v Wednesbury Corporation* [1948] 1 KB 223, although it would seem that the courts now believe the test should be replaced by something more modern and appropriate to contemporary administrative law (see *ABCIFER v Secretary of State for Defence* [2003] EWCA Civ 473). However, the Court of Appeal in the *ABCIFER* case, whilst wounding the principle severely, declined to kill it off completely, believing that the mortal wound could be inflicted only by the House of Lords. Consequently, the principle may be around for some time to come and, even if it is dispatched, it is likely to remain in lawyers' vocabulary. It is therefore still important to be aware of what *Wednesbury* unreasonableness does mean. In *Wednesbury*, Lord Greene explained that: 'the exercise of a discretion must be a real exercise of

**12.
ACCOUNTABILITY
& CHALLENGE**

the discretion. If, in the statute confirming the discretion, there is to be found expressly or by implication matters which the authority exercising the discretion ought to have regard to, then in exercising the discretion it must have regard to those matters. Conversely, if the nature of the subject matter and the general interpretation of the Act make it clear that certain matters would not be germane to the matter in question, the authority must disregard those irrelevant collateral matters.'

Lord Greene felt that the word 'unreasonable' had often been used to cover a wide range of unlawful administrative acts as a general description of things that must not be done. 'For instance a person entrusted with a discretion must direct himself properly in law. He must call his own attention to the matters which he is bound to consider. He must exclude from his consideration matters which are irrelevant to what he has to consider. Similarly, there may be something so absurd that no sensible person could ever dream that it lay within the powers of the authority [...] Warrington LJ in Short v Poole Corporation [1926] Ch. 66 gave the example of the red-haired teacher, dismissed because she had red hair. It is so unreasonable that it might almost be described as being done in bad faith and, in fact, all these run into one another....'

Lord Greene summarised the position as follows:

'The court is entitled to investigate the action of the local authority with a view to seeing whether they have taken into account matters which they ought not to take into account, or, conversely, have refused to take into account or neglected to take into account matters which they ought to take into account. Once that question is answered in favour of the local authority, it may still be possible to say that, although the local authority have kept within the four corners of the matters which they ought to consider, they have nevertheless come to a conclusion so unreasonable that no reasonable authority could ever have come to it. In such a case, again, I think the court can interfere. The power of the court to interfere in each case is not as an appellate authority to override a decision of the local authority, but as a judicial authority which is concerned and concerned only, to see whether the local authority have contravened the law by acting in excess of the powers which Parliament has confided in them.'

The principles were again considered in the *Council of Civil Service Unions v Minister for the Civil Service* [1985] 1 AC 374. Lord Diplock identified three principles: 'illegality', 'irrationality' and

12.
ACCOUNTABILITY
& CHALLENGE

'procedural impropriety'.

- Illegality implies that the decision-maker has not correctly understood, or acted in accordance with, the law that regulates his decision-making power.

- Irrationality was, in Lord Diplock's view, the equivalent of *'Wednesbury* unreasonableness' and applies to a decision which is so outrageous in its defiance of logic or accepted moral standards that no sensible person who has applied his mind to the question to be decided could have arrived at it.

- Finally, procedural impropriety covers a failure to observe procedural rules that are expressly laid down in the statutory framework and which regulate the decision under challenge and also a failure to observe the basic rules of natural justice or to act with procedural fairness.

Following implementation of the Human Rights Act 1998 in October 2000, the courts have looked beyond these traditional concepts to include, first, as another ground of challenge that an authority has acted in a way which is incompatible with one or more of the rights set out in the European Convention on Human Rights (Convention Rights) and, second, to consider whether, even in cases where Convention Rights do not apply, the courts will set aside a decision or action which is disproportionate. The trend towards the test of proportionality (enunciated in, for example, *R (Alconbury Ltd) v Secretary of State for the Environment, Transport and the Regions* [2001] 2 WLR 1389 at p. 1406) is recognised by the Court of Appeal's decision in *ABCIFER v Secretary of State for Defence* ([2003] EWCA Civ 473), albeit that the Court was not prepared to say that the test had yet displaced that of *Wednesbury* unreasonableness. In future, though, this may become an important ground of challenge for, while *Wednesbury* unreasonableness is effectively a very difficult test for any claimant to satisfy, proportionality is less strict and, perhaps more importantly, may require a court to look more closely at the merits of a decision.

12. ACCOUNTABILITY & CHALLENGE

For the time being, however, it is challenges alleging breaches of the Human Rights Act that are likely to be more common. The 1998 Act requires all primary and subordinate legislation to be read and given effect in a way which is compatible with the Convention Rights listed in the schedule to the Act, so far as it is possible to do so (s. 3(1) of the Human Rights Act 1998). More importantly for LEAs, the Act renders it unlawful for public authorities to act in a way that is incompatible with one or more of the Convention Rights (s. 6(1)).

The meaning of 'public authorities' clearly includes public bodies, such as LEAs, exercising statutory functions, but the definition can also extend to quasi-public bodies and even private limited companies that are carrying out a function on behalf of a local authority. The breadth of the definition is still unclear and will depend on the circumstances, but the situation appears to be that where an authority contracts with a private organisation to enable the authority to discharge its functions, the private body will not be considered a public authority (see *R (ota Heather) v Leonard Cheshire Foundation* [2002] EWCA Civ 366) but where the authority's functions are transferred or delegated to a private company, if the company 'steps into the shoes' of the authority, that private company will be treated as a public authority (see *Hampshire County Council v Beer (t/a Hammer Trout Farm)* [2003] EWCA Civ 1056). This may be of significance to LEAs which either wish to work with private partners or have had outsourcing to private firms forced upon them. In education terms, what the cases suggest is, for example, that if a child with SEN is placed in an independent school, the school will not necessarily be treated as public authority, but if the LEA were to outsource its SEN functions to a private company, that company would be treated as a public authority and would therefore be subject to the duties in the Human Rights Act.

What the ultimate effect of the 1998 Act will be in the education field has been the subject of much debate and dispute, although the case law to date has not seen the Act having a significant impact on LEA work. Though warnings were initially given that the Act could change the culture of decision-making in local authorities, the foretellers of significant litigation and liability have been proved mainly wrong and the 1998 Act might be regarded as having an effect not dissimilar to that of the Millennium Bug.

The principal Convention Rights that affect education are summarised below.

- Article 6 – The right to a fair trial, which provides that everyone, in the determination of his civil rights and obligations, is entitled to a fair and public hearing within a reasonable time by an independent and impartial tribunal established by law. Judgment should be given in public, but the press may be excluded in certain specified circumstances.

- Article 8 – The right to respect for private and family life, which includes the right to respect for a person's home and correspondence.

- Article 9 – Freedom of thought, conscience and religion, which can be limited only in a way prescribed by law and necessary for reasons of public safety, public health or morals, public order or the rights or freedom of others.

- Article 10 – Freedom of expression, by which everyone is entitled to the rights of freedom of expression and to receive and impart ideas without interference.

- Article 14 – Prohibition on discrimination. This is not a stand-alone Convention Right, but provides that the enjoyment of other Convention Rights should be secured without discrimination on grounds such as sex, race, colour, language, religion, political or other opinion, national or social origin, association with a national minority, property, birth or other status.

- First Protocol, article 2 – No one shall be denied the right to education. In the exercise of any functions which it assumes in relation to education and to teaching, the state shall respect the right of parents to ensure such education and teaching in conformity with their own religious and philosophical convictions.

Although the last Convention Right appears to be most relevant to LEAs as it specifically talks of the right to education, it has turned out not to be the most influential right or indeed the one cited most effectively in challenges brought to date. This is because, first, the right is subject to a derogation secured by the United Kingdom Government which provides that the right applies only insofar as it is compatible with the provision of efficient instruction and training and the avoidance of unreasonable public expenditure, i.e. the same qualification which applies to the obligation to educate children in accordance with their parents' wishes (s. 9 of the Education Act 1996). Second, European Court of Human Rights case law has limited its potential effect.

The right, in effect, comprises two parts: the first, the right of a child or other beneficiary of education, not to be denied education; the second, the right given to parents to have their religious and philosophical convictions taken into account.

**12.
ACCOUNTABILITY
& CHALLENGE**

The article and earlier ECtHR jurisprudence was considered in detail in the Scottish case of *Dove and Dove (In the Petition of Dove and Dove for judicial review of the acts of Scottish Ministers in relation to St Mary's Episcopal Primary School, Dunblane*, 31 July 2002, unreported), a decision of the Court of Session relating to an objection to a school reorganisation. The Court of Session concluded that: 'The general right to education in the first sentence of Article 2, it has been said, dominates the article. For that reason, any interpretation given to the right of parents to have philosophical convictions taken into account must not conflict with the primary right to education enjoyed by the child [...]'

Incorporated within that general right are the four separate rights (none of which is absolute) namely:

1. a right of access to such educational establishments as exist,

2. a right to effective (but not the most effective possible) education,

3. a right to official recognition of academic qualifications, and

4. a right, when read with the freedom from discrimination guaranteed by Article 14 of the Convention, not to be disadvantaged in the provision of education on any ground such as sex, race, colour, language, religion, political or other opinion, national or social origin, association with a national minority, property, birth or other status without reasonable and objective justification.

The state is entitled to regulate these rights, taking account of individual and community needs and resources, provided this does not 'injure the substance of the right to education nor conflict with other rights enshrined in the Convention'. Lord Cameron, delivering the Court's judgment, summed up by saying (at para 26): 'It follows that measures such as [those relating to reorganisation of schools] which are concerned only with regulation of the constitution of the management and control of the management and administration of a school and which do not affect the curricula or teaching at the school, that is to say, the effectiveness of the education offered there, or limit access to the school or the education offered at it, do not fall within the scope or ambit of the right to education guaranteed by the first sentence of Article 2. They do not constitute a disadvantage to any of the modalities of the exercise of that right nor are they linked to the exercise of that right.'

That Article did not, he pointed out, require each state to establish a general and official educational system, but merely allows citizens to have access to whatever systems are in place at the time.

The second limb of the article was not infringed by the ban on corporal punishment in schools (*Williamson v Secretary of State for*

Education and Skills [2002] EWCA Civ 1820) but it does mean that LEAs should always have regard to parents' religious and philosophical convictions and where appropriate, for example on an application form for admissions, enable parents to express those convictions (see *R (on the application of K) v Newham LBC* [2002] EWHC 405 (Admin)).

The right enshrined in article 6 (fair trial) has also been shown to be of limited relevance to LEAs, particularly with regard to admission and exclusion appeals, largely because the courts have relied on old European Court of Human Rights case law to the effect that a 'right' to a place or not to lose a place at school is not a 'civil right'.

To fall within the article, the aggrieved citizen must show that there has been a determination of his civil rights or obligations. At first sight it would appear natural to assume that the admission or exclusion of a child would be a matter involving that child's civil rights. The European Court of Human Rights, however, took a different view in *Simpson v United Kingdom* (1989) 64 D & R 188. This case concerned a dyslexic child who complained at an LEA's decision not to place him in a special school. The child had appealed to an old-style local appeal panel, in the days before the Special Educational Needs [and Disability] Tribunal. It had dismissed his appeal. The Commission held that the right not to be denied education was not a civil right within article 6 and thus the requirement for a fair and impartial hearing, etc. was not a requirement under the Convention.

Although the decision in *Simpson* is quite old in terms of the development of education law and the rights of parents and pupils under UK law, English courts have followed *Simpson* and for the time being article 6 does not apply to admission appeal panels, even those dealing with infant class size appeals (see, for example, *R v Richmond upon Thames London Borough Council, ex parte JC* [2000] ELR 565 CA and *R v School Admissions Appeals Panel for Hounslow LBC ex parte Hounslow LBC*) or exclusion appeals (see *S, T and P v Brent LBC and Others*), although the *Brent* case provided a warning that the courts might in the future consider the right not to be excluded as a civil right to which article 6 might apply.

**12.
ACCOUNTABILITY
& CHALLENGE**

Other administrative decisions, applications for assistance under s. 518 of the 1996 Act for example, are also unlikely to fall within article 6 so long as aggrieved individuals can seek redress through judicial review. Although a judicial review cannot look at the merits of the case, the courts have been disinclined to impose an unreasonable burden on administrative bodies by requiring an independent and impartial appeal mechanism in respect of every decision (see, in particular, *R (Beeson) v Dorset County Council* [2002] EWCA Civ 1812).

In criminal cases, however, article 6 will apply to all proceedings. Initially, this was thought to mean that prosecutions for non-attendance, which for all intents and purposes are offences of strict liability, would fall foul of the article. However, the court in *Barnfather v Islington LBC* ([2003] EWHC 418 (Admin), [2003] ELR 263) held that non-attendance prosecutions under s. 444 of the 1996 Act were compatible with article 6.

Any action, or failure to act, on the part of an LEA which infringes a person's Convention Rights can lead to challenge by way of judicial review or, if proceedings are being brought by the LEA against the aggrieved individual, can be raised by way of collateral challenge to those proceedings. In principle, the Human Rights Act 1998 will allow individuals aggrieved by breach of their Convention Rights to seek damages, but damages recoverable under the Act are significantly limited. In comparison to damages recoverable under private law actions, the amounts that may be awarded will be significantly less and consequently any damages claim for breach of Convention Rights is likely to be made in types of proceedings other than judicial review.

Although some elements of the European Convention had started to creep into UK law before the Human Rights Act came into force (see, for example, the decision of the House of Lords in *Barrett v Enfield LBC* [1999] 3 WLR 79), the majority of the jurisprudence on the Convention Rights was found in decisions of the European Commission and Court of Human Rights and this still continues to be relevant as English Courts must have regard to this case law. Such cases include the following.

- *Simpson v UK* – see above.

- *The Belgian Linguistics Case* (1979-80) 1 EHRR 252. Article 2 to the First Protocol guarantees a right of access to educational institutions and teaching which exists in a state. It does not require the state to establish at state expense, or to subsidise, education of a particular type or at any particular level. In other words, where a parent has a particular philosophical view about the way their child should be taught, the Convention does not require the establishment at public expense of tuition or schooling to ensure that those views are met.

- *Sulak v Turkey* 17 January 1996. The Convention does not prevent a state introducing rules to allow the suspension or expulsion of pupils.

- *Costello-Roberts v UK* [1994] ELR 1. Corporal punishment involving three whacks with a gym shoe at an independent school did not infringe the Convention and did not amount to degrading or inhumane treatment.

- *Vogt v Germany* [1996] ELR 232 Consideration of the legality of dismissing a teacher because of her political activities. Ms Vogt won some points of her case against her dismissal from teaching for membership of the Communist Party, e.g: '[D]ismissal of V as a disciplinary sanction was disproportionate to the legitimate aim pursued' (at p. 234E).

- *X v United Kingdom* (application 7782/77, unreported). There is no positive obligation on the state to subsidise any particular form of education in order to respect the religious and philosophical beliefs of parents. It is sufficient for the state to evidence respect for the religious and philosophical beliefs of parents within the existing and developing system of education.

- *Valsamis v Greece* [1998] ELR 430. Parents who were Jehovah's Witnesses requested that their daughter be excused from school RE lessons and any event which was contrary to their religious beliefs, including national celebrations. The pupil refused to take part in a school parade on a national day and was punished with a one-day suspension. The parents claimed a violation of article 2 of the First Protocol. The court held that there was no breach of article 2 of the First Protocol on its own but there was a breach of the Convention, as there was no mechanism in Greek law to enable the parents to seek redress for what they perceived to be a breach of the article.

However, since the 1998 Act's introduction, the domestic case law is starting to build up and the following are examples of decisions made by the English courts which have not been considered already.

- *R v Department of Education and Employment ex p Begbie* [1999] ELR 471. A case in which it was held that article 2 of the First Protocol did not guarantee a right to an assisted place.

- *R (O) v J Roman Catholic School Appeal Panel* 4 December 2000. The right to respect for family life under article 8 can be engaged by an admission decision to a denominational school, where one sibling is already attending and equally the right to respect for parents' religious convictions can be engaged. However, article 8 confers no absolute right to have a child admitted to a school already attended by a sibling. A school will act compatibly by having a sibling connection as a criterion in its admission policy, but it does not have to be an overriding criterion.

- *T v SENT and Wiltshire County Council* [2002] EWHC 1474 (Admin). The wish of parents that their autistic child should receive Lovaas provision was not a religious or philosophical conviction.

- *CB v Merton LBC and SENT [2002] EWHC 877 (Admin)*, [2002] ELR 441. Placing a child in a residential school would infringe article 8 (private and family life) but, in the circumstances, the infringement was justified.

- *Abdul Hakim Ali v Head Teacher and Governors of the Lord Grey School* [2003] EWHC 1533, [2003] ELR 517, QBD. A claim for damages against a school for what the judge found to be an unlawful exclusion was dismissed. A claim for damages for breach of the pupil's right not to be denied education under article 2 of the First Protocol of the European Convention also failed. Neither the school's decision to exclude the pupil whilst awaiting the outcome of a police investigation nor the LEA's failure to provide tuition, in circumstances where the pupil's family declined its offer, gave rise to any liability for a denial of his education.

3.2.2. The judicial review process

Only those with sufficient interest, often referred to as those persons having *locus standi* in a matter, can make an application to the court. Within the educational field, it is usually quite clear whether a parent or a parent taking action on behalf of their child has sufficient interest in a decision of an LEA.

The court may, in certain circumstances, decline to allow a judicial review to go ahead if alternative statutory remedies are available. This immediately produces an issue in the educational field where the Secretary of State retains default powers to deal with complaints about the performance of an LEA. Generally, the courts will take the view that only in exceptional circumstances will a judicial review be allowed if a suitable, effective alternative remedy is available. For example, in *R v Newham LBC ex parte R* [1995] ELR 156, it was held that the appeal mechanism to the Secretary of State was more appropriate and effective than judicial review. Similar principles were applied in *R v Special Educational Needs Tribunal ex parte F* [1996] ELR 213, where it was held that there must be exceptional circumstances for a judicial review of the SEN Tribunal to be allowed, if there was an alternative, statutory right of appeal. Some judges, however, are stricter in the application of these principles than others. There have been cases, particularly where concern has been expressed at the delay inherent in a complaint to the Secretary of State, where judicial review has been allowed to go ahead in spite of the alternative statutory remedies. Other examples of the courts ignoring alternative remedies have arisen where the court has decided that matters of law arise which the court and only the court can interpret or decide (see, for example, *R v Barnet LBC ex part B* [1994] ELR 357).

Judicial reviews should be brought promptly after the decision being challenged but in any event within three months from the date of the decision or failure. The period can be extended but exceptional grounds need to be shown. If the court believes that there has been undue delay, it may refuse to allow permission for a judicial review to go ahead or may refuse relief if it considers that to do so would be likely to cause substantial hardship to or substantially prejudice the rights of any person or would be detrimental to good administration (s. 31(6) Supreme Court Act 1981).

Judicial review consists of a two-stage process. The first is an application for permission. At this point, it is necessary for the claimant to show that they have an arguable case and for the court to be convinced that they have sufficient interest and are not vexatious. The application for permission is usually heard *ex parte*, that is, the public body whose action is under challenge is not notified of the application. If permission is granted, the second stage, a full hearing, follows, at which both the applicant and the challenged authority present their cases.

A number of discretionary remedies are available to the court, including the following:

**12.
ACCOUNTABILITY
& CHALLENGE**

- a quashing order – an order that the decision under challenge be quashed, often followed by an order that the matter should be remitted back for the body to reach a conclusion in accordance with the court's findings;

- a mandatory order – an order requiring the performance of a specified act or duty. This is normally granted only where the authority is under an absolute duty to do something or else the facts make it clear that the authority concerned has failed to perform its duty at all;

- prohibition – an order which prevents the authority concerned acting or continuing to act unlawfully;

- declaration – which is as it says simply a declaration by the court of the law and/or the rights of the parties concerned;

- injunction – an order restraining a particular act or acts;

- damages – an order very rarely made in judicial review proceedings. It can be awarded only if the court is satisfied that if a claim had been brought in a private law action the applicant would have been entitled to damages. In practice, because of the short time limits, it is rarely possible to provide evidence to support a claim for damages; therefore, applicants normally pursue compensation by way of private-law remedies.

Judicial reviews brought against LEAs have been numerous and although most have concerned children with special educational needs, virtually all areas of LEA responsibility have, at one time or another, been considered. Most of the important decisions affecting the functions of LEAs have been considered under the relevant sections in this book. The following, including some less well-known judgments, provide a brief illustration of the types of cases which the courts have considered in judicial review proceedings.

- *R v Hampshire County Council ex parte Martin* (1982) *Times*, 20 November. The court reviewed the decision of the LEA concerning the ordinary residence of a minor who had applied for an educational award. (The LEA had misinterpreted the rules of ordinary residence.)

- *R v Secretary of State for Wales and Clwyd County Council ex parte Russell* 28 June 1983, unreported. Whether objectors to a statutory proposal to modify a school were entitled to see the response to their objections. (They were not.)

- *R v Hertfordshire County Council ex parte Cheung* (1986) *Times*, 4 April. A challenge to an LEA's interpretation of the ordinary residence of an applicant for a mandatory award. (The challenge was successful.) [Though it should be noted that neither Martin (above) nor Cheung proved to be the leading case that led to a change in the law, through the Education (Fees and Awards) Act 1983.]

- *R v Liverpool City Council ex parte Professional Association of Teachers* (1984) 83 LGR 648. A review of a decision of the LEA to remove the Professional Association of Teachers from the LEA's recognised negotiating bodies. (The decision of the LEA was invalid and an injunction was granted.)

- *R v Liverpool City Council ex parte Ferguson* (1985) *Times*, 20 November. A challenge to the decision of the LEA to issue notices of dismissal to all teachers and headteachers. (As the dismissals followed a decision to set an illegal rate, they were not for educational purposes and were in breach of the LEA's statutory duties.)

- *R v Hampshire Education Authority ex parte J* 28 November 1985, unreported. A challenge to the LEA's decision that dyslexia did not constitute a learning difficulty. (It did.)

- *R v Kirklees MBC ex parte Molloy* (1987) *Independent*, 28 July. A challenge to a decision to close a school, with the court examining what was meant by a duty to consider a report from an education committee and what such a report needed to contain. (It needed to be reasonably self-explanatory.)

- *R v Croydon LBC ex parte Leney* (1986) 85 LGR 466. Considered the meaning of 'persons of experience in education'.

- *R v Lancashire County Council ex parte M* [1989] 2 FLR 279. Whether an LEA was under a duty to provide speech therapy. (It was.)

- *R v Greenwich LBC ex parte Governors of the John Ball Primary School* [1990] Fam Law 469. Consideration of the legality of an admissions policy which discriminated against out-of-LEA-area pupils. (It was not lawful.)

- *R v Brent LBC ex parte Assegai* (1987) *Times*, 18 June. Whether a governor had been removed from office fairly in accordance with correct procedures. (He had not.)

- *Brunyate v ILEA* [1989] 2 All ER 417. Whether governors had been removed unlawfully by an LEA. (They had not.)

- *R v Camden LBC ex parte S* (1990) *Times*, 7 November. Whether an appeal hearing could adjourn and resume with different members. (It could not.)

- *R v Bradford MBC ex parte Sikander Ali* (1993) *Times*, 21 October. Whether an LEA could take account of traditional links between primary and secondary schools especially if it discriminated against ethnic minorities. (It could.)

- *R v Northamptonshire County Council ex parte K* (1993) *Times*, 27 July. A challenge to school closure on grounds it might cause

**12.
ACCOUNTABILITY
& CHALLENGE**

potential sex discrimination. (The decisions of the LEA and Secretary of State were not unreasonable or unlawful.)

- *R v Lancashire County Council ex parte West* 27 July 1994, unreported. Whether allotting places at schools by lottery was lawful. (Surprisingly, the judge agreed that it was.)

- R *v East Sussex County Council ex parte Tandy* [1998] ELR 251. The legality of blanket reduction in hours of home tuition provided. (The arbitrary reduction as part of a cost cutting exercise was unlawful.)

- *R v Birmingham City Council Education Appeals Committee ex p B* [1999] Ed CR 573, QBD. An appeal committee was required to decide whether an appellant lived at an address within a catchment area or an address outside. The appeal committee issued a standard-form decision letter which did not address this key issue. (The decision letter should have made specific reference to the Committee's decision on this issue; as it had not, the decision was quashed.)

- *R v Kirklees MBC ex p Beaumont* [2001] ELR 204, QBD. A decision to issue a notice closing School X and expanding School Y was challenged on the basis that two governors from School Y were councillors on the committee making the decision. Neither councillor declared a pecuniary or non-pecuniary interest. (They did have a private or personal interest capable of giving rise to a clear and substantial interest which should be declared. The decision was therefore quashed as the councillors should not have voted.)

- *R v St Mary's College, ex p Metropolitan Borough of Wirral* [2000] All ER (D) 229 QBD. The LEA altered its admission arrangements to allow parents to express preferences for admission, after the outcome of selection exams for selective schools in the area was known. The adjudicator found the new arrangements were unfair as they gave the parents of grammar-school pupils two first preferences. The LEA challenged this decision. (The adjudicator had not behaved irrationally.)

- *R v Birmingham City Council, ex p Y (a child)* [2000] All ER (D) 2231, QBD. The LEA denied assistance under s. 518 of the 1996 Act to a pupil to attend a dance school on the basis the parents had not demonstrated there were no other sources of finance or that the child needed to attend a non-mainstream school to obtain the dance qualifications. (The LEA had not behaved unreasonably; under the Scholarship and Other Benefits

Regulations 1977, the LEA had to be satisfied certain criteria were met and the child was not being denied a right to education.)

- *R (Rhodes) v Kingston upon Hull City Council* [2001] 2 ELR 230, QBD. Parents of children sought a declaration from the court that the LEA was not providing efficient education. (The court held that it was for the LEA to decide what was efficient education; the parents had already complained to the Secretary of State, who had dismissed the complaint and so the court took that into account.)

- *R v Schools Organisation Committee of Lambeth London Borough Council, ex p B* [2001] All ER (D) 302 (Jun), QBD – a SOC's decision to close a number of special schools and replace them with one primary and one secondary special school for children with 'complex needs' was challenged by pupils at a closing school. The LEA stated that whilst children with challenging behaviour could be educated alongside severely physically disabled pupils, children with EBD would not be sent to the new schools. (LEA's and SOC's decision not unreasonable.)

- *R v Secretary of State for Education, ex p Robyn Bandtock (a Minor)* [2001] 3 ELR 333, QBD. This was a challenge to the consultation process relating to proposals to close a special school for deaf children. (Process was not faulty.)

- *R v Walsall Metropolitan Borough Council, ex p the Transport and General Workers' Union* [2001] All ER (D) 85 (Jun), QBD. Three parent governor members of a committee were prevented from voting on a decision to outsource a school meals contract. (They should not have been: provision of school meals was a matter of direct concern to schools and under reg 10 of the Education (Parent Governor Representatives) Regulations 1999 (SI 1999 No. 1949) and the representatives were entitled to vote on it.)

- *R v Governing Body of Gateway Primary School, ex p X* [2001] 3 ELR 321, QBD. A pupil in an infants' class had been absent from her oversubscribed school for the last weeks of the summer term and the first of the autumn term primarily to attend a wedding in Morocco. Her father had not sought permission and the school deleted her name from the roll and filled her place. On returning, the child was refused a place and her appeal was unsuccessful. (The deletion of the child's name was unlawful:

reg 9(1)(e) of the Education (Pupil Registration) Regulations 1995 (SI 1995 No. 2089) (under which it had purportedly been done) did not apply, as there had been no leave of absence and consequently no exceeding its end date or period of grace. The court did not order that the child be re-admitted as the case was brought substantially out of time and it would not be in the interest of good administration for an order to be made [re-] admitting the pupil.)

- *R v Chair and Governing Body of Cwmfelinfach Primary School on the application of G* [2001] EPLI vol 6, issue 2, pp. 49–50 (Case Synopsis), QBD. A governing body refused to allow a child who persisted in wearing earrings contrary to school policy to participate in certain activities e.g. P.E. (Decision was lawful; the rule was a legitimate regulation on health and safety grounds.)

- *R (C) v Waltham Forest London Borough Council* [2002] All ER (D) 450 (Jul), QBD. An LEA passed on details of allegations (unproven) of paedophilia against a teacher to a prospective employer which led to an offer of employment being withdrawn. (The LEA should not have passed on the information and acted improperly in disclosing it, without notifying C or putting the document in context, to the prospective employer.)

- *R (H) v Brent London Borough Council* [2002] All ER (D) 348, QBD. The LEA decided to cease providing a pupil with transport after he transferred to an out-borough special school. (The LEA failed to have regard to the pupil's individual circumstances.)

- *R (T) v Leeds City Council* [2002] ELR 91, QBD. The LEA refused requests to fund transport for three sisters from an ultra-orthodox Jewish family to their parents' preferred school 45 miles away. (The LEA had had regard to the religious basis of the parents' preference and did not discriminate against Jews in its policy of funding transport to Anglican or RC schools (up to 5.9 miles beyond its boundaries) if such schools were the nearest to the pupils' homes.)

- *R (B) v Leeds School Organisation Committee* [2002] All ER (D) 72 (Sep), (2002) *Times*, 22 October, QBD. A SOC considered objections to reorganisation proposals and resolved that the amalgamation should proceed. The SOC did not call for further representations. (It was open to a SOC to call for or hear representations from interested parties, but it was not obliged to do so, though in the instant case it was regrettable that inadequate notice had been given of the SOC's meeting, which was held in public.)

- *R (Louden) v Bury School Organisation Committee* [2002] EWHC 2749 (Admin). A parent challenged a decision by the LEA and SOC to close a primary school on grounds including that the chairman of the SOC had previously sat as a member of the review panel examining the proposals and had voted in favour of closure. (He was not disqualified and the evidence showed he had properly performed his duties as chairman of the SOC and had not sought to use his position to influence other members.)

3.3 Civil liability – enforcement of private law rights

3.3.1 Introduction

Having considered the public law aspects of LEAs' functions and the remedies available, it is now necessary to turn to liabilities of LEAs in private law.

Local authorities, and LEAs in particular, enjoy no special status in law and may be held liable in the courts for damages if they infringe the private law rights of individuals or other organisations.

LEAs will owe obligations under their contracts and, like any other organisation or person, will be directly liable for certain wrongful actions, as well as assuming vicarious liability for their employees' wrongs. This section will therefore examine these issues, although, given the emphasis on claims for compensation in recent years, particular attention will be paid to the tortious liability of LEAs.

3.3.2 Contracts

An LEA, as manifestation of a local authority, has a general power to enter into contracts for the discharge of any of its functions (s. 111 of the Local Government Act 1972). In a number of Acts, specific power to contract is given (for example, the power to contract with careers service providers for a limited period (s. 10A of the Employment and Training Act 1973)). Under the Local Authorities (Goods and Services) Act 1970, a local authority can enter into agreements with a number of prescribed public bodies for the authority to supply goods, materials, services, transport and equipment and to carry out maintenance work. Included within the prescribed bodies are, for example, Education Action Forums (by virtue of para 2 of sched 30 to the School Standards and Framework Act 1998) and institutions within the further and higher education sectors (by virtue of para 71 of sched 8 to the Further and Higher Education Act 1992).

**12.
ACCOUNTABILITY
& CHALLENGE**

The decision of the Court of Appeal in *R v Yorkshire Purchasing Organisation ex p British Educational Suppliers Ltd* [1998] ELR 195 confirmed that LEAs either individually or through trading consortia could enter into contracts with maintained schools with delegated budgets under local management. As the court recognised, to decide otherwise would have meant that LEAs could enter into contracts with grant-maintained and independent schools (which were prescribed public bodies) but not the LEAs' own schools. It is submitted that this decision is of equal effect with regard to all maintained schools under the School Standards and Framework Act 1998.

Another issue which affected local authorities in the 1990s was the problem of some contracts being subsequently held by the courts to have been outside the local authority's powers. This particularly applied to a series of cases where local authorities had entered into contracts on the financial markets, which had gone very wrong, leaving the authorities facing huge debts. To avoid paying these debts, a number of authorities successfully argued that the original contracts had been outside their powers and unlawful. If the contracts were unlawful, they were void *ab initio* and therefore the other party to the contract could not recover the sums due to them.

Not unnaturally, this prompted considerable concern about the contractual reliability of local authorities. To meet these concerns, the Local Government (Contracts) Act 1997 was introduced. The Act makes clear that local authorities have power to enter into contracts with others for the provision, or making available, of assets, services or both (s. 1(1)). The Act also allows local authorities to enter into certain finance contracts, but to protect the other party from the local authority's subsequently reneging on the contract, a contract certification procedure is introduced (s. 2). Once certified, the contract has effect as if the local authority had power to enter into it and had exercised that power properly (s. 2(1)). Thus, in principle, provided a contractor has a certificate from the local authority, there should be no question of the authority's arguing at a later stage that the contract was unlawful and therefore void.

The contractual provisions set out above are of specific application to local authorities, including LEAs. Within this work, however, we could not hope to deal with the general principles of contract law and, therefore, on issues of the contractual liability of LEAs, reference should be made to the general works on the subject.

3.3.3 Torts

A tort is a civil wrong, the redress for which is usually in the form of legal action for damages or an order of the court, such as an injunction. Although the most common types of action are for breach of statutory duty and/or negligence, this area of the law embraces such matters as trespass to persons, goods and land, nuisance, defamation and misfeasance in public office.

Before turning our attention to actions for negligence and/or breach of statutory duty, we will first briefly consider the other types of tort and the potential for their commission by LEAs.

It is first necessary, however, to examine the difference between the direct liability of LEAs and their vicarious liability for the acts of their staff, a distinction which has been at times confusing, not least for the courts.

i. *Direct and vicarious liability*

In *X v Bedfordshire County Council*; *M (A Minor) v Newham LBC*; *E (A Minor) v Dorset County Council*; *Christmas v Hampshire County Council*; *Keating v Bromley LBC* [1995] 2 AC 633, [1995] ELR 404 (frequently cited or referred to as *X (Minors) v Bedfordshire County Council* or simply *X*), the House of Lords drew a distinction between the direct liability of a local authority and the liability which can be incurred vicariously for the acts of its employees in the context of claims for breach of statutory duties and/or negligence. Lord Browne-Wilkinson identified a number of areas where a local authority might owe direct duties of care to a claimant, either because the tort was committed through the action of the authority corporately (for example, as a result of a committee decision) or through the act of an officer which constituted a breach of a direct duty, an authority being able to act only through its servants in the majority of cases. These were, in his Lordship's view, to be distinguished from the separate, additional, usually professional duties, which an individual officer owed personally to a claimant and where the authority would not necessarily be directly liable, but where it would be vicariously liable. Indeed, in the education cases under consideration in *X*, the Lords held that vicarious liability, as opposed to direct liability, might arise in respect of the professional duties owed by educational psychologists and headteachers to pupils in their care.

In view of this 'definitive' analysis of the differences, it is perhaps no wonder that people are confused. The distinction is, however, not so important in respect of the first categories of torts discussed below. It is when we consider negligence and breaches of statutory duties that it takes on an added significance and we will therefore return to the issue when we look at those torts.

ii. *Trespass to persons*

Trespass to persons covers a range of torts including assault, battery and false imprisonment. These are not usually committed directly by an LEA, but an LEA may find itself vicariously liable for its staff's actions which constitute these torts.

Battery is the intentional and direct application of force to another person; assault is an act which causes another person to apprehend the infliction of battery upon him by that other person.

In the world of LEAs, these torts are of particular significance in the school setting where a number of claims have been made against teachers who have come into physical contact with their pupils for one reason or another. Corporal punishment, now outlawed, would clearly constitute battery, but what is often overlooked is that a mere touching can amount to the tort, a particular problem for staff in schools, especially where physical restraint may be required. To alleviate certain fears amongst school staff, s. 550A of the Education Act 1996 was introduced by the Education Act 1997. This section provides reassurance by making clear that any teacher who works at the school and any other person who, with the authority of the headteacher, has lawful control or charge of pupils at the school, may use reasonable force to prevent a pupil committing an offence, causing personal injury to himself or others or damage to property, or engaging in behaviour prejudicial to the maintenance of good order and discipline at the school or among any of its pupils. This power applies both to actions on the school premises and off site where the member of staff has lawful control or charge of the pupil. Guidance on the use of restraint by school staff can continue to be found in DfEE Circular 10/98 *The Use of Force to Control or Restrain Pupils.*

LEAs are unlikely, if at all, to incur direct liability for assault or battery, but they may do so through the acts of their staff. Previously, LEAs were not held liable for the acts of teachers who had been guilty of deliberate criminal misconduct, on the grounds that such acts were outside the scope of the employee's employment. (See, for example, *Trotman v North Yorkshire County Council* [1998] ELR 625, now overruled, in which an LEA was held not to be vicariously liable for a sexual assault by a deputy headteacher on a handicapped teenager in his charge whilst on a school trip abroad.) Since the House of Lords decision in *Lister v Hesley Hall Limited* ([2001] UKHL 22; [2001] 2 All ER 769), however, an LEA is likely to be held vicariously liable for the acts of teachers and other employees, even if they amount to criminal misconduct, where there is a sufficiently close connection between the misconduct and the employment involved. In *Lister*, a warden employed by the proprietor of an independent school for maladjusted and vulnerable children, sexually assaulted a number of children attending the school. He was subsequently convicted and the children sued the proprietor. The proprietor was held liable on the basis that there was a close connection between the guilty party's misconduct and the nature of his employment: the proprietor had undertaken to care for the children; and in doing so had employed the abuser and put him in the position where he could commit the abuse; the acts had been committed in the time when and on the premises where the abuser was employed to perform his duties. It follows, therefore, that if a similar situation were to occur in the maintained sector, the LEA (in the case of community or voluntary controlled schools) or governing bodies (in the case of voluntary aided and foundation schools) are also likely to be held liable so long as there is that close connection between the act and the nature of the employment. (See also chapter 6.E.9.8).

False imprisonment is another tort which would appear to be of little relevance to LEAs. However, claims have arisen in respect of the detention of pupils. In general terms, false imprisonment is the infliction of bodily restraint which is not expressly or impliedly authorised by law. In 1980, an attempt was made to claim false imprisonment in respect of a class detention, but in an unreported decision, the judge in the Blackpool County Court would have none of it and dismissed the claim on the grounds that the school had lawful authority to impose the punishment.

The position, though, became confused where parents refused to allow their children to take detentions. Could schools detain children against their parent's wishes? To avoid some of these problems, the Education Act 1997 tried to clarify the position by inserting a new section into the Education Act 1996 (s. 550B). This provides that where a pupil is required on disciplinary grounds to spend a period of time in detention at school after the end of the school day, his detention shall not be rendered unlawful by virtue of the absence of his parent's consent provided certain conditions are met (s. 550B(1)). These conditions are that the headteacher must have made generally known within the school and to all parents that detentions will be used; that the detention must be imposed by the headteacher or a teacher specifically authorised to do so; the detention must be reasonable in all the circumstances and the pupil's parent must have been given at least 24 hours' notice, in writing, of the detention (s. 550B(2)). If these conditions are met, the headteacher and, vicariously, the LEA, should have a defence to a claim for false imprisonment.

iii. *Trespass to land*

Trespass to land is the unjustified interference with the possession of land. This rarely affects LEAs, certainly not deliberately. On occasion, an LEA may accidentally trespass on the land of another, for example where there may be confusion over the boundary of a school. Usually, though, the trespass is committed against the LEA.

iv. *Trespass to goods and conversion*

Trespass to goods takes the form of a wrongful physical interference with a person's goods. Conversion is similar, but involves a dealing with the goods of a person so as to deny his rights in them, for example the wrongful taking of goods. Again, these are torts with which LEAs will rarely be sued, but they may arise, vicariously, in the school environment when a teacher confiscates an item from a pupil. The usual defence, though, is that if the confiscation is justified, either because the possession of the item is against school rules or is detrimental to discipline in the school, the interference or taking of the item will not be wrongful and hence not unlawful.

Having been taken into possession, though, the goods will be considered as having been bailed into the care of the teacher. If the goods are then negligently lost or damaged, the teacher and, vicariously, the LEA will be liable.

v. *Nuisance and* **Rylands v Fletcher** *liability*

To many neighbours, schools are always a nuisance. However, the general noise and inconvenience caused does not normally constitute a nuisance in law. For there to be a nuisance in private law, there must be an unlawful interference with a person's use or enjoyment of land, or some right over, or in connection with, it (*Read v Lyons & Co Ltd* [1945] KB 216). A school, provided that it has been established in accordance with the correct statutory procedure, should not therefore simply by being there constitute a nuisance as, even if it does interfere with a neighbour's enjoyment of their land, it will not be an unlawful interference. If, however, an unlawful activity is committed on the school site which does so interfere, liability may arise.

A tort associated with nuisance is strict liability under the rule in the case of *Rylands v Fletcher* (1865) 3 H & C 774. This applies where a person for his own purposes brings on his land and collects and keeps there anything likely to do mischief if it escapes. That person must keep it at his peril and, if he does not do so, is *prima facie* answerable for all the damage which is the natural consequence of its escape. The case itself concerned the collection of water in a reservoir, which burst and flooded a neighbour's mines, but it has been subsequently applied to the escape of fire, oil, gas and in one, possibly unreliable case, the discharge of a noxious person (*Attorney General v Scott* [1933] Ch 89). A number of statutes provide a defence to a claim, for example, where water companies are required to construct reservoirs, but no such defences are likely to assist LEAs. Thus, for example, if an oil tank on a school site were to leak and cause damage to adjoining property, the LEA may well be liable under this rule.

vi. *Defamation*

Defamation comprises the publication of a statement which reflects on a person's reputation and tends to lower him in the estimation of right-thinking members of society generally or tends to make them shun or avoid him. Libel is the written or broadcast form of the tort, slander the spoken form.

Although LEAs, as public bodies, cannot sue for defamation (*Derbyshire County Council v Times Newspapers Ltd* [1993] AC 534), they can be sued either as an organisation if they publish defamatory material or, vicariously, if one of their employees in the course of his employment does so.

Certain defences are available, however, and these include justification (i.e. what was said was true), fair comment on a matter of public interest or that the statement was privileged. In the case of LEAs, the privilege most frequently relied on is the qualified privilege which arises where a statement is made in council or committee meetings or is made in circumstances where the maker of the statement is under a legal, moral or social duty to communicate the information in the statement to the recipient. If the statement is made maliciously, the privilege will not apply; otherwise the defence should stand to protect the maker and, if an employee of an LEA, the LEA from liability (as a good example of where the defences will and will not apply, see *Lillie and Reed v Newcastle City Council and Barker, Jones, Saradjian and Wardell* [2003] EWHC 1600 (QB)). Thus, for example, if a teacher were to pass on their concerns about a child to the social services department, they would enjoy the second type of qualified privilege. If, however, that statement were made maliciously, because the teacher did not like the child's parent, then the privilege would disappear.

vii. *Misfeasance in public office*

This tort is committed by a local authority and/or by individual officers where they perform an *ultra vires* act maliciously. The person acting needs to know that he or his authority had no power to act in the way against which complaint is made and that he either intended to injure or probably knew that so acting would injure the complainant. In recognition of the seriousness of the tort, the Court of Appeal (*Three Rivers DC v Governor and Company of the Bank of England (No. 3)* [1998] All ER 558) held that deliberate and dishonest abuse of power is necessary in every case in which misfeasance is alleged.

Where the tort is alleged against a decision of a council or committee, as opposed to the act of an individual, it is necessary to show that a majority of the members voting in favour of the decision did so with the object of damaging the claimant's interests (Jones v Swansea CC [1990] 1 WLR 1453).

To the authors' knowledge, a claim of misfeasance in public office has been pursued against an LEA officer in only one case (*Jarvis v Hampshire County Council* [2000] ELR 36, [2000] EdCR 1) where it was alleged that an LEA officer had committed the tort when arranging for a child with special educational needs to be placed in a special school. The Court of Appeal struck out the allegation as misconceived on the grounds that the placement was made, first, not by the officer against whom the allegations were made, but by a multi-disciplinary panel and, second, because it was an abuse of the process of the court to make allegations of dishonesty which were inconsistent with all the known facts. Although an appeal was made in this case to the House of Lords, the Court of Appeal's conclusions on misfeasance were not challenged.

viii. *Breach of statutory duty and/or negligence*
The effect of this area of law on public authorities has troubled the courts over the last few years and a relatively high number of cases have been considered by the Court of Appeal and House of Lords. The liability of the police (*Hill v Chief Constable of West Yorkshire* [1989] AC 53), ambulance services (*Kent v Griffiths* [1998] EWCA Civ 1941), fire services (*Capital and Counties v Hampshire County Council* [1997] 2 All ER 865, (1997) 95 LGR 831), highway authorities (*Stovin v Wise (Norfolk County Council (Third Party)* [1996] AC 923) and social services (*X v Bedfordshire County Council* [1995] ELR 404) have all been subject to judicial scrutiny, but, unfortunately, not necessarily with consistent or unambiguous conclusions.

The same can be said of those cases which have addressed the alleged failings of schools and LEAs. Add to this a number of cases which have been decided as strike-out applications, i.e. without the courts having the benefit of seeing any evidence and the whole question of the liability of public authorities for breach of statutory duty and/or common law negligence can at times become difficult to fathom.

a. Breach of statutory duty

On the issue of breach of statutory duty, *X* ([1995] 2 AC 633, [1995] ELR 404 HL,) is the leading authority. As reference to this decision recurs throughout this section, it is worth examining the facts, such as there were, involved in this decision.

X was five cases in one, two involving claims against social service authorities and three against LEAs. The social services cases concerned allegations in *X v Bedfordshire* that social workers had failed to take action to protect children at risk of abuse and in *M v Newham LBC* that children were taken into care when they should not have been. The three education cases, *Christmas v Hampshire County Council*, *E v Dorset County Council* and *Keating v Bromley LBC*, involved claims respectively against a headteacher and advisory teacher for failing to spot and address a child's dyslexia, an educational psychologist on similar grounds and an LEA for placing a child in a special school and not mainstream education. In all five cases, the claims were based either on breaches of statutory duties by the various authorities and/or negligence on the part of the authorities and/or their staff (as to the latter, see below).

So far as breach of statutory duties was concerned, Lord Browne-Wilkinson, in the leading judgment, made clear that the circumstances in which such claims could be successfully pursued would be rare. 'The basic proposition,' he said ([1995] ELR 404 at p. 415) 'is that in the ordinary case a breach of statutory duty does not, by itself, give rise to any private law cause of action.' Thus if an LEA were to breach any of its various duties, although it might lead to challenge by way of judicial review, it would not normally lead to a claim for damages. Lord Browne-Wilkinson continued:

> 'However, a private law cause of action will arise if it can be shown, as a matter of construction of the statute, that the statutory duty was imposed for the protection of a limited class of the public and that Parliament intended to confer on members of that class a private right of action for breach of the duty... [I]t is significant that [we] were not referred to any case where it had been held that statutory provisions establishing a scheme of social welfare for the benefit of the public at large had been held to give rise to a private right of action for damages for breach of statutory duty. Although regulatory or welfare legislation affecting a particular area of activity does in fact provide protection to those individuals particularly affected by that activity, the legislation is not to be

12. ACCOUNTABILITY & CHALLENGE

treated as having been passed for the benefit of those individuals but for the benefit of society in general [...]The cases where a private right of action for breach of statutory duty have been held to arise are all cases in which the statutory duty has been very limited and specific as opposed to general administrative functions imposed on public bodies and involving the exercise of administrative discretions.'

On this basis, in the education cases, the House of Lords struck out a claim that the LEA in the *Bromley* case had been in breach of the relevant education legislation. The Lords held that a claim that an LEA had failed to provide sufficient school places (contrary to what is now s.14 of the 1996 Act) could not give rise to a private law claim for damages. Lord Browne-Wilkinson also held that, although the legislation relating to children with special educational needs protected individual children ([1995] ELR 404 at p. 454), Parliament did not intend to give those children a right of action for damages if the duties in the legislation were not met.

This position was confirmed in *Holtom v Barnet LBC* ([1999] ELR 255) where it was held that an alleged breach of the duties in respect of children with special educational needs in the 1996 Act could not give rise to a private right of action for damages. The position was reaffirmed by the House of Lords in Phelps ([2000] ELR 499, HL).

In *Phelps* the House of Lords considered that although the various duties under the education legislation were intended to benefit a particular group, for example children with particular educational needs, the legislation was essentially providing a general structure for LEAs in respect of all children who fell within the legislation's ambit. 'The general nature of the duties imposed on local authorities in the context of a national system of education and the remedies available by way of appeal and judicial review indicate that Parliament did not intend to create a statutory remedy by way of damages. Much of the [legislation] is concerned with conferring discretionary powers or administrative duties in an area of social welfare where normally damages have not been awarded when there has been a failure to perform a statutory duty' (Phelps [2000] ELR 499, HL *per* Lord Slynn at p. 515).

The occasions when an LEA will be sued for a direct breach of its statutory duties are therefore likely to be rare. To stand a chance of succeeding a claimant must be able to show that Parliament has imposed the statutory duty for the benefit of a limited class of the public and intended that breach of that duty should lead to a claimant's having a private right of action for damages. Given the circumstances considered in *X*, *Phelps* and *Holtom* it is suggested that few claims (if any) for breach of statutory duty will be successful against an LEA. Claims for negligence are, however, a different matter.

b. Common law negligence

In simple terms, negligence is the breach of a duty to take care which results in damage. For the tort to arise, the damage must result from a duty which the law will impose, there must have been a breach of that duty and damage or injury must result from that breach.

So far as establishing a duty of care is concerned, the law will not impose duties on all occasions. The circumstances where duties may arise were outlined by Lord Atkin in the landmark case of *Donoghue v Stevenson* ([1932] AC 562). 'You must take reasonable care to avoid acts or omissions which you can reasonably foresee would be likely to injure your neighbour. Who, then, in law is my neighbour? The answer seems to be persons who are so closely and directly affected by my act that I ought reasonably to have them in contemplation as being so affected when I am directing my mind to the acts and omissions which are called in question.'

Even if a duty of care can be established, a claimant then needs to show that there has been a breach of that duty. In most cases the test is whether there has been 'an omission to do something which a reasonable man, guided upon those considerations which ordinarily regulate the conduct of human affairs [in more modern language, in all the circumstances], would do, or doing something which a prudent and reasonable man would not do' (*Blyth v Birmingham Waterworks Co* (1856) 11 Ex 781).

This principle is slightly modified where the actions of professionals (for example, doctors, psychologists, solicitors and headteachers) are called into question. In these cases, the so-called *Bolam* test applies. Thus the standards to be applied in these circumstances are not those of the ordinary man, but the standards of reasonably competent fellow professionals at the time (*Bolam v Friern Hospital Management Committee* [1957] 1 WLR 582).

Assuming that a duty is owed and that there has been a breach of the duty, damage of a type recognised by law has to be thereby caused.

**12.
ACCOUNTABILITY
& CHALLENGE**

This therefore requires a claimant to show that the act or omission which constitutes a breach of duty caused the injury for which the claimant is seeking compensation and was not so remote that it could not have been a contributory factor.

The claimant must also show that physical damage resulted and, except in a very few cases, that economic loss was not the only consequence of the act or omission. This latter point causes some difficulties but is important in the context of the educational cases discussed below. An example was provided in *Murphy v Brentwood DC* [1991] AC 398, where it was alleged that the local authority had negligently approved defective building plans, causing a reduction in the value of the claimant's house. It was held that a duty of care could be owed in respect of personal injury or damage to property arising from a defect (i.e. physical damage), but no such duty was owed to those who acquired the house and suffered economic loss because of the effect of the defects on its value. Only if the local authority had accepted some additional responsibility, akin to that of an independent surveyor retained by a purchaser, would the local authority have been liable for any such economic loss. As it was, all it had done was carry out its statutory functions and no more and that could not give rise to any liability for the diminution in value.

Those, then, are the general principles applying in simple cases of negligence. Needless to say, negligence, so far as it affects local authorities and LEAs in particular, is not so simple. This is principally because a number of other factors come into play to recognise the discretionary nature of much decision-making and public policy issues concerning the imposition of liability on public bodies.

These factors contributed to the general analysis by Lord Browne-Wilkinson in *X* of the circumstances where liability for common law negligence might arise in respect of local authority functions. His Lordship (at p. 418) identified three categories of situation where a common law duty of care (i.e. the first requirement of negligence) might arise:

1. where a statutory duty gives rise to a common law duty of care owed to a claimant by a local authority to do or refrain from doing a particular act;

2. where, in the course of carrying out a statutory duty, a local authority has brought about such a relationship between itself and the claimant as to give rise to a duty of care at common law; or

3. where, whether or not the authority is itself under a duty of care to the claimant, its officers or employees in the course of performing the statutory functions of the authority were under a common law duty of care for a breach of which the authority would be vicariously liable.

Whether duties will actually arise in these circumstances will depend on a number of other factors.

a) Under categories (1) and (2) above, it is possible that common law duties of care may arise in the performance of statutory functions, but a distinction has to be made between, first, cases in which it is alleged that the authority owes a duty of care in the manner in which it exercises a statutory discretion (for example, a decision whether or not to exercise the discretion to close a school) and, secondly, cases in which a duty of care may arise from the manner in which the statutory duty has been implemented in practice (for example, the running of a school pursuant to statutory duties). In the first case, no common law duty of care should arise, but in the second case it will.

b) A local authority cannot be held liable for doing what Parliament authorised in legislation. To establish liability for negligence in the exercise of a discretion, it is necessary to show that the decision was outside the ambit of the discretion altogether; if it was not, a local authority cannot itself be directly in breach of any duty of care.

c) A common law duty of care in relation to the taking of decisions involving policy matters cannot exist, for Parliament will have conferred the discretion on the authority, not the courts. Nothing which falls within the ambit of the statutory discretion can be actionable. If the matter complained of falls outside the statutory discretion, it may give rise to liability. If, however, factors relevant to the exercise of the discretion include matters of policy, the court cannot adjudicate on such policy matters and therefore cannot reach the conclusion that the decision was outside the ambit of the statutory discretion.

**12.
ACCOUNTABILITY
& CHALLENGE**

d) If, however, the allegations concern negligence, not in the taking of a discretionary decision to do some act but in the practical manner in which that act has been performed, the question of whether or not a common law duty of care arises is determined by the general principles.

e) In circumstances where no direct duty of care arises, local authorities may be vicariously liable for the acts or omissions of their officers and employees. However, where there is no allegation of a separate professional duty of care being owed by an individual employee, the negligent acts of that employee are capable of constituting a breach of a duty of care (if any) owed directly by the authority to the claimant. This follows only from the fact that the authority can act only through its staff.

Although Lord Browne-Wilkinson's judgment was intended to be a definitive statement of the duties of care that may be imposed on public authorities, it is fair to say that it caused some confusion and a number of other cases have had to be considered by the higher courts in order to flesh out the basic principles, not all either successfully or consistently. For example, it is hard to see why a firefighter who decides not to attend a fire is immune from liability for his inaction, but a firefighter who risks his life trying to deal with a fire, but gets it wrong, can be held liable (*Capital & Counties v Hampshire County Council* [1997] 2 All ER 865, (1997) 95 LGR 831); or why an ambulanceman can be held liable both for not attending and for making a mistake whilst tending a patient (*Kent v Griffiths* [1998] EWCA Civ 1941).

Further discussion on this topic, though, is a matter for academics and works on the general liabilities of local authorities. It is, though, important to look at the, albeit confused, general principles in order to help understand specific educational issues and the effect this all has on the liability of LEAs.

Negligence cases involving LEAs can best be split into two categories: cases involving physical injury and cases where the allegation is of educational malpractice leading to an inadequate education or attainment (sometimes referred to as educational well-being or failure-to-educate cases).

b.i *Physical injury*
The first category is relatively straightforward. Such cases have been brought successfully against LEAs for years; they all arise from operational actions, so there is no need to worry about the ambit of statutory discretions and there is usually clearly ascertainable injury. If a chemistry teacher poisons a whole classroom by combining the wrong chemicals, reference to Lord Browne-Wilkinson's carefully reasoned judgment is somewhat redundant.

In these cases, the duty can best be expressed as a duty to take reasonable care for the health and safety of pupils (and, for that matter, other employees and visitors). In certain circumstances, the duty may extend to require the taking of positive steps to protect a pupil from physical harm (see *Hippolyte v Bromley LBC* [1995] PIQR 309).

The standard of care to which all staff must aspire in cases of physical harm (as opposed to educational malpractice cases, where the standard is different) is that of a careful and/or reasonable parent (*Williams v Eady* (1893) 10 TLR 41; *Rich v London County Council* [1953] 2 All ER 376 and *Martin v Middlesborough Corporation* (1965) 63 LGR 385). The standard should, though, take account of the fact that a teacher will, unlike the reasonable parent, usually be responsible for a whole class or a large playground (*Beaumont v Surrey County Council* (1968) 66 LGR 580 and *Lyes v Middlesex County Council* (1962) 61 LGR 443). The courts have also been disinclined to wrap children in cotton wool or require schools to be turned into secure fortresses (*Nwabudike v Southwark LBC* [1997] ELR 35).

Much press interest has recently been raised by claims for injury caused by bullying. One of the first of these attracted considerable press attention, when a claim against *Richmond LBC* was settled by insurers ('Bullying case may bring new claims', *TES*, 22 November 1996), but as it never came to court, it did not create a legal precedent. As it is part of a teacher's duty to take reasonable steps to protect pupils from injury (see *Beaumont v Surrey County Council* (1968) 66 LGR 580), there is no reason why bullying claims will not succeed if, for example, supervision has been negligent.

However, although schools are required to have anti-bullying policies, these claims should not fall into any special category, but should be considered in line with the general principles. Whether many such claims will succeed, however, is debatable, given the failure of the two 'bullying' cases which have been heard since the *Richmond* settlement. In *Bradford-Smart v West Sussex County Council* [2002] EWCA Civ 07, [2002] All ER(D) 167 (Jan), the LEA was not liable where the acts of bullying, although committed by fellow pupils of the victims, had taken place off the school premises and where the school had put in place adequate bullying and internal disciplinary policies and had responded appropriately when the bullying was brought to its attention. Two sister victims also failed to establish liability in *Faulkner and Faulkner v Enfield LBC and Lea Valley High School* [2003] ELR 426, QBD. The court accepted that a school and LEA owed a duty to take reasonable care to protect pupils from bullying and other mistreatment by other pupils and also, where parents were reasonably concerned about the continued safety of their children, had a duty to act reasonably by providing the parents with information that would enable them to make properly informed decisions about whether to continue sending their children to the school. However, on the facts, the school had responded appropriately to the incidents of bullying which had been reported. Further incidents had allegedly taken place, but in the absence of any complaint being made to the school about these, the school could not be held liable for them.

Despite attempts to claim the contrary, duties of care may extend beyond the school gate and beyond the school day. Obviously, duties of care arise during break and lunchtimes in respect of the adequacy of supervision for ensuring safety and similar duties will be owed when ensuring the safe arrival and departure of children. In *Barnes v Hampshire County Council* [1969] 3 All ER 746, it was held that a school which had released a class of five-year-olds five minutes before the end of the school day was negligent.

If a school or LEA arranges school transport, it will be under a duty to take reasonable care of the children during the journey, including entering and leaving vehicles. Organised school trips will also involve similar duties, but, given the potentially dangerous nature of some activities, greater supervision may be required as the potential for injury may be greater (as shown by, for example, the Land's End and Lyme Bay tragedies).

A number of the cases involving injury to pupils have been discussed in chapter 6.C.6 (on schools and school buildings and injuries to staff; for example, *Purvis v Buckinghamshire County Council* [1999] ELR 231 and *Moore v Kirklees MBC* 30 April 1999, unreported). The following, however, provide examples where the duties of care owed by teachers to protect pupils from harm, and vicariously by LEAs or governing bodies as appropriate, have been considered by the courts. Some are possibly unreliable and may be considered creatures of their time, reflecting as they do different attitudes to the protection of pupils than exist today.

12. ACCOUNTABILITY & CHALLENGE

Smith v Martin and Kingston-upon-Hull Corporation [1911] 2 KB 775. A teacher ordered a pupil to attend to an open fire in the staff common room. The pupil's clothes caught fire and she was injured. The teacher was liable, but so was the LEA as the order to attend to the fire was given in the course of the teacher's employment.

Chilvers v London County Council (1916) 80 JP 246. A pupil was allowed by a teacher to bring his toy soldiers to school. Another pupil fell on a soldier, with the result that her eye was pierced. The court found that there was no negligence and this was an accident which might happen in any nursery where children play with toys. The age of the case may suggest it is unreliable, but the sentiments expressed contain, it is suggested, a degree of common sense which is as applicable now as then.

Jones v London County Council (1932) 96 JP 371. A student participating in an organised game of riders and horses was injured. The game involved one boy riding on the back of another trying to cause another mounted fellow pupil to fall. At the time, the court held that it was a common game and no negligence was involved. It is doubted that a court would reach the same conclusion today.

Gibbs v Barking Corporation [1936] 3 All ER 115. A teacher failed to assist a pupil vaulting over a gym horse. The pupil was injured. The teacher was found not to have taken reasonable care and the LEA was therefore held liable.

Rawsthorne v Ottley [1937] 3 All ER 902. Pupils were left alone to play in a playground at a time when a lorry was delivering. The court held that the headteacher had not been negligent in failing to supervise or in allowing the lorry on to the site – again, a potentially dubious decision to rely on today.

Ricketts v Erith Borough Council [1943] 2 All ER 629. A child in a playground fired a toy arrow which injured the plaintiff child. A teacher did check the playground from time to time, but the supervision was not continuous. The court held that continuous supervision was not required and that in the circumstances the level of supervision was adequate.

Wright v Cheshire County Council [1952] 2 All ER 789 (another gym case). A pupil was assigned to catch a pupil using the vaulting horse, but that pupil wandered off whilst the other pupil was in mid-flight. The plaintiff fell and was injured. The teacher was supervising other pupils at the time. It was found that this was a generally approved practice and that the teacher had not been negligent in allowing a child to be a catcher.

12.
ACCOUNTABILITY
& CHALLENGE

Rich v London County Council [1953] 2 All ER 376 (another allegation of failing to supervise pupils in the playground). The court held that the level of supervision was adequate and a constant monitoring in the circumstances was not required.

Lewis v Carmarthenshire County Council [1955] AC 549. The House of Lords affirmed a decision of the Court of Appeal that a teacher had not been negligent after a pupil escaped from a classroom whilst the teacher was attending to an injured child. However, after the child had escaped, he was able to pass out of the school and on to a busy road, causing a lorry to crash, killing the driver. The LEA was held liable to the driver's widow as it had not taken reasonable precautions to prevent the pupil escaping into the road.

Clark v Monmouthshire County Council (1954) 52 LGR 246. Again, the court held that there was no obligation to ensure constant supervision in the playground. All that was required was reasonable supervision.

Crouch v Essex County Council (1966) 64 LGR 240. During a chemistry lesson, two pupils squirted some liquid into the eyes of another pupil, not knowing that it was double-strength caustic soda. The court held that in the circumstances (the pupils were 15) it was reasonable to allow the pupils to use caustic soda without direct supervision provided they had been given adequate warning and instruction. The standards of discipline imposed by the teacher were found to have been sufficient from the point of view of safety and he could not be held liable for the irresponsible acts of pupils in the circumstances.

Beaumont v Surrey County Council (1968) 66 LGR 580. A teacher put a three-metre length of elastic in a wastepaper bin. It was removed by some pupils and used in horseplay which resulted in a pupil being hit in the eye. It was held that it was a headteacher's duty, bearing in mind the known propensities of children, to take all reasonable and proper steps to prevent any of the pupils suffering injury from inanimate objects and the actions of other pupils. The placing of the elastic in the bin was unreasonable as it was foreseeable it would be taken and used by the pupils. Further, there were inadequate levels of supervision, which meant the horseplay had not been spotted and stopped before the accident occurred. The LEA was therefore liable.

Barnes v Hampshire County Council [1969] 3 All ER 746. A class was dismissed five minutes before the normal going home time. The plaintiff's parent was therefore not by the school gate as usual to meet her. The girl ran into a road and was knocked down. The LEA was held liable: releasing the children early was negligent.

Ward v Hertfordshire County Council [1970] 1 All ER 535. A child, who had arrived early at school, ran into a wall and injured his head. The LEA was held not to be liable as the wall was not inherently dangerous. As the accident occurred in the normal course of play, it was irrelevant that there was no supervision and it was anyway impossible to supervise children so that they never fell down and injured themselves.

Moore v Hampshire County Council (1981) 80 LGR 481. A disabled child, who was forbidden from doing PE, persuaded a new teacher that she could take part and tried to do a handstand. She fell and broke her ankle. The teacher was supervising other children at the time. The court held that the teacher had not met the standard of care required, as the girl's special condition required a greater level of supervision and that she should not have allowed her to take part in the first place without checking.

Affutu-Nartoy v Clarke (1984) *Times*, 9 February. A teacher took part in a game of rugby with 15 year-old pupils and tackled the plaintiff causing injury. The teacher was held liable.

Nwabudike v Southwark LBC [1997] ELR 35. A case brought by another child who had escaped from school and was subsequently injured. It was held that, although the standard of care was high, a school that had taken all proper and reasonable steps to ensure such safety was not in breach of its duty of care. On the evidence, it was found that there had been only one similar accident in six years, demonstrating that all proper and reasonable steps had been taken.

Jenny v North Lincolnshire Council [2000] ELR 245, CA. A pupil had left the school during a break without permission and without anyone noticing him. He was hit by a car approximately 1,000 metres from the school, on a major road and was seriously injured. The driver of the car was not at fault. The judge concluded and, on appeal the Court of Appeal agreed, that the school, being in charge of children at risk if unaccompanied in the trafficked world, was in breach of its duty to establish a system for ensuring, so far as was practicable, that all five school gates were kept closed and fastened during school hours and especially during breaks; that the school's system was somewhat haphazard and insufficiently stringent for a playground with so many exits and that the breach caused the accident.

Gough v Upshire Primary School [2002] ELR 169, QBD. A pupil was injured after sliding down a stair banister. The school had properly assessed the risks and had a good standard of discipline. The school was not negligent in failing to take steps against a possibility that, although foreseeable, was considered no more likely than many other risks which may befall children at school.

Waugh v Newham LBC [2002] EWHC 802, QBD. The LEA was held liable for injuries to a teacher, where, because it had failed to provide adequate prior information and instruction about a pupil who exhibited challenging and dangerous behaviour to a school escort, the child escaped from the escort and assaulted the teacher.

Chittock v Woodbridge School [2002] EWCA Civ 915, [2002] All ER (D) 207 (Jun), CA. An independent school was held not to be liable for an accident to a pupil on a skiing trip where the school staff had taken reasonable precautions.

Kearn-Price v Kent County Council [2002] EWCA Civ 1539, [2003] ELR 17. The duty of care owed to pupils included a duty to take reasonable steps to enforce a playground ban on full-sized leather footballs and to carry out regular spot checks to ensure that school rules imposed for health and safety reasons were being enforced.

Simonds v Isle of Wight Council, 23 September 2003, unreported. Contrary to school rules and his mother's instructions, a pupil used a swing that was out of bounds but had not been immobilised. He sustained injury. The court held that it would not be reasonable to impose a legal duty on the LEA to eliminate every potential hazard from a playing field.

b.ii *Educational malpractice or educational well-being cases*
The second category of cases, educational malpractice or educational well-being cases, is a much more recent phenomenon and, although the first one or two cases were seen as groundbreaking successes for campaigners for pupils' rights, subsequent cases appear to have emphasised the difficulties aggrieved pupils will have in successfully bringing such claims.

The catalyst for the development of these claims was the decision of the House of Lords in respect of the education cases in *X*. As has been seen, claims for physical injury had a long history, but, before *X*, no claim for a failure to educate or a failure to remedy an educational need had been brought in the courts.

In the *X* cases, it was alleged that LEAs, through their educational psychologists (*E v Dorset County Council*) or headteachers and advisory teachers (*Christmas v Hampshire County Council*) or education officers (*Keating v Bromley*) owed duties to detect the special educational needs of pupils, provide appropriate remedial tuition or support and ameliorate those needs. No actual physical injury was alleged. Instead, it was claimed that the children had suffered an educational detriment so that their future career prospects were affected. In addition, in the Dorset claim, the recovery of the costs of educating the pupil in a private school was attempted.

It must be remembered, however, that the appeals before the House of Lords were against applications to the lower courts to strike out claims. These were presented on the basis that, as a matter of law, none of the claims should succeed. As a consequence, no evidence had been given as to either the arrangements for educating pupils with special educational needs in the respective LEAs or on the specific details of what had happened to these particular pupils. The decision of the Lords therefore needs to be read in light of the fact that, because there was no evidence, they had to make certain assumptions about the work of the education professionals involved. In particular, Lord Browne-Wilkinson probably did misunderstand the role of the educational psychology service, an error which he subsequently corrected in *Barrett v Enfield LBC* [1999] 3 WLR 79.

Nonetheless, the Lords held the following.

a)   A headteacher, being responsible for a school, is under a duty of care to exercise the reasonable skills of a headteacher in relation to a pupil's educational needs. If it comes to the attention of a headteacher or teacher that a pupil is underperforming, he owes a duty to take such steps as a reasonable teacher would consider appropriate to try to deal with such underperformance. If a headteacher gives advice to parents, he should exercise the skills and care of a reasonable headteacher in giving such advice. To hold that, in such circumstances, the headteacher could properly ignore the matter and make no attempt to deal with it would fly in the face, not only of society's expectations of what a school will provide, but also of the fine traditions of the teaching profession itself (per Lord Browne-Wilkinson at p. 451).

b)   An advisory teacher brought in to advise on the educational needs of a specific pupil, if he knows his advice will be communicated to the pupil's parents, owes a duty to the pupil to exercise the skill and care of a reasonable advisory teacher.

c)   Where educational psychologists carry out an assessment of an individual pupil as part of the statutory process, even though their advice is directed to the LEA, they could owe a duty of care to use reasonable professional skill and care in the assessment and determination of the pupil's educational needs. This view was, however, at the time based on Lord Browne-Wilkinson's mistaken belief that an educational psychology service was offering a service to the public, in the same way as medical psychologists in the NHS. Nonetheless, though for different reasons, the House of Lords in *Phelps* confirmed that educational psychologists should and did owe a duty of care to those children they assess (see below).

d) Actions for common law negligence should not, however, be brought where the imposition of a common law duty of care might cause a conflict with the LEA's statutory responsibilities.

e) Damages might, in principle, be recoverable for educational detriment, but that was a matter for the trial judge when in possession of all the facts.

f) LEAs would be vicariously liable for the breaches of duty committed by their teaching, advisory and educational psychology staff.

Although the Lords' decision seemed to quash any notion of damages being recovered from LEAs for breach of statutory duty and emphasised that any claim would be difficult to pursue successfully, the decision was seen as a green light for a number of claims against LEAs for the negligence of their staff.

This view was diminished, albeit briefly, by the decision of Kennedy J in *Christmas v Hampshire County Council* [1998] ELR 1, the first of the education cases considered in *X* to come to trial. Having heard the evidence, the judge concluded that neither the headteacher nor the advisory teacher had been negligent and therefore dismissed the claim.

Next day, however, Garland J gave judgment at first instance in *Phelps v Hillingdon LBC* [1998] ELR 38 and found the LEA to be liable for what he considered were the negligent acts of the LEA's educational psychologist. The judge found that the educational psychologist owed a duty of care to a pupil and should have known that her findings in respect of the pupil would have been acted upon by the pupil's parents. There had been, in the judge's view, a failure to diagnose the claimant's dyslexia and a failure by the educational psychologist to review her opinion after she was aware that the claimant had failed to make progress. This amounted to negligence. Further, in failing to mitigate the adverse consequences of dyslexia, a congenital defect, the claimant had been injured, for which she

12.
ACCOUNTABILITY
& CHALLENGE

should be compensated with damages. The LEA was therefore held liable for the educational psychologist's negligence and was ordered to pay £46,000 damages.

That decision was overturned by the Court of Appeal (see [1998] ELR 587), but was reinstated by the House of Lords (see *Phelps v London Borough of Hillingdon*; *Anderton v Clwyd County Council*; *G v London Borough of Bromley*; *Jarvis v Hampshire County Council* (referred to as *Phelps*) [2000] ELR 499).

Of the other three cases heard with *Phelps*, only the decision of the Court of Appeal in *Gower v Bromley LBC* ([1999] ELR 356) had gone against the LEA. However, in light of the House of Lords' decision and their endorsement of the propositions set out by the court in that case, it is worth considering that case before focusing on the judgment of their Lordships.

In *Gower*, allegations of negligence were made against teachers at a maintained special school who were accused of being professionally incompetent and failing to provide a pupil with the computer teaching or aids necessary to enable him to communicate adequately in order to learn or socialise with his fellow pupils. The Court of Appeal declined to strike out the claim and set out the following propositions applicable to claims against teaching staff in schools.

Headteachers and teachers have a duty to take such care of pupils in their charge as a careful parent would have in like circumstances, including a duty to take positive steps to protect their well-being.

Headteachers and teachers have a duty to exercise the reasonable skills of their calling in teaching and otherwise responding to the educational needs of their pupils. Those responsible for teachers who break that duty may be vicariously liable for it.

The justiciability of such a claim for vicarious responsibility is the same whether or not headteachers and teachers are operating under a statutory scheme, such as that for children with special educational needs and whether or not the school is in the public or private sector.

The duty is to exercise the skill and care of a reasonable headteacher and/or teacher, i.e. whether the teaching and other provision for a pupil's educational needs accords with that which might have been acceptable at the time by reasonable members of the teaching profession.

It is plainly reasonably foreseeable by a headteacher and his staff that if they do not properly teach or otherwise provide for a pupil's educational needs he may suffer educationally and possibly psychologically.

In normal circumstances of the headteacher and teacher/pupil relationship, there should be little difficulty in establishing proximity where, as in *Gower*, it is alleged that the teaching staff held themselves out as specialists in the teaching of pupils with special educational needs.

The principles set out by the Court of Appeal in *Phelps* had been, however, preferred by the Court of Appeal in the next case to be considered (*Jarvis v Hampshire County Council* [2000] ELR 36; [2000] EdCR 1), albeit that that case involved educational psychologists and education officers as opposed to teachers. This was another application to strike out a claim. In addition to alleging misfeasance in public office, compensation had been sought in respect of the LEA's alleged failure to provide the claimant with the education it should have done. The claimant accordingly sought to recover the cost of remedial tuition and the loss of prospective future earnings. Relying on *Phelps*, the LEA applied for the claim to be struck out as disclosing no cause of action.

In summary, the claim in *Jarvis* was that, during the course of assessment and statementing under the Education Acts, an LEA educational psychologist had negligently offered advice to the LEA as to the appropriate placement for the claimant and that the LEA's officers had been negligent in arranging the claimant's placement at a school which it was alleged was inappropriate to meet his needs. The Court of Appeal found that none of the allegations of negligence made against the educational psychologist and LEA officers was capable of giving rise to a duty of care. Nor could any of them be liable to the claimant so as to give rise to any vicarious liability on the part of the LEA.

Appeals were lodged in respect of all these cases and the linked case of *Anderton v Clwyd County Council* ([1999] ELR 1) and all four appeals were heard together by the House of Lords. Their Lordships overturned the decisions of the Court of Appeal in *Phelps*, *Anderton* and *Jarvis* and upheld the decision in *Gower* ([2000] ELR 499) and held that the various educational professionals could owe common law duties of care towards children for whom they were responsible and that their employers (LEAs or schools) could be vicariously liable for those breaches of duty.

The Lords could find no reason for finding some form of immunity as these were not cases where the LEA had had to weigh competing interests or which related to considerations which Parliament could not have intended to be justiciable. The question therefore was whether the damage alleged to have occurred was foreseeable and proximate and it was reasonable to recognise a duty of care. The Lords did not accept that a duty was prevented from arising simply because the advice was given only because an LEA, through its officers, had a statutory power to do so. Adopting the judgment of Lord Browne-Wilkinson in *X*, the Lords felt that only where the imposition of a common law duty would be inconsistent with the exercise of a statutory duty or power should the courts be wary of creating such a duty.

In the Court of Appeal, it had been suggested that to establish liability there had to be some 'acceptance of responsibility' on the part of the educational professional, the court treating the damage as being in the nature of economic loss and therefore applied the principles required to found such a claim. The House of Lords, however, rejected that argument and considered that the damage in issue could amount to personal injury: psychological damage and a failure to diagnose a congenital condition and to take appropriate action as a result of which a child's level of achievement is reduced (which leads to a loss of employment and wages) were capable of being personal injuries to a person ([2000] ELR 499, HL per Lord Slynn at p. 529).

That being the case, the acceptance of responsibility was no longer a determinative factor. Instead, Lord Slynn, with whom the other Lords agreed, held ([2000] ELR 499 at p. 516) that it was elementary that persons exercising a particular skill or profession may owe a duty of care in its performance to people who it can be foreseen will be injured if due skill and care are not exercised. This would include doctors, accountants or engineers. It would also include an educational psychologist or psychiatrist or a teacher (including a teacher in a specialised area, such as a teacher concerned with children having special educational needs). Lord Slynn agreed (at p. 517) with Lord Browne-Wilkinson (*X* [1995] ELR 404 at p. 451) that a headteacher or teacher owed duties of care to specific pupils. There was no reason why similar duties on specific facts should not arise for others engaged in the educational process, for example, an educational psychologist. The fact that the psychologist owed a duty to their employer to exercise skill and care should not oust any duty to the child.

In an attempt to offset criticism that the decision would 'open the flood gates', Lord Slynn (at p. 517) pointed out that this was only the start of the enquiry. 'It must still be shown that the educational psychologist is acting in relation to a particular child in a situation where the law recognises a duty of care. A casual remark, an isolated act may occur in a situation where there is no sufficient nexus between the two persons for a duty of care to exist. But where an educational psychologist is specifically called in to advise in relation to the assessment and future provision for a specific child and it is clear that the parents, acting for the child and the teachers will follow that advice, *prima facie* a duty of care arises.'

Applying these principles to the *Phelps* case, the Lords reinstated the decision of Garland J and the award of damages to the claimant. In the other cases, they decided that the claims should not be struck out and that full argument should occur.

As a consequence, in *Phelps* the Lords clarified the law after *X* and made clear that teachers, headteachers and all other educational professionals involved with school children, especially those having special educational needs, may owe duties of care which, if broken, may enable a claim to be made for compensation. The logic of the decision and the need for equivalence between professionals cannot be doubted, but the potential effect, especially when applied to all pupils as it must be, could be a cause of concern. However, given the strict criteria which have to be met and which have been highlighted in both *X* and *Phelps*, the flood gates are unlikely to open too wide.

Indeed, claims post-*Phelps* have not been extensive or numerous. Most have involved questions of limitation, with claims being brought long after the child finished education. For example, in *Robinson v St Helens MBC* ([2002] EWHC Civ 1099), a claim that a school failed to provide appropriate teaching to a dyslexic pupil failed because on the facts the pupil's condition was not found to be a personal injury as categorised in *Phelps* and the claim had been lodged outside the relevant time limit. Similarly, in *Meherali v Hampshire County Council* ([2002] EWHC 2655 (QB), [2003] ELR 338), a claim was held to be statute-barred and the judge declined to extend the time limit, especially as he thought the claimant had no real prospect of succeeding in her claim. In *Rowe v Kingston upon Hull City Council* (26 March 2003, unreported, QBD) the court at first instance allowed a claim to proceed although it was issued out of time, although that decision was recently overturned by the Court of Appeal (*Rowe v Kingston upon Hull City Council and Essex County Council* [2003] EWCA Civ 1281, [2003] ELR 771). In contrast, however, in *Adams v Bracknell Forest BC* ([2003] EWCA Civ 706, [2003] ELR 409), the court held that a similar claim had been made in time. All these cases do, though, depend on their individual circumstances and the actions taken to issue proceedings.

With two exceptions, the substantive post-*Phelps* cases, i.e. those where courts have considered if LEAs have been negligent on the evidence, have found in favour of the authority and its staff. In *H v Isle of Wight Council* [2001] All ER(D) 315 (Feb) QBD, Wright J considered the claimant's claim and the witnesses in her support to be unconvincing and dismissed proceedings against the LEA. In *Liennard v Slough BC* ([2002] EWHC 398 QBD), the pupil also failed. The pupil in this case had an unusual condition which meant it was not obvious that he had a difficulty which required a response. He performed well in many subjects and did not appear to have a learning difficulty requiring special provision. Consequently, applying the standards expected of teachers at the relevant time, the court considered that the staff involved had been reasonably competent and were therefore not negligent. Similarly, in *Button v Norfolk County Council* (11 April 2003, unreported, QBD), a claim against an educational psychologist failed as his conduct was held not to have fallen below the relevant professional standard. Finally, in *Keating v Bromley LBC* ([2003] EWHC 1070 (QB)), one of the original cases involved in the *X* decision and which took eight years to come to trial, the claim was dismissed. This case clearly involved difficulties between the pupil's parents, the various schools he attended or did not attend and the LEA which, the court appears to have considered, had more detrimental impact on the pupil's education than anything either the schools or the LEA had done. Consequently, nothing having a detrimental effect on the pupil's education could be attributable to the LEA or its staff, who were accordingly not negligent.

In contrast, the two successful cases, which have not been extensively reported, were first *Johnson v Stockport MBC* (February 2002, unreported, Stockport County Court). Limited details of the claim are available, but the Court found that the LEA had not spotted the claimant's dyslexia between 1983 and 1988. The dyslexia was found to have been undiagnosed until he was 11 and, on the basis that his condition was permanent and he could not be employed in any job which required him to work with or produce documents, he was awarded £52,500 in compensation.

The second case is *DN (by his litigation friend WN) v Greenwich LBC* [2003] All ER(D) 401(Dec) QBD. At the time of writing the case had not been fully reported, but it concerned a claim that the

LEA's educational psychologist had failed, when assessing the claimant (who had Asperger's Syndrome), to identify his complex communication and social needs and that the LEA failed to place him in a suitable school. Having heard and accepted expert evidence on behalf of the claimant, the judge found that the educational psychologist's assessment fell below the standard of a competent member of the profession and that the school did not provide for his needs, a fact the psychologist should have identified. As a result, the judge held that the claimant had lost the opportunity to improve his social skills, of learning how to cope with autism and of gaining educational qualifications..

The cases post-*Phelps* show that, after the House of Lords has established the general principles for these cases, actual trials depend very much on the individual circumstances of the case, the professionals involved and the professional standards expected at the relevant time. Each case is therefore of limited precedent value. Perhaps the object lesson of all the litigation is that, rather than adopt 'defensive education' as was suggested might occur during argument in the Lords, as long as proper procedures are followed and the guidance in the relevant codes of practice adhered to, there should be few failures that may give rise to litigation.

12.
ACCOUNTABILITY
& CHALLENGE

BIBLIOGRAPHY

References for Chapters 1 and 3–12

ALEXANDER, A. (1985). 'Structure, centralization and the position of local government.' In: LOUGHLIN, M., GELFAND, M.D. and YOUNG, K. (Eds) *Half a Century of Municipal Decline 1935–1985*. London: Allen & Unwin.

ARDEN, A., MANNING, J. and COLLINS, S. (1999). *Local Government Constitutional and Administrative Law*. London: Sweet & Maxwell.

ARNOLD, M. (1908). *Reports on Elementary Schools 1852–1882*. London: HMSO.

ASSOCIATION OF PRINCIPAL YOUTH AND COMMUNITY OFFICERS, CONNEXIONS, DEPARTMENT FOR EDUCATION AND SKILLS, LOCAL GOVERNMENT ASSOCIATION and NATIONAL YOUTH AGENCY (2002). *Working Together: Connexions and the Statutory Youth Service*. London: DfES.

AUDIT COMMISSION (1989). *Losing an Empire, Finding a Role: the LEA of the Future* (Audit Commission Occasional Papers No. 10). London: Audit Commission.

AUDIT COMMISSION (1998). *Changing Partners: a Discussion Paper on the Role of the Local Education Authority* (Audit Commission Occasional Papers No. 9). London: Audit Commission.

AUDIT COMMISSION (1999). *Held in Trust: the LEA of the Future. National Report*. London: Audit Commission.

AUDIT COMMISSION (2002). *Special Educational Needs: a Mainstream Issue*. London: Audit Commission.

AUDITING PRACTICES BOARD (1990). *Guidance for Internal Auditors*. London: Institute of Chartered Accountants of England and Wales.

BANNOCK CONSULTING (2003). *Evaluation of New Ways of Working in LEAs* [online]. Available: http://www.indepen.co.uk/panda/docs/DfES_Report_May_2003-Vol_III.pdf [24 March, 2004].

BARRELL, G.R. (1970). *Legal Cases for Teachers*. London: Methuen.

BEATTIE, D.J. and TAYLOR, P.S. (1944). *The New Law of Education*. London: Butterworth & Co.

BIBLIOGRAPHY
WEBSITES

BILLINGTON, S. (2000). 'Education Action Zones: a progress report', *Education Law Journal*, **1**, 1, 9–12.

BIRKINSHAW, P. (2001). *Government and Information: the Law Relating to Access, Disclosure and Their Regulation*. London: Butterworth & Co.

BOARD OF EDUCATION (1943). *Educational Reconstruction* (Cmd. 6458). London: HMSO.

CHARTERED INSTITUTE OF PUBLIC FINANCE AND ACCOUNTANCY (1995). *Application of the Auditing Practices Board's Guideline 'Guidance for Internal Auditors'*. London: CIPFA

CHILDREN & YOUNG PEOPLE'S UNIT (2003a). *IRT: Guidance on Information Sharing and Information Sharing Protocols* [online]. Available: http://www.cypu.gov.uk/corporate/docs/Legal%20Guidance%20v[1].8.12-01.pdf [24 March, 2004].

CHILDREN & YOUNG PEOPLE'S UNIT (2003b). *IRT: Information Sharing to Improve Services for Children – Guidance* [online]. Available: http://www.cypu.gov.uk/corporate/docs/IRTGuidance%20v%208%2005-02%20doc.pdf [24 Marcy, 2004].

CHILDREN & YOUNG PEOPLE'S UNIT (2003c). *IRT: Information Sharing to Improve Services for Children – Technical Issues Report* [online]: Available: http://www.cypu.gov.uk/corporate/docs/Technical%20Issues%20Report%20v8[1].12-01.pdf [24 March, 2004].

CLARK, T. (2003). *Public Service Agreements at the Local Level* (EMIE Report No.70). Slough: NFER, EMIE.

COMMISSION FOR LOCAL ADMINISTRATION IN ENGLAND (2001). *Annual Report 2000/2001*. London: Commissioner for Local Administration.

COMMISSION FOR LOCAL ADMINISTRATION IN ENGLAND (2002). *Digest of Cases 2001*. [online]. Available: http://www.lgo.org.uk/digest.htm [26 March, 2004].

COMMISSION FOR LOCAL ADMINISTRATION IN ENGLAND (2003a). *Annual Report 2002/03*. [online]. Available: http://www.lgo.org.uk/pdf/LGOreport2003.pdf [26 March, 2004].

COMMISSION FOR LOCAL ADMINISTRATION IN ENGLAND (2003b). *Digest of Cases 2002/3*. [online]. Available: http://www.lgo.org.uk/digest.htm [26 March, 2004].

COMMISSION FOR LOCAL ADMINISTRATION IN ENGLAND (2004). *Special Report: School Admissions and Appeals. Advice and Guidance from The Local Government Ombudsmen*. London: Commission for Local Administration England.

COUNCIL ON TRIBUNALS (2003). *School Admission and Exclusion Appeal Panels. Special Report* (Cm. 5788) [online]. Available: http://www.council-on-tribunals.gov.uk/files/eap.pdf [29 March, 2004].

DE SMITH, S.A. and BRAZIER, R. (1989). *Constitutional and Administrative Law*. Sixth edn. Harmondsworth: Penguin.

DENT, H.C. (1944). *Education in Transition: a Sociological Study of the Impact of War on English Education, 1939–1943* (International Library of Sociology and Social Reconstruction). London: Kegan Paul, Trench, Trubner & Co.

DEPARTMENT FOR CONSTITUTIONAL AFFAIRS (2002a). *Lord Chancellor's Code of Practice on the Management of Records Issued Under Section 46 of the Freedom of Information Act 2000* [online]. Available: http://www.dca.gov.uk/foi/codemanrec.htm [24 March, 2004].

DEPARTMENT FOR CONSTITUTIONAL AFFAIRS (2002b). *Privacy and Data-Sharing: the Way Forward for Public Services* [online]. Available: http://www.dca.gov.uk/foi/sharing/ [24 March, 2004].

DEPARTMENT FOR EDUCATION (1992). *Choice and Diversity: a New Framework for Schools* (Cm. 2021). London: HMSO.

DEPARTMENT FOR EDUCATION AND EMPLOYMENT (1996a). *Nursery Education Scheme: the Next Steps.* London: DfEE.

DEPARTMENT FOR EDUCATION AND EMPLOYMENT (1996b). *Self-government for Schools* (Cm. 3315). London: The Stationery Office

DEPARTMENT FOR EDUCATION AND EMPLOYMENT (1997). *Excellence for All Children: Meeting Special Educational Needs* (Cm. 3785). London: The Stationery Office.

DEPARTMENT FOR EDUCATION AND EMPLOYMENT (1997a). *Excellence in Schools* (Cm. 3681). London: The Stationery Office.

DEPARTMENT FOR EDUCATION AND EMPLOYMENT (1998). *The Learning Age: a Renaissance for a New Britain* (Cm. 3790). London: The Stationery Office.

DEPARTMENT FOR EDUCATION AND EMPLOYMENT (1998a). *Fair Funding: Improving Delegation to Schools May 1998* (Consultation Paper). London: DfEE.

DEPARTMENT FOR EDUCATION AND EMPLOYMENT (1998b). *Meeting the Childcare Challenge: a Framework and Consultation Document* (Cm. 3959). London: The Stationery Office.

DEPARTMENT FOR EDUCATION AND EMPLOYMENT (1999). *From Exclusion to Inclusion: a Report of the Disability Rights Task Force on Civil Rights for Disabled People*. London: DfEE.

505

DEPARTMENT FOR EDUCATION AND EMPLOYMENT (1999a) *Learning to Succeed: a New Framework for Post-16 Learning* (Cm. 4392). London: The Stationery Office.

DEPARTMENT FOR EDUCATION AND EMPLOYMENT (1999b). *Learning to Succeed: the Learning and Skills Council Prospectus.* London: DfEE.

DEPARTMENT FOR EDUCATION AND EMPLOYMENT (1999c). *Social Inclusion: the LEA Role in Pupil Support. Supplementary Guidance for Local Education Authorities* (Circular 10/99). London: DfEE.

DEPARTMENT FOR EDUCATION AND EMPLOYMENT (1999d). *Work Experience: Legal Responsibility and Health and Safety.* London: DfEE.

DEPARTMENT FOR EDUCATION AND EMPLOYMENT (2000). *Asset Management Plans* (DfEE/095/2000). London: DfEE.

DEPARTMENT FOR EDUCATION AND EMPLOYMENT (2000a). *Connexions: the Best Start in Life for Every Young Person.* London: DfEE.

DEPARTMENT FOR EDUCATION AND EMPLOYMENT (2000b). *Education of Children and Young People in Public Care: Guidance.* London: DfEE.

DEPARTMENT FOR EDUCATION AND EMPLOYMENT (2000c). *The Connexions Service: Prospectus and Specification.* London: DfEE.

DEPARTMENT FOR EDUCATION AND EMPLOYMENT (2000d). *The Role of the Local Education Authority in School Education.* London: DfEE.

DEPARTMENT FOR EDUCATION AND EMPLOYMENT (2000e). *SEN and Disability Rights in Education Bill: Consultation* [online]. Available: http://www.disability.gov.uk/archive/senbc/ [24 March, 2004].

DEPARTMENT FOR EDUCATION AND EMPLOYMENT (2001). *Transforming Youth Work: Developing Youth Work for Young People.* London: DfEE.

DEPARTMENT FOR EDUCATION AND SCIENCE (1984). *Parental Influence in School: a New Framework for School Government in England and Wales* (Cmnd. 9242). London: HMSO.

DEPARTMENT FOR EDUCATION AND SCIENCE. REVIEW GROUP ON THE YOUTH SERVICE IN ENGLAND (1982). *Experience and Participation* (Cmnd. 8686). London: HMSO.

DEPARTMENT FOR EDUCATION AND SKILLS (2001a). *Assessing the Net Capacity of Schools.* London: DfES.

BIBLIOGRAPHY WEBSITES

DEPARTMENT FOR EDUCATION AND SKILLS (2001b). *Consultation on School Admissions*. London: DfES.

DEPARTMENT FOR EDUCATION AND SKILLS (2001c). *Health and Safety: Responsibilities and Powers* [online]. Available: http://schoolsportal.suffolkcc.gov.uk/hands/Responsibilites_Powers _DfES_0803_2001.pdf [29 March, 2004].

DEPARTMENT FOR EDUCATION AND SKILLS (2001d) *Schools Achieving Success* (Cm. 5230). London: The Stationery Office.

DEPARTMENT FOR EDUCATION AND SKILLS (2001e). *SEN Toolkit*. London: DfES.

DEPARTMENT FOR EDUCATION AND SKILLS (2002a). *Accessible Schools: Planning to Increase Access to Schools for Disabled Pupils*. London: DfES.

DEPARTMENT FOR EDUCATION AND SKILLS (2002b). *Accessible Schools: Summary Guidance* [online]. Available: http://www.teachernet.gov.uk/_doc/2215/Accessible_Schools.pdf [29 March, 2004].

DEPARTMENT FOR EDUCATION AND SKILLS (2002c). *Delivering Results: Education and Skills. A Strategy to 2006*. London: DfES.

DEPARTMENT FOR EDUCATION AND SKILLS (2002d). *Guidance on School Uniforms* [online]. Available: http://www.teachernet.gov.uk/management/atoz/index.cfm?component=topic&id=84 [29 March, 2004].

DEPARTMENT FOR EDUCATION AND SKILLS (2002e). *School and LEA Funding in 2002-04: Guidance Letter No. 2*. London: DfES.

DEPARTMENT FOR EDUCATION AND SKILLS (2002f). *School Staffing (England) Regulations 2003 No.1963 and Staffing Guidance under Sections 35(8) and 36(8) of the Education Act 2002* [online]. Available: http://www.governornet.co.uk/linkAttachments/ACF3B38.doc [29 March, 2004].

DEPARTMENT FOR EDUCATION AND SKILLS (2002g). *Transforming Youth Work: Planning for the Local Authority Youth Service. 2003–04 Guidance*. London: DfES.

DEPARTMENT FOR EDUCATION AND SKILLS (2002h). *Transforming Youth Work: Resourcing Excellent Youth Services*. London: DfES.

DEPARTMENT FOR EDUCATION AND SKILLS (2002i). *Work Experience: a Guide for Employers*. London: DfES.

DEPARTMENT FOR EDUCATION AND SKILLS (2002j). *Work Experience: a Guide for Secondary Schools*. London: DfES.

DEPARTMENT FOR EDUCATION AND SKILLS (2002k). *Working Together: Giving Young People a Say (The Participation Guidance)* [online]. Available: http://www.transformingschools.org.uk/POOLED/ARTICLES/BF_N EWSART/VIEW.ASP?Q=BF_NEWSART_68943 [29 March, 2004].

DEPARTMENT FOR EDUCATION AND SKILLS (2003) *14-19: Opportunity and Excellence* (DfES/0744/2002). London: DfES.

DEPARTMENT FOR EDUCATION AND SKILLS (2003a). *A Consultation Document on Changes to Plans Required of Local Education Authorities: Amending the School Standards and Framework Act 1998 and the Education Act 1996*. London: DfES.

DEPARTMENT FOR EDUCATION AND SKILLS (2003b). *Building Schools for the Future: Consultation on a New Approach to Capital Investment*. London: DfES.

DEPARTMENT FOR EDUCATION AND SKILLS (2003c). *Consultation on the Draft Education (Maintained Special Schools) (Amendment) (England)*. Regulations (DfES/0531/2003). London: DfES.

DEPARTMENT FOR EDUCATION AND SKILLS (2003d). *Consultation on the Education–Related Provisions Included in the Anti-Social Behaviour Bill* (DfES/0710/2003). London: DfES.

DEPARTMENT FOR EDUCATION AND SKILLS (2003e). *Departmental Report 2003* (Cm. 5902). London: The Stationery Office.

DEPARTMENT FOR EDUCATION AND SKILLS (2003f). *Ensuring Regular School Attendance. Guidance on the Legal Methods Available to Secure Regular School Attendance*. London: DfES.

DEPARTMENT FOR EDUCATION AND SKILLS (2003g). *Funding for LEAs to Support Schools in Workforce Remodelling – Standards Fund Grant 508c* (Letter to CEOs, LEA/0140/2003, 9 April). London: DfES.

DEPARTMENT FOR EDUCATION AND SKILLS (2003h). *Improving Behaviour and Attendance: Guidance on Exclusion from Schools and Pupil Referral Units* [online]. Available: http://www.teachernet.gov.uk/wholeschool/behaviour/exclusion/guidance [30 March, 2004].

DEPARTMENT FOR EDUCATION AND SKILLS (2003i). *Raising Standards and Tackling Workload: a National Agreement. Time for Standards*. London: DfES.

DEPARTMENT FOR EDUCATION AND SKILLS (2003j). *School Teachers' Pay and Conditions Document 2003 and Guidance on School Teachers' Pay and Conditions*. London: The Stationery Office.

BIBLIOGRAPHY WEBSITES

DEPARTMENT FOR EDUCATION AND SKILLS (2003k). *Special Grant Report* (No. 122). London: DfES.

DEPARTMENT FOR EDUCATION AND SKILLS (2003l). *Sure Start Guidance 2004-2006: Overview and Local Delivery Arrangements*. London: DfES.

DEPARTMENT FOR EDUCATION AND SKILLS (2003m). *Travelling to School: a Good Practice Guide* [online]. Available: http://www.dft.gov.uk/stellent/groups/dft_susttravel/documents/pag e/dft_susttravel_023992.pdf [29 March, 2004].

DEPARTMENT FOR EDUCATION AND SKILLS (2003n). *Travelling to School: a Good Practice Guide*. London: DfES.

DEPARTMENT FOR EDUCATION AND SKILLS (2003o). *Twigg Encourages Parents, Local Community and Other Interested Parties to Set Up New Secondary School* (Press Notice 2003/0224) [online]. Available: http://mirror.eschina.bnu.edu.cn/Mirror1/dfee/www.dfes.gov.uk/pns /DisplayPN4cd6.html?pn_id=2003_0224 [24 March, 2004].

DEPARTMENT FOR EDUCATION AND SKILLS (2004). *Children Bill*. London: The Stationery Office.

DEPARTMENT FOR EDUCATION AND SKILLS (2004a). *Clarke Welcomes LEAs' Decisions on School Funding 13.1.2004* (Press Release) [online]. Available: http://www.teachernet.gov.uk/docbank/index.cfm?id=5943 [7 May, 2004].

DEPARTMENT FOR EDUCATION AND SKILLS (2004b). *Performance Data Framework for LEAs* (DfES/0148/2004). London: DfES.

DEPARTMENT FOR EDUCATION AND SKILLS (2004c). *Raising Standards and Tackling Workload: Implementing the National Agreement*. London: DfES.

DEPARTMENT FOR EDUCATION AND SKILLS (2004d). *Removing Barriers to Achievement: the Government's Strategy for SEN*. London: DfES.

DEPARTMENT FOR EDUCATION AND SKILLS (2004e). *School Travel Schemes – Draft Bill and Prospectus*. London: DfES

DEPARTMENT FOR EDUCATION AND SKILLS (2004f). *Travelling to School: an Action Plan* [online]. Available: http://www.dfes.gov.uk/publications/pdf/Travelling%20to%20School. pdf [29 March, 2004].

DEPARTMENT FOR EDUCATION AND SKILLS and CABINET OFFICE (2003). *'Making a Difference': Reducing Red Tape and Bureaucracy in Schools – Second Report*. London: Cabinet Office, Public Sector Team, Regulatory Impact Unit.

DEPARTMENT FOR TRANSPORT (2003). *Beating the Traffic? A New Approach to the School Run?* (News Release 2003/0113) [online]. Available: http://www.dft.gov.uk/pns/DisplayPN.cgi?pn_id=2003_0113 [24 March, 2004].

DEPARTMENT FOR TRANSPORT, LOCAL GOVERNMENT AND THE REGIONS (2001). *Strong Local Leadership: Quality Public Services* (Cm. 5237). London: DTLR.

DEPARTMENT FOR TRANSPORT, LOCAL GOVERNMENT AND THE REGIONS (2002). *Your Region, Your Choice: Revitalising the English Regions* (Cm. 5511). London: The Stationery Office.

DEPARTMENT FOR TRANSPORT, LOCAL GOVERNMENT AND THE REGIONS, AUDIT COMMISSION and HOME OFFICE (1999). *Best Value and Audit Commission Performance Indicators for 2000–2001. Vol. 1: The Performance Indicators.* London: DTLR.

DEPARTMENT OF HEALTH (1998). *Modernising Social Services: Promoting Independence, Improving Protection, Raising Standards* (Cm. 4169). London: HMSO.

DEPARTMENT OF HEALTH (2002). *Safeguarding Children: a Joint Chief Inspectors' Report on Arrangements to Safeguard Children* [online]. Available: http://www.dh.gov.uk/PublicationsAndStatistics/LettersAndCirculars/ChiefInspectorLetters/ChiefInspectorLettersArticle/fs/en?CONTENT_ID=4004286&chk=PZKIDJ [30 April, 2004].

DEPARTMENT OF THE ENVIRONMENT, TRANSPORT AND THE REGIONS (1998). *A New Deal for Transport: Better for Everyone* (Cm. 3950). London: The Stationery Office.

DEPARTMENT OF THE ENVIRONMENT, TRANSPORT AND THE REGIONS (2000). *Modernising Local Government Finance: a Green Paper.* London: DETR.

HER MAJESTY'S INSPECTORATE FOR EDUCATION AND TRAINING IN WALES (2003). *Local Education Authorities in Wales: a Framework for Inspection.* Cardiff: Estyn.

HER MAJESTY'S TREASURY (2003a). *Every Child Matters* (Cm. 5860). London: The Stationery Office.

HER MAJESTY'S TREASURY (2003b). *Public Services: Meeting the Productivity Challenge. A Discussion Document.* London: The Stationery Office.

HOME OFFICE (1968). *The Law on Performances by Children: a Guide to the Children (Performances) Regulations 1968 and Related Provision.* London: HMSO.

HOME OFFICE (2002). *Referral Orders and Youth Offenders Panel: Guidance for Courts, Youth Offending Teams and Youth Offender Panels* [online]. Available:
http://www.homeoffice.gov.uk/docs/referral_orders_and_yop.pdf [30 March, 2004].
http:// www.wales.gov.uk/subieducationtraining/content/Consultation/ maintainedschools-consultation-e.pdf [24 March, 2004].
http://www.elwa.ac.uk/elwaweb/elwa.aspx?pageid=1612 [25 March 2004].

HOME OFFICE (2003). *The Victoria Climbié Inquiry Report* (Cm. 5730). London: The Stationery Office.

HOUSE OF COMMONS. EDUCATION AND SKILLS COMMITTEE (2003). *Public Expenditure: Schools' Funding. First Report of Session 2003–04* (HC 112). London: The Stationery Office.

HUNTER, P. and MADEN, M. (2000). *A New Governance for Education.* London: Institute for Public Policy Research.

INFORMATION COMMISSIONER (1998). *Data Protection Act 1998: Legal Guidance* [online]. Available:
http://www.dataprotection.gov.uk/dpr/dpdoc.nsf [30 March, 2004].

INFORMATION COMMISSIONER (2001). *Advice Note – Local Authorities and Data Sharing.* Wilmslow: Office of the Information Commissioner

INFORMATION COMMISSIONER (2003). *The Freedom of Information Act: An Introduction.* Wilmslow: Office of the Information Commissioner.

LEARNING AND SKILLS COUNCIL (2002). *Trust in the Future. The Report of the Bureaucracy Task Force: November 2002.* London: LSC.

LIELL, P.M., COLEMAN, J.E. and WOLFE, D. (2004). *The Law of Education* [CD ROM]. Croydon: LexisNexis Butterworths.

LOCAL GOVERNMENT ASSOCIATION (2000). *Has the LEA Had its Day?* London: LGA.

LORD CHANCELLOR'S DEPARTMENT (2002). *Lord Chancellor's Code of Practice on the Discharge of Public Authorities' Functions Under Part I of the Freedom of Information Act 2000, Issued Under Section 45 of the Act* [online]. Available:
http://www.dca.gov.uk/foi/codepafunc.htm [24 March, 2004].

MACLURE, S. (1984). *Educational Development and School Building: Aspects of Public Policy 1945–73.* London: Longman.

MCLEOD, J. (1990). 'Church and state: the religious settlement in the Education Reform Act 1988.' In: MORRIS, R. (Ed) *Central and Local Control of Education After the Education Reform Act 1988.* London: Longman.

MINISTRY OF EDUCATION (1945). *The Purpose and Content of the Youth Service*. London: HMSO [Reproduced in the informal education archives] [online]. Available: www.infed.org/archives/e-texts/minofed_purpose_youth_service.htm [30 March, 2004].

MORRIS, R. (1994.) *The Functions and Roles of Local Education Authorities*. Slough: NFER, EMIE.

NATIONAL ASSEMBLY FOR WALES (1999). *School Admissions: Welsh Office Code of Practice* [online]. Available: http://www.wales.gov.uk/subieducationtraining/content/guidance/admiss/admssns_e.pdf [5 May, 2004].

NATIONAL ASSEMBLY FOR WALES (1999). *School Admission Appeals: the National Assembly for Wales Code* [online]. Available: http://www.wales.gov.uk/subieducationtraining/content/guidance/admiss/appeals_e.pdf [5 May, 2004].

NATIONAL ASSEMBLY FOR WALES (2003). *Consultation on the Replacement of the Financing of Maintained Schools Regulations 1999 (as amended)* [online]. Available: http://www.wales.gov.uk/subieducationtraining/content/Consultation/maintained-schools-intro-e.htm

NATIONAL ASSEMBLY FOR WALES (2003). *Pupil Involvement in Decisions that Affect Them and Establishment of School Councils in Primary Secondary and Special Schools* [online]. Available: http://www.wales.gov.uk/subieducationtraining/content/Consultation/school-councils-e.pdf [30 March, 2004].

NEW LOCAL GOVERNMENT NETWORK (2002). *Future Models of Local Education*. London: NLGN.

OFFICE FOR STANDARDS IN EDUCATION (2000). *Inspection of Sheffield Local Education Authority*. London: Ofsted.

OFFICE FOR STANDARDS IN EDUCATION (2002). *LEA Support for School Improvement: Framework for the Inspection of LEAs* (HMI 345). London: Ofsted.

OFFICE FOR STANDARDS IN EDUCATION (2003a). *Excellence in Cities and Education Action Zones: Management and Impact* (HMI 1399). London: Ofsted.

OFFICE FOR STANDARDS IN EDUCATION (2003b). *Key Stage 4: Towards a Flexible Curriculum* (HMI 517) London: Ofsted.

OFFICE FOR STANDARDS IN EDUCATION (2003c). *The Annual Report of Her Majesty's Chief Inspector of Schools: Standards and Quality in Education 2001/02*. London: The Stationery Office.

OFFICE FOR STANDARDS IN EDUCATION (2004). *Framework for the Inspection of LEAs* (HMI 1770). London: Ofsted.

BIBLIOGRAPHY
WEBSITES

POOLE, K.P. (1988). *Education Law: an Outline of the Law Relating to the Public System of Education in England and Wales.* London: Sweet & Maxwell.

RICHARDS, P.G. (1980). *The Reformed Local Government System* (The New Local Government Series. No. 5). Fourth edn. London: Allen & Unwin.

SOCIAL EXCLUSION UNIT (1999). *Bridging the Gap: New Opportunities for 16–18 Year Olds Not in Education, Employment or Training* (Cm. 4405). London: The Stationery Office.

STEERING GROUP ON THE INSPECTION OF CHILDREN'S SERVICES (2004). *Every Child Matters Inspecting Services for Children and Young People. A Discussion Paper* [online]. Available: http//www.ofsted.gov.uk [25 March 2004].

WORKING GROUP ON 14-19 REFORM (2003). *Reforming the 14-19 Curriculum and Qualifications*: Progress Report (DfES/0489/2003). London: DfES.

WORKING GROUP ON 14-19 REFORM (2004). *14-19 Curriculum and Qualifications Reform. Interim Report of the Working Group on 14-19 Reform.* London: DfES.

YOUTH ADVISORY COUNCIL (1943). *The Youth Service After the War.* London: HMSO.

References for Chapter 2

(In order of citation)

NATIONAL ASSEMBLY FOR WALES (2001). *Plan for Wales 2001* [online]. Available: http://www.planforwales.wales.gov.uk/pdf/plan_for_Wales_English.pdf [25 March, 2004].

GREAT BRITAIN. PARLIAMENT. HOUSE OF COMMONS (1997). *Building Excellent Schools Together* (Cm. 3701). London: The Stationery Office.

FURTHER EDUCATION FUNDING COUNCIL FOR WALES (1999). *Education and Training Action Plan for Wales: Submission to the Post-16 Education and Training Committee* [online]. Available: http://www.wfc.ac.uk/education/fefcw/pub99/action_plan.html [17 March, 2004].

FUTURE SKILLS WALES (1999). *FSW 1998 Skills Survey* [online]. Available: http://www.futureskillswales.com/eng/content.php?cID=5&pID=1&zID=8&nhID=40 [17 March, 2004].

NATIONAL ASSEMBLY FOR WALES (2001). *Plan for Wales 2001*. Cardiff: National Assembly for Wales.

BASIC SKILLS AGENCY (2001). *The National Basic Skills Strategy for Wales*. London: Basic Skills Agency.

NATIONAL ASSEMBLY FOR WALES (2001). *The Learning Country: a Paving Document. A Comprehensive Education and Lifelong Learning Programme to 2010 in Wales*. Cardiff: National Assembly for Wales.

NATIONAL ASSEMBLY FOR WALES (2002). Made in Wales Support for Teachers (Press Release: Education and Lifelong Learning, 19 April) [online]. Available: http://www.wales.gov.uk/servlet/PressReleaseBySubject?area_code=37D4D35C000B6B0C000005D400000000&document_code=3CC031760000672E000063FA00000000&p_arch=null&module=dynamicpages&month_year=4|2002 [5 May, 2004].

NATIONAL ASSEMBLY FOR WALES (2000). *Children and Young People: a Framework for Partnership* [online]. Available: http://www.childpolicy.org.uk/dir/index.cfm?ccs=1096&cs=620 [17 March, 2004].

NATIONAL ASSEMBLY FOR WALES (2000). *Extending Entitlement: Supporting Young People in Wales. Report by the Policy Unit*. Cardiff: National Assembly for Wales.

NATIONAL ASSEMBLY FOR WALES (2002). *Extending Entitlement Support for 11 to 25 Year Olds in Wales: Direction and Guidance* [online]. Available: http://www.childpolicy.org.uk/presources/indexhtm.cfm?ccs=1967&cs=2877 [17 March, 2004].

WELSH DEVELOPMENT AGENCY (2000). *Entrepreneurship Action Plan for Wales – Strategy Document. The Sky is the Limit* [online]. Available: http://www.wda.co.uk/resources/ent_actionplan_en.pdf [17 March, 2004].

NATIONAL ASSEMBLY FOR WALES (2000). *Implementation Plan for Entrepreneurship. Action Plan for Wales: Making It Happen.* Cardiff: National Assembly for Wales.

NATIONAL ASSEMBLY FOR WALES (2002). *A Winning Wales: the National Development Strategy of the Welsh Assembly Government.* Cardiff: National Assembly for Wales.

NATIONAL ASSEMBLY FOR WALES (2003). *Skills and Employment Action Plan for Wales. Progress Report July 2003* [online]. Available: http://www.wales.gov.uk/subieducationtraining/content/employment/skills-empl-action-plan-03-e.pdf [17 March, 2004].

NATIONAL ASSEMBLY FOR WALES (2002). *Reaching Higher: Higher Education and the Learning Country. A Strategy for the Higher Education Sector in Wales.* Cardiff: National Assembly for Wales.

NATIONAL ASSEMBLY FOR WALES (2002). *Well Being in Wales: Consultation Document.* Cardiff: National Assembly for Wales.

NATIONAL ASSEMBLY FOR WALES (1999). *The Children First Programme in Wales: Transforming Children's Services* (Circular 20/99) [online]. Available: http://www.wales.gov.uk/subisocialpolicy/content/circulars/2099/wo_circular_20-99_e.htm [17 March, 2004].

NATIONAL ASSEMBLY FOR WALES (2002). *Languages Count: the Welsh Assembly Government' s National Modern Foreign Languages Strategy.* Cardiff: National Assembly for Wales.

QUALIFICATIONS, CURRICULUM AND ASSESSMENT AUTHORITY FOR WALES (2000). *Personal and Social Education Framework. Key Stages 1 to 4 in Wales.* Cardiff: ACCAC

QUALIFICATIONS, CURRICULUM AND ASSESSMENT AUTHORITY FOR WALES (2000). *Personal and Social Education: Supplementary Guidance.* Cardiff: ACCAC.

QUALIFICATIONS, CURRICULUM AND ASSESSMENT AUTHORITY FOR WALES (2000). *A Framework for Work-Related Education for 14 to 19-Year-Olds in Wales.* Cardiff: ACCAC.

QUALIFICATIONS, CURRICULUM AND ASSESSMENT AUTHORITY FOR WALES (2000). *Work-Related Education for 14 to 19-Year-Olds in Wales. Supplementary Guidance.* Cardiff: ACCAC.

QUALIFICATIONS, CURRICULUM AND ASSESSMENT AUTHORITY FOR WALES (2003). *Credit and Qualifications Framework for Wales July 2003: Implementation Plan.* Cardiff: ACCAC.

NATIONAL COUNCIL FOR EDUCATION AND TRAINING FOR WALES (2002). *Credit and Qualifications Framework for Wales* [online]. Available: http://www.elwa.ac.uk/elwaweb/elwa.aspx?pageid=1612 [23, June 2004].

ASSOCIATION OF TEACHERS AND LECTURERS 2003). *The Learning Country: Foundation Phase 3-7 years* [online]. Available: http://www.askatl.org.uk/pdfs/110603.pdf [17 March, 2004].

QUALIFICATIONS, CURRICULUM AND ASSESSMENT AUTHORITY FOR WALES (2000). *Desirable Outcomes for Children's Learning Before Compulsory School Age.* Cardiff: ACCAC.

NATIONAL ASSEMBLY FOR WALES (2002). *Learning Country: Learning Pathways 14-19.* Cardiff: National Assembly for Wales.

WELSH BACCALAUREATE QUALIFICATION (2004). *The Welsh Bac* [online]. Available: http://www.wbq.org.uk/ [17 March, 2004].

INDEPENDENT INVESTIGATION GROUP ON STUDENT HARDSHIP AND FUNDING IN WALES (2001). *Investing in Learners: Coherence, Clarity and Equity for Student Support in Wales: a Report of the Independent Investigation Group on Student Hardship and Funding in Wales.* Cardiff: Cardiff University School of Social Sciences.

WELSH OFFICE. EDUCATION DEPARTMENT (1999). *Code of Practice on LEA-School Relations.* Cardiff: Welsh Office, Education Department.

HER MAJESTY'S INSPECTORATE FOR EDUCATION AND TRAINING IN WALES and AUDIT COMMISSION (2003). *Local Education Authority Services in Wales: a Framework for Inspection.* Cardiff: Estyn.

NATIONAL ASSEMBLY FOR WALES (2001). *Cymru ar Lein: the Welsh Assembly Government's Information Age Strategic Framework for Wales* [online]. Available: http://www.cymruarlein.wales.gov.uk/pdf/strategy.pdf [17 March, 2004].

WELSH LOCAL GOVERNMENT ASSOCIATION (2002). *Raising Standards for a Better Wales: the Future Role of Local Authorities in Education in Wales.* Cardiff: Welsh Local Government Association.

NATIONAL ASSEMBLY FOR WALES (2003). *LEA/School Partnership Agreements. Consultation Document.* Cardiff: National Assembly for Wales.

BIBLIOGRAPHY WEBSITES

USEFUL WEBSITES

Central government

Cabinet Office
www.cabinet-office.gov.uk/

Department for Culture, Media and Sport, DCMS
www.culture.gov.uk/default.htm

Department for Constitutional Affairs
www.dca.gov.uk/

Department for Work and Pensions
www.dwp.gov.uk/

Department of Health
www.dh.gov.uk/Home/fs/en

DfES
www.dfes.gov.uk/index.htm

Department of Trade and Industry, DTI
www.dti.gov.uk/

Education and Skills Committee
www.parliament.uk/parliamentary_committees/education_and_
skills_committee.cfm

House of Commons
www.parliament.uk/about_commons/about_commons.cfm

Learning Wales
www.learning.wales.gov.uk/

National Assembly for Wales
www.wales.gov.uk/index.htm

Office of the Deputy Prime Minister, ODPM
www.odpm.gov.uk/

United Kingdom Parliament
www.parliament.uk/index.cfm

Government department units

Children and Young People's Unit, CYPU
www.cypu.gov.uk/

Value for Money Unit
www.dfes.gov.uk/valueformoney/

Disability Unit
www.disability.gov.uk/

Schools' Innovation Unit
www.standards.dfes.gov.uk/innovation-unit/

Standards and Effectiveness Unit, SEU
www.standards.dfes.gov.uk/seu/

Statutory and public bodies

Qualifications, Curriculum and Assessment Authority for Wales, ACCAC
www.accac.org.uk/

Adult Learning Inspectorate
www.ali.gov.uk/htm/index.htm

Audit Commission
www.audit-commission.gov.uk/

British Educational Communications and Technology Agency, Becta
www.becta.org.uk/

Centre for Public Scrutiny
www.cfps.org.uk/home/index.php

Commission for Social Care Inspection
www.csci.org.uk/default.htm

Connexions
www.connexions.gov.uk/

Council on Tribunals
www.council-on-tribunals.gov.uk/

Disability Rights Commission
www.drc-gb.org/

Education and Learning Wales, ELWa
www.elwa.ac.uk/elwaweb/portal.aspx

Her Majesty's Inspectorate for Education and Training in Wales, Estyn
www.estyn.gov.uk/home.asp

General Teaching Council for England
www.gtce.org.uk/

General Teaching Council for Wales
www.gtcw.org.uk/

Health and Safety Executive
www.hse.gov.uk/

Health Development Agency
www.hda-online.org.uk/

Information Commissioner
www.informationcommissioner.gov.uk/eventual.aspx

Learning and Skills Council
www.lsc.gov.uk/National/default.htm

Learning and Skills Development Agency
www.lsda.org.uk/home.asp

Legal Services Commission
www.legalservices.gov.uk/

Local Government Ombudsman (England)
www.lgo.org.uk/

Local Government Ombudsman (Wales)
www.ombudsman-wales.org

National Grid for Learning, NGfL
www.ngfl.gov.uk/

Office of the Schools Adjudicator
www.schoolsadjudicator.gov.uk/index.cfm

Ofsted
www.ofsted.gov.uk/

Qualifications and Curriculum Agency, QCA
www.qca.org.uk/

Special Educational Needs and Disability Tribunal
www.sendist.gov.uk/index.cfm

Standards Board for England
www.standardsboard.co.uk/

The Disclosure Service
www.disclosure.gov.uk/index.asp

Teacher Training Agency, TTA
www.tta.gov.uk/php/read.php?sectionid=1

Welsh Joint Education Committee, WJEC
www.wjec.co.uk/

Youth Justice Board
www.youth-justice-board.gov.uk/YouthJusticeBoard/

Professional associations and groups

Association of Directors of Education and Children's Services, ADECS (password protected on Confed's site)
www.confed.org.uk/ACEO/aceohomepage.htm

Association of Directors of Social Services, ADSS
www.adss.org.uk/

British Educational Leadership, Management and Administration Society, BELMAS
www.shu.ac.uk/bemas/index.html

Chartered Institute of Public Finance and Accountancy
www.cipfa.org.uk/

Confederation of Education Service Managers, ConFed
www.confed.org.uk/

National Association of Educational Inspectors, Advisers and Consultants, NAEIAC
www.naeiac.org.uk

Society of Chief Inspectors and Advisers, SCIA (password protected on Confed's site)
www.confed.org.uk/SCIA/sciahomepage.htm

Services for local government

Dialog
www.lg-employers.gov.uk/diversity/

EMIE at NFER
www.nfer.ac.uk/emie/

Employers' Organisation for Local Government, EO
www.lg-employers.gov.uk/

EURYDICE
www.nfer.ac.uk/eurydice/

Improvement and Development Agency, IDeA
www.idea.gov.uk/

IDEA-Knowledge
www.idea-knowledge.gov.uk/idk/core/page.do?pageId=1

Local Government Association, LGA
www.lga.gov.uk/

Local Government Information Unit, LGIU
www.lgiu.gov.uk/

National Consortium for Examination Results
www.ncer.org/

New Local Government Network
www.nlgn.org.uk/nlgn.php

The Education Network, TEN
www.ten.info

Virtual Staff College, VSC
www.virtualstaffcollege.co.uk/

Welsh Local Government Association, WLGA
www.wlga.gov.uk/

General reference sites

4 Nations Child Policy Network
www.childpolicy.org.uk/enghome/index.cfm

British Official Publications Current Awareness Service, BOPCAS
www.bopcas.com/

DfES publications
www.dfes.gov.uk/publications/

DfES statistics
www.dfes.gov.uk/rsgateway/contents.shtml

DirectGov
www.direct.gov.uk/Homepage/fs/en

HMSO
www.hmso.gov.uk/

Info4local
www.info4local.gov.uk/

Learning Wales publications
www.learning.wales.gov.uk/scripts/fe/news_list_doctype.asp

Learning Wales statistics
www.wales.gov.uk/keypubstatisticsforwales/topicindex/topicindex
-e.htm#E

National Statistics
www.statistics.gov.uk/

Public Bills before Parliament
www.parliament.the-stationery-office.co.uk/pa/pabills.htm

Tagish directory of local government websites
www.tagish.co.uk/links/

Trends in education and skills
www.dfes.gov.uk/trends/

UK Parliament's world wide web service
www.parliament.the-stationery-office.co.uk/

UK statutory instruments
www.hmso.gov.uk/stat.htm

Subject specific government information sites

14-19 gateway
www.dfes.gov.uk/14-19/

Adult learning
www.waytolearn.co.uk/

Behaviour and attendance
www.dfes.gov.uk/behaviourandattendance/

Cutting burdens
www.teachernet.gov.uk/wholeschool/remodelling/cuttingburdens/

Education Action Zones
www.standards.dfes.gov.uk/eaz/

Ethnic minority achievement
www.standards.dfes.gov.uk/ethnicminorities/

Governornet
www.governornet.co.uk

Information Management Strategy
www.teachernet.gov.uk/management/tools/ims/

LEA gateway
www.dfes.gov.uk/leagateway/

Leadership and management (A-Z of school leadership)
www.teachernet.gov.uk/management/atoz/

Learning and skills gateway
www.dfes.gov.uk/learning&skills/index.shtml

LEAs' area (Standards site)
www.standards.dfes.gov.uk/lea/

Lifelong learning
www.lifelonglearning.co.uk/

Parent Centre
www.parentcentre.gov.uk/

Pay and performance (teachers)
www.teachernet.gov.uk/management/payandperformance/

Public private partnerships
www.dfes.gov.uk/ppppfi/

School admissions
www.teachernet.gov.uk/management/atoz/A/admissions/

School attendance
www.dfes.gov.uk/schoolattendance/

School buildings and design
www.teachernet.gov.uk/management/resourcesfinanceandbuilding/
schoolbuildings/

School diversity
www.standards.dfes.gov.uk/schooldiversity/

School funding
www.teachernet.gov.uk/management/schoolfunding/

School improvement
www.standards.dfee.gov.uk/sie/

School organisation changes
www.dfes.gov.uk/schoolorg/

School security
www.dfes.gov.uk/schoolsecurity/

Sick children (children with medical needs)
www.dfes.gov.uk/sickchildren/

Special educational needs and disability
www.teachernet.gov.uk/wholeschool/sen/

Specialist schools
www.standards.dfes.gov.uk/specialistschools/

Standards site
www.standards.dfes.gov.uk/

Sure Start
www.surestart.gov.uk/

Teachernet
www.teachernet.gov.uk/

Young people's gateway
www.dfes.gov.uk/youngpeople/index.shtml

Youth justice
www.youth-justice-board.gov.uk/PractitionersPortal/

Trusts, charities

Basic Skills Agency
www.basic-skills.co.uk/site/page.php?cms=2

ContinYou
www.continyou.org.uk/

Centre for Studies on Inclusive Education
www.inclusion.uwe.ac.uk/csie/csiehome.htm

National Association of Governors and Managers
www.nagm.org.uk/

National Association for SEN
www.nasen.org.uk/

National Literacy Trust
www.literacytrust.org.uk/index.html

National Children's Bureau
www.ncb.org.uk/

National Foundation for Educational Research, NFER
www.nfer.ac.uk

National Governors' Council
www.ngc.org.uk/contents.htm

National Institute of Adult Continuing Education
www.niace.org.uk/

National Youth Agency
www.nya.org.uk/Homepage.asp?NodeID=Ô88833

Who Cares? Trust
www.thewhocarestrust.org.uk/

These and other links are regularly updated on the EMIE website, www.nfer.ac.uk/emie.

GLOSSARY, INCLUDING ACRONYMS AND ABBREVIATIONS

Introduction

This book attempts a synthesis of educational and jurisprudential thinking on the LEA as prominent role-player in the public education service. To put it less loftily, the jargons of two large professional groups come together here in a way in which the authors have tried to demystify and to explain as they go on. Lawyers and educators not only do things differently: they speak in different codes. But we have tried to be guided by a vision in which the legal educator and practitioner, on the one side, and the education officer, headteacher and elected member alert to legal implications of administrative reality, on the other, can equally make sense of Government's policies on education and local government, the huge volume of legislation, and the growing corpus of case law on education.

To be blunt: educators have allowed abbreviations and acronyms to proliferate, and have fallen to saying 'learning situation' when they mean 'classroom' or 'facilitator of the learning situation', for 'teacher'. To our shame, it was an LEA which Mr Hoggart (*The Guardian*, 1 November 2003) excoriated for claiming that it had 'developed a successful pilot scheme at X School that demonstrates its commitment to developing partnerships through integrated teamwork, a high-quality driven agenda and a commitment to people to drive a cultural change to minimise risk while maximising client value.' Academic writers use the Harvard notation to tell us that such-and-such was said by Bloggs (1990, p.310); so seductive is this formulary that we have seen articles in which authorship of, say, the Education Reform Act is ascribed to 'E II R (1988)'. Lawyers, though, have developed systems of citing decided cases (including, of course crucially important precedents) in a string of Latinity and abbreviation not explained in the books in which they appear *but in other works, which the reader must use as directories.*

This is not to say that our pages are free from the odd *per* (instead of some clumsiness like 'as given in the judgment of') or *inter alia* (meaning that the list is not exhaustive). The citation of judicial review judgments (see chap. 12.D.3.2.1) can be a little confusing:

the traditional form *R[egina] v Sadshire CC ex parte Bloggs* [1990] QBD had the merit of brevity. The *'ex parte'* signifies that the Crown has adopted (but not actually brought) the case in the Queen's Bench Division of the High Court on behalf of the aggrieved Bloggs. From January 2001 in the Court of Appeal, and thereafter in the Lords and the High Court, so-called neutral citation has been introduced, without retrospection, and some Anglicisation has appeared. Thus, the attempt by Bloggs to challenge Sadshire's action or omission would read, if determined nowadays: *R* [or Queen] (*on the application of Bloggs* [or, *ota Bloggs*]) *v Sadshire CC* [2003] EWHC 2061 (Admin), indicating that the Administrative Court had taken and decided *Bloggs* as its 2061st case of that year. In the new notation, the Court of Appeal (Civil Division) is logged as EWCA Civ, and the dignity of the highest appellate court is condensed to UKHL. Still, the abbreviations point up the distinction that the jurisdiction of the former is England and Wales (see chap. 2.A) whereas that of the latter is the United Kingdom. See also the Notes to the Table of Cases.

Neutral citation is handy for the practising lawyer who has [paid for] access to the texts of decided cases. For others' benefit, it is helpful to add reference to the commercially-produced volume of appropriate law reports after the neutral citation. In the Table of Cases, we expand references to law reports, and we have cited those in Jordans' *Education Law Reports* (ELR) more than others' because ELR is the set to which the non-lawyer in an education department or head's study is most likely to have access. There are also references to the useful, but short-lived, *Education Case Reports* (Sweet & Maxwell, [1988]–[2000]). On the distinction between square and round brackets in citations of cases, the reader is directed to the explanation in ATH Smith's Glanville Williams: *Learning the Law* 12th edition (2002) Sweet & Maxwell, p.48. It concludes: 'The reader should spared this pedantry; it is explained here simply to save bewilderment.'

We have explained technical terms as the text has unfolded. Thus *'Wednesbury* unreasonableness' is dealt with in detail in chapter 12.D.3.2.1, but briefly explained earlier as it occurs. 'Fair Funding' is discussed in chapters 1.C.6 and 6.D.2 (and subsequent sections of that part of chapter 6). A statemented child should be no mystery to the reader of chapter 8; and the LEA's all-important *vires* are examined in chapters 1.A.1 and 12.B.7 (and D.3.2) – not to say *passim* (or 'all over the place', as the modernisers might have it).

GLOSSARY
ACRONYMS &
ABBREVIATIONS

We should add that, in this book, the LEA is an 'it' and not a 'they'; though the latter is preferred by the Parliamentary draftsperson, we have thought it inappropriate to a corporate body. Similarly, the governing body 'is' to us: not 'are'. As is proper, however, we must concede that we are not of one mind on the point. We have attempted so-called inclusive grammar, but have drawn the line at 'his or her' on every relevant occasion, and have hidden behind: (a) the Interpretation Act 1978 to wield the gender-unspecific he/him/his; and/or (b) they/them/their etc, as singular in context.

ACRONYMS AND ABBREVIATIONS

ACCAC	Awdurdod Cymwysterau, Cwricwlwm ac Asesu Cymru Qualifications, Curriculum and Assessment Authority for Wales
ALI	Adult Learning Inspectorate
BSF	Building Schools for the Future
BVPI	Best Value Performance Indicator
BVPP	Best Value Performance Plan
BVR	Best Value Review
CCIS	Connexions Customer Information System
CCTA	City College for the Technology of the Arts
CEO	Chief Education Officer
CERA	Capital expenditure charged to revenue account
CFR	Consistent Financial Reporting
CILT	The National Centre for Languages
CIPFA	Chartered Institute of Public Finance and Accountancy
CPA	Comprehensive Performance Assessment
CTC	City Technology College
CYPU	Children and Young People's Unit
DES	Department of Education and Science
DFC	Devolved Formula Capital
DFE	Department for Education
DFEE	Department for Education and Employment
DFES	Department for Education and Skills
DTLR	Department for Transport, Local Government and the Regions
EAF	Education Action Forums

EAZ	Education Action Zone
EBD	Emotional and Behavioural Difficulties
EDP	Education Development Plan
EFS	Education Formula Spending
EFSG	Education Finance Strategy Group
EFSS	Education Formula Spending Share
ELWa	National Council for Education and Training for Wales – Education and Learning Wales
EMA	Education Maintenance Allowance
ESO	Education Supervision Order
ESP	Education Strategic Plan (Wales)
ESS	Education Standard Spending
ESTYN	Her Majesty's Inspectorate for Education and Training in Wales
EYDP	Early Years Development Plan
EYDCP	Early Years Development and Childcare Partnership
FE	Further Education
FEFC	Further Education Funding Council
FSS	Formula Spending Shares
GEST	Grants for Education Support and Training (Wales)
GM	Grant Maintained
GTCE	General Teaching Council for England
GTCW	General Teaching Council for Wales
HC	House of Commons
HE	Higher Education
HL	House of Lords
HMCI	Her Majesty's Chief Inspector
ICS	Integrated Children's System
ICT	Information and Communications Technology
IEB	Interim Executive Board
IEM	Interim Executive Member
IPPR	Institute for Public Policy Research
IRT	Identification, Referral and Tracking
ISB	Individual Schools Budget
J	Justice
LCVAP	LEA Co-ordinated Voluntary Aided Programme
LGA	Local Government Association
LJ	Lord Justice
LPSH	Leadership Programme for Serving Heads

GLOSSARY ACRONYMS & ABBREVIATIONS

LSB	Local Schools Budget
LSC	Learning and Skills Council
LSCB	Local Safeguarding Children Board
NAW	National Assembly for Wales
NLGN	New Local Government Network
NPQH	National Professional Qualification for Headship
ODPM	Office of the Deputy Prime Minister
Ofsted	Office for Standards in Education
OSA	Office of the Schools Adjudicator
PFI	Private Finance Initiative
PHIP	Professional Headship Induction Programme (Wales)
PI	Performance Indicators
PIU	Performance and Innovation Unit
PRU	Pupil Referral Unit
PSA	Public Service Agreement
QCA	Qualification and Curriculum Authority
RSPT	Recreation and Social and Physical Training
SACRE	Standing Advisory Council on Religious Education
SEN	Special Educational Needs
SENDIST	Special Educational Needs and Disability Tribunal
SEP	Single Education Plan
SI	Statutory Instruments
SOC	School Organisation Committee
SOP	School Organisation Plan
SSA	Standard Spending Assessment
SSFA	School Standards and Framework Act
TEC	Training and Enterprise Council
TSC	Training Standards Council
TTA	Teacher Training Agency
WAG	Welsh Assembly Government
WJEC	Welsh Joint Education Committee
WLGA	Welsh Local Government Association
YIP	Youth Inclusion Programme
YISP	Youth Inclusion Support Programme/Panel
YOT	Youth Offending Team

Acronyms are regularly updated on the EMIE website, **www.nfer.ac.uk/emie**.

GLOSSARY
ACRONYMS &
ABBREVIATIONS

INDEX

Q

R